OXFORD MEDICAL PUBLICATIONS

An Atlas of Clinical Neurology

An Atlas of Clinical Neurology

JOHN D. SPILLANE MD, FRCP

Consulting Neurologist to the University Hospital of Wales

SECOND EDITION

LONDON

OXFORD UNIVERSITY PRESS

NEW YORK   TORONTO

1975

Dedicated to the memory of
DR. MILTON DAVIES

*A country practitioner in Pembrokeshire
for half a century, to whom the art of
clinical observation was a source of
constant delight*

First Edition 1968
Second Edition 1975

Oxford University Press, Ely House, London W.1
GLASGOW NEW YORK TORONTO MELBOURNE WELLINGTON
CAPE TOWN IBADAN NAIROBI DAR ES SALAAM LUSAKA ADDIS ABABA
DELHI BOMBAY CALCUTTA MADRAS KARACHI LAHORE DACCA
KUALA LUMPUR SINGAPORE HONG KONG TOKYO

© Oxford University Press 1968, 1975

ISBN 0 19 264172 7

Printed in Great Britain by BAS Printers Limited, Wallop,
Hampshire

CONTENTS

PREFACE TO THE SECOND EDITION

When I was preparing the first edition of this book for publication, I kept on fearing that it would be too old-fashioned for this ultra-scientific age—a mothy arbour of neurological lore—and that the modern student might well feel it was more suited for the museum than for the library. But I also kept on saying to myself that this was the very stuff of Medicine, and that if the reader did not know it then I had better see to it that he did.

Ten thousand buyers of the ensuing product of this conflicting state of mind, and its translation into Japanese and Spanish, have reassured me that all is not yet lost and that our future doctors still wish to be something more than technicians, speaking only the language of the laboratory. British medicine has always stressed the dangers in the over-development of the scientific at the expense of the humanistic approach to the healing art, and if no home for such a philosophy can be found here, it might well be lost forever.

The general format has been retained. I have resisted suggestions which would simply turn it into another textbook, and I have tried to keep my students rather than my colleagues in mind when withdrawing some illustrations, inserting new ones, amending and adding to the text, and correcting errors (of which the majority passed undetected, or should I say undisclosed, by reviewers).

'It is the duty of a clinical teacher', said Sir William R. Gowers many years ago, 'to bring out of his treasury things old and new'.

Once again, to Mr. Ralph Marshall and his staff in the Department of Medical Illustration, University Hospital of Wales, I express my thanks for years of happy collaboration.

PREFACE TO THE FIRST EDITION

This book is the outcome of a chance meeting with Dr. J. C. Gregory of the Oxford University Press, at a cocktail party in Penang. He inquired about the illustrations I had just used in a lecture there, and this led, by the end of an evening of particular enchantment, to a gay promise on my part to try and arrange my collection of clinical photographs for publication.

The initial idea was merely to put them in some order and append suitable legends. But I soon found that there were things I wanted to say about the patients portrayed and their illnesses and about the art of clinical neurology. The aim has been to try and show the student how far the use of his senses will take him when struggling with the burdens of diagnosis at the bedside. The formidable array of modern diagnostic technical procedures are not here considered, except in passing. Neither have I included methods of clinical examination nor systematic accounts of the pathology and manifestations of diseases of the nervous system as a whole. There are many good texts already. This atlas, therefore, is not to be regarded as a formal introduction to diseases of the nervous system.

Medicine is all-consuming. Its practitioners have the opportunity of cultivating an endless range of interests. The art and the history of medicine have, for me, held a particular appeal, not just in recent years, fostered by age and experience, but indeed since my student days. The memory is still vivid of my Professor of Medicine, Alexander Mills Kennedy, a meticulous clinical observer, running a pin up the limbs and trunk of a woman paralysed below the waist and marking the upper level of sensory loss across her chest. A spinal cord tumour was diagnosed, and following its removal by the late Professor Lambert Rogers, the patient was soon walking again. All this, of course, before the days of myelography. Clinical skill of this nature is now commonplace enough but the wonderment induced in the student, seeing it for the first time, is still remembered.

The same talent at the bedside was shown by Charles

Elsberg, of New York, one of the American pioneers of neurosurgery, with whom I worked for a year. His monograph on tumours of the spinal cord, published in 1925, is a classic. The case histories and records of his one hundred patients are models of their kind.

Although it is in the ward that the student learns the elements of his craft, the whole of clinical neurology cannot be taught at the bedside. Neither time nor staff is available. Fortunately, many neurological phenomena, such as disorders of motion, sensation and reflex activity, can be demonstrated in amphitheatre or lecture room. Television can be used to enlarge the scope of the lecture-demonstration and enable the student to see signs such as ptosis, nystagmus or wasting of the small muscles of the hands, which he would not otherwise observe. For over twenty academic years I have held a weekly demonstration of two neurological patients. Slides of similar cases and other appropriate illustrations are projected, to exemplify and enlarge upon points that arise. And so, over the years, I have acquired a collection of slides, running into several thousands, which forms the material on which this atlas is based. Former students and assistants may recognize some of the patients and recall the interest, perplexities and sympathy they once aroused. The case histories of another clinician can never be as interesting as one's own but the value of a clinical photograph is usually enhanced by a brief abstract and this procedure has been generally adopted.

The human visual cortex is larger than the auditory and the processes of learning and memory are predominantly visual. The lecture-demonstration is not as intimate as ward teaching, in which the student is an active participant, but it does enable larger numbers of students to see and hear regularly something of neurology. In three years they can learn a great deal.

I have often been my own photographer but nearly all the illustrations chosen for publication in this book were taken in the Department of Medical Illustration in my hospital, under the direction of Mr. Ralph Marshall, F.R.P.S. To him and to his staff I wish to acknowledge with gratitude the expert assistance I have enjoyed for the past fifteen years.

Lastly, it may seem odd that the first chapter in a book of this sort should be of an historical nature. It reflects an approach to medicine which I have always found valuable and one which was encouraged by Dr. Paul D. White, of Boston, in whose Department of Cardiology I spent another year. One of the great clinicians of this century he is deeply immersed in the history of his specialty and indeed my very first assignment that year was to search out and present at a weekly staff meeting the contribution to cardiology of one Giovanni Maria Lancisi (1654–1720), one of the earliest writers on cardiac aneurysms. Each new student in his department had a similar task.

It has often been said that a man can only write the book that is within him, or, as Henry Thoreau, the New England naturalist and philosopher, once said, 'A man should step to the music which he hears'.

I am most grateful to Dr. J. C. Gregory for his expert advice in the preparation of this book for publication.

Cardiff   J. D. S.
September 1967

1 AN INTRODUCTION TO CLINICAL NEUROLOGY

A medical student entering a hospital ward for the first time, eager for contact with patients after years of preparatory studies, is about to experience a new method of instruction—bedside clinical teaching. He has probably assumed that it is as old as medicine itself that students were always so taught. Did not Hippocrates advocate the observational method for the study of disease, enjoining his pupils 'to be skilled in nature . . . to know those things which are to be seen, touched and heard'? He did indeed, but for many centuries books, not patients, were the source of medical knowledge. Theories and philosophies of medicine were pursued in university faculties. The student did not visit the sick. Not until, that is, the flowering of clinical medicine in the 18th century. Then, for a time, the influence of university medical faculties waned. They came into their own again in the 19th century when physics and chemistry, physiology and microscopy enlarged pre-clinical studies and ushered in the modern era of scientific medicine.

Meanwhile it was Sydenham, an English physician of the 17th century, who introduced the method of observation at the bedside, who taught that 'speculation and fictitious reasonings, borrowed from books, contribute no more to the cure of diseases, than painting does to the improvement of navigation'. He virtually originated clinical medicine. It took another century before the English medical student benefited from this revolutionary development.

Teaching at the bedside was introduced and developed in Leyden in the 17th century reaching Great Britain in the 18th century, where it was first practised in Edinburgh. It achieved great success in Dublin at the end of the 18th and in the early years of the 19th centuries where men such as Graves and Stokes, Cheyne, Corrigan and Adams made clinical observations of classical renown. In London they were followed by physicians like Bright, Addison and Hodgkin—names enshrined eponymously in the literature of medicine.

Thus by 1858, the year of the Medical Act which officially recognized the general practitioner (now fortified with a stethoscope but as yet without the short clinical thermometer and the sphygmomanometer), clinical medicine and bedside teaching had together created the apprenticeship system of medical education.

The clinical student, with some knowledge of human biology and some training in the scientific method, becomes an apprentice. Supervised by his teachers he sets out to learn about diseases and people. For Medicine concerns people, not things. Its practice is a craft or skill to be learned by participating. No book, no lecture, no demonstration, conference or symposium can compare with, let alone replace, the hour at the bedside. It is the whittling away of the time devoted to ward teaching that dilutes experience and endangers the future standards of clinical practice. If sound clinical habits are not acquired at this stage they may never be learned. The case record—the written account of the patient's history, his interrogation and examination—should be a thing of excellence, sympathetic, discriminating, unambiguous and accurate.

In his pre-clinical years the student's mind has been disciplined by the study of scientific subjects presented to him in a planned, organized fashion. He may have found much of it tedious and wondered about its relevance but he has at least been struggling with a coherent body of knowledge based on observation, measurement and experiment. He has learned how hypotheses should be formulated, analysed and, if necessary, rejected. How to preserve this attitude of mind in his new clinical environment poses a problem in which the outlook of teacher as well as student is involved. Some generality of approach is helpful to the student in gaining orientation and perspective.

One way is to consider how the classical procedures of observation and experiment are used in his new sphere. A hospital ward is a very different place from a laboratory but in both of them observation and recording of data are essential activities. In the laboratory, of course, phenomena may be selected and even isolated for study in a way which is not practicable in the ward. The symptoms and signs observed by the clinician are the random manifestations of disease. They can only be studied in the context of their environment. Measurement, a routine and vital technique in the laboratory, is often crude or even impossible in the clinical field, although considerable advances have been made in recent years. On the other hand the experimental method, in its strict scientific sense, is not a routine procedure in clinical investigation although it can be used for purposes of research, providing it is not harmful to the patient and permission has been obtained. On further consideration, however, it may be reasoned that the clinician is actually experimenting when he uses certain procedures in the course of his examination of a patient.

First, he observes the natural phenomena of disease, such as loss of movement or sensation. Secondly, he endeavours to elicit further information by using certain clinical tests. These may be designed to observe the response to stimuli such as the effect of light on the pupils, the effect of stroking the sole of the foot on the movement of the toes, and the effect of stretching a tendon on movement of its associated muscle. These manifestations of reflex activity may be regarded as experimentally induced observations. In other cases the object of a test is to see what effect is produced on the patient by altering or modifying his relationship with the environment. Thus, the clinician observes the influence of posture on blood pressure and on the orientation of the body in space. He may induce a symptom, such as syncope or vertigo, or a sign, such as bradycardia or nystagmus, by a positional manoeuvre. Lastly, there are clinical tests in which the aim is to see how symptoms and signs are influenced by the physical state of the patient. In myasthenia gravis, for example, the effect of physical fatigue on the eyelids, voice and muscle strength is examined.

The difficulties and limitations of this sort of approach are evident enough. They illustrate both the potential value of the scientific approach to medicine and the handicaps under which the clinician works. Clinical science is still a restricted field; clinical judgement remains a necessary qualification of practice.

Another way of approaching clinical studies is the historical one. The history of medicine is often regarded as a hobby, a topic for retirement, a subject which is riddled with aphorisms, anecdotes and trivial pomposities of all kinds and unsuitable for students. There is some truth in these criticisms. On the history of medicine a textbook can indeed be the dullest tome a student will ever handle, a lecture the driest account of some of the ancient apothecaries and their remedies, and a museum a place only for the collector of incunabula and a repository of medical lore. No wonder the history of medicine is rarely mentioned in medical school syllabuses or in symposia on the curriculum. One may search in vain for a reference to it even in the deliberations of those responsible for establishing new medical schools. But, like archaeology in recent years, it may yet flourish.[1]

The history of medicine is an aspect of the history of

man. The clinician may only study man for a short span of time; if he had only that to go upon he would learn very little indeed. The knowledge won by his predecessors, and often forgotten, would seem to provide an indispensable background. In point of fact one finds that the majority of one's colleagues have acquired a considerable knowledge of the origins and development of their specialties. It is usually not used except in the most incidental fashion, such as in enlivening a lecture by anecdote or illustration.

The superficial cult of the collector of eponymous syndromes should not be confused with advocacy of the historical approach to clinical studies. That is like comparing a habit with a line of thought, a hobby with a way of life. There is a glibness and worthlessness about the former fad which has irritated many and prejudiced judgement. For my part I believe we have neglected the history of medicine and have failed to exploit its rich resources. Few would deny that medicine has been revolutionized in the past 30 years and that there is every indication that progress will bring problems as well as benefits. A sense of direction and perspective will be invaluable to the medical profession as a whole and to its individual members. Surely, the past experience of the profession, its knowledge and its thinking, must be used to guide and educate its future members. The historical line of thought should permeate the curriculum with the object of assisting in the judgement of contemporary problems, the assessment of current claims and the formulation of new concepts. It is the general influence of the historical outlook which could be so valuable, as it should also be in sociology and psychiatry.

A student once asked me why it was that the carpal tunnel syndrome was only so recently described. Presumably, over the centuries, the median nerve had not been immune to pressure at the wrist. What, if anything, had happened? This raises the whole question of nosology and the discovery and recognition of syndromes and diseases. Why, later, some syndromes are seen to be spurious, without foundation in terms of disordered structure or function, while others vanish with the passing of time, as if they were due to some environmental or cultural influence of the period. Visceroptosis and chlorosis are two examples that come to mind. Have we come to the end of an era of clinical nosology? Do present textbooks of neurology describe all the disorders of the nervous system? Are there really none still undiscovered?

There is a general belief that this is largely true and that future research is going to be mainly concerned with discovering the causes of the diseases we already know, and their prevention and cure. So far as neurology is concerned the student who asked the question mentioned above, should he continue his inquiries, would find that

[1] In September, 1966, it was announced that the *first* university department of the history of medicine in Great Britain was being established in University College, London.

the various forms of disease of the nervous system he sees in hospital were nearly all described in Europe during the last and present centuries. Yet most neurologists admit that they can only put a name to about 60 per cent. of the disorders which afflict their patients. There may be nothing wrong with some of them but are all the rest neurotic? Isn't it probable that hiding away, as it were, in this group, waiting to be identified and described, there are syndromes as clear cut, for example, as '*restless legs*', '*periodic migrainous neuralgia*', '*vestibular neuronitis*' and '*micturition syncope*'—ailments of recent 'vintage', often tardily diagnosed? And what of the tropical regions of the world? Do no 'new' diseases of the nervous system lurk there? And who can say that 'old' diseases will not continue to turn up, not merely in different guises, but arising from new causes—natural or man-made?

In neurology we are dealing with that part of man which is most distinctively human—his brain. In its cortex we see the highest achievement of evolution. Some acquaintance with the story of man's endeavour to comprehend the nature of his own nervous system, and its ills should assist the student and guide him in his studies.

The Evolution of Clinical Neurology

Today, one of the commonest lesions of the brain is concussion resulting from head injury. Trephining for cranial injury and for purposes which remain conjectural, is the oldest operation of which we have any record. The latter, in this instance, consists of the neolithic skulls themselves, first unearthed, curiously enough, a mere 100 years ago. The first *written* neurological record we have was made by the ancient Egyptians about 3000 B.C. We find the term 'brain' was first used by them. They described paralysis of a lower limb after injury to the opposite side of the head. The writings of Hippocrates and others in the 5th and 4th centuries B.C. contain accounts of neurological disorders such as epilepsy (including the aura, visual and olfactory accompaniments, post-ictal amnesia, status epilepticus and Jacksonian convulsions), spinal injuries (paraplegia, tetraplegia and sphincter paralysis), head injuries (fissured and depressed fractures of the skull, blunt and penetrating injuries with dural tears) and there were early descriptions of the brain, its hemispheres, cerebral and cerebellar, and its ventricles and membranes.

Despite observations of this kind the ancient Greeks, guided by the philosophies of Plato and Aristotle, failed to recognize any physiological function of the nervous system. The brain was only a gland which excreted 'phlegm' into the pituitary gland and nose. The heart was the central organ of the body and the blood vessels, not the nerves, were the channels by which motion and sensation were transmitted, a belief even shared to some degree by William Harvey 2,000 years later. Not for the last time did the philosophers construct dogmas to suit their theories instead of basing them on the available data. Logic, Aristotle had every right to invent, but not physiology.

The true role of the nervous system was first suspected by Galen, of Rome (A.D. 130–210). He sectioned the spinal cord of new-born pigs and noted the loss of movement and feeling in the limbs. He considered that the brain was the seat of intelligence and imagination, the principal organ for sensory perception. But the brain, he taught, was the source of one of his vital spirits which flowed down the nerves in invisible channels, transmitting motion and sensation.

Although the anatomists of the Renaissance—Vesalius, Fallopius, Willis, Sylvius and Morgagni—laid the foundations of our knowledge of the structure of the nervous system, it was not until the 19th century that the mode of transmission in nerves was discovered.

The two dogmas which bedevilled neurological studies were those concerning the humours and the soul. The former likened the brain and nerves to the heart and vessels; one contained a hypothetical fluid and the other, blood. The brain, moreover, contained man's soul. But there were new philosophies appearing, those of Bacon, Locke and Newton, and the principles of observation, experiment and inductive reasoning were fostered. By the middle of the 18th century these methods were being directed to the physiology of nerve and muscle, to the conducting properties and reflex activity of the spinal cord and to the general functions of the brain.

The Nerves. Experimental stimulation of the exposed tissue of animals and man by mechanical, thermal and chemical means was performed. Some tissues responded by pain or movement, others did not. A muscle contracted, a nerve remained motionless. Tendons and ligaments were less sensitive than nerves and could thus be differentiated. The concepts of 'sensitivity', 'irritability' and 'contractility' emerged. Nevertheless, the wasting of tissues distal to a nerve section could still be explained by the loss of the nourishing nerve juices which were thought to flow from the brain, although the microscope (1674) failed to reveal the nerve channels through which they were said to pass.

The quest took a new form, physical instead of humoral, as a result of the discovery of the new physical laws of the age. Descartes (1596–1650) had already conceived the human body to be a machine and had postulated the movement of nerve 'threads', connecting brain and periphery, as the basis of the phenomena of movement and sensation. Notions of 'commotion', 'vibration' and 'pressure waves' in nerves were expressed. But it was the discovery of electricity which led to the final solution of nerve conduction. Until the end of the 18th century only the static form of electricity was known but it was appreciated that the shock from certain forms of fish and eel was electrical so that 'animal electricity' and the possibility of electrical conduction in nerves were in the air. Frictional machines to produce electricity were devised and condensers (e.g. the Leyden jar) to store it. It was left to Galvani (1737–1798) to apply this knowledge to neurophysiology using the humble nerve-muscle preparation of the frog to demonstrate that nerve conduction was electrical in nature.

For a time there was debate about the interpretation of Galvani's experiments, whether the electricity was a natural or artificial excitant, and where it resided in the nerve-muscle preparation. It was indeed found in muscle as well as nerve and during the first half of the 19th century it became possible to measure conduction rates and potentials at rest and during activity. Just a

century ago it was shown that the nerve impulse results from a self-propagating depolarization of nerve membrane. With more sensitive instruments it became possible to measure grades and speeds of responses so that by the first decade of the present century the 'all or nothing' law and the refractory period were described and modern electrophysiology had arrived.

The story of the chemical factors in the transmission of the nerve impulse is an offshoot of the main theme. The synapse was unknown until Sherrington's day (1897) but the peculiar histology of motor end-plates and the delays in conduction which occurred there raised the question of some form of transmission which was not electrical. Pharmacological experiments with smooth muscle, denervated and perfused, showed this to be true. The roles of adrenaline and acetylcholine in the sympathetic and parasympathetic synapses were discovered by the physiologists—Elliott, Loewi and Dale. In the end, the ancient neurohumoral theory proved to contain a particle of truth.

The Spinal Cord. Gazing at one of the multicoloured diagrams of a modern neuroanatomical text the student may be forgiven if he pauses in wonderment and dismay at the spectacle of those lines coming and going, crossing, shunting and relaying in the fashion of a switchboard. Trying to commit them to memory is a sterile and unprofitable approach. He should rather try to gain a view of how such diagrams came to be drawn at all, how they were created, not by draughtsmen, but by anatomists, physiologists and clinicians using the methods of observation, experiment and inductive reasoning. The value of this approach is well illustrated in the case of the spinal cord. Names with which the student is familiar, such as Flechsig and Gowers, Schwann and Purkinje, Marchi, Golgi, Cajal, Waller and Brown-Séquard come to mean something more than a tract or cell, stain, sheath, apparatus or phenomenon. What these men accomplished, and how, is more interesting and instructive.

The studies which enabled Horsley in 1887 to be the first to remove a spinal cord tumour (diagnosed by Gowers) and which allowed Martin in 1911 to be the first to perform cordotomy for the relief of pain, were almost entirely carried out in the 19th century. For long the spinal cord was viewed as some form of prolongation of the brain or a bundle of nerves but its anatomy and function were not known. The double roots and ganglia were noted, the fasciculi were crudely dissected and the crossing of the pyramids identified, but there was little else. The first important step, early in the century, was the discovery by Magendie and Bell that the spinal roots possessed different functions. By section and stimulation they showed that the anterior were motor and the posterior were sensory. This proved to be the first indication of separate conducting elements within the cord.

1. The spine (Gowers)
This illustration, drawn by Gowers, appeared in the first edition of his textbook in 1886 and was the first one to show clearly the relationships between the spinous processes, the vertebral bodies and the segments of the spinal cord. It was based on dissections prepared for him at University College Hospital by a young demonstrator of anatomy named Victor Horsley. A year later, in 1887, Gowers and Horsley were the first surgeons to diagnose and successfully remove a spinal cord tumour.

The next steps were made possible by the elaboration of the microscope and the techniques of staining the nervous system. These developments, moreover, were taking place at a time when men like Purkinje (who invented the term protoplasm) were noting the resemblance between plant and animal cells. Schwann went back to the cells of the ovum of these forms of life and built up the doctrine of cellular life which, by the end of the century, had led to the concept of the neurone as the basis of nervous activity. The nuclei, and other intracellular particles were identified, together with the membranes and extensions of the cell bodies. In their wake came the neurohistologists, Golgi, Marchi, Weigert and Cajal, portraying with their silver and gold impregnations, their aniline dyes and osmic acid techniques, the extraordinary complexity of nervous tissue. It is not surprising that the intricate ramifications and arborizations of the axones and dendrites and the web of the glia should have lent support to the reticular, as opposed to the neuronal, theory of nervous function. The concept of the synapse was still to come.

The source and termination of axones were traced by two methods. Studies were made of the formation of myelin in the newborn and also of the manner in which it disintegrated after injury and disease. This enabled Flechsig to trace the pyramidal and dorsal spinocerebellar tracts. Waller discovered that section of an axone caused its peripheral portion to degenerate—deprived of the nourishment from its cell body. Section of the anterior nerve roots indicated that their cells of origin were in the grey matter. When the posterior roots were cut, it was the central portion of the axone which entered the spinal cord that died and not the peripheral, which remained connected to the root ganglion.

Türck of Vienna and others followed tracts in the spinal cord and showed that their degeneration took place in the direction in which they conducted. He traced the motor pathway up the spinal cord, decussating in the medulla, to the basal grey matter of the brain. He called it the pyramidal tract because of the pyramids of the brain stem. It was Betz of Kiev who described and named the pyramidal cells of the motor cortex which we now know to be the origin of the pyramidal tracts. He is said to have studied 5,000 human brains.

A picture emerged of white tracts, composed of descending motor fibres, the majority of which crossed in the medulla, and ascending, relaying sensory routes, packed around a central core of grey matter. The functions of these structures were examined and in particular the pathways for the sensory modalities of touch, pressure, pain and temperature were worked out. For a time there was no evidence of more than one sensory pathway—that in the posterior columns—and the grey matter also seemed to be involved in sensory function. But by the middle of the century the procedure of selective partial section of the spinal cord, single and multiple, horizontal and vertical and at different levels, had disclosed that there were at least two pathways for sensation. From clinical observations came confirmation that pain and temperature sensations were transmitted by fibres which decussated and ascended in the lateral columns and that touch and postural sensibilities travelled by way of the ipsilateral posterior columns. Penetrating wounds of the cord, cases of compression and syringomyelia, with its zones of dissociated anaesthesia, provided increasing evidence that the spinothalamic tract, as it came to be known, traversed the grey matter of the cord as it passed upwards to the brain.

2a   2b

2. The knee jerk
An illustration from *Diseases of the Nervous System* by W. R. Gowers, published in 1886 and affectionately known as the 'Bible of Neurology'. Gowers was an artist and was able to illustrate his classical text. The mode of rising from the ground in pseudo-hypertrophic muscular dystrophy became known as Gowers' sign. He coined the term 'knee jerk', of which he wrote: 'It has been called the "knee phenomenon" by Westphal, the "patellar tendon reflex" by Erb, the "knee jerk" by myself.' Other words he coined were 'amyotatic', 'abiotrophy' and 'fibrositis'. (*a*) The dotted line indicates the movement which follows the blow on the patellar tendon. (*b*) Method of obtaining it when it is not readily produced in the ordinary way.

It remains to refer to the reflex activity of the spinal cord. A suggestion, through the centuries, that there was more than one form of movement was implied by the notion that some movements were controlled, not by the will, but by the 'appetite', or emotions. The involuntary actions of the pupils and eyelids under the influence of light and threat respectively, and the convulsive movements of the decapitated fowl (and perhaps of the executed criminal) were, by the 16th century, referred to as 'automatic'. Animal experiments demonstrated that they depended on an intact spinal cord and the word 'reflexion' came into use. Marshall Hall (1790–1857), a London physician, used clinical and experimental experience to develop his conception of spinal reflex activity. He coined the terms 'reflex arc' and 'spinal shock', and found that there were remote as well as segmental aspects of some reflexes and that they could be influenced by the will. He said, 'The spinal cord has a life of its own'—the brain might sleep but the spinal cord never slept.

Babinski (1857–1932) first described his sign in a short note of only 28 lines in 1896. 'In a certain number of cases of hemiplegia or crural monoplegia secondary to organic involvement of the central nervous system, I have observed an alteration of the cutaneous plantar reflex which I shall describe briefly. Pricking of the sole of the foot on the unaffected side causes flexion of the thigh on the pelvis, of the leg on the thigh, of the foot on the leg, and of the toes on the metatarsus. This is the same response that takes place in the normal state. A similar stimulus on the paralysed side also causes flexion of the thigh on the pelvis, of the leg on the thigh and of the foot on the leg, but the toes show a movement of extension on the metatarsus instead of the usual flexion.' Gowers in 1886 considered the plantar reflex to be among the most important of the cutaneous reflexes.

During the 19th century there came the discovery of reflex inhibition through the investigation of the vagus nerves and their influence on the mechanisms of respiration and swallowing. Lastly, Sherrington (1857–1952) and his school, in a whole series of classical studies provided the basis for our understanding of reflex activity at all levels of the nervous system. Sherrington's *The Integrative Action of the Nervous System*, published in 1906, is one of the major scientific treatises of history.

The Brain. The removal of an intracranial meningioma, now a commonplace procedure in most parts of the world, is not just a triumph of surgical skill and technique; it may be justifiably regarded as a pinnacle of achievement in the history of man's study of the human brain. The centennial anniversary of the birth of neurosurgery has yet to be celebrated. The operation of removing a meningioma was first performed in 1879 by Sir William MacEwen, Regius Professor of Surgery at the University of Glasgow. Five years later, in 1884, at the Hospital for Epilepsy and Paralysis, Regent's Park, London, Rickman Godlee removed the first glioma. These achievements were based solely on anatomical, physiological and clinical observations—before the days of radiology (1891) and lumbar puncture (1895). MacEwen's patient presented with a supra-orbital hyperostosis; Godlee's patient with left-sided focal convulsions and bilateral papilloedema.

The student who wishes to trace the historical growth of our knowledge of the anatomy of the brain could take as his landmarks some of the names he learns in the dissecting room. Many parts of the brain are still referred to by the names of those who first described them. The torcular of Herophilus (the confluence of the sinuses) and the vein of Galen (the great cerebral vein) are examples from antiquity. Also known to the Ancients were the pulsation of the brain, its convolutions, coverings and cavities. Indeed, until dissection was introduced in Bologna in the 16th century, it was not so much the substance of the brain which attracted attention, as its membranes and ventricles. These structures preoccupied anatomists and philosophers for 2,000 years. The terms 'dura mater' and 'pia mater' came into use in medieval times and are thought to derive from the concept of protecting 'mother' membranes—the 'hard' and the 'devoted'. The 'spidery' arachnoid membrane was not described until the 17th century, when Pacchioni also described the 'granulations' of the dura mater. He believed these membranes were not merely protective in function, but that by muscular contraction they forced nervous fluid to the periphery.

The ventricles were thought to be concerned in the processes of respiration and excretion, essential to the Galenical doctrine of the three spirits. Medieval anatomists described three ventricles and attributed certain mental faculties to them. In general, thought, imagination and memory were distributed in anteroposterior fashion, but there were many variants. The casts of the ventricles made by Leonardo da Vinci about the year 1500, and the drawings made from them were, like most other products of this genius, centuries ahead of his time. But as they remained hidden for hundreds of years, they were without influence. It was probably the persistence of theories of spirits or humours in the brain which hampered anatomists, preventing them from making unbiased observations and delaying the discovery of those passages through which the content of the ventricles flowed. The aqueduct of the midbrain was described by Sylvius, Professor of Medicine in Leyden in the 17th century, who was one of the first to teach medicine at the bedside. The interventricular foramina were described in the 18th century by Alexander Monro, *secundum*, Professor of Anatomy at Edinburgh. It was his father, having studied in Leyden, who introduced bedside teaching to Great Britain. The exit foramina of the fourth ventricle were not described until the 19th century, by Magendie and Luschka.

The fluid that filled the ventricles was thought by Willis, the 17th-century physician who described the arterial anastomosis at the base of the brain, to come from the choroid plexuses. The illustrations in his *Cerebri Anatome* were drawn by Christopher Wren. The nature and distribution of the cerebrospinal fluid were first adequately described by the man who also gave us the first account of sciatica, Cotugno, Professor of Medicine in the University of Naples, at the end of the 18th century. Many lesser contributions have gained for their authors eponymous 'immortality'. The diagrams which in modern texts chart the source, flow and fate of the cerebrospinal fluid are thus the outcome of centuries of investigation. But although we now also know the chemical and cellular constitution of this fluid, its function remains a mystery. When this is discovered, it may, like many other cerebral structures, enjoy an eponymous title, instead of remaining a 'liquor innominatum'.

The reader may also be surprised to learn that the identification of the cranial nerves as they emerge from the base of the brain, was yet another perplexing problem. The present classification of the cranial nerves into twelve numbered pairs has only been generally adopted since the middle of the 19th century. Vesalius in his *Fabric of the Human Body* (1543) had continued to accept and depict the seven cranial pairs of Galen. The olfactory nerves were excluded. The fourth and sixth nerve pairs were only identified later in the 16th century; the destination of the fourth in the superior oblique muscle of the eyeball was described by Fallopius, of uterine tube fame. Willis added the olfactory pair, making the total nine. His first six pairs were the same as our modern ones. He spoke of the 'smelling nerves' (1), the 'seeing nerves' (2) and the 'moving nerves of the eyes' (3). The grouping of the lower cranial pairs con-continued to be a confused subject. The modern classification of twelve cranial pairs was proposed in 1778 by a medical student, von Sömmerring of Göttingen, in his doctorate thesis.

In the first edition of *Gray's Anatomy*, published in 1858, this method had not yet been adopted; only nine cranial nerve pairs were described. The first six were as we now know them; the seventh was the combined facial and auditory nerves; the eighth comprised the ninth, tenth and eleventh nerves; the ninth was the hypoglossal. The proposal made by the German medical student that the cranial nerves be numbered in accor-

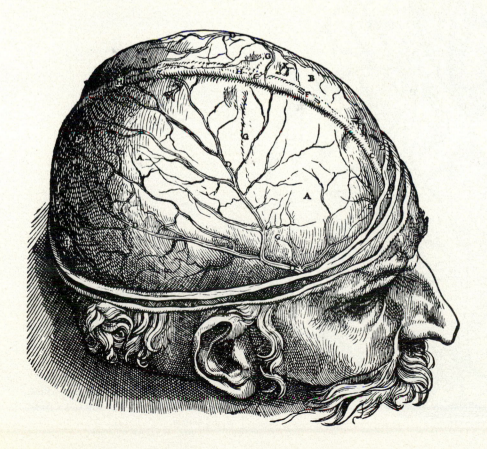

3. The brain (Vesalius)
The surface of the brain as depicted in the *Fabric of the Human Body* by Vesalius, 1543.

dance with the foramina in the base of the skull through which they pass, is now universally accepted. Its usage is likely to continue even longer than the 1,500 years of Galen's seven pairs.

If we turn now to the brain itself—'its stuff and substance'—we learn that the preoccupation and philosophizing about the ventricles and their presumed mental functions, declined after the time of Vesalius. In the 17th century William Harvey was asking 'Is the substance of the brain or the ventricle the chief part?' Willis was thinking in terms of cerebral rather than ventricular localization of function. He thought the 'sensus communis' (the meeting place of the five senses, from which we derive our modern term 'common sense'), resided in the corpus striatum; imagination in the corpus callosum and memory in the cortex. He coined the word *neurologie*, 'the doctrine of the nerves'. Malpighi, one of the first biological scientists to use the microscope, the creator of microscopic anatomy, began to consider the composition of brain substance.

The cerebral convolutions were quite neglected by anatomists until the early 19th century. Indeed, it was not until the middle of that century that the terms 'convolutions' and 'gyri' came into use. For centuries the cerebral convolutions had been likened to the coils of the intestine and had usually been referred to as 'enteroid processes' or 'gut-like prominences'. They were often described as resembling 'a plate of macaroni' or 'a bank of clouds in the sky'. The first structure on the surface of the brain to be given a name was the fissure of Sylvius, in the 17th century. The island of Reil was named in 1809, and the fissure of Orlando in 1831.

The significance of the cortex was first stressed by Gall, founder of phrenology, at the end of the 18th century. His physiology, which associated different mental faculties with bumps on the skull, was a myth, but his anatomical studies—differentiating grey and white matter, identifying the large commissures of the brain and the decussation of the pyramids and his notion of an anterior speech area—mark him as one of the

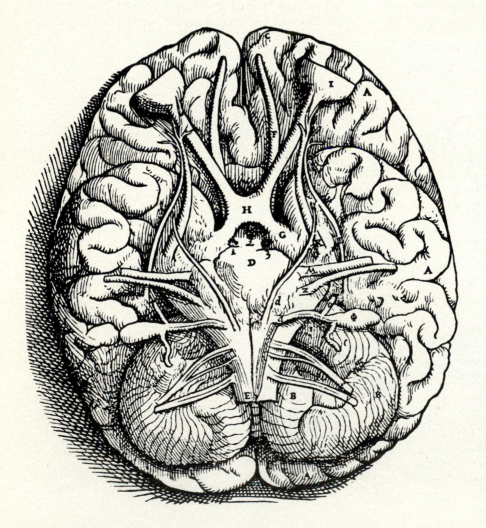

4. The brain (Vesalius)
The base of the brain as depicted in the *Fabric of the Human Body* by Vesalius. Although this classic work is renowned for its beautiful illustrations, this drawing is crude in comparison with that by Christopher Wren in FIG. 5. Note how the pons is united with the temporal lobes. Vesalius numbered the cranial nerves in seven pairs, as did Galen.

originators of the theory of the localization of cerebral functions.

Examination of the minute structure of the brain became possible in the 19th century with the advent of the achromatic microscope and the techniques of hardening and fixation of brain tissue. The semi-fluid grey matter of the nervous system could be studied in no other way. These methods permitted men like Purkinje, Reil and Rolando, whose names are familiar to modern students, to make their distinctive contributions. By 1840 the cells in various parts of the nervous system had been recognized and described. Myelinated and unmyelinated fibres had been demonstrated. But it took another 20 years before it was firmly established that all fibres were connected to cells. Virchow coined the term 'neuroglia' in 1856. The neurone, the unit structure of the nervous system, was named by Waldeyer in 1890. He established the neurone theory of nervous activity. This was the culmination of three main lines of research. His used histogenetic methods and observed the growth of the nerve cells and processes in embryo, showing that fibres grew from single cells. He coined the term 'dendrites'. Forel, using the technique of Wallerian and retrograde degeneration, showed that the axone was an extension of the cell. Cajal's brilliant histological studies proved, once and for all, that the nervous system was not a simple network. By the end of the century staining methods had been developed which formed the basis of the many splendid atlases of gross and microscopic anatomy of the brain. For their work, Golgi and Cajal shared the Nobel Prize for Medicine in 1906.

The Functions of the Brain. The primacy of the brain was recognized by Hippocrates. In his treatise on *The Sacred Disease*, namely epilepsy, he wrote:

'And men ought to know that from nothing else but the brain come joys, delights, laughter and sport, and sorrows, griefs, despondency and lamentations. And by this, in an especial manner we acquire wisdom and knowledge, and see and hear . . . and by the same organ we become mad and delirious, and fears and terrors assail us . . . and ignorance of present circumstances, desuetude and unskilfulness. All these things we endure from the brain when it is not healthy . . . It is the brain which is the messenger to the understanding. . . . It is the brain which interprets the understanding. . . . All the most acute, most powerful and most deadly diseases and those which are the most difficult to be understood by the inexperienced, fall upon the brain.'

Throughout the ages the only 'studies' which could be viewed as being directed towards the localization of brain function were those concerned with the doctrine of the seat of the soul. This provided philosophers as well as clinicians and anatomists with endless material for argument and discussion until modern times. The broad principles of the localization of function within the brain were not established until the 19th century.

Contributions were of two kinds—clinical and experimental.

The features of brachial and crural monoplegia, hemiplegia, hemianopia and hemianaesthesia were described and correlated with the pathological findings at autopsy. The effects of penetrating wounds and discrete foci were particularly noted. The terms 'Broca's convolution' and 'Jacksonian epilepsy' remind us of those days. There were areas of the brain, moreover, in which lesions did not cause paralysis. Thus the frontal lobes, which were so strikingly involved in general paresis, were discovered to be concerned with intellectual functions. Injuries and disease of the cerebellum were found to produce effects like alcoholic intoxication; the function of equilibrium was conceived as cerebellar in nature. Disorders of the basal ganglia were seen to cause difficulties of movement and locomotion which were not due to actual paralysis.

From clinical studies also came evidence of the cortical localization of visual and auditory functions in the occipital and temporal lobes respectively. Recognition of the sensory loss consequent on a lesion of the thalamus was slow in emerging because in many cases the sensory fibres in the adjacent internal capsule were involved. In the brain stem—ophthalmoplegia, alternate paralysis and bulbar and respiratory paralysis—came to be associated with lesions of the midbrain, pons and medulla respectively.

The tracing and identification of motor and sensory pathways within the brain was a necessary corollary to these clinicopathological studies. In the first edition of *Gray's Anatomy* the pyramidal pathways were still portrayed as originating in the basal ganglia; they were not traced to the motor cortex until later in the century. There were similar difficulties in identifying the thalamic and cortical destinations of the ascending sensory fibres. As in the case of the peripheral nerves and spinal cord, the two chief methods which were used were the study of myelin formation in the foetus and the Wallerian technique of tracing the paths of degeneration induced by artificial or pathological lesions.

Meanwhile, two experimental methods of investigation of brain function in animals—ablation and stimulation—were being explored. Cortical excisions, cerebral and cerebellar hemispherectomies were performed in a wide variety of animals and with improved techniques. Many of them survived long enough for observations to be made on movement, sensation, vision, hearing and equilibrium. Over the years, the extrapolation of these data to the problem of cerebral functions in man was a matter of constant discussion.

Stimulation of the cerebral cortex of animals had been attempted in the latter half of the 18th century, and throughout the first half of the 19th century there were great differences of opinion about the excitability of the cortex. The matter was not finally settled until the 1870's when Fritsch and Hitzig in Berlin and Ferrier in London, using galvanic and faradic currents, finally demonstrated the electrical excitability of the 'motor cortex'. When the first glioma of the brain was removed in 1884, the predominantly motor and sensory functions of the precentral and postcentral convolutions had been established. In reporting their success, the physician and surgeon concerned paid tribute to the experimentalists who had contributed to this 'mapping' of the cortex.

The doctrine of cerebral localization was now in its heyday. Claims were exaggerated, there was absurd parcelling of function, but Hughlings Jackson's penetrating observations and reasoning eventually prevailed. The 'positive' and 'negative' effects of a cerebral lesion, the notion of 'discharging' and 'destroying' lesions were propounded and, eventually, the importance of his concept of 'levels' within the nervous system was a major influence. The latter derived from the notion that evolution led to the development of better brains in

higher species. As they evolved, higher brain centres gradually took control over lower ones, achieving more unity and efficiency of brain function as a whole. In disease of the nervous system the manifestations of dissolution would first be revealed in failure of those skills most recently acquired during the processes of evolution. Thus, in progressive paresis of an upper limb, consequent on a lesion of the motor cortex, skilled, highly differentiated movements of the fingers would suffer earlier and more severely than the coarser, more 'primitive' movements of the proximal portions of the limb. In restoration of function the process would be reversed.

The mode of production of symptoms came to be regarded not only in the light of the anatomical lesion itself. An acute lesion would have an immediate effect—shock or 'diaschisis'—which would be temporary. The ensuing paralysis was a 'direct' result of the lesion, sooner or later to be followed by 'indirect' effects, as

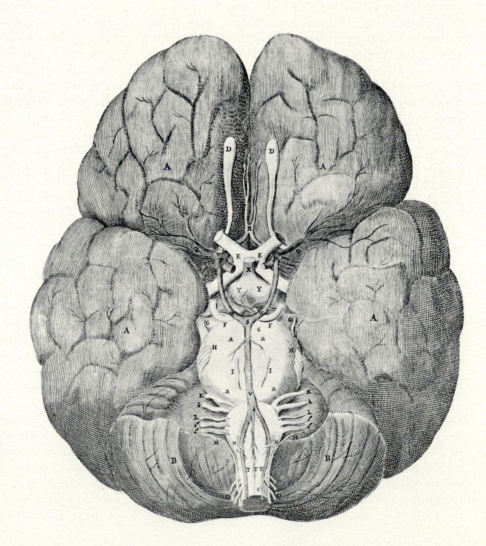

5. The brain (Willis)
The base of the brain as depicted in the *Cerebri Anatome* of Thomas Willis, 1664. One of the first accurate descriptions of the human brain, the illustrations in his book were drawn by Sir Christopher Wren. Willis recognized that the first pair of cranial nerves were the olfactory. He numbered nine cranial nerve pairs.

lower levels of the nervous system were 'released' from the control of higher centres. The factor of time, therefore, became important in the interpretation of physical signs.

At the end of the 19th century, direct electrical stimulation of the cerebral cortex in man was being undertaken, but it required the techniques of 20th-century neurosurgery to develop this field. Although the electrical currents of the brains of animals were discovered nearly 100 years ago, the electroencephalographic potentials in man were first recorded only in 1929. Their value in the diagnosis of epilepsy and brain tumour was discovered just over 30 years ago.

The chemistry of the nervous system is a recent field of neurological study. Knowledge of the chemical constituents of nerve tissue, their distribution and metabolism, is a necessary prelude to investigations of a pathological nature. The activity of electrolytes, enzymes and lipids, the role of the neuroglia and the blood-brain barrier, assume increasing importance. The concept of a biochemical lesion arose from a study of the chemical changes in the nervous system in beriberi. It has had a profound influence on the whole field of medical research, contributing to our knowledge of genetics and hereditary diseases, and to pharmacology and therapy. There is every indication that the neurochemical lesion will have a rich history.

Neurological Nosology. A systematic classification of diseases of the nervous system is not yet possible. We are as ignorant of the cause of many of them as when they

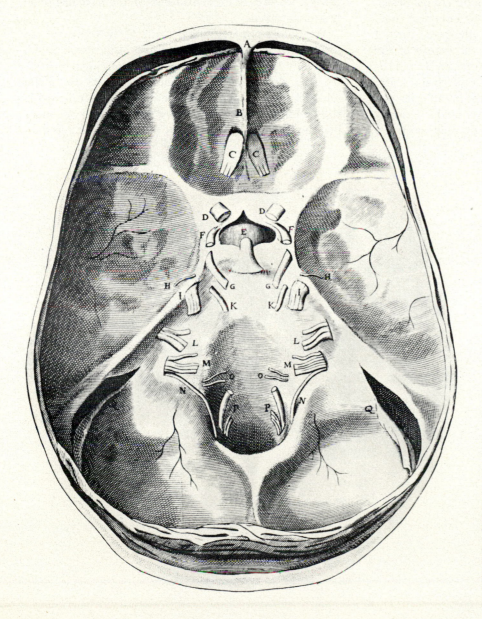

6. The base of the skull (Willis)
From *Cerebri Anatome*. CC, the olfactory nerves; DD, the optic nerves; E, the pituitary gland; FF, the carotid arteries; GG, 'the moving nerves of the eye'; HH, 'the pathetic nerves'; II, 'the fifth pair'; KK, 'the sixth pair'; LL, 'the seventh pair'; MM, 'the eighth or wandering pair seen to grow together with an accessory nerve of many fibres, NN, as it goes out of the skull'; OO, 'the ninth pair'.

were first described one hundred or so years ago. The names we give to those which we now distinguish often reflect the methods used in their identification, which were largely pathological. Examples are multiple sclerosis, tabes dorsalis and syringomyelia. On the other hand, some disorders have been named according to the nature of the principal clinical feature, as in chorea, torticollis and myasthenia gravis. In still others the disease is called by the name of its discoverer—Parkinson, Friedreich, Wilson, Pick and Huntington. Syndromes are also given eponymous titles, as in the cases of Wernicke, Landry, Korsakow, Horner, Brown-Séquard and Guillain-Barré. The term 'syndrome' is often also used in an anatomical sense, as in the carpal tunnel syndrome, the thalamic syndrome and the chiasmal syndrome.

Naturally, with the growth of knowledge, classifications will change. Locomotor ataxy, a functional designation, became tabes dorsalis, a pathological one. Subacute combined degeneration of the spinal cord, a title which gave some indication of the nature of the neural lesion, is giving way to that of vitamin B_{12} neuropathy, which indicates the aetiology of the cord disease. A hundred years ago the aetiology of the paraplegias was practically unknown. Today we are still unable to identify the cause of many of them—multiple sclerosis, motor neurone disease and the hereditary types—but vitamin B_{12} neuropathy, cervical spondylosis and spinal cord tumour are examples in which the cause has been discovered. On the other hand we are still ignorant of the causes of vitamin B_{12} deficiency, spondylosis, and meningioma. Polyneuritis is a term which covers a group of disorders of widely differing aetiology.

Despite its drawbacks and deficiencies, classification is necessary, not only for educational and descriptive reasons, but in the interests of therapy. If the distinction had not been made between such diseases as tabes dorsalis, subacute combined degeneration and diabetic neuropathy, examples in which in the lower limbs there are sensory complaints, objective sensory loss and absent reflexes, then the discovery of penicillin, vitamin B_{12} and insulin could not have been so widely and correctly applied in therapy. The long task of unravelling the distinctive features of these disorders would have had to be first undertaken.

We should not forget that many of the terms we use today, such as 'neuralgia', 'migraine' and 'myoclonus', are really little better than the 'nervous distempers', 'spasms' and 'exhaustion' of our forefathers. But if the scientific basis of many common nervous complaints is still unknown, the patients are with us and we must practise our art until such time as they can be cured.

A SELECTED BIBLIOGRAPHY

General

CASTIGLIONI, A. (1947) *A History of Medicine*, trans. and ed. Krumbhaar, E.B., 2nd ed., New York.

COPEMAN, W. S. C. (1965) The evolution of clinical method in English medical education, *Proc. roy. Soc. Med.*, **58**, 887.

FABER, K. H. (1930) *Nosography in Modern Medicine*, 2nd ed., New York.

MEDICAL CLASSICS (1936–1940) Vols. I–IV, Baltimore.

SIGERIST, H. E. (1932) *Man and Medicine; an Introduction to Medical Knowledge*, London.

SIGERIST, H. E. (1951) The historical approach to medicine, in *A History of Medicine*, Vol. I, New York.

SINGER, C. (1925) *The Evolution of Anatomy to the Time of Harvey*, London.

SINGER, C. (1941) *A Short History of Science to the Nineteenth Century*, Oxford.

WALSHE, F. M. R. (1948) *The Structure of Medicine and its Place among the Sciences*, Edinburgh.

Neurological

BRAIN, LORD (1964) William Harvey, neurologist, in *Doctors Past and Present*, London.

BRAZIER, M. A. (1959) The historical development of neurophysiology, in Neurophysiology, section I, Vol. I, *A Handbook of Physiology*, ed. Field, J., Magoun, H. W., and Hall, V. E., American Physiological Society, Washington D.C.

CLARKE, E., and DEWHURST, K. (1972) *An Illustrated History of Brain Function*, Oxford.

CLARKE, E., and O'MALLEY, C. D. (1968) *The Human Brain and Spinal Cord*, Berkeley, Cal.

FERRIER, D. (1878) *The Localisation of Cerebral Disease*, London.

FERRIER, D. (1886) *The Functions of the Brain*, 2nd ed., London.

FOSTER, M. (1970) *Lectures on the History of Physiology during the 16th, 17th and 18th Centuries*, New York.

HAYMAKER, W., ed. (1953) *The Founders of Neurology*, Springfield, Ill.

KEELE, K. D. (1957) *Anatomies of Pain*, Oxford.

LIDDELL, E. G. T. (1960) *The Discovery of Reflexes*, Oxford.

McHENRY, L. C. (1969) *Garrison's History of Neurology*, Springfield, Ill.

MEYER, A. (1971) *Historical Aspects of Cerebral Anatomy*, London.

PETERS, SIR R. A. (1963) *Biochemical Lesions and Lethal Synthesis*, Oxford.

POYNTER, F. N. L., ed. (1958) *The History and Philosophy of Knowledge of the Brain and its Functions*, Oxford.

RIESE, W. (1945) The history and principles of classification of nervous diseases, *Bull. Hist. Med.*, **18**, 465.

RIESE, W. (1950) *The Principles of Neurology; in the Light of History and their Present Use*, New York.

RUCKER, C. W. (1966) The history of the numbering of the cranial nerves, *Proc. Mayo Clin.*, **41**, 453.

SINGER, C. (1952) *Vesalius on the Human Brain*, London.

VEITH, I. (1965) *Hysteria. The History of a Disease*, Chicago.

WALKER, A. E., ed. (1951) *A History of Neurological Surgery*, Baltimore.

WOOLLAM, D. H. M. (1957) The historical significance of the cerebrospinal fluid, *Med. Hist.*, **1**, 91.

ZILBOORG, G., and HENRY, G. W. (1941) *A History of Medical Psychology*, New York.

2 STATURE

Many factors, genetic and environmental, determine the stature of an individual. Growth may be impaired as a result of malnutrition, or as a consequence of disease of the heart, lungs, kidneys or liver. Certain inborn errors of metabolism may impair growth. Short stature may be a consequence of glandular deficiency, as in the cretin or the patient with a pituitary lesion. Various disorders of the skeleton may impair growth.

Dwarfism is not a scientific term and can scarcely be regarded as a diagnosis. It is best viewed as a physical sign which may or may not be accompanied by other abnormalities. Individuals with certain types of dwarfism are prone to develop various neurological abnormalities. Thus, in achondroplasia, compression of the cauda equina or the spinal cord may cause paresis of the lower limbs in middle life. Hydrocephalus is common. In Morquio–Brailsford disease, tetraparesis may develop as a result of atlanto-axial subluxation.

Similarly, tall stature may be a consequence of hyperpituitarism, chromosome disorder or bone disease. Neurological disorders in association with excessively tall stature are not common.

Short Stature

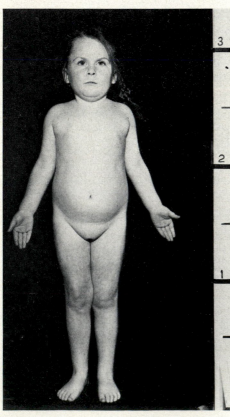

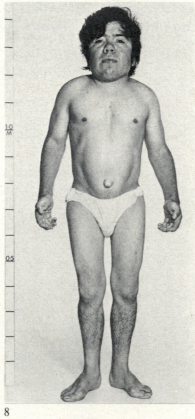

7. Craniopharyngioma
Age 6 years. Height 3 ft. 2 in. Negative family history. Birth weight 6½ lb. Apparently well, attending school, no complaints. Parents had noted lack of growth; none for 18 months. Examination: intelligent, head circumference 55 cm., slight obesity. Pale optic discs. V.A.R. 6/36, V.A.L. 6/24. Left temporal hemianopia. Skull radiographs disclosed calcified suprasellar mass. Radiographs of wrist revealed a bone age of 3 years. Craniotomy: large 6 cm. × 6 cm. cystic craniopharyngioma. Failure of growth is a very uncommon presenting symptom in craniopharyngioma.

8. Hurler's syndrome
Male, aged 20 years. Dwarfism with large head, saddle nose, thick lips and gaping nostrils. Short neck, broad hands with clawed and spatulate fingers. General restriction of joint movements. Protuberant abdomen with umbilical hernia. Mental retardation. This patient has had bilateral papilloedema for at least 2 years. No other neurological abnormality. This is a rare occurrence in Hurler's syndrome and is sometimes associated with hydrocephalus. Air studies not undertaken. (Courtesy of Dr. P. S. Harper.)

7

8

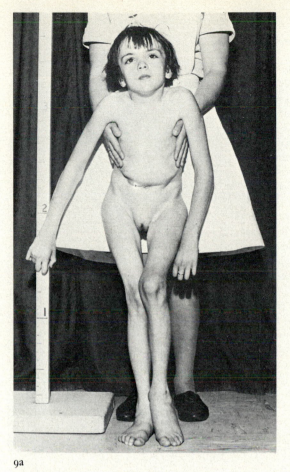

9a

9. Morquio–Brailsford syndrome with spastic tetraparesis

Age 14 years. Progressive paresis of 2 years' duration. (*a*) Short stature, short neck, normal head. No hepatosplenomegaly. Gross spastic tetraparesis with hyperactive reflexes and bilateral extensor plantar responses. Vibration lost up to C.3; distal superficial sensory impairment. Note short spine, long limbs and hip deformity. (*b*) Platyspondyly with anterior beaking of the bodies of the vertebrae. (*c*) and (*d*) Cervical spine in extension and flexion, showing dislocation of C.1 on C.2 and abnormal shape of the bodies of the vertebrae. (Courtesy of Dr. J. G. Graham.)

Short Stature

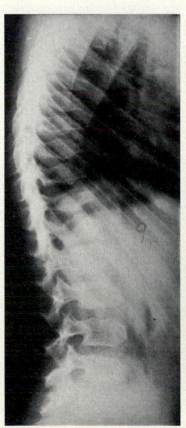

9b

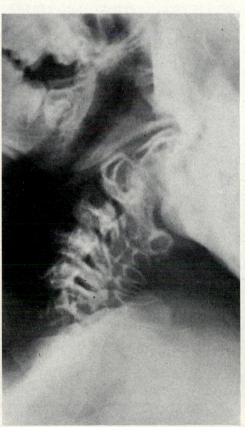

9c

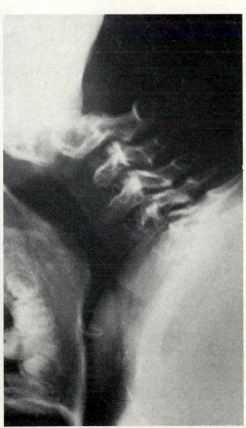

9d

Short Stature

10. Achondroplasia; bilateral foot drop

Age 37 years. Height 4 ft. 5 in. Head circumference 24 in. No family history of dwarfism. Two years' history of sciatica with bilateral foot drop, absent right knee jerk, absent ankle jerks. L.4–S.1 sensory impairment bilaterally. Lumbar puncture: manometric block, CSF protein 575 mg./100 ml. Cisternal air encephalography showed general ventricular dilatation. Radiology of spine showed dorsolumbar kyphosis, concave posterior surfaces of the bodies of the vertebrae, with arrest of *Myodil* opposite disc spaces; partial block at L.4, complete block at L.3. Laminectomy disclosed a narrow spinal canal with multiple disc protrusions and cauda equina compression. Moderate improvement in the right leg. Ten years later still severely disabled but able to walk about house unaided.

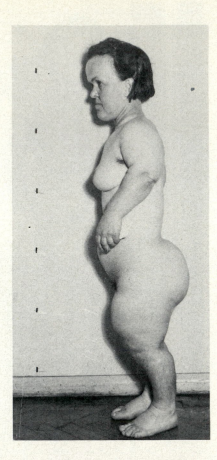

Tall Stature

11. Klinefelter's syndrome

Age 25 years. In maximum security hospital for 6 years. Originally suspected of having temporal lobe epilepsy, but later proved to be a case of schizophrenia. Height 6 ft. 4 in.; hypogonadism. Neurological examination negative. Chromosomes: chromatin positive, 47 XXY.

12. Marfan's syndrome

Age 15 years. Positive family history. Height 6 ft. 4 in., long extremities, high arched palate, pectus excavatum (partially corrected by surgery), kyphoscoliosis, bilateral iridodonesis due to subluxation of lens. Arachnodactyly, muscular weakness and hypotonia. Pansystolic murmur but no aortic dilatation. The neurological complications in this disorder usually result from aortic dissection with cerebral and spinal cord vascular syndromes. Convulsions may occur. In childhood, muscular dystrophy may be suspected because of muscular hypoplasia and weakness. (Courtesy of Dr. P. S. Harper.)

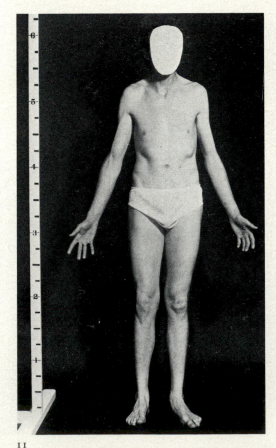

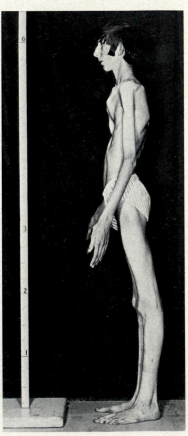

11   12

3 THE HEAD AND NECK

The Face and Head

'Of all the branches of political economy' wrote Hazlitt, 'the human face is perhaps the best criterion of value.' The physician instinctively examines his patient's face when they first meet and he continues to observe it while taking the history. Formal examination of the face and scalp may follow when necessary. Signs of many types of disorder may be seen and some are of particular interest to the neurologist. They may point the way to a correct diagnosis when the complaints of the patient are vague or the routine examination by the clinician is not illuminating. A disorder may be recognized rather than diagnosed—as for example in Parkinsonism and myxoedema.

Some signs are congenital in nature as in oxycephaly, craniovertebral anomalies and in the Klippel–Feil syn-drome. These are skeletal abnormalities which alter the contour of the head and neck. The skull may also alter in shape as a result of disease, as in osteitis deformans (Paget's disease). The facial bones and soft tissues change in acromegaly. The facial skin may be marked by a rash as in adenoma sebaceum (epiloia) or naevus as in the Sturge–Weber syndrome.

Particularly important are the hyperostoses of the skull in meningiomas. The thickening of a supra-orbital ridge, the bulge of a temple or local prominence on the vertex of the skull may indicate diagnosis at a stage when other signs are still absent and the prospects of surgical treatment are better.

Facial expression should be noted. We have, for example, the alertness and anxiety of the patient with

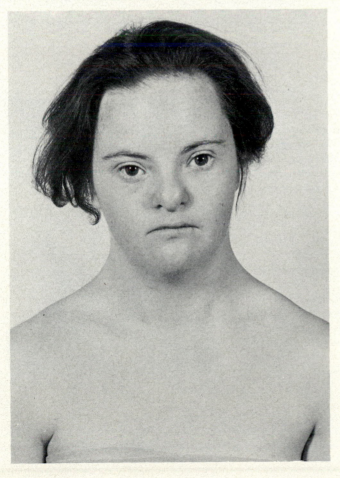

The Facial Appearance

13. Down's syndrome (mongolism) Age 22. Transient attacks of loss of consciousness, usually without falling; no convulsion; sudden pallor and loss of awareness. E.E.G. normal. Exertional dyspnoea; systolic ejection murmur with splitting of second sound in pulmonary area. E.C.G.: left axis deviation, Wolff–Parkinson–White syndrome. Probably small atrioventricular defect. Chromosomes: 47, trisomy 21. Congenital cardiac defects are not uncommon in Down's syndrome, and these attacks were probably syncopal and not epileptic. Note webbing of neck.

neurosis or thyrotoxicosis; the sad, quiet face of depression; the flat dullness of the myopathic facies; the immobile yet anxious face in Parkinsonism; the euphoria of multiple sclerosis; the emotional lability in cerebral arteriosclerosis; the weak look in general paresis; the foolish face and the fatuous remarks in frontal lobe tumour; the puzzled, lost look of the dementing individual and the insane expression in advanced dementia. These diseases do not of course always leave their mark on the human face. The patient with multiple sclerosis may be worried and depressed; Parkinsonism may spare the face (Parkinson did not record any facial abnormality in his original description of the disease); and depression may be very difficult to identify. It is surprising how often in dementia from cerebral atrophy the face looks normal and the body remains lively. In some cases of this disorder one has the impression that the body is unusually preserved.

In describing a pain not only the words but the patient's facial expression should be noted. In the case of chronic headache or facial pain, there are usually no signs to be discovered. Much depends on the interpretation of the complaints. The eagerness of the neurotic patient, determined that you appreciate the intolerable nature of the suffering, is characteristic. The 'agony, even now doctor' is not mirrored in the face. On the other hand, the fear of the patient with trigeminal neuralgia, dreading the next attack, is there to be seen.

The student should note and record the mood of a patient. There are degrees of anxiety and depression and the English language is rich in adjectives which he can use to convey his impression. In grading anxiety he can choose from the following scale: nonchalant, calm, composed, uneasy, fretful, tense, apprehensive, tremulous, agitated, panicky and terrified. Some features of anxiety may be observed such as impaired concentration, distractability, fidgeting, muscular tension, tremor, speed of movement, flushing, sweating, dry mouth, rapid breathing and pulse rate. Between black melancholy and maniacal excitement there is a continuum of mood: hopeless, despondent, disconsolate, dejected, gloomy, solemn, serious, placid, cheerful, buoyant, elated and euphoric. (The poet Thomas Gray used to refer to his 'leucocholy', his natural melancholy.)

Hyperostosis in Meningioma

The peculiar tendency of certain meningiomas to cause thickening of the overlying calvarium has been known for many years. The hyperostosis may be diffuse or nodal. It is not necessarily confined to one bone and the suture lines of the skull do not act as a limiting boundary. Cushing and Eisenhardt, in their

The Facial Appearance

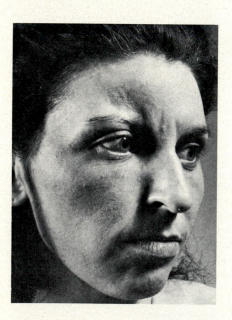

14. Scleroderma ◁
Localized scleroderma giving the *coup de sabre* appearance on the forehead. The scar had been present since the age of 12 and there was recent epilepsy and memory deterioration. Clinical examination, air encephalography and carotid arteriography were normal.

15. Subacute combined degeneration of the spinal cord ▷
An old clinical impression is that pernicious anaemia is prone to affect blue-eyed persons whose hair has turned prematurely grey. It must be admitted that this is rare, but in this particular case the appearance suggested the diagnosis.

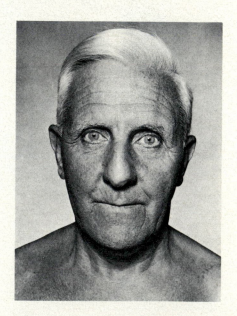

classical monograph on the meningiomas, divided the reactions of bone into eight varieties [FIG. 40]. In the first variety there is merely increased vascularity of the overlying bone. In the second the bone is thinned slightly by tumour pressure. In the third variety there is a slight endostosis. In the fourth variety there is a palpable swelling of the outer table of the skull. In the fifth variety there is an ivory mound of bone produced by the *en plaque* tumour. The outward appearance is quite similar in the sixth variety; the diploë are widened. In the seventh variety the tumour extends extracranially. In the rare eighth variety a core of tumour extends into the hyperostosis.

Naturally these types of bone reaction can be detected earlier and studied more accurately by the radiologist. They are important to the clinician because they may point to the diagnosis at a stage when symptoms are few and slight. The only symptom of a convexity meningioma might be a tendency to somnolence. This may be followed by a simple dementing process without focal symptoms or signs. In pterion and sphenoidal ridge meningiomas, headache may be slight indeed. Discomfort around one eye and puffiness of the eyelid may be the first manifestations. Ptosis, diplopia and proptosis follow. The resulting ocular asymmetry is accentuated by temporal or supra-orbital thickness which may be seen and felt. Writing of the pterion *en plaque* tumours, Cushing wrote 'from case to case, they are surprisingly alike—possibly more alike than are the members of any other single group of meningiomas, not excepting the suprasellar lesions'. The patient is nearly always a woman.

The Facial Appearance

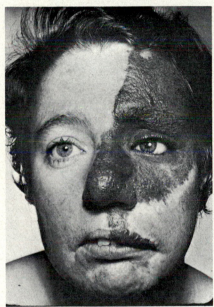

16a

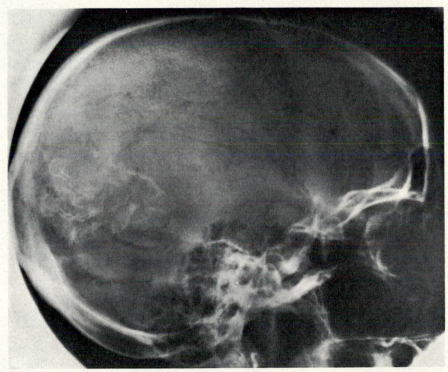

16b

16. Sturge–Weber syndrome

Facial naevus, epilepsy and intracranial calcification. The cutaneous vascular naevus or 'port wine stain' is associated with a cortical angioma—often in the occipital region. The calcification is in the cortex and not in the abnormal vessels. The cutaneous and intracranial naevi are usually on the same side. Various forms of congenital abnormality may be found in the eye of the affected side (glaucoma, strabismus, buphthalmos or ox eye, angiomata of the choroid).

(*a*) In this patient the left eye was removed in childhood, probably because of buphthalmos.

(*b*) Note characteristic intracranial calcification in parieto-occipital region (L); convolutional calcification with double contours. Arteriography failed to reveal any intracranial angioma.

The Facial Appearance

17. Left frontal mucocele
Six weeks' history of pain in the left eyeball associated with ptosis and diplopia. Marked depression of the left eyeball with partial left third nerve palsy, absent corneal reflex, and trigeminal sensory impairment in the first division territory. Radiographs showed loss of the superior orbital margin and a translucency in the left frontal sinus. At operation there was a large left frontal mucocele. (Courtesy of Dr. J. G. Graham.)

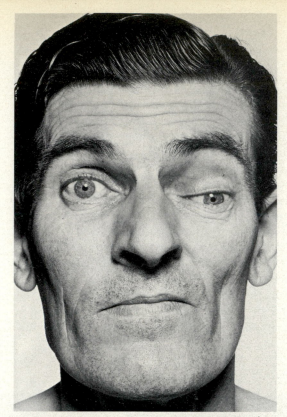

18. Idiopathic gustatory sweating
A wide variety of foodstuffs have been incriminated in gustatory sweating: chocolate, cheese, alcohol and pickles are commonly mentioned. In this case strong cheese was the chief culprit and had to be avoided. Migraine can also be provoked by such foods as cheese and chocolate, but this appears to be the result of absorption of tyramine. This is not the case in gustatory sweating, where there is no evidence that the condition is due to the absorption of any pharmacologically active substance. In diabetics, gustatory sweating seems to be a manifestation of autonomic neuropathy. Brown-Séquard suffered from chocolate-induced gustatory facial sweating.

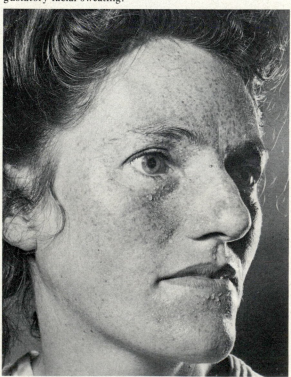

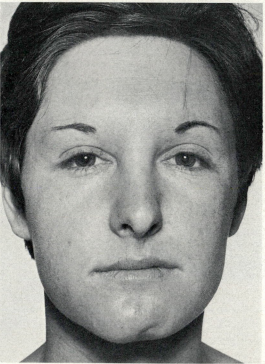

19. Early progressive facial hemiatrophy
Age 26. A dimple appeared on her chin 3 years previously. It has enlarged and is now a small cleft just to the left of the midline. Another cleft is appearing to the left of the philtrum and she thinks her left upper lip is shrinking. She has pain and paraesthesiae in the cheek. This is her main complaint. No sensory loss, but slight pigmentation over the left cheek. Radiographs and E.E.G. were normal.

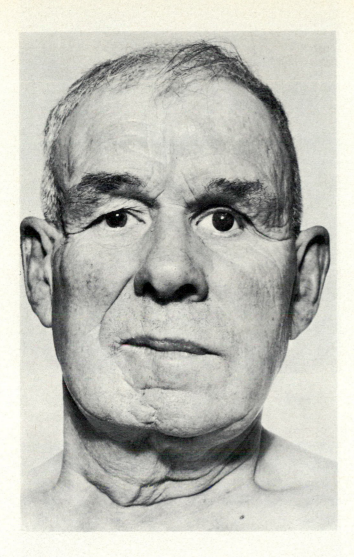

The Facial Appearance

20. Facial hemiatrophy ◁
Age 66. This man thought that a deepening hollow in his right temple had resulted from a trivial injury. There was diffuse right facial hemiatrophy. Air encephalography showed quite gross but symmetrical cerebral atrophy. This is a so-called trophic disorder of unknown causation, in which there is progressive wasting of the tissues on one side of the face. Skin, subcutaneous tissues, muscles and bone may all be involved. Trigeminal neuralgia may occur but facial movements remain relatively unaffected. It may coexist with scleroderma elsewhere in the body.

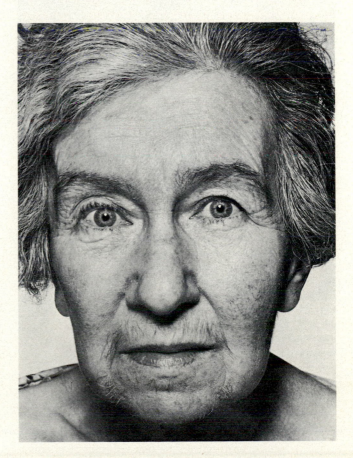

The Facial Expression

21. Early Parkinsonism ▷
This lady complained of a painful left 'frozen' shoulder. Clumsiness of the left arm was attributed to limitation of movement at this joint. But there was periodic tremor of the fingers, cogwheel rigidity at the wrist and a facial expression characteristic of Parkinsonism. James Parkinson (1755–1824), a London practitioner, did not describe the characteristic facies or 'mask' which has become associated with his name.

*The Facial
Expression*

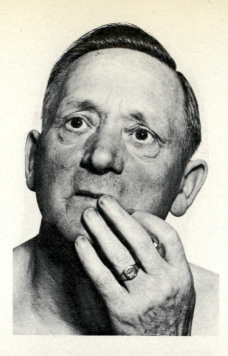

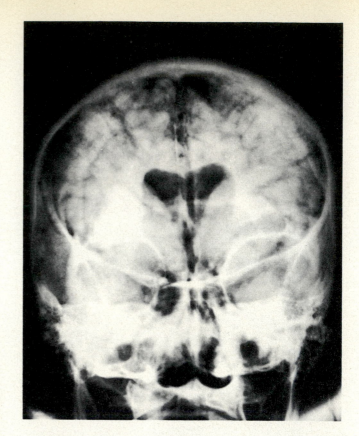

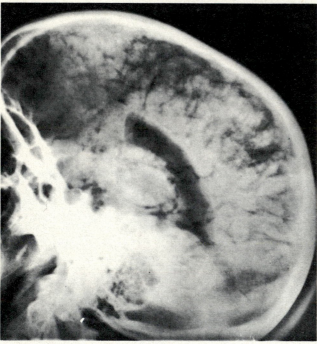

22. Organic dementia due to cerebral atrophy △
Impairment of cerebration and loss of recent memory. Quiet, pleasant, tidy and outwardly alert. Good physical condition. No abnormal neurological signs but psychometry revealed considerable intellectual loss and air encephalography demonstrated dilated ventricles and convolutional atrophy. His puzzled and vacant look when given simple tests is illustrated.

23. Presenile dementia ▷
Increasingly slovenly in dress and habits. Somnolent by day, dysarthric and disoriented for time and place. Hopelessly demented.

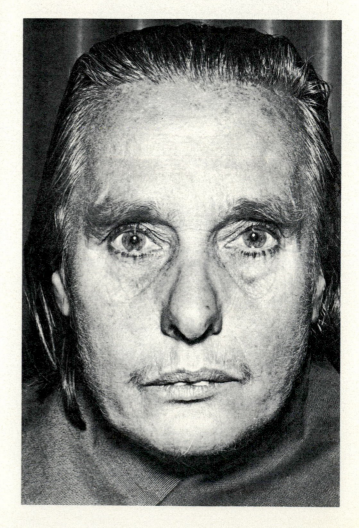

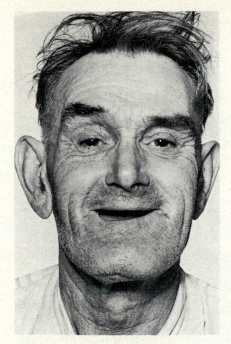

24. Right frontal lobe glioma
Failing at his work and admitting only to
mild headache. Completely lacking in
insight, for ever laughing, joking and
facetious. Every morning he felt
'champion'.

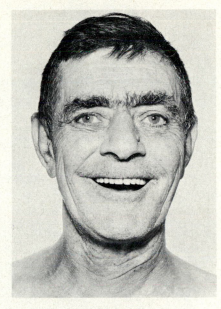

25. Right frontal lobe glioma
Two recent epileptic attacks. No complaints. 'Feeling fine' and only waiting to
get back to his work. His euphoria, according to his family, was a gross exaggeration
of a pre-existing trait.

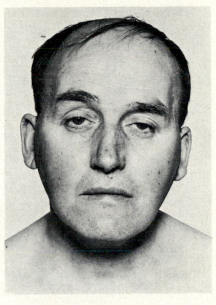

26. Myotonia atrophica
A flat, lifeless face with drooping eyelids
and sad mouth. Note the baldness.

*The Facial
Expression*

27. Emotional lability
Post-traumatic dementia. Old head injury.
Note right frontal scar and broken nose
(not an ex-boxer). A word of sympathy and
he would dissolve into tears. Recovery was
equally abrupt and he would be smiling
and wiping away his tears the next minute.

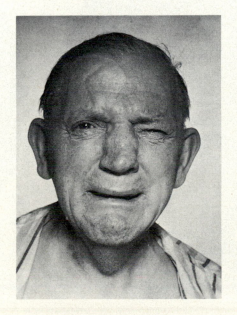

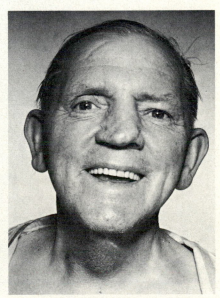

The Facial Expression

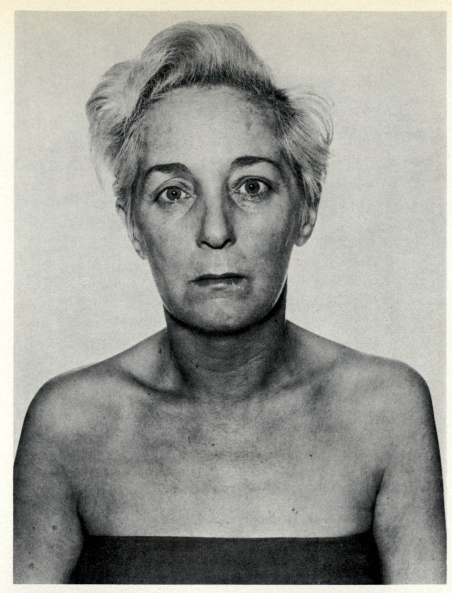

28. Thyrotoxicosis ▷
Age 40. Three-year history of lassitude, somnolence, vivid dreams and episodes of amnesia and cataplexy. Central nervous system normal apart from obvious anxiety and finger tremor. Pulse 100, raised jugular venous pressure, loud systolic ejection murmur conducted into neck. Thyroid normal. Eyes normal. B.M.R. +80. Protein-bound iodine 16·0 µg./100 ml. I^{131} uptake typical of thyrotoxicosis. Satisfactory response to treatment with carbimazole.

Neither the history nor the facial appearance suggested the correct diagnosis. The suspicion was of temporal lobe epilepsy in an unstable person.

29. Petit mal ▽
Two photographic exposures, at 4-second intervals, in the case of a boy suffering from petit mal. Note the glazed look and open mouth which altered his appearance in the second photograph.

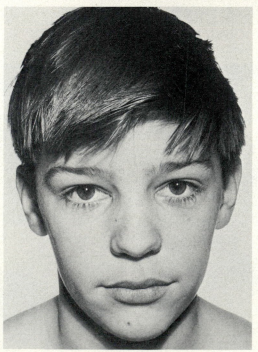 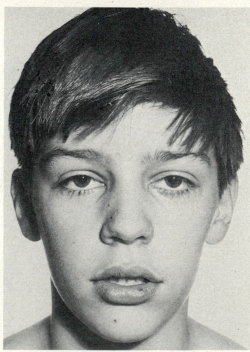

The Skull

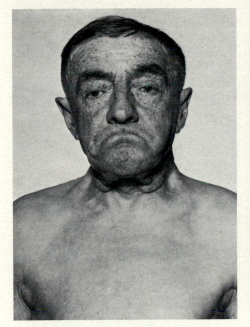

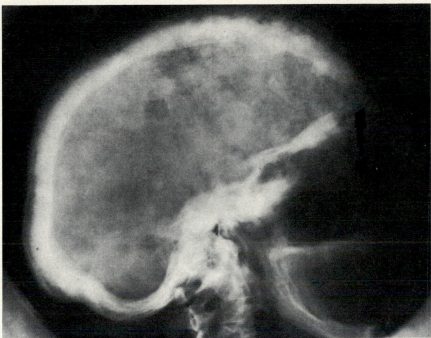

30. Osteitis deformans (Paget's disease) △

Recent onset of epilepsy and complaint of head pains. He had noted an increase in the size of his hats. Note bulging of both sides of the skull in the parietotemporal regions. The scalp felt unusually warm to the touch. Radiographs showed the thickened 'woolly' calvarium and associated basilar impression.

31. Oxycephaly (turricephaly; tower skull) ▽

A congenital abnormality of the skull due to premature synostosis of the sutures, especially the coronal. Convolutional atrophy from pressure of the growing brain may occur, as also optic atrophy. Here there was a recent onset of epilepsy. Note the flat, high forehead, the shallow orbits and the prominent right eye. There was bilateral anosmia and moderate right nerve deafness.

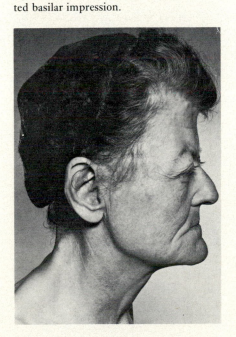

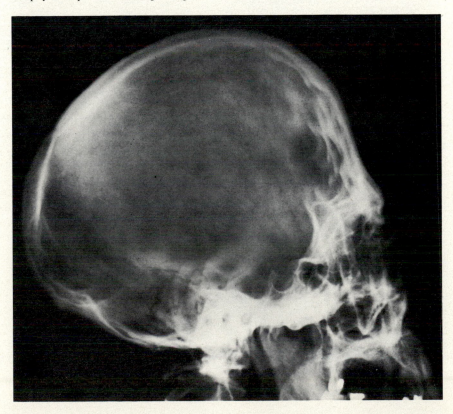

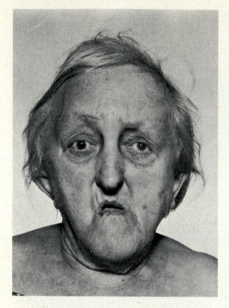

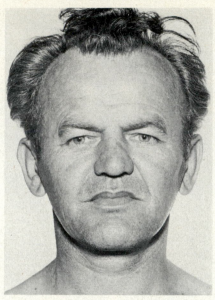

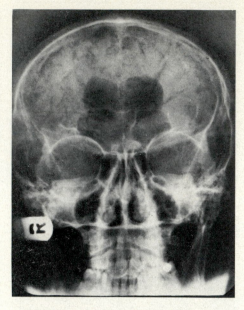

32. Osteitis deformans
Bilateral deafness and obscure head pains. Note frontal and temporal bulging. There was bilateral anosmia and a mild organic dementia.

33. Arrested hydrocephalus
Age 44, former paratrooper. One child with minor epilepsy. Five year history of headache. No relation to posture or physical activity. Sometimes associated with transient blurring of vision. Large head (circumference 61 cm.), normal optic discs and fundi, and negative neurological examination. E.E.G. normal.

Air encephalogram showed large lateral ventricles lying symmetrically; normal third and fourth ventricles and cortical sulci. Communicating hydrocephalus due either to a disturbance in the formation and absorption of cerebrospinal fluid or to an obstruction to its circulation in the subarachnoid space itself.

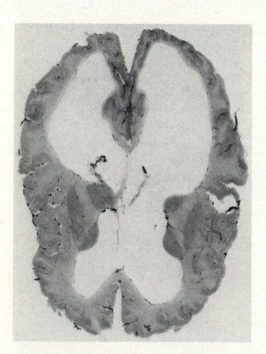

34. Congenital communicating hydrocephalus
Horizontal brain section of a patient aged 26 years who died 10 days after lumbar air encephalography. Low average intelligence, two recent major convulsions, head circumference 64 cm. Negative neurological examination. C.S.F. pressure 200 mm. The cerebral cortex at the frontal pole measured 13 mm. and at the occipital pole 18 mm. Such investigations are dangerous and can result in rapid decompensation.

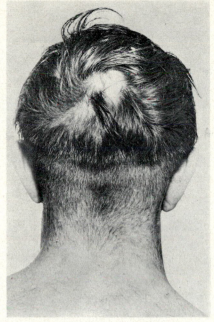

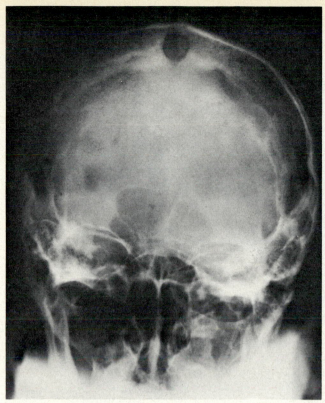

35b

35. Encephalocele △

Male, aged 35. Mental defective, ataxic since childhood. Confined to a wheelchair for 3 years. Spastic tetraparesis with coarse nystagmus and ataxic slurring dysarthria. Large head; circumference $23\frac{1}{2}$ inches.

(*a*) Encephalocele.

(*b*) Skull radiograph showing circular bone defect over lambdoid suture.

Facial and Cranial Hyperostosis

36. Right sphenoidal ridge meningioma ▽

Age 51. Trigeminal numbness and paraesthesiae of one year. Recent morning headache; temporal lobe epilepsy. Partial right third nerve palsy, absent corneal reflex, sensory impairment over the second and third divisions of the right trigeminal nerve. Right optic disc normal; field nor-

mal. Radiographs showed an enlarged right orbital fissure and erosion of the lesser wing of the sphenoid.

(*a*) Note the right ptosis and paralysis of upward gaze of the right eye. The right supra-orbital margin and adjacent frontal bone was prominent and thickened.

(*b*) Right carotid arteriogram; meningioma 'blush'.

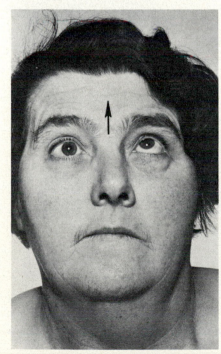

36a

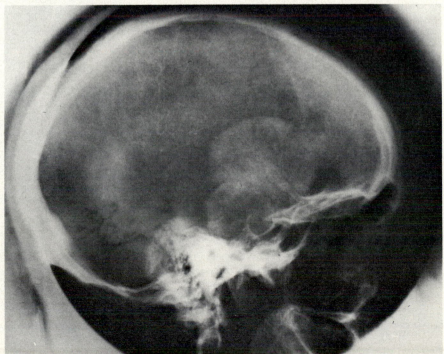

36b

Facial and Cranial Hyperostosis

37. Parasagittal meningioma
This photograph was taken in Cairo in 1942. A soldier in the 8th Army, he reported sick 'because I can't keep my forage cap on'! He was in excellent health and had no complaint of headache. There were no abnormal neurological signs, yet the extent of the slowly growing hyperostosis on his vertex may be seen. He was deemed worthy of a berth on the next hospital ship returning home.

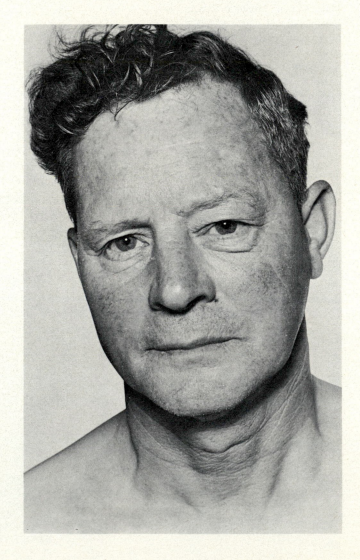

38. Left frontal meningioma
Age 53. Eighteen month history of drooping left upper eyelid, blurring of vision on the left and diplopia. Note the ptosis, proptosis and thickening of the left supraorbital ridge and temple on the left side. Early temporal defect in the left visual field. (Courtesy of Dr. C. E. C. Wells.)

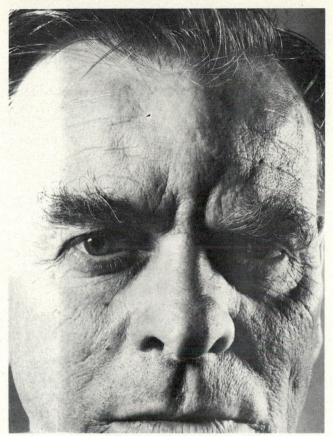

39a

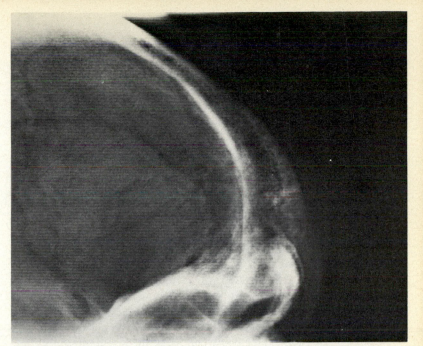

39b

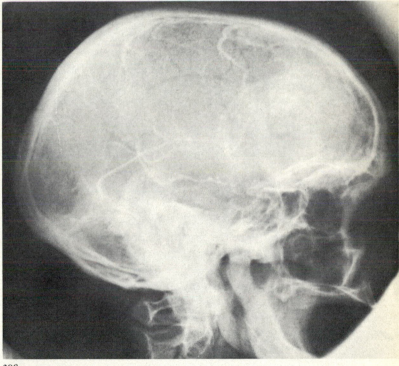

39c

39. Left frontal meningioma

Age 54. Progressive organic dementia of one year's duration. Slow, somnolent, forgetful. Driving a railway engine until 3 months previously; complained of little headache. The only abnormal neurological signs consisted of the dementia and some unsteadiness of gait. Senses of smell and vision were normal.

(*a*) and (*b*) Note the midline frontal hyperostosis.

(*c*) Left carotid arteriogram; meningioma 'blush'. (Courtesy of Dr. C. E. C. Wells.)

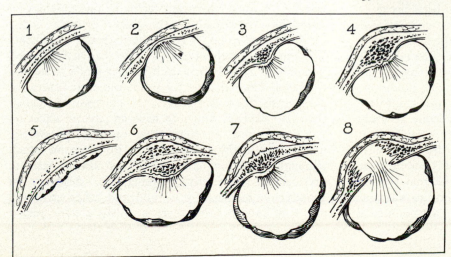

40. Cranial hyperostosis

Eight varieties of hyperostosis from meningiomas; Cushing, H. W., and Eisenhardt, L. (1938) *Meningiomas*. (Courtesy of Hafner Publishing Co. Inc., New York.)

The Neck

Visible abnormalities of the neck are uncommon, although, as in many other parts of the human body, there is a wide range of normality. In the infant the cervical spine is straight, but with growth and the full development of the intervertebral discs, which become thicker anteriorly, a lordosis appears. In middle age the cervical spine tends to become straight again, and thinning of the discs in old age may even render it kyphotic.

The movements which take place in the cervical spine are complex; mobility is dependent on the composite motion between all the vertebrae and not upon the small amount of motion which takes place between any two of them. The head and atlas move essentially as one unit on the axis in rotation and lateral flexion. In nodding movements of the head most of the motion occurs at the atlanto-occipital joints. Generally speaking, stresses and strains are probably greatest in the lower parts of the cervical spine. The greater part of rotation occurs at the junction between the first and second cervical vertebrae.

Cervical Spondylosis

In spondylosis, which is the commonest lesion of the cervical spine, the outward appearance of the neck is usually normal. Restriction of the range of movement of the neck is no guide to the degree of disc degeneration. The degree of radiographic abnormality in the cervical spine is no indication of disability. Some elderly people with gross spondylotic changes have no complaints; others with persistent pain and stiffness may show only slight changes.

The so-called 'whiplash' injury of the cervical spine has achieved for itself a status in medico-legal circles as popular as the 'strained back', the 'post-concussional syndrome', and the 'railroad spine' of the last century.

In a condition which is so common, it is very difficult to be sure what part cervical spondylosis plays in the production of symptoms such as headache, giddiness, vertebrobasilar ischaemia and drop attacks. Some clinicians believe that spondylotic headache presents quite distinctive features; it is usually occipital and spreading to the forehead or eye on the same side, nagging or wearing in character, not throbbing or bursting. Pain in the arm on the same side may accompany the headache, the two pains tending to wax and wane together. Movement and posture may influence

both. The causation of such headache remains obscure. Pressure on posterior nerve roots is unlikely, because sensory impairment on the scalp is exceptional and because it would not explain pain in the forehead and eye.

Analysis of the origin of vertigo in cervical spondylosis is equally difficult. In many forms of vertigo, posture can be influential; the patient's account, as such, does little to help the examiner locate the cause of the vertigo. In spondylosis it is usually provoked by head movement and conceivably could result from interference with the circulation in the vertebrobasilar system consequent on compression or stretching of the vertebral arteries which, in this age group, may be hardened, kinked and more tortuous. Neck movements may have been noted to trigger off transient episodes of unsteadiness, hemiparesis, dysphasia, diplopia, loss of vision or hemianopia. These episodes are clearly ischaemic in nature and it is likely that vertigo is due to ischaemia of the brain stem or cerebellum. Equally, vertigo initiated by movement of the head may arise in the labyrinth. Passive rotation of the head, with the patient in a supine posture, is the usual way of eliciting positional vertigo and nystagmus. However, this movement also distorts the vertebral and carotid arteries in the neck, and therefore circulatory effects should be excluded by rotating the patient in such a way that the position of the head relative to the shoulders remains constant. A person over 55 with postural vertigo and deafness is also likely to have cervical spondylosis, but labyrinthine ischaemia can then scarcely be attributed to the spondylosis.

In the aetiology of spondylotic myelopathy, compression of the spinal cord by osteophytes and bars is often considered an unsatisfactory explanation because of the lack of correlation between the severity of the spondylosis and the severity of the paraparesis, the infrequency of manometric block and the frequently disappointing results of surgery. Interference with the blood supply to the cord, and the effects of subluxation and of hypertrophy of the ligamentum flavum, have also been invoked. A most important factor in the aetiology of spondylotic myelopathy is the sagittal diameter of the cervical spinal canal. It is usually narrower in patients with cervical spondylotic myelopathy than in the general population. Spondylosis itself further tends to narrow the canal. The narrower the canal, the more severe the paraparesis that ensues. Also, the narrower the canal, the more likely is injury to have an adverse effect on the spinal cord. It seems that cervical spondylotic myelopathy is always associated with a narrow canal, although a narrow canal does not always lead to myelopathy. Generally speaking, the disability in spondylotic myelopathy is mild and, after an initial period of deterioration, there is usually a static period lasting for a number of years. In old age there is a tendency to a progression of symptoms. Surgical treatment should be reserved for patients whose disability is progressing.

If a fall or an accident causes an unexpected paraparesis, one is likely to find one of the following: cervical spondylosis, a narrow cervical spinal canal, fused cervical vertebrae or some craniovertebral anomaly. I have not seen a cervical spine with a canal narrower than 10 mm. in anteroposterior diameter. In 70 per cent. of adults it is between 16 mm. and 19 mm.

Another aspect of cervical spondylosis needs mention. Radiculopathy and myelopathy are the usual forms of neurological presentation. The symptoms and signs are those of a cervicobrachial neuritis and a paraparesis, singly or in combination or sequence. But there is a small group of patients, usually elderly, who complain of numb, useless hands and fingers. No pain, no lower limb complaints. They say 'Look, my hands are not weak, I can clench my fists, I can carry things, I can lift things, but I have lost the feeling in my fingers and hands, I can't handle small things or pick them up, I drop them, I fumble'. Unpleasant sensations in the hands accompany their disability and many of these patients are tormented and lose sleep. Dressing, shaving, cooking, writing and a hundred and one little activities become a source of complaint and distress. Inability to use toilet paper is particularly unpleasant. On examination the hands are found to be fairly strong, there is usually no muscular wasting, reflexes are brisk and superficial forms of sensation are largely preserved, but during the examination the observer may think that the patient is restless and fidgety because the fingers move erratically. When the patient's eyes are closed, the fingers are seen to wander in a writhing manner—'pseudo-athetosis' or 'sensory wandering' [FIGS. 41a and 373]. The sensory loss is practically confined to the modalities of posture and vibration, and objects placed in the hand cannot be identified by touch. These elderly people, with bilateral astereognosis, always have marked cervical spondylosis and I suspect that here again the narrowness of the canal is the crucial factor. Certainly, most of them have narrow canals. Varying degrees of subluxation and posterior compression from a thickened ligamentum flavum probably contribute to interference with the posterior root entry zones. Nerve conduction rates are normal. Decompressive laminectomy helps some; carpal tunnel surgery does not. Steroids fail.

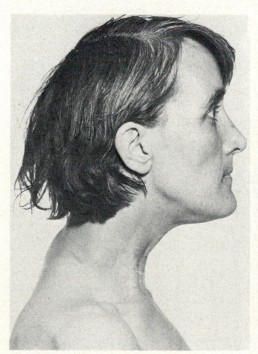
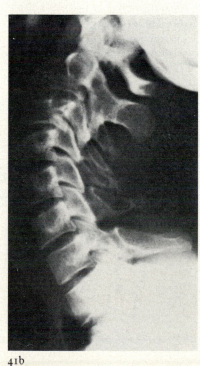

41a
41b

41. Spinal subluxation, C.3–4

(*a*) Age 38. Following partial thyroidectomy for a non-toxic nodular goitre 4 years previously, she noticed increasing numbness and clumsiness of the fingers and hands. Pseudo-athetosis; superficial sensation normal; postural sense absent in fingers, retained at wrist; vibration sense absent to wrists. She subsequently developed bilateral extensor plantar reflexes with characteristic pyramidal signs in lower limbs. Note posture of head and neck.

(*b*) Radiography showed subluxation of C.3 on C.4 in extension. Myelography showed almost complete obstruction at C.3–4 on extension. Radiographs of her neck taken before her thyroidectomy were inspected and these showed that the subluxation was already present. Her first symptoms followed this operation and began while she was still in hospital.

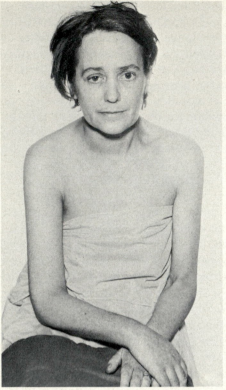

42a

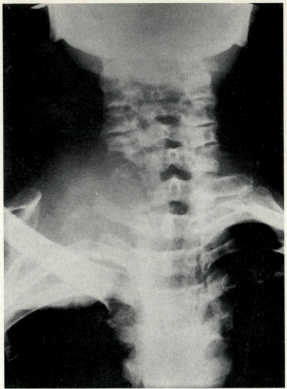

42b

42. Right apical pulmonary carcinoma (Pancoast's tumour or superior sulcus tumour)

(*a*) Age 45. Nine months' history of pain, weakness and numbness of the right hand and forearm. Loss of weight, 3 stone. The pain in the fingers and the palm of the hand was exceptionally severe, burning in character, and unrelieved by ordinary analgesics. Note the right Horner syndrome, the swelling at the root of the neck on the right side, the puffiness of the dorsum of the weak right hand and the ill appearance of the patient. The mass in the right supraclavicular fossa could be felt, the trachea was central, the breasts were normal. Reflexes in the weak and numb upper limb were retained and there was diffuse hyperalgesia of the right hand; appreciation of touch, vibration and posture was retained.

(*b*) Radiography revealed gross bony destruction in the root of the neck involving the lower cervical vertebrae, the clavicle and the upper ribs.

Cervical Spinal Canal

43. Sagittal diameter of the cervical spinal canal

(*a*) In 70 per cent of adults this measurement is between 16 and 19 mm., but it may vary from 12 to 22 mm. (*b*) The upper and lower limits of the normal variation can be depicted on a graph. The black line shows the diameter in the case shown in Fig. 44.

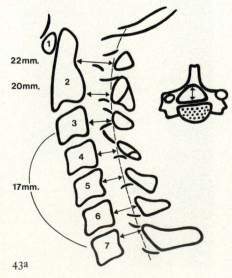

43a

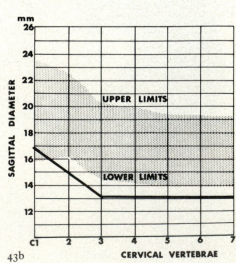

43b

Cervical Spinal Canal

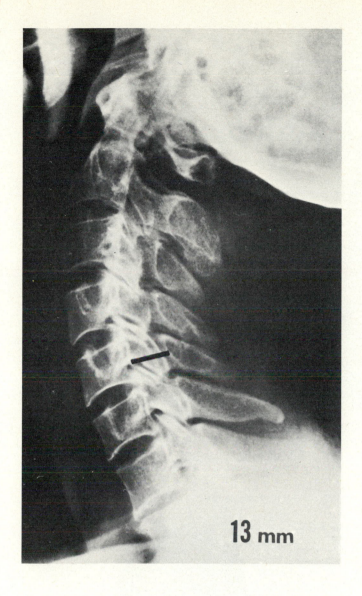

13 mm

44. Acute spastic tetraparesis
Male aged 54 was heaving a bag of cement on to a truck and experienced a sudden 'electric-shock-like' sensation through his limbs. 'Paralysis'. Hospital admission 2 weeks later revealed a moderate spastic tetraparesis. Radiograph of cervical spine: no spondylosis; sagittal diameter 13 mm. CSF protein 70. Manometry normal in the neutral position but with a block when the neck was extended. Myelography showed partial block at C.5–6. Posterior decompressive laminectomy revealed a disc protrusion at C.5–6. Recovery was slow and incomplete.

Torticollis

Twisting, tilting or rotation of the neck to one side, 'wry neck', may be due to various conditions. It may be congenital or acquired, spasmodic or continuous.

There are two types of congenital torticollis: (1) that due to a developmental bony abnormality, such as fusion of the atlas and the occipital bone, fusion of the atlas with the axis or wedge-shaped malformations of the cervical vertebrae. This is sometimes referred to as 'bony torticollis'. It is usually symptomless but bouts of pain and stiffness of the neck are not uncommon and may be precipitated by injury. (2) A commoner type in which there is a congenital contracture of the sternomastoid muscle, usually on the right side. It is prenatal and analogous to congenital talipes and congenital elevation of the scapula. The abnormal muscle may rupture during birth but the haematoma which forms is not responsible for the actual torticollis. Facial asymmetry is commonly associated.

Torticollis

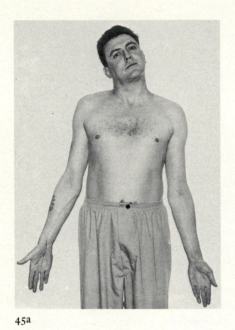

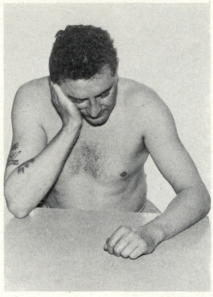

45a

45b

45. Torticollis and right ulnar palsy ◁
(*a*) Age 40. Accountant with torticollis of
7 years' duration. Recent numbness of
inner border of right hand and forearm
with clumsiness of fourth and fifth fingers.
Area of objective sensory impairment
suggested diagnosis of cervical neurofibroma (C.8), but investigations were
negative. Nerve conduction studies showed
that the numbness in the right hand was
due to an ulnar nerve lesion at the right
elbow.
(*b*) Explanation: to keep his head still
as he sat at his desk, he learned to write
with his left hand while supporting his
head with his right hand, with resultant
compression of the ulnar nerve at the
elbow. The upper limit of sensory loss
subsequently proved to be at the wrist.

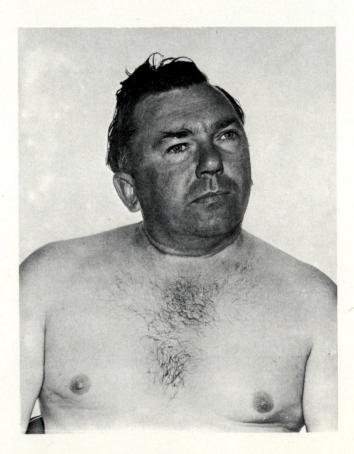

46. Congenital wry neck
Prenatal lesion of right sternomastoid
muscle; contracture; head turned to left.
Note smaller right palpebral fissure.

Torticollis

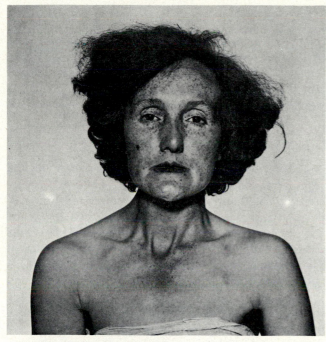

47. Congenital bony torticollis
Slight tilt of the head to the left in association with basilar impression and fusion of the first and second cervical vertebrae. Pain, stiffness of neck and shoulders with periodic numbness of fingers.

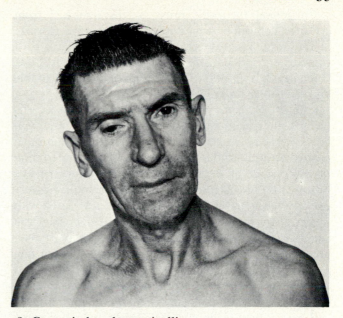

48. Congenital ocular torticollis
Congenital paresis of right extra-ocular muscles with resulting diplopia. This was avoided by the adoption of a compensatory head posture which minimized the movements called for from the affected muscles. Note squint and ptosis on the right.

49. Spasmodic hysterical torticollis
Immature, anxious individual with neurotic attitudes. Persistent torticollis resistant to psychotherapy and narcosis. (Courtesy of Dr. J. P. Spillane.)

Congenital torticollis must be distinguished from acquired conditions which disturb the normal carriage of the head, such as cerebellar tumour, cervical cord tumour or various affections of the cervical spine. Occasionally a tilt of the head is adopted to avoid double vision—ocular torticollis.

One of the commonest varieties of acquired torticollis is the spasmodic type. Clonic or tonic contraction of the cervical muscles is responsible for the abnormal rotated attitude of the head. It may be a manifestation of hysteria or of organic neurological disorder. The posture may be sustained or intermittent. In the hysterical variety the onset is often acute and associated with recent anxiety or some form of mental distress. Firm suggestion is more likely to reduce the jerking movement temporarily in the hysterical variety. When torticollis develops insidiously over a period of years, it is usually a manifestation of progressive dystonia (torsion spasm). The movements may be tonic or clonic, or both, and may spread to involve one upper limb. For many years the movements are noticed only by the patient, emotion, observation or fatigue aggravating them. Relief is often obtained by a finger placed against the chin. So far as I know they subside in sleep. The degree of discomfort or torment experienced varies considerably; some patients describe much pain, while others are only embarrassed by the movement. Hypertrophy of a sternomastoid muscle is common. The responsible lesion in this organic type of spasmodic torticollis is not known, but there are presumed to be degenerative changes in the basal ganglia. Other members of the family and relatives may exhibit tremor, nodding movements of the head or various signs of mild ataxia.

Lastly it should be remembered that the phenothiazines may be responsible for the acute development of dystonic movements about the face and neck. I have seen torticollis in a boy of 10 who had swallowed a dozen tablets of trifluoperazine (*Stelazine*) over a weekend and which he had found under his mother's pillow.

Craniovertebral Anomalies

Various forms of anomalous development at the craniovertebral junction and in the neck have been described. The abnormality may be a simple and unimportant one such as lack of fusion of the posterior arch of the atlas, or gross and extensive, affecting bony and nervous tissues. Disability, however, is not solely a reflection of the grossness of the malformation. Some individuals with extensive derangement at the craniovertebral junction and pronounced visible deformity may pursue their lives with little or no difficulty. In other cases, with a normal configuration and seemingly moderate disturbance of skeletal structures, disability may be progressive and reach serious proportions. A further puzzling feature of these disorders is that neurological

Torticollis

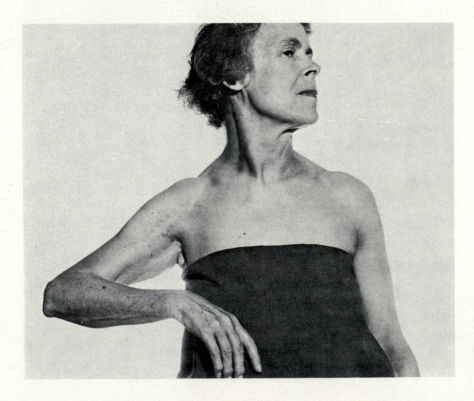

50. **Spasmodic torticollis (dystonia)** Spasmodic turning of head to left with spasmodic contraction of right deltoid muscle. The movements were part of a developing torsion dystonia. Note hypertrophied right sternomastoid muscle. Surgical scar from excision of head of the humerus—before correct diagnosis was established.

complications may not make their appearance until adult life; this in turn may lead to incorrect diagnosis. Finally, it is sometimes only at operation that the pathological explanation for the dominant symptoms and signs is revealed. Thus a syringomyelic syndrome in a patient with a skeletal anomaly at the craniovertebral junction, may result from intramedullary cavitation (representing true syringomyelia, hydromyelia, or ischaemic necrosis) or from compression of the neuraxis (by a stenosed foramen magnum, a displaced odontoid process, a dural band or by cerebellar herniation).

The outward appearance is often quite normal but an unusual posture of the head, an abnormal configuration or restricted mobility of the neck, or an altered position of the hair line, may suggest an underlying malformation. If the neck is grossly short then the probability is that several of the cervical vertebrae are fused (Klippel-Feil syndrome). Otherwise an abnormally short neck cannot be correlated with any specific type of craniovertebral anomaly. Occipitalization of the atlas nearly always alters the outward appearance. A low hairline is not a sign of much value. In the majority of cases it is a clinical corollary of a short neck and does not actually represent an extension of the hair-producing properties of the scalp to the posterior parts of the upper cervical dermatomes. A small tuft of hair in the midline, somewhere down the back of the neck, should raise the possibility of an underlying spina bifida.

Webbing of the neck is occasionally seen in craniovertebral anomalies. The term has been used to indicate either a thin sheet of soft tissue stretched between the region of the mastoid and the shoulder, or alternatively to describe the triangular appearance of the neck resulting from abnormal splaying of the upper fibres of the trapezius muscles. I have never seen webbing of the first type in craniovertebral anomalies, but abnormal splaying of the trapezii is not uncommon. Other associated stigmata are facial asymmetry, malformation of the ears, abnormalities of the palate, congenital absence of thenar muscles or of digits.

In platybasia there is an increase of the basal angle of the skull which is made by the intersection of the plane of the sphenoid and the plane of the clivus. It has no known clinical significance but may be associated with basilar impression.

In basilar impression the bones surrounding the foramen magnum are invaginated into the cranial cavity resulting in deformity of the contents of the posterior fossa. Basilar impression may be congenital or result from bony disease, such as osteomalacia, rickets or Paget's disease.

Occipitalization of the atlas, chronic atlanto-axial dislocation, or a separate odontoid process are all relatively rare anomalies which may be found with or without basilar impression.

In Klippel and Feil's (1912) original patient there

Craniovertebral Anomalies

51. Ovarian agenesis; Turner's syndrome
Ovarian maldevelopment; shortness of stature, webbing of neck, cubitus valgus and coarctation of the aorta. Usually presents after puberty with primary amenorrhoea. In 80 per cent. there is a chromatin-negative nuclear sex, an XO instead of an XX sex chromosomal complement and only 45 chromosomes per cell.

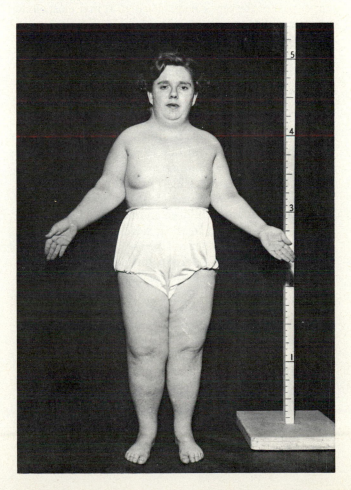

were only four cervical vertebrae fused into a single column of bone but the term is now used to describe any congenital fusion or reduction of the cervical vertebrae producing a shortening of the neck. The classical symptoms described by Klippel and Feil were: (1) shortening of the neck; (2) lowering of the hairline; and (3) limitation of motion of the neck. The Klippel–Feil syndrome is frequently associated with other congenital anomalies of the spine and other portions of the skeleton, and in some cases with neurological disturbances. Serious involvement of the medulla or cervical cord is probably almost always due to the presence of anomalies at the craniovertebral junction. Congenital fusion of cervical vertebrae may be symptomless until the patient sustains an injury and suffers pain in the neck and one or both upper limbs. In children syncopal attacks caused by a sudden movement of the neck are occasionally encountered. A curious and annoying abnormality is mirror movements of the upper limbs in an otherwise harmless Klippel–Feil malformation. It is usually noticed by parent or teacher when the child is writing. Mirror movements in an adult are rarely troublesome but such activities as riding a bicycle or climbing a ladder can be hazardous.

The Arnold–Chiari malformation is a congenital anomaly of the hindbrain. There is herniation of the tonsils of the cerebellum and the distal portion of the medulla through the foramen magnum and into the upper part of the cervical spinal canal. It may exist alone or it may be associated with skeletal craniovertebral anomalies or with various forms of spina bifida. It is a frequent and important malformation in infants with hydrocephalus and spina bifida. In the adult the malformation may lead to compression of the upper cervical spinal cord and mimic a tumour. This type (Chiari type 1) may be present when there is no outward abnormality of the neck and where the routine X-rays are normal. It is often said that Arnold described the cerebellar and Chiari the medullary components of the malformation. This is not true. It was Chiari of Prague, in 1891, who described in great detail the many features of this malformation in infants, children and adults. The paper by Arnold of Heidelberg, in 1894, was based solely on one autopsy and did not refer to Chiari's original work. The term 'the Arnold–Chiari malformation' was subsequently coined by two pupils of Arnold, Schwalbe and Gredig, in 1907.

The neurological syndromes associated with these craniovertebral anomalies are of five main types; syringomyelic syndrome, compression of medulla and upper cervical cord, cerebellar syndrome, intracranial hypertension and lower cranial nerve palsies.

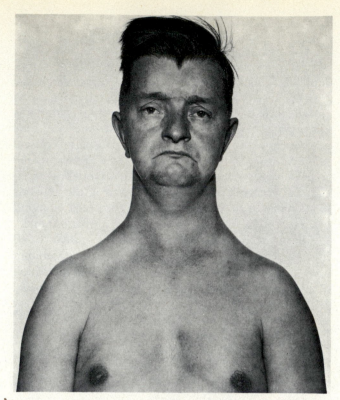

52. Cleidocranial dysostosis
Congenital absence of the middle portions of the clavicles. Abnormal development of the skull, mental retardation and spasticity. The disorder is often familial. Note the prominent forehead. There is no evidence of increased intracranial pressure as in craniostenosis. This patient presented with epilepsy and there were signs of spastic paraparesis.

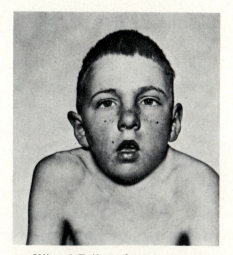

53. Klippel–Feil syndrome
Family history of serious forms of spina bifida and myelodysplasia. This patient suffered from epilepsy, incontinence of faeces and a speech defect. There was external ophthalmoplegia from nuclear agenesis; mirror movements of hands. Cervical and lumbar spina bifida.

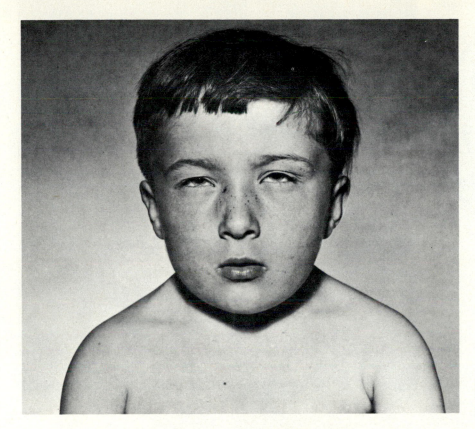

Craniovertebral Anomalies

54. Klippel–Feil syndrome
No family history; bilateral 6th nerve palsies.

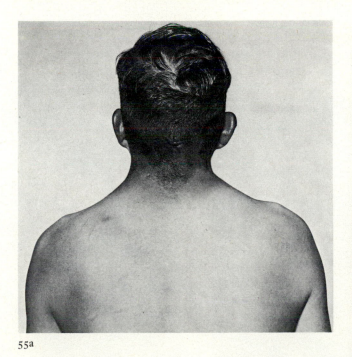

55a

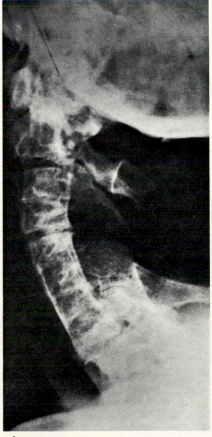

55. Klippel–Feil syndrome
(*a*) Operation for cervical meningocele in infancy (note scar). A soldier, aged 22, with weakness of lower limbs after route marches. (*b*) All cervical vertebrae were fused; minimal spastic signs in lower limbs and slight dilatation of lateral ventricles. Ten years later, no progression.

55b

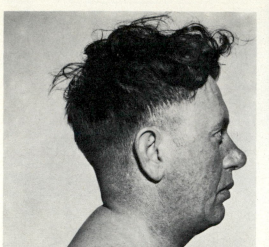

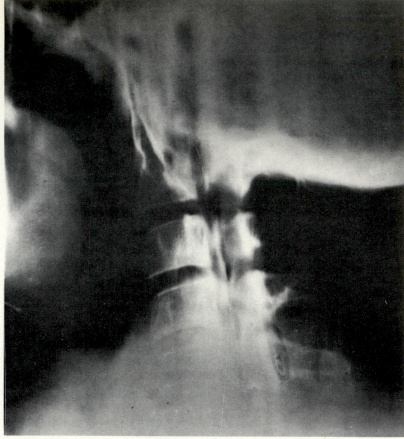

56a

56. Craniovertebral anomaly
Syringomyelic syndrome, (*a*) short neck:
(*b*) A–P tomogram; basilar impression,
elevation of rim of the foramen magnum:
(*c*) lateral tomogram; anterior arch of atlas
fused to clivus, no posterior arch identified. Beaked odontoid process protrudes
through the foramen magnum into the
posterior fossa.

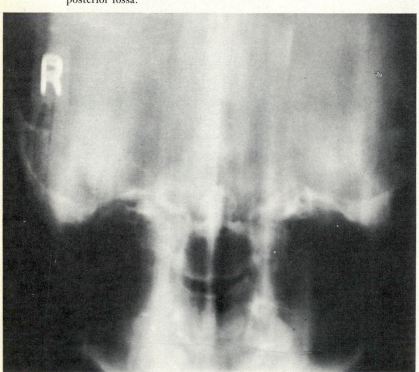

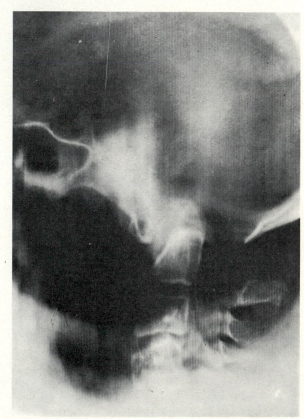

56b   56c

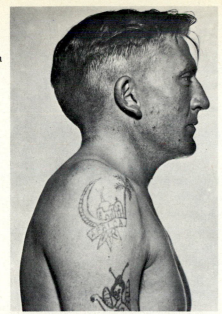

57a

57. Craniovertebral anomaly
Stiffness of neck, weakness of upper limbs,
mirror movements, nystagmus. (*a*) Note
short neck. Operation; Chiari malformation. (*b*) Post-operative tomogram; steep
clivus fused to anterior arch of atlas and
odontoid; occipitalized posterior arch of
atlas.

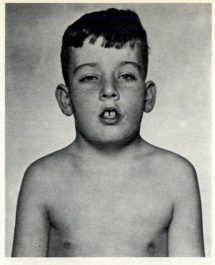

58a

Craniovertebral Anomalies

58. Arnold–Chiari malformation
Age 7. Cervical meningocele removed at
one year. (*a*) Short neck, ataxia, mirror
movements of the hands, vibration loss in
limbs. (*b*) Myelogram: large foramen
magnum and capacious upper cervical
canal. Note neck of meningocele filled with
Myodil.

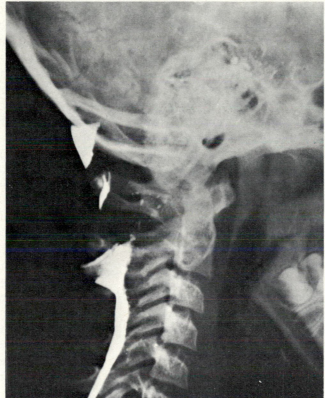

58b

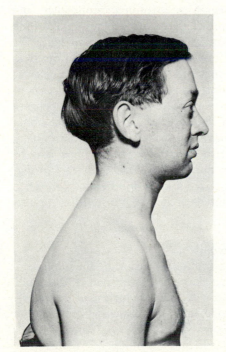

59. Basilar impression
Many patients with craniovertebral
anomalies have a normal appearance and
configuration of the head and neck. This
patient presented with oscillopsia, ataxia
and nystagmus. He walked with his head
flexed forwards to diminish the oscillopsia.
There was basilar impression and at
operation a Chiari type 1 malformation.

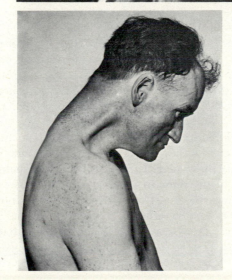

60. Syphilitic meningomyelitis
Weakness and wasting of trapezii and
extensor muscles of the neck in a case of
chronic syphilitic cervical meningo-
myelitis.

The Cranial Nerves

THE EYES

Loss of Vision

The majority of complaints of visual failure are due to faults in the eye as an optical instrument—errors of refraction, opacities of the media or disease of the retina. The commonest causes of blindness in Britain are intrinsic diseases of the eye such as senile cataract, macular degeneration, diabetic retinopathy, glaucoma and retinal detachment. In their absence or, more important, when they cannot be held to account for the symptom, there must be some interference with the conduction of impulses at some point between the retina and the occipital cortex. Further, if the loss of vision is progressive a cerebral tumour is the probable explanation. Visual failure may be transient, acute or progressive and in each case, unilateral or bilateral.

Amblyopia is a consequence of arrested physiological development after an untreated visual handicap. The macula is not formed until the sixth month of life. Visual acuity does not reach normal adult standards until the fourth or fifth year, at which time binocular vision is also established. A squint, a unilateral error of refraction, or congenital hypermetropia or astigmatism will result in weak or absent binocular vision. A squint may lead to amblyopia because the eye is suppressed by the visual cortex in order to avoid confusion and diplopia. When a unilateral error of refraction or dissimilar refractive errors are present, amblyopia may occur without any squint; the normal eye comes to dominate the other, the blurred retinal image being suppressed by the visual cortex. If there is congenital bilateral hypermetropia or astigmatism, early bilateral amblyopia may develop in the absence of squint.

Normal visual acuity is accepted as 6/6. An acuity of about 6/12 is needed to read a car number plate at 25 yards (a legal requirement for drivers). When acuity is too poor for the use of test-types, it is useful to document the ability to count fingers (CF), the ability to see hand movements (HM), and whether the patient has perception of light (PL).

The pinhole test is a simple and effective way of determining whether depressed visual acuity is the result of a refractive error. By making the patient observe the test-type through a pinhole, the effects of any refractive error are minimized, and patients who achieve better vision in this test should be referred for refraction rather than neurological investigation. A discrepancy between distance acuity and near acuity is nearly always the result of a refractive error. A myope may read quite well but cannot see the test-type across the room. A presbyope cannot read at 30 cm. yet has clear distance acuity.

In *glaucoma* there is increased intra-ocular pressure resulting from an obstruction to the escape of aqueous from the eye. The upper limit of normal for intra-ocular pressure is difficult to determine, so that the early detection of glaucoma presents a problem. Chronic glaucoma is usually hereditary and visual acuity may remain good until blindness is imminent. The eye is normal externally, but the raised intra-ocular pressure produces changes in the optic nerve which result in characteristic visual defects and a cupped optic disc. The earliest defect consists of small scattered scotomata, which later fuse to form an arcuate scotoma. An acute form of glaucoma is the angle-closure type. In this there are episodes of severe pain in the eye, appreciable visual deterioration, haziness of the cornea and an inactive, semi-dilated pupil.

A *cataract* is an opacity within the lens of the eye. Some degree of cataract formation is almost inevitable after the age of 70. The vast majority of cataracts represent a simple senile change, but they may also be a consequence of injury, diabetes, or local disease of the eye such as uveitis or retinal detachment. Cataracts occur in such diseases as myotonia, mongolism and hypoparathyroidism. The presenting symptom is failing vision and the condition will be most obvious when the central area of the lens is affected. The rate of progress of cataract formation is rarely predictable and a cataract may remain apparently stationary for years. Occasionally a patient with a cataract complains of a positive scotoma, a central defect which does not float about with normal eye movements as in the common 'musca volitans'. The whitish opacity within the pupil may be evident on close examination, but early cataract formation is usually recognized during ophthalmoscopy when there is a dark silhouette against the reddish fundus reflex.

Transient Amaurosis

The fleeting obscuration of vision in the adolescent on getting up from a chair, the 'swimminess' described by the anxious housewife and the blurring in the elderly individual are well-known examples. The cause of accompanying syncopal sensations may not always be obvious, as in melaena and heart block. Amaurosis in migraine is not inevitably associated with teichopsia (scintillating scotomata, fortification spectrum) or hemianopia and may sometimes cause anxiety.

But the two most important causes of transient loss of vision are retinal ischaemia and papilloedema.

Recurrent attacks of loss of vision in one eye are most commonly due to stenosis of the ipsilateral internal carotid artery. Symptoms of transient cerebral ischaemia may accompany or follow the attacks. Many last only a few minutes and recovery is complete, while others may last a few hours and leave a scotomatous defect. I have never been fortunate enough to see anything untoward in the optic fundus in such attacks on the few occasions when the opportunity has arisen. But venous stasis and arterial emboli in transit have been described. The emboli may be white or red and are presumably platelets or fragments of red thrombus. Following repeated attacks of retinal ischaemia, there may be visual impairment and fundus changes. In mild cases the retina is usually unchanged. In moderate cases a few cotton-wool patches may be all that remains in the anoxic retina. But in severe cases optic atrophy may follow and cholesterol-containing embolic fragments have been found in the retinal arteries.

Transient blindness or amaurosis fugax occurs far more frequently in one eye than in both. The patient is usually over 50. The monocular blindness persists for several minutes and the attacks tend to be repeated, but their frequency, duration and severity vary considerably even in the same patient. Most commonly the patient describes a curtain coming down over the field of vision. Even if no emboli are seen travelling through the retinal arterioles, the arteries may look narrow and the pupil is often inactive to light during the attack. A bruit may be heard over the carotid artery. Many patients with episodes of carotid insufficiency of this nature develop a stroke within a few years, but the published figures, both for the incidence of strokes after transient visual failure and for the history of transient visual failure in cases of strokes, vary considerably. It is very difficult to evaluate the advisability of carotid arteriography and surgical treatment of occluded internal carotid arteries.

Transient loss of vision, even amounting to blindness, may also result from cortical ischaemia. This is found in paroxysmal hypertension, in migraine, in porphyria, and in severe postural hypotension and anaemia. Bilateral dimness of vision may be encountered, with obstruction of the great vessels at or near their origin from the aortic arch, and these episodes may occur when the patient changes his position from the supine to the erect. Transient anaurosis after a hot bath, exercise or a heavy meal may be an excessive physiological response in healthy persons, but it may be particularly striking in patients with multiple sclerosis as a sequel of retrobulbar neuritis. Most of these disorders which produce transient blindness may on occasions cause permanent blindness.

It should be remembered that transient loss of vision may be a striking feature after head injury in children. Vision usually returns within a few hours and the injury may have been quite mild, without loss of consciousness.

In migraine the visual loss, usually beginning with a central scotoma, is soon followed by shimmering teichopsia spreading to the periphery. It usually lasts from 15 to 30 minutes and there may be flashing or coloured lights, field defects or fortification spectra. Persistent field defects are rare in migraine.

Optic disc oedema or papilloedema is usually symptomless in the early stages. When brief attacks of blurring or loss of vision do occur, the swelling of the disc head is usually severe. The attacks usually pass off within a few seconds but may last longer and recur frequently during the day. The patient may say that when he stoops or strains his vision is temporarily obscured. Visual acuity, except during these transient episodes, is usually normal. In this respect papilloedema differs from optic or retrobulbar neuritis in which condition loss of vision is early and pronounced. It is best to regard papilloedema as a physical sign, the existence of which must be discovered with the ophthalmoscope. It cannot be anticipated by the clinical history and it bears no direct relationship to the intracranial pressure. It is not infrequently an unexpected finding.

Acute Loss of Vision

When this is the only symptom there are few causes. In the young adult it is usually monocular and due to retinal detachment or optic neuritis. In the middle-aged or elderly person it may result from cranial arteritis.

But acute bilateral loss of vision may be a striking feature of some illnesses—acute toxic encephalopathy of infants and children, the hypertensive encephalopathy of the adult. It is occasionally an alarming complication of blood transfusion and haemorrhage. Curiously, in the latter case, it is more likely to occur after repeated small haemorrhages than after a large one. Gastro-intestinal and uterine haemorrhages are most frequently responsible and the loss of vision may occur several days later and be permanent.

Obstruction of the central retinal artery by embolus or thrombosis causes complete blindness in the affected eye. There may or may not have been premonitory spells of amaurosis. There is immediate pallor of the optic disc and the retinal arteries are narrowed to mere threads and the blindness is nearly always permanent. Obstruction to branches of the central retinal artery produces various field defects. The patient is usually suffering from heart disease or arteriosclerosis.

Optic neuritis is a common cause of acute loss of vision in one eye in a healthy adult. Although textbooks often provide lists of causes, practical experience is that the patient either remains well or develops multiple sclerosis. The loss of vision is usually maximal in a few days and begins to improve in a few weeks. Pain in the eyeball is usually absent or slight, but the affected eyeball may be tender to touch. The pupil is usually dilated and the light reflex impaired or lost, according to the degree of loss of vision. There is a central scotoma which may be identified more readily with a red object than a white one. In multiple sclerosis this central scotoma may be very small and not revealed by the confrontation test. On ophthalmoscopy, especially in the early stages, the optic disc and fundus are normal. Swelling of the disc is seen when the demyelinating lesion in the optic nerve is near the disc head. There is a great variability in the extent of visual loss, the swelling of the optic disc and the degree of recovery. The majority of patients usually recover normal or near normal vision within 2 or 3 months, by which time pallor of the temporal half of the optic disc may be seen. Optic neuritis can recur and occasionally it is bilateral. No one knows what proportion of patients with optic neuritis subsequently develop multiple sclerosis, but in the young adult it is certainly a grave warning. It is less frequent as the initial symptom of this disease in middle-aged patients and it is possible that some of these carry a less serious prognosis. The optic nerve is a vital pathway, but there must be many fibre tracts in the nervous system where a single small lesion would pass unnoticed.

Not infrequently in optic neuritis there is a history of recent dental infection or extraction, sinus infection or an attack of influenza. There is little to suggest they ever cause optic neuritis. There is no harm in the patient thinking this and in ordinary circumstances nothing further need be said to the patient.

Cranial arteritis is seen in middle-aged and elderly persons and is characterized by subacute inflammation of the arteries of the scalp. The patient may or may not appear ill. Pain in the head, face, neck and jaw is the main complaint and sometimes there is general systemic disorder with loss of weight, weakness, aching limbs and depression. The most serious complication is a sudden loss of vision in one or both eyes resulting from occlusion of the arteries to the optic nerve or the central artery of the retina. It is a most dangerous development. I have seen total permanent blindness develop in 24 hours. Pain in the head is usually severe and the patient will sometimes mention the soreness of the scalp, the difficulty in wearing a hat or in placing the head on a hard pillow. Often the prominence and tenderness of the superficial temporal arteries has already been noted by the patient. Affected occipital arteries are often difficult to feel with the finger-tips. Immediate treatment with steroids is indicated.

Acute blindness can occur without any abnormality being discovered in the eye or on ophthalmoscopy. This type of acute blindness is found in lesions of the calcarine cortex of the occipital lobes or of the chiasmal pathways. In cortical blindness the pupillary reactions to light are retained. Commonly the patient is an elderly person with hypertension or arteriosclerosis;

occlusion of the basilar artery at the origin of the posterior cerebral arteries may be found. A large aneurysm of the basilar artery may also present in this way, with blindness following a subarachnoid haemorrhage. In the latter case, blindness may also result from bilateral vitreous haemorrhages. Pituitary apoplexy, in which there is sudden infarction and swelling of the pituitary gland, may cause sudden blindness of chiasmal origin. Aneurysms in the chiasmal region, arising from either the carotid or the basilar artery, may cause rapid loss of vision and may even enlarge the sella so that a pituitary tumour is suspected.

It has been pointed out that optic neuritis due to demyelinating disease usually affects only one eye at a time. In the syndrome known as Devic's disease or neuromyelitis optica (probably a form of acute multiple sclerosis), rare in this country but common in Japan, loss of vision may be sudden and bilateral.

In old people it is important to remember that complaints of unusual and periodic disturbances of vision may have grave significance. In acute glaucoma the patient may be troubled by 'haloes' seen around naked light sources, usually in the evening. They generally take the form of rainbow-hued circles. In retinal detachment the initial symptoms often include flashes of light followed by black streaks rising up from the lower visual field. These are the result of vitreous haemorrhage consequent on blood leaking from a torn retinal vessel. Retinal detachments and acute glaucoma are ophthalmological emergencies.

Progressive Loss of Vision

In the neurological clinic this is usually due to compression of the optic nerves or chiasma by tumour. The patient may lose sight in one or both eyes from optic atrophy and yet suffer little headache. All the characteristic features of intracranial hypertension—headache, vomiting, papilloedema, mental impairment and so on —may be completely absent. Loss of vision in one eye may pass unnoticed for a time. Disc pallor may not be marked, but visual field studies reveal the evidence of encroachment on the visual pathways. The importance of the confrontation test has already been stressed. As in the case of papilloedema, optic atrophy is a physical sign and not a diagnosis. In children, congenital and genetic causes explain the majority of cases. In the elderly person, probably arteriosclerosis. But in middle age, chiasmal compression from a meningioma or a pituitary adenoma should be the first consideration.

The pupil of a blind eye does not react to light, but constricts when the opposite eye is stimulated. In minor degrees of optic nerve involvement there is inequality in the briskness and extent of the pupillary reaction when the two eyes are stimulated separately. When the pupillary light reaction is being examined, the patient should gaze into the far distance so that accommodation reaction is excluded. Normally the consensual response is identical with the direct response. In unilateral disease of the retina or of the optic nerve, the sound pupil contracts normally if the sound eye is illuminated and the other eye covered; but if the affected eye is illuminated and the other eye is covered, there is a small constriction of the former which is followed by dilatation. This parodoxical reaction to light on the affected side is due to the normal consensual reflex dilatation to darkness masking the impairment of the direct light reflex in the affected eye. The dilatation that occurs is caused by removal of the light from the normal side. This curious phenomenon is commonly called the Marcus Gunn pupillary sign. It may be the earliest indication of a lesion of the optic nerve. If an optic disc looks pale but there is no pupillary defect, it can be concluded there is no early optic atrophy.

Functional Disturbances of Vision

Visual symptoms of one sort or another are common manifestations of neurosis. The floating specks ignored by the healthy person become a source of preoccupation and distress to the neurotic. Wearing tinted glasses in the consulting room is nearly always a sign of neurosis, rarely of fashion, and it is practically never an indication that the sun is shining outside. When asked about them the patient usually says that they are worn on the advice of an optician. Blepharospasm is usually said to be a common functional complaint although I usually find that the patient does not mention it, presumably having long accepted it. Hysterical ptosis resulting from spasm of the palpebral fibres of the orbicularis oculi may be recognized when the spasm increases as the examiner attempts to raise the lid. Complaints of 'eye-strain' with headache, especially among students and teachers, is often accompanied by spasm of accommodation or excessive or defective convergence.

In the hysteric visual failure may be only one of many complaints or it may be the chief one. The young girl from the factory who has sustained some minor blow to the head may say she is more or less blind in one eye. The pupillary light reflexes and the optic discs are normal and confrontation often discloses progressive constriction of the visual field with each circuit of the test object. In making a sudden feint with the hand to detect a blink reflex, it is important not to evoke a response by creating a draught of air. When hysterical visual failure is bilateral, complaint exceeds performance. In accident neurosis it is often alleged that visual failure resulted from concussion. Many such plaintiffs then purchase, and sometimes wear, spectacles for the first time.

In young schoolchildren, impairment of visual acuity which cannot be attributed to refractive error is a common problem. Over-accommodation may diminish distance vision, causing periodic difficulty in reading from the blackboard in school. The various forms of retinal degeneration may cause serious loss of vision, with little change in the optic fundi. Signs of macular degeneration or pigmentary retinal disorder may be late in appearing. Optic nerve atrophy in children, especially of the hereditary variety, may be accompanied by little pallor of the optic disc at a stage when there is noticeable visual defect. The emotional problems that not uncommonly accompany visual failure in children might point in the direction of hysteria if it were not appreciated that visual loss may precede fundus changes. Refined tests such as colour vision charts, perimetry, dark adaptometry, optokinetic tests and electroretinography may be required before a firm exclusion of organic visual disorder can be made.

There are a variety of visual symptoms and disorders, some of them bizarre in nature, which might suggest a functional disorder but which are, in fact, organically determined.

Visual hallucinations may result from lesions of the occipital or parieto-occipital lobes or from lesions in the temporal lobes. In the former case the hallucinations are unformed and the patient has difficulty in describing them; he may mention a sensation of colours or of bright lights moving about in one visual field. Formed visual hallucinations usually arise in the temporal lobe. Blindness consequent on bilateral occipital lesions may actually be denied, the denial being accompanied by a remarkable confabulation about surrounding objects. In occipital–parietal lesions, primary visual perception may be maintained but the recognition of the meaning of objects is lost. Dyslexia is a particular form of this visual agnosia in which the meaning of written material is not understood. A general visual agnosia may be thought to be hysterical. Prosopagnosia, the failure to recognize faces, may be mistaken for loss of memory or a general dementing process. These visual agnosic defects are commonly associated with lesions in the dominant hemisphere and are sometimes accompanied by receptive dysphasia.

Lesions in the parieto-occipital area may render it difficult to judge relationships in space. The patient may be unable to orientate himself correctly, so that certain movements are poorly executed; laying a table, adjusting furniture, or taking some familiar route may reveal his difficulties. Neglect of one half of the visual space is another example.

Cortical lesions, usually parietal, may also cause apraxia of eye movements. The involuntary ocular movements are normal, but the patient is not able to fix his gaze voluntarily on an object. Any emotional accompaniment to the patient's difficulty in voluntary gaze may suggest a functional rather than an organic disorder.

These visual agnosias are disorders of recognition and not of perception. One speaks of visual agnosia, visual spatial agnosia and topographical agnosia.

A complaint of 'double vision' does not always mean there is true diplopia. To most patients double vision is something that is readily understood, unlike the visual fields. A complaint of double vision should always be subjected to careful inquiry. It often turns out to be something quite vague and unimportant. The words 'double vision' should not be used by the doctor in suggestion or explanation of the proffered complaint. The patient then takes up the theme and much time is wasted. Monocular diplopia is more often functional than organic; but it can occur in cataract, corneal opacities, dislocation of the lens and high degrees of astigmatism. With the encouragement of the examiner functional diplopia can often be elaborated to triplopia and so on and occasionally the patient who complains of 'double vision' will volunteer the information that she sees 'three or four of everything'. The inconsistencies and absurdities which arise during objective tests for diplopia should dispel doubt.

The Field of Vision

An individual with normal vision who looks at an object directly in front of him, realizes that surrounding objects are seen less clearly or perhaps not at all. His field of vision is limited by the structure of his eye and the size of the retina and also by the prominence of his nose and supra-orbital ridges. He is not subjectively aware of his blind spot—the negative scotoma which is the projection in the visual field of his optic disc. But he is aware that acuity of vision is not uniform throughout the field. It is sharpest in the centre and declines peripherally, so that a small object in the outer part of his field may go undetected unless it moves. By turning his head he enlarges his field of vision and by fixing his gaze on an object and using the macula, he achieves maximum perception of vision.

The average patient does not know about visual fields, that they overlap and that there is bilateral representation of vision in the cerebral hemispheres. When something goes wrong with his vision he thinks in terms of one or both eyes. The patient with a right homonymous hemianopia complains, if at all, of loss of vision in the right eye. This eye may be normal on examination.

The patient with a visual field defect may or may not be aware of it. In unilateral optic neuritis he may not only complain of the rapid loss of vision but be able to describe the positive central scotoma. The centre of a page of print may be blurred, but not the periphery. As he looks at the doctor, with his normal eye covered, he may say 'I can see your ears and chin but not your nose and eyes'.

Awareness of a hemianopic defect depends to a considerable extent on the rapidity with which it developed. In acute cerebrovascular lesions the patient may only complain of some visual disorder. He may not even be able to say whether it is right or left. In the absence of disturbance of speech or of movement or sensation of limbs, a sudden onset of visual disorder in an elderly subject should always lead to the examination of the visual fields. In such cases an homonymous hemianopia is frequently found. The time which elapses before a patient recognizes a hemianopia varies considerably, it is often a reflection of age and activity, but I am sure there are other factors which are ill-understood.

Hemianopia of insidious onset is another problem altogether. If it is unilateral it may never be appreciated by the patient, but if it is bilateral then, sooner or later, the patient will complain. But even then his complaints may not be primarily visual. The housewife might say 'I seem to be getting clumsy, I always seem to be bumping into things'. As she moves about her house she is puzzled by trivial collisions with various articles of furniture, by encounters with doorposts, by the narrowness of passages and the not infrequent vocal protests from domestic pets on whom she has trodden. When she is out shopping she is surprised by the sudden appearance or disappearance from her view of a neighbour walking down the street. Traffic frightens her, 'it seems to come from nowhere'. Jostling with shoppers in busy stores becomes unpleasant and embarrassing and her efficiency in the supermarket may suffer. Back home again she may think she is 'absent-minded' because she misplaces her purchases. When her husband notices that the table is incompletely laid for a meal, that she misses her saucer or even the table, when putting down her cup, that when laundering her iron keeps falling from the ironing board, or that at kitchen range or sink accidents happen, he too shares her concern.

In my experience the male patient is more likely to provide the sharper clues to the existence of a hemianopia. This is not only because, as a car driver, he is more likely to have experiences which immediately suggest visual disorder. He seems better able to describe and analyse his trouble. But it must be confessed that it is the car driver, male or female, who is most likely to suspect the existence of hemianopia. Trivial accidents in parking, manoeuvring and reversing may occur. He may notice that he 'loses' his near-side wing mirror. The serious accident usually occurs in the patient with a homonymous hemianopia who fails to see traffic or a pedestrian approaching on the blind side.

The great majority of the fibres in the optic nerve are concerned with macular function, and the fibres from the macula to the optic nerve (the papillomacular bundle) enter the temporal border of the disc. The macula represents the centre of the visual field. The nasal and temporal visual fields are represented by a vertical line drawn through the macula and not through the disc. Fibres from the temporal half of the retina relay to the ipsilateral occipital cortex; nasal fibres cross in the chiasm to relay to the contralateral cortex. There is no defect in visual acuity in homonymous hemianopia; with half the macula functioning, visual acuity remains normal.

In the confrontation test the patient looks at the examiner's eyes and the examiner—holding out his hands about 18 inches apart, midway between himself and the patient—enquires whether both hands are seen and whether there is any difference between them. If there is a dense hemianopia, only one hand will be seen; if it is not dense, there will merely be a subjective difference in the clarity of the two hands. Visual defects from parietal lesions tend to be denser below the horizontal meridian, while temporal lobe defects tend to be denser above this meridian. If there is any suspicion of hemianopia in the confrontation tests, finger counting can be done after hand movement. The examiner holds out both his hands with the fists closed, then briefly exposes one or two fingers of one hand and asks the patient how many fingers he saw. Each quadrant of each visual field can be checked in this manner. After hand movements and finger counting have been tested, white and red hatpins of 5 mm. diameter may be used, and the difference in the quality of redness on each side of the fields may be assessed. Red pins are especially useful in chiasmal and tract lesions. The finger counting and finger moving method can also be employed for detecting inattention hemianopia in occipital or parieto-occipital lesions. In this case the examiner uses the fingers of both his hands simultaneously.

Loss of central vision characterizes optic nerve and macular lesions. A persistent, progressive, central visual disturbance, with defective colour vision and a relative afferent pupillary defect, should always suggest the possibility of compression of an optic nerve. In macular disease the loss of central vision is often accompanied by complaints of distortion (metamorphopsia), micropsia or macropsia.

Visual field defects are not produced by corneal lesions, by cataracts, or by lesions of the aqueous or vitreous. A constricted pupil rarely reduces the visual field.

Discovery of a unilateral central scotoma should always lead to a careful watch on the visual field of the other eye. A compressive lesion of an optic nerve usually causes a central scotoma in its early stages because central vision is conveyed by the papillo-macular bundle, the part of the optic nerve most vulnerable to compression. In progressive unilateral compression of an optic nerve, a defect in the upper temporal field of the opposite eye may appear; this is due to involvement of the crossing fibres that loop forward into the opposite optic nerve.

In chiasmal lesions the essential defect is a bitemporal hemianopia. This commonly develops in an insidious and unnoticed manner until there is sudden deterioration of visual acuity. The commonest cause is an expanding pituitary tumour pushing upwards out of the sella and compressing the chiasm. A large aneurysm may act likewise. Craniopharyngiomata compress the chiasm from behind. In the child there may be resultant failure of growth and failure of vision; in early adult life any endocrine features may be obscure; and in the elderly the presentation may take the form of dementia.

In homonymous hemianopia there may only be a general awareness by the patient of some visual disturbance. In a left homonymous hemianopia, the patient may have trouble in reading because of difficulty in finding the new line. In a right homonymous hemianopia, reading may be difficult because the line cannot be scanned in the normal way. Homonymous hemianopias are either 'macular splitting' or 'macular sparing'. In the former type the defect bisects the fields, while in the latter a small ring of central vision is preserved on the hemianopic side, but it is not easy to demonstrate these features by simple confrontation. Occlusion of a posterior cerebral artery is the commonest cause of a macular sparing hemianopia.

Lesions of the optic tract are rare causes of homonymous hemianopia. The hemianopic defects are not identical, as the arrangement of the fibres in the tract makes involvement asymmetrical. There is an incongruous homonymous hemianopia, the field defect on the side of the lesion usually being slightly larger than on the other side.

The visual fibres of the optic tracts relay in the lateral geniculate bodies. From there they enter the posterior limb of the internal capsule, emerging as the optic radiation running to the calcarine cortex of the occipital lobe. The visual fibres run below and behind the capsular region, so that field defects are not a characteristic feature of capsular thrombosis or haemorrhage. Fibres from the upper temporal fields sweep forward into the temporal lobe. Lesions of this lobe tend to produce an incomplete but congruous quadrantic hemianopia. Parietal lobe lesions tend on the other hand to involve all the fibres of the optic radiation, producing a more complete hemianopia. Lesions affecting the whole optic radiation tend to produce homonymous field defects which are congruous.

The cortical visual area is situated above and below the calcarine sulcus with the upper quadrants of the retina represented in the upper part of the visual cortex, above the sulcus, and the lower quadrants below it. Lesions of one visual cortex cause crossed homonymous field defects. If the upper half of the cortex is affected the field defects will be inferior, and vice versa. A lesion restricted to the occipital pole, where the macula is represented, produces a central or paracentral scotoma.

Although, strictly speaking, the confrontation test is a crude procedure, there is no doubt that in experienced hands it is a remarkably useful test. A rough estimate of the size and density of a scotoma may be made and quadrantic and hemianopic defects recognized. A few words of explanation to the patient will nearly always improve the degree of co-operation. The examiner can see at once if the eye of the patient moves and during the test he is comparing his own field with that of the patient.

The importance of the confrontation test is not in the detection of early field disturbances. These must be searched for by quantitative perimetry. But the patient with gross disturbance of his visual fields, and who retains good acuity of vision, may never be sent for quantitative perimetry if the clinical history or the confrontation test has not unmasked this form of visual failure.

The Field of Vision

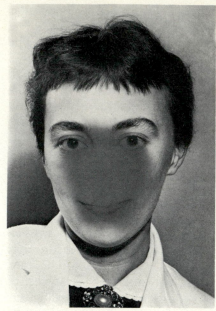

61. Central scotoma
A patient with a dense unilateral scotoma, on covering the sound eye will see the house physician's face in this way. The ears, forehead and chin may be clear, but not the centre of the face.

62. Right homonymous hemianopia
The patient in bed with a right homonymous hemianopia sees the doctor at the foot of the bed, on the left, but not the ward sister on the right.

63. Bitemporal hemianopia
The lateral half of each field of vision is obscured.

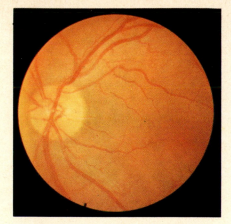

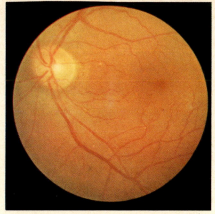

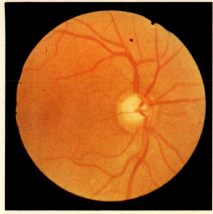

64. The normal fundus
Patient aged 20 years. The optic disc is paler than the surrounding fundus. In its centre may be seen the excavation caused by the central dipping of nerve fibres into the optic nerve. Veins and arteries radiate from the disc. The veins are darker and broader than the arteries. There are usually four main branches of both the arteries and the veins—superior and inferior nasal, and superior and inferior temporal. The dark macular region of the disc lies to the temporal side and is relatively free of vessels. In examining the fundus one should note the colour of the optic disc, the physiological cup, the disc margin, the arteries and veins, the macula, and the presence or absence of exudate or haemorrhage.

65. Normal fundus
A patient aged 55 years with normal vision. A smaller optic disc, with straighter and somewhat attenuated vessels which are the result of age. With the ophthalmoscope there was a loss of sheen and the retina was more opaque than in FIGURE 64.

66. Deep physiological cup
Normal optic discs show variations of the physiological cup. This is the central pit of the optic disc, from which the central retinal vessels emerge. Its depth and diameter vary considerably. At the bottom of the cup one may see the lamina cribrosa, the perforations through which the nerve fibres pass to form the optic nerve.

The Optic Fundi

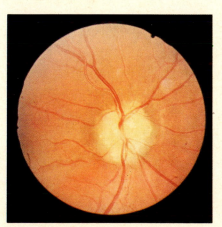

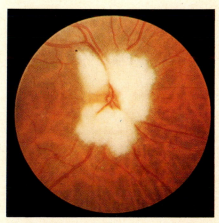

67. Drüsen of the optic disc
Rounded irregular whitish deposits on the disc surface. Drüsen rarely interfere with vision but may be mistaken for swellings of the optic disc.

68. Opaque nerve fibre
Normally the fibres of the optic nerve lose their myelin sheath as they enter the eye. Occasionally it persists for some distance after the fibres leave the optic disc. It produces white patches with frayed margins at the edge of the disc. If extensive it can obscure the disc and the emerging vessels. It does not affect vision.

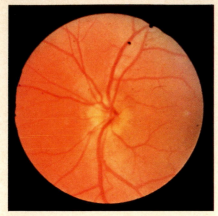

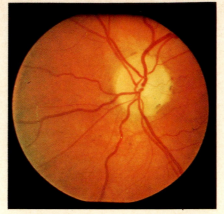

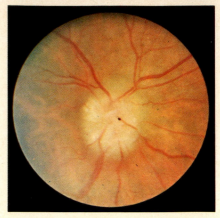

69. Normal discs resembling papilloedema

A man aged 50 with epilepsy of recent onset. The appearance of his optic discs was thought to indicate early papilloedema, and intensive investigations were undertaken with negative results. Five years later the discs were unchanged, but again they led to a suspicion of papilloedema and to hospital admission. Pseudopapilloedema may be due to hypermetropia, to a congenital abnormality of the disc, or to deposits of Drüsen.

70. Unilateral primary optic atrophy

Failure of sight on the right side for 5 years. Repeated changes of lenses. The left optic disc was normal. On the right side the visual acuity was 6/60. The optic disc is dead white and its margins are sharp. A right subfrontal meningioma.

71. Secondary optic atrophy

Blindness due to atrophy following long-standing papilloedema in a case of meningioma. The discs are grey and the margins blurred.

The Optic Fundi

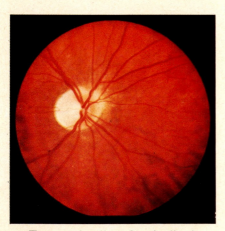

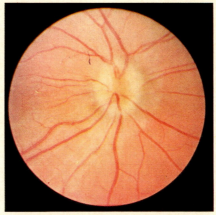

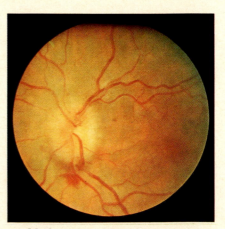

72. Temporal pallor of optic disc in multiple sclerosis

This is not pathognomonic of this disease. It may be seen in normal individuals.

73. Early papilloedema

A youth aged 18 with one month's history of episodes of transient amaurosis and diplopia. Paresis of upward gaze and early papilloedema. Note the filling in of the centre of the discs, the blurring of the margins and the irregular radial streaks. Ventriculography demonstrated aqueduct stenosis.

74. Moderate papilloedema

Male, aged 50, presenting with dementia. Glioblastoma. The margins of both optic discs were blurred and congested. There are haemorrhages on the inferior margin of the disc.

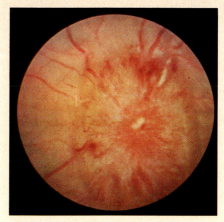

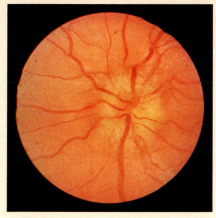

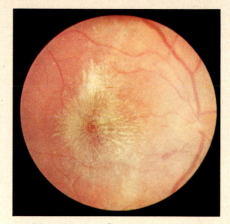

75. Gross papilloedema (choked discs)
Male aged 52 with 4 weeks' history of headache, vomiting, failing vision and left hemiparesis. Visual acuity bilaterally was 6/12. The enlarged blind spot could be detected by confrontation. Note the 'angry' appearance of the disc, with mushrooming upwards of the disc head and radial streaking with haemorrhages and exudates. Right frontal astrocytoma.

76. Unilateral optic neuritis
Acute loss of vision on the right of 6 days' duration. No other abnormality. The left eye was normal. The pupil of the right eye was slightly dilated and reacted poorly to light. There was a small dense central scotoma. There is moderate swelling of the optic disc.

77. Macular star figure
The nerve fibres in the macular region have a radial arrangement and in conditions producing oedema of the disc head or retina, a macular fan or star figure may develop. This was a case of hypertensive retinopathy.

The Optic Fundi

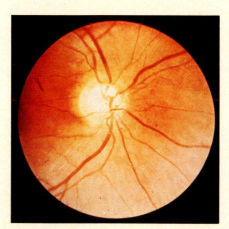

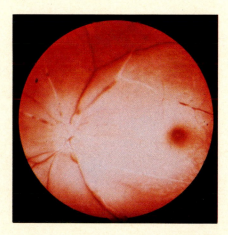

78. Chronic glaucoma
Painless, insidious, progressive bilateral visual failure. Pathological cupping of the optic disc.

79. Central retinal artery occlusion
This lesion presents with sudden loss of vision. It may be due to local thrombosis or to embolism from the heart, aorta or carotid artery, or it may result from cranial arteritis. In a few hours the affected vessel becomes narrow and bloodless and the ischaemic retina looks pale and milky. The 'cherry red spot' in the macula appears when the vascular choroid is visible through the thin retina. There is sometimes oedema of the optic disc and the surrounding retina. Loss of vision is usually permanent if it persists for more than a few minutes, but occasionally emboli have been seen to traverse a vessel so that blood flow may then be restored. Many of these patients suffer from hypertension, arteriosclerosis and diabetes mellitus.

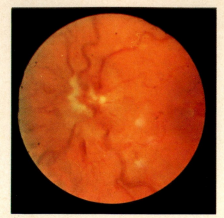

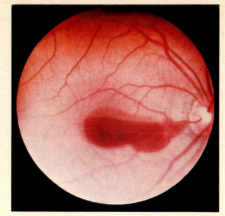

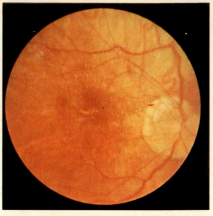

80. Central retinal vein occlusion
Here also there is sudden loss of vision, but it is not usually as complete as in occlusion of the central retinal artery. There are striking engorgement of retinal veins, linear haemorrhages, soft exudates and perhaps oedema of the optic disc. The occlusion is usually near the lamina cribrosa where the artery and the vein are in contact. Sclerosis of the artery may involve the vein. Retinal vein thrombosis occurs in hypertension, in arteriosclerosis and in hyperviscosity syndromes.

81. Subhyaloid haemorrhage
The haemorrhage is pre-retinal, in the space between the retina and the posterior face of the vitreous, in front of the retinal vessels. If the haemorrhage is small, it has a nest shape when the patient is upright. Small haemorrhages are usually absorbed with full restoration of vision. Pre-retinal haemorrhages occur in hypertension, in diabetes and in subarachnoid haemorrhage.

82. Arteriosclerotic retinopathy
Male aged 67 years, hypertensive (200/110), with left ventricular hypertrophy. No visual symptoms. The optic discs are normal, but the retinal arteries are straightened and narrow. There are hard glistening exudates at the macula.

The Optic Fundi

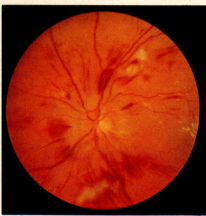

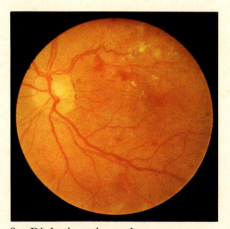

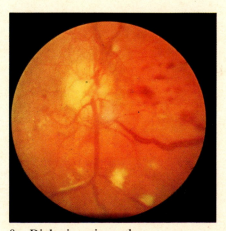

83. Hypertensive retinopathy
Female aged 40 years with malignant hypertension. Failing vision. The optic disc is swollen and there are haemorrhages and hard and soft retinal exudates.

84. Diabetic retinopathy
This is essentially a disorder of the retinal blood vessels. The pathological lesions which appear in the optic fundi comprise micro-aneurysms, haemorrhages, soft and hard exudates, venous abnormalities, vitreous changes, and new blood vessel and connective tissue formation. They are not specific to diabetes, but their progressive development forms a highly characteristic picture. In this fundus there are dot and blot haemorrhages and hard exudates.

85. Diabetic retinopathy
Here we see venous tortuosity, haemorrhages, exudates and neovascularization around the optic disc.

The Ophthalmoscope and the Optic Fundi

The ophthalmic instrument devised by Ludwig von Helmholtz in 1851 has never achieved the popularity and status of the stethoscope of René Théophile Hyacinthe Laennec, invented in 1817. Every school-boy is familiar with the stethoscope yet few adults know anything of the ophthalmoscope. This is probably because they only catch fleeting glimpses of this instrument in the darkened rooms of the optician or ophthalmologist. It is a common experience in the neurological clinic to read in a doctor's referring note such phrases as '? discs—but battery run down', '? fundi—ophthalmoscope not working properly!!!' or '? papilloedema—glimpse only'. The difficulties experienced in using an ophthalmoscope are often due to its neglect. Many a good instrument has quietly rusted away in drawer or cabinet. It is also a delicate instrument; it cannot be dropped on the floor as can a stethoscope. Even in out-patient clinics one may be handed an ophthalmoscope which would have released a fine string of Prussian oaths from the lips of its inventor.

Emphasis on the value of the ophthalmoscope in teaching hospitals should not be left to neurologists and ophthalmologists. The student then gets the notion that it is a very specialized instrument that he need not worry about. Only if he becomes familiar with it in his student days will he purchase and use one when he is in practice.

Familiarity with the range of normal variation of the optic fundus can only be gained by practical experience. The essential feature is the optic nerve head with its radiating blood vessels. The silken surface sheen of the retina of a young person gives way, with age, to a duller appearance. The general colour of the fundus depends on the degree of pigmentation. If there is dense pigmentation in the retina, the fundus appears darker in colour. In a lightly pigmented retina the fundus appears lighter in colour and the underlying choroidal detail is more visible. In the optic nerve head itself there are considerable normal anatomical variations. Refractive errors influence the size and configuration of the disc; the margins may be well or poorly demarcated; crescents are also a normal variation. Vascular anomalies and embryonic remnants are common in the disc head. The temporal side of the optic disc is often pinker than the nasal side because it contains more nerve fibres with their nutrient blood vessels. Emerging from the nerve head is the central retinal artery, which branches into superior and inferior divisions which in turn divide into temporal and nasal branches. There is a capillary circulation on the surface of the disc. Retinal veins have very thin walls with a larger lumen. At arteriovenous crossings the vein may be nipped, especially when there is arteriolar sclerosis. A normal retinal arteriole is virtually invisible because its wall is transparent; what one sees is the column of blood. The wall becomes visible as a result of sclerosis producing a 'copper wire' or 'silver wire' appearance. Ultimately a severely sclerosed arteriole takes on an opaque white or yellowish colour. Sclerosed retinal arterioles also become straighter and their branches become attenuated.

On the temporal side of the optic disc, one to two disc diameters away, is the fovea, lying at the centre of the macular area. Here the fundus is darker and relatively free from blood vessels. Macular lesions cause serious loss of visual acuity as the macula is the most sensitive part of the retina and is concerned in central vision. Here one may see signs of pigmentation, degeneration, oedema, and haemorrhages and exudates.

The two most important signs to be seen through the ophthalmoscope are optic atrophy and papilloedema. Because the colour, shape, size and marginal clarity of the optic discs are so variable in the normal individual, errors of interpretation are practically inevitable. The optic disc is paler than the surrounding fundus because it does not contain a layer of pigment epithelium nor a vascular choroid. This pallor of the disc may be quite marked, but if the visual acuity and fields are normal, it cannot be inferred that there is degeneration of the optic nerve. Alternatively, loss of vision from optic nerve degeneration is sometimes attended by little pallor of the disc. In the case of papilloedema the problem is much the same—namely, one of recognizing the wide range of normal appearances. Blurred disc margins, irregularly emerging vessels, a 'heaping up' of one sector of the disc, hyaline deposits and veins which look overfilled are among the observations which may mislead. The 'pink' disc is not necessarily hyperaemic. Particularly in hypermetropia the discs may look hyperaemic and the margins obscured. There is a tendency to pallor in myopia, but the disc appears larger and there is often a crescent of pallor to one side. The depth of the optic cup, in the centre of the disc, varies greatly. When it is deep it may give the impression of optic atrophy and it may still be clearly seen in cases of frank papilloedema.

Optic atrophy is said to be 'primary' when the disc is dead white and its margins clearly delineated. If the disc is greyish in colour and the margin is blurred, the optic atrophy is said to be 'secondary'. To some the latter term signifies that the optic atrophy is not due to a lesion of the nerve itself; to others it means that the atrophy is consecutive to papilloedema. Primary optic atrophy is usually due to local lesions of the optic nerve. It may be damaged by head injury, compressed by tumour or aneurysm or involved in such diseases as multiple sclerosis and tabes dorsalis. Primary optic atrophy may also be a familial disorder. The temporal half of an optic disc is often paler than the nasal. This is not necessarily pathological. It is often seen in multiple sclerosis, with or without a previous history of optic neuritis, and is due to a lesion involving the papillomacular bundle.

Optic atrophy in childhood may be hereditary or may result from a head injury, from lead poisoning, or from an optic nerve glioma or a craniopharyngioma. It may occur in cerebral palsy, in hereditary ataxia or in hydrocephalus. In the adult, optic atrophy may be due to compressive lesions of the optic nerve (pituitary tumour, meningioma, craniopharyngioma, aneurysm, orbital tumour), or it may be caused by diabetes or by vitamin deficiency or be associated with some of the hereditary disorders of the nervous system. Optic atrophy may be consequent on papilloedema, optic neuritis or retinal disease. Whatever the cause of the condition, its essential features are gliosis, demyelination and ischaemia.

When oedema of the optic disc is developing rapidly, it is less likely to be missed. The impression of swelling and engorgement may be quite vivid. On the other hand, papilloedema which is developing insidiously or which has been present for some months or years, may be very difficult to recognize. It is in such patients, often harbouring a meningioma, that symptoms are slight and few and the changes in the disc unimpressive. Mistakes can occur both ways. I once diagnosed chronic bilateral papilloedema in the same patient on two occasions—separated by an interval of 5 years. His discs were 'normal'.

Bilateral papilloedema usually means cerebral tumour, but it may also result from meningitis or intracranial abscess. Unilateral papilloedema may result from optic neuritis or thrombosis of the central vein of the retina. In cerebral tumour there is no direct relationship between papilloedema and the level of intracranial pressure. Lumbar puncture may reveal a high pressure when the optic discs are still normal. Brain swelling from oedema is no doubt an important factor in the production of papilloedema.

When it is uncertain whether the appearance of the optic discs is due to chronic low-grade papilloedema or not, the presence of other signs and symptoms should determine the timing of further investigations.

Fluorescein angiography is of particular value in the study of papilloedema. In early papilloedema, when there is only oedema and some hyperaemia of the disc, fluorescein angiography reveals a fine vascular network on the surface of the disc. In acute papilloedema there is venous engorgement and the angiogram shows early leakage of dye into the surrounding retina. In chronic papilloedema the vascular network which develops on the optic disc may be visible with the ophthalmoscope. In general the optic disc is not only elevated but enlarged by the spreading of the oedema beyond the disc margins. Pulsation of retinal veins is commonly seen in the normal fundus and tends to disappear in papilloedema. If there is questionable oedema of the disc head, the presence of venous pulsation usually means that the optic nerve is not abnormal, but its absence in such a case has no diagnostic significance. Occasionally papilloedema is seen in patients without raised intracranial pressure; it has been described in spinal cord tumours, in chronic pulmonary disease, in the Guillain-Barré syndrome, in Paget's disease, and in Hurler's syndrome [Fig. 8].

It is important to remember that in recent years, cases of papilloedema have developed as a result of therapy. Steroids, oral contraceptive agents, and excessive treatment with vitamin A, tetracyclines and nalidixic acid have been indicted from time to time. Children seem most susceptible to these agents. In children especially, the ophthalmoscopic features of papilloedema and optic neuritis are essentially identical. Optic neuritis in children is often bilateral.

In the condition of benign intracranial hypertension, papilloedema is often gross and unexpected. The obese girl or young woman who feels and looks well and complains only of headache and blurring of vision is more likely to be suffering from this disorder than a tumour in the posterior fossa. Naturally it is a diagnosis which should not be made without ventriculography, but the disparity between the alarming degree of papilloedema and the obvious health of the patient is perhaps its most characteristic feature.

Just as the optic discs vary greatly so do the retinal arteries and veins. Tortuous or kinking arteries and pulsating veins are not signs of disease. Although it is common to speak of the retinal 'arteries', structurally and functionally they fall into the category of arterioles. Neither is it certain to what extent their state reflects that of the rest of the arterial tree. But the retinal and cerebral arteries share a common origin and it was hoped that the appearances of the former might reflect the state of the cerebral arteries, but it is now known there is little correlation between them, probably because atheroma usually attacks arteries of larger calibre than the retinal. By contrast, in conditions such as hypertension and diabetes, it is the small vessels that are mainly affected and in which such striking changes may be seen in the fundus with the ophthalmoscope. In hypertensive retinopathy there is narrowing and 'beading' of the retinal arteries which may compress veins at points of crossing. The 'silver wire' appearance due to intensification of the arterial light streak is not necessarily pathological. Sheathing of arteries after they have emerged from the discs is pathological. Micro-aneurysms are probably the most early and important sign of hypertensive retinopathy. The diameter of retinal arterioles varies enormously not only among individuals but even within the same fundus. They are also difficult to measure. Unless arteriolar narrowing is extreme it cannot be considered a reliable guide to the presence of early hypertension.

In diabetic retinopathy the earliest changes also include micro-aneurysms, dot haemorrhages and small white spots. But it seems that the retinopathy is not dependent on hypertension for its existence. The soft exudates of hypertension are less conspicuous than in hypertensive retinopathy. A diabetic form of optic neuritis has been described, but I have never seen it.

Grading of the fundus changes in arteriosclerosis and hypertension I have always found difficult. The apparent ease with which many of my junior colleagues grade the changes I–IV has been a source of envy. It is probably more important to distinguish between those cases with and without papilloedema. There is no hard and fast dividing line between arteriosclerotic retinopathy and hypertensive retinopathy, but bilateral papilloedema is surely the ultimate distinguishing feature of the latter. Soft exudates in a young woman with hypertension carry a graver prognosis than spotty glistening deposits in an elderly person.

Cotton-wool retinal spots, so called because of their fluffy appearance, are seen in diseases associated with hypertension, in certain diseases of arterioles such as polyarteritis nodosa and systemic lupus erythematosus and in retinal embolism and severe anaemias. They are usually restricted to the posterior part of the fundus and disappear without trace in a few months. The cotton-wool spot is a focal ischaemic reaction of injured axons.

Fluorescein angiography has shown that cotton-wool spots occur in the vicinity of leaking arterioles. The lesions consist of swellings in the nerve fibre layer of the retina. They develop more rapidly in hypertension than in diabetes, and when the hypertension is controlled the leaking spots on the arterioles disappear within a few days. In diabetes the local areas of capillary non-perfusion persist longer and the essential retinal lesion is in the capillaries, while in hypertension it is in the terminal arterioles.

The Eyelids

The position of the lids is governed by the degree of protrusion of the eyeball and the tone of the lid muscles. These are the levator palpebrae superioris, the orbicularis oculi and the corrugator. The levator, innervated by the third nerve, raises the upper lid and is the direct antagonist of the orbicularis oculi, the sphincter muscle of the eyelids, which is innervated by the seventh nerve. In eye closure the levator relaxes. On upward gaze there is additional aid by the contraction of the frontalis muscle. The smooth muscle of the orbit includes fibres to the upper eyelid and their nerve supply comes from the cervical sympathetic.

Ptosis or drooping of the upper eyelid may be due to paralysis of the levator as a result of a third nerve lesion or to paralysis of the smooth muscle as a result of a sympathetic lesion. The ptosis is nearly always slighter in the latter case, but it can be marked. To distinguish between the ptosis resulting from a third nerve lesion and a sympathetic lesion, the patient should be asked to look upward. Raising of the eyelid normally occurs with elevation of the eyeball. The amplitude of this associated movement remains normal in the sympathetic lesion; it is diminished when the levator is paralysed. In bilateral ptosis the frontal muscles contract to overcome the drooping and the eyebrows may be permanently raised and the forehead wrinkled. This occurs in tabes dorsalis.

Ptosis may also result from disease of the muscles as in myasthenia gravis and ocular myopathy. It may be induced or increased in myasthenia gravis by asking the patient to maintain upward gaze. In ocular myopathy there may be a notable absence of soft tissue in the lids and periorbital region. The skin and subcutaneous

The Eyelids

86. Congenital unilateral ptosis
In the normal Marcus Gunn phenomenon (jaw-winking) elevation of the ptosed eyelid occurs on opening the mouth or on lateral movements of the jaw. In reverse jaw-winking, the partially closed lid becomes further drooped when the mouth is widely opened, as in (*b*). Protrusion of the tongue produces the reflex elevation of the ptosed eyelid (*c*). Swallow-winking has also been described. When Gunn described this phenomenon in 1883, a committee was appointed to examine the case. The Chairman was Gowers. They thought that the simplest explanation was that the levator of the lid was innervated from both the third and fifth cranial nerve nuclei.

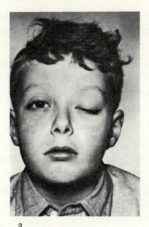 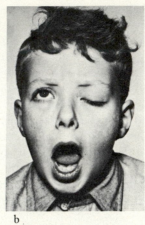 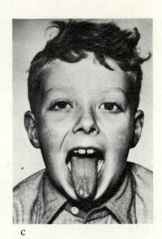

a   b   c

Age 20   Age 37

 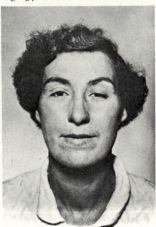

87. Congenital unilateral ptosis
A red herring in a case of headache.

tissue of the upper lids is often thin and semitransparent.

Varying degrees of unilateral or bilateral ptosis of a congenital nature are not infrequent. In some the degree of ptosis apparently increases with age. It may be necessary to study past photographs of the patient when the significance of ptosis is in doubt.

Sometimes there is a family history of ptosis, suggesting a dominant inheritance. It is often unilateral and there may be associated weakness of the superior rectus muscle on the same side.

Unilateral ptosis can, of course, be voluntary, suppressing diplopia. Pseudoptosis results from mechanical factors in which there is thickening of the lids following

recurrent inflammation, or extreme thinning of the lids after repeated episodes of angioneurotic oedema.

Lid retraction is most frequently seen in thyrotoxicosis but exophthalmos is not necessarily present. It is due to spasm or overaction of the smooth or striated muscles of the upper lids. The term 'lid retraction' usually implies some form of spasm; it is not used to refer to the position of the upper lids which mechanically follow the presence of exophthalmos. Paresis of elevation of the eyeball may be associated with lid retraction. It may be seen in lesions of the upper midbrain, as in multiple sclerosis, post-encephalitic Parkinsonism and tumour. The superior rectus and levator palpebrae have

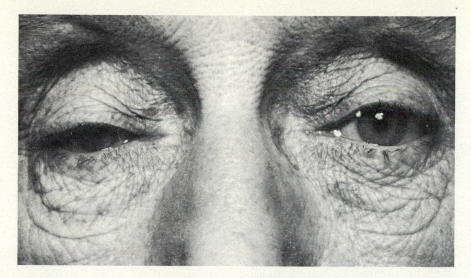

88. Unilateral ptosis in a lady of 80
No cause was found and there was no
response to *Tensilon*. There were no other
abnormal neurological signs.

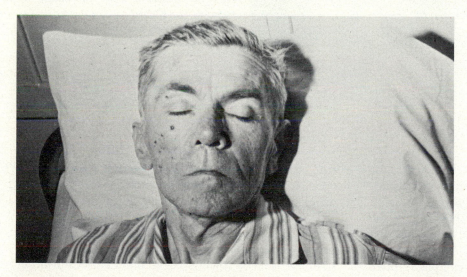

89. Apraxia of lid opening
Bedridden respiratory cripple (chronic
bronchitis and emphysema). Slight
Parkinsonian features in last 2 years.
Very distressed at inability to open his
eyes on waking in the morning. Similar
difficulty after firm voluntary closure of
eyelids. Manual depression of one or both
lower eyelids effectively released elevation
of upper lids.

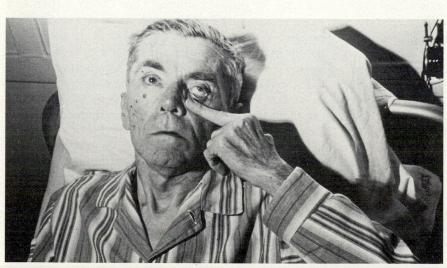

The Eyelids

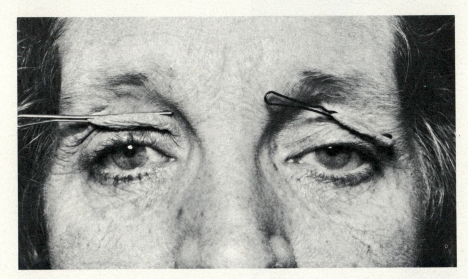

90. Ocular myopathy
This middle-aged lady with severe drooping of her lids had for many years pinned
them up with Kirbigrips. There was
moderate bilateral external ophthalmoplegia.

a common nerve supply and it has been thought that the effort required to hold the eyes in a position of horizon-tal gaze in such cases causes an overinnervation of both muscles. When the superior rectus is paralysed only the levator is capable of response. The lid retraction dis-appears on depression of gaze.

Blepharospasm is commonly a mild complaint, often associated with photophobia. It may be troublesome when ocular movements are being examined. Severe blepharospasm with firm closure of the eyes is most frequently seen in female hysterics. There is then obvious contraction of the orbicularis oculi. The patient may complain of inability to open his eyes and sometimes this provides an excuse for not venturing out of doors when there is agoraphobia [FIG. 557].

An entirely different problem is presented by the patient with apraxia of lid opening [FIG. 89]. Here the patient complains that at certain times he cannot open his eyes voluntarily. This may occur on waking from sleep, after voluntary closure of the eyes, or even after blinking. It may be momentary or persistent. The patient is unable to initiate or has difficulty in initiating the act of lid elevation. Lid closure is normal and there is no blepharospasm. Some patients learn certain tricks

that enable them to overcome the initial difficulty in opening their eyes, such as tilting back the head, opening the mouth, or pressing down the lower lid. In the patients whom I have examined there has usually been evidence of involvement of the basal ganglia. There may be some degree of lid retraction, but there is no ophthalmoplegia. It is a curious disorder and can be quite disabling. One of my patients, a woman with slight Parkinsonism, had many an alarming experience after dozing on a park bench. It is certainly not an hysterical disorder. In the few patients I have treated with levodopa, there was no significant response.

It should not be forgotten that the state of the eyelids in health and disease usually reflects the state of consciousness. The lids close in sleep, stupor and coma. The degree of ptosis parallels the reduction in conscious-ness. In deep sleep there is also contraction of the orbicularis oculi, and in some states of stupor passive elevation of the upper eyelid induces brisk blepharo-spasm. Blinking or reflex closure of the eyelids is characteristic of the conscious patient; a person falling asleep ceases to blink, but blinking can continue when the eyelids are closed as in drowsiness or stupor. The patient with ptosis or a Bell's palsy continues to blink.

The Eyelids

91. Carcinoma of the thyroid gland ▷
Retraction of the upper eyelids. His sole
complaint was severe right hip pain which
proved to be due to an osteolytic deposit.

92. Multiple sclerosis ▽
Retraction of left upper eyelid in association with bilateral ophthalmoplegia.

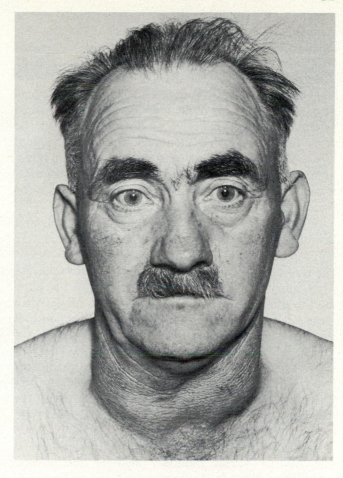

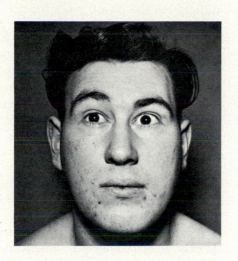

The Pupils

The size of the pupils is controlled by the muscles of
the iris. The circular fibres, the sphincter pupillae, are
innervated by the third nerve and constrict the pupil.
The radial fibres dilate the pupil and are innervated by
the cervical sympathetic. The size of the pupil depends
on the balance between them, the sphincter probably
being the more powerful. The normal pupil is about
4 mm. in diameter, but it is never completely at rest. Its
size at any one moment is dependent mainly on the surrounding illumination and on convergence-accommodation. It is also influenced by the age of the individual; it
is smaller in old age.

A small constricted pupil signifies a lesion at some
point in the pathway taken by the sympathetic supply
to the pupillary dilator muscles. It may be in the cervical
sympathetic ganglia or chain, or within the upper cervical spinal cord, brain stem, hypothalamus or in the
fibres which run to the eye with the first division of the
fifth cranial nerve. A dilated pupil results from involvement of the parasympathetic supply through the third
nerve. The lesion usually lies in the midbrain, in the

nerve itself or in the ciliary ganglion in the orbit. It
should be remembered that pupillary abnormalities are
sometimes congenital or the result of previous injury or
disease. The pupil may be small in iritis and occasionally a fixed dilated pupil results from the presence of
adhesions or synechiae. The latter can usually be identified quite readily if they are anterior with attachment to
the cornea, but dilatation of the pupil, if possible, may
be necessary to identify posterior adhesions to the lens
capsule.

The normal pupillary light reflex is brisk and bilateral.
We speak of a direct and a consensual reaction. When a
light shines on one eye and neither pupil constricts, then
the lesion must be in the afferent portion of the reflex
arc, namely in the retina, optic nerve or chiasma. In
such cases, when the lesion is completely unilateral, both
pupils will react when the normal side is stimulated. If
the lesion is in the efferent side of the reflex arc, for
example in the third nerve, the affected pupil is not able
to constrict whichever side is stimulated. If vision is retained and neither pupil reacts to light, the lesion is

usually in the midbrain. In testing the pupillary light reaction it is essential to use a bright light and take into account the age of the person. Many an unnecessary lumbar puncture has been undertaken because of alleged defective pupillary light reflexes.

Constriction of the pupils also occurs during convergence, so that the patient should gaze into distance when the pupillary light reflex is being tested. It may be lost with the light reaction in a third nerve lesion. When the light reflex is preserved but the accommodation reflex of the pupil is lost, the lesion is in the midbrain. In post-encephalitic Parkinsonism this may be accompanied by paresis of convergence.

When there is a complaint of unilateral visual loss, it is important to examine both pupils very closely. In unilateral optic neuritis the pupillary light reflex is often surprisingly brisk on that side. However, by alternating the light between the two eyes, the pupil on the affected side may be seen to dilate slowly when exposed to the light. This paradoxical response is actually a normal dark response. The optic nerve lesion results in a diminished pupillomotor stimulus compared with that produced when a light is directed into the healthy eye. Thus, direct light produces less pupillary constriction than does the consensual reflex, and the pupil may actually be seen to dilate as it changes from an intact consensual to a relatively impaired direct response. This phenomenon is sometimes known as the Marcus Gunn pupillary sign or the afferent pupillary defect. It is an important one in lesions of the optic nerve because it may be the earliest sign.

The Argyll Robertson Pupil

Douglas Argyll Robertson (1837–1909), an Edinburgh ophthalmic surgeon, was 31 years of age when he published his papers on pupillary reaction to light and accommodation. In these famous papers he not only described the pupils and their abnormalities, but also their significance in relation to the diagnosis of syphilis of the spinal cord. We must remember that they were written many years before the Wassermann test was introduced. Today an Argyll Robertson pupil is almost pathognomonic of neurosyphilis. The pupil is small, irregular, inactive to light, reacting on accommodation, but dilating poorly to mydriatics. Argyll Robertson did not emphasize the irregularity of the pupil; it is by no means constant. Sometimes the pupils are not small and may even be dilated. They may be unequal in size. Some writers would not use the eponym when the pupils are large, although otherwise conforming to the qualifications described by Argyll Robertson. In the rare non-syphilitic case the pupil is often dilated. In some cases atrophy of the iris can also be recognized. It is obvious that the various features of the Argyll Robertson pupil must take some time to develop and that slow response

to light stimulation may antedate loss of the reflex. I have seen 'sluggish' and readily fatigued pupillary light responses in neurosyphilis. The signs may be more advanced in one eye than in the other. A unilateral Argyll Robertson pupil, in which the other pupil is quite normal, has never in my experience been the result of neurosyphilis. It sometimes occurs in diabetes. The site of the lesion or lesions in the Argyll Robertson pupil remains unknown.

The Myotonic Pupil

This syndrome is associated with the names of Moore, Holmes and Adie. The pupil fails or almost fails to react to light but the disorder is a benign one and differs in some important respects from the Argyll Robertson pupil. It is nearly always unilateral, the affected pupil is dilated and it reacts normally to mydriatics. The reaction to light, both direct and consensual, is partially or completely abolished, but the pupil dilates slowly in a dark room and contracts slowly on prolonged exposure to light. Moreover, during accommodation-convergence, after a delay which may last several minutes, the abnormal pupil constricts slowly until it may become smaller than the normal pupil.

It is most often encountered in young women. It is often symptomless and the patient or friend simply notices the large pupil. In some cases the onset is acute and associated with blurring of vision or photophobia. It may be associated with absent lower limb reflexes. When it is unilateral and the affected pupil is dilated, it is not difficult to distinguish from the abnormality of the pupils in neurosyphilis. But considerable difficulty may be encountered in the chronic stages of the disorder, especially when both pupils are affected. I have seen a patient in whom the second eye was affected 7 years after the first. In the interval the first pupil, which was originally dilated, gradually constricted. Reverse diagnostic errors are rare but on one occasion I saw a case of juvenile taboparesis with large pupils failing to react to light, and areflexia, mistakenly considered to be an example of the myotonic pupil syndrome.

There are many minor variants of the classical myotonic pupil syndrome. The failure to react to light is certainly commoner than the delayed constriction on convergence. The responsible lesion is probably in the ciliary ganglion.

The pupil is actually hypersensitive to cholinergic substances, so that a lesion of the parasympathetic postganglionic fibres can be inferred. The myotonic pupil has also been observed in association with segmental sudomotor denervation. This observation also supports the notion of a lesion in the parasympathetic outflow of the autonomic system. But the absence or loss of tendon reflexes which may be associated with this pupillary abnormality has not been explained. I have not encountered orthostatic hypotension in patients with the myotonic pupil, but other autonomic disturbances might well occur.

Horner's Syndrome

Paralysis of pupillary dilatation is due to a lesion of the cervical sympathetic. The pupil is constricted by the unopposed sphincter pupillae and fails to dilate when the eye is shaded or when the sympathetic is stimulated as in states of pain and excitement. Myosis is accompanied by varying degrees of ptosis and enophthalmos; this sympathetic ophthalmoplegia is called Horner's syndrome. Ipsilateral vasodilatation and anhidrosis of the head and neck are two less constant features of Horner's syndrome.

The activity of the oculo-sympathetic system is controlled by the hypothalamus, from which fibres descend in the tegmentum of the brain stem and in the cervical cord, from which they emerge by the anterior roots of the eighth cervical and first and second dorsal segments. They join the sympathetic chain and ascend to enter the skull in the sheath of the carotid artery. After passing through the wall of the cavernous sinus they join the ophthalmic division of the trigeminal nerve and reach the iris by way of the long ciliary and the nasociliary nerves. The fibres innervate the involuntary levator of the upper lid, the dilator pupillae and the involuntary muscle of Müller which helps maintain the normal position of the eye. Lesions can occur at several points in this oculosympathetic pathway, but the syndrome is rarely if ever seen in disease above the level of the hypothalamus. It is most often seen in disease of the cervical cord (syringomyelia, tumours) and in conditions involving the ascending cervical sympathetic trunk. Carcinoma of the apex of the lung and cervical glandular enlargement or metastases are common causes. Injury to the brachial plexus or avulsion of the roots of the eighth cervical and first thoracic nerves are at times responsible. Some degree of oculosympathetic palsy may also occur in thrombosis of the internal carotid artery.

The site of the lesion in Horner's syndrome is usually determined by the analysis of associated symptoms and signs. The patient may or may not be aware of the ptosis and myosis. The former varies considerably and is not usually as marked as in a third nerve paralysis. Enophthalmos is variable and it is often more apparent than real. In carcinoma of the lung apex the patient may notice lack of sweating on the affected side of the face or excessive sweating in the ipsilateral arm. But there seems to be an idiopathic variety of this syndrome where the site of the lesion is unknown and from observation it must be benign. The patient is usually a female and the signs of the syndrome may be observed during the course of a routine examination. In other cases the patient comes complaining of ptosis or has noticed that the pupil on that side is smaller. I have known cases where the syndrome has developed after an episode of brachial neuritis on the same side. The lesion is probably ganglionic as in the myotonic pupil.

The physical signs of Horner's syndrome may fluctuate. I have observed this in cases of neurogenic orthostatic hypotension, where the lesion was within the cervical spinal cord. This fluctuation may be quite remarkable. I have not observed it in autonomic failure in polyneuritis.

Horner, a Swiss ophthalmologist, described the syndrome in 1869. The lesion in his patient was not discovered. He noticed episodes of ipsilateral facial vasodilatation. Paget, in 1864, noticed myosis and ptosis in cases of cervical root injury on the same side. He quoted Hughlings Jackson's suggestion that injury to the ciliospinal fibres was probably responsible for the ocular signs.

In the paratrigeminal syndrome of Raeder, there is involvement of the first division of the fifth nerve and the oculosympathetic fibres with the exception of the sudomotor fibres to the face. There is usually trigeminal pain and first division sensory impairment, with myosis and ptosis. Raeder's first case was due to a paratrigeminal tumour, but the nature of the lesion in many cases remains unknown. It has been suggested that dilatation of the internal carotid artery may be responsible. Ophthalmic pain is usually a prominent symptom which persists for several months and then subsides gradually leaving the patient with a mild degree of ptosis and myosis. Raeder's syndrome may occur as a feature of cranial arteritis or nasopharyngeal carcinoma.

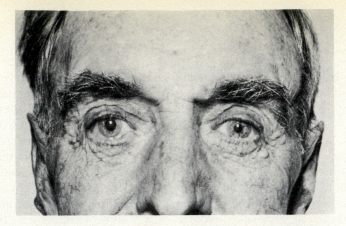

The Argyll Robertson Pupil

93. General paresis
Note slight bilateral ptosis and pupillary inequality. Neither pupil reacted to light.

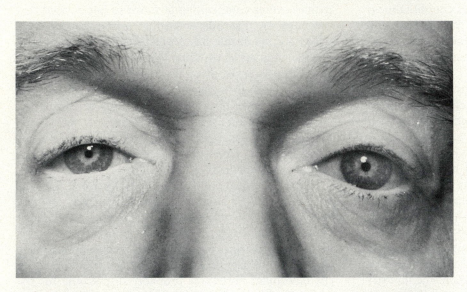

94. Diabetic pseudotabes
Age 55. Backache and unsteadiness of gait. Small inactive pupils; ptosis on right. Absent lower limb reflexes with sensory ataxia; loss of Achilles pain sense. Negative serology. Glycosuria 3 per cent.; fasting blood sugar 220 mg./100 ml. Diabetic retinopathy.

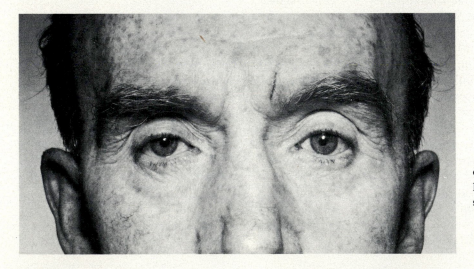

95. Tabes dorsalis
Bilateral ptosis, small irregular pupils, slight inequality and not reacting to light.

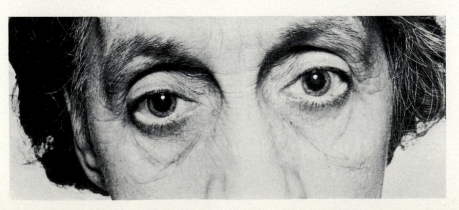

96. Tabes dorsalis
Marked bilateral ptosis with dilated pupils which were fixed to light.

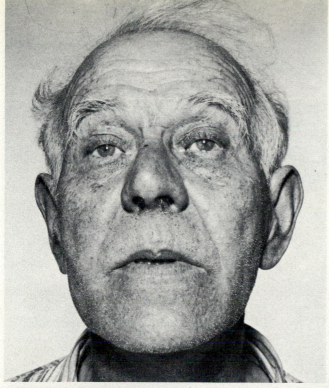

The Argyll Robertson Pupil

97. Tabes dorsalis
Bilateral ptosis, small unequal pupils, which were fixed to light. Note over-action of frontalis muscle to counteract the ptosis.

98. Tabes dorsalis
Argyll Robertson noted that the pupils dilate slowly and imperfectly to mydriatics. In this case homatropine dilatation progressed for an hour.

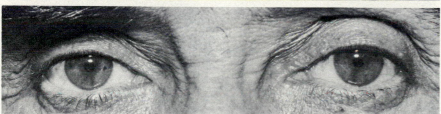

0 min

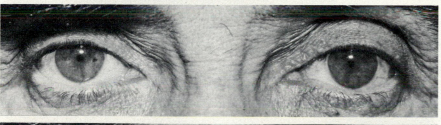

10 min

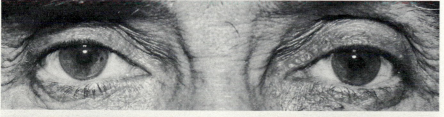

20 min

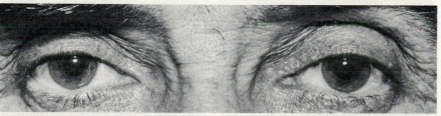

30 min

40 min

The Holmes–Adie Syndrome or Myotonic Pupil

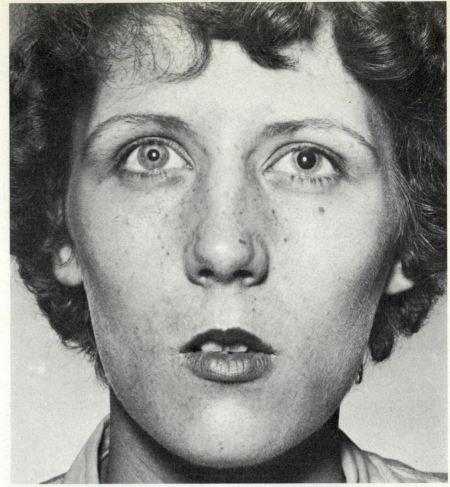

99. The myotonic pupil
The condition is usually seen in young women. The onset is often acute and the dilatation of the pupil may be quite striking and is often associated with unilateral blurring of vision.

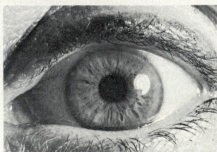
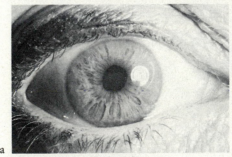

100a

100. The myotonic pupil
In this young woman with absent knee and ankle jerks and no serological evidence of neurosyphilis, the pupils (*a*) did not react to light, or on accommodation. They dilated promptly to homatropine (*b*) and constricted to *Mecholyl* (*c*). Minute doses of 2 per cent. *Mecholyl* do not constrict a normal pupil.

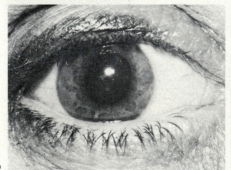
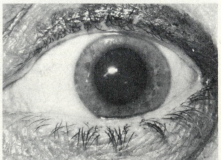

100b

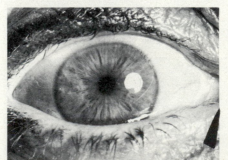
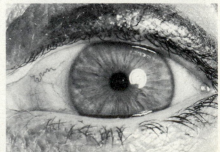

100c

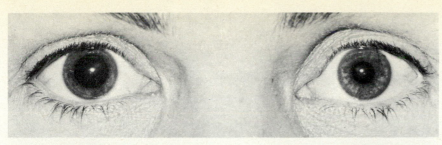

a

101. The myotonic pupil

Dilated right pupil is seen in (*a*). It responds normally to cocaine drops (*b*), to eserine (*c*) and homatropine (*d*). Drops were placed in both eyes.

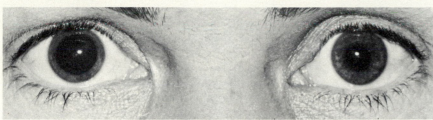

b

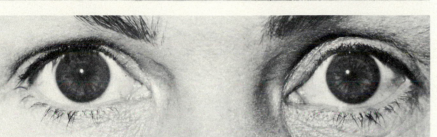

c

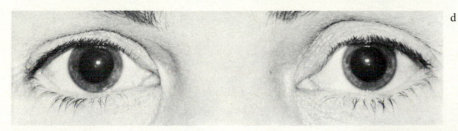

d

103. Horner's syndrome, 'idiopathic' variety ▽

The patient is usually a female and the site of the lesion is unknown. In this case signs persisted unchanged for many years without disability.

Horner's Syndrome

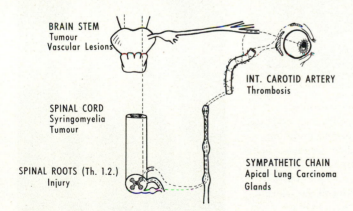

BRAIN STEM
Tumour
Vascular Lesions

INT. CAROTID ARTERY
Thrombosis

SPINAL CORD
Syringomyelia
Tumour

SPINAL ROOTS (Th. 1.2.)
Injury

SYMPATHETIC CHAIN
Apical Lung Carcinoma
Glands

102. The oculo-sympathetic pathway and the sites of lesions in Horner's syndrome △

Lesions in the brain stem and spinal cord; the spinal roots of C.8 and T.1; the sympathetic chain; the internal carotid artery. In the idiopathic variety and in neurosyphilis the site of the lesion is not known.

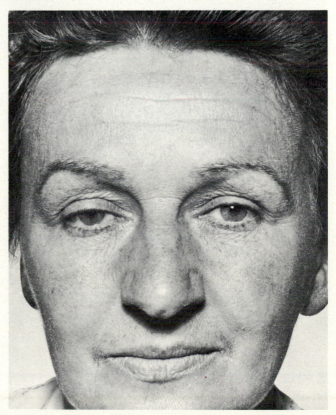

Horner's Syndrome

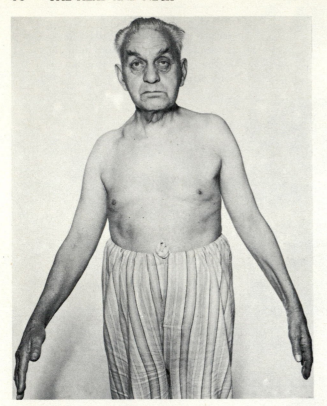

104. Left Horner's syndrome
Carcinoma of the apex of the left lung. His complaint was of pain, numbness and weakness in the left forearm. Note wasting of the muscles of the left upper limb, especially of the forearm and of the first dorsal interosseous.

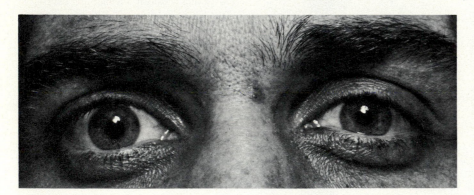

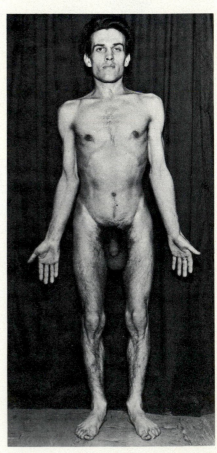

105. Left Horner's syndrome
The presenting symptoms were weakness, loss of weight and drooping of the left upper eyelid. He had not mentioned to his wife or his doctor that he had had a swelling in his scrotum for the previous 3 months. Note narrowing of the palpebral fissure due not only to ptosis of the upper eyelid, but to elevation of the lower eyelid. Malignant tumour of the testis (seminoma).

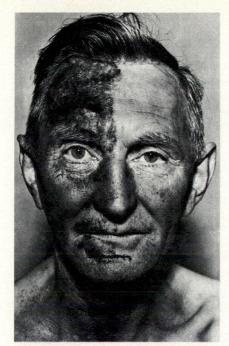

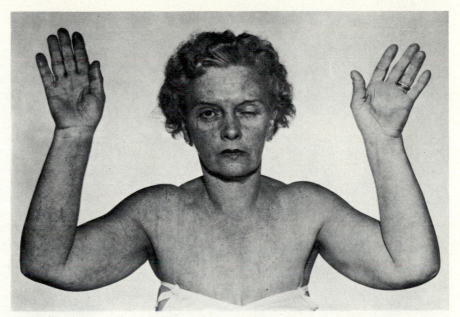

106. Left Horner's syndrome
Left ptosis and myosis one month. Sweat test showed excessive sweating in the left hand and absence of sweating over left side of face. Thrill and bruit over left sub-clavian artery. Operation revealed a small metastatic carcinomatous lesion at the left lung apex. Subsequently the primary lesion was discovered in the oesophagus.

107. Horner's syndrome in syringo-myelia
The degree of ptosis varies in Horner's syndrome; it is particularly marked in this case. Note discoloration of the index and middle finger of the right hand due to

cigarette stains and burns. The right hand was cold and cyanosed and there was wasting of the intrinsic muscles, although the outline of the thenar and hypothenar eminences remained fairly normal.

The Eyeballs

Proptosis or exophthalmos is seen in thyrotoxicosis, exophthalmic ophthalmoplegia (endocrine exophthalmos), orbital tumours and retro-orbital intracranial tumours. Primary tumours of the orbit may arise from the optic nerve or sheath and the orbit may be invaded by malignant neoplasms arising in the paranasal sinuses. A retro-orbital meningioma or aneurysm may cause protrusion of the eyeball. In the adult an orbital space-occupying lesion often turns out to be a granuloma.

In thyrotoxicosis the exophthalmos is usually mild and paralysis of the external ocular muscles is rare. By contrast, in the exophthalmos associated with exophthalmic ophthalmoplegia, thyrotoxicosis is usually mild or has been relieved by treatment or been replaced by frank myxoedema. But the ophthalmoplegia is often pronounced. There may be ptosis or lid retraction. The protrusion of the eyeball is the result of an increase in the bulk of the retrobulbar tissues. There is fatty and cellular infiltration of the extra-ocular muscles. The dis-order arises in middle life and is usually bilateral. The conjunctiva is oedematous and movements of the eyeballs outwards and upwards suffer earliest. The pupils remain normal. The disorder seems to remain active for several years before burning out. Usually there are some residual signs—a staring of the eyes and some limitation of ocular movement.

Patients with endocrine exophthalmos may be clinically hyperthyroid or euthyroid. In thyrotoxicosis the eye symptoms comprise stare, soreness, watering, lid retraction and lid lag. These are due to excessive activity of the thyroid hormone. But the associated exopthalmos is caused by pituitary factors. Lid retraction is more common in thyrotoxicosis than actual exophthalmos and may give the illusion of exophthalmos. The most severe cases of exophthalmos are euthyroid, but there is no fundamental difference between the exophthalmos of thyrotoxicosis and that associated with normal thyroid function.

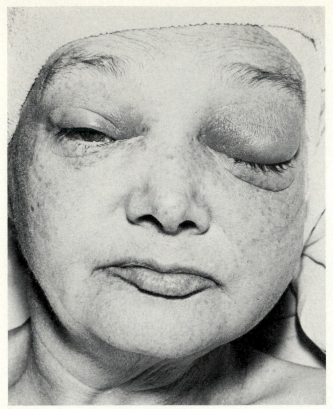

108a

The Eyeballs: Proptosis

108. Cavernous sinus thrombosis
Age 48. Occipital carbuncle for 3 weeks. Sudden headache, vomiting, mental confusion. On admission (*a*) moribund, pyrexia 39·2°C, cyanosed, polymorph leucocytosis 30,000; E.S.R. 128; blood culture grew *Staphylococcus aureus*. (*b*) Bilateral orbital oedema and chemosis, proptosis on left, bilateral incomplete external ophthalmoplegia; pupils unequal and unresponsive. No papilloedema. Good response to antibiotic treatment.
Now a rare illness, cavernous sinus thrombosis was formerly almost always fatal. (Courtesy of Dr. J. G. Graham.)

108b

In severe cases of endocrine exophthalmos there may be so much ocular displacement that visual impairment is caused by papilloedema and stretching of the optic nerves. Involvement of the external ocular muscles results in diplopia, but the severity of the ophthalmoplegia is not directly related to the degree of proptosis. Visual loss may also occur where inability to close the eyes (lagophthalmos) leads to corneal exposure and ulceration.

Endocrine exopthalmos may begin unilaterally, and if the patient is euthyroid it is most important to exclude other causes of proptosis of the globe. If there is lid retraction, endocrine exophthalmos is the probable explanation. Usually there is no visible difference between the degree of proptosis in the erect and supine positions. However, it has been shown with the exophthalmometer that the eyeball does normally sink back slightly in the supine position, and this postural change in the eyes does not occur in endocrine exopthalmos. In a unilateral orbital tumour, the normal postural difference is preserved in the other eye.

There are non-endocrine causes of exophthalmos. The eyeball may be enlarged in severe myopia and in certain forms of childhood glaucoma (buphthalmos). The eyes may be displaced forwards, and also downwards, when there is malformation of the skull as in craniostenosis, hypertelorism and hydrocephalus [FIG. 33]. Proptosis of an eyeball may result from vascular lesions such as cavernous sinus thrombosis [FIG. 108] or caroticocavernous fistula. In the former case the patient is very ill and febrile, there is no cranial or orbital bruit and the exophthalmos is non-pulsatile. There is usually some suppurative lesion in the head or face. Caroticocavernous fistula may result from trauma or from spontaneous rupture of a sclerotic internal carotid artery into the cavernous sinus. The proptosis may be reduced by digital occlusion of the carotid artery in the neck. The exophthalmos is pulsatile and there is an associated bruit.

Lesions of the frontal and ethmoidal sinuses may result in proptosis. Occlusion of the sinus orifices may lead to distension of the sinus and the formation of a mucocele, and the latter may encroach into the orbit and cause proptosis.

When proptosis is unilateral, the first consideration should always be that of a tumour of the orbit. These tumours are sometimes benign ones such as the dermoid cyst. However, many malignant lesions can involve the orbit, including sarcomas, lymphomas and leukaemias. There may be a tumour of neural origin such as a neurofibroma, meningioma or optic nerve glioma.

The orbital pseudotumour is a mysterious lesion which often presents unilaterally. Biopsy reveals that the proptosis is due to a granuloma. The condition simulates a genuine orbital tumour, but the outlook is good and vision is not usually lost.

The Eyeballs: Proptosis

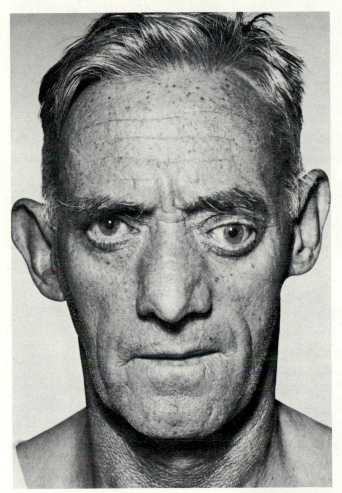

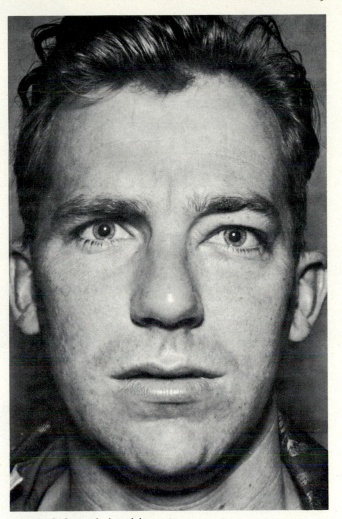

111. Left frontal sinusitis △
Chemosis of left upper eyelid, slight depression of eyeball and slight proptosis. Left frontal pain, orbital pain, diplopia on upward gaze and three epilepic fits probably the result of an associated intra-cranial thrombophlebitis.

109. Orbital granuloma △
Proptosis and downward displacement of left eyeball. One year's history of misty vision with diplopia and left orbital pain. Bony erosion of orbital roof on X-ray. Granulomatous mass removed from orbit via left frontal craniotomy. No recurrence.

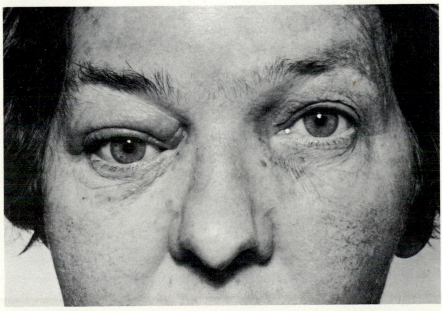

110. Orbital carcinoma ▷
Chemosis of right upper eyelid; proptosis and depression of right eyeball. Malignant invasion of right ethmoid sinus and orbit. (Courtesy of Mr. C. Langmaid.)

The Eyeballs: Proptosis

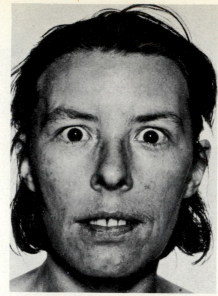

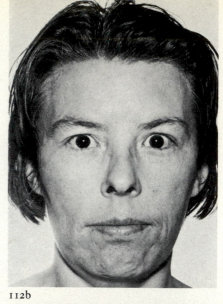

112a   112b

112. Thyrotoxicosis
Prominent eyes with lid retraction and lid-lag. Anxiety and weight loss. Before treatment (*a*); after 2 months' treatment (*b*).

113. Proptosis of the right eye on bending forward
He had noticed that his right eye bulged forwards on bending (*b*). It resumed its normal position in 3 minutes (*a*). Symptomless, no other signs, no bruit. It had been present for many years. Refused investigation.

113a   113b

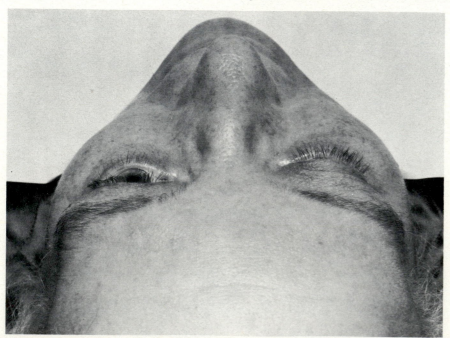

114. Unilateral (R) proptosis
Proptosis can often best be seen if the observer looks down on the patient's face from behind. Headache, right-sided ptosis of 5 years' duration; partial right third nerve palsy; weak left external rectus. X-rays and arteriography normal. *Tensilon* tests negative. Euthyroid. Probably endocrine exophthalmos.

The Eye Movements

The six pairs of muscles which move the eyes normally act in a perfectly co-ordinated manner. Except in convergence the movements are conjugate, both eyes moving together in the same direction. In convergence the movements are said to be disjunctive. Horizontal movements are effected by the internal and external recti; their action is simple. But all the other muscles have primary and subsidiary movements so that their actions are more complex. For all practical purposes we can say that the elevators and depressors of the eye are the superior and inferior recti when the eyeball is abducted and the inferior and superior oblique muscles when it is adducted.

These six ocular muscles are arranged in pairs and inserted into the eyeball in such a way that the principal action of each muscle is antagonistic to that of the second member of the pair. The lateral and medial recti possess only a horizontal action, but the paired superior and inferior recti and the paired superior and inferior obliques possess not only elevatory or depressor actions but also horizontal and torsional functions. Elevation of the eye is performed by the superior rectus and inferior oblique muscles acting together.

The lower motor neurones which innervate these muscles arise in the nuclei of the third and fourth cranial nerves which lie in the midbrain and of the sixth cranial nerve in the pons. Each nucleus receives cortical direction from both sides—from the middle frontal convolutions. This bilateral upper motor neurone control explains why paralysis of conjugate lateral movement is usually only a transient feature of an acute unilateral hemisphere lesion. Bilateral cortical disease on the other hand can paralyse voluntary conjugate movements of the eyes. Co-ordination of left and right is effected by nuclear connexions through the medial longitudinal bundle in the brain stem.

It is obvious therefore that paralysis of the ocular muscles or ophthalmoplegia may result from lesions in the hemispheres, in the brain stem and pons, in the third, fourth and sixth cranial nerves and in the ocular muscles themselves.

Paralysis of lateral conjugate movement may be seen in the patient unconscious from a stroke; his eyes are turned away from the paralysed limbs by the unopposed activity of the other cerebral hemisphere. In pontine haemorrhage or tumour conjugate movement of the eyes to the side of the lesion may be paralysed. Spasmodic conjugate deviation of the eyes is seen in epilepsy, post-encephalitic Parkinsonism and, rarely, as a side-effect of certain tranquillizers. A discharging lesion in the left frontal lobe turns the eyes to the other side. In the oculogyric crises of post-encephalitic Parkinsonism the deviation of the eyes is usually upwards. In midbrain lesions, such as tumours or haemorrhages, conjugate paralyses of vertical movements may be seen.

There are three supranuclear systems which influence conjugate movements of the eyes. First, vestibular and tonic neck reflexes influence the continual adjustment of the eyes in relation to the position of the head in space. These postural reflexes are inborn and are mediated through centres in the brain stem: co-ordination of vertical movements in the pre-tectal area, and co-ordination of horizontal movements in the pons. Secondly, so that the eyes can reflexly follow moving objects, influences are derived from information received in the visual occipital cortex. Thirdly, there are influences initiated in the frontal lobes whereby the eyes are moved voluntarily or in search, exploration, and reflex fixation. These second and third supranuclear systems are now generally referred to as the occipital pursuit and the frontal saccadic system respectively. The eye movements of the former are slow, while those of the latter are rapid.

Supranuclear opthalmoplegia is commonly an acute development resulting from lesions, often vascular, in frontal or parietal lobes. In a supranuclear gaze palsy, although the patient may be unable to turn his eyes vertically or horizontally to order, he may still be able to fix his gaze on a moving object and follow it. He is also able to maintain fixation on an object when his head is passively turned in a vertical or a horizontal direction. On the other hand, when the lesion responsible for conjugate gaze palsy is in the midbrain or pons, not only is the patient unable to direct his gaze on request, but he cannot follow a moving object, nor can he fix his gaze on a stationary object when his head is passively turned. In the condition called progressive supranuclear palsy there is a degenerative process which results in mild dementia, abnormalities of posture and Parkinsonian features in addition to the striking supranuclear ophthalmoplegia. That the basal ganglia are also involved in eye movements can be deduced from the occurrence of oculogyric crises in post-encephalitic Parkinsonism, and the impairment of upward gaze in both Parkinsonism and Huntington's chorea.

Dissociation of conjugate lateral movements is seen in internuclear ophthalmoplegia which is nearly always due to multiple sclerosis. On right and left lateral gaze it will be seen that there is unequal action of the external and internal recti. Usually there is fair outward deviation of one eye with defective inward deviation of the other. It is not always possible to be sure that, as often stated, contraction of the internal recti on convergence is spared. The lesion in internuclear ophthalmoplegia is said to lie in the medial longitudinal bundle.

Sometimes, as in the case illustrated in FIGURE 132, there is not just weakness of convergence of the eyes, but actual paresis of both medial recti. At rest the eyes are diverged. In the classical variety of internuclear ophthalmoplegia there is ataxic nystagmus of the abducting eye. The function of the medial rectus of the adducting eye may be revealed as normal when the abducted eye is covered. Occasionally the reverse situation is observed: there is weakness of abduction on each side, but adduction is normal. Ataxic nystagmus in the abducting eye distinguishes this condition from a bilateral sixth nerve palsy. In these internuclear ophthalmoplegias there is blurring of vision and diplopia as a consequence of the disconjugate movements of the eyes and the asymmetrical nystagmus. The gaze palsies are disconjugate. In conjugate gaze palsies the eyes maintain their relative positions during movements so that blurring of vision, diplopia and nystagmus are not encountered.

Ophthalmoplegia resulting from nuclear lesions is uncommon. In the case of the sixth nerve it is not possible to distinguish a nuclear from an infranuclear paralysis. Bilateral asymmetrical involvement of the muscles supplied by the third nerve is sometimes nuclear in origin and the lesion is usually a tumour. In this country Wernicke's encephalopathy is now a rare manifestation of lack of thiamine (vitamin B_1).

Ocular paralyses due to lesions of the third, fourth and sixth cranial nerves are described on pages 77–84. Ophthalmoplegia due to muscular disorders is found in myasthenia gravis, exophthalmic ophthalmoplegia and ocular myopathy.

Diplopia

As in the case of 'giddiness' it is vital to know what the patient means when complaining of 'double vision'. It does not necessarily mean the seeing of two images of an object instead of one. Questioning may disclose that the term is only used because the patient is not sure how otherwise to describe the visual complaint. It is wise at first to say little and listen. It is surprising how often an attentive nod of the head is all that is required to secure a description which exonerates the ocular muscles. Spots, specks, floats, squiggles and such like are common experiences which the neurotic may start worrying about. 'I didn't mind them until they started crossing over' or 'they make me want to squint'. But it must be admitted that some patients seem to have so much difficulty in describing what they see that it is not until they say they still see it with the eyes closed or that it goes if they close one eye, as the case may be, that one can sigh with relief and proceed to inquire further along functional or organic lines.

Even when the patient complains only of blurred vision and is unaware of any diplopia, it is advisable to check the effect of closing either eye because if there is a minimal separation of the images the patient may not appreciate that he is seeing double. Horizontal separation of the images usually means sixth nerve paresis; the diplopia may then be apparent only on distance fixation; when the palsy is complete there is diplopia with near vision. A vertical separation of images points to involvement of one of the vertically acting muscles supplied by the third or fourth cranial nerves. Where the patient says that when he tilts his head the diplopia is abolished, this often indicates a fourth cranial nerve paresis. Transient cerebral ischaemia is a common cause of transient diplopia, but the latter arises not with carotid artery but with vertebrobasilar insufficiency. Lesions of the temporal and parietal lobes practically never cause unilateral diplopia. Permanent diplopia can arise from many types of lesion in the orbit, in the ocular nerves or in their brain stem nuclei. Conjugate gaze palsies, which are essentially disorders of movement, do not cause diplopia because there is no misalignment of the eyes. Sometimes in supranuclear and internuclear ophthalmoplegias there is obvious deviation of the eyes, but the patient does not complain of diplopia. Even so, he may tend to close one eye during the examination.

Distortions of vision, so that an object looks larger, smaller, or tilted, are known as metamorphopsias. Persistent distortions usually indicate a retinal lesion, commonly macular. Metamorphopsias may also arise from temporal lobe lesions and may be a feature of temporal lobe epilepsy. In oscillopsia there is an illusory movement of the environment which accompanies nystagmus of peripheral origin; it is less often seen with nystagmus of brain stem origin. A patient who dislikes looking to one side may have horizontal diplopia or nystagmus or both, but the patient with a homonymous hemianopia may also have difficulty in looking to the blind side.

Monocular diplopia can arise from disease of the eye such as early cataract, corneal opacities, dislocation of the lens and marked unilateral astigmatism; I have never seen it in disease of the nervous system. But what is said by the patient to be 'double vision' of one eye may turn out to be a distortion of vision or field defect. I have met it in children with migraine especially of the hemiplegic variety.

Monocular diplopia of cerebral origin is exceedingly rare, but it has been described in association with a field defect due to an occipital lobe lesion. Neon signs at night and fluorescent street lighting are known sources of occasional monocular diplopia in normal individuals. It is thought that the diplopia is caused by the upper part of the lens acting as a weak prism.

Similarly, seeing more than double, 'four or five doctor, it's terrible' although usually hysterical, sometimes turns out to be organic (polyopia). The phrase is intended to mean a jumble or overlapping of images, an example of the bizarre visual distortions that may occur in cortical lesions.

Another reason for being careful in taking the history is that the clinical examination often reveals nothing abnormal. There is no squint and ocular movements appear normal.

It is a matter of surprise that genuine diplopia is not commoner. Eye co-ordination has to be perfect to produce a single mental impression. The two images must fall on exactly corresponding retinal points. If the images are disparate there is diplopia. This can take place in the normal individual in extreme lateral conjugate deviation. Any pathological process which causes the image to fall on the fovea of one eye and on extra-foveal retina of the other eye, will result in diplopia. If the disturbance is transitory, examination of eye movements usually discloses nothing abnormal. In the young person myasthenia gravis and multiple sclerosis come to mind. In the elderly it is customarily attributed to arteriosclerosis, but whether the lesion is in muscle, nerve or brain stem it is rarely possible to learn. It usually subsides.

In multiple sclerosis diplopia during or after physical effort may be the presenting symptom. It must be distinguished from myasthenia gravis. Transitory diplopia may also be a presenting complaint in benign intracranial hypertension although I have never seen it before the appearance of papilloedema.

When testing ocular movements the reactions of the patient should be observed. The neurotic will often first request to wipe her eyes and fidget before saying 'There, that's right!' indicating that she is now 'ready'. After one circuit of the fields she might blink, sniff, sigh or sway. Sometimes she asks to sit down feeling 'funny' or 'giddy'. Responses that are consistent and unequivocal are the exception. Not so in genuine diplopia. Here the patient quickly indicates whether the two images are still present and in which direction of gaze they are most apparent. The unpleasantness of seeing double in one or more definite directions of gaze is registered unemotionally and does not unduly distress.

The identification of the eye, nerve or muscle at fault can often be made without the need of coloured lenses and charts. It is necessary only to remember two things. First, separation of the images is greatest in the direction of primary action of the weak muscle. Second, the false image is displaced in the direction of action of the paralysed muscle. When the position has been ascertained in which the separation of the images is greatest, the more peripherally placed image is the false one, belonging to the affected eye. It is often less distinct. The patient will usually be able to say which image disappears when each eye is covered separately.

In horizontal diplopia the images are side by side and the weak muscle is the external or internal rectus. In vertical diplopia the images are one above the other and the weakness is in either of the obliques or the superior and inferior recti. As an example of the former: if the right external rectus is weak diplopia will be maximal on looking to the right and the peripheral image will disappear if the right eye is covered. As an example of vertical diplopia: if the right inferior rectus is weak diplopia will be maximal on looking downwards and to the right and the lower image will disappear on covering the right eye.

While analysing the diplopia in this way the movements of the eyeballs are noted. One eye may lag behind the other; a movement may be poor or absent; there may be nystagmus. Lateral movements of the eyes are easier to study than vertical. The range of the latter varies considerably and in elderly people upward movement is often not only reduced but disliked. 'Paresis of upward gaze' must have figured on many a case sheet of an aspiring neurologist. I have always found observations of head turning and tilting in diplopia to be tiresome and unrewarding. In long-standing ocular palsies the effects of secondary contractures also make clinical analysis difficult.

Lesions of the third, fourth and sixth nerves account for the majority of cases of diplopia. Isolated lesions of these nerves are commoner than multiple lesions. The commonest is the isolated sixth nerve lesion, major causes of this being trauma, vascular disease, multiple sclerosis and tumours. Aneurysm is a rare cause, and many cases remain unexplained. Next in order of frequency comes third nerve palsy, for which aneurysm, vascular disease, tumour and trauma are all equally often responsible. An isolated fourth nerve palsy is not common; if trauma can be excluded, it is rare to find an explanation for this. A complete unilateral ophthalmoplegia usually indicates a lesion in the cavernous sinus, most commonly a carotid aneurysm. Any pathological process in the parasellar region or near the superior orbital fissure can cause a unilateral painful ophthalmoplegia. The pain is due to involvement of the first or second division of the trigeminal nerve and there may be appropriate sensory loss. A vascular aetiology is the usual explanation when the onset is acute and the ocular palsies remain static or improve. Tumour is more likely when symptoms and signs are insidious in onset.

A unilateral painful ophthalmoplegia, sometimes intermittent or recurrent, may prove to be inflammatory in origin. In such cases the pain subsides, the ophthalmoplegia slowly clears, and tumour and aneurysm can be excluded by appropriate studies. A raised sedimentation rate, slight fever and a satisfactory response to steroid therapy will assist in identi-

The Eye Movements

115. Paralysis of conjugate lateral gaze to the right; glioma of pons
Age 50. Four months' headache; recent vomiting and ataxia. Papilloedema (left). Pupils normal. Trigeminal function normal. Slight left lower facial weakness. Paralysis of conjugate gaze to the left; he could not direct his gaze towards the pen held to the left. Normal conjugate lateral gaze to the right. Reflex conjugate lateral gaze to the left was also lost; he could not follow a moving finger with his gaze to that side, but could do so to the right. A pontine lesion usually impairs reflex conjugate lateral deviation as well as the voluntary movement. In this case the right medial rectus contracted normally on convergence.

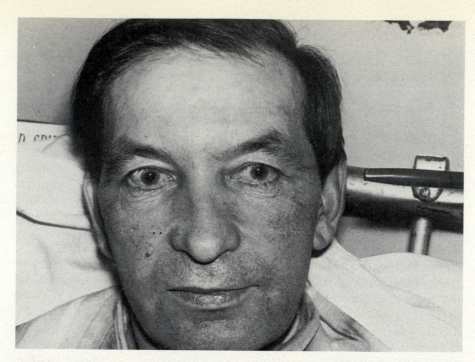

116. Spasm of conjugate lateral gaze; vertebrobasilar ischaemia
Episodes of transient dysarthria, vertigo and numbness of the right side of the face. In addition, longer episodes, sometimes lasting 1–3 hours, in which the patient's eyes were 'pulled to the right like a magnet'. One such attack occurred in hospital and was photographed. The patient remained fully conscious and could not turn her eyes to the left. Episodic deviation of one or both eyes may occur in transient ischaemic attacks due to vertebrobasilar insufficiency.

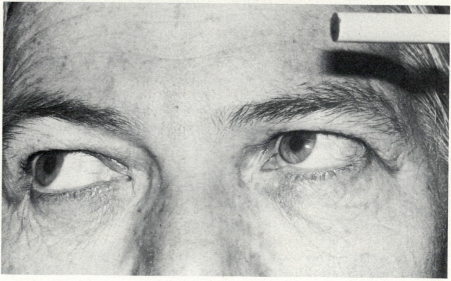

fying the inflammatory nature of the lesion. It should be remembered, however, that remissions on steroid therapy can occur in tumour cases.

Squint

It sometimes arises whether a squint is concomitant (spasmodic) or paralytic. The patient is often a child who has had a head injury. The mother or grandmother (the father rarely) avers that there was no squint before the injury. In concomitant squint there is no diplopia, the position of the eyes does not influence the squint and the movement of the squinting eye will be found to be complete if the fixing eye is covered.

Full binocular vision is normally attained in the fifth year of life. Acuity of vision, bifoveal fixation and binocular projection of the retinal image, and the develop-

ment of fusion enable the eyes to be used simultaneously so that each eye contributes to a single, common perception. In squint there is a deviation of the normally parallel visual axes. In concomitant squint there is a failure of development of accurate co-ordination of ocular movements. The squint may be constant or intermittent, manifest or latent, convergent or divergent. Normally, when the eyes are directed at an object and one of them is covered, there is no deviation. If a squint is present the affected eye deviates in relation to the other eye (primary deviation). If the sound eye is covered and the affected eye fixates on the object, then the eye which is covered deviates (secondary deviation). In concomitant squint these deviations are equal. In paralytic squint the secondary deviation is greater than the primary one. Heterotropia is a manifest squint; heterophoria is a latent squint. In the former case there is obvious deviation of one visual axis, but in the latter the tendency to deviate is corrected by the desire for fusion. If one eye is covered, fusion is no longer possible and deviation will occur. The terms esotropia and esophoria indicate convergent deviation; the terms exotropia and exophoria indicate divergent deviation. A neglected concomitant squint results in supression of the image of the deviating eye and resulting amblyopia.

The adult with a congenital ocular muscle weakness may adopt a head tilt which minimizes the use of the weak muscle, thereby controlling the deviation. It may be exceedingly difficult to differentiate such cases from acquired squint, because in middle age there may be a breakdown to manifest deviation. In the child, if there is obvious deviation, diagnosis is not likely to be delayed. If the weakness is missed, amblyopia may develop before a diagnosis is made. In both types there is commonly a refractive error and the child may be noticed to rub his eyes, tilt his head, and hold a book close to his eyes when reading. There may be irritation of the eyes and photophobia. Rarely, a concomitant squint in a child arises from a more serious lesion such as optic atrophy or retinal tumour. In the adult with a long-standing paralytic squint, secondary changes in non-paralysed muscles may convert this into a concomitant squint.

Nystagmus

I do not know which physical sign puzzles students the more—nystagmus or the extensor plantar response of Babinski. A few jerks at the extremes of lateral deviation of the eyes are often seen in normal individuals, but I have also seen them in multiple sclerosis before sustained nystagmus appears. The jerks are often of large amplitude and the eyes become steady when the deviation is slightly reduced. It may well be scientifically correct to say that nystagmus must be present or absent but it is also necessary to add that the decision is often difficult.

The involuntary rhythmic movements or oscillations of the eyeballs that characterize nystagmus, may be unilateral or bilateral, fine or coarse, rapid or slow, horizontal, vertical or rotary, spontaneous or on ocular deviation, transitory or constant and congenital or acquired. The patient may or may not be aware of the movement and may or may not experience symptoms as a result.

Nystagmus which can be seen across the consulting room desk is usually congenital, unrelated to the story which emerges, and symptomless. Despite the striking nature of the movements, which are usually horizontal and pendular, there is no oscillopsia and the patient can read, but the visual acuity is nearly always reduced. When the patient looks in a mirror he is puzzled that he cannot see the movements which are so obvious to his family and friends.

Why oscillopsia or the apparent movement of objects is a complaint by some patients with acquired nystagmus and not others remains obscure. It can be a distressing symptom in cerebellar tumour, craniovertebral anomalies and in streptomycin toxicity.

In the miner, oscillopsia is only one of many symptoms which, in addition to vertigo, include night blindness, photophobia and general anxiety. Miner's nystagmus is now rare in this country, although according to one of the foremost American textbooks of neuro-ophthalmology 'it is such a serious problem in Great Britain that it gravely threatens the future of the coalmining industry because of the huge sums that are paid out in compensation'!

Nystagmus is usually found to be pendular or jerky. It is not usually present in the position of rest, but appears on deviation of the eyes in one or more directions. In pendular nystagmus the movement is of the same rate in both directions, but this feature often diminishes with increasing deviation. Pendular nystagmus is due to imperfect ocular fixation and is seen in cases of congenital cataract, macular degeneration and in optic atrophy.

In jerky nystagmus there are slow and fast components of the movements, whether these are horizontal, vertical or rotary. It is seen in disease of the labyrinth, the brain stem and the cerebellum. Acquired nystagmus may, therefore, be classified as ocular, vestibular or central in origin.

The cardinal feature of nystagmus is that there is weakness in sustaining conjugate ocular deviation, or imbalance of the postural control of eye movements. The eyes tend to drift back to the central position; this is the essential pathological component of the movement and it is slow. The original position of gaze is regained by a fast movement which traditionally records the direction of the nystagmus. In addition to the qualitative terms used to describe nystagmus which have already been mentioned, there are terms commonly used to record degrees of nystagmus. First degree nystagmus is a minor form manifested on full lateral gaze to the weak side, second degree nystagmus appears on the slightest deviation to the weak side, while third degree nystagmus may be observed even when the eyes are directed away from the affected side. It is not known whether the quick movement is entirely the result of attempts to restore fixation.

Evoked nystagmus may be physiological or pathological. In the normal person nystagmus can be induced by caloric stimulation of the semicircular canals, by rotation tests or by gazing at moving objects (optokinetic nystagmus). One variety of the last type is railway nystagmus. The absence of optokinetic nystagmus is pathological, indicating a lesion of one of the supranuclear gaze pathways or the cortex. Optokinetic nystagmus is retained if only a small amount of vision remains; if it is present in a patient who claims to be completely blind, it is evidence of malingering.

In practice the problem is usually one of deciding whether the nystagmus is the result of disorder in the labyrinth or the brain stem and cerebellum. In the former it is usually intermittent and associated with the episodes of vertigo. It is usually rotary in character with the quick phase and the greater amplitude away from the side of the lesion. Movement and posture have more effect than in central lesions. In one variety of labyrinthine nystagmus, so-called positional nystagmus, the movement of the eyeballs may only be seen in one particular position of the body. Here we are dealing with an induced form of nystagmus which is pathological.

The procedure for eliciting positional nystagmus is illustrated in FIGURE 171. There are two varieties, the commoner type being known as 'benign paroxysmal nystagmus'. After a short interval in the critical position the nystagmus starts. The patients feels giddy and often closes his eyes and protests. The nystagmus usually lasts only a few seconds before it subsides, but the giddiness may return when the patient sits up. Repeating the test a few minutes later may fail to provoke vertigo and nystagmus. In the second variety, known as the 'central type', there is no latent interval before the appearance of the nystagmus, it does not subside spontaneously and there is no fatigability. The patient does not usually feel giddy and the nystagmus persists as long as the posture is maintained.

In the benign type of positional nystagmus the fast component is directed downward towards the lower ear, whereas in the central type the direction of the nystagmus is typically upward towards the upper ear. The benign type is thought to be due to a disturbance of the otolith and the prognosis is good. It is a common disorder in the middle-aged and elderly, but usually subsides in a few weeks. It can be particularly troublesome and may be the sole consequence of concussion, in which case it may persist for a year. The central type of positional nystagmus is not so clear-cut as the benign form. Each bout usually lasts longer and there may be nausea and vomiting. Multiple sclerosis or a metastasizing bronchogenic carcinoma may present in this fashion. Other symptoms and signs of involvement of the central nervous system may be present. Brain stem ischaemia may be responsible. All forms of vertigo are aggravated by movement, so that the clinical history in the benign and the central types of positional nystagmus may be similar. However, generally speaking the patient with the benign type is in good health, the attacks are clear-cut and stereotyped and there are no other physical signs. The central type is less common,

the patient is often very ill, there is not the same tendency to improvement and there may be other symptoms and signs.

In the patient with disease of the brain stem or cerebellum, usually multiple sclerosis or tumour, nystagmus is a common sign. In a unilateral cerebellar tumour the nystagmus is present in both eyes but is most marked on deviation to the side of the tumour. The quick phase is usually to the periphery and the slow phase to the position of rest. The nystagmus of cerebellar tumour is often more asymmetrical than in multiple sclerosis and in posterior midline cerebellar tumours it may be absent. In progressive cerebellar degeneration, nystagmus may be absent although the patient is grossly ataxic.

There is no type of nystagmus which is pathognomonic of multiple sclerosis. It does not come and go in such a striking manner as in Ménière's disease, but it can certainly be intermittent in the early stages. It is not true to say that when once established in this disease it is permanent. The movements are usually horizontal, rapid and jerky. The fine, quivering movements of 'jelly' nystagmus, best seen with the ophthalmoscope, are characteristic but not diagnostic of multiple sclerosis. Similarly the 'ataxic' nystagmus in internuclear ophthalmoplegia, while nearly always due to multiple sclerosis, may also be seen in brain gliomas and vascular lesions. In this condition when the eyes are turned laterally, the outer eye shows coarse nystagmus and the inner eye moves weakly.

Nystagmus is often said to occur in tumour of the frontal lobe or disease of the cervical spinal cord. I have never seen it in the former condition and when nystagmus has been present with cervical cord disease, the diagnosis has been syringomyelia, craniovertebral anomaly or tumour at the foramen magnum. All those are disorders in which structures above the foramen magnum may be involved.

Errors of observation and interpretation are common in nystagmus. It has always been the most over-diagnosed sign by my house physicians. By its very nature there will always be bedside disagreements on this topic. It should be remembered that a weak ocular muscle may cause nystagmus. This is often seen in paralysis of an external rectus muscle. Nystagmus is uncommon in myasthenia and nearly always excludes a diagnosis of neurosyphilis. It is well known to result from alcohol, anticonvulsants and barbiturates and many a fine nystagmus observed in a morning clinic disappears after lunch. Paradoxically, I have known alcohol to reduce congenital nystagmus temporarily. A patient of mine with gross congenital nystagmus lost many a dancing partner after a turn around the ballroom, only to discover when he was older that two pints of beer before the dance assured him temporary freedom from his spontaneous nystagmus. Still later, after marriage, he soon discovered that to his wife absence of nystagmus meant that he had taken at least two pints of beer on his way home.

There are a few distinctive types of nystagmus which may be mentioned because they have diagnostic significance. Latent nystagmus elicited by covering one eye is congenital and usually associated with some form of squint; it has no neurological significance. Seesaw nystagmus, a very rare clinical sign in which downward movement of one eye is associated with upward movement of the other, is most commonly due to a parasellar lesion or craniopharyngioma. Down-beat nystagmus, a vertical nystagmus present only on downward gaze, is usually due to a lesion in the posterior fossa; it has been recorded in basilar impression and cerebellar ectopia. Ocular bobbing, a somewhat similar spontaneous downward jerking of the eyes, I have not seen. In contrast to down-beat nystagmus, the slow–fast sequence is in opposite directions: a quick downward jerk and a slow return to the mid position. It has usually been noted in pontine haemorrhage. Opsoclonus is a grossly irregular, non-rhythmic, chaotic motion of the eyeballs, most often seen in encephalitis.

Voluntary nystagmus is a curiosity. I have only seen it on two occasions and must confess I was quite impressed.

The Third Cranial Nerve

The nucleus of the third cranial nerve lies in the midbrain just anterior to the Sylvian aqueduct. Its efferent fibres emerge from the medial side of the cerebral peduncle. The nerve runs forward between the posterior cerebral and superior cerebellar arteries, lateral to the posterior communicating artery, to pierce the dura lateral to the posterior clinoid process. It then lies in the lateral wall of the cavernous sinus, above the fourth nerve and lateral to the intracavernous portion of the internal carotid artery. The nerve enters the orbit through the superior orbital fissure. It supplies the levator of the upper lid and all the extrinsic ocular muscles except the lateral rectus and the superior oblique. Parasympathetic fibres innervate the constrictor of the pupil and the ciliary muscle of accommodation.

In complete paralysis there is ptosis; lateral deviation of the eye due to the unopposed action of the external rectus; wide dilatation of the pupil with loss of the direct and consensual light reflexes; paralysis of accommodation; and paralysis of all ocular movement except laterally and inferomedially. There is internal and external ophthalmoplegia.

Diplopia at onset is soon masked by the ptosis or it may only be experienced during recovery or on passive raising of the lid by the examiner. Overaction of the frontalis muscle (innervated by the facial nerve) raises the lid slightly.

Partial paralysis is common. Fibres in the nerve may escape involvement or recovery may proceed unequally. The iridoconstrictor fibres often escape in diabetic third nerve palsy. Simultaneous involvement of the ocular sympathetic behind the orbit explains some examples of pupillary non-dilatation. An *acute, isolated, painful* third nerve palsy is nearly always due to an *unruptured* intracranial aneurysm. The spinal fluid usually remains clear. Syphilis is no longer the commonest cause of a painless third nerve palsy. Midbrain vascular and demyelinating lesions, parasellar neoplasms, sphenoidal wing meningiomas and carcinomatous lesions of the skull base are other causes. Transient incomplete third nerve palsies in the elderly are 'vascular' in origin, recovery is usual and angiography is meddlesome. *Recurrent* third nerve palsies often defy solution.

In the aneurysmal cases the onset is not always sudden. Even the characteristic pain in the forehead and eyeball and sometimes the cheek, may be felt increasingly for some weeks before oculomotor paralysis. It is a referred pain usually confined to the first branch of the trigeminal nerve. Actual anaesthesia is rare. In cases of spontaneous recovery there may only remain an absent corneal reflex, a narrowed palpebral fissure and some limitation of vertical movements of the eyeball. Lateral movements tend to recover more completely.

In 'ophthalmoplegic migraine' angiography rarely reveals the presence of an intracranial aneurysm. The story may be similar in both but in migraine it begins in childhood or adolescence, recovery is more rapid and, lastly, it is always complete. In the aneurysmal cases there may be some periodicity or relapse but recovery after an attack is never complete.

The Third Cranial Nerve

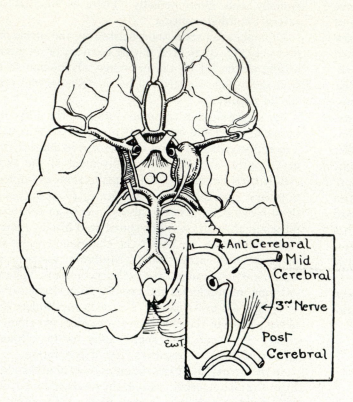

117. Third cranial nerve palsy
The common cause of an acute, painful, unilateral, third cranial nerve palsy: aneurysm of the internal carotid artery. Note the involvement of the nerve in the wall of the aneurysm. This drawing is of some historical importance. It was made by the late Dr. E. W. Twining of Manchester in 1927. It was the first case in which a direct attack was made on an intracranial aneurysm. The pioneer surgeon was the late Sir Geoffrey Jefferson. (Courtesy of the Editor, *Proceedings of the Royal Society of Medicine*.)

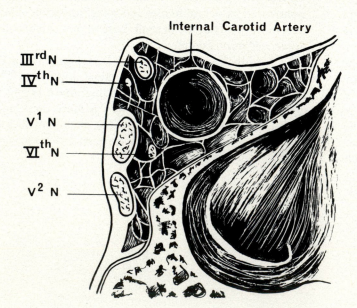

118. The third, fourth and fifth cranial nerves
The relationship of the third, fourth and fifth cranial nerves to the wall of the cavernous sinus and the internal carotid artery.

The Third Cranial Nerve

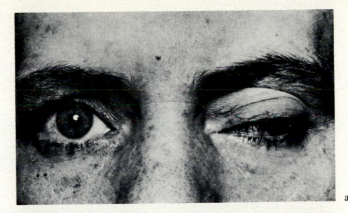

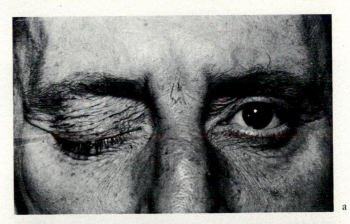

119. Left third nerve palsy
Partial left third nerve palsy; carcinoma
of nasopharynx. (*a*) Ptosis and lateral
deviation of left eye. (*b*) Upward gaze;
slight elevation of left lid reveals
dilated pupil and paralysis of elevation
of left eyeball.

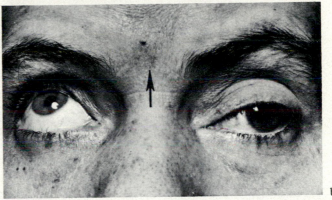

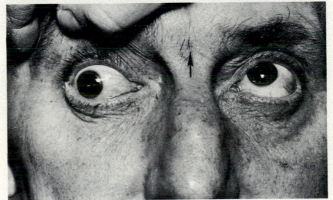

120. Right third nerve palsy
Complete right third nerve palsy.
Aneurysm of internal carotid artery. (*a*)
Complete ptosis. (*b*) Raising the paralysed
lid reveals the dilated pupil and the
abducted position of the eyeball. The
patient is asked to look upwards but only
the left eye moves.

The Third Cranial Nerve

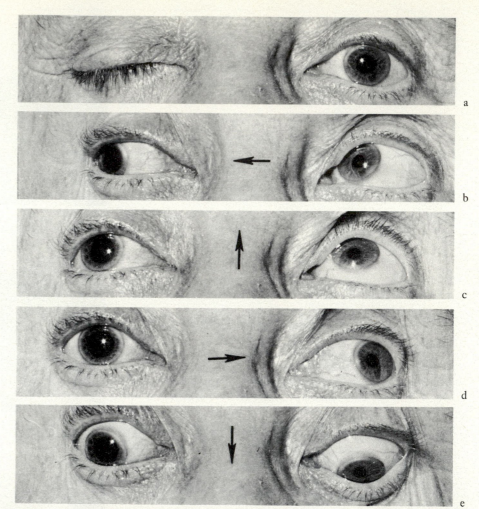

121. Right third nerve palsy
Complete right third nerve palsy.
Aneurysm of the right posterior communicating artery. (*a*) Right ptosis. (*b*) Right lateral gaze; intact right lateral rectus. (*c*) Upward gaze; absent on right. (*d*) Left lateral gaze; paralysis of right medial rectus. (*e*) Downward gaze; absent on right. Note widely dilated right pupil which was fixed to light and on accommodation. (*f*) and (*g*) Right carotid arteriogram showing the aneurysm.

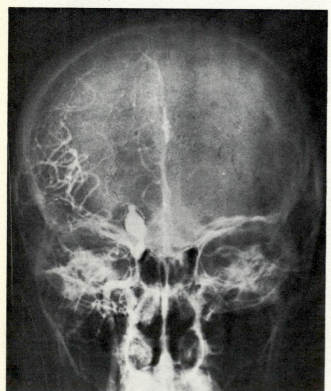

121f

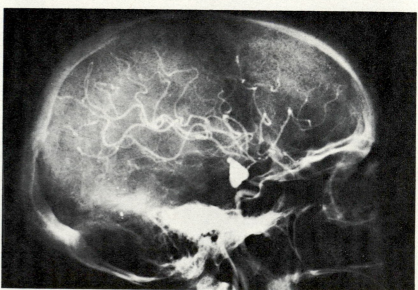

121g

The Third Cranial Nerve

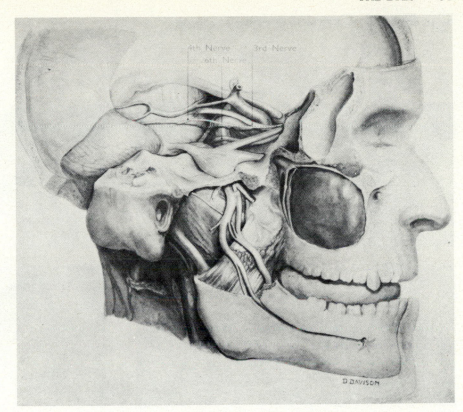

122. The third, fourth, fifth and sixth **cranial nerves**
The relationship of the third, fourth, fifth, and sixth cranial nerves to the carotid syphon. (Courtesy of Pitman Medical Publishing Co. Ltd., *Selected Papers of Sir Geoffrey Jefferson*.)

The Fourth Cranial Nerve

The trochlear nucleus is situated in the midbrain, in the floor of the aqueduct, below the third nerve nucleus. It is the most slender of the cranial nerves and it is unique in that it crosses the midline as it emerges from the brain stem to wind round the peduncle. It traverses the interpeduncular cistern and enters the lateral wall of the cavernous sinus to supply the superior oblique muscle of the eyeball. Because of the decussation a nuclear lesion affects the opposite superior oblique muscle. A unilateral lesion of the midbrain may involve the fourth nerve of the opposite side and the third nerve of the same side.

The action of the superior oblique muscle is not a simple one, but its primary function is depression of the eye; this is maximal in the position of adduction and nil in abduction. A secondary action is to abduct the eye and rotate the vertical meridian. When the muscle is paralysed there is impairment of downward movement of the eye in the adducted position, with vertical diplopia and tilting of the false image. Diplopia which arises on depression of the eyeballs is always particularly troublesome during reading or descending stairs.

Opinions differ concerning the frequency of an isolated fourth nerve palsy, but diplopia on depression of the eyeballs is not an uncommon complaint in elderly people although it is usually temporary. In the presence of a third nerve palsy it is particularly difficult to detect paralysis of the superior oblique muscle. The eye is then in the abducted position and as a result the superior oblique muscle cannot produce a downward movement of the eye; its contraction results only in torsion, a movement which is very readily overlooked.

Injury is a not uncommon cause of a fourth nerve lesion. It is rarely possible to determine the site of the injury in general concussion, but an orbital injury may fracture the superior orbital rim, dislocate the trochlear pulley, or injure the superior oblique muscle itself. The nerve may be injured at the tentorial edge. Diabetes and vascular lesions are other causes of this palsy.

A diagnostic clue to paralysis of one superior oblique muscle is the position of the head adopted by the patient. The diplopia is vertical and is worse on downward gaze. It is minimized by turning the head to the other side and depressing the chin.

The Fourth Cranial Nerve

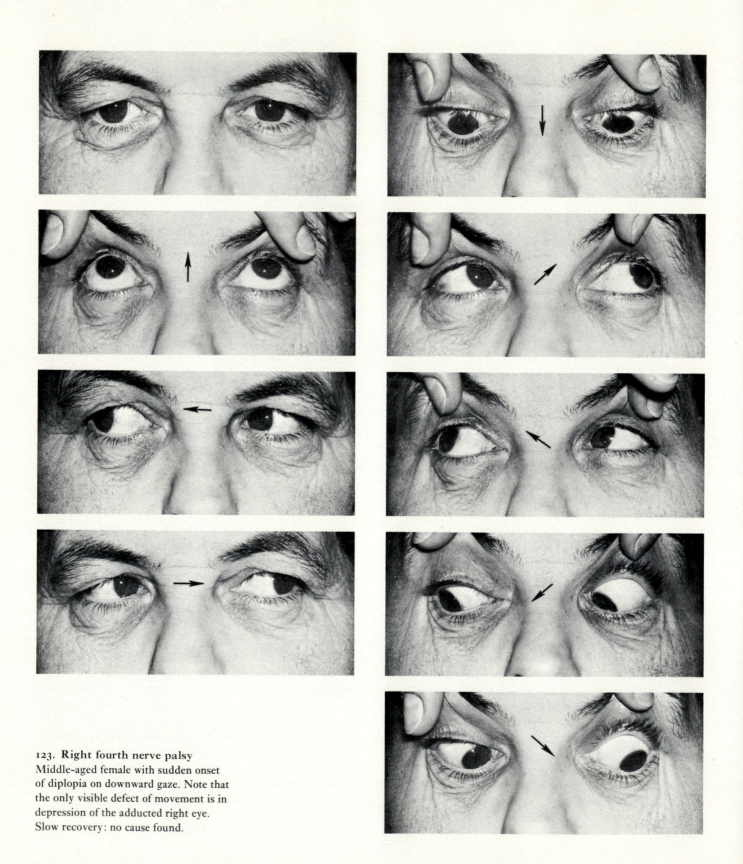

123. **Right fourth nerve palsy**
Middle-aged female with sudden onset
of diplopia on downward gaze. Note that
the only visible defect of movement is in
depression of the adducted right eye.
Slow recovery: no cause found.

The Sixth Cranial Nerve

The nucleus of the abducens nerve lies in the lower part of the pons beneath the floor of the fourth ventricle. The nerve fibres run forward through the pons to emerge near the pontomedullary junction. The nucleus is close to that of the facial nerve and consequently nuclear affections of the sixth nerve are sometimes associated with facial paralysis. In congenital facial diplegia there is sometimes an associated paralysis of the external recti: there is aplasia of the nuclei of these cranial nerves. Multiple sclerosis or a pontine tumour can present with unilateral sixth and seventh cranial nerve palsies. The nerve itself has a long extracerebral course at the base of the brain. It arches over the apex of the petrous bone near the inferior petrosal sinus, entering the lateral wall of the cavernous sinus and passing through the superior orbital fissure to the orbit. It supplies the external rectus muscle. A lesion of the sixth nerve causes paralysis of this muscle with loss of abduction of the eye, which may be deviated inwards by the unopposed action of the internal rectus muscle. Diplopia is experienced on turning the eyes to the affected side, the false image lying lateral to and parallel with the true image.

It is not possible to distinguish nuclear paralysis of the sixth nerve from an infranuclear paralysis unless there are associated signs indicating the situation of the lesion. The nucleus may be involved in virus infections of the brain stem, in tumours and vascular lesions of the pons. The majority of sixth nerve palsies are due to lesions of the nerve after it emerges from the pons. The nerve may be compressed directly by a tumour; an isolated palsy from intracranial aneurysm is uncommon. Syphilis is occasionally responsible. In the majority of cases of an isolated palsy the cause is not known. The majority of subjects are elderly and naturally 'vascular' lesions are suspected. Diabetes is another possible cause of sixth nerve palsy. Recovery is the rule, investigations should be restricted and admission to hospital is rarely necessary. The patient is usually arteriosclerotic and weekly clinical observation is more important than anything else. It is important to remember that a sixth nerve palsy, unilateral or bilateral, may be a false localizing sign in the presence of raised intracranial pressure. The explanation lies in the long course of the nerve and its liability to stretching when there is an expanding lesion with downward displacement of the brain stem.

A recurrent, relapsing or fluctuating sixth nerve palsy in a young person is usually due to multiple sclerosis or myasthenia gravis. The latter condition should not be forgotten even in elderly subjects, where cerebral arteriosclerosis may come too readily to mind.

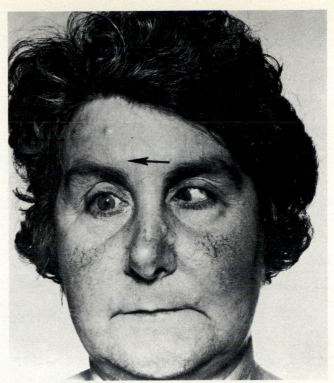

124. Right sixth nerve palsy
Sudden onset of diplopia while watching television. No other symptoms. Note paralysis of right external rectus on right lateral gaze. Pupils normal; neurological examination negative. Positive serology in blood and spinal fluid; the latter was otherwise normal.

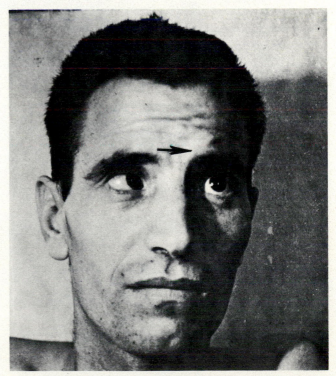

125. Left sixth nerve palsy
Left external rectus paralysis in a patient with a tuberculoma of the cerebellum; a false localizing sign resulting from raised intercranial pressure. Later, the right external rectus muscle became paralysed. Bilteral papilloedema was already present when first seen.

84

The Sixth Cranial Nerve

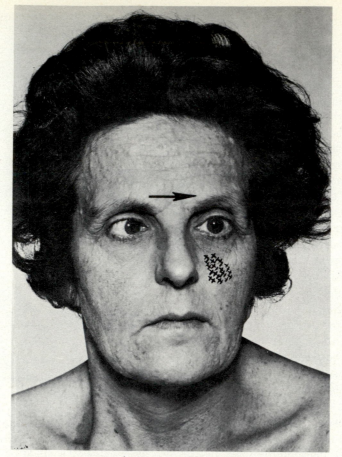

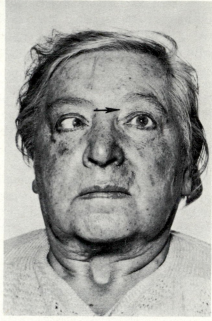

126. Left sixth nerve palsy ◁
Sudden onset of diplopia. One month later headache, vertigo and vomiting. Cutaneous signs of neurofibromatosis. Left external rectus paralysis, numbness of left cheek, normal hearing. X-ray showed normal auditory meati. Normal cerebrospinal fluid. Normal air encephalography and carotid arteriography. Pontine glioma at autopsy.

127. Left sixth nerve palsy △
Isolated left sixth nerve palsy in a patient with hypertension and diabetes mellitus. Recovery was complete.

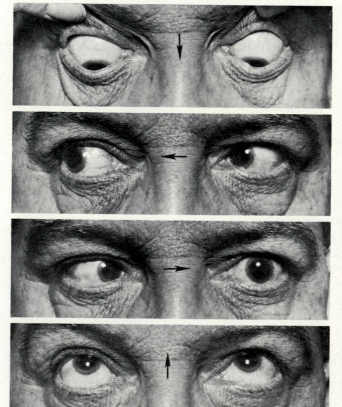

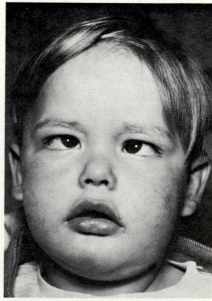

128. Left sixth nerve palsy △
Isolated left sixth nerve palsy. All movements of the affected eyeball are normal except abduction. Recovery was complete but the patient subsequently developed multiple symptoms and signs due to multiple sclerosis.

129. Bilateral sixth nerve palsy △
Convergent strabismus in congenital bilateral sixth nerve paralysis. This is sometimes seen in association with congenital bilateral facial paralysis—congenital facial diplegia, due to nuclear aplasia.

Unilateral Ophthalmoplegia

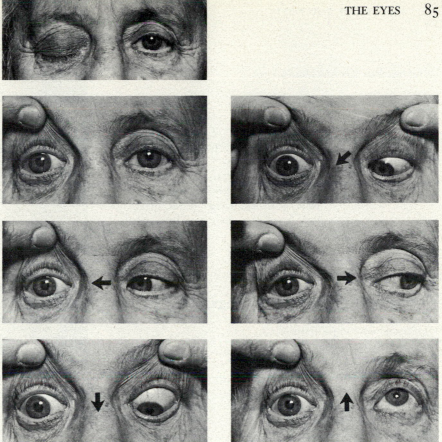

130. External ophthalmoplegia ▷
Complete right external ophthalmoplegia. Left eye normal. The right pupil was only slightly dilated and still reacted sluggishly to light. There was also anaesthesia over the distribution of the first branch of the right trigeminal nerve. Intracranial aneurysm arising from the right internal carotid artery.

Internuclear Ophthalmoplegia

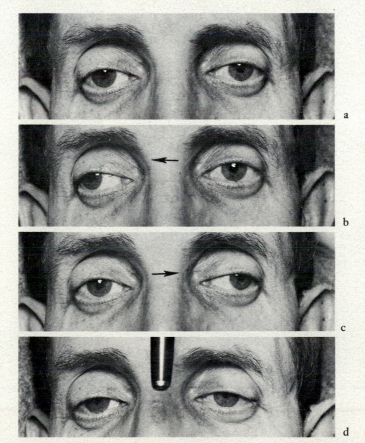

131. Internuclear ophthalmoplegia in multiple sclerosis ▷
In (*a*) note slight right divergent strabismus. In (*b*), right lateral gaze; paresis of the left internal rectus. In (*c*), left lateral gaze, paresis of the right internal rectus. In (*d*) there is slight contraction of the internal recti on convergence-accommodation.

Internuclear Ophthalmoplegia

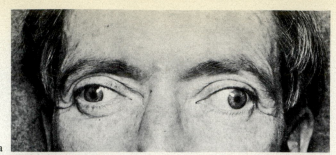

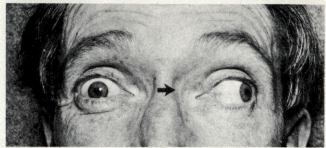

132. Internuclear ophthalmoplegia in multiple sclerosis ▷
In (*a*) there is bilateral divergent strabismus. In (*b*), left lateral gaze, paralysis of right internal rectus. In (*c*), right lateral gaze, there is paralysis of left internal rectus.

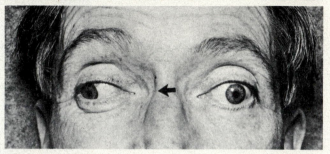

Endocrine Ophthalmoplegia

133. Endocrine exophthalmos ▽
In (*a*), note retraction of upper eyelids and the glistening appearance of the conjunctivae. There was no diplopia. In (*b*), 3 months later, the patient had developed characteristic myxoedema. Note the oedema of the upper eyelids and the suffusion of the conjunctivae.

a

b

c

133a

133b

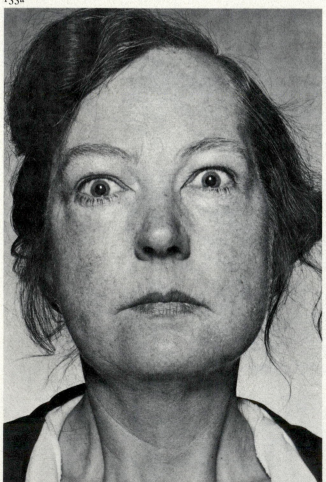

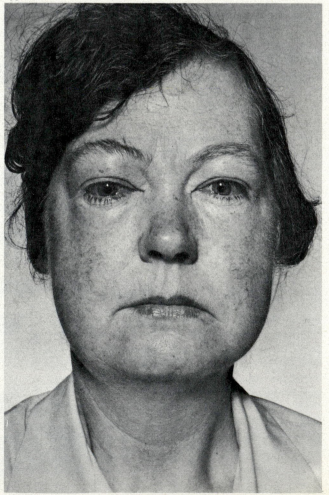

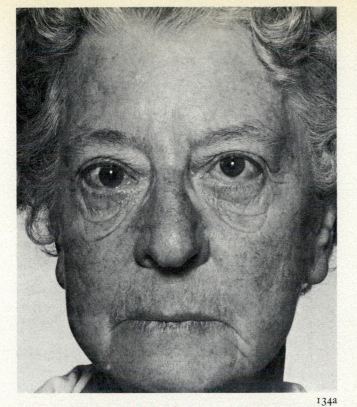

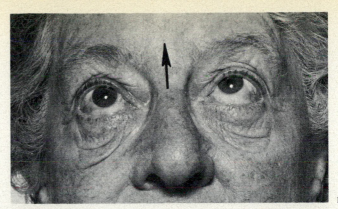

134b

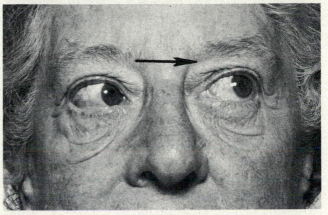

134c

134a

134. Endocrine exophthalmos △
Complaints were of diplopia and protrusion of left eyeball (*a*). Note defective upward gaze (*b*) of right eye and abduction (*c*) of left eye. Movements of elevation and abduction suffer earliest.

Endocrine Ophthalmoplegia

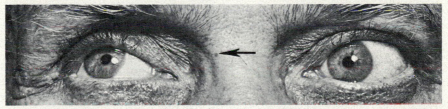

a

b

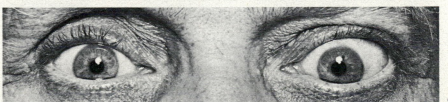

c

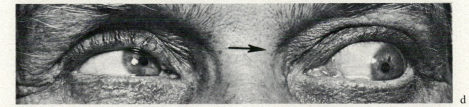

d

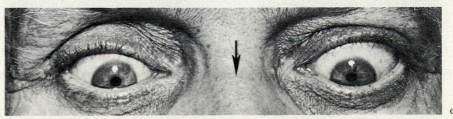

e

135. Endocrine exophthalmos ▷
This patient, a male aged 47, was mildly hyperthyroid and complained of diplopia. In (*c*), forward gaze, note right divergent strabismus and retraction of upper lids. In (*b*), right lateral gaze, note weakness of left internal rectus. In (*d*), left lateral gaze, note weakness of right internal rectus. Fluctuating ophthalmoplegia over a period of observation of 10 years.

Ocular Myopathy

The extra-ocular muscles are not affected in the majority of patients with muscular dystrophy. Progressive external ophthalmoplegia was for many years considered to be nuclear in origin. But there was never any convincing autopsy evidence that this was the explanation. Ocular muscle biopsy revealed that the paralysis of the ocular muscles was due to myopathic degeneration. Ocular myopathy may be congenital or familial, but it may start at any age. It probably accounts for some of those cases of ptosis which appear in infancy and actually increase during lifetime. Many cases appear to start in middle life.

The distinction between neuropathic and myopathic ophthalmoplegia may be difficult. The majority of patients with progressive ophthalmoplegia and ptosis seem to be examples of progressive ocular myopathy, although serum enzymes may not be raised as in other myopathies. Electrophysiological and histological studies indicate a myopathic process. Rarely, the ocular myopathy may be accompanied or followed by oculopharyngeal or general myopathy. Such cases should not of course be confused with dystrophia myotonica, in which there is ptosis as well as a myopathic facies. On the other hand there are cases of progressive ptosis with ophthalmoplegia in which, although muscle biopsy reveals an apparent myopathic process, at autopsy degenerative neurological disease is found. The interpretation of ocular muscle biopsy specimens must be difficult because section of the oculomotor nerve can result in changes in the denervated muscles which are indistinguishable from those of myopathy. Ocular muscles are not merely small slips of skeletal voluntary muscle; they have anatomical, physiological and pharmacological differences. In a limb one axone supplies 100 to 200 muscle fibres, whereas in the eye one axone supplies only a few fibres. In summary, it is probable that as yet, in the disease of ocular myopathy, there are insufficient neuropathological studies to establish with certainty whether the ophthalmoplegia is neurogenic or myogenic in origin.

Males and females are about equally affected. In my experience ptosis is invariable, although there are reports which state otherwise. The ptosis is usually bilateral but it may be unilateral for a long time. Diplopia is an uncommon complaint and in large part this is due to the ptosis. Passive elevation of the eyelids may unmask the diplopia. In other cases the progressive immobility of the eyeballs is so symmetrical that the visual axes remain parallel. Some patients state that they were aware of the inability to move their eyeballs for several decades. The pupils are spared and react normally to light. Because of the ptosis the eyebrows are usually elevated above the supra-orbital ridges and in severe cases the head is thrown back to permit vision. The wasting of the eyelids and ocular muscles often results in a paperlike texture to the upper lids with the eyes sinking into apparently empty orbits. Occasionally there is some degree of myopathic degeneration in the upper facial and temporal muscles.

The disorder is progressive but may become arrested at any stage. The ptosis and ophthalmoplegia do not fluctuate or remit as in myasthenia gravis. However, the patient may complain that there is occasional intermittent diplopia and that fatigue aggravates the ptosis. This often raises the suspicion of myasthenia gravis. A *Tensilon* or *Prostigmin* test is then necessary. In both myasthenia gravis and ocular myopathy the pupil reactions are normal. Sometimes the *Tensilon* or *Prostigmin* tests temporarily aggravate the condition of ocular myopathy.

Although facial weakness occurs in some cases of ocular myopathy, bulbar palsy is rare. In motor neurone disease ptosis and ophthalmoplegia are rare.

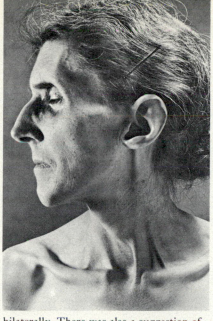

Ocular Myopathy

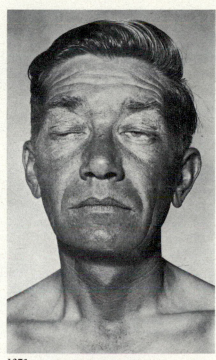

137a

136. Ocular myopathy
This patient presents the characteristic
facies. The sleepy look, the thin upper lids,
the sunken eyes and in addition wasting of
the temporal and masseter muscles

bilaterally. There was also a suggestion of
early wasting and weakness of the cervical
muscles. *Tensilon* test negative. Duration
20 years.

137
c

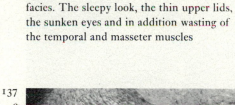

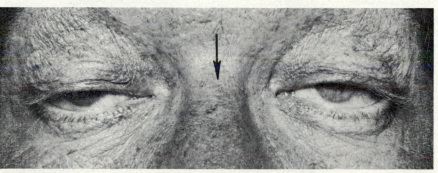

d

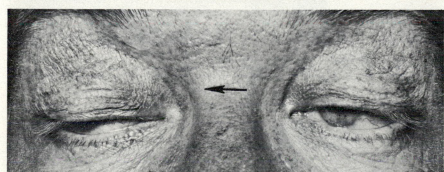

e

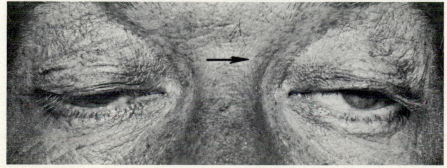

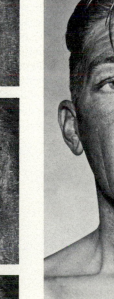

137b

137. Ocular myopathy
Forward gaze in (*a*). Upward gaze in (*b*);
note that although eyeballs do not turn up
the lids open. In (*c*), downward gaze, the
eyeballs do not move. In (*d*) and (*e*), right
and left lateral gaze, there is minimal
movement. Onset in early 20's. Family
history negative. *Tensilon* test negative.

Ocular Myopathy

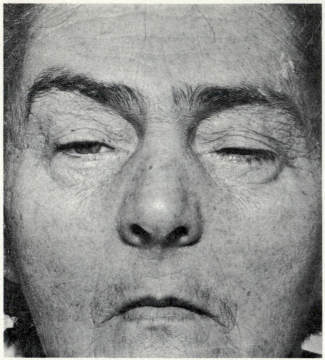

138a

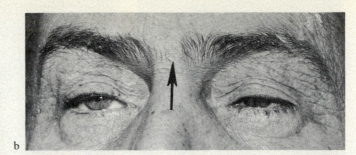

b

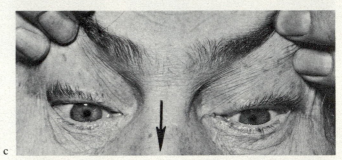

c

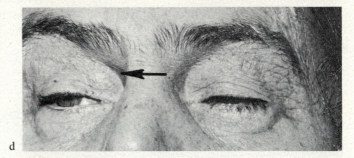

d

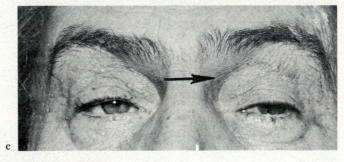

e

138. Bilateral external ophthal-moplegia (cause unknown) △ ▷
A 10-year history of progressive dementia, diplopia, dysarthria and ataxia. Absent lower limb reflexes with bilateral extensor plantar responses. Originally said to have had a megaloblastic anaemia but there was normal gastric acidity. No response to B_1 or B_{12} therapy. Possibly an irreversible Wernicke's encephalopathy. Pupils normal. In (a), forward gaze, note bilateral ptosis and drooping of mouth. In (b), (c), (d) and (e) almost complete bilateral external ophthalmoplegia.

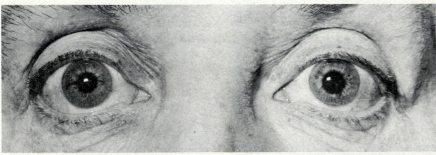

139a

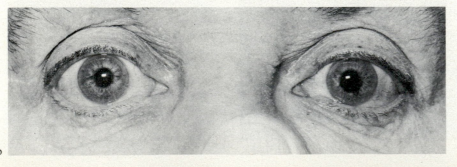

139b

139. Post-encephalitic Parkinsonism ◁
Paresis of convergence-accommodation. In (a), distant gaze, note pupillary inequality. In (b) the patient is attempting to focus on the finger of the examiner; note lack of convergence bilaterally and lack of pupillary constriction on the left.

THE FIFTH CRANIAL NERVE

The trigeminal nerve consists of a motor and a sensory element. The motor nucleus lies in the tegmental portion of the pons, its fibres passing forwards to emerge from the ventral aspect of the pons with the sensory root. The motor root passes below the Gasserian ganglion to join the third or mandibular division of the sensory nerve. It supplies the muscles of mastication; the temporals and masseters and the internal and external pterygoids. The two former muscles serve to raise the mandible, close the mouth and clench the teeth. The pterygoids assist in opening the mouth, protruding the mandible and effect side-to-side movements of the jaw.

Lesions of the motor root cause weakness and wasting of these muscles and there may be flattening or hollowing above and below the zygoma. Palpation of the anterior border of the masseter on each side, when the patient is asked to clench his teeth, reveals the defective contraction. On fully opening the mouth the jaw deviates to the paralysed side as a result of the unopposed action of the external pterygoid on the opposite side. In bilateral paralysis of the masticatory muscles, which may be seen in bulbar poliomyelitis, in the late stages of motor neurone disease and in myasthenia gravis, the jaw hangs open.

In the majority of healthy males one cannot obtain a visible jaw jerk—a reflex contraction of the masseter—but it may accompany general hyper-reflexia in nervous patients. When it is obviously hyperactive it may help in determining the level of a lesion in the pyramidal pathways. It may assist in distinguishing between a pontine and a cervical cord lesion. In a case of tetraparesis or paraparesis a brisk jaw jerk may be the only indication that the lesion or lesions involve pontine or suprapontine levels.

The sensory fibres of the trigeminal originate in the Gasserian ganglion which lies in a dural recess at the apex of the petrous bone, lateral to the internal carotid artery and behind the cavernous sinus. The peripheral axons form the ophthalmic, maxillary and mandibular divisions of the nerve which carry all forms of sensation from the face, the anterior portion of the scalp, the eye and the anterior two-thirds of the tongue. The second cervical segments meet the trigeminal area of supply at the vertex of the scalp and above the jaw line. The side of the nose is innervated by branches from the first and second divisions of the trigeminal nerve. Anatomical texts differ in the extent to which they depict the trigeminal innervation of the pinna. Some show the mandibular division supplying only the tragus; others the anterior upper half of the whole pinna. There may be some normal variation but in the writer's experience section of the sensory root of the trigeminal nerve usually results in sensory loss involving only the tragus and sometimes a strip along the upper and anterior margin of the pinna.

The central fibres from the Gasserian ganglion pass to the pons in the sensory root. Those bearing touch and proprioception enter the principal sensory nucleus in the pons, while those fibres conveying pain and temperature turn downwards to end in the spinal nucleus of the trigeminal nerve, which runs through the medulla and into the upper two or three cervical segments of the spinal cord. The sensory fibres of this trigeminal system may be involved within the brain stem or along the course of the nerve itself. The presence of pain fibres from the trigeminal nerve in the cervical cord possibly explains why pain from lesions in the neck can be referred to the forehead. Dissociated sensory loss in the face, with impairment of appreciation of pain and temperature and preservation of that of light touch, results from the anatomical rearrangement of the sensory fibres within the brain stem. Examples of this type of sensory loss are seen in cases of syringobulbia and in occlusion of the posterior inferior cerebellar artery. Multiple sclerosis is a common cause of temporary unilateral paraesthesiae and numbness of the face. I have seen at autopsy a plaque in the emerging sensory root. The site of the lesion in multiple sclerosis which causes trigeminal neuralgia is probably within the pons. Why the majority of sclerotic lesions produce paraesthesiae and numbness and a minority produce paroxysmal trigeminal pain is not known.

Dense total trigeminal anaesthesia indicates a lesion of the ganglion or sensory root, usually a tumour. A meningioma or neurofibroma growing from the sensory root may produce a 'stone dead face' without pain. Other lesions in this vicinity, for instance malignant metastases and granulomatous processes such as sarcoid, tend to produce pain, paraesthesiae and progressive sensory loss. There is an 'idiopathic' form of trigeminal sensory neuropathy. Numbness of the face usually develops in an insidious fashion. At times there may be slight pain and some paraesthesiae, but on the whole it is of a simple loss of sensation that the patient complains. This is located over the cheek and on the inside of the mouth and may spread to involve all three divisions of the nerve. Occasionally it involves both sides of the face. I have seen two cases in which eventually there was total trophic erosion of the nose [FIGS. 144 and 146]. These two cases may represent something exceptional*. Usually in trigeminal sensory

---

* Lord Elgin (1772–1841), of Parthenon fame, contracted a disorder of the face with a painful tic and gradual destruction of his nose, so that he was monstrously disfigured for the rest of his life. A rhyme of the day said, 'Noseless himself he brings here noseless blocks, to show what time has done and what the pox'.

neuropathy the numbness progresses for some weeks or months and then subsides. The corneal reflex is often retained. Taste may be lost on the affected side of the tongue if the mandibular division is involved. Usually the sensory loss affects both pinprick and light touch. The motor root is only rarely involved. The numbness of the face is often very unpleasant and the patient may complain bitterly of feelings of stiffness, coldness and deadness of the whole side of the face. In other instances the sensory loss is milder, less extensive and less bothersome.

A lesion in the Gasserian ganglion or root would explain this disorder. Its nature is not known. Trigeminal sensory neuropathy can be a feature of systemic lupus erythematosus, but in many such case reports there were indications in the clinical history that the trigeminal sensory neuropathy was not an isolated and presenting symptom. For the present it is best to look on this condition as a syndrome with a varying aetiology. In my experience the majority of patients recover and do not develop other signs of disease, but the diagnosis should not be made until compressive lesions of the sensory root have been carefully excluded. Multiple sclerosis, nasopharyngeal carcinoma, sarcoid and even syphilis must be remembered as possible explanations.

Invasion of the Gasserian ganglion by the virus of herpes zoster is well known. The ophthalmic division of the nerve is most commonly involved, but the lesions can be curiously selective [FIG. 143]. Equally obscure is the cause of post-herpetic neuralgia. This is particularly troublesome in the elderly, and there is some evidence that very severe pain at the onset is an ill omen. This is by no means always the case, however, and some elderly people with a characteristic and brisk attack of shingles of the face weather the storm without subsequent neuralgia. Some clinicians have reported that early treatment of the shingles with ACTH or steroids by mouth in large doses diminishes the likelihood and the severity of subsequent neuralgia. In contrast to tic douloureux the pains, although they wax and wane and occur in bouts and crises, are not brief and paroxysmal, but last for minutes or hours at a time. They are not reflexly excited by trigger mechanisms as in tic douloureux, and this possibly explains why they do not cease during sleep. Fortunately the pain tends to subside, but I have known it persist indefinitely. It is entirely unrelieved by ordinary analgesics including carbamazepine (*Tegretol*), a drug so useful in trigeminal neuralgia. The elderly or aged patient should not be allowed to suffer continuously or offered useless surgical treatment because of fears of addiction, since powerful euphoriant analgesics are available and would make his life tolerable. Gowers recorded the case of Sir William Jenner's patient with post-herpetic neuralgia who 'before the days of

anaesthetics endured the excision of the skin to which the pain was referred in the hope of relief, but found none and then, unable to bear the continuous agony, he shot himself'.

If the trigeminal sensory root is compressed by a tumour arising from the auditory nerve, paraesthesiae, numbness and impairment of the corneal reflex are then much commoner than pain. When pain does occur it is rarely paroxysmal, and perceptive hearing loss and ipsilateral facial paresis suggest the diagnosis. Investigations should then proceed to determine the precise nature of the deafness; radiological examination of the internal auditory meatus is necessary, and the protein content of the spinal fluid must be measured.

Pain in any division of the trigeminal nerve, or in all three divisions, may be caused by structural disease long before any sensory loss can be detected. Particularly important in this respect is nasopharyngeal carcinoma. Facial neuralgia from metastasizing lesions may be severe and intractable. The absence of clinical signs and the depressed appearance of the patient may tempt the clinician to think in terms of a depressive illness. Ocular movements, hearing, the nose and sinuses, the buccal mucous membrane, the tongue, the gums (with dentures removed), the tonsils, pharynx and throat must all be carefully and repeatedly examined. Only in this way and by radiological studies can these cases be identified.

More peripherally, injury is the commonest cause of lesions of the supra-orbital or infra-orbital nerves. Following a blunt head injury the convalescent or discharged patient begins to complain of numbness and pain on the forehead or cheek. The symptoms can be remarkably persistent and at times fluctuating and unless careful sensory testing is carried out, a diagnosis of post-concussional syndrome or neurosis may be made. Local tenderness and referred pain is sometimes present on palpation of the emerging nerves. Occasionally these post-traumatic neuralgias draw attention to previously missed orbital or maxillary fractures. Infra-orbital neuralgia may also follow antrostomy. Pain is usually continuous, aching, and often made worse by heat so the patient will tell you that he dare not sit close to a fire. A causalgic type of pain in the distribution of the inferior dental nerve sometimes follows dental extraction.

In *trigeminal neuralgia* there are no objective physical signs. Diagnosis must be based on the clinical history. Salient features of the pain are its unilaterality, its confinement to the trigeminal territory, its paroxysmal quality and its precipitation by talking, eating and washing the face. The pain occurs in bouts which may be separated by intervals of freedom lasting months or years. One moment the patient is well and the next moment the pain explodes in his face. With each paroxysm the face may be contorted with spasm (hence the term 'tic douloureux'). Oddly, the majority of patients with this disease sleep soundly. The stimuli which can trigger off a paroxysm of pain may be minimal. One patient plucked a hair from his head and with it had only to touch a tiny spot on the upper lip to produce a flash of pain. As in tabetic lightning pains the patient may feel that the pain lasted a minute or so, when in reality it was over in several seconds. One of my patients did not realize this until he timed his pain by the clock on his television screen at a horse jumping competition; each paroxysm lasted 5 or 6 seconds. Some patients feel a dull continuous ache in the face after severe paroxysms.

James Hogg (1770–1835) 'the Ettrick Shepherd', a friend and contemporary of Walter Scott, gave a graphic description of trigeminal neuralgia.

'I never fan [felt] ony pain like the Tick Dollaroose. Ane's no accustomed to a pain in the face. For the toothach's in the inside o' the mouth, no in the face; and you've nae idea hoo sensitive's the face. Cheeks are a' fu' o' nerves— and the Tick attacks the hail bunch o' them screwing them up to sic a pitch o' tension that you canna help screeching out, like a thousand ools, and clappin' the pawms o' your hauns to your distrackit chafts [jaws], and rowin' yoursell on the floor on your groff ['on the groffe'=flat on the ground], wi' your hair on end, and your een [eyes] on fire, and a general muscular convulsion in a' your sinnies; sae piercin', and searchin', and scrutinisin', and diggin', and houkin', and tearing is the pangfu' pain that keeps eatin' away and manglin' the nerves o' your human face divine. Only think o' the Tick Dollaroose in a man's face continuing to a' eternity!'

The doctor who is first consulted by a patient with pain in the face has an important responsibility. In the majority of cases there are no physical signs. The diagnosis is going to depend on the history. The doctor should record this carefully: first what the patient says about the pain, and secondly his answers to questions put to him. Mistakes are common in this field and very often it is exceedingly difficult later on to establish the truth. Even in hospital clinics, where records are kept, the difference between the first story and the last may be unbelievable. The general practitioner who merely records 'pain in the face' and the drug he prescribed at the time has missed the best diagnostic opportunity. The neurotic patient, with his sheaf of reports, may have acquired something which bears no more relation to a genuine clinical history than does a rumour to an event. What began as an account of a quite non-specific type of pain in the face becomes over the years, with its localizations, paroxysms and triggers, indistinguishable from tic douloureux except that it does not respond to treatment.

On the other hand, especially in the very elderly, the characteristic features of tic douloureux may be exceedingly difficult or quite impossible to elicit. The pain is not paroxysmal but apparently 'continuous';

'it never stops'. It spreads beyond the trigeminal territory or to the other side of the face. It disturbs sleep. It is 'in the head' as much as in the face. Chewing and swallowing are not triggers. Nevertheless even the frailest old person has noticed some sort of trigger. Most commonly it is a simple touch at some point on the face, usually the nasolabial fold. Blowing the nose or putting in dentures first thing in the morning may be the sole triggers which provide the clue to the diagnosis.

The student will probably not see a patient suffer the paroxysm of tic douloureux in hospital. It is one of the little dramatic scenes in the neurology clinic and has been vividly described by Edwards* (1973) in the following way.

'The patient, past middle age, often looks older than she is. She will walk gingerly and slowly into the consulting room looking jaded. She is afraid to make a sudden jarring movement and lowers herself gently into the chair with a sigh. She has the look of a person filled to the brim with recent suffering. If the examiner is lucky he may see an attack and be able to weigh roughly its severity and minutely its length. He will then see a physical sign portrayed in the form of a unique momentary vignette. Suddenly the patient will stop talking and moving except for her arms and one side of the face. The rest of her will freeze in a second or two into complete immobility. Her eyes will seem to fix at a distance. Then her face will screw up on the side of the pain and remain contorted. Usually the hands will slowly come up towards the face but not touch it. Having assumed this position in a matter of seconds, she will remain statuesque but emitting a prolonged groan whilst the pain lasts. Then the rigidity and grimace will melt in seconds, the groan replaced by a sigh or the words; "that was one". The whole affair will have lasted seconds or a minute or so.'

In my experience it is rare for a patient over the age of 70 to complain of any severe form of unilateral facial pain that does not turn out to be trigeminal neuralgia.

A form of hemicrania which is of particular interest is *periodic migrainous neuralgia*. During the past 50 years it has been given many names, sphenopalatine ganglion neuralgia; ciliary migrainous neuralgia; Vidian neuralgia; erythromelalgia of the head; histaminic cephalalgia; petrosal neuralgia and cluster headaches. The patient is usually an adult healthy male. He is subject to attacks of pain of the most intolerable severity in and around one eye, spreading to the forehead, temple and cheek. It has a prolonged, boring and often a throbbing character, entirely different from trigeminal neuralgia. The pain usually lasts 1 or 2 hours and during the attack the eye on the affected side becomes reddened and there is lacrimation. Congestion of the ipsilateral nostril is common. The attacks of pain occur in bouts lasting several weeks and often wake the patient from his sleep in the early hours of the morning. As in trigeminal

* Edwards, C. H. (1973) *Neurology of Ear, Nose and Throat Diseases*, London.

neuralgia, there are no physical signs to be detected, but knowledge of the disorder and its characteristic features enables a diagnosis to be made. Prophylactic ergotamine preparations, orally or hypodermically, are most effective.

When all is said and done, the great majority of patients with facial pain are suffering either from toothache or from a disorder which is unknown. It is true that the provocation of dental pain by eating, especially sweet, cold or hot foods, may in the elderly be interpreted as trigeminal neuralgia. But dental pain is so common and so variable in its clinical manifestations that no patient with continuous or recurrent facial pain should fail to have appropriate dental examination.

In contrast to the clearly defined entities we have described—such as post-herpetic neuralgia, trigeminal neuralgia, migrainous neuralgia, and those disorders in which the pain is a consequence of a structural lesion involving the trigeminal sensory system—there is a much larger group of patients with facial pain who, for want of a better term, are said to be suffering from 'atypical facial pain'. Despite the prefix 'atypical', some clinicians believe that these patients nevertheless represent a well recognized entity. It is generally acknowledged that the majority of them are women, usually middle-aged. They may or may not be depressed. In some the pain is a feature of an endogenous depression, but it may not respond to antidepressive treatment. In others the depression seems to be reactive, a consequence of their pain, though this is a distinction I find exceedingly difficult to make. The majority of my patients are not depressed as far as I can judge. They do not respond in any satisfactory way to anti-depressive treatment. They allege that their pain is severe, but they do not look ill. Some are quite cheerful [Fig. 569]. No analgesic offers them relief. Indeed, they usually do not look disappointed when they tell you that your latest prescription is no better than the previous one. There is a curious perversity about their complaint. They do not look as if they are 'suffering'. So far as I know they are incurable, and they serve to remind one of the remark made by Sigmund Freud to one of his patients, 'I am afraid we can't cure your hysterical misery, but we will try to turn it into ordinary human unhappiness'.

The Fifth Cranial Nerve

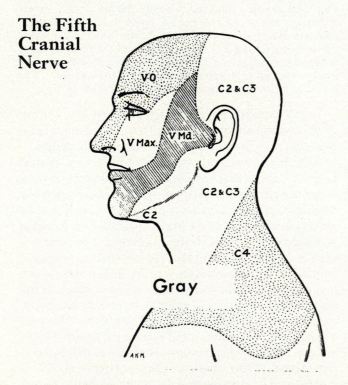

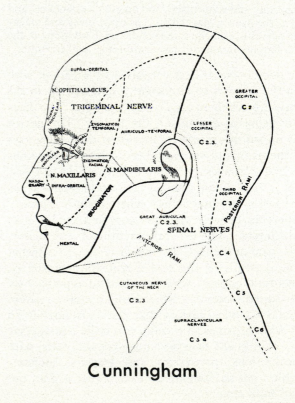

140. The fifth cranial nerve
The differing extent of the distribution of the mandibular nerve to the upper anterior
pinna is portrayed in these two diagrams from well-known textbooks of anatomy.

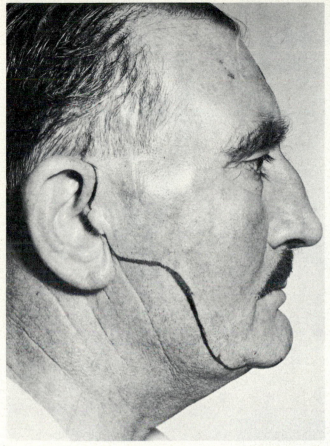

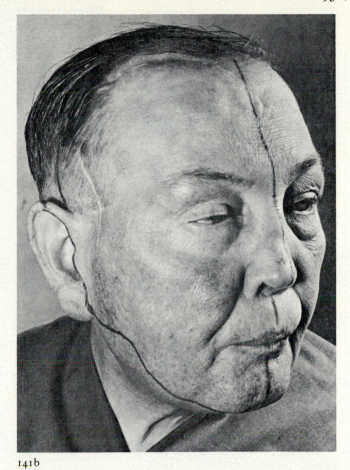

141a   141b

141. Trigeminal anaesthesia
Both these patients had complete section of the trigeminal sensory root for trigeminal neuralgia. The extent of the anaesthesia is outlined and it will be seen that only the tragus of the external ear is involved in (a) and in (b).

The Fifth Cranial Nerve

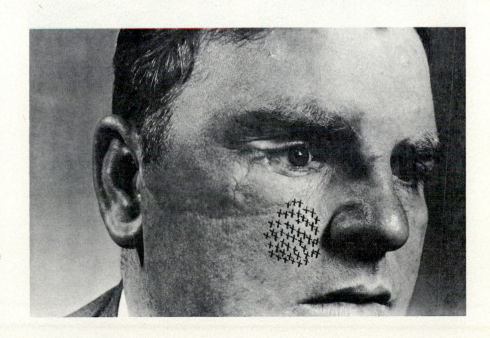

142. Infra-orbital nerve injury
Head injury with fracture of the right maxilla and slight residual flattening of the cheek. Persistent, troublesome pain and paraesthesiae in the distribution of the infra-orbital nerve. Sensory impairment was still present 8 months later.

143a

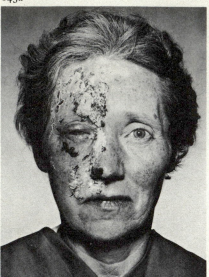

143b

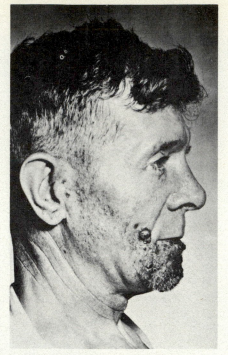

143c

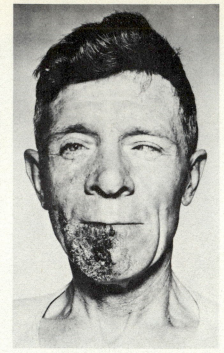

143. Herpes zoster
(*a*) Herpes zoster of the right Gasserian ganglion involving the first and second divisions of the nerve. Note the chemosis of the right eye and the sparing of the mandibular division.

(*b*) and (*c*). Herpes zoster of the right Gasserian ganglion involving only the third division of the nerve. (The left squint is congenital.)

The Fifth Cranial Nerve

144a

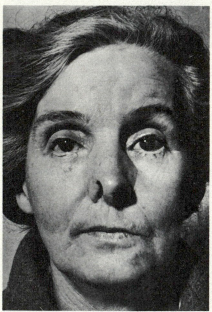

144b

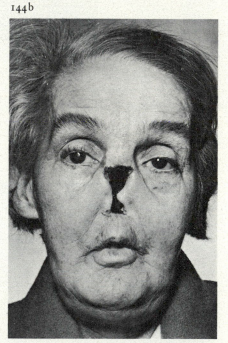

144c

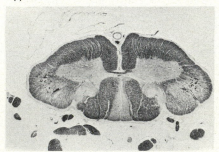

144. Trigeminal neuropathy
Age 58. Obscure bilateral progressive trigeminal anaesthesia, probably due to 'degenerative' lesions of the Gasserian ganglia. Corneal anaesthesia.
The patient was followed for 20 years until her death at the age of 78. In the second decade of the illness she gradually developed signs of pyramidal and posterior column involvement of the spinal cord.

At autopsy there was widespread involvement of the trigeminal sensory system, the posterior root ganglia, and the pyramidal tracts and posterior columns in the spinal cord. Professor H. Urich considered that the lesions were in the nature of some obscure form of vascular amyloidosis which was curiously systematized within the nervous system.

(*a*) Erosion of the ala nasi in an early stage of the disease. Progressive trigeminal anaesthesia with neuropathic keratitis.
(*b*) The same patient 8 years later with total trophic destruction of the nose.
(*c*) Transverse section of the cervical spinal cord showing involvement of the pyramidal tracts and the posterior columns (Luxol fast blue stain).

145. Erosion of left ala nasi in post-encephalitic Parkinsonism

Age 52 years. A psychotic vagrant whose complete medical history is not known. Abnormal behaviour since adolescence; speech disorder and characteristic tremor and cogwheel rigidity, mainly in the left limbs. No response to L-dopa. One year's history of progressive erosion of the left nostril. Unreliable sensory witness, but probable impairment of all modalities of sensation on the left side of the face; corneal reflex retained.

Erosion of the nose in post-encephalitic Parkinsonism has been described and is usually attributed to constant picking of the nostril when there is analgesia. It has also been described in the acute stage of the illness and then attributed to the friction of a nasal feeding tube.

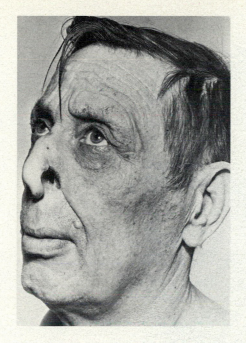

The Fifth Cranial Nerve

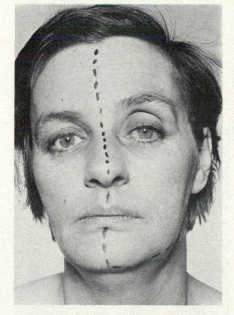

146a

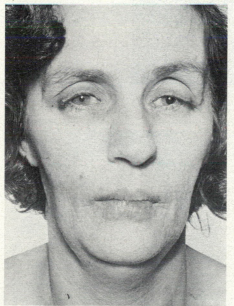

146b

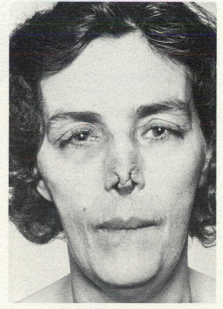

146c

146. Bilateral trigeminal neuropathy

(*a*) Female aged 38 years. Six months' history of *left*-sided paroxysmal trigeminal pains, followed by progressive trigeminal anaesthesia and subsidence of pains. Left Horner syndrome; clinical examination otherwise negative. Extensive investigations, including air encephalography and left vertebral angiography, were all negative.

(*b*) One year later, onset of similar pains and anaesthesia in *right* trigeminal field. Neuropathic keratitis on the left required tarsorrhaphy. Complete loss of taste bilaterally.

(*c*) Fourth year of illness; bilateral nasal erosion, right tarsorrhaphy for neuropathic keratitis. Questionable wasting of masseter and temporal muscles. Steroid treatment ineffective.

No other cranial nerve involvement; no evidence of any systemic disorder. Sarcoidosis, systemic sclerosis and systemic lupus have all been excluded. Serum proteins, electrophoresis, spinal fluid and biopsy of nose all normal. A raised sedimentation rate has been the only positive laboratory finding: 15, 48, 52, 45 and 50 in successive years.

The Fifth Cranial Nerve

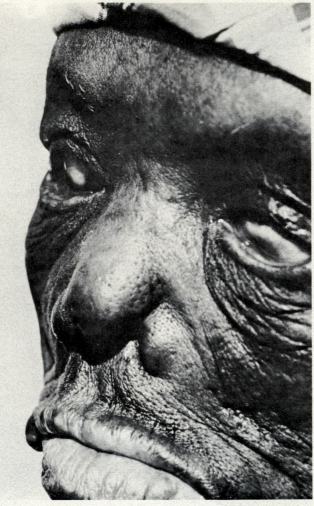

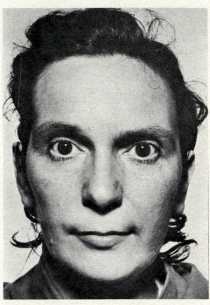

149. Trigeminal paralysis
Right trigeminal motor paralysis showing
hollowing above and below the right
zygoma. Carcinoma of breast with metastatic involvement of the mandibular
nerve.

147. Leprosy
Leprosy with trigeminal anaesthesia,
neuropathic keratitis and erosion of the
left ala nasi. (Erosion of the anterior nasal
spine is an early sign of leprosy and can be
detected by appropriate radiographs. It is
said that the skeleton of Robert the Bruce,
who is supposed to have died of leprosy,
showed this sign.)

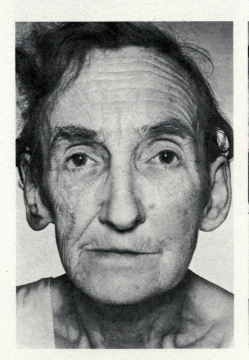

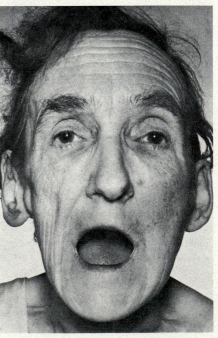

148. Trigeminal paralysis
Right trigeminal motor paralysis showing
flattening of right cheek due to atrophy of
underlying masseter. Deviation of jaw to
the right on opening the mouth, due to the
unopposed action of the left external
pterygoid muscle. Isolated trigeminal
lesion (motor and sensory); followed for 5
years; aetiology unknown.

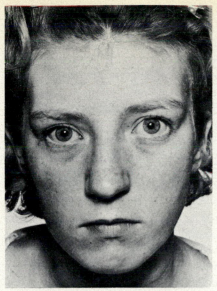

150a

150b

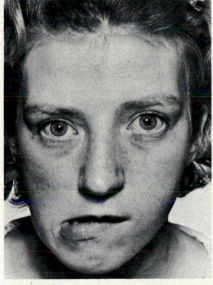
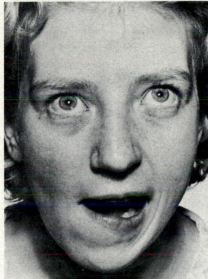

150c

150d

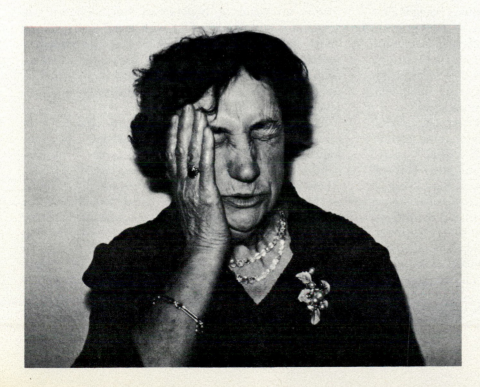

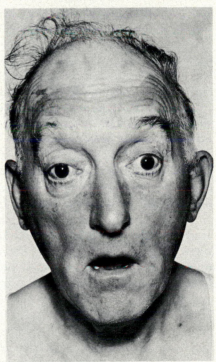

The Fifth Cranial Nerve

150. Trigeminal paralysis ◁
Cystic astrocytoma of the right cerebral hemisphere which presented as an acute, painful, right trigeminal motor and sensory paralysis (a rare false localizing sign). Deviation of the jaw to the right on opening the mouth (*b*). She could protrude her jaw to the right with the intact left external pterygoid muscle (*c*). In (*d*) she is trying to protrude her jaw to the left but cannot do so because of the paralysed right external pterygoid muscle.

151. Myasthenia gravis △
Drooping jaw due to bilateral paralysis of the muscles of mastication. Such a patient often holds his chin up with his hand when speaking or chewing. Contraction of frontalis compensates for ptosis.

152. Trigeminal neuralgia ◁
A paroxysm of pain.

THE SEVENTH CRANIAL NERVE

The facial nerve proper contains motor fibres only, although in part of its course it is associated with sensory fibres from the external auditory meatus and fibres carrying the sensation of taste from the anterior two-thirds of the tongue. It also conveys secretory fibres destined for the lacrimal and salivary glands, excluding the parotid gland which receives fibres from the auriculotemporal branch of the mandibular division of the trigeminal nerve.

The motor nucleus is in the lower pons and the emerging fibres first hook around the nucleus of the sixth nerve before turning forward to emerge at the lower border of the pons close to the eighth nerve. The nerve crosses the subarachnoid space and enters the internal auditory canal, passing medial to the middle ear and emerging from the skull at the stylomastoid foramen. It divides within the parotid gland into a number of branches which innervate the muscles of facial expression and the platysma. The former comprise the muscle of the scalp (occipitofrontalis), the sphincter muscles of the eyelids (orbicularis oculi) and the muscles of the cheek (buccinator), nose and mouth. The frontalis raises the eyebrows. The corrugator is the 'frowning' muscle. The small nasal muscles effect wrinkling movements of the nose and widening of the nostrils. Movements of the lips and mouth are effected by a number of muscles which elevate, depress, retract and compress the upper and lower lips. The zygomaticus major is the principal muscle used in laughing and the buccinator muscles compress the cheeks against the teeth as in mastication. It is through the interaction and selective control of these various facial muscles that the human being is able to register voluntarily and involuntarily the gamut of human emotions; grief, surprise, suffering, contempt and disdain, irony, laughing and crying and so on. Immobility of these muscles causes a lack of ordinary expression. Dissociation of voluntary and emotional facial movements may result from central lesions.

Unilateral facial paralysis may result from a peripheral or a central lesion. A peripheral lesion may be nuclear or, more commonly, infranuclear, as in Bell's palsy. Then there is paralysis of the upper and lower parts of the face, so that the eye cannot be closed or it can easily be opened by the examiner; the eyeball turns up on attempted closure (Bell's phenomenon) and the patient is unable to elevate his eyebrow on that side. The corner of the mouth droops, the nasolabial fold is smoothed out and voluntary and involuntary movements of the affected side of the mouth are paralysed. The lips and philtrum may be drawn to the opposite side and the protruded tongue may then deviate as well, so that unilateral

hypoglossal paralysis is suspected.

In testing voluntary facial movements it should be remembered that there is a wide variation in the degree of control. Not all people can whistle or even elevate their eyebrows. If these natural limitations are marked, bilateral facial paresis may be suspected in error.

The site of the lesion in the commonest type of peripheral facial palsy (Bell's palsy) is said to be in the stylomastoid foramen. The aetiology is not known. The onset is usually acute and painless but pain behind the ear is not uncommon and it sometimes leads to suspicion of mastoiditis and emergency admission to hospital. More or less complete recovery takes place in 75 per cent. of cases of Bell's palsy. If paralysis remains complete after two weeks full recovery is virtually impossible. A pontine lesion, due usually to multiple sclerosis, tumour or a vascular lesion, is often associated with an ipsilateral, trigeminal, or sixth nerve paresis and a contralateral hemiplegia. Compression of the nerve in its intracranial course may occur in the cerebellopontine angle by an acoustic neuroma or meningioma and there is then associated deafness and loss of taste in the anterior two-thirds of the tongue. After the nerve has emerged from the stylomastoid foramen, it may be involved in a tumour of the parotid gland or by pathological processes such as sarcoidosis and polyneuritis. Trauma to the nerve may occur as a result of the fracture of the temporal bone or during forceps delivery at birth. If taste, salivation and tear production are not affected, so that the lesion does not appear to involve the chorda tympani, a lesion in the pons or the stylomastoid foramen may be suspected. If lacrimation is normal, but taste and salivation are impaired, the lesion is in the facial canal below the branching off of the superficial petrosal branch, but proximal to the departure of the chorda tympani. Distortion of sound or hyperacusis (phonophobia?) is sometimes complained of in high facial nerve lesions above the departure of the branch to the stapedius muscle. Together with the tensor tympani the stapedius contracts in response to high-pitched sounds and is thought to exert a protective damping effect upon sound vibrations reaching the internal ear.

The level of the lesion affecting the facial nerve in idiopathic Bell's palsy has been investigated by techniques which measure lacrimation, degrees of impairment of taste, and the activity of the stapedius reflex. These have indicated that the nerve is usually involved in the lower part of the facial canal. Swelling of the nerve in this confined space is considered to be the cause of the paralysis. The aetiology of the swelling remains unknown. It affects young and old, there is no particular seasonal incidence or history of recent infection, and a story of exposure to a draught is uncommon. Cold air is more likely to figure in the story when litigation is involved. Bell's palsy occurs in cold weather and in hot weather; it occurs in the tropics, and one report disclosed that it was twenty times more common in a teaching hospital in Alexandria than in London (El-Ebiary, 1971)*. A person may suffer recurrent attacks of Bell's palsy on the same or on the other side [FIG. 154]. There is a small familial incidence. The disorder is sometimes said to be more common in diabetic and hypertensive patients, but this has not been established.

The patient with Bell's palsy is invariably alarmed and wishes to be reassured. One can tell him that in about 90 per cent. of cases there is complete or nearly complete recovery. The patient will naturally enquire how soon one can say that he will be one of the majority. If the facial paralysis is partial, then he can be assured of complete recovery. A young patient usually does better than an elderly one. The presence or absence of pain at the onset does not in itself assist in prognosis, but severe pain is a warning of denervation. Loss of taste has no early prognostic significance, but recovery of taste in the first week is a good sign. Electrophysiological tests have shown that complete denervation of facial muscles occurs in some 10 to 15 per cent. of cases. It is among these that residual paresis, associated movements and varying degrees of contracture appear; a few develop crocodile tears.

Head injuries are an increasing source of traumatic facial paralysis. Here again, about 90 per cent. recover spontaneously and regain normal facial function. Facial paralysis which is an immediate consequence of head injury suggests direct trauma to the nerve, but when the paralysis develops some hours or days after the injury, the process is probably a secondary one by way of oedema or haematoma within the nerve sheath. The prognosis in the second type is better than in the first. Fractures of the temporal bone involving the base of the skull are the main cause of the condition. The petrous bone around the internal auditory canal is thick and resistant; fractures in this region tend to involve the tegmen tympani, the labyrinth or the middle ear. Most injuries of the facial nerve occur within its intralabyrinthine course. Loss of hearing and vertigo are common accompaniments. The prognosis of facial nerve injuries is better in longitudinal than in vertical fractures of the temporal bone. The former are commoner.

In unilateral facial paralysis of central type, the lesion involves the supranuclear pyramidal pathways from the opposite frontal lobe. Because of the bilateral innervation of the forehead, the upper part of the face is much less affected than the lower. In addition, emotional and associated movements of the face may be more or less unaffected. Occasionally the reverse occurs, namely,

there is loss of emotional movements and retention of voluntary movements, so-called mimic paralysis. Dissociation between voluntary and emotional facial movements is sometimes of considerable localizing significance. Cortical lesions tend to spare emotional movements; deep-seated lesions tend not to do so.

In an old peripheral facial palsy, when the face is in repose it may be difficult to say on which side was the original paralysis. Contractures can lead to accentuation of the nasolabial fold on the paralysed side and to deviation of the angle of the mouth to that side. In addition, annoying synkinetic or associated movements due to misdirection of regenerating nerve fibres may occur during voluntary, emotional and reflex movements.

In the Ramsay Hunt syndrome it is uncertain whether the geniculate ganglion is always involved. In the original cases described by the Philadelphian neurologist (1874–1937), facial palsy was associated with an herpetic eruption in the external auditory meatus. Later, he recorded further cases in which the rash developed behind the ear, in the nose, on the palate, fauces or one side of the tongue, face or neck. Thus the facial palsy can be associated with trigeminal, occipital or cervical herpes with or without auditory involvement. Autopsies are rare and in some at least the geniculate ganglion has been spared. But clinically it is important to remember that herpetic vesicles should be looked for in these sites in cases of Bell's palsy. The paralysis is usually complete, there is ipsilateral loss of taste and recovery is often partial.

If the term 'Ramsay Hunt syndrome' is restricted to those cases of facial paralysis in which the zoster is confined to the region of the external auditory meatus, involvement of the geniculate ganglion is quite probable. This has been confirmed at autopsy. The fact that the geniculate ganglion escapes involvement in some cases of zoster of the face, neck, or mouth in association with facial paralysis, does not imply that there is no such condition as geniculate zoster. In herpetic facial palsy of any of these types, the incidence of denervation is much greater than in ordinary Bell's palsy. Recovery is commonly incomplete.

Electrodiagnostic tests in the idiopathic and herpetic types of facial palsy can, within four or five days from the onset, differentiate between patients with simple conduction block who recover and those with nerve degeneration. Yet it remains difficult to predict the degree of recovery likely to be achieved in the important latter group. Treatment remains empirical, but there is gradually accumulating evidence that oral prednisolone is effective. Naturally the earlier treatment is commenced the better, but it is probably worth while starting treatment at any time during the first week.

In *bilateral facial paralysis*, immobility and not asymmetry is the main clinical feature. Because of this

---

* El-Ebiary, H. M. (1971) *Rheumatol. phys. Med.* 11, 100.

it may pass undetected. The congenital form of bilateral lower motor neurone paralysis of the face due to nuclear agenesis has already been mentioned. Acquired forms of bilateral flaccid paralysis occur in polyneuritis, myasthenia gravis and some forms of muscular dystrophy. It is relatively rare in motor neurone disease. Bilateral supranuclear lesions usually result from cerebrovascular disease when there may be pseudobulbar palsy. In this condition slight stimuli may provoke forced laughter and crying distressing to relatives and friends. A word of sympathy, a handshake or pat on the back, a portrait, a few bars of music or an item of news or gossip may cause the patient to dissolve into tears or laughter. This story of 'emotional incontinence' in an elderly person with a shuffling gait is virtually diagnostic of diffuse cerebral arteriosclerosis. They are important points in diagnosis, because the patient's actual complaints may be misleading and formal clinical examination may disclose nothing of note.

Facial Tic (Habit Spasm)

This condition is most commonly seen in children. There are sudden brief recurrent movements of one or more parts of the face; a blink of the eyes, a grimace or sniff. They do not look involuntary and the child is usually overactive and fidgety. When questioned the child usually grins, shrugs a shoulder and says 'I can't help it'. The disorder is psychological.

Facial Myokymia

This is an unusual form of involuntary movement of the facial muscles. The onset is usually acute, unilateral, and diffusely affecting the musculature of the face. It lasts for some days or weeks and then subsides. It is a curious form of rippling, flickering or quivering that passes over the face in rapid undulating waves. It involves the frontalis as well as the platysma and may semi-close the eye, draw up the angle of the mouth or purse the lips. There are no associated paraesthesiae or pain. The condition does not occur after facial palsy and is most commonly encountered in patients with multiple sclerosis. The lesion is probably in the pons close to the facial nucleus. Unfortunately the term 'myokymia' has also been given to that benign form of fasciculation which one sees in healthy limbs or in the lower eyelid.

Hemifacial Spasm

This is a disorder which chiefly affects middle-aged or elderly people and is organic in nature. It usually begins as a twitching of an eyelid or a corner of the mouth. In the early stages it may only appear towards the end of the day and there may be long periods of freedom. As the years pass the spasms become more frequent and severe and the whole of one side of the face may be momentarily contorted. In many cases some degree of weakness appears in the facial muscles. It is curious that the patient may also suffer from trigeminal neuralgia on the same or the opposite side.

Very rarely hemifacial spasm may be confused with a focal convulsive seizure.

The disorder is usually idiopathic but has been described in lesions involving the facial nerve such as an auditory neuroma, an aneurysm of the basilar artery, or arachnoiditis of the posterior fossa. It has been postulated that in the idiopathic cases there is a state of chronic irritation of the facial nerve in an unusually narrow facial canal. Surgical decompression of the affected facial nerve gives variable results; paresis may recover and the movements return. A better outlook is afforded in those cases where selective division of terminal branches of the facial nerve is undertaken. Twitching of an eyelid or of the corner of the mouth may be arrested without causing any facial paresis.

The Seventh Cranial Nerve

153a

153b

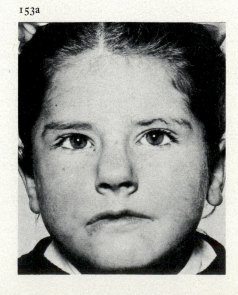 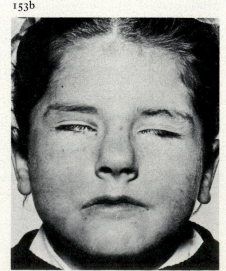

153. Congenital facial diplegia
Bilateral sixth and seventh cranial nerve paralysis due to nuclear agenesis.
(*a*) Note slight bilateral internal strabismus, the expressionless face and the lax, drooping mouth.
(*b*) She is trying to close her eyes but the orbicularis oculi are paretic. The upper eyelids can be raised and lowered because of the intact levators (supplied by the third cranial nerve). Note the upward turning of the eyeballs (Bell's phenomenon), an involuntary synkinetic movement.

The Seventh Cranial Nerve

154. Recurrent Bell's palsy ▷
Age 26 years. She has had six attacks of
acute peripheral facial palsy since the age
of 13. Personally seen in five of them.
The first attack affected the right side
and all subsequent attacks the left side
of her face. Recovery from the first took
1 year; recovery from the others about
6 months. In the last attack she was
admitted to a fever hospital with suspected
meningitis because of pain behind the
left ear and some neck stiffness. A lumbar
puncture was normal, and within 48 hours
she had the sixth attack of facial palsy.
This photograph was taken 6 weeks later
and shows slight residual weakness of eye
closure and retraction of the lips on the
left side. No evidence of any systemic
disorder on numerous investigations.
Family history negative.

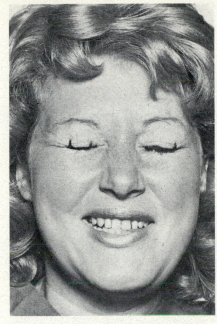

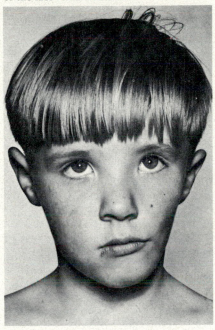

**155. Traumatic peripheral facial palsy
at birth** ▽
Note lack of growth of left side of face. In
progressive facial hemiatrophy movements
of the face remain normal.

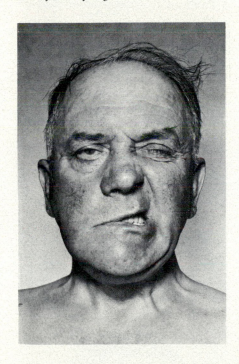

156. Acute Bell's palsy ◁
A hypertensive patient who woke one
morning with right facial paralysis. He
thought he had had a stroke and because
of dysarthria his doctor concurred. Note
the smoothing of the furrows on the right
side of his forehead, the sagging of the
right eyebrow, the eversion of the lower
eyelid (with troublesome epiphora or over-
flowing of tears), the disappearance of the
nasolabial furrow and the drooping of the

mouth on the right.
   He is trying to close his eyes and bare
his teeth. Observe the complete immobility
of the right side of the face, the failure to
close the right eye and the *absence* of Bell's
phenomenon. In health the eyeballs
usually, but not invariably, turn up in
sleep or on closing the eyes. In patients
with facial paralysis this variability is
manifested.

157a

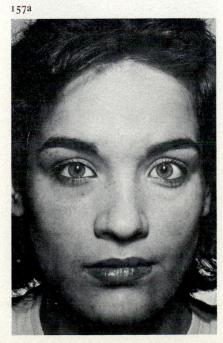

157b

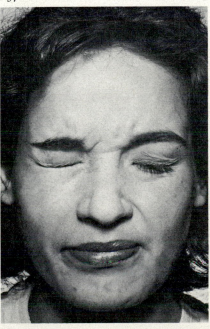

157. Old Bell's palsy ▷
(*a*) In repose there is often no visible
asymmetry. Here there is a hint of laxity
of the left lower eyelid.
(*b*) Closing the eyes reveals the weakness
of the orbicularis oculi on the left side.

*The Seventh
Cranial Nerve*

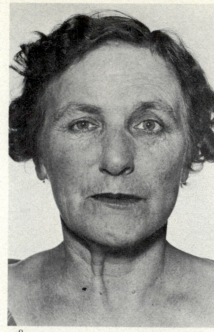
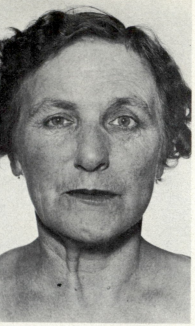

158a   158b

158. Old Bell's palsy ▷

(*a*) At rest it might be thought that the left corner of her mouth was drooping but the narrowed palpebral fissure on the right (due to contracture in the orbicularis oculi), and the inability to retract the right angle of the mouth (*b*), show that the original paralysis was on the right side. Note also the 'winking' of the right eye during the attempted movement. She was embarrassed by this 'winking' when she smiled.

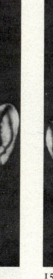

159a   159b

159. Central facial palsy ▷

A mild stroke.

(*a*) Voluntary effort to retract the angles of the mouth reveals the weakness on the left side.

(*b*) Retention of involuntary movement of the left side of the mouth and cheek during the act of smiling. Occasionally the reverse occurs—loss of emotional movements and retention of voluntary movements—mimic paralysis. Unilateral *exaggeration* of emotional movements (there is a hint of it here) is called paradoxical hypermimia. Similarly, there may be dissociated action of the facial expressions of sorrow and disappointment in these central facial palsies.

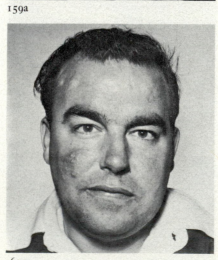

160a   160b

160. Central facial palsy ▷

Central facial palsy on the left side due to a gunshot wound in the right frontal region.

(*a*) Left lower facial weakness with the left eyebrow at a slightly lower level than that on the right.

(*b*) The *involuntary* movement of the mouth on the left side, on smiling, is good.

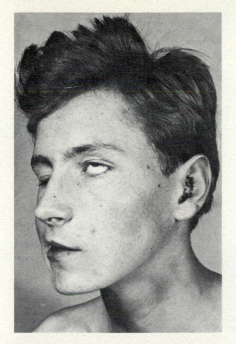

161. The Ramsay Hunt syndrome
Facial paralysis and ipsilateral otitic herpes zoster. He attempts to close his eyes and bare his teeth. Left peripheral facial paralysis, involuntary upward turning of the left eye and paralysis of orbicularis oculi. Note the crusting lesions of herpes zoster in the meatus of the ear. There was moderate deafness on the left side. Pain in the ear, vesicles and loss of hearing preceded the facial palsy by 3 days. Taste was lost on the left side of the tongue anteriorly.

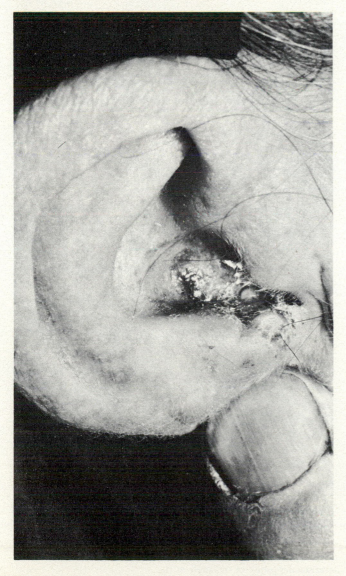

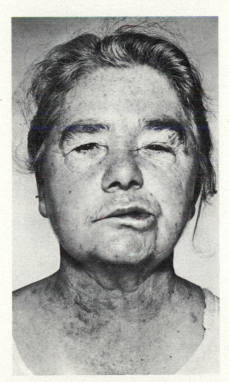

162. The Ramsay Hunt syndrome
Right facial palsy of peripheral type with ipsilateral auricular zoster. Taste was lost in the anterior part of the tongue on the same side. There was no tinnitus or deafness.

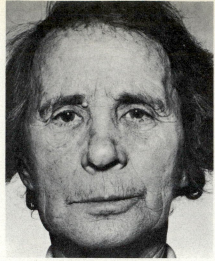

163a

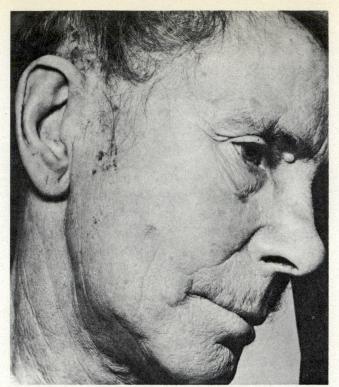

163b

163. The Ramsay Hunt syndrome △ ▷
(*a*) Drooping of the right corner of the
mouth, smoothing out of the right nasolabial groove and sagging of the right lower
eyelid.
(*b*) Zoster lesions in front of and above the
ear (trigeminal field). There were also
zoster lesions behind the ear (C.2).

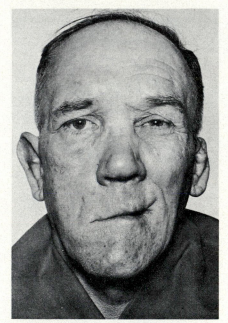

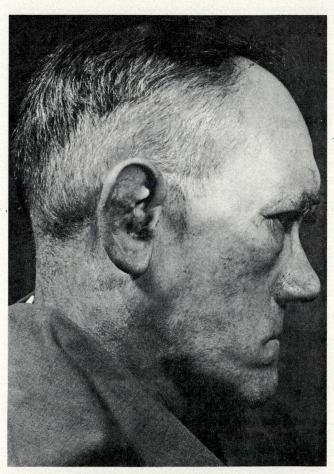

164. Traumatic facial palsy △ ▷
This collier's right facial nerve was
severed behind the ear by a penetrating
wound. It serves to recall the famous case
described by Sir Charles Bell in 1827. A
Middlesex Hospital medical student,
observing the facial paralysis of an old
street sweeper, brought him to Bell. There
was a story of the man being tossed by an
ox 12 years previously. 'The point of the
horn entered under the angle of the jaw
and came out before the ear.' Bell
observed that on the affected side 'the
nostril has no motion in breathing' and
the old sweeper explained that when he
took snuff 'I can draw it in but I cannot
make it mount.' Bell visited the patient's
wife to confirm that the right eye turned
up when he slept. Bell thought nature
arranged this so that the eye in sleep would
be moistened as it 'dipped in the lacrimal
fountain'. The cheek on the paralysed side
'puffed out on each cachinnation'.

In this illustration the scars of the ear
and over the mastoid may be seen. Note
also the deformity of the angle of the
mandible which was fractured.

The Seventh Cranial Nerve

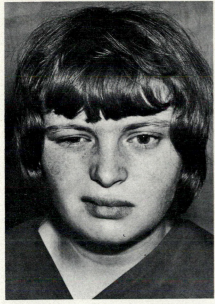

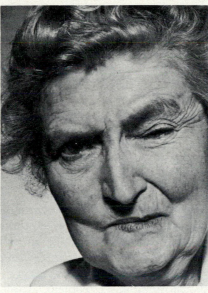

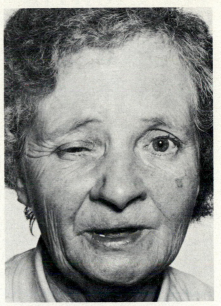

165. Facial tic (habit spasm) △
Sudden brief recurrent movements of the
right side of the face, ceasing when her
attention was diverted and increasing when
she was embarrassed. Periodic sniffing,
shrugging movements of the shoulder and
moodiness.

166. Hemifacial spasm
Clonic hemifacial spasm associated with
ipsilateral trigeminal neuralgia.

167. Hemifacial spasm
Right hemifacial spasms were almost
continuous and there was slight weakness
and wasting of the facial musculature on
the right side. Taste was lost over the
anterior two-thirds of the tongue on the
affected side.

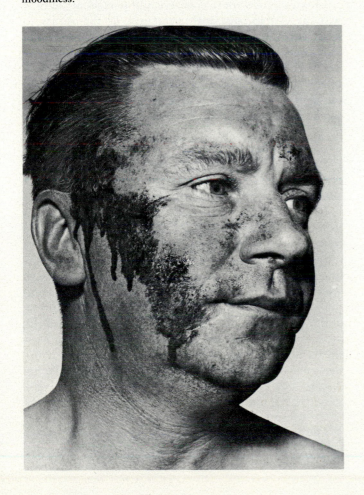

168. The auriculotemporal syndrome
Old gunshot wound of the face. Tasting
or eating food provokes flushing and
sweating of the side of the face—gustatory
sweating syndrome. The auriculotemporal
nerve is a branch of the mandibular nerve
and it communicates with the facial nerve
and the otic ganglion. The syndrome
arises from faulty regeneration after injury
to the face in the region of the parotid
gland.

THE EIGHTH CRANIAL NERVE

The auditory nerve has two components, cochlear and vestibular, subserving hearing and equilibrium. These nerves originate in separate central connexions.

Sound vibrations are transmitted through the tympanic membrane and auditory ossicles to the oval window (air conduction) or by direct bone transmission to the inner ear (bone conduction). The fluids of the cochlea are set in motion and stimuli are set up in the hair cells of the organ of Corti. The cochlear nerve transmits the impulses to the cochlear nuclei in the pons with bilateral upward transmission in the lateral lemnisci to the medial geniculate bodies and the superior gyrus of each temporal lobe. This auditory decussation precludes deafness from a unilateral cerebral cortical lesion. On the other hand, central lesions may be responsible for auditory hallucinations; epileptic auras may include the auditory sphere. Persistent tinnitus usually arises from a lesion in the organ of Corti or the auditory nerve and is accordingly often accompanied by deafness.

An estimate of the type and degree of hearing loss can be made with simple tests of hearing, using the voice and tuning forks. A conversational voice can normally be heard in quiet surroundings at 6 metres; with slight deafness it can be heard at 4 metres, and with moderate deafness at 1 metre. If the raised voice is heard only when close to the ear, there is severe loss.

There are two principal varieties of loss of hearing. There is 'conductive deafness' as in middle ear disease, where there is primarily a loss of air conduction; bone conduction may be preserved or even exaggerated. The Rinne test is then said to be negative. In the normal response to the Rinne test the vibration of the tuning fork is still heard at the meatus after it becomes inaudible on the mastoid. In the Weber test, with tuning fork on the vertex, the sound is referred to the affected side. In conductive deafness low tones are lost, so that certain vowel sounds may not be recognized.

In 'nerve' or perceptive deafness air conduction and bone conduction are both diminished, but they may retain their normal relationship so that the Rinne test is positive. In the Weber test the sound is referred to the healthy side. The hearing loss is especially marked for high tones and the patient has difficulty in hearing sibilants and sharp consonants. The presbycousis of the elderly person usually involves a progressive loss of high tones.

More complete assessment of a patient with hearing loss will require various types of audiometry: pure tone, speech, and impedance audiometry. A high tone fade indicates presbycousis. A low tone loss suggests the possibility of Ménière's disease or of acoustic neuroma. A sudden drop at 4,000 Hz indicates noise trauma deafness. Perceptive deafness may result from injury from infection (e.g. mumps) or from the toxic effects of drugs, but the most common form of perceptive deafness is degenerative. The lesion is either in the organ of Corti or in the neurones supplying the cochlea. Perceptive deafness may be unilateral or bilateral. Unilateral cases of acute onset are usually due to a virus infection or to vascular lesions. Progressive unilateral deafness is suggestive of Ménière's disease or acoustic neuroma. There are audiometric tests which help to distinguish between cochlear and neural deafness, such as recruitment and Békèsy audiometry.

Speech audiometry is useful in deciding upon the value or otherwise of a hearing aid. A sound may be audible but not accurately recognized. Speech consists of complex sound waves with a great range of frequency. Vowel sounds are mainly strong and of low frequency content, while consonant sounds are weaker and contain higher frequencies. In high tone loss the intelligibility of speech is impaired because consonants are not heard and these carry much more information than vowels.

In otosclerosis there is severe and persistent tinnitus without vertigo, but with paracusis, or the ability to hear better in the presence of loud noises. This is an important point in the differential diagnosis from nerve deafness, for most patients with that condition complain of profound inability to hear in the presence of noise. In otosclerosis the loss of hearing is mainly for the lower tones. The deafness is of the conductive type and is progressive and bilateral. Tinnitus is common, especially in the older age group.

Excluding trauma the two most important causes of nerve deafness are Ménière's disease and auditory neuroma. Determining the level of an auditory nerve lesion, whether it is in the cells of the organ of Corti as in Ménière's disease, or in the cerebellopontine angle as in auditory neuroma, may be very difficult. The loudness recruitment test assists in the differentiation. When a deaf person complains of being shouted at when voices are raised a little, he is, roughly speaking, experiencing the phenomenon of loudness recruitment. The deafness of the affected ear is reduced at higher intensities of the same frequency. Under standard test procedures with the electric audiometer, the degree of loudness recruitment may be measured. It does not occur in middle ear disease but is found in Ménière's disease and otosclerosis, but not as a rule in acoustic neuroma or lesions of the nerve trunk.

The patient with deafness may not mention it and a hearing aid may not be visible across a consulting room desk. If deafness is not detected by the examiner, diagnostic errors may arise. A few examples may be quoted. Conductive type deafness in an elderly person with an obscure limb pain, may turn out to be Paget's disease. The detection of nerve deafness in a patient whose symptoms are few and vague may direct attention to the activity of the thyroid gland. Loss of hearing after a head injury is frequently missed. The patient with an auditory neuroma may forget to mention deafness because it has been there so long, or he may consciously omit to refer to it because it seemed irrelevant to the current complaints of headache, diplopia or unsteadiness.

Loss of hearing is usually an insidious process; when it is sudden and severe, it is always alarming, whether it affects one ear or both. It is usually accompanied by loud tinnitus and vertigo is not uncommon. It is nearly always of perceptive type and it is surprising how often the cause remains unknown. In such infections as measles, mumps and herpes, it results from a toxic neuritis. The cochlear branches of the internal auditory artery are end arteries and it is possible that vascular occlusions account for some cases.

Sudden loss of hearing is usually unilateral. Acute bilateral loss of hearing may occur in multiple sclerosis, although rarely; vascular lesions are the usual explanation in middle-aged and elderly people, and there may be evidence of atrial fibrillation, embolism or hypertension. Similar lesions may occur in polycythaemia, in leukaemia and in polyarteritis nodosa. Ototoxic drugs usually cause progressive hearing loss, but in certain circumstances, notably the presence of renal failure, the deafness may be sudden and bilateral. The tinnitus which occurs in the majority of cases of acute loss of hearing may be as dramatically sudden in onset as the deafness. Vertigo varies in frequency and is probably most often encountered in vascular lesions. There is commonly a feeling of pressure and fullness in the ear, with distortion of sound and loudness discomfort. Sophisticated audiological tests are necessary if the site of the lesion, whether cochlear (sensory) or retrocochlear (neural), is to be established. It is said that if cases in the latter group are seen early enough, within two weeks of the onset, steroid treatment is effective. Vascular lesions do not often respond to treatment.

Trauma, both direct and indirect, is playing an increasingly important role in the aetiology of deafness. Direct trauma to the head may cause either perceptive or conductive deafness. The former is much more frequent, and in both types fracture of the temporal bone is common. In recent years there has been a growing appreciation that it is not always the inner ear that is damaged, but sometimes the ossicular chain. There are appropriate methods of reconstructing these injuries with good results, so that it is important to iden-

tify them. In the acute stage of the head injury, the presence of blood in the ear canal suggests injury to the tympanic membrane or the middle ear. There may be cerebrospinal fluid otorrhoea. It is in these cases that careful subsequent investigations may reveal ossicular injury.

Deafness due to indirect trauma, induced by noise, is an increasing problem in industrial environments. It is almost invariably bilateral and is characteristically a pure perceptive deafness of insidious onset. It is maximal at 4,000 Hz. The hearing levels at 4,000 Hz of retired coal miners are related to the number of years they spent at the coal face. Audiometric surveys on people employed in noisy industries have shown a characteristic 'acoustic dip' in the region of 4,000 cycles per second. Noise-induced hearing loss is not yet a prescribed disease. It is not known what part noise plays in the development of presbycousis, but the degenerative changes in the two conditions are said to be different: in noise-induced deafness the changes are confined to the spiral organ, whereas they are more diffuse in presbycousis.

'Discotheque deafness' is a form of noise-induced deafness found, as one would expect, among the young. There is no real evidence that exposure to non-amplified music is a source of acoustic trauma. Noise-induced deafness was noted among blacksmiths and bell-ringers more than a hundred years ago.

The vestibular division of the eighth nerve arises from cells of the vestibular ganglion in the floor of the internal auditory meatus. It transmits sensation from the three semicircular canals, the utricle and saccule. Changes in the rate of movement, particularly rotary movement, of the head result in displacement of endolymph and stimulation of the hair cells in the ampullae of the semicircular canals and of the otoliths in the saccule and utricle. The vestibular nuclei in the medulla have important connexions with the oculomotor nuclei, the cerebellum, the spinal cord and the temporal lobes. The function of the vestibular apparatus is to maintain balance and to steady vision. Vestibular failure leads to vertigo and ataxia with nystagmus and, sometimes, oscillopsia.

The value of unhurried history-taking is nowhere better exemplified than in the case of the patient who complains of sudden giddiness. In the majority of cases a proper analysis and interpretation of the complaint can be achieved by taking a careful history and performing a clinical examination. The patient who has experienced sudden giddiness usually has little difficulty in conveying to his doctor the fact that there has been some upset of equilibrium. The difficulty is not that giddiness goes unrecognized by doctor or patient, though this may happen, but that some other sensation is misleadingly described or interpreted as giddiness.

Giddiness is a sensation of disturbed equilibrium. It is not just 'faintness', 'queer feelings', 'muzzy feeling', 'lightheadedness', 'floating', 'sick feeling', or any of the many unpleasant sensations that some people experience under certain circumstances, such as on heights or in busy city streets. The person who experiences giddiness nearly always experiences a sensation of movement. His senses are deceived into seeing or feeling movement of one sort or another. This abnormal sensation of movement is not necessarily one of rotation (vertigo). Vertigo is, of course, one of the commonest forms of giddiness; there is a sensation of turning (*vertere*, to turn), either in self, of self or of the environment. The patient may feel a swirling sensation in his head; he may feel that his body is spinning; he may see or feel his surroundings are turning about him. Vertigo is often used in this strict sense—to denote that the sensation of movement is one of rotation. But there is nothing to be gained by adhering to this definition, for we know that other equally distressing forms of giddiness, of identical aetiology and significance, may be characterized not by a revolving sensation, but by a sense of falling through space or by some movement of self or surroundings in any other plane.

Whatever form the giddiness actually takes the patient will try to catch hold of something or lie down. He may close his eyes in an attempt to shut off the distressing impression of movement. Pallor, sweating, nausea and vomiting may follow. The patient not only feels very ill and prostrated, but his appearance may be alarming. The total picture may suggest some catastrophic illness or food poisoning, not a transient upset in one ear. During an attack of aural vertigo, the patient usually lies on the sound side. If he opens his eyes and looks upwards to the affected ear, nystagmus will be seen. If he is lying on his back, the nystagmus is increased in amplitude when the eyes are turned to the sound side.

The lesion responsible for acute rotatory vertigo is usually a peripheral one, in the labyrinth itself in Ménière's disease, and in the vestibular nerve in so-called vestibular neuronitis. In Ménière's disease the attacks recur and are associated with tinnitus and increasing deafness. There is usually some degree of deafness already present when the patient is first seen. An increase in tinnitus with some distortion of hearing often heralds an attack of acute vertigo. The patient often learns to heed these premonitory warnings.

The pathology of vestibular neuronitis is not known, but it is thought to be in the nature of a selective lesion of the vestibular system. It affects a younger age group than those afflicted with Ménière's disease and as there is no involvement of the cochlea there is no tinnitus or deafness. It is not usually a recurrent disorder but full recovery may take weeks or months.

In postural vertigo the patient complains that giddiness is provoked by certain movements or positions of the head. He may find that he is giddy if he lies down or if he looks upwards. Nausea and vomiting are rare and there is no impairment of hearing. The cause is not known, but it is important to remember that it may occur after concussion. It tends to persist for some weeks or months and then subside. In view of the positional character of the stimulus needed to evoke the disturbance, it is thought that the lesion is in the otolith apparatus. Transient nystagmus may be observed by the examiner in the clinical test procedure portrayed in FIGURE 140. When the patient is brought rapidly into a supine position with the head low and turned to one side, gross nystagmus may be seen. A negative result to this test must not be taken to exclude the diagnosis if a characteristic history has already been obtained. When positive the patient will confirm that the movement induced the complaint for which he sought advice. Although temporarily distressed, he is usually relieved that his complaint, often thought to be neurotic, is understood. It is usually a benign disorder and the patient can be reassured. Occasionally postural vertigo results from a cerebellar or brain stem lesion. The nystagmus is then usually induced in more than one position of the head and persists until normal posture is restored. Positional nystagmus of this nature may be an early sign of posterior fossa tumour.

In posterior fossa tumours vertigo is a common symptom but it tends to be less paroxysmal than in the conditions above described. Disturbance of gait tends to be progressive and independent of vertiginous episodes. The tumour patient may recognize that this loss of balance is due to lack of control over his limbs and not to some disturbance in his head. This should be put to him. He may also have noticed that one upper limb is clumsy when there is no question of disturbed balance —as when he is sitting down or reclining. In the tumour case the vertigo may or may not be related to any particular position of the head. In the early stages of the growth of an auditory neuroma, the deafness may pass unrecognized and tinnitus may be negligible. It is not surprising that the diagnosis is rarely made at this stage. Numbness of the face resulting from the involvement of the trigeminal nerve, diplopia as a result of sixth nerve paresis, and clumsiness of the homolateral limbs from cerebellar compression, are the developments which usually draw attention to the serious nature of the illness.

Vertigo of central origin occurs in lesions of the brain stem, cerebellum and temporal lobes. Sudden involvement of the vestibular connexions in the brain stem may occur in multiple sclerosis and in thrombosis of a vertebral artery or of the posterior inferior cerebellar branch. In multiple sclerosis the patient is usually young, there is no evidence of cochlear disease and the vertigo and nystagmus are usually, but not always, accompanied by signs of involvement of other nuclei and tracts. There may be diplopia and sensory symptoms. Recovery is less prompt than in aural vertigo. Thrombosis of the posterior inferior cerebellar artery may lead to ptosis with impairment of sense of pain and temperature on the same side of the face and on the opposite side of the body. These signs may be noticed by the patient when he shaves or takes a bath. In elderly and arteriosclerotic subjects acute vertigo, sometimes evoked by a movement of the head, may occur against a background of a sensation of more or less continuous unsteadiness or insecurity. Episodes of transient brain stem ischaemia commonly account for vertigo in elderly subjects, but it is usually impossible to decide whether they are a direct result of atheroma or whether cervical spondylosis and compression of the vertebral artery plays a part. Digital compression of a sclerotic internal carotid artery may induce vertigo and movements of the head can certainly interfere with the flow of blood in the vertebral arteries lying in their bony canals in the cervical spine.

Vertigo of cortical origin is less impressive and frequent, but may be seen in various forms of epilepsy, in temporal lobe tumours and as a result of intracranial hypertension.

In the differential diagnosis of these patients with deafness, tinnitus and vertigo, it may be necessary to proceed to more elaborate tests of auditory and vestibular function. Pure tone audiometry will usually differentiate between perceptive deafness, conductive deafness and otosclerosis. It may reveal a degree of deafness unsuspected by the doctor. The function of each labyrinth may be investigated by caloric tests. Abnormal responses are obtained in almost all cases of Ménière's disease and auditory nerve tumour. They are often normal in postural vertigo. These tests of auditory nerve function are now standardized procedures and are as important and necessary for full investigation and diagnosis as are the longer established visual field studies in diseases of the optic system.

But when all is said and done it must be admitted that many who complain of giddiness are not suffering from any organic disability. It may be but one expression of an anxiety state of which there is ample evidence, but these patients may describe their 'giddiness' with such insistence and graphic terms of phrase, that the inexperienced may fear the worst. It is not unnatural that the newly qualified physician, listening to a patient, usually a woman, who says that when walking in the street she is pulled or veers to the left, that she is for ever bumping into people or objects, that she fears her sense of balance has gone, should begin to think in terms of a lesion of the cerebellum. There may be no other complaint and the patient's husband may confirm and indeed elaborate the story. The subsequent fear of falling may render her virtually housebound. Formal examination reveals no abnormality but the diagnosis is not usually difficult. You get to recognize the type, the flood of words, the voluntary enacting of the 'drunkenness'. Curiously, the patient may not appear alarmed and may actually smile as she describes her difficulties. She often appears to recognize that there is nothing seriously amiss and she may confess 'it's silly really, isn't it?' In such patients it is often said that the Romberg test is positive. When she is asked to stand with her feet together, her eyes closed and her arms outstretched in front of her she usually smiles nervously, runs for her handkerchief and, immediately the eyes are closed, she sways, opens her eyes, looks alarmed, and seeks to clutch at the nearest piece of furniture. Yet, with persistence and encouragement, she will soon be doing it normally. A similar sequence of events is observed when she is asked to walk in straight line, especially in heel–toe fashion.

All this does not mean that anxiety cannot follow acute vertigo. Recurrence of an alarming experience may be feared and is quite understandable. Diagnostic errors may be made in two ways. The anxiety may be so profound that, unless a careful history is taken, the organic nature of the initial vertiginous episode may not be identified. Secondly, as sometimes occurs in young epileptic girls, super-added hysterical features may go unrecognized. Tests of labyrinthine function are vital in such cases.

The Eighth Cranial Nerve

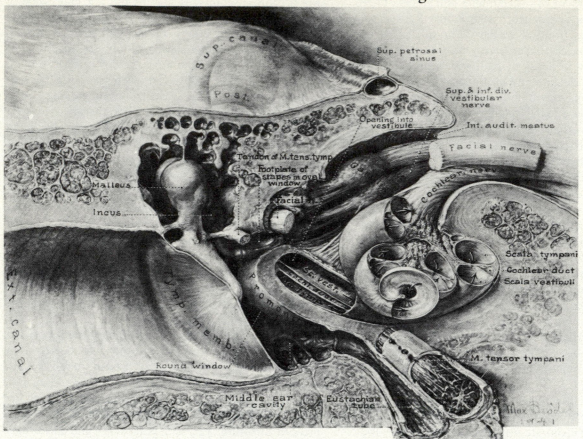

169. The inner ear by the late Max Brödel △
This drawing was made by the late Max Brödel (1870–1941) and is an outstanding example of the art of medical illustration. It is reproduced by permission of W. B. Saunders Company Ltd.

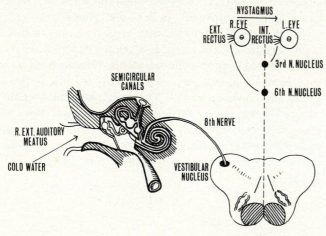

170. Diagram of mechanism of caloric nystagmus ◁
Cooling of the right horizontal semicircular canal by irrigating the ear with cold water. This sets up currents in the endolymph, the labyrinth is stimulated and the resulting nystagmus is horizontal with the quick phase to the left.

171. Diagram to illustrate method of inducing positional nystagmus ◁
The vertigo and nystagmus usually cease within a minute or so, but may recur transiently when the patient sits up. (Reproduced from Hallpike, C. S. (1955) *Postgrad. med. J.*, **31**, 330, by courtesy of the Editor.)

THE NINTH CRANIAL NERVE

The glossopharyngeal nerve has motor, sensory and vegetative functions. The motor fibres arise in the cells of the nucleus ambiguus in the medulla, emerge from the skull through the jugular foramen and innervate the stylopharyngeus muscle. Paralysis of this slender muscle cannot be detected on clinical examination and section of the nerve for glossopharyngeal neuralgia causes no detectable weakness in palate or pharynx. The nerve carries sensation from the nasopharynx and pharynx, Eustachian tube, middle and inner ear, and the posterior third of the tongue. It also transmits the sensation of taste from the same part of the tongue. Secretory fibres are also carried to the parotid gland. When the nerve is involved in any pathological process, it is practically always in association with the tenth and eleventh cranial nerves.

Glossopharyngeal neuralgia is much rarer than trigeminal neuralgia, but is very similar in the quality of the pain and the paroxysmal nature of the disorder. The pain is felt in the tonsil region and in the side of the throat; it may radiate to the angle of the jaw and to the ear. It is usually precipitated by the act of swallowing or clearing the throat and may be triggered off by the examiner on touching the tonsil of the affected side. As in trigeminal neuralgia there are no abnormal sensory signs. It is sometimes difficult to distinguish it from the rare case of trigeminal neuralgia confined to the third division. Careful examination is also necessary to exclude any compression of the glossopharyngeal nerve by tumour or gland in the neck.

THE TENTH CRANIAL NERVE

The vagus nerve is closely associated with the glossopharyngeal nerve and carries sensory and motor fibres. It conveys somatic sensation from the pharynx and larynx and innervates the muscles of the palate, pharynx and larynx. The nerve emerges from the skull through the jugular foramen with the ninth and eleventh cranial nerves and descends in the neck deep to the large vessels and enters the thorax.

Lesions of the nerve produce varying degrees of paralysis of the palate, pharynx and larynx. A unilateral palatal paralysis is symptomless. When there is bilateral palatal paresis the patient usually talks with a nasal twang and may complain of nasal regurgitation of fluids on swallowing. A typical example of palatal paresis is to be seen in the case of the young woman with myasthenia gravis whose nasal intonation and 'snarling' or 'sneering' smile, due to defective movements of the lips, together present a characteristic picture.

Unilateral pharyngeal paralysis is symptomless but the person with bilateral weakness will experience dysphagia and the pharyngeal reflex will be absent. Talking is often haltingly interrupted to enable the patient to swallow accumulating saliva. In unilateral laryngeal paralysis the voice is usually hoarse and the vocal cord takes up a position intermediate between abduction and adduction. When the paralysis is bilateral phonation and coughing are impossible and there may be inspiratory stridor. There may be selective paralysis of the abductors of the vocal cords in bilateral lesions. Bilateral adductor paralysis reduces the voice to a whisper. When the cause of a whispering voice is hysteria the patient is able to cough.

Supranuclear lesions of the vagus are unimportant clinically; the vocal cords are not affected in hemiplegia. Nuclear lesions are common and comprise tumours, vascular lesions, syringomyelia, motor neurone disease and poliomyelitis and polyneuritis. Primary and secondary tumours at the base of the skull not infrequently involve the ninth, tenth, eleventh and twelfth emerging nerves in various combinations. In the neck and mediastinum also compression from tumours and enlarged glands are common causes of pharyngeal and laryngeal paralyses. It is rare nowadays to see paralysis of the recurrent laryngeal nerve from aortic aneurysm.

Occasionally defective movement of one or both vocal cords results from arthritis involving the crico-arytenoid. This complication sometimes occurs in patients with chronic rheumatoid arthritis.

THE ELEVENTH CRANIAL NERVE

The spinal accessory is a purely motor nerve whose cells of origin lie in the lower end of the nucleus ambiguus of the medulla and in the anterior horn of the grey matter of the upper five segments of the cervical cord. The cranial roots emerge from the side of the medulla and run laterally to the jugular foramen, where they separate from the spinal portion and are principally distributed to the pharyngeal and recurrent laryngeal branches of the vagus nerve. The ascending spinal root enters the skull through the foramen magnum behind the vertebral artery and passes laterally through the jugular foramen to emerge from the skull with the vagus. It enters the neck between the internal carotid artery and the internal jugular vein, passing beneath the sterno-mastoid muscle, which it supplies, crossing the posterior triangle of the neck to end in the trapezius muscle. The sternomastoid is also supplied by the second cervical nerve and the trapezius by branches from the third and fourth cervical nerves.

The action of one sternomastoid is to tilt the head towards the shoulder of the same side and to rotate the head so as to carry the face towards the opposite side. Acting together the sternomastoids help in flexing the neck forwards as in the act of raising the head in the supine position. The trapezius, in association with other muscles inserted into the scapula, aids in maintaining the level and poise of the shoulder and controlling the position and movements of the scapula during active use of the arm. It elevates and braces back the shoulder and draws the head backwards and laterally.

Wasting of one sternomastoid muscle may be seen on frontal inspection; turning of the head to the opposite side produces a visible contraction. Comparisons can also be made during the action of raising the head from the pillow against resistance. Wasting of the upper part of the trapezius accentuates the normal curve from occiput to the point of the shoulder; the latter is lowered and the scapula is tilted so that the lower angle is nearer the midline than the upper. With the shoulder at rest there may be slight winging of the scapula which is obliterated on contraction of the serratus anterior. When both trapezii are paralysed there is weakness of extension of the neck and the head tends to fall forward.

In supranuclear lesions, as in hemiplegia, there is weakness but not paralysis of the sternomastoid and trapezius muscles. Unilateral lesions may be seen in syringomyelia, craniovertebral anomalies, tumours near the jugular foramen and after severe injuries to the head or neck. Formerly, dissection of tuberculous cervical glands was a common cause of injury to the nerve in the neck. As with other cranial nerves it may be involved in metastatic carcinoma anywhere along its course.

Bilateral paralysis of these muscles may be seen in poliomyelitis, polyneuritis, in nuclear lesions such as motor neurone disease and in various forms of muscular dystrophy. In dystrophia myotonica bilateral sterno-mastoid atrophy is particularly characteristic.

The Eleventh Cranial Nerve

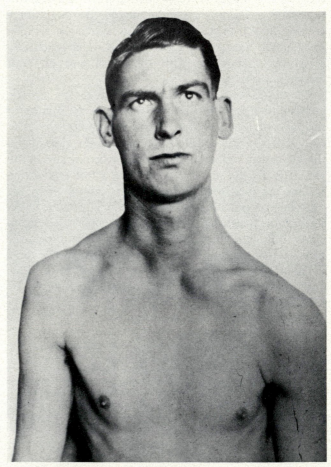

172. Isolated unilateral spinal accessory nerve palsy
Note the marked dropping of the affected shoulder girdle and the absence of the sternomastoid muscle on the same side. The cause in this case was unknown. It was of long-standing and he was referred to a military hospital during the Second World War, complaining of aching in the affected shoulder when wearing kit. It was obviously long-standing, his tailor having commented on the shoulder asymmetry in his early teens.

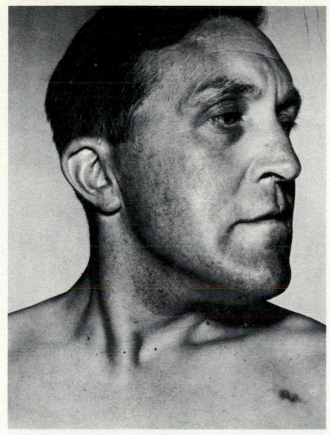

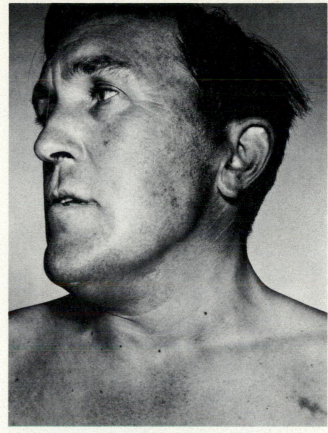

173. **Syringomyelia** △
Wasted left sternomastoid muscle can be
seen when he turns his head to the right.

174. **Carcinoma of the lung** ▽
This patient complained of hoarse voice,
cough, pain in the left side of the neck
and numbness of the left side of the face.

There were signs of involvement of the
left fifth and eighth, and the right tenth
and eleventh cranial nerves. Note wasting
of the right sternomastoid.

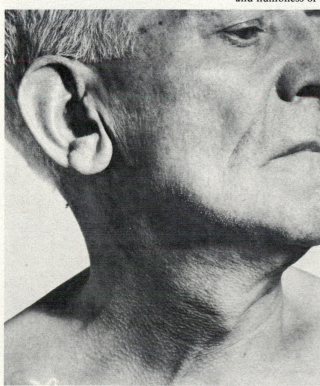

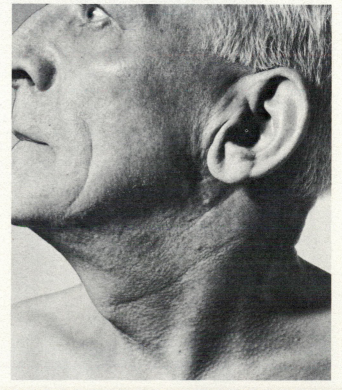

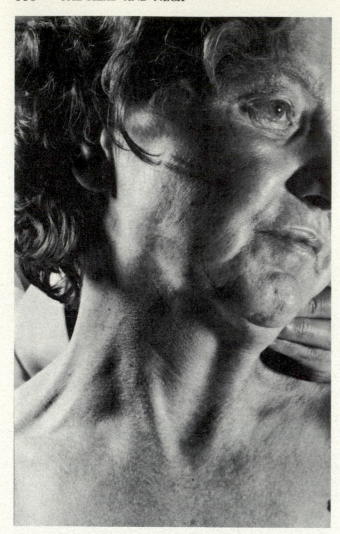
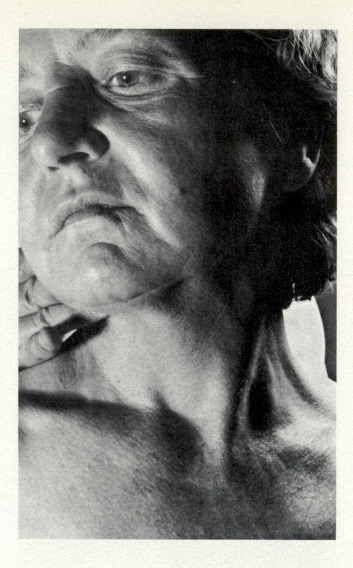

The Eleventh Cranial Nerve

175. Tumour of the right glomus jugulare

The latter is part of a chemoreceptor system which includes the carotid and aortic bodies. Glomera are situated on the dome of the jugular bulb and on the tympanic branch of the glossopharyngeal nerve. Tumours arising from these bodies tend to invade the middle ear and the posterior fossa causing multiple lower cranial nerve palsies. In this case there was deafness, vertigo, weakness of the palate and wasting of the sternomastoid muscle, all on the right side.

THE TWELFTH CRANIAL NERVE

The hypoglossal nerve is the motor nerve to the tongue; it contains no sensory fibres. From the hypoglossal nucleus in the medulla rootlets emerge on its frontal aspect between the olive and the pyramid. They pass across the posterior fossa of the skull uniting in the hypoglossal foramen, just lateral to the foramen magnum, to emerge from the skull. The nerve supplies the intrinsic and extrinsic muscles of the tongue and the depressors of the hyoid bone. The root of the tongue is attached to this bone and to the mandible. In each half of the tongue there are two sets of muscles, intrinsic and extrinsic. The former are mainly concerned in altering the shape of the tongue; movements of narrowing, elongating, flattening and broadening the tongue such as are concerned in speech, mastication and deglutition. There are four main extrinsic muscles; the genioglossus draws the tongue forwards and protrudes the tip from the mouth; the hyoglossus depresses the tongue; the chondroglossus also depresses the tongue; the styloglossus draws the tongue upwards and backwards.

Paralysis of the tongue, as with any other group of voluntary muscles, may result from a lesion in the upper or the lower motor neurone. In the former the lesions are often bilateral and contribute to the syndrome known by the unsatisfactory title of 'pseudobulbar palsy'. There is slurring of speech, the jaw jerk is exaggerated, the patient cannot protrude the tongue, which lies on the floor of the mouth, small and tight. There is loss of voluntary control over emotional expression. The syndrome usually results from cerebral arteriosclerosis, multiple sclerosis, motor neurone disease and high brain stem tumours.

In lesions of the lower motor neurone, the tongue wastes. If the lesion is unilateral the tongue on that side is wrinkled and furrowed and the median raphe curves in a concave manner to the paralysed side. The protruded tongue deviates to the side of the lesion as a result of the unopposed action of the opposite genioglossus. Unilateral lesions can result from disease in the medulla such as syringomyelia, motor neurone disease and tumours. Occasionally one hypoglossal nerve is involved in a disease process at the base of the skull, but in the neck itself lesions are uncommon. By far the commonest cause of bilateral wasting and weakness of the tongue is motor neurone disease. Wasting of the intrinsic muscles of the tongue throws the mucous membrane, to which some of them are attached, into folds. Fur collects on the surface of the tongue and sticky mucus accumulates posteriorly. The whole tongue may be markedly reduced in size or the wasting may be asymmetrical. Fasciculation is usually present and may be marked. These fine vermiform movements may not be visible in all positions of the tongue. Thus they may not be seen when the tongue is wholly within the mouth or on strong protrusion. They are often best seen if the patient can be made to relax the floor of the mouth or just protrude the tip of the tongue beyond the lower lip. Maintaining tongue protrusion is tiring and tremors may appear; they are not to be confused with fasciculation. Similarly the surface of many normal tongues is corrugated and furrowed; this does not mean intrinsic atrophy. Paralysis of the tongue can often be suspected before the examination while the patient is describing his symptoms. Articulation of some consonants and vowels is defective and the patient may be observed to pause frequently in order to swallow accumulating saliva.

The Twelfth Cranial Nerve

176. Hypoglossal paralysis
Isolated right hypoglossal nerve palsy due to head injury; a rare consequence of concussion. The day after a road accident this motor cyclist noticed his articulation was different but it was not until several months later when brushing his teeth that he observed his tongue deviated to the right on protrusion. He had persistent right occipital pain but radiographs did not reveal any fracture of the base of the skull. Articulation of some consonants and vowels was defective, which is rare in unilateral paralysis of the tongue. Alcohol aggravated his dysarthria. Presumably the hypoglossal nerve was injured in the anterior condylar (hypoglossal) foramen. A recurrent meningeal branch is given off by the nerve in this canal and it is thought to be sensory. It may have accounted for the persistent occipital pain in this patient.

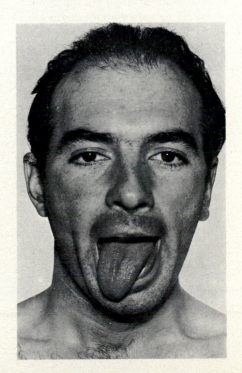

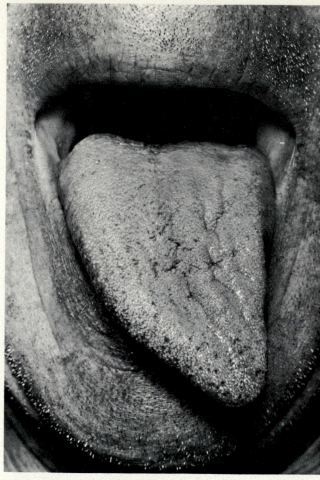

177. Hypoglossal paralysis △
Left hypoglossal nerve palsy showing
deviation of the protruded tongue to the
left. The left genioglossus muscle is
paralysed and the protruded tongue is
pushed to the left by the unopposed action
of the right genioglossus. The paired
genioglossi normally draw the tongue forward and protrude the tip from the mouth.
The anterior half of the left side of the
tongue is wasted.

    The patient had a bronchogenic carci-
noma with cervical glandular metastases.

178. Hypoglossal paralysis ▽
Left hypoglossal nerve palsy showing
wrinkling and furrowing of the left side of
the tongue and deviation to the left. The
patient complained of pain in the left ear
and temple, tinnitus and deafness on the
left and hoarseness of voice. She was
found to have a tumour of the left glomus
jugulare with a polypoid lesion in the
external auditory canal and erosion of the
petrous temporal on radiography. This is
one of the non-chromaffin paragangliomas.

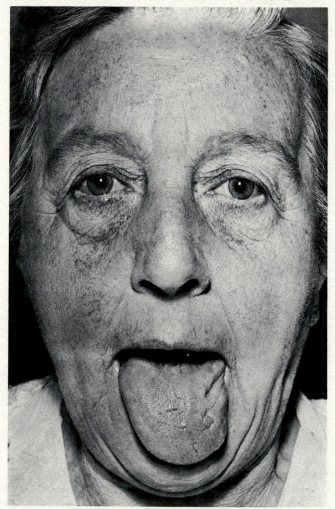

*The Twelfth
Cranial Nerve*

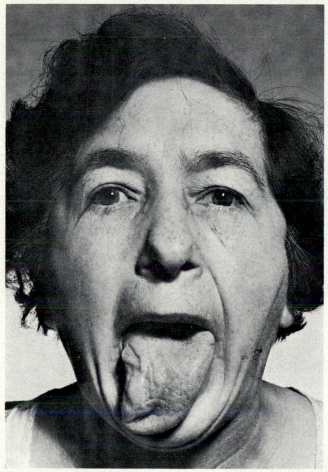

179a

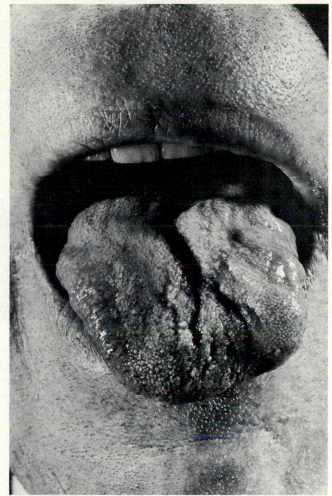

179b

179. Motor neurone disease
(*a*) Unilateral wasting of the tongue. It is
wrinkled and furrowed on the right and
the median raphe curves in a concave
manner to the paralysed side.
(*b*) Bilateral paralysis of the tongue showing the characteristic shrinking of the intrinsic muscles and the throwing of the
mucous membrane into folds.
(*c*) *and* (*d*) Bilateral paralysis of the tongue.
In (*c*) the patient was asked to depress the
tongue (hyoglossus) but could not do so:
in (*d*) to protrude the tongue, but the
movement is limited.

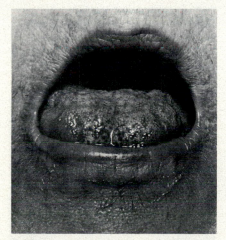

179c

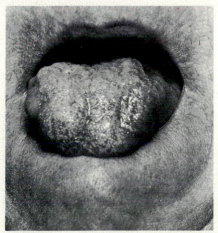

179d

Multiple Cranial Nerve Palsies

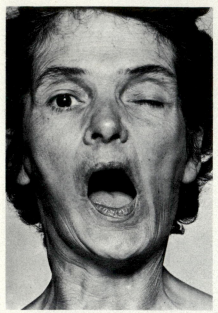

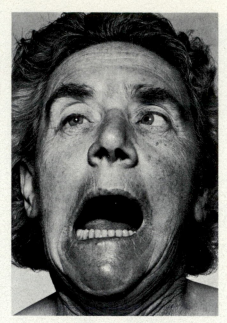

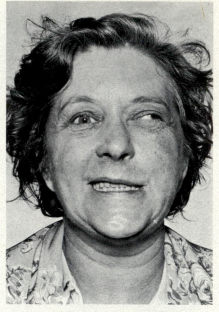

180. Paget's disease of the skull △
Bilateral nerve deafness with paresis of the
left third, fourth, fifth and sixth cranial
nerves. Note ptosis and deviation of the
jaw to the left on opening the mouth, due
to left pterygoid paralysis.

**181. Acute left pontine lesion;
probably encephalitis** △
Left internal strabismus due to paralysis
of left external rectus; left lower facial
weakness. Asymmetry on opening the
mouth was *not* due to a right trigeminal
motor paralysis.

182. Nasal diphtheria △
Epistaxis, nasal discharge and fever were
followed by partial left third and seventh
nerve paralyses. Note left external strabismus due to paralysis of left internal rectus
and unopposed action of left external
rectus.

183. Glioma of the pons ▽
Deafness, vertigo, ataxia, diplopia and
episodes of headache and vomiting. In (*a*)
note slight right internal strabismus,
flattening of the furrows on the right side
of the forehead and slight drooping of the
right corner of the mouth. In (*b*) he is

attempting to close his eyes and bare his
teeth; note peripheral facial palsy on the
right. In (*c*) he is looking to the left;
note paresis of right internal rectus and
left external rectus. Shaded area denotes
area of sensory impairment (left second
and third trigeminal zones).

183a

183c

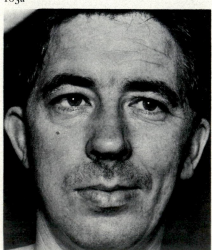

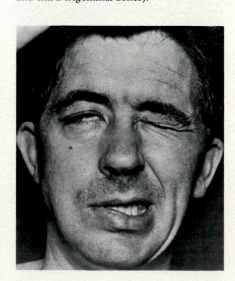

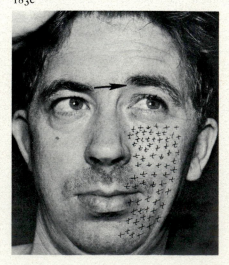

Multiple Cranial Nerve Palsies

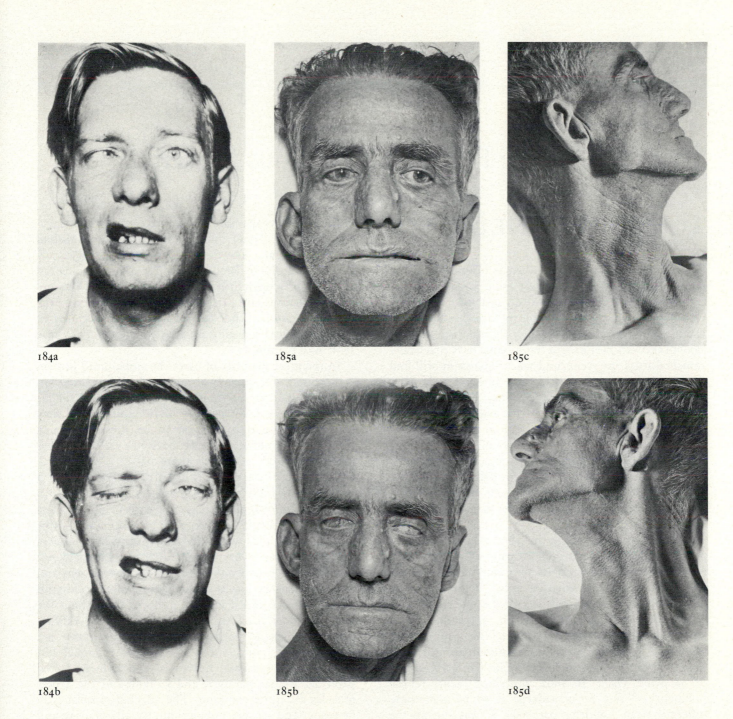

184a

185a

185c

184b

185b

185d

184. Multiple sclerosis
In (*a*) note paralysis of the right external rectus with internal strabismus, left lower facial paresis with deviation of the philtrum to the right. In (*b*) he is trying to bare his teeth and close his eyes; note paralysis of left orbicularis oculi and left zygomaticus.

185. Carcinomatosis of the basal meninges; primary lesion in the caecum
In (*a*) he is trying to bare his teeth; note loss of furrows in forehead and of naso-labial grooves; left ptosis with slightly dilated pupil and external strabismus due to weakness of the left internal rectus. In

(*b*) he is trying to close his eyes; bilateral paralysis of orbicularis oculi. His nostrils did not move when he sniffed and he could not purse his lips. (*c*) Note wasting of right sternomastoid muscle due to spinal accessory nerve lesion. In contrast, the left sternomastoid muscle contracts normally (*d*).

4 THE LIMBS

Disorders of the Peripheral Nervous System

ACUTE POLYNEURITIS

Today a medical student is not long in hospital before he realizes that most patients with acute polyneuritis are suffering from a disease of entirely unknown aetiology. He will search in vain for examples of the causative agents listed in his textbooks. Arsenic, diphtheria, beriberi, alcohol and various forms of septicaemia have practically vanished from the scene, and what remains he will find described under various titles such as acute toxic polyneuritis, acute febrile polyneuritis, acute infective polyneuritis, acute polyneuropathy, acute polyradiculoneuritis, acute polyneuronitis and so on; and everywhere he will encounter the names of Landry, Osler, Guillain, Barré, Strohl, Holmes and Bradford. The student will profit more from a knowledge of the history of this disorder than from memorizing the endless lists of causes of polyneuritis which he is unlikely to encounter.

The story really began in 1859 when Landry, a physician of Paris, described 10 patients who suffered from an illness characterized by numbness and weakness of the limbs and what he called 'acute ascending paralysis'. Two of his patients died from respiratory failure. It was Westphal of Berlin, of patellar reflex fame, who in 1876 first referred to the syndrome of 'Landry's ascending paralysis', differentiating it from poliomyelitis. In the first edition of his famous *Textbook of Medicine*, Osler, in 1892, described 'acute febrile polyneuritis' but he considered it to be something different from Landry's paralysis. It was during the First World War that the disease became generally recognized following the accounts of Guillain, Barré and Strohl in 1916, Holmes in 1917 and Bradford and his colleagues in 1918. The French workers described for the first time the elevation of the cerebrospinal fluid protein; Holmes examined the spinal fluid in 2 of his 12 cases and found it to be normal. Bradford examined it in 4 of his 30 cases and also found it to be normal. Neither of these authors specifically referred to the protein content of the fluid, nor did they mention the published French accounts. The term 'acute infective polyneuritis' was adopted by Bradford and his associates, instead of the term 'acute febrile polyneuritis' used by Osler and Holmes, because they believed they had transferred the disease to monkeys and showed it was a virus infection. This has never been substantiated but an infective cause remains a possibility.

In the great majority of cases the spinal fluid protein is increased; occasionally also the cells. The changes in the spinal fluid are no measure of the severity of the illness and the protein content of the spinal fluid may continue to rise after the peak of the illness has been reached. The clinical picture does not differ whether the spinal fluid is normal or abnormal.

The onset of the illness is usually rapid, often with a sore throat or influenza-like complaint, the neurological symptoms following a few days or a week or so later. The paralysis may begin in all four limbs simultaneously or may first affect the lower limbs. Complaints of numbness and paraesthesiae vary considerably in their incidence and severity. Usually they are mild and transient and objective sensory loss is slight. Paralysis is flaccid with loss of reflexes and it may be uniform throughout the limbs or more marked proximally or distally, varying from one case to another. Sphincter symptoms are usually slight, consciousness is usually retained, but involvement of cranial nerves is well known. Facial paralysis, bulbar paralysis and weakness of the ocular muscles are quite common. The affected muscles may be tender and sensory impairment, usually of glove and stocking distribution, is slight. Sometimes despite the complaint of paraesthesiae there may be no objective sensory loss.

As in all cases of acute polyneuritis, notably in beriberi and in diphtheritic paralysis, tachycardia is common and there is always the danger of acute myocardial failure. Many a young patient convalescent from acute polyneuritis has died suddenly of heart failure. Respiratory failure, on the other hand, is most likely to occur during the first 3 weeks of the illness. It must be treated vigorously because the outlook of the patient, if he survives the period of respiratory failure, is as good as that of other patients. The onset, development of paralysis, and the course of the illness and its convalescence vary considerably. In many the paralysis progresses for 1 or 2 weeks, remains stationary for a few weeks and then begins to recede. In other patients, whether the onset was acute or subacute, recovery and convalescence are very slow and it may be a year or more before the patient is fully ambulant. Occasionally there are residual changes by way of weak atrophic muscles with contractures. Very rarely a patient may experience recurrences of the disorder. One of my patients has had three episodes in 30 years, each of which disabled him for a period of about 6 months. He was originally invalided home from Egypt in the First World War with a diagnosis of diphtheritic paralysis.

Acute ascending paralysis is usually due to acute polyneuritis, the principal lesion being in the spinal nerve roots, but myelitis and poliomyelitis may present in a similar fashion. In myelitis the plantar reflexes are usually extensor, despite absent reflexes in the early stages, sensory loss is more extensive and sphincter disturbances more marked. In poliomyelitis the onset is more sudden, paraesthesiae are rare, there is no sensory loss and examination of the spinal fluid usually shows an increase of cells. In acute porphyria, the commonest neurological manifestation consists of a flaccid paralysis of the limbs with loss of reflexes and sensory disturbance. Abdominal pain is frequent and often severe, cerebral symptoms may be present and there may be a history of previous similar episodes. Attacks may be initiated by a variety of drugs, including barbiturates, sulphonamides and alcohol.

Modern drug-induced peripheral neuropathies do not usually present in such a dramatic manner as acute polyneuritis. Their onset is slower, pains and paraesthesiae are prominent and paralysis less widespread. The heavy metals such as arsenic, lead and mercury no longer enter the field because Fowler's solution, lead-containing pastes and lotions, and teething powders have disappeared. Drugs such as isoniazid, nitrofurantoin, chloroquine and insecticides have taken their place in the causation of peripheral neuropathy. Thalidomide neuropathy was mainly of a sensory kind and paralysis was rare. An alerted profession may not be completely able to prevent the occurrence of iatrogenic neuropathy in the future, but it should aid in early recognition.

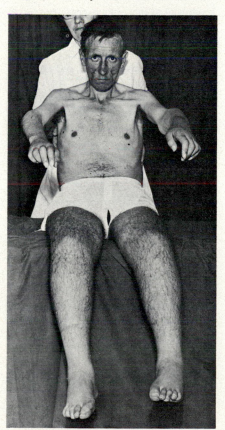

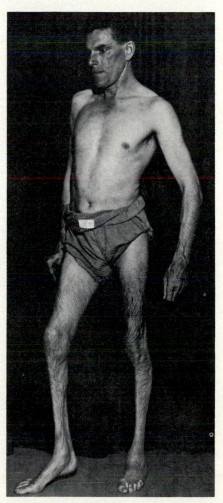

186. Acute polyneuritis one year after onset ◁

No preceding infection, onset subacute. No cranial nerve involvement; complete flaccid paralysis of the limbs, minimal sensory impairment; complete areflexia. From the outset the lower limbs were flushed and cyanosed and perspired excessively. Bilateral femoral vein thrombosis complicated the illness and there was little sign of recovery for 6 months. Still unable to stand but he can feed himself.

187. Acute polyneuritis with incomplete recovery ▷

Age at onset, 13 years. Acute febrile illness with dyspnoea, palpitation, tachycardia and flaccid peripheral paralysis with numbness, paraesthesiae and fasciculation. Full recovery in upper limbs in 2 years. Permanent wasting, weakness and loss of reflexes in lower limbs. Ataxic gait, bilateral foot drop. Now aged 40 years with recent deterioration in lower limbs. Cranial nerves normal. Upper limbs: power normal, no wasting, absent reflexes. Glove and stocking type of sensory loss, more marked in the lower limbs, where joint position and vibration sensibilities were absent. There was also an obscure chronic cardiomyopathy. Extensive laboratory investigations failed to reveal any metabolic disturbance but the CSF protein was 149 mg./100 ml. No evidence of amyloidosis.

Acute Polyneuritis

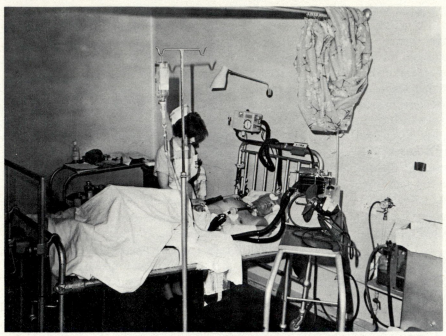

188a

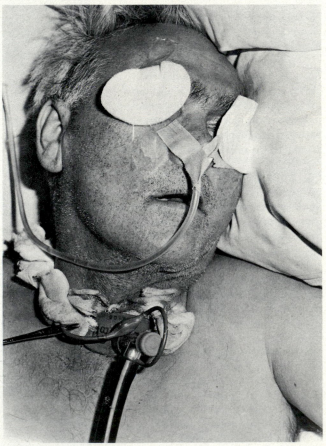

188b

188. Acute polyneuritis

Age 53. Acute polyneuritis with respiratory paralysis 3 weeks after an acute upper respiratory tract infection. Paraesthesiae of hands and feet began 5 days before admission to hospital; weakness of the legs for 3 days; right peripheral facial palsy, 1 day. Despite ACTH from the day of admission the paralysis progressed, he developed a left peripheral facial palsy 4 days after admission, respiratory failure on the sixth day and tracheostomy and artificial respiration were necessary from the seventh day. Continuous artificial ventilation was necessary for 11 days; the respirator was required for 5 weeks; the tracheostomy for 2 months. There was complete flaccid peripheral paralysis of the limbs, with total loss of reflexes, but the only objective sensory disturbance consisted of defective joint position sense in the toes. CSF protein was 312 mg./100 ml.; cells 5/mm^3.

(a) Continuous artificial ventilation.

(b) Tracheostomy, nasal feeding, exposure keratitis necessitated tarsorrhaphy.

(c) Eight weeks after admission; tracheostomy closed, power returning to limbs.

(d) Twelve weeks after admission, note atrophy of interossei muscles and residual lower right facial weakness.

(e) Nine months after admission to hospital. Complete physical recovery but deep reflexes still absent. Residual amnesia of 3 weeks' duration. Acute polyneuritis is an example of an illness in which a patient may recover completely, although death may have appeared imminent for some days. Expert intensive care is vital.

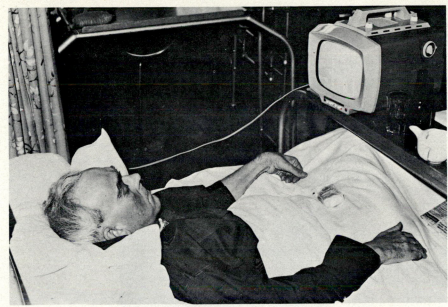

188c

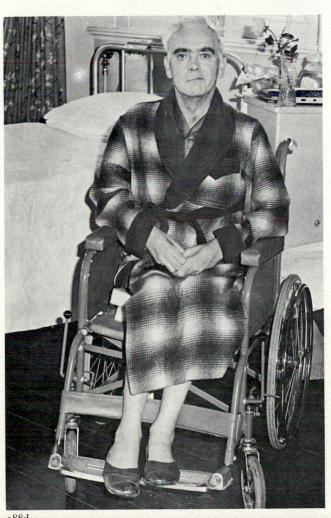

188d

188e

CHRONIC POLYNEURITIS

The commonest form of neuritis in the world is leprosy. It is a true infective neuritis; the bacterium invades the peripheral nerves. The human leprosy bacillus (*Mycobacterium leprae*) was the first bacterium to be identified under the microscope as the cause of disease in man. It was discovered by Hansen in 1874. It is nearly 200 years since leprosy died out in Great Britain; the last indigenous case is said to have died in the Shetland Islands in 1798. There are more than 10 million lepers in the world and since the disease was made notifiable in Great Britain in 1952, more than 600 cases have been registered. I have seen two coloured immigrants with leprosy in the past year. How many were there in the 4 million immigrants from hot countries who have entered northern Europe in the past 3 years?

In this country, however, diabetes is probably the commonest cause of chronic peripheral neuropathy, although it does not take the form of a multiple symmetrical peripheral neuritis. Alcoholic polyneuritis is a relatively rare disease here but in southern France and in Boston and New York it is still common. The increase in carcinomatous neuropathy is a reflection of the increased incidence of bronchogenic carcinoma.

Inevitably, there are forms of chronic polyneuritis which are idiopathic—sporadic or familial. The latter are an obscure group of disorders in some of which there is interstitial hypertrophy of the nerves. In Refsum's syndrome there is in addition an atypical retinitis pigmentosa and cerebellar ataxia. An abnormal fatty acid (phytanic acid) accumulates in the tissues. In a similar syndrome, that of Déjérine and Sottas, no biochemical disorder has been discovered although similar pathological changes in the nerves occur in both these syndromes. In the absence of hypertrophy of nerves it may be impossible to distinguish them clinically from peroneal muscular atrophy. These familial neuropathies seem to merge gradually into the syndromes of peroneal muscular atrophy, the Roussy–Levy syndrome (pes cavus and absent tendon jerks), and Friedreich's and other hereditary ataxias.

190. **Chronic idiopathic polyneuritis** ▷
Age 35 years, onset at 15 years. Negative family history, all investigations negative except abnormal pyruvate tolerance test. The onset was subacute and deterioration has been more or less progressive; there have been periods during which the progress of the disease has seemed to halt for several months or a year at a time. There was complete anaesthesia of glove and stocking distribution. Note the wasting of the distal musculature, the clawing of the fingers and toes, the wasting of the small muscles of the hand and the scarred knuckles. Despite the complete anaesthesia, radiographs revealed no sign of absorption of the terminal phalanges. No nerve hypertrophy.

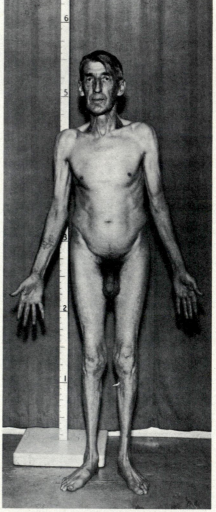

Chronic Polyneuritis

189. **Chronic idiopathic polyneuritis** Age 70. Two-year history of pains and paraesthesia in feet and calves followed by weakness of lower limbs. Sensory but no motor symptoms in the upper limbs. Absent reflexes, glove and sock type of sensory impairment with fasciculation in calves and thighs. General health excellent, no evidence of carcinoma; observed so far for 2 years. Note wasting of forearms and lower limbs.

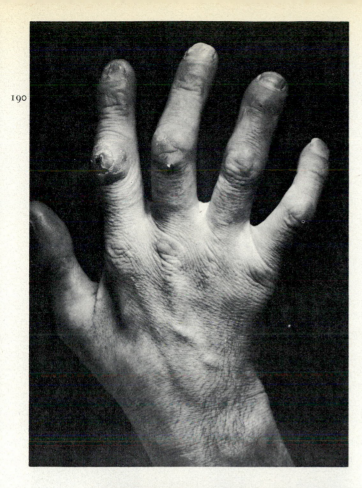

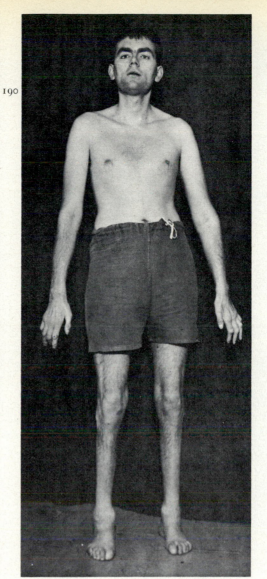

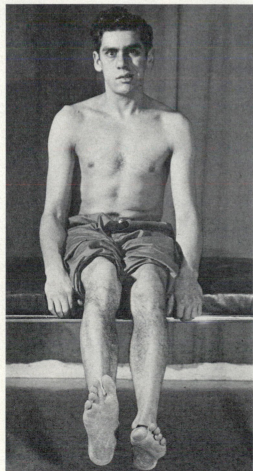

191. Mononeuritis multiplex; acute leukaemia 2 years later ◁

Age 29. As an asthmatic, had been taking prednisone 10 mg. daily for many years. One year previously had a partial right third nerve palsy; complete recovery except for residual enlargement of the pupil. Eight weeks before hospital admission he developed a left foot drop with paraesthesiae. Ten days before admission, a right facial palsy. No sensory disturbance; normal reflexes, flexor plantar responses. No clinical or laboratory evidence of sarcoidosis. Kviem test negative. One year later developed headache, vomiting and papilloedema; extensive investigations revealed no evidence of an intracranial space-occupying lesion. One further year later he became rapidly ill with acute lympho-blastic anaemia which proved fatal. Incomplete recovery of the palsies of the facial and common peroneal nerves. (Courtesy of Dr. C. E. C. Wells.)

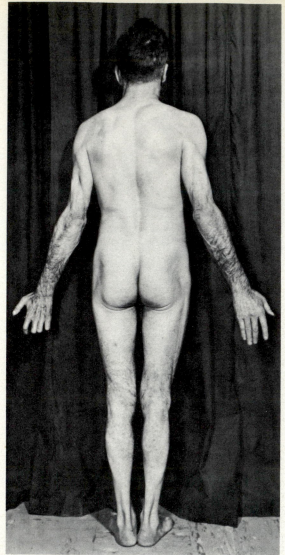

192a

192. Chronic progressive hypertrophic polyneuritis

Age 56; negative family history. Onset at 46 with pain, numbness and cramp in the left hand. Four years later similar symptoms appeared in the left leg, a year later in the right leg and 2 years later in the right hand. At that time there was evidence of chronic polyneuritis. Palpable enlargement of peripheral nerves (the left ulnar, the left median, the left common peroneal and the musculocutaneous branches of both common peroneal nerves) was not detected until the tenth year of his illness. (*a*) Shows general appearance with clawing of the fingers of the left hand in the sixth year of the illness. The appearance of this hand in the tenth year of illness is shown in (*b*). The musculocutaneous branch of the left common peroneal nerve may be seen in (*c*). This nerve is exposed at operation on the left side (*d*). Histology showed the characteristic features of the disease. It is usually familial, with onset in childhood.

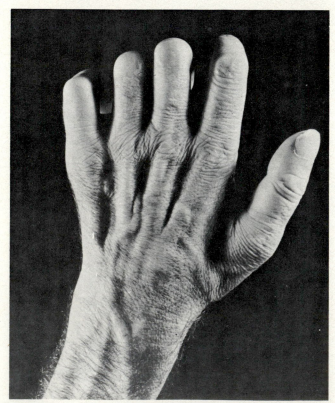

192b

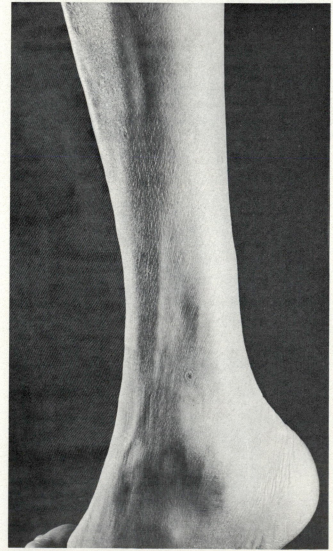

192c

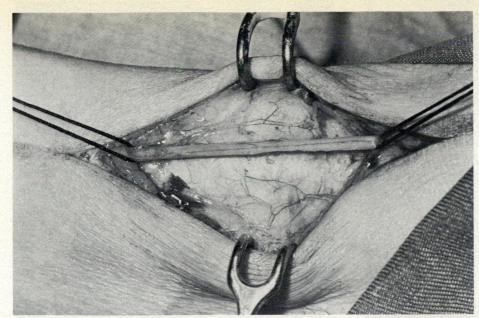

192d

**193. Hereditary hypertrophic poly-
neuropathy: father and son**

Father aged 50 (a). Bilateral pes cavus,
steppage gait, atrophied calf muscles,
areflexia. No thickened nerves. Electromyography: severe sensorimotor
neuropathy.

Son aged 14 (a and b). Two years' history
of clumsiness in the gymnasium;
abnormal gait. Recent paraesthesiae,
numbness and clumsiness of the fingers.
Examination: steppage gait, weakness of
abduction of the fingers, thin calf and
peroneal muscles; no pes cavus. Areflexia,
distal sensory impairment in all four limbs.
Visible and palpable thickening of some
subcutaneous nerves (cervical—arrowed
in (b)—and sural). Phytanic acid normal.
Electromyography: similar to that of his
father. Sural nerve biopsy: hypertrophic
demyelinating neuropathy with Schwann
cell proliferation.
Two brothers also affected.

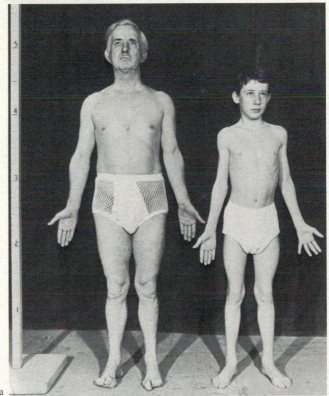

193a

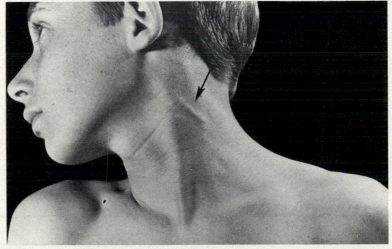

193b

*Chronic
Polyneuritis*

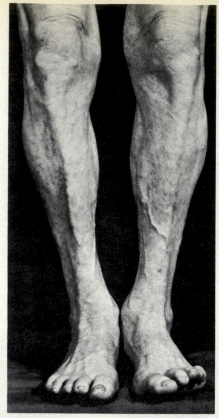

194a

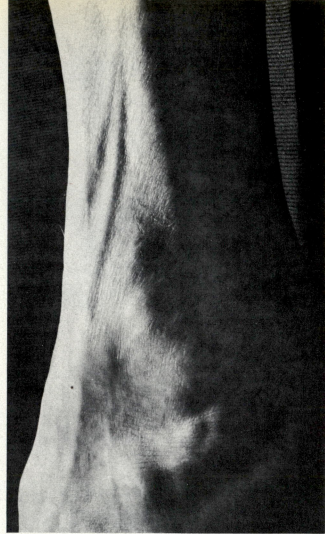

194b

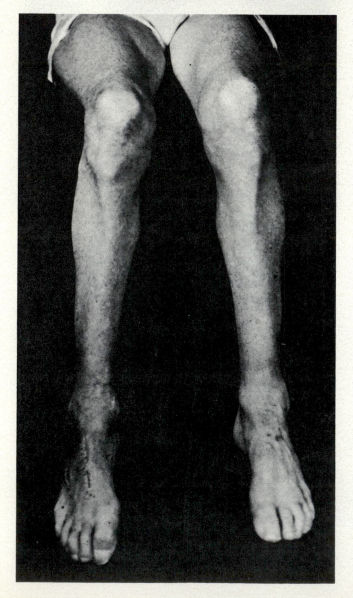

194. Chronic polyneuritis △
Male, aged 63; negative family history.
Six-year history of numbness and weakness of distal parts of lower limbs. Bilateral
flaccid foot drop: sensory loss of stocking
distribution; absent knee and ankle jerks.
Abnormalities of nerve conduction in
lower and upper limbs.

Nerve biopsy showed no signs of
amyloid neuropathy nor of hypertrophic
polyneuritis. There was considerable
perineural fibrosis and segmental demyelination.
(*a*) Wasting of anterior tibial muscles.
(*b*) Visible enlargement of musculocutaneous branch of common peroneal nerve.

195. Chronic polyneuritis (beriberi) ◁
A British soldier in the Second World War
who developed bilateral retrobulbar neuropathy, bilateral nerve deafness and dry
beriberi while a prisoner of war in the Far
East. There was residual bilateral optic
atrophy (visual acuity, 6/36 bilaterally);
the deafness was moderate and there was
apparently permanent ataxia resulting from
the beriberi. This picture was taken 2 years
after his return from the Far East in 1948.
Note wasting of the muscles below the
knees, especially of the anterior tibial
group; bilateral foot drop.

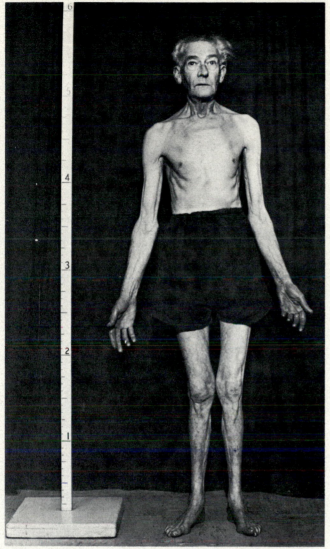

196a

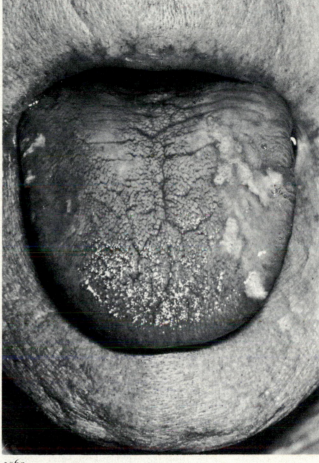

196c

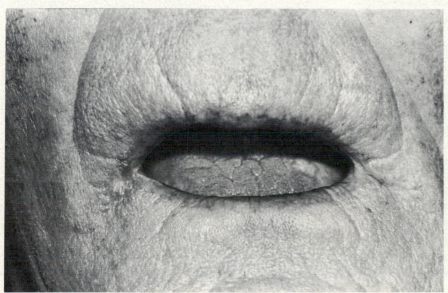

196b

196. Chronic polyneuritis

Malabsorption syndrome, 20 years after gastrectomy. Seven-year history of numbness and weakness of hands and feet. Cramps in legs, ataxic gait, impaired lower limb reflexes, loss of vibration sense to knees, superficial sensory loss of sock distribution. No anaemia; normal values for serum B_{12} and folate. Osteoporosis, weight loss. Serum calcium 8 mg./100 ml.

(*a*) General loss of weight, thin legs.

(*b*) *and* (*c*) Angular stomatitis and smooth, raw tongue.

Leprosy

In this country the patient is likely to come from the Middle East, Asia or Africa and may have acquired the illness in childhood. Infection probably occurs through the skin when there are active lesions, but the patient may be unaware of having had any contact with the disease. It principally involves the skin and subcutaneous nerves and there are two reasonably well-defined types —the lepromatous and the tuberculoid—with every variety of intermediate lesion. The first type develops when there is little resistance to the disease, the bacilli multiply and disseminate freely and the lepromin reaction is negative. In the second type there is a pronounced tissue reaction, the bacilli spread locally and the lepromin reaction is positive.

There is a period of incubation of several years and the first signs of the disease comprise some form of skin lesion. But mucous membranes, viscera and bones may be involved. In the tuberculoid type the neural elements of the dermis are completely destroyed and clinically there are anaesthetic cutaneous macules and patchy polyneuritis. The neural lesions in the lepromatous type result from ischaemia and compression of nerve twigs.

The patient is likely to draw attention to an area of skin which is the site of thickening or nodule formation, or to areas where the skin is dry, depigmented and anaesthetic. Small nerves are thickened in the vicinity of the skin lesions and they may be visible and palpable. The patient may present with the symptoms and signs of a progressive lesion of an individual nerve in the upper or lower limbs—the ulnar, the radial or the peroneal. The skin over the cutaneous distribution of the affected nerves may be shiny, inelastic and dry. Vasomotor and trophic disturbances may be prominent. Perforating ulcers result at points of pressure, especially over the heads of the metatarsals; digital ulceration and destruction occurs. Superficial sensation is usually involved before vibration and position sensations are affected. Sometimes the leprous neuritis produces sensory dissociation similar to that seen in syringomyelia. The commonest cranial nerves to be affected are the fifth and seventh, producing patchy facial anaesthesia and partial facial paralysis. The great auricular nerve may be visibly thickened where it crosses the sternomastoid muscle.

Diagnosis is easier in the lepromatous type because the organisms are readily found in biopsy material or smears of scrapings from the nasal mucosa. The bacilli are rarely found in the skin or mucosal scrapings in tuberculoid leprosy and biopsies of cutaneous nerves may be necessary. When a suspicion of leprosy arises, usually in the dermatology or neurology clinic, expert opinion should be sought without delay. In a coloured patient an area of altered skin, questionably insensitive, should be enough to alert the physician.

Leprosy

197. Leprous neuritis
An area of anaesthesia about the elbow of an Indian immigrant to England in 1966. He presented in a neurological outpatient department complaining of numbness of the elbow and ulnar paraesthesiae. No cutaneous lesions, no thickened nerves.

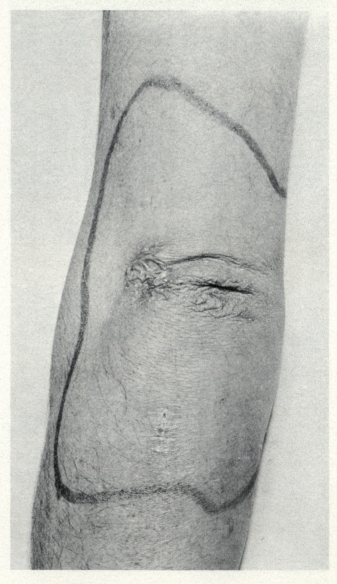

198

198. Leprosy ◁
A Jamaican leper with mutilated hands from chronic leprous neuritis.

199. The skull of King Robert the Bruce ▽
He is said to have died from leprosy. This is a drawing from a cast of his skull which was disinterred in 1819. Erosion of the anterior nasal spine and adjacent portions of the maxillae are indicated by the arrows. (Courtesy of the Editor, *Med. Hist.* (1958) **11**, 287.)

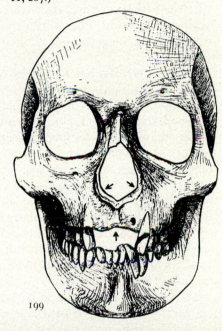

199

200. Leprosy
(*a*) Jamaican leper. Clawing of hands and right peripheral facial palsy.
(*b*) Phalangeal osteolysis.

200a

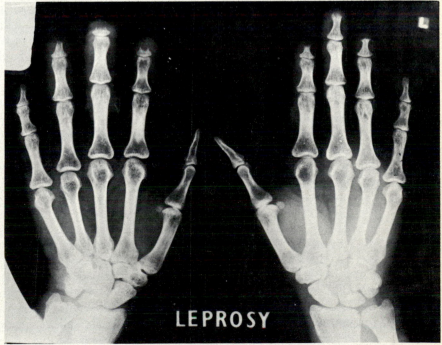

LEPROSY

200b

Alcoholic Neuropathy

Fortunately now uncommon in this country, it is still particularly important to recall it, because it may present when it is least expected and diagnostic delay may have grave consequences. Formerly it was not difficult to recognize the development of neuropathy in an alcoholic but nowadays the alcoholic addiction may be completely disguised and known only to the patient. The latter is often a lonely widow or an elderly solitary person. Relatives are usually unsuspecting and the neighbours who see the furtive purchasing trips or the regular deliveries to the house are rarely available to the clinician seeking information. The young parson or social worker may think the suggestion of alcoholism is wide of the mark.

Alcoholic neuritis has long been considered to be a nutritional neuropathy due to dietary deficiency rather than a direct toxic effect of the alcohol taken. It is rare in the working man who regularly drinks large quantities of beer and yet enjoys his food. It is usually found in the underweight person, with a poor appetite who drinks some form of spirits. The fact that in its chronic form it may not respond to injections of vitamin B_1 is no proof that deficiency of that vitamin is not involved. In the latest studies from the United States it has been shown there is an actual deficiency of members of vitamin B complex in the blood of patients with alcoholic neuritis. It may well be that alcohol is more neurotoxic in the presence of a deficiency state.

It is a disorder that begins in an insidious manner but it is usually painful. The patient complains of tingling, numbness and pains in the feet and later in the hands, often attended by cramps, complaints of coldness, various dull and sharp pains in the distal extremities. Sleep may be disturbed because these sensory symptoms are worse at night. The patient may prefer to wear slippers, there is general distress and, with lack of sleep and food, the general appearance deteriorates. Difficulty in walking from weakness and ataxia follow after some months.

Because these symptoms are most pronounced in the feet, physical examination is first directed to them. When they are handled the patient may withdraw the legs and cry out with pain; there is exquisite tenderness of the soles of the feet and frequently also of the calf muscles. Despite this there is impairment of superficial modalities of sensation, so that the touch of a finger or the prick of a pin are not felt. At this stage the ankle jerks are impaired and weakness may be slight. Later, there is progressive paresis with foot drop, wrist drop, a steppage type of gait and loss of reflexes. As in diabetic neuropathy trophic and vasomotor changes in the hands and feet are common. When the disease becomes chronic, pain and tenderness tend to subside and sensory signs may be limited to loss of deep pressure, position and vibration resulting in a sensory ataxia—alcoholic pseudotabes. Bladder and rectal control are not affected, but some degree of mental disturbance is invariable. Usually this merely amounts to general neglect, impairment of memory and irritability. The confabulatory amnesia of Korsakow's psychosis is not very common.

Alcoholic neuritis must be distinguished from subacute combined degeneration of the spinal cord and from diabetic neuropathy. In vitamin B_{12} deficiency distal numbness and paraesthesiae are characteristic but it is less painful and tenderness of the feet and calf muscles less evident. Nevertheless examination of the blood and an estimation of the serum B_{12} level should be routine investigations. In diabetes the onset of neuropathy may precede the diagnosis of diabetes, the latter may be very mild so that there are no other complaints. Signs of neuropathy—loss of vibration sense and reflexes—may precede symptoms. The neuropathy is usually largely sensory, nocturnal pains are common and there are autonomic disturbances.

Diabetic Neuropathy

The disease known as diabetes mellitus gains in complexity with each passing decade. It can no longer be regarded a simple matter of insulin deficiency. Whether it is a disease or a syndrome or a variety of related disorders of metabolism the sufferer is exposed to a whole series of possible complications. Arterial degeneration affecting the cerebral, coronary, renal, retinal and peripheral vessels is a particular liability and in one form or another arteriosclerosis seems to be an almost inevitable accompaniment of the diabetic state. Presumably these vascular lesions are irreversible but may be delayed by effective control. The position is somewhat different in the case of diabetic neuropathy. Not only are the changes reversible but it has often been observed that the onset of neuropathy may precede the diagnosis of diabetes or may even appear shortly after the introduction of treatment. It must be admitted it may also develop at any period during the course of the disease. It does not depend on the severity of the diabetes nor on its duration. The neurologist is not really in a position to judge whether poor control is the responsible factor leading to the development of neuropathy. His patients tend to represent a special group—those in whom neuropathy dominates the clinical picture. It is well known that diabetics, regardless of their age at onset, the duration of their disease, or its severity, show a diminution of vibratory sense at an earlier age than normal individuals—often two decades earlier. The neuropathy may not be directly related to the disorder of carbohydrate metabolism.

Whatever its nature there appear to be several ways in which neurological signs actually appear. Mention has already been made of loss of vibration sense in the lower limbs. This is usually symptomless, insidious and often associated with loss of the ankle jerks; there is no superficial sensory loss or muscle weakness. Treatment usually has no effect on these signs.

A different clinical picture is seen when there is an acute or subacute mononeuropathy. The lower limbs suffer more frequently than the upper and lesions affecting the femoral, sciatic, ulnar and median nerves are encountered. There are pains and paraesthesiae and examination reveals the appropriate disturbances of sensation and muscle function. It is often said that the third, fifth and sixth cranial nerves can suffer in this way but it is by no means certain.

In a third type there is a form of subacute polyneuritis but it rarely progresses to involve all four limbs in a marked manner. It is most commonly confined to the lower limbs. Upper limb involvement if it occurs, is usually less marked. The characteristic symptom is of burning pains and paraesthesiae in the feet, often aggravated by heat and when the patient is at rest, so disturbing his nights. There is hyperaesthesia, superficial tenderness, muscular tenderness and, after a time weakness and wasting. The reflexes are usually impaired or absent when the patient is first seen. Sensory loss may be slight or profound. Similarly muscle weakness may be slight or disabling. Generally speaking, after some months of suffering, the neuritis subsides and there is partial or complete recovery.

The existence of an autonomic neuropathy is debated from time to time but with little pathological foundation. Urinary difficulties, nocturnal diarrhoea, disturbances of sweating, impotence and postural hypotension are some of the clinical symptoms which have suggested this explanation. Trophic changes in the feet are well known and the painless ulcer which develops over a pressure point contrasts with the lesions which result from ischaemia.

Whatever the mode of presentation of diabetic neuropathy, whether it is painful or insidious, distal or proximal, predominantly sensory or motor, confined to one limb or affecting all limbs, the pathological findings are said to be similar in all cases, varying only in extent and severity. The degeneration affects the lower motor and primary sensory neurones. Diabetic neuropathy may simulate many neurological disorders. An acute mononeuritis in one upper limb may be misdiagnosed as 'brachial neuritis', cervical spondylosis, an ulnar 'friction' neuritis arising at the elbow, or it may pass as an example of the carpal tunnel syndrome. In the lower limb the pain may be viewed as ischaemic in origin or arising from lumbar spondylosis or disc prolapse. Painless wasting of thigh muscles might be interpreted as some form of late myopathy, while paralysis of the bladder may lead to myelography and a suspicion of tumour of the cauda equina. Sensory ataxia with appropriate disturbance of gait and absent reflexes may suggest subacute combined degeneration of the spinal cord. If there is also pupillary abnormality tabes dorsalis may be suspected. In these circumstances testing the urine for sugar becomes a matter of vital importance.

201. Diabetic neuropathy
Wasting of the dorsal interossei muscles of the right hand in a poorly controlled diabetic who complained of unsteadiness of gait. There was no weakness of the lower limbs, but there was loss of knee and ankle jerks and sensory ataxia. There were no sensory complaints referable to the right hand and the hypothenar muscles were normal.

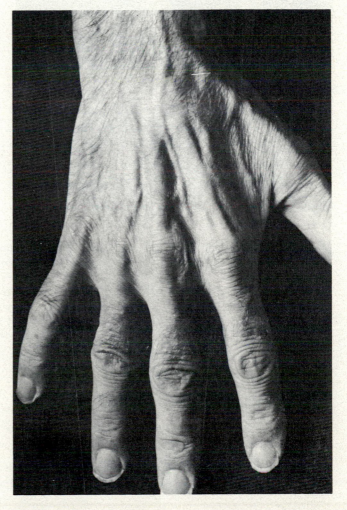

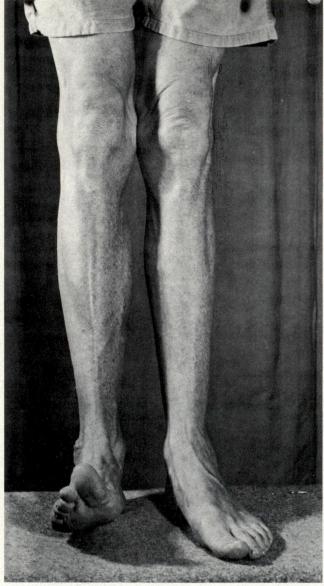

202a

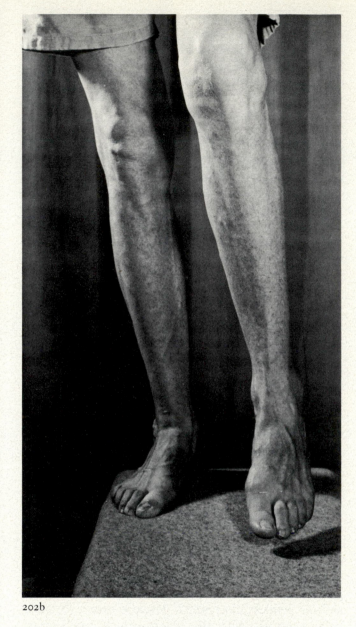

202b

Diabetic Neuropathy

202. Diabetic neuropathy; left common peroneal nerve palsy in a chronic diabetic

Pain, paraesthesiae and numbness in the left foot with subacute onset of foot drop. In (*a*) he is trying to stand on his heels; note inability to dorsiflex left foot. In (*b*) he is trying to elevate the left foot. There were nocturnal cramps, his feet were tender, both ankle jerks were absent and the left knee jerk was impaired. There was distal superficial sensory loss in the left leg and vibration sense was absent below both knees.

The Sensory Neuropathies

In this category of chronic polyneuritis the principal clinical feature consists of distal sensory loss. The disorder may occur sporadically or it may be familial. Motor involvement may be absent, slight, or considerable. In some cases it has been established that the main lesion consists of degeneration in the posterior spinal root ganglia and afferent nerve fibres. The pattern of the sensory loss varies. In some it consists of loss of all modalities of sensation in a glove and sock distribution. In others it is clearly radicular in character. The sensory loss may involve all forms of sensation but it is frequently dissociated in character, mainly involving loss of pain and thermal sensation in the lower extremities. The upper extremities are less frequently involved.

The most striking clinical feature of these cases lies in the progressive 'trophic' changes which occur in the extremities. Recurrent perforating ulcers, terminal phalangeal osteolysis and digital necrosis combine to present a picture of mutilating acropathy. Such changes may occur of course in leprosy, tabes dorsalis, diabetes mellitus and porphyria, but all of these can be excluded by appropriate investigations. Primary amyloidosis can be identified by biopsy. Rarely, trophic lesions of the feet accompanied by sensory loss, occur as a late manifestation in some patients suffering from peroneal muscular atrophy. In hereditary sensory neuropathy deafness is not uncommon. Lumbosacral syringomyelia has no firm foundation in neuropathology and it seems certain that most cases formerly described as such were examples of hereditary radicular sensory neuropathy. The sensory dissociation which may be prominent at some stage of the disease, is a result of this radicular involvement; it tends to diminish as more nerve roots are affected.

Some form of sensory neuropathy may have been present in the fatal illness of King Edward VI in 1553. He died at the age of 15 after an illness in which there were skin eruptions, loss of hair and nails and 'a falling off of the fingers and toes'. He may have been poisoned.

The word 'trophic' means 'concerned with nourishment or food', a derivation from the Greek word 'trophe', meaning food. Trophic lesions in the extremities may arise from a variety of lesions of the nervous system. It is difficult to determine how much of the destruction of tissue results from repeated painless trauma and how much from loss of nutrition of the tissue owing to injury to autonomic fibres and secondarily of blood supply. The notion, 70 years ago, that these lesions were nutritional in origin led observers to postulate anatomical structures without taking the steps necessary to establish whether or not they existed. There are no known trophic nerves and many a famous clinician of the 90's would be bewildered to learn that the word 'trophic' cannot be found in many modern textbooks of physiology. But if the nerves have vanished the lesions are still with us. So the term is merely descriptive; the lesions are well known but their pathogenesis is obscure.

Against the theory that trophic lesions in analgesic states result from disregard of injuries, is the observation that section of the spinothalamic tracts (cordotomy) does not cause trophic disturbances. That trophic lesions result from vascular disturbance—directly or through the autonomic nervous system—is also questionable. Certainly the vascular supply to a part may be altered without causing any trophic disturbance. Similarly, various forms of sympathectomy can be carried out without danger of trophic lesions.

Sensory Neuropathy

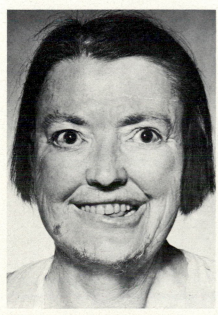

203a

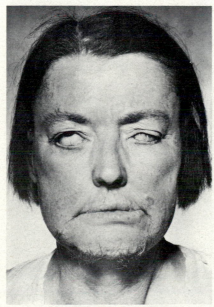

203b

203. Progressive sensory neuropathy Onset at 37 years, death at 59. Negative family history. Recurrent blisters and ulcers of feet and subsequently of the left hand over a period of 20 years. Progressive phalangeal osteolysis and many amputations of digits. No paraesthesiae but progressive loss of temperature and pain appreciation in the feet from the outset. Recent bilateral facial weakness. Slight diffuse weakness of both arms and marked weakness of the legs with bilateral foot drop. Impaired upper limb reflexes, brisk knee reflexes, absent ankle reflexes. Sphincters unaffected. Light touch sensation absent below both knees and in the left hand. Pain and temperature sensation

[continued overleaf

203—*continued from p. 137*

absent below both knees and posterior
aspect of thighs and buttocks (L.4–5 and
S.1–S.5). Pain and temperature sensation
also absent over the left forequarter of the
body (C.4 to T.4). Autopsy revealed
degeneration in the cervical, thoracic and
lumbar posterior spinal root ganglia. There
was also a reduction in the number of
anterior horn cells in the lumbar and
cervical regions. (*a*) and (*b*) show the
bilateral facial weakness, with failure to
retract the right corner of the mouth and
to close the eyes. The mutilated appearance of the left hand is shown in (*c*) and
of the feet in (*d*).

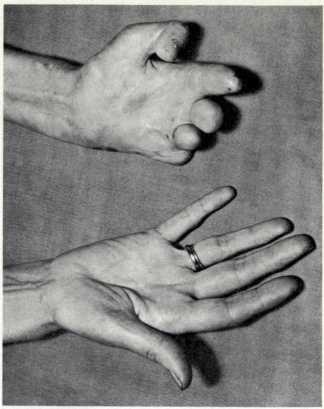

203c

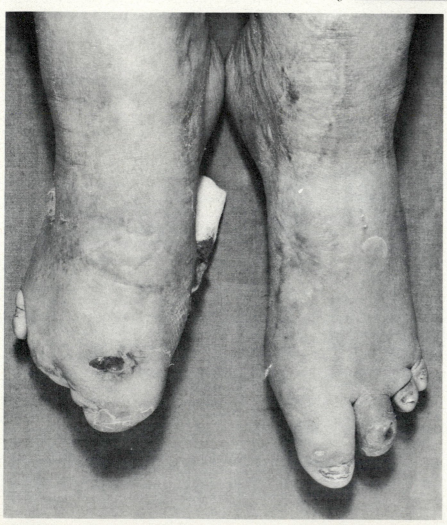

203d

Sensory
Neuropathy

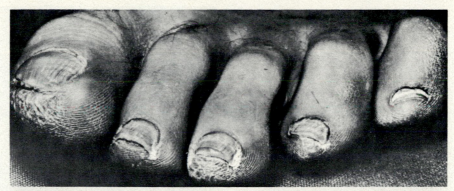

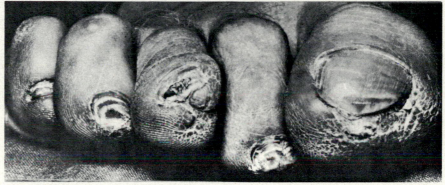

204. Progressive sensory neuropathy
Male, aged 29, with recurrent blisters and numbness and pains in the toes and feet since the age of 17. Normal peripheral circulation; normal femoral arteriography. Power, tone and reflexes normal, but progressive impairment of superficial sensation in the toes and distal portions of the feet; no dissociation. Nerve biopsy showed fibrous replacement. The illustrations show the progressive dry necrosis of the digits; radiographs revealed extensive osteolysis of the terminal phalanges. Observed for 5 years; little deterioration.

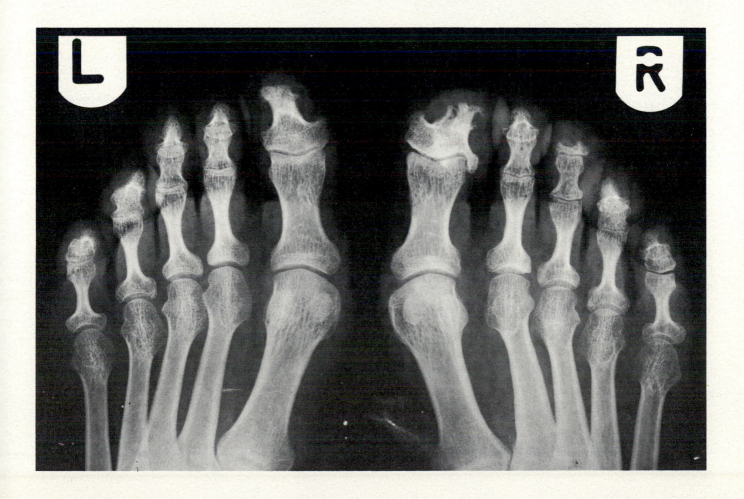

Sensory
Neuropathy

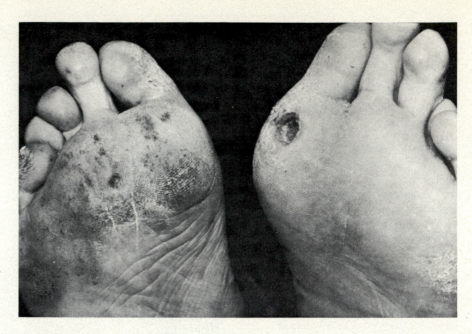

205. **Progressive sensory neuropathy**
Male, aged 50. Uncle of the patient in
Figure 172. Recurrent pains, discomfort
and perforating ulcers on the soles of both
feet for some years. No significant motor
disability. Ankle jerks impaired. Distal
sensory impairment.

Carcinomatous Neuropathy

The carcinomatous neuromyopathies are a group of
disorders associated with visceral carcinoma. They include dementia, cortical cerebellar degeneration, multi-
focal leuco-encephalopathy as well as peripheral
neuropathy and myopathy. They may be associated
with carcinoma of the lung, breast, ovary or uterus and
usually give rise to a slowly progressive asymmetrical
polyneuropathy of mixed motor and sensory type. Sometimes the disorder is primarily motor or sensory. The
neurological disorder may precede, coincide with or
follow the first manifestations of the visceral tumour. It
may run a variable course, but spontaneous remission
is rare. Sometimes there are myasthenia-like symptoms.
Spinal fluid protein level is often high. The cause of these
non-metastatic neurological disorders in patients suffering from carcinoma is not known.

In the cerebellar form ataxia of gait may be severe and
is often associated with dysarthria; nystagmus may be
minimal or absent and there are no signs of an expanding cerebellar lesion. The onset is usually gradual but it
can be rapid. Ataxia may also be the presenting symptom
in sensory neuropathy due to loss of position sense.
Motor neurone disease may be mimicked by motor
neuropathy. In the myasthenic-myopathic type the
proximal muscles of the limbs and even the bulbar
muscles may be principally involved and the weakness
aggravated by fatigue. The response to anti-myasthenia
drugs is incomplete and variable. In some cases it is
difficult to be certain whether progressive weakness of
the proximal muscles of the limbs is neural or muscular
in origin.

At autopsy only a careful examination may reveal the
presence of the tumour. Multiple microscopic metastatic
emboli are found in only a minute proportion of the
cases. Occasionally there are inflammatory features
affecting the brain, anterior horn cells and posterior
ganglia resembling an encephalomyelitis, suggesting
that a virus is responsible. There is no correlation between the size of the tumour and the degree of neural
disorder. It is possible that toxins are secreted by the
tumours, but none have been found.

In clinical practice it should be remembered that a
middle-aged man, presenting with ataxia of cerebellar or
sensory type or with weakness of proximal limb muscles,
may be harbouring a hidden neoplasm.

Carcinomatous Neuropathy

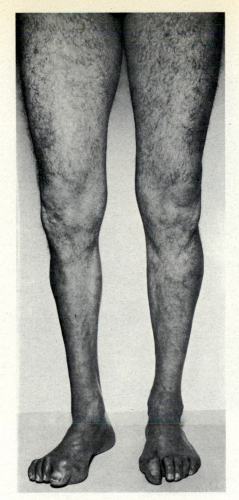

206. Carcinomatous neuropathy
Male, aged 53. Four months' history of cramp, paraesthesiae, numbness and weakness of the right lower limb. The only visible sign was of moderate diffuse wasting of the muscles below the right knee; the right foot was cold and cyanosed; both ankle jerks absent; right knee jerk impaired. Distal superficial sensory impairment on the right side, with bilateral impairment of vibration and postural sensibilities in both feet. Extensive investigations, including bronchoscopy failed to reveal any sign of malignancy.

The disability did not progress, but one year later he developed a right haemothorax which proved to be due to a bronchogenic carcinoma.

Rheumatoid Neuropathy

Neuropathy in rheumatoid arthritis is relatively rare; the majority of patients with this disease suffer no neurological complications. But it has long been known that peripheral nerve involvement may occur as a complication of the disease. Gowers in his *Manual of Diseases of the Nervous System* (1886) commented that nerves may be involved when they 'pass by a joint that is the seat of rheumatic inflammation'. Compression of the median nerve in the carpal tunnel is probably the commonest example of this type of neurological complication. The common peroneal and ulnar nerves may be similarly involved by local pressure. On the other hand frank polyneuritis is rare and when it does occur it is usually associated with systemic vasculitis. There is constitutional disorder with fever, anaemia and leucocytosis. It is subacute and asymmetrical in evolution, presenting rather as a 'mononeuritis multiplex', differing in these respects from the typical acute, infective or toxic polyneuritis. It is probably ischaemic in origin, a result of the generalized arteritis of rheumatoid arthritis and it is commoner in steroid-treated patients. It is a grave complication.

More commonly one encounters patients with rheumatoid arthritis in whom there is a sensory neuropathy which carries a good prognosis. Upper and lower limbs may be involved and the complaints are of numbness, coldness, clumsiness and perhaps weakness of the extremities. Sometimes the symptoms are confined to one or more digits of a limb; in such cases the only abnormality consists of digital hypo-aesthesia and hypalgesia. When the neuritic involvement is more marked there may be vibrational and postural loss with consequent clumsiness of movement. Digital neuropathy may be combined with various degrees of involvement of major peripheral nerves in the limb. In the lower limbs loss of reflexes is common. The symptoms fluctuate, tend to remit and there is no particular association with steroid treatment. Local nerve pressure from a swollen joint and occlusion of the vasa nervorum by the arteritis which occurs in rheumatoid arthritis are probably responsible for these benign forms of neuropathy.

Rheumatoid Neuropathy

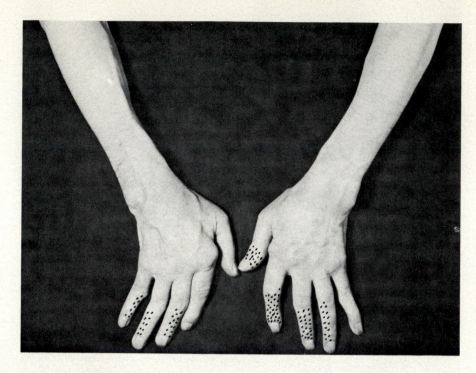

207. Rheumatoid neuropathy ▷
Male, aged 47, with rheumatoid arthritis
for 11 years. No steroid therapy. He had
always complained of cold feet, which were
arthritic, but now complained of cold
fingers, numbness of the tips and clumsiness. There was no additional weakness
and the abnormal neurological findings
consisted solely of digital hypo-aesthesia
and hypalgesia as shown. There was no
vibration or postural loss. The arm reflexes
were normal and there were no signs of
neuropathy in the lower limbs.

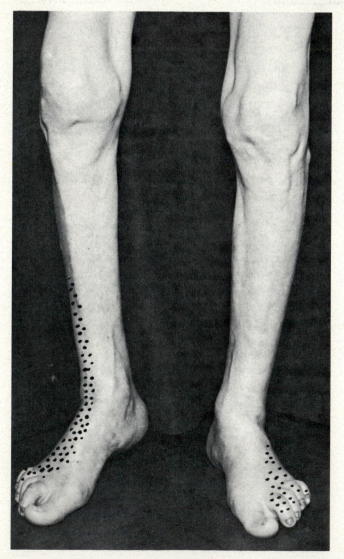

208. Rheumatoid neuropathy ◁
Male, aged 53. Rheumatoid arthritis 7
years. Steroid treatment 2 years. Recent
weakness in legs, coldness and numbness
of feet and swelling of the right knee.
Partial right foot drop, tenderness over the
right common peroneal nerve and impairment of superficial sensation as outlined.
No weakness on left side. Ankle pulses
normal. Recovery of foot drop in 7 weeks.

Ischaemic Neuropathy

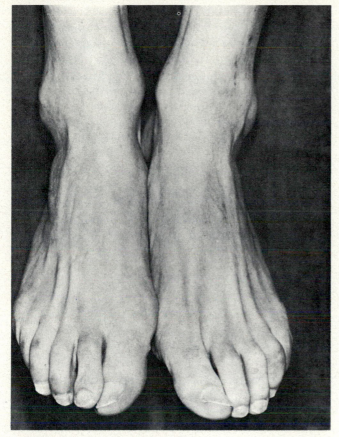

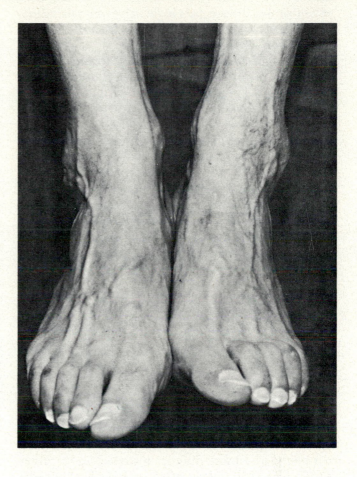

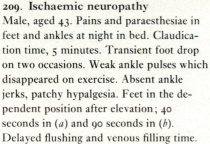

209. Ischaemic neuropathy
Male, aged 43. Pains and paraesthesiae in feet and ankles at night in bed. Claudication time, 5 minutes. Transient foot drop on two occasions. Weak ankle pulses which disappeared on exercise. Absent ankle jerks, patchy hypalgesia. Feet in the dependent position after elevation; 40 seconds in (*a*) and 90 seconds in (*b*). Delayed flushing and venous filling time.

Ischaemic Neuropathy

In progressive, obliterative vascular disease of the lower limbs, neuropathy may result from occlusion of the vasa nervorum or it may result from stenosis of major arteries. Foot drop from ischaemia of the common peroneal nerve is a not uncommon sequel to poor anastomotic circulation. Ischaemic neuropathy may also arise during the course of polyarteritis.

There is usually a story of intermittent claudication and with the onset of neuropathy the pain becomes continuous and severe. There is a burning superficial pain and a deep gnawing pain in the feet and calves which usually come on at night when the patient gets warm in bed. Relief is often obtained by hanging the foot down-

wards out of bed. There is often some degree of muscular weakness and wasting with impairment or loss of ankle jerks, but sensory testing usually discloses only patches of hypo-aesthesia or hypalgesia. Stimulation of the soles of the feet often gives rise to delayed unpleasant responses. When there has been acute arterial occlusion signs of involvement of the tibial or common peroneal nerves may be present.

Vascular disease is not likely to be overlooked if the patient's complaint has been pain in the calf on walking, rapidly relieved by rest. But if the pain has been in the buttock or thigh, osteo-arthritis of the hip or lumbosacral vertebral disc degeneration may have been diagnosed. Claudication in the small foot muscles may be diagnosed as metatarsalgia, and pain in the os calcis, ascribed to a spur. In spondylolisthesis and in some cases of lumbar disc disease, pain in the calves on walking may be the presenting symptom, but it is usually associated with various forms of paraesthesiae.

Inquiry concerning the appearance, temperature and comfort of the extremities, particularly on exposure to cold or on exercise, is necessary if peripheral vascular disease is suspected. Particular attention should be paid to the appearance of the feet in the horizontal, elevated and dependent positions. The ankle pulses are frequently absent, but it should be remembered that dorsalis pedis pulsation is absent in about 10 per cent. of normal young adults. The ankle pulses may become imperceptible following exercise and gradually return with rest. As a corollary, a palpable pulse at rest does not exclude a diminished blood flow. With the patient at rest tests for plantar pallor, flushing time and venous filling time should be carried out. The lower limb is raised to an angle of 45 degrees and the colour of the plantar surface is observed. Normally, pallor should not develop. If the patient then sits up and the previously elevated limb is allowed to hang in a dependent position, the time taken for the circulation to return to the toes may be measured. In the normal warm limb this should take a few seconds, but in vascular disease it may be increased to half a minute or longer. Normally, the veins on the dorsum of the foot fill in less than 20 seconds. In occlusive arterial disease the venous filling time may be prolonged to 1 or 2 minutes.

Digital ischaemia commonly leads to nail changes—distortion of growth, thickening and roughening from ridging, loosening of the nail—but they are not necessarily associated with atrophy of the finger pulp nor are they a good reflection of the state of the arterial supply.

Classification of Neuropathies

From an anatomical viewpoint one can speak of the following types of neuropathy. (1) A *mononeuropathy* is a motor or sensory disorder restricted to the distribution of a single nerve trunk or branch of a nerve. The lesions are commonly compressive. In mononeuritis multiplex they are discrete and multiple as in diabetes, leprosy and polyarteritis nodosa. (2) In *radiculoneuropathy* there is an inflammatory lesion of nerve roots, spinal or cranial, and there may be an associated myelitis. The Guillain–Barré syndrome is an example of a widespread radiculoneuropathy. (3) Lastly there is *symmetrical peripheral neuropathy*, usually due to metabolic or toxic disorders: a symmetrical sensori-motor neuropathy of subacute onset and slow progression, e.g. alcoholic neuropathy.

From the pathological point of view, neuropathies fall into three categories. First, a neuropathy may be primarily axonal as in beriberi, porphyria, or poisoning with lead or triorthocresyl phosphate. Secondly, it may be primarily a segmental demyelinating lesion as in diabetes, diphtheria, carcinoma and the Guillain–Barré syndrome. Thirdly, the essential pathology may be one of interstitial hypertrophy, infiltration or allergic swelling: such lesions occur in hypertrophic polyneuritis, in amyloidosis and in acute infective polyneuritis.

The two main abnormalities in polyneuritis are segmental demyelination of the nerve fibre sheath and axonal degeneration. Demyelination tends to reduce conduction velocity in nerves, whereas axonal degeneration has a greater tendency to produce patterns of denervation and falling out of motor unit potentials on electromyography. These tests are not infallible and it is well known that although a reduced conduction velocity usually means polyneuritis, a normal result does not exclude the diagnosis. Nerve conduction measurements are most reliable in the compressive or entrapment neuropathies where a short segment of the nerve is compressed and the resultant ischaemia slows conduction.

Using the combined techniques of nerve biopsy and electrodiagnostic tests, two main categories of neuropathy can be recognized. In the first there is a combination of segmental demyelination and a substantially reduced nerve conduction velocity; the Guillain–Barré syndrome, diabetic neuropathy and hereditary hypertrophic neuropathy come in this category. The disease processes seem primarily to affect the Schwann cells. In the second group there is axonal degeneration with little or no segmental demyelination, combined with only mild reduction of conduction velocity; examples are alcoholic and porphyric neuropathy, triorthocresyl phosphate poisoning and isoniazid neuropathy. General experience has shown that in the majority of neuropathies there is a combination of axonal degeneration and segmental demyelination. No doubt the Schwann cells and the axons differ in their degree of vulnerability to the various agents responsible for the neuropathies.

The Upper Limb

The upper limb is innervated by the brachial plexus which normally derives its supply from the fifth, sixth, seventh and eighth cervical roots and the first thoracic root. The obliquity of the roots as they emerge from the spinal cord is sufficient for at least part of the anterior root exit zone to lie at one disc level higher than the intervertebral foramen through which the radicular nerve leaves the spinal canal. On the other hand the dural pouches, enclosing the roots, emerge from the spinal dura at right angles. Fibrosis of the dural sheaths or deformity or absence of a pouch may cause angulation of the corresponding nerve. With advancing years, there is loss of intervertebral disc space and a reduction of the degree of obliquity of the intrathecal roots. Injury to, degeneration and herniation of, the intervertebral discs are the commonest causes of root lesions.

The posterior roots carry the afferent sensory fibres and the efferent fibres subserving vasodilatation. The anterior roots carry efferent motor, sudomotor, pilomotor and vasoconstrictor fibres and also afferent sensory fibres. The area of skin which is supplied by the fibres of a certain spinal root is called a dermatome. Dermatomes are arranged along the pre-axial and post-axial borders of the limb. The group of muscles supplied from a single spinal segment is referred to as a myotome. Sclerotomal innervation is not important in clinical practice. Sclerotomes (the bony and ligamentous segmental zones) usually extend distally throughout the whole length of the limb. In cervical root syndromes the interpretation of the distribution of pain, paraesthesiae, objective sensory loss and muscular weakness and the pattern of reflex abnormality, necessitates a knowledge of the segmental innervation of the limb. There is probably considerable variation in the dermatome distribution, with much overlap, especially of the fifth and sixth dermatomes on the outer side of the arm. The C.8 dermatome on the ulnar side of the hand, may end at the wrist or extend some distance up the forearm, and it may involve the middle finger. The upper and lower limits of the first and second thoracic dermatomes, on the inner side of the forearm and arm, are also variable. The armpit is the centre of the third cervical dermatome with a variable triangular prolongation to the inner side of the upper arm.

Resection of one single root in man is not followed by loss of sensibility as ordinarily tested. Tactile dermatomes are larger than the pain and the thermal dermatomes. It seems that each fibre in a nerve root is distributed over the entire dermatome, so that sensibility may be preserved despite the destruction of the majority of fibres in a posterior nerve root.

In the motor innervation of the upper limb there is also variation and overlap. Movements of the shoulder, elbow, wrist and fingers should be methodically examined. The strength of groups of muscles and of individual muscles should be assessed, if necessary against resistance.

At the shoulder, forward thrust is carried out by contraction of the serratus anterior, supplied by the long thoracic nerve of Bell (C.5–7). Abduction of the arm is carried out by the supraspinatus (C.5) and the deltoid (C.5–6). Lateral rotation of the arm is effected through the infraspinatus (C.5–6) and the teres minor (C.5). Medial rotation and adduction require the action of latissimus dorsi, teres major and the subscapularis (C.5–8).

At the elbow flexion of the forearm is performed by contraction of the biceps and brachialis (C.5–6). The biceps also assists in supination. Extension is performed by the triceps (C.6–8) and pronation by the pronator teres (C.6–7). The brachioradialis (C.5–6) assists in flexion and supination of the forearm.

Movements of flexion and extension at the wrist (C.6–8) and at the fingers (mainly C.8) may be weakened in a manner that is liable to escape detection unless they are tested against resistance. The thenar and hypothenar muscles are supplied by C.8 and T.1. The interossei and lumbricals are also innervated by C.8 and T.1 segments.

Pain in cervical root lesions may be severe and radiate from the neck across the shoulder and down the whole length of the limb into the fingers. Quite frequently there are intervening pain free zones, so that the patient will describe sharp pain across the front of the shoulder, at the elbow and in the thumb and index. Paraesthesiae are usually distal in site on the radial or ulnar side of the hand or, perhaps, restricted to one finger, as in the case of the middle finger (C.7). The acute, sharp, darting superficial pain from a root lesion may occur against a background of dull aching pain of myotome distribution. Thus, in a C.7 root lesion, there may be sharp pain and paraesthesiae in the middle finger, with a dull aching pain over the pectoral muscle, mimicking angina.

In the course of their distribution to the upper limb, nerve fibres may be injured or involved in disease processes at various points. Certainly, one of the commonest is the root involvement caused by prolapsed discs and cervical spondylosis. Compression of the median nerve in the carpal tunnel comes next in frequency. Ulnar nerve lesions are commoner than costoclavicular syndromes. Injury is an increasingly common agent and takes many different forms—avulsion of the cervical roots, contusion or rupture of the brachial plexus, and damage, directly or indirectly, of individual peripheral nerves.

Tests of Upper Limb Movement

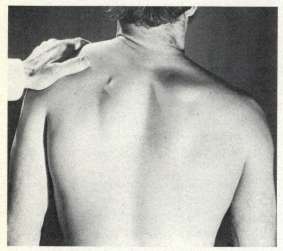

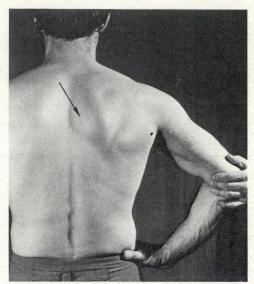

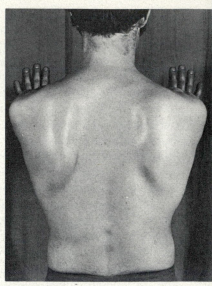

210. Trapezius (accessory nerve and C.3, 4)
This is the elevator of the scapula and shoulder girdle. With the rhomboids it retracts the scapula and braces back the shoulder. Photograph shows elevation of the shoulder against resistance.

211. Rhomboids (nerve to rhomboids; C.5)
The patient, with his hand on his hip, tries to brace his shoulder backwards against resistance.

212. Serratus anterior (nerve to serratus anterior; C.5, 6, 7)
The patient pushes hard against a firm structure. This muscle draws the scapula forward and is the chief one concerned in forward pushing, thrusting and punching movements.

Muscles of the Shoulder Girdle and Scapula

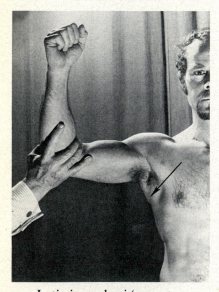

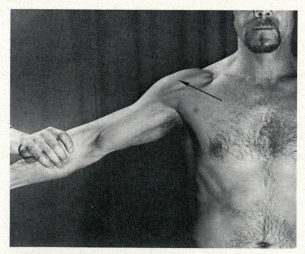

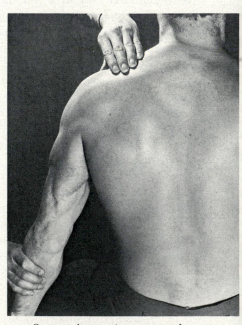

213. Latissimus dorsi (nerve to latissimus dorsi; C.7)
When the patient coughs, the muscle bellies can be felt. It can also be seen and felt, as in the photograph, when the patient attempts to adduct the arm from the abducted position against resistance.

214. Deltoid (circumflex nerve; C.5)
The patient holds his arm abducted against the examiner's resistance.

215. Supraspinatus (suprascapular nerve; C.5)
The patient begins to abduct the arm from the side against resistance. Contraction of the muscle can be felt and sometimes seen.

*Muscles of the
Shoulder Girdle
and Scapula*

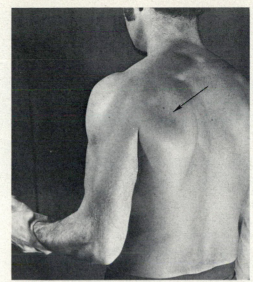

**216. Infraspinatus (suprascapular
nerve; C.5)**
With his elbow at his side, the patient
is trying to turn the flexed forearm
backwards against resistance. External
rotation at the shoulder joint. The
contracting muscle can be felt and
sometimes seen.

**217. Pectoralis major (lateral and
medial pectoral nerves; C.6, 7, 8)**
With his hand on his hip the patient
presses inwards, and the muscle can be
seen and felt to contract. This tests the
sternocostal portion of the muscle. The
clavicular portion contracts when the
patient raises his arm forward above the
horizontal and tries to adduct it against
resistance.

216

217

Muscles of the Elbow Joint

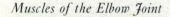

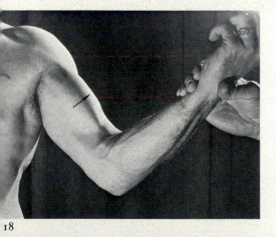

**218. Biceps (musculocutaneous
nerve; C.5)** ◁
The patient is trying to flex the supinated
forearm against resistance.

18

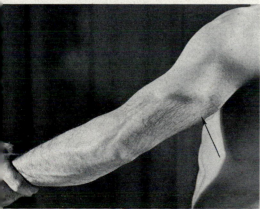

219. Triceps (radial nerve; C.7)
The patient extends the elbow and holds
it there against the examiner's attempt to
flex it. Alternatively, the patient attempts
to extend the elbow against resistance.

**220. Brachioradialis (radial nerve;
C.5, 6)**
With the forearm midway between
pronation and supination, the patient is
trying to flex the forearm against
resistance.

19   220

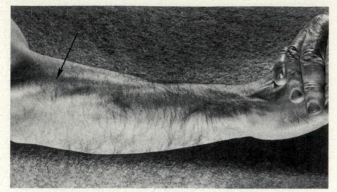

221. Extensor carpi radialis longus (radial nerve; C.6, 7)
With his fingers extended, the patient is trying to dorsiflex the wrist to the radial side against resistance.

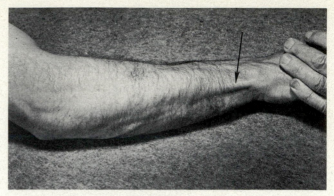

222. Extensor carpi ulnaris (radial nerve; C.7)
The patient is trying to dorsiflex his wrist to the ulnar side against resistance.

Muscles of the Forearm and Wrist Joint

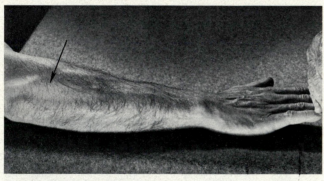

223. Extensor digitorum (radial nerve; C.7)
The patient is resisting an attempt to flex the fingers at the metacarpophalangeal joints.

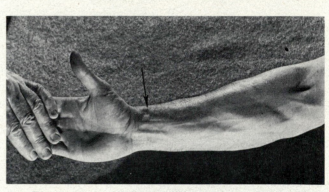

224. Flexor carpi radialis (median nerve; C.6, 7)
The patient is trying to flex his wrist towards the radial side against resistance.

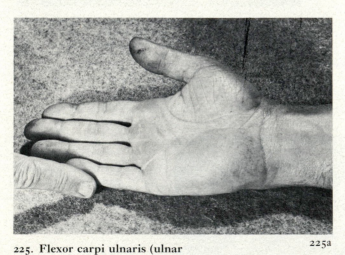

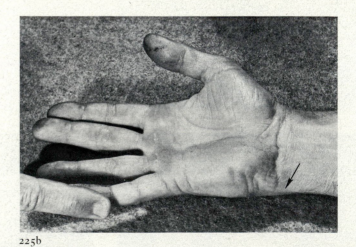

225a   225b

225. Flexor carpi ulnaris (ulnar nerve; C.8)
(a) The patient lays his hand palm upwards on the table with fingers extended. The examiner holds a finger against the patient's fifth finger. (b) The patient abducts his fifth finger against resistance. The tendon of flexor carpi ulnaris can be seen and felt to contract as it fixes the point of origin of abductor digiti minimi. This action can be noted even when abductor digiti minimi is paralysed.

Muscles of the Hand and Fingers

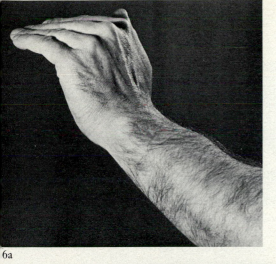

6a

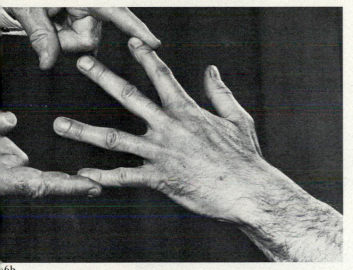

6b

**226. Lumbricals and interossei
(median nerve—lumbricals I and II;
ulnar nerve—interossei, lumbricals
III and IV)** ◁
(*a*) The patient flexes his extended fingers
at the metacarpophalangeal joint (lumbricals). (*b*) The patient holds his fingers
in the abducted position against resistance
(interossei).

**227. First dorsal interosseous muscle
(ulnar nerve; T.1)** ▽
With fingers and palm on a flat surface
the patient is trying, against resistance,
to abduct the index finger.

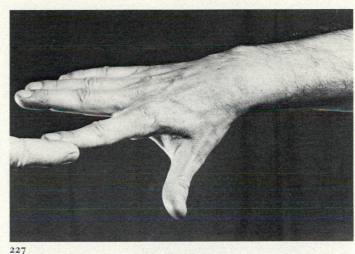

227

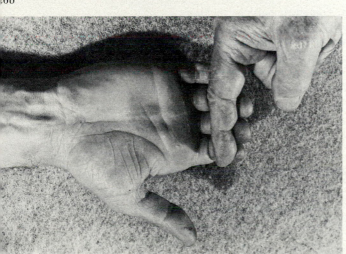

8

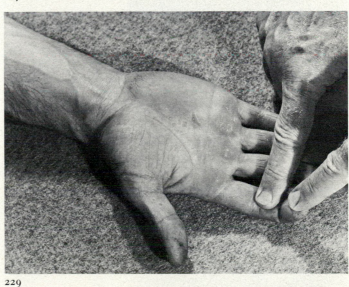

229

**228. Flexor digitorum sublimis
(median nerve; C.8)** △
The four tendons of this muscle are
inserted into the middle phalanges. The
action of the muscle is to flex first the
middle and then the proximal phalanges.
It can also act as a flexor of the wrist.
The patient flexes his fingers at the
proximal interphalangeal joints against
resistance.

**229. Flexor digitorum profundus I
and II (median nerve; C.8)** △
This muscle flexes the distal phalanges
after flexor digitorum sublimis has flexed
the middle phalanges. It also can assist
in flexing the wrist. The patient resists

an attempt to extend the terminal phalanx
of the index finger while the middle
phalanx is fixed. The medial part of
flexor digitorum profundus is supplied
by the ulnar nerve, the lateral part by
the anterior interosseous branch of the
median nerve.

Muscles of the Thumb

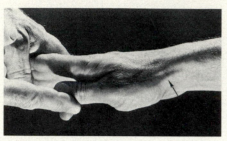

230. Abductor pollicis longus (radial nerve; C.8)
The patient is trying to abduct his thumb in a plane at right angles to the palm.

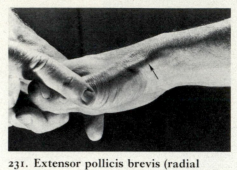

231. Extensor pollicis brevis (radial nerve; C.8)
The patient is resisting an attempt to flex his thumb at the metacarpophalangeal joint.

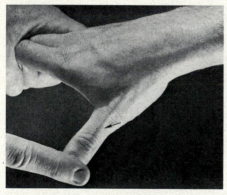

232. Extensor pollicis longus (radial nerve; C.8)
The patient is resisting an attempt to flex his thumb at the interphalangeal joint.

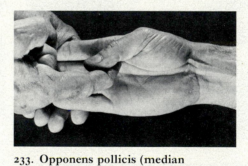

233. Opponens pollicis (median nerve; T.1)
The patient attempts to touch his fifth finger with his thumb against resistance. The thumb nail should remain in a plane parallel to the palm.

a

234. Abductor pollicis brevis (median nerve; T.1)
(*a*) With the patient's hand palm upwards, his thumb is placed so that the nail is in a plane at right angles to the

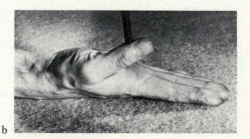

b

palm. The examiner holds a pencil on the patient's thumb as shown. (*b*) The patient raises his thumb vertically against resistance.

Muscles of the Thumb

235. Flexor pollicis longus (median nerve; C.8)
The patient resists an attempt to extend the terminal phalanx of his thumb while the proximal phalanx is fixed.

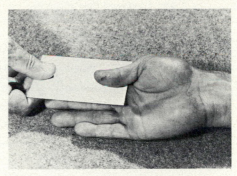

236. Adductor pollicis (ulnar nerve; T.1)
With his thumb in a plane at right angles to the palm, the patient attempts to hold a card between the thumb and the index finger.

Nerves of the Upper Limb

237. Innervation of the upper limb
(Reproduced from *Aids to the Investigation of Peripheral Nerve Injuries*, 1943, by permission of the Controller of Her Majesty's Stationery Office.)

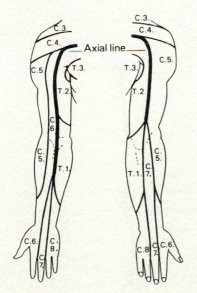

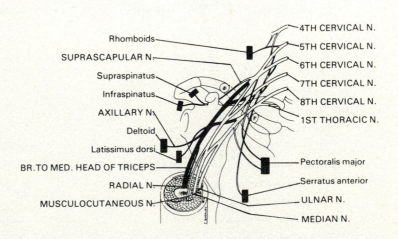

(*a*) Distribution of spinal segments in the upper limb.

(*b*) Diagram of the brachial plexus, its branches and the muscles which they supply.

[*continued overleaf*

Nerves of the Upper Limb
237—*continued from p. 151*

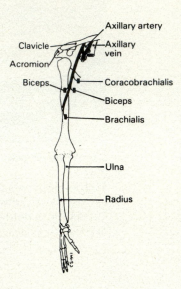

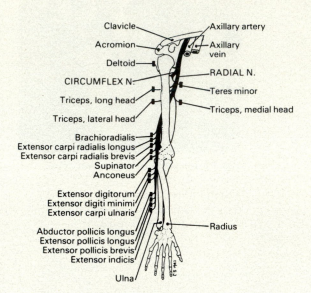

(*c*) Diagram of the musculocutaneous nerve and the muscles which it supplies. (Modified from Petres and Testut.)

(*d*) Diagram of the circumflex and radial nerves and the muscles which they supply. (Modified from Petres and Testut.)

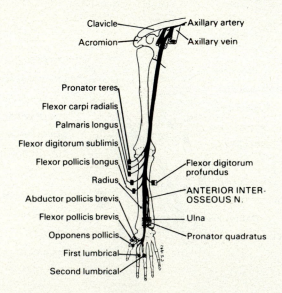

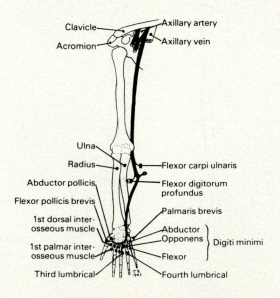

(*e*) Diagram of the median nerve and the muscles which it supplies. (Modified from Petres and Testut.)

(*f*) Diagram of the ulnar nerve and the muscles which it supplies. (Modified from Petres and Testut.)

Cervical Root Lesions

Injury to the neck is a common cause of cervical root irritation. It has been known for many years that traumatic tetraplegia may occur without apparent injury to the cervical spine. No doubt the great flexibility of the cervical spine protects it somewhat from fractures and dislocations, but this flexibility also renders it liable to hyperflexion and hyperextension as in the 'whiplash injury' in automobile accidents. There may be no evident damage to the cervical vertebrae or joints. In addition to pain referred to the upper limbs there may be headache, dizziness, tenderness about the neck and a reluctance to move it and some restriction of the range of movement. Paraesthesiae in the hands, aggravated by neck movement, is described. Usually there are no objective neurological findings in the upper limbs. In many cases litigation and neurosis make analysis of the disability wellnigh impossible. It is surprising how often the patient is a young healthy person with a normal cervical spine and not, as might be expected, the elderly car passenger with considerable cervical spondylosis. Lesions in the sympathetic ganglia, of the vertebral artery, and 'neurovascular structures' are invoked to explain some of the more bizarre symptoms, such as vertigo, blurring of vision, nausea, tinnitus, unsteadiness of gait and, that all too familiar complaint, 'lack of concentration'. It was inevitable that electroencephalographic 'abnormalities' would be described in whiplash injury without concussion. This is not to say that violent movement of the neck cannot produce a sprain or strain, as it were, of the cervical joints with persisting symptoms. But, like the 'slipped disc', the term 'whiplash injury' is now more of a cliché than a syndrome. Repeated radiological examination, the too early prescription of a collar, local injections and ultrasonic therapy, serve usually to exaggerate and prolong the disability.

In cervical disc protrusions, the onset of pain may be gradual or sudden and it is not necessarily attended by any painful stiffness of the neck. The mid-cervical roots are most commonly involved and the pain, radiating down the arm, may be aggravated by coughing or sneezing or by movements of the neck. Rest may relieve the pain in the arm, but not the stiffness of the neck. Paraesthesiae are common and are usually distal, in the thumb and index in a sixth root lesion, in the middle finger when the seventh root is involved and in the ring and little fingers and along the ulnar border of the hand when the eighth root is affected. Sixth root involvement is commonest. There is usually some restriction of neck movement and signs of a radicular lesion in the arm. Points of tenderness may be detected in the proximal muscles of the limb, with varying degrees of weakness, sensory impairment and diminished reflexes. In a sixth root lesion biceps and radial reflexes are reduced or absent and there is tingling and numbness of thumb and index. The triceps reflex is lost in seventh root lesions.

In the cervical region root involvement from disc disease is much more commonly due to progressive protrusion of the annulus fibrosus than to acute nuclear prolapse. In cervical spondylosis there is progressive degeneration of the discs, bulging of the annulus, and osteophyte formation at the margins of adjacent vertebrae. Pressure upon an emerging root in an intervertebral foramen or involvement of the root by a local fibrous reaction in its sheath often at several levels or bilaterally, are a common cause of brachial neuritis. The discs between the fifth, sixth and seventh cervical vertebrae are those most commonly affected and pain in the arm may be diffuse and persistent. There is pain and stiffness of the neck, paraesthesiae, muscle weakness and wasting, and depression of reflexes. Fasciculation may be seen but is never as prominent and diffuse as in motor neurone disease. Significant wasting of the small muscles of the hand (C.8 and T.1) is uncommon but, according to the level and extent of root involvement, wasting of the deltoid, biceps, triceps and supinator muscles may result. The biceps, radial and triceps reflexes may be selectively or uniformly depressed or the two former may be depressed and the triceps jerk exaggerated. Sometimes the phenomenon of 'inversion' of these reflexes may be observed. Percussion of the tendon of the biceps may provoke contraction of the triceps; flexion of the fingers may replace contraction of the brachioradialis when the latter reflex is tested by tapping the lower end of the radius. In such cases there are often signs of spinal cord disturbance in the lower limb—exaggerated reflexes, extensor plantar responses and some form of sensory disturbance. This pattern of reflex abnormality in the upper limbs is often the clue to the level of the lesion responsible for signs discovered in the lower limbs.

It should be unnecessary to say that radiographic evidence of cervical spondylosis should not be assumed to explain all forms of 'brachial neuritis'. Cervical spondylosis is common and usually symptomless; it is likely to be present in the middle-aged woman with the carpal tunnel syndrome, in the patient with ulnar neuritis from arthritis of the elbow and in diabetic neuropathies.

Irreversible injury to cervical nerve roots occurs when they are avulsed from the spinal cord by forcible separation of the head and shoulder. For many years it has been realized that traction lesions of the brachial plexus carry a much graver prognosis compared to lesions of the peripheral nerves in general. This is explained in part by the knowledge, now at our disposal as a result of the development of opaque myelography, that unsuspected avulsion of the individual rootlets at their exits from the spinal cord occurs in many of these traction injuries. At first detected on post-mortem examination and surgical exploration, they can now be identified by myelography. It is obvious that the violence which ruptures the nerve roots may also damage the peripheral portion of the axones. The injured person is usually a young man who has fallen from a motor cycle. Following recovery from concussion he has a paralysed flail arm. There is little or no recovery and the muscles waste, the reflexes are absent and the only remaining zone of sensation is from T.2 and 3 on the inner side of the upper arm and the axilla. There is often a Horner syndrome and its presence is a grave prognostic sign. Causalgia is common. If, in such cases, there is a fracture or dislocation of the clavicle, direct injury to the plexus may be assumed. Rehabilitative measures and exploration may be undertaken, whereas myelography might have shown the damaged root pouches and *Myodil*-filled sacs characteristic of root avulsion. The root pouches may sometimes be torn without damage to the roots themselves.

A useful, though not diagnostic sign in root avulsion is the retention of the normal histamine-induced axone reflex. It is based upon the production of cutaneous flare by the intradermal introduction of histamine. The flare response depends upon the integrity of peripheral cutaneous axones, and is present in normal individuals and in patients with purely root lesions, in which the peripheral axone or its cell body in the dorsal root ganglion has not been injured. It obviously gives no indication of the extent of motor root avulsion and they are said to be more liable to this form of injury than the posterior roots. Obviously also there may be axone damage distal to the ganglia as well as proximally.

The condition of the serratus magnus muscle and the rhomboids should be tested when root avulsion is suspected. These muscles are supplied by nerves which arise directly from the nerve roots and their paralysis is presumptive evidence of root injury. The presence of Horner's syndrome does not necessarily mean root avulsion, although injury to the T.1 sympathetic outflow or in the communicating rami must have occurred. The poor prognosis in cases with a Horner's syndrome is probably a reflection of the severity of the neural injury.

Cervical Root Lesions

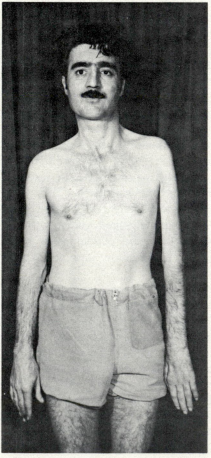

238a

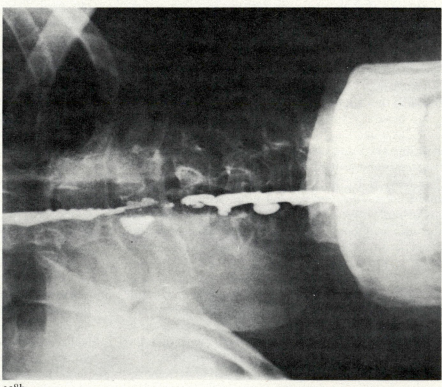

238b

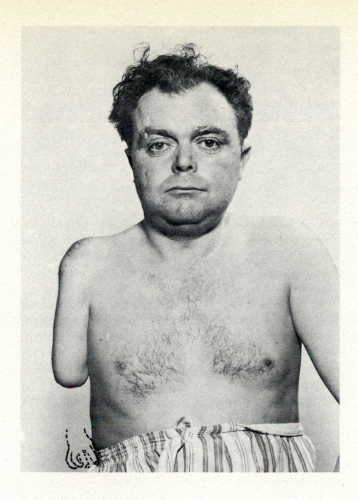

239. Cervical root avulsion ◁
Motor cycle accident 14 years previously.
Fractures of the transverse processes of
C.4 and 5 (R), paralysis of the right arm.
Amputation 3 years later. Paralysis of
right diaphragm and paradoxical movement. Opaque myelography showed large
diverticulae at C.7, C.8 and T.1 with
absent root pouches C.4, 5, 6, 7. Note
right Horner syndrome. Position of
residual phantom hand is indicated in
outline.

240. Cervical root avulsion ▽
Motor cycle accident, fracture of right
humerus, fracture dislocation of right
clavicle. Immediate paralysis of the right
arm which was subsequently amputated.
Painful phantom limb. Note absence of
right Horner syndrome. Opaque myelography showed root avulsion and diverticulae C.5, 6, 7, 8.

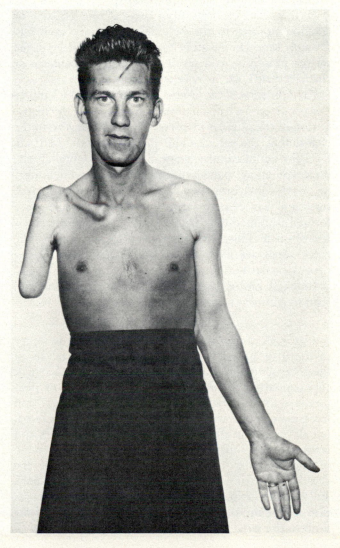

238. Cervical root avulsion ◁
Motor cycle accident. Unconscious 5
minutes. Immediate paralysis of left arm
with fracture of left clavicle and of first,
second and third left ribs. Six months
later there was a partial left Horner's
syndrome, complete flaccid paralysis of
the left upper limb, with loss of reflexes
and anaesthesia—from C.4 to T.1 (*a*).
There was a positive histamine axone
reflex on each forearm. Radiographs revealed marked elevation of the left dome of
the diaphragm with paradoxical movement of that side on sniffing. Opaque
myelography (*b*) showed the typical
appearance of an avulsion injury with
Myodil-filled dural sacs on the left side
at C.6, 7 and T.1. Anteroposterior projection, patient lying on his left side.

Persistent pain in the hand and the flail
arm led to an above-elbow amputation one
year later. Subsequently developed an
intensely painful phantom hand held in a
partially clenched position. This was
relieved 4 years after the injury by cordotomy (Mr. R. D. Weeks). The phantom
hand also assumed a more 'relaxed'
position.

Brachial Plexus Lesions

The five roots (C.5, 6, 7, 8 and T.1) of the brachial plexus unite to form upper, middle and lower trunks about $1\frac{1}{2}$ inches from the lateral border of the cervical vertebral bodies. The trunks enter into cord formation about 3 inches from the vertebrae. The posterior cord is the first to be formed, followed by the lateral and then the medial. Cord formation extends beneath the clavicle and the coracoid process to the upper part of the axilla. As it courses through the posterior triangle of the neck and beneath the clavicle into the axilla, the brachial plexus may be injured by penetrating wounds, by fracture of the clavicle or dislocation of the shoulder or it may be compressed by a cervical rib, a tumour, enlarged glands or an aneurysm. Direct damage to the plexus may be inflicted during surgical operations and indirect damage as a result of traction and pressure in operations, such as thoracotomy, when the upper limb is abducted. Fibrosis may involve the brachial plexus following radical mastectomy and radiotherapy.

Birth palsies resulting from cervical root avulsion or traction injuries to the brachial plexus are now fortunately rare. On the other hand, traction injuries of the plexus in adults, as a result of industrial accidents or road accidents, are increasingly encountered.

An indication of the level in the plexus at which injury has occurred may be obtained by a study of the distribution of the muscles involved. *Root* branches go to the rhomboids, the serratus and the diaphragm. At *trunk* level the suprascapular nerve is the first to branch off; if the spinati are paralysed, the level of the lesion must lie above trunk formation; if the spinati are preserved, the lesion is more peripheral. The *cords* of the plexus are formed at about the level of the clavicle, so that infraclavicular injuries must always have a cord distribution. The three cords are close to the subclavian artery in the neurovascular bundle.

Brachial plexus lesions are usually incomplete and tend to conform to one of the following types.

Upper plexus paralysis (*Erb's palsy*). There is injury to the fifth and sixth cervical roots with paralysis of the biceps, deltoid, brachioradialis (supinator longus), supraspinatus, rhomboids, clavicular portion of pectoralis major, serratus anterior, latissimus dorsi and teres major. The arm cannot be abducted or elevated, nor flexed at the elbow; movements of the fingers and wrist are not impaired. There is weakness of bracing of the shoulder (rhomboids), of depression of the shoulder (latissimus dorsi), adduction (pectoralis major), and rotation (spinati). The biceps reflex is lost and sensation is impaired or lost along the outer border of the limb to the wrist, thumb and index finger.[1]

Lower plexus paralysis (*Klumpke's palsy*). There is a lesion of the eighth cervical and first thoracic roots or of the trunk which forms the median and ulnar nerves. There is paralysis of the flexors of the wrist and fingers and the small muscles of the hand; the zone of sensory loss comprises the hand and the inner border of the forearm to the elbow. In a root lesion there is an accompanying Horner's syndrome.

Complete lesions of the brachial plexus are rare; the commonest being due to avulsion of the roots from the cord. The whole of the limb is paralysed, all reflexes are lost and sensation is only retained on the inner side of the arm in its upper third.

In non-traumatic, progressive lesions of the brachial plexus, palpation in the supraclavicular fossa and in the axilla may disclose tenderness, fullness or glandular enlargement. Swelling of the hand from lymphoedema may be present for some years in cases of brachial plexus involvement following mastectomy and radiotherapy. A carcinoma of the superior pulmonary sulcus (Pancoast's tumour) may present with symptoms and signs of a progressive brachial plexus lesion. The pain is often severe, radiating down the arm, with disturbances of sweat secretion and often a Horner's syndrome. A fullness above the clavicle may be detected.

[1] German medical students used to refer to an upper brachial plexus disability as due to injury to the 'nervus poculomotorius', poculus meaning 'drinking cup'. The movements by which a glass is brought to the lips are effected by the biceps, brachialis, brachioradialis and deltoid muscles.

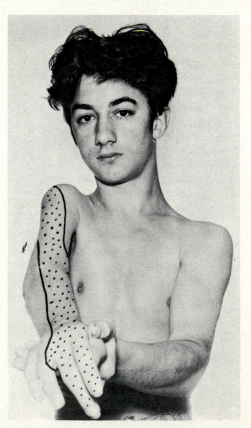

241

Brachial Plexus Lesions

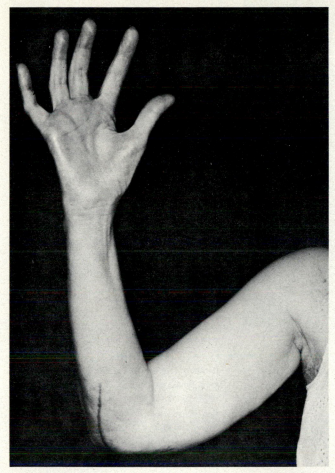

242a

242. Brachial plexus injury
Right brachial plexus palsy following
radical mastectomy and radiotherapy.
Onset of progressive pain, numbness,
weakness and stiffness of the right hand 3
years after treatment. Transplantation of
the right ulnar nerve 1 year later when a
mistaken diagnosis of ulnar paralysis was
made. When first seen by me 6 months
later there was global atrophy of the small
muscles of the right hand, wasting of the
forearm, (*a*), absent biceps and radial reflexes on the right; impaired right triceps
reflex. Diffuse sensory impairment
C.6–T.2 (*b*).

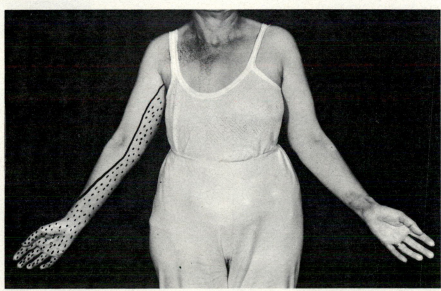

242b

241. Brachial plexus injury ◁
Six months after a motor cycle accident in
which he fractured his right radius and
ulna. Almost complete paralysis of right
arm involving deltoid, spinati, latissimus
dorsi. Rhomboids, trapezius and pectoralis
major were intact. No movement at elbow,
minimal movements at wrist, thumb, index
and middle fingers Sensory loss of C.5, 6 ·
and 7 distribution. Myelography normal.
Histamine–induced axone reflex normal.

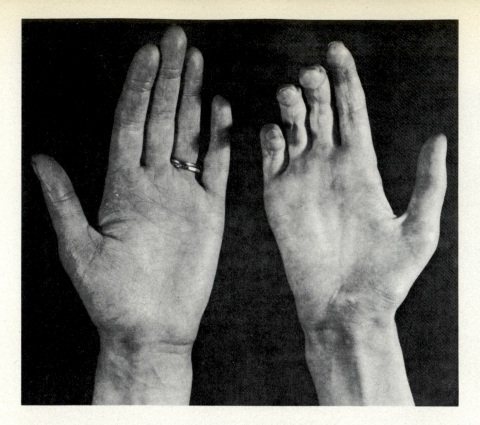

243. Brachial plexus injury ◁
Right brachial plexus palsy following right thoracotomy. Weakness and numbness of the affected hand was noticed on recovery from anaesthesia. Three months later there was global atrophy of the intrinsic muscles of the right hand, clawing of the fingers, diffuse, mild sensory impairment of C.6, 7, 8 and T.1, and glossy, cyanosed skin of the hand. Such lesions result from traction of the abducted limb in the prone position. Incomplete recovery after 2 years.

245. Brachial plexus lesion ▽
Partial brachial plexus palsy due to carcinoma of the apex of the left lung. There was global wasting of the intrinsic hand muscles of the left hand; wasting of the flexor muscles of the forearm and loss of the radial reflex. The biceps and triceps reflexes were preserved, sensory loss was slight and diffuse (C.6, 7 and 8) and the hand was puffy, moist and cyanosed.

244. Brachial plexus injury ▽
Paresis of the right upper limb in a youth after 2 weeks' humping sacks of coal. Returned home one evening complaining of pain and weakness about the right shoulder; paresis of the arm followed while at work the next day. Wasting of right deltoid, biceps, triceps and slight winging of the right scapula. The spinati were weak; reflexes absent. Recovery began 3 weeks after onset and 6 weeks later was nearly complete. There was no definite sensory loss; he had felt some paraesthesiae in the right hand and stroking the hand and forearm produced a tingling sensation.

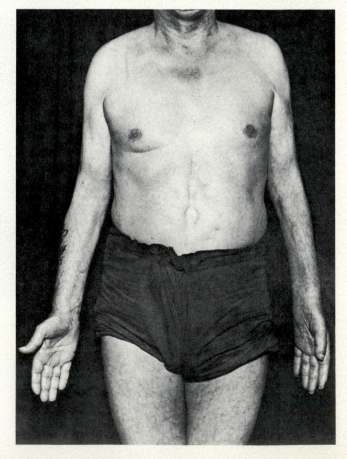

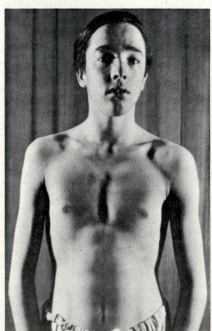

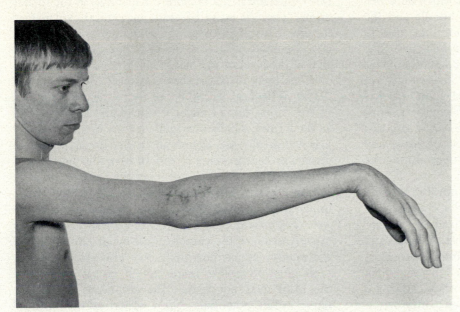

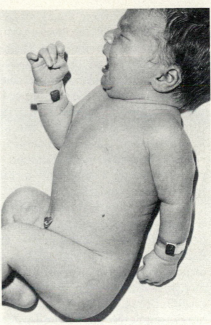

246. Right brachial plexus injury
Right wrist drop 1 month after an operation for excision of the head of the right radius, following a comminuted fracture. A supraclavicular brachial plexus block with 30 ml. 1 per cent. lignocaine was used. The following day there was paresis of the right deltoid, paralysis of the biceps and triceps and of the muscles of the forearm and hand. Profound sensory loss. Rapid recovery of power in the deltoid, slower in biceps and triceps. Three months later there was still moderate weakness of movement at the wrist and of the fingers.

247. Left Erb's palsy in a newborn infant
This condition results from cervical root avulsion or from traction injuries to the brachial plexus during a difficult delivery. Note position of left arm, internally rotated at the shoulder, with the elbow extended and the forearm pronated. Recovery was complete in 6 months.

Cervical Ribs

The neurovascular bundle—comprising the brachial plexus and the subclavian artery and vein—passes through the thoracic inlet (or outlet) on its way to the axilla. The detailed anatomy of this area varies considerably and it is the precise relationship of the brachial plexus to the first rib which largely determines the development of symptoms. Only a minority of patients with cervical ribs have symptoms; the ribs may be bilateral but the symptoms unilateral; the onset of symptoms is usually delayed until adult life is reached. Women are much more likely to be affected than men. The onset of symptoms occasionally follows trauma to the shoulder, but more commonly the delay in appearance of symptoms is attributed to the gradual drooping of the shoulder that tends to occur during life, especially in women.

It is well known that the innervation of the muscles of the upper limb may vary by as much as a spinal cord segment. Anatomists consider that the degree of pre-fixation or post-fixation of the brachial plexus is the main factor in determining the mode of development of the ribs at the thoracic inlet. It is said to be pre-fixed when there is a contribution from the fourth cervical root and that from the first thoracic root is small. It is said to be post-fixed when the contribution to the plexus from the fourth and fifth cervical roots is small, and that from the first and second thoracic roots is considerable. Pre-fixation allows the development of a supernumerary rib from the seventh cervical vertebra. In post-fixation the first rib, over which the lower trunk of the plexus arches, may be deformed and rudimentary in appearance. Compression of the neurovascular bundle may thus result from the presence of an extra rib or a rudimentary first rib. In either case the rib may be incomplete and compression effected by a fibrous prolongation. These skeletal abnormalities at the thoracic inlet must necessarily influence the development and attachments of the three scalene muscles to the first and second ribs.

It is clear that there are many factors which influence the relationship of the neurovascular bundle and the thoracic inlet. To describe them under the title of 'cervical rib' is an obvious over-simplification. The terms 'costoclavicular compression' and the 'scalenus anterior syndrome' have been used for many years, but the identification of the carpal tunnel syndrome has thrown doubt on much of the older interpretations. Compression of the median nerve in the carpal tunnel is certainly a much more common cause of pains and paraesthesiae in a hand and forearm than any of the thoracic inlet syndromes.

The patient with the cervical rib syndrome is likely to be a young or middle-aged female. She complains of pain, weakness and numbness in one hand or forearm. Pain is not usually severe and may consist of sharp darts of pain in certain positions of the limb or, more commonly, a diffuse ache in the forearm muscles and a dragging sensation in the whole limb when carrying a heavy weight. Numbness and paraesthesiae may be felt on the inner side of the forearm and hand or about the thumb and index. The whole hand may at times feel cold and numb and look pale, but paraesthesiae are rarely referred to all finger-tips. Symptoms are often provoked by some particular posture or movement, such as sleeping on the affected limb, cleaning a window, carrying a bag or using a tool or instrument. There may be a long story of such discomfort before symptoms are really troublesome. Discomfort or pain in the neck, or pain radiating from the neck across the shoulder and into the upper limb is not a characteristic feature. Naturally some discomfort about the shoulder and clavicle may accompany the limb symptoms, but the dominant complaints are referred to the periphery of the arm. The woman who complains that the pain in her hand and forearm is much worse at night and improves during the day, is not usually suffering from a cervical rib but from compression of the median nerve in the carpal tunnel.

Despite the pronounced nature of the sensory complaints, objective sensory loss is usually slight. Most commonly it involves the inner side of the forearm and perhaps the hand. It may be confined to the fourth and fifth fingers. In many of the older descriptions, sensory loss on the radial side of the hand was mentioned, but in all probability many such cases were actually examples of compression of the median nerve in the carpal tunnel. Both in cervical rib and in the carpal tunnel syndrome there may be partial thenar atrophy. This atrophy, usually of the radial side of the thenar eminence, is due to wasting of the abductor pollicis brevis and opponens pollicis. In other cases there may be a mild global atrophy involving thenar, hypothenar and interossei muscle groups, but even in

this type the wasting is more conspicuous in the thenar group. There is no satisfactory anatomical explanation for the susceptibility of the abductor pollicis brevis and opponens pollicis to the effects of nerve compression at the level of the first rib.

When there is partial thenar atrophy, the differential diagnosis lies between compression of the median nerve in the carpal tunnel and costoclavicular compression. In the former, which is certainly commoner, the sensory loss will involve the thumb and index finger. In costoclavicular compression it will involve the fourth and fifth fingers, or the ulnar border of the hand or forearm. Where there is no certain sensory loss in the hand, impairment of conduction in the median nerve at the wrist can usually be detected if the thenar atrophy is a manifestation of the carpal tunnel syndrome. Study of the sensory action potentials may also assist in diagnosis. An intraspinal lesion which causes wasting of the hand does not reduce the amplitude of sensory nerve action potentials, but a lesion at the brachial plexus level may, by producing degeneration distal to the lesion, affect sensory conduction in the peripheral parts of the ulnar nerve. This sometimes happens in cases of cervical rib.

A curious feature of this syndrome is the tendency for the symptoms and signs to be either neural or vascular. When there are obvious ischaemic digital changes, muscular atrophy and sensory disturbance are often absent. Alternatively, there may be striking muscular atrophy and sensory disturbance without any indication of circulatory insufficiency. Raynaud's phenomenon affecting one hand of a young woman is usually due to a cervical rib. There are recurrent episodes of coldness, pallor and cyanosis of the digits with pain in the muscles of the hand and forearm, often aggravated by exercise of the limb or preventing its use for a time. It is in such cases that obliteration of the radial pulse may be observed. Compression of the subclavian artery is the explanation for these developments and there may be tenderness over the dilated or thrombosed artery above the clavicle, with repeated embolic detachment of clot and digital gangrene. Minor diminution of the radial pulse by various manoeuvres of abduction, depression or bracing of the shoulder girdle of the same side, is not necessarily abnormal; it may be found in many young adults. A supraclavicular bruit may be heard in some cases of cervical rib.

Surgery can be expected to relieve the patient of pain and paraesthesiae and she may be able to use the arm more energetically. Power in the hand may also improve and wasting be arrested, but I have never actually seen any significant return of bulk to wasted thenar or hypothenar muscles.

Cervical Ribs

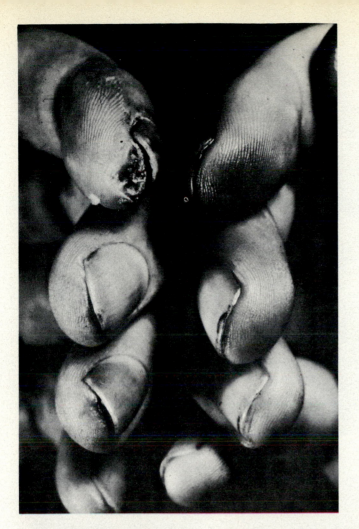

248. Cervical rib
Ischaemic necrosis at tip of left index
finger from compression of brachial artery
by large cervical rib.

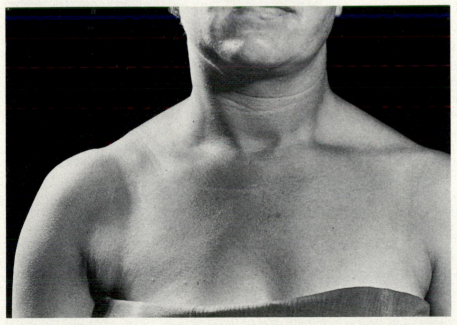

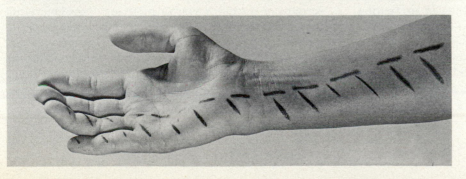

249. Bilateral cervical ribs
Periodic aching and sharp pains in the
right upper limb since childhood,
especially after exercise. Increasing of
late, with weakness of thumb and index
finger and noticeable atrophy of thenar
muscles for 6 months. Fingertips often
white. All symptoms worse during cold
weather. Fullness and tenderness in right
supraclavicular fossa; compression there
caused pain in the right arm. No bruits.
No Horner's syndrome. Reflexes normal;
C.8—T.1 sensory impairment. Atrophy
of lateral half of thenar eminence;
interossei and hypothenar group normal.
Bilateral cervical ribs with anomalous
development of partially fused C.3–4
vertebrae. Arch aortogram showed no
evidence of subclavian compression.

Cervical Ribs

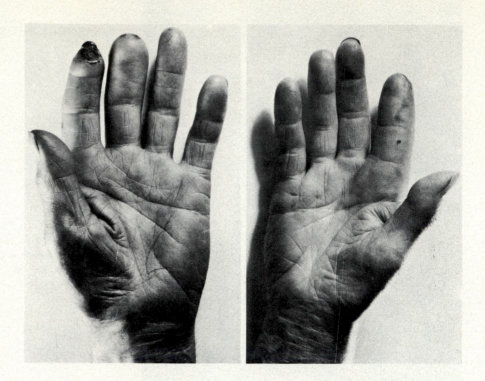

250. Bilateral cervical ribs
Male, aged 50. Diffuse aching pain in both upper limbs, especially the ulnar borders of the forearms. Worsened by movements, carrying heavy weight; relieved by rest. Weakness of thumb movements. Numbness and pallor of index and middle fingers. Note wasting of thenar muscles and ischaemic changes on tips of index and middle fingers on both sides.

Shoulder-girdle Neuritis

This is a form of brachial neuritis which is sometimes known as localized neuritis of the shoulder girdle or neuralgic amyotrophy. It came into prominence during the Second World War and many patients were already in hospital suffering from some minor infectious disorder of the respiratory or alimentary tracts, or recovering from some minor operation. It is indistinguishable from the brachial neuritis which may follow the injection of sera and vaccines. The cause is unknown and the pathology has not been established. Clinical analysis points to a mononeuritis in some cases, a plexus lesion in others, a root lesion in still others, or a combination of such lesions.

There is an acute onset of pain in the shoulder and side of the neck, over the scapula and down the affected arm, usually not further than the elbow. In the hand and forearm there may be some pain and paraesthesiae but the brunt of the attack is felt in the shoulder. The pain is commonly worse at night, disturbing or preventing sleep. It is aggravated by lying on the affected side and usually persists for a week or 10 days. Thereafter it rapidly subsides, but sometimes there is a chronic ache which may persist for 6 or 7 weeks. The pain is usually most severe in those muscles which subsequently show paralysis and atrophy. There is little or no general upset,

no stiffness of the neck and the upper limb reflexes may remain unaltered. After a few days or when the pain is subsiding, paralysis supervenes. The muscles most commonly affected are the serratus, the spinati, the deltoid and the trapezius in that order. The neuritis may be bilateral. Frequently the muscle or muscles supplied by one nerve only are affected; various combinations of paralysis are found, the commonest being of the deltoid and spinati of the same side. Muscles that are usually spared are the pectorals, latissimus dorsi, biceps, triceps and the muscles of the forearm and hand. Sensory loss is, as a rule, slight or absent; the commonest sensory sign being a small zone of hypo-aesthesia over an affected deltoid muscle in the area of cutaneous supply of the axillary nerve.

It differs from poliomyelitis in the absence of general signs of infection and of meningeal irritation, the normal cerebrospinal fluid, and a tendency for the paralysis to be peripheral rather than segmental in character. The prognosis is good but affected muscles often waste rapidly and recovery is slow. In the cases of a paralysed serratus or deltoid, a year or more may pass before full power is restored. Rarely, there may be a recurrence in the same or opposite shoulder. One of my patients had a second attack in the right shoulder, 20 years after the first episode affecting the left shoulder. In the first attack he was in a military hospital with tonsillitis; in the second attack he was recovering from influenza.

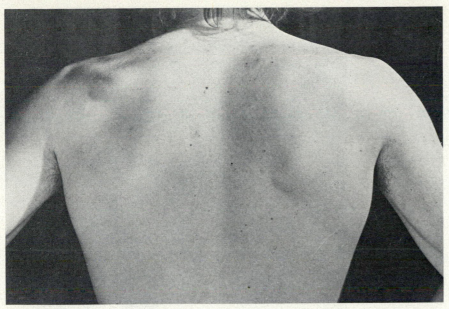

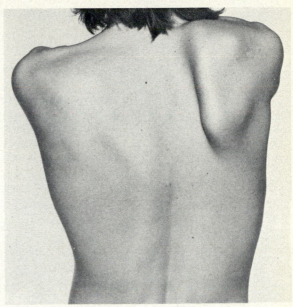

251a

251b

251. Recurrent shoulder-girdle neuritis

Age 18 years; international swimming champion. Three years ago, at end of swimming season, acute onset of severe pain in the *right* shoulder, followed by weakness and wasting of the spinati on that side. Gradual recovery. Two years later, again at the end of the swimming season, a similar episode affecting the *left* side. (*a*) Note wasting of spinati on the *left*. Good recovery from both attacks. (*b*) One year later, paralysis of *right* serratus magnus. Incomplete recovery.

This swimmer specialized in the butterfly style, and it is conceivable that he may have injured his suprascapular nerves and the long thoracic nerve of Bell by stretching. I have seen one other national schoolboy swimming champion with paralysis of the spinati on one side. The scalenus anticus syndrome has been described in competitive freestyle swimmers by Frankel, S. A., and Hirata, I. (1971) *J. Amer. med. Ass.*, **215**, 1796.

Shoulder-girdle Neuritis

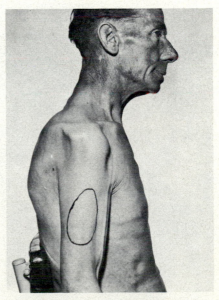

252. Shoulder-girdle neuritis △
Right deltoid paralysis and wasting 8 weeks after acute onset. Pain lasted 10 days; minimal residual sensory loss over axillary nerve zone. Almost complete recovery in 18 months.

Shoulder-girdle Neuritis

253. Shoulder-girdle neuritis
Left deltoid paralysis and wasting 4 weeks after acute axillary neuritis; 7 days after Jennerian vaccination. Complete recovery in 4 months. He is trying to abduct the left arm.

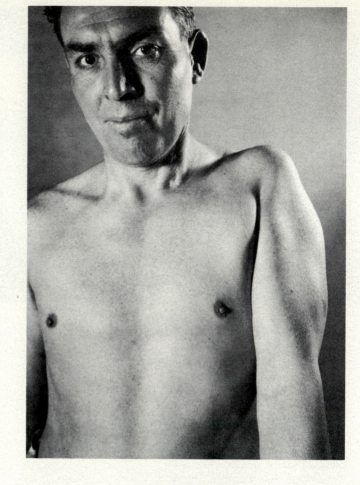

254. Shoulder-girdle neuritis ▽
Right serratus magnus palsy 1 month after onset. Acute pain behind shoulder for 7 days. With arms at rest (a) there is slight displacement of the right scapula towards the midline. Winging of the scapula occurs on forward raising of the right arm, accentuated when he presses against a wall. (b) Trapezius paralysis may also cause slight winging of the scapula at rest. In serratus palsy the lower angle of the scapula tilts towards the midline; in trapezius paralysis the scapula tends to droop downwards and outwards.

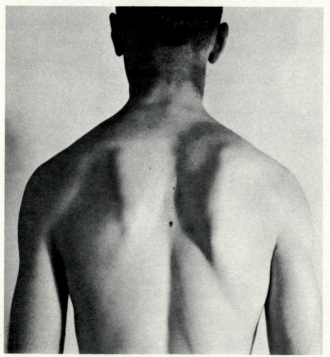

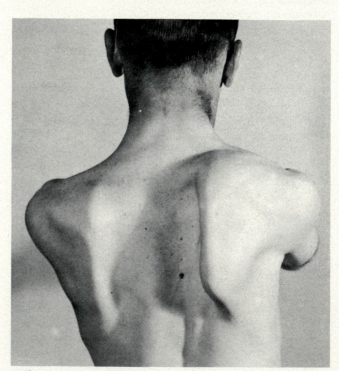

254a

254b

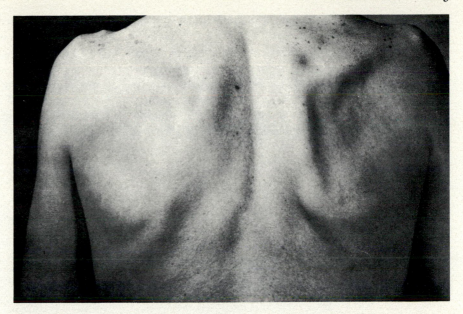

255. Shoulder-girdle neuritis; paralysis of supraspinatus and infraspinatus on the right
Six months previously severe pain behind right shoulder lasting 1 week. Residual weakness of certain shoulder movements, slow recovery. Note atrophy of right spinati. There was weakness of early abduction at the right shoulder and external rotation. Neuritis of the suprascapular nerve.
Complete recovery took a year.

LESIONS OF INDIVIDUAL NERVES

The Radial Nerve (C.5, 6, 7, 8)

The radial nerve is a continuation of the posterior cord of the brachial plexus. It descends from the axilla, winding around the posterior aspect of the humerus to supply the triceps and anconeus, the brachioradialis, the extensors of the wrist and fingers, and the extensors and long abductor of the thumb. It supplies the skin over the dorsum of the wrist and hand, the first interosseous space, the dorsum of the thumb and of the proximal two phalanges of the index and middle fingers. Despite this extensive cutaneous distribution, the overlapping supply from the adjacent median and ulnar nerves is such that in actual lesions of the radial nerve, sensory loss can usually only be detected in the space between the first two metacarpals.

The nerve may be injured in fractures of the shaft of the humerus, it may be compressed by callus formation, by a tourniquet or crutch, or, during sleep or anaesthesia, against the sharp edge of a chair, couch or operating table. It may follow an imperfectly placed intramuscular injection. Transient paralysis may follow a blow to the back of the upper arm, or to the outer side of the elbow. The radial nerve is not subject to the forms of compression or entrapment which are such a common cause of pain and paraesthesia in the distribution of the median and ulnar nerves. Cases are encountered in which a neuritis of the superficial branch appears to explain the distribution of pain and discomfort; it may mimic a tenosynovitis or an arthritis of the first carpometacarpal

joint. The deep branch of the radial nerve—the posterior interosseous nerve—penetrates the posterior compartment of the forearm and runs down the dorsal aspect of the interosseous membrane. Pain in this distribution with weakness of abduction and extension of the thumb, may result from a lesion of this nerve. Lead poisoning is now an extremely rare cause of wrist drop. I have never actually seen a case.

The cardinal feature of paralysis of the radial nerve is wrist drop. The hand hangs limply at the wrist and the patient is unable to lift the wrist or straighten out the fingers. If the wrist is passively dorsiflexed, the fingers remain flexed at the metacarpophalangeal joint; the patient is unable to straighten them at this joint. He is able to straighten the interphalangeal joints as these movements are carried out by the lumbricals and interossei through the ulnar nerve. If the patient grasps an object with the affected hand, he reports that his grip is weakened. This must not be mistaken for an indication of paralysis of the long flexors of the fingers. The grip is weak because the normal associated extension of the wrist does not take place. If the wrist is passively dorsiflexed the grip improves. Occasionally some degree of extension of the terminal phalanx of the thumb is possible through the action of abductor pollicis brevis, innervated by the median nerve. In such cases a slip from this muscle is inserted in the radial side of the tendon of extensor pollicis longus. Abduction and adduction of the fingers may appear weak when there is wrist drop; these movements should be tested when the palm of the hand rests flat on a table with the fingers extended.

Extension at the elbow is lost and the triceps reflex abolished when the lesion is in the axilla. Commonly the triceps escapes. Paralysis of the brachioradialis may be detected when the forearm is flexed against resistance, midway between pronation and supination. Supination is impossible if the elbow is extended; if the elbow is flexed some degree of supination is obtained through the action of the biceps.

In cases of obscure progressive paralysis of the radial nerve, without sensory loss, surgical exploration and inspection of the posterior interosseous nerve is sometimes necessary. Small benign tumours (lipoma, fibroma or neuroma) are sometimes responsible for the symptoms.

The Radial Nerve

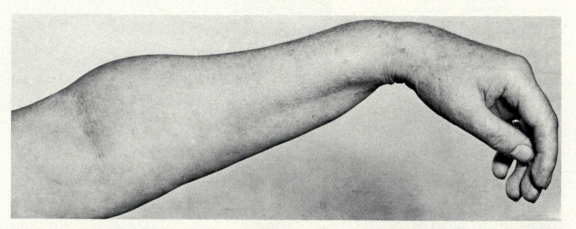

256. Radial nerve palsy; lipoma of the left forearm with radial nerve compression △
Female, aged 57. Five-year history of progressive difficulty in extending the fingers of the left hand—fourth, third, fifth, first and second, in that order. Two-year history of weakness in extending the left wrist. First noticed swelling of the dorsum of the left forearm on the appearance of the early symptoms. There was complete wrist and finger drop but no detectable sensory deficit. The enucleated tumour proved to be a lipoma over which the radial nerve was stretched. (Courtesy of Dr. D. W. Farquhar.)

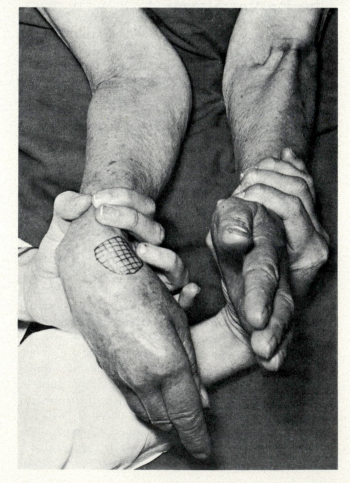

257. Acute right radial nerve palsy ▷
Female, aged 66. Two weeks previously, following a day spent clipping a hedge with a shears, she developed wrist drop with numbness on the dorsum of the hand. The triceps was normal, the brachioradialis was paralysed, right radial reflex was absent and there was a small area of hypaesthesia as indicated. No diabetes, slow recovery.

258. Radial nerve palsy (idiopathic)
(*a*) Left wrist drop with weakness of grip
owing to loss of synergic extension of the
wrist. Note contrasting position of the
wrist on the sound side (*b*).

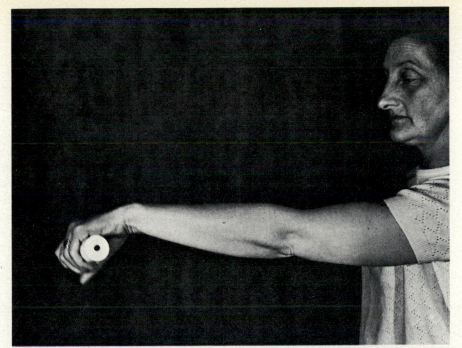

258a

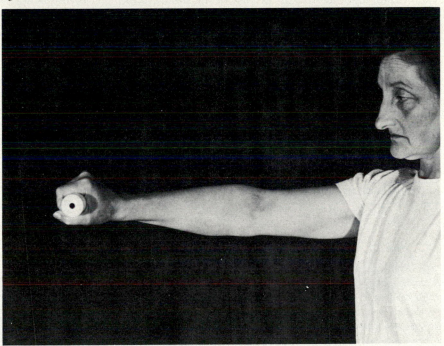

258b

The Median Nerve (C.7, 8; T.1)

The median nerve is formed by the union of branches
from the lateral and medial cords of the brachial plexus.
It is closely related to the brachial artery in the upper
arm and penetrating injuries frequently damage both
structures. There are no branches of the median nerve
in the upper arm; nearly all the important branches
arise high in the forearm, just before the nerve dips
beneath the pronator teres. It lies deep to the superficial
forearm muscles, becoming more superficial as it
approaches the palm, which it enters by passing beneath
the transverse carpal ligament. It supplies the pronators,
the long flexors of the forearm (excluding the ulnar
flexor of the wrist and the ulnar half of the deep flexor),
the muscles of the thenar eminence (abductor, opponens
brevis and the outer head of the flexor pollicis brevis) and
the two lateral lumbricals. Complete paralysis is a
crippling disability because it paralyses the grip,
weakens pronation and, in addition, renders the two
terminal phalanges of the index and middle fingers
anaesthetic. Moreover, partial lesions of the median
nerve are usually painful.

In civilian practice the commonest cause of paralysis

of the median nerve is a laceration at the wrist; occasionally the nerve may be damaged during intravenous injections at the elbow. Injuries at the wrist such as fractures of the carpus and distal end of the radius may involve the nerve directly or subsequently. But by far the commonest example of a median nerve lesion is that known as the carpal tunnel syndrome in which the nerve is compressed as it enters the palm.

In complete lesions of the nerve the appearance of the hand and forearm is characteristic. There is flattening of the flexor surface of the forearm and wrist, slight ulnar deviation, flattening of the thenar eminence, tapering of the affected fingers and loss of pulp, and vasomotor and trophic changes in the area of cutaneous distribution. The skin of the index and middle fingers is dry, smooth and reddened, while the nails are dull and brittle. The extended thumb and index, the flattening of the thenar eminence, with the thumb on a level with the fingers, together give the picture of the simian hand.

On attempting pronation of the forearm the patient usually rotates the upper arm internally at the shoulder. When the wrist is flexed against resistance, the hand deviates to the ulnar side and contraction of the ulnar flexor tendon may be seen and felt. In trying to clench the fist the ulnar two fingers flex, although imperfectly, into the palm; the third finger moves slightly, while thumb and index are gravely paralysed. Flexion of the distal phalanges of thumb and index is impossible. The proximal phalanges can still be flexed through the action of the interossei and lumbricals. Opposition and abduction of the thumb are impaired. The thumb may be adducted but it cannot be opposed to the tip of the fifth finger or abducted at right angles to the palm.

The actual extent of sensory loss is variable, but it is most dense and disabling on index and middle fingers; it is not usually completely lost over the terminal portion of the thumb. The total effect of weakness and numbness of thumb and index finger is particularly disabling.

Variations of muscular innervation are particularly well known in the hand. Thenar and hypothenar muscles share the supply from median and ulnar nerves in a variable manner. These anomalies explain the apparent incompleteness of lesions of these nerves when they are divided and in the case of median nerve paralysis, many of the lost movements, except for flexion of the distal phalanx of the index finger and movements of the thumb, can be performed by ulnar innervated muscles. They should not be mistaken for signs of recovery.

The Median Nerve

259. Median nerve palsy
Female aged 18 years. On leaving a cinema with her boy friend she had paraesthesiae in the left hand and could not use her fingers when buttoning up her coat. No pain. Some recovery of movement in the third, fourth and fifth fingers during the next few days. When seen on the seventh day after onset, she was unable to flex her thumb and index finger due to paresis of flexor pollicis longus and of flexor digitorum profundus. In addition there was weakness of abduction and opposition of the thumb. Residual sensory impairment on volar aspect of thumb and index finger. Nerve conduction studies revealed no abnormality below the elbow; the anterior interosseous nerve was normal. However, there was a motor conduction block in the median nerve at the axillary outlet. She made a good recovery from this compressive lesion.

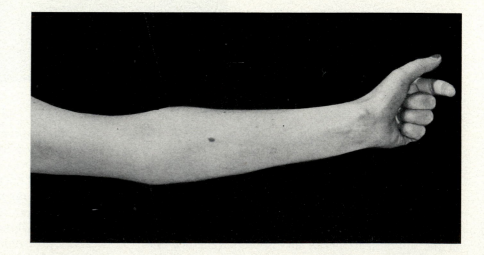

The Median Nerve

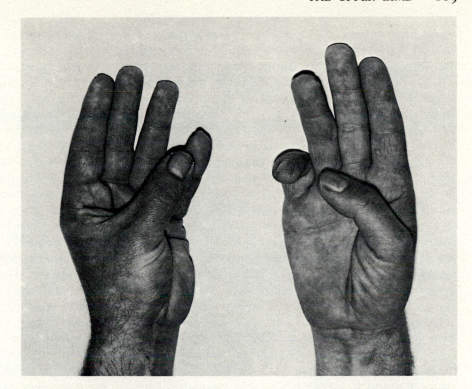

260. Median nerve palsy; weakness of opposition of the thumb in a right median nerve lesion
In weakness of opponens pollicis the patient may be able to oppose the thumb to the middle or ring fingers, but not to the little finger. Note contrast with normal action on left side; and the thenar atrophy on the right side.

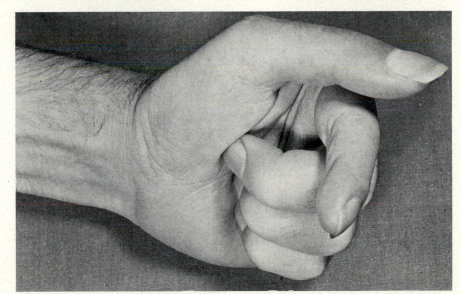

261. Anterior interosseous nerve palsy
Three years previously the patient fell and fractured the left scaphoid. This injury was followed by inability to make a complete fist. He was unable to flex the terminal phalanx of his thumb and index finger. No sensory loss.
These movements are effected by flexor digitorum profundus and flexor pollicis longus. The anterior interosseous nerve arises from the median nerve deep in the middle of the forearm, so that the wrist injury which fractured the scaphoid was not responsible for the nerve lesion. When the median nerve is injured at the wrist, the paralysis is confined to the small hand muscles.

The Carpal Tunnel Syndrome

This is one of the commonest painful conditions of the upper limb. It is caused by compression of the median nerve as it runs in its tunnel under the transverse carpal ligament. The latter is a thick, relatively inelastic structure which extends from the distal crease at the wrist for a variable extent into the palm. The motor branch to the opponens muscle hooks over the distal edge of the ligament to run proximally into the opponens muscle. This branch of the median nerve may be constricted at this point. The condition is usually seen in stout middle-aged women engaged in vigorous manual work; the housewife with a large family and few of the appliances of a modern kitchen, or the wife who also works in a local laundry or factory. It may also be encountered in the young wife, busy with unaccustomed activity in a new home, or during her first pregnancy. The general appearance of the hand in the middle-aged female patient usually bears witness to much manual labour, yet it is so uncommon in the male that there must be other factors at work—presumably endocrine and indeed it may be encountered in myxoedema and acromegaly. Occasionally symptoms appear some time after a fall on the wrist or the nerve may have been compressed as a result of rheumatoid arthritic changes, in which case correct diagnosis may be delayed.

The patient complains of pain, numbness and paraesthesiae in the palm and fingers of the affected hand. She usually indicates the middle fingers, but may also stroke the forearm when describing her discomfort. The symptoms are particularly troublesome at night, often preventing sleep or disturbing it throughout the night; she may withdraw her hand from under the bedclothes, hang it over the bed, elevate it, rub it or she may be forced to sit up and even walk about the bedroom, shaking, rubbing and 'bringing back life into the hand'. In the morning the fingers feel swollen and clumsy and she has difficulty in handling objects on her dressing table, in clothing herself and preparing breakfast. By the time the children have gone to school the symptoms are subsiding. In due course she finds that the tips of the thumb, index and middle finger are getting numb and causing clumsiness. Pains and tingling come and go during the day, while she is at her work, and she usually finds that a day's rest, a holiday, or a mild illness which puts her to bed, relieves her nocturnal suffering. She may sleep well on a Saturday and Sunday night after a period of relative rest, but if Monday is a washing day she is invariably troubled that night. If she is admitted to hospital for any reason, or has to wait there for an operation, the symptoms usually subside.

In early cases there may be no abnormal physical signs but usually one can detect some impairment of sensation over the affected fingers. Tenderness on compression of the nerve in the wrist, and thenar atrophy are relatively rare. If the story is characteristic the absence of physical signs should not deter one from advising surgical decompression of the carpal tunnel. Therapeutic failures are now rare and the discovery, 20 years ago, that compression of the nerve is responsible for the nocturnal pain and paraesthesiae of middle-aged women, has brought relief to many. It has been the explanation for much that was obscure about thoracic inlet syndromes and there has been a sharp drop in the number of operations at the latter site.

The Carpal Tunnel Syndrome

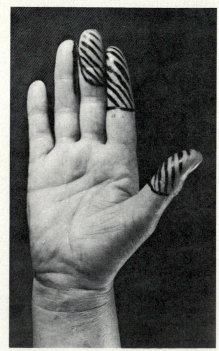

262. Bilateral carpal tunnel syndrome
Wasting of the left thenar eminence and bilateral sensory impairment of median nerve distribution. The sensory loss in this case was more extensive than usual.

The Carpal Tunnel Syndrome

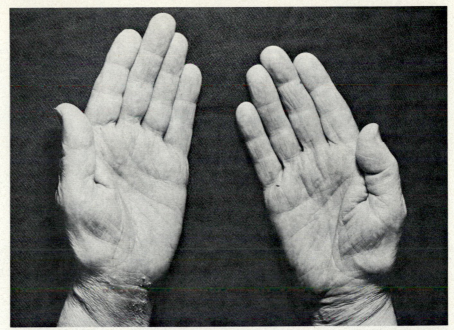

263a

263. Bilateral carpal tunnel syndrome (*a*) A few weeks after surgical decompression of the nerve on the left side; (*b*) 18 months after the second operation on the right side. Her symptoms were relieved but there was still marked bilateral thenar atrophy.

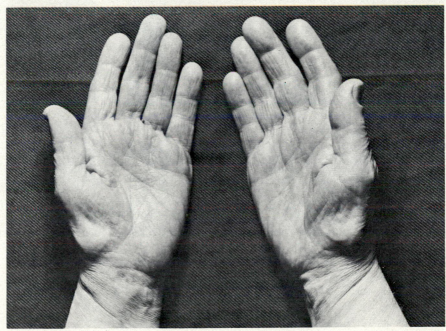

263b

The Carpal Tunnel Syndrome

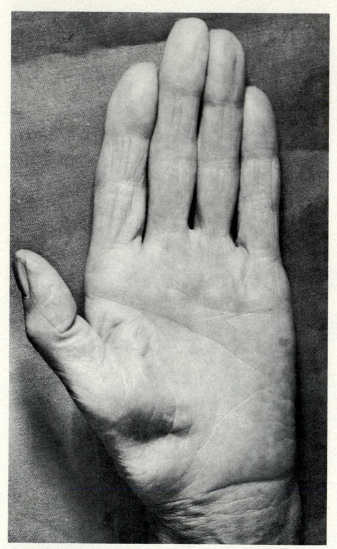 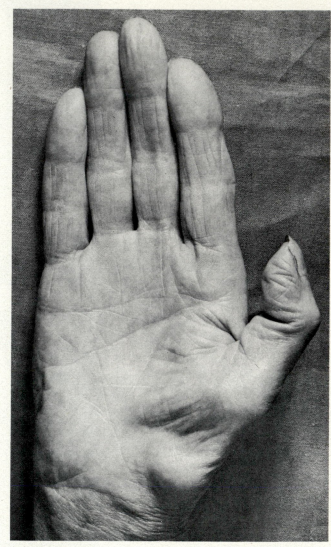

264. The carpal tunnel syndrome
This, and the preceding photographs were taken nearly 20 years ago; nowadays thenar atrophy is not usually seen in this syndrome, owing to earlier diagnosis. The wasting of the thenar muscles leads to concavity and grooving of the outer and proximal end of the eminence, due to atrophy of the opponens and abductor muscles. The branch of the median nerve to the opponens can be trapped separately as it crosses over the edge of the transverse carpal ligament where it turns proximally to enter the opponens muscle.

The Ulnar Nerve (C.7, 8)

This nerve is the continuation of the medial cord of the brachial plexus. In the upper arm it is in close relation to the brachial artery and the median nerve, between the biceps and the triceps muscles. Below the middle of the arm it passes posteriorly through the medial intermuscular septum to reach a groove behind the medial epicondyle. It enters the forearm by passing between the humeral and ulnar heads of the flexor carpi ulnaris continuing down the forearm between this muscle and the flexor digitorum profundus. It is normally retained in the olecranon groove by a fibrous expansion of the common flexor origin over the groove. At the wrist the nerve enters the hand beneath the volar carpal ligament, between the pisiform bone and the hook of the hamate bone, where it bifurcates to a deep and superficial branch.

The ulnar nerve has no important branches in the upper arm. In the forearm it supplies the ulnar flexor of the wrist, the ulnar half of the deep flexor of the fingers, the muscles of the hypothenar eminence (the abductor, opponens and short flexor), the interossei, the two inner lumbricals and the adductor and inner head of the short flexor of the thumb. The superficial terminal branch also supplies the palmaris brevis muscle; digital compression of the ulnar nerve against the pisiform bone produces visible wrinkling of the ulnar side of the palm due to contraction of the palmaris brevis muscle. The ulnar sensory area comprises the ulnar border of the hand, the fifth finger and the inner half of the fourth finger.

The nerve may be injured by penetrating wounds at any point in its course, in fractures and dislocations at the wrist and elbow and as a late sequel to injury, callus, scar formation at these sites, or as a result of arthritis.

In complete paralysis, arising from a lesion at or above the elbow, paralysis of the ulnar flexor of the wrist results in deviation to the radial side when the wrist is flexed against resistance; palpation fails to reveal any contraction of the tendon of the flexor carpi ulnaris. The grip is weak, as flexion at the interphalangeal joints of the fifth finger is abolished, while those of the fourth finger are weakened. Paralysis of the hypothenar muscles abolishes lateral movements of the fifth finger and impairs flexion of this finger at the metacarpophalangeal joint. Paralysis of the interossei abolishes abduction and adduction of the fingers. Movements of the thumb are also impaired as a result of paralysis of the adductor and short flexor. This weakness is revealed by the test known as the *signe de journal* of Froment; the patient is instructed to hold a sheet of paper between thumb and index finger while the examiner attempts to withdraw it. The patient tries to retain the paper by flexing his thumb at the interphalangeal joint.

The affected hand takes on a characteristic appearance; the hypothenar eminence is flattened and the ulnar contour of the palm is lost. In manual workers with thickened skin this contour may be retained for some time, but palpation should reveal 'the empty purse'. There is hollowing of the palm, guttering of the grooves between the metacarpals of the dorsum of the hand and clawing of the fingers. This deformity is a consequence of the paralysis of the interossei and the inner two lumbrical muscles. Their combined action is to flex the fingers at the metacarpophalangeal joints with the distal joints extended. When these muscles are paralysed the unopposed action of the long flexors and extensors of the fingers produces the opposite posture—hyperextension at the metacarpophalangeal joints and flexion of the distal phalangeal joints. Since the two outer lumbrical muscles are supplied by the median nerve, the clawing is seen only in the ulnar fingers, which also take up a position of slight abduction.

In addition to the characteristic zone of cutaneous anaesthesia of the ulnar border of the hand, the fifth finger and the inner half of the fourth finger, there is vibration and postural loss in the fifth finger.

In civilian practice the commonest type of ulnar paralysis results from compression and irritation of the nerve in the olecranon groove at the elbow. The nerve can be disturbed by anything that alters the angular relationship at the elbow. The carrying angle is normally greater in women than in men and in cubitus valgus, as the result of old injury or disturbance of growth, this may lead to a stretching and irritation of the ulnar nerve as it passes into the forearm. A constant irritation over the years produces a tardy ulnar palsy. In other cases a too shallow olecranon groove allows abnormal movement and dislocation of the nerve from the groove in movements of flexion and extension of the elbow. These mechanical flaws at the elbow are frequently bilateral, but involvement of the ulnar nerve may not develop and progress in a simultaneous manner. It is surprising how painless arthritis of the elbow can be. The joint may be thickened and gnarled and the range of flexion and extension considerably reduced without the patient having taken much notice. He is usually surprised when informed that the wasting, weakness and numbness of his hand is the result of a longstanding arthritis of an elbow. Sensory symptoms usually precede motor; pain and paraesthesiae of ulnar distribution, aggravated by movements of the elbow, pressure on it during sleep and discomfort when it rests on a hard surface. Thus the occupation of the patient may determine the circumstances under which these symptoms appear—the clerk at his desk, the secretary at the telephone with her flexed elbow resting on the desk, or the carpenter, bricklayer, painter and decorator constantly flexing and extending the elbow. But in many cases discomfort and sensory symptoms are slight and not until weakness or atrophy is noticed does the patient come to the doctor. Moreover, muscular wasting may be quite marked before it is recognized and the patient may believe that the on-set was recent. There is often local tenderness over the nerve at the elbow, with referred paraesthesiae (Tinel's sign) to the ulnar two fingers on tapping and in some instances abnormal mobility and thickening of the ulnar nerve in the olecranon groove may be detected.

Ulnar nerve paresis can, however, arise at the elbow with little local discomfort or sign and it must then be distinguished from the effects of lesions involving the spinal cord, the eighth cervical or first thoracic root, or the brachial plexus. In syringomyelia there may be wasting of the small hand muscles which mimics ulnar paralysis but there is likely to be dissociated sensory loss extending beyond the ulnar zone, loss of arm reflexes

and perhaps a Horner's syndrome. An eighth cervical root lesion will weaken the small muscles of the hand, but the sensory loss will also involve the radial side of the fourth finger and again there may be a Horner's syndrome. In a cervical rib the paraesthesiae may be referred to the ulnar or radial side of the hand and fingers but wasting tends first to appear in the muscles of the hand supplied by the ulnar nerve. But objective sensory disturbances are usually slight or absent and without characteristic peripheral distribution.

Less commonly the ulnar nerve or its terminal branches may be injured or compressed at the wrist or in the palm. The superficial branch of the nerve supply-ing sensation to the skin and innervating the palmaris brevis muscle, leaves the ulnar nerve in the distal portion of the forearm. In ulnar nerve paresis with normal

The Ulnar Nerve

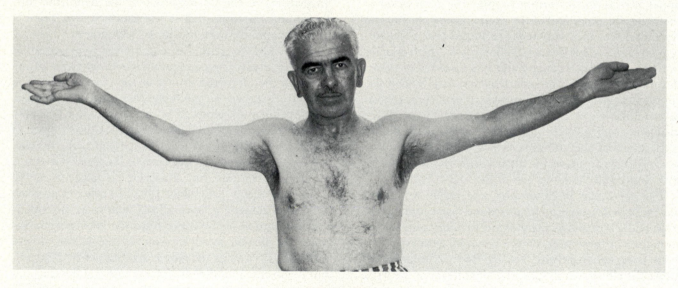

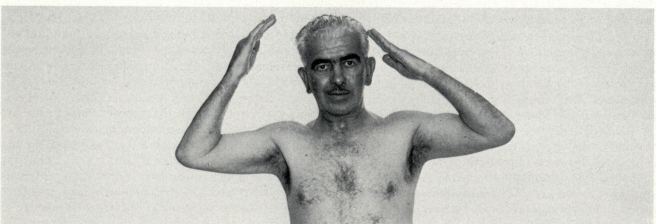

265. Ulnar nerve palsy; chronic arthritis of the elbow
Restriction of the full range of movement of the right elbow joint may be seen; the photographs were taken to illustrate the range of flexion and extension on each

side. This is the commonest cause of a chronic ulnar nerve lesion and in many cases the patient has not noticed any significant abnormality of the elbow. A trivial blow may draw his attention to it because of undue sensitivity and referred

pain and paraesthesiae. In rheumatoid arthritis the nerve may be compressed by a thickened arcuate ligament between the two heads of flexor carpi ulnaris. But usually the elbow is the seat of osteo-arthritis.

sensation the lesion must be distal to the superficial palmar branch. If all the ulnar-supplied muscles are paralysed, the lesion must be in the short interval between the separation of the superficial sensory branch and the point where the deep branch divides to supply individual muscles. This short section of nerve lies on the outer side of the pisiform bone, winding beneath the hook of the hamate to reach the deeper structures of the palm. A pressure neuritis of the deep palmar branch of the nerve occurs in individuals whose occupation subjects them to pressure on the ulnar side of the base of the palm. The force may be a repetitive one from the use of a particular tool or instrument, such as pliers or screwdriver; machinists and metal polishers are liable to this lesion. In some instances the duration of pressure has been surprisingly short—a day in the garden or on a racing cycle. The nerve is rarely involved in a Colles' fracture, but it may be compressed by the proximal end of a metal hand splint. Drivers of heavy vehicles, cranes, refuse collectors and street cleaning machines with heavy gear levers are also liable. The pressure is usually such that the branch of the nerve to the hypothenar muscles relatively escapes, only the interossei and adductor pollicis are affected. The absence of sensory loss may suggest a diagnosis of early motor neurone disease; a horny palm, a callosity or tenderness should lead to inquiry about occupation.

In rheumatoid arthritis some of the wasting of the small hand muscles may be due to interference with this deep palmar branch of the ulnar nerve, consequent on subluxation of the carpal bones on the radius and ulna.

The Ulnar Nerve

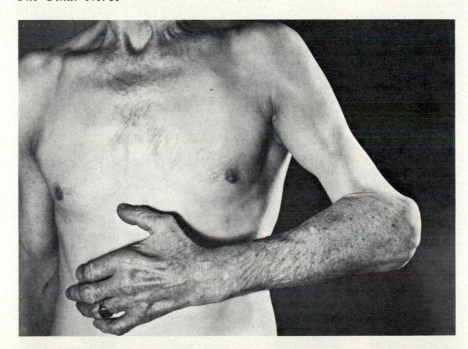

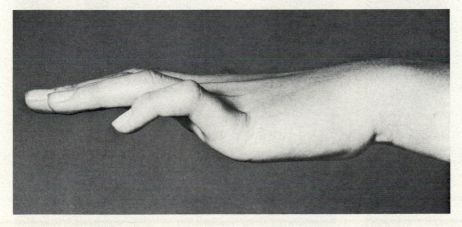

266. Ulnar nerve palsy
Severe osteo-arthritis of the left elbow joint with atrophy of the interossei from ulnar nerve involvement. Note the flexed abducted position of the fifth finger.

267. Ulnar nerve palsy
Paralysis of the deep palmar branch of the left ulnar nerve in an amateur racing cyclist after a long run. She woke the following morning and found she had little movement of the fourth and fifth fingers. There was no ulnar sensory loss, the hypothenar muscles functioned practically normally, but there was paralysis of the adductor, the interossei and inner two lumbricals. The clawing posture of the fourth and fifth fingers is seen, with hyperextension at the metacarpophalangeal joint, flexion of the interphalangeal joints and abduction of the fifth finger. This posture is seen only in the ulnar fingers because although all the interossei are paralysed, the radial lumbricals supplied by the median nerve are not involved. There is unopposed action of the long extensors of the fingers, which overextend at the metacarpophalangeal joints. Similarly, the unopposed action of the long flexors of the fingers produce flexion of the interphalangeal joints. In this case the photograph was taken 48 hours later. There was full recovery in the course of 4 or 5 weeks.

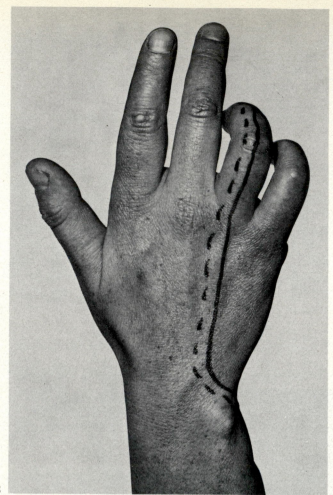
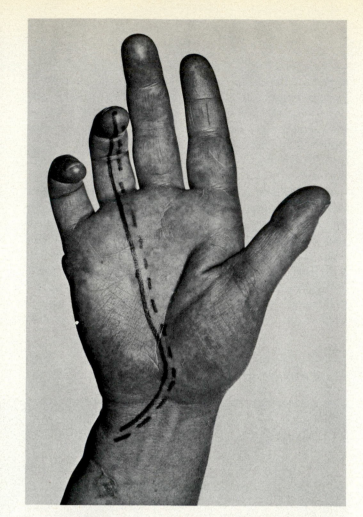

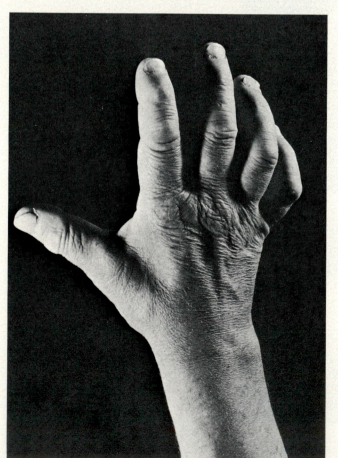
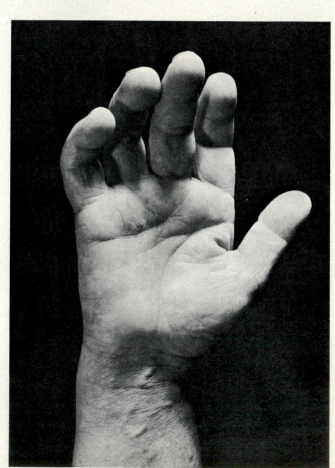

The Ulnar Nerve

268. Ulnar nerve palsy ◁
The area of sensory loss in an ulnar nerve lesion from a laceration at the wrist. Analgesia (continuous line); anaesthesia (interrupted line). The nerve was severed.

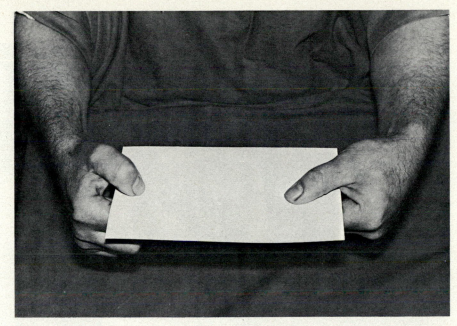

270. Ulnar nerve palsy
Froment's 'thumb sign' in a right ulnar nerve palsy. Weakness of the adductor pollicis and flexor pollicis brevis makes gripping between thumb and index difficult. If the patient pulls on the paper he has to flex the affected thumb and 'pinch-grip'. Froment, Professor of Neurology in Lyons, described this sign in 1915. He called it the 'thumb sign'; it is often referred to as the 'journal sign'.

269. Ulnar nerve palsy ◁
Right ulnar nerve palsy arising at the elbow showing that although there is obvious wasting of the dorsal interossei, with abnormal posture of the fourth and fifth fingers, there is no discernible flattening of the hypothenar eminence. Nevertheless, palpation of the ulnar border of the palm revealed wasting of the underlying muscles. It was like handling an empty leather purse. In manual workers with thickened skin, the contour of the ulnar border of the palm may be retained for a time despite atrophy of the hypothenar muscles. If hypothenar involvement goes undetected, some other cause, such as motor neurone disease, may be suspected.

271. Ulnar nerve palsy and hysteria
Hysterical contracture of the fourth and fifth fingers, accompanying mild injury to the ulnar nerve at the wrist during intravenous drip. There was pain and swelling of the arm and hand and the ulnar fingers were flexed into the palm within 3 days.

The only signs of ulnar nerve injury were obtained by nerve conduction studies. In addition there were gross signs of motor and sensory hysterical paralysis. The lines at the elbow indicate the upper levels of anaesthesia in successive testing during one examination.

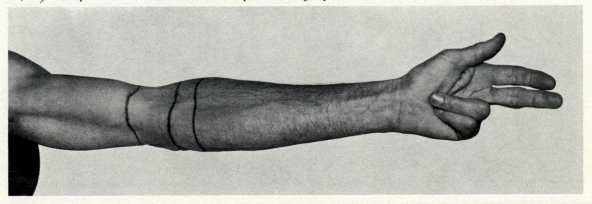

Miscellaneous

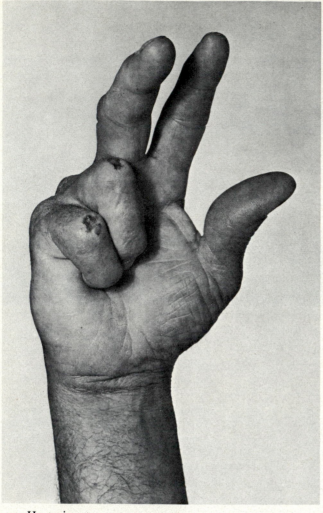

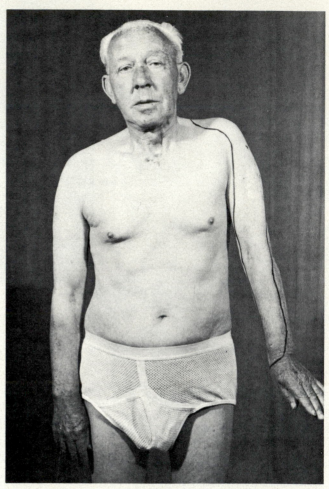

272. Hysteria △
Hysterical contracture of fourth and fifth
fingers of the right hand following a fall
on the right elbow. Photograph taken 2
years after injury. Abrasions on knuckles
were not due to anaesthesia; 'accident
neurosis'.

274

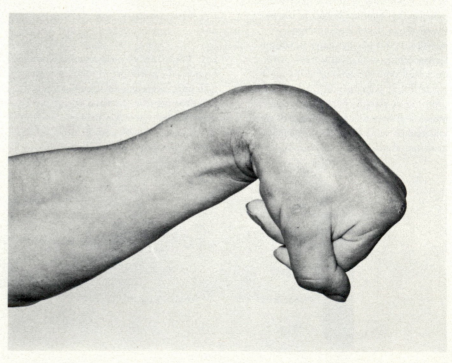

273. Hysterical contracture of hand ▷
Hysterical contracture of the left hand of a
young man after a minor electrical burn of
the palm of the hand 3 years previously.

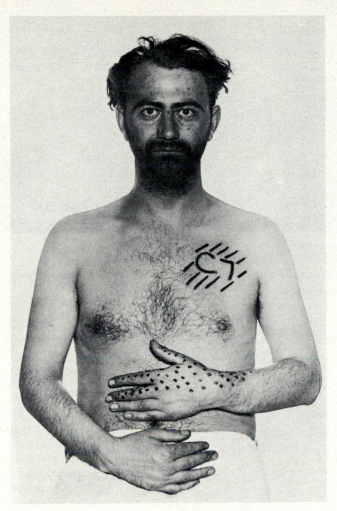

274. Herpes zoster ◁
Herpes zoster of C.5–6 posterior root ganglia with paralysis and wasting of deltoid and biceps muscles; note distribution of rash and area of sensory impairment. He is trying to abduct the left arm. The zoster virus usually only appears to invade the sensory ganglia and roots, but the anterior roots and horn cells are sometimes involved and paralysis results. (Courtesy of Dr. K. Lloyd.)

275. Brachial neuritis ▷
Acute brachial pain due to protrusion of intervertebral disc. Six-weeks' story of stiff neck with pain radiating down the outer border of the left arm. Paraesthesiae and slight impairment of sensation over C.6–7 dermatome (dotted area) with deep pain and some tenderness in left pectoral muscle (C.7 myotome).

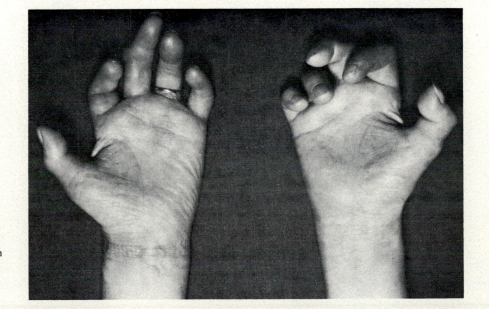

276. Scleroderma; systemic sclerosis of connective tissues ▷
It began here with Raynaud's phenomenon and skin changes in the hands: progressive sclerodactyly. Early sclerodactyly may mimic a carpal tunnel syndrome.

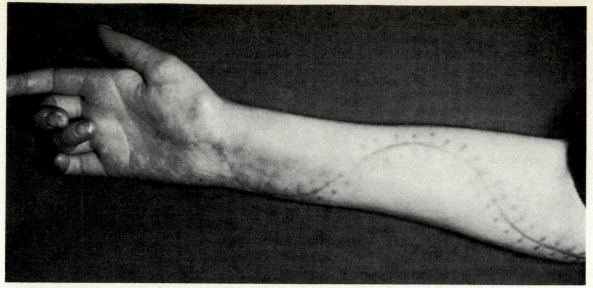

277. Volkmann's contracture △
This followed surgical treatment of aortic coarctation. There is wasting and contracture of the small muscles of the hand which was cold and cyanosed. A muscle sliding operation has been performed. The syndrome is primarily due to vascular injury, but motor and sensory nerves are secondarily involved. The nerves are probably compressed during the phase of acute swelling of the forearm muscles. These photographs were taken 2 years after the cardiac operation.

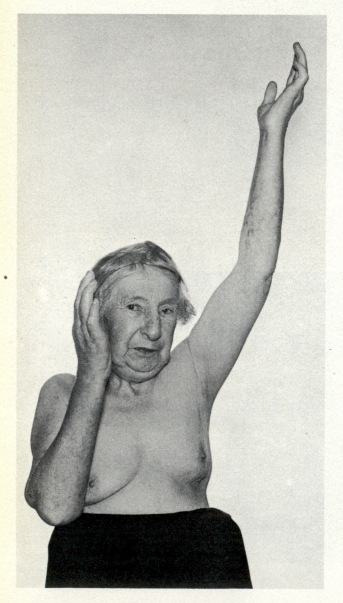

278. Right 'shoulder-hand syndrome'
This may be initiated by injury or may follow a cerebrovascular accident or myocardial infarction. There is pain and stiffness of the shoulder with swelling, redness and stiffness of the hand and fingers. Note difficulty in movement of the shoulder, the swollen right hand with scaling red skin.

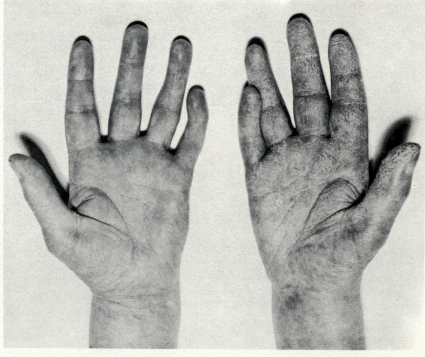

The Lower Limb

The lower limb is innervated by the lumbosacral plexus which derives its supply mainly from the five lumbar and five sacral spinal nerves. The roots of the lower lumbar and upper sacral nerves are the largest of all the spinal nerves. They run vertically downwards to their respective exit foramina in the lower part of the spinal subarachnoid space. The resemblance of this sheaf of nerves to a horse's tail gives it the term of the cauda equina. The roots pierce the theca one segment above their respective foramina. They then course downwards and lateralwards, crossing the outer portion of the posterior surface of the corresponding disc. The fifth lumbar and first sacral roots, so often involved in sciatica, usually emerge just above the level of the discs, L.4–5 and L.5–S.1 respectively. The lumbar plexus lies in the psoas major muscle, in front of the transverse processes of the lumbar vertebrae. The sacral plexus lies on the posterior wall of the pelvic cavity. The morphological arrangement of the nerves of the lumbosacral plexus is not so apparent as in the brachial plexus. The skin of the lower limb is largely innervated by the first, second, third, fourth and fifth lumbar nerves and the first and second sacral nerves. The buttocks are innervated by the third, fourth and fifth sacral nerves. Owing to the torsion of the lower limb during its early development, the pre-axial and post-axial borders around which the dermatomes evolved, have not been so readily recognized as in the upper limb. Accordingly, there is a wider range of variation to be seen in diagrams illustrating the distribution of dermatomes in the lower limb than in the upper. For practical purposes L.2 covers the front of the thigh and L.3 the knee. The inner and outer sides of the legs are served by L.4–5 respectively, the latter including the dorsum of the foot, the great toe and the inner border of the sole of the foot. S.1 supplies the outer border of the foot, the small toe and the lateral aspect of the sole. S.2 is a zone running up the posterior aspect of the leg and thigh to the buttock. S.3, 4, 5 are in concentric rings around the anus.

Pain due to root irritation is felt in dermatome and myotome distribution. It is not always possible to differentiate between these two types of referred pain, but the former may be sharp, superficial and well localized, while the latter is 'deep' and of a dull aching character and poorly localized by the patient. Deep pain from a lesion of the fifth lumbar root is felt in the anterior tibial and peroneal muscles; that from lesion of the first sacral root is felt in the muscles of the calf. Both superficial and deep pain may be felt only in one portion of the corresponding dermatome or myotome. There may be a patch of superficial sensory loss over the zone of superficial pain, and tenderness on palpation over a zone of deep pain. As in the upper limb, there is probably considerable variation and overlap in neural segmentation; anomalies of vertebral segmentation are common in this region. How often neural segmental anomalies occur when the vertebrae are normal is not known.

Root involvement caused by prolapsed lumbosacral discs is one of the commonest causes of pain in the lower limb—sciatica. The roots of the cauda equina may also be involved in tumours within the spinal canal. The lumbosacral plexus may be compressed by tumours arising in the vertebrae or pelvis, and paralysis of the lumbosacral cord (L. 4–5) and of the obturator nerves may result from pressure of the foetal head during parturition. Injuries to the individual nerves of the lower limbs are common in wartime but in civil practice they occur less frequently than those of the upper limb; sciatica and foot drop are the commonest examples.

Maintenance of the erect attitude, the stability of the hip and knee joints and the movements of walking may be disturbed in various ways as a result of weakness of the muscles of the lower limb. A wide range of movements is possible at the hip joints and the upright posture is dependent on a balanced tonus between the flexors (iliopsoas and rectus femoris) and the extensors (gluteus maximus and the hamstrings). These muscles may act from above or from below. They may be used to flex and extend the trunk at the pelvis or to flex and extend the lower limbs when the trunk is in the erect or horizontal position. Weakness of the hip flexors or extensors impedes walking and running. Forward motion is dependent on the 'push off' of the toes, plantar flexion at the ankle and forward swing of the hips and pelvis. The glutei stabilize the pelvis when the opposite lower limb is in motion, and when these muscles are paralysed there is a characteristically lurching gait. When they remain intact in the presence of weakness of other muscles which move the hip, the act of walking is less disturbed. The three adductors of the thigh also assist in walking and running by drawing forwards the lower limb. Abduction of the thigh is performed by the gluteus medius and minimus assisted by the tensor. Lateral rotation of the hip is principally performed by the gluteus maximus and medial rotation principally by the iliopsoas.

At the knee joint the principal movements are flexion, performed by the hamstrings assisted by gracilis, gastrocnemius and sartorius; and extension by the quadriceps femoris. The latter is the principal extensor muscle of the leg and when it is weak the stability of the knee is reduced and the leg tends to give way when walking. The hamstring muscles vary considerably in length. When they are short they restrict flexion of the trunk at the hip joints while the knees are extended.

Stooping is then largely carried out by flexion of the spine and may be a source of strain.

Movements of the ankle comprise flexion and extension (plantar- and dorsiflexion). Dorsiflexion is performed through the anterior tibial muscle, assisted by the long extensor muscles of the toes. Plantar flexion is carried out by the action of the gastrocnemius and soleus, assisted by the posterior tibial muscle and the long flexor muscles of the toes. Inversion of the foot is brought about by the anterior and posterior tibial muscles assisted by the long extensor and flexor tendons of the great toe. Eversion is performed by the peronei. Together with the intrinsic muscles of the foot, these muscles are concerned in the maintenance of the arches of the foot. The feet have to function not only in forming a rigid support for the weight of the body in a standing position, but also as a mobile springboard during walking and running. On commencing to walk, the heel is raised from the ground, the foot becomes inverted, the longitudinal arch is increased, there is flexion at the metatarsophalangeal joints, so that push-off is possible; the foot is raised and dorsiflexed to clear the toes. Just before the toes of one foot leave the ground, the heel of the other makes contact. There are various types of abnormality of gait which result from weakness of one or more muscle groups in the lower limbs. They will be referred to later.

Tests of Lower Limb Movement

Muscles of the Hip Girdle

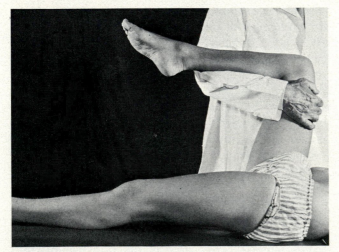

279. Iliopsoas (femoral nerve; L.1, 2, 3)
With the patient in the supine position and the flexed leg supported by the examiner, the patient attempts to flex his thigh against resistance.

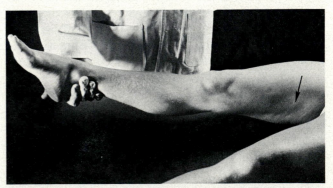

280. Adductors (obturator nerve; L.2, 3)
The patient lies supine with his knee extended and attempts to adduct the limb against resistance.

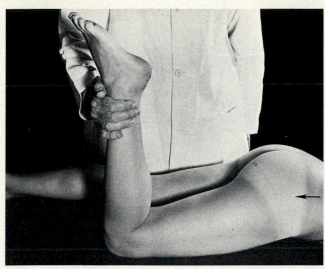

281a

281b

281. Gluteus medius and minimus (superior gluteal nerve; L.4 and 5, S.1)
(*a*) Internal rotation at the hip joint. The patient lies prone with his knee flexed to a right angle and attempts to move his foot laterally against resistance.
(*b*) Abduction at the hip. The patient lies supine with his leg extended and is trying to abduct it against resistance.

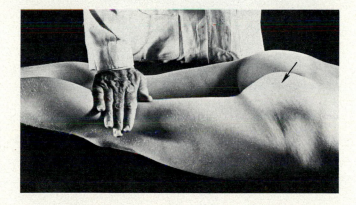

282. Gluteus maximus (inferior gluteal nerve; L.5, S.1)
The patient lies prone and tries to lift one knee against resistance. Comparison between right and left can also be made by asking the patient to tighten both buttocks.

Muscles of the Thigh and Knee

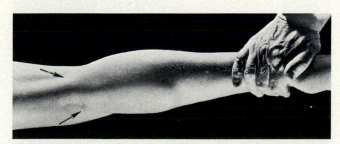

283. Hamstrings; biceps, semitendinosus, semimembranosus (sciatic nerve; L.4 and 5, S.1 and 2)
The patient lies prone and attempts to flex his right knee against resistance.
Upper arrow: biceps tendon, laterally.
Lower arrow: semitendinosus, medially.

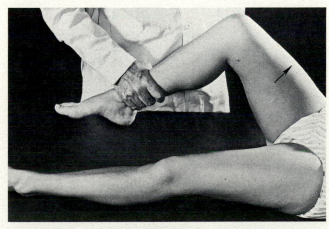

284. Quadriceps femoris (femoral nerve; L.3, 4)
The patient lies supine and attempts to extend his knee against resistance.

Muscles of the Leg and Ankle

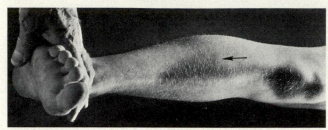

285. Tibialis anterior (anterior tibial nerve; L.4, 5)
The patient is trying to dorsiflex his foot against resistance.

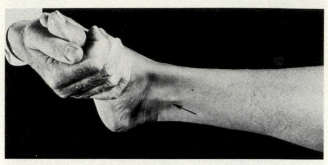

286. Tibialis posterior (posterior tibial nerve; L.4)
The patient lies supine and is trying to invert the plantar-flexed foot against resistance.

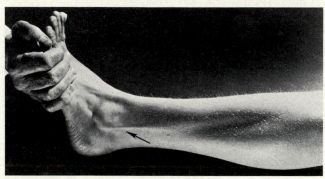

287. Peronei (common peroneal nerve; L.5, S.1)
The patient is trying to evert his foot against resistance.

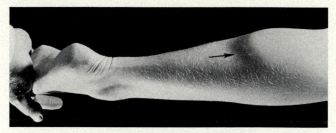

288. Gastrocnemius (posterior tibial nerve; S.1)
The patient lies prone and attempts to plantar-flex his foot against resistance.

Muscles of the Foot and Hallux

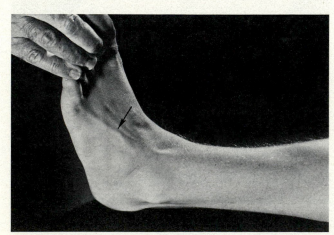

289. Extensor digitorum longus (anterior tibial nerve; L.5)
The patient is trying to dorsiflex his toes against resistance.

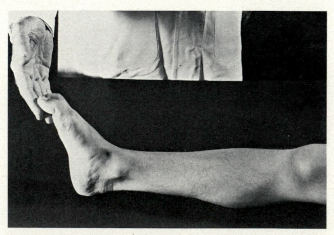

290. Flexor digitorum longus (posterior tibial nerve; L.5, S.1)
The patient is trying to flex the terminal phalanges of his toes against resistance.

Muscles of the Foot and Hallux

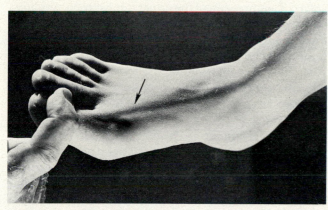

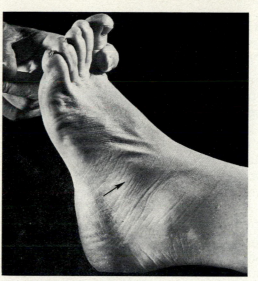

291. Extensor hallucis longus
(anterior tibial nerve; L.5, S.1)
The patient is trying to dorsiflex the
hallux against resistance.

292. Extensor digitorum brevis
(anterior tibial nerve; S.1)
The patient dorsiflexes the hallux against
resistance.

Nerves of the Lower Limb

293. Innervation of the lower limb
(Reproduced from *Aids to Investigation of
Peripheral Nerve Injuries*, 1943, by
permission of the Controller of Her
Majesty's Stationery Office.)

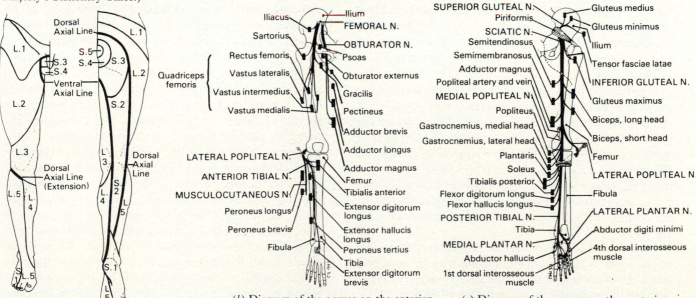

(*a*) Distribution of spinal segments in the
lower limb.

(*b*) Diagram of the nerves on the anterior
aspect of the lower limb, and the muscles
which they supply. (Modified from Petres
and Testut.)

(*c*) Diagram of the nerves on the posterior
aspect of the lower limb, and the muscles
which they supply. (Modified from
Petres and Testut.)

LUMBOSACRAL ROOT LESIONS

The nerve roots of the cauda equina may be compressed by tumour or protruded intervertebral disc, or they may be involved in inflammatory lesions (arachnoiditis) or congenital defects (spina bifida). By far the commonest root lesion is that which occurs in sciatica due to posterolateral intervertebral disc protrusion. Here one or more roots are compressed in their extrathecal course. Compression of lumbosacral roots before their emergence from the theca may result from massive posterior protrusion of a disc; it behaves like a tumour. Occasionally a small disc protrusion is associated with the formation of dense adhesions within the theca which strangle the roots of the cauda equina. Tumours of the cauda equina may be primary or secondary.

Tumours of the Cauda Equina

Although they are relatively rare, tumours of the cauda equina are usually benign and removable—neurofibromas and meningiomas. Gliomas and ependymomas are rarer. Pain is the most important early symptom and it may be severe when there are still no abnormal physical signs. When the latter appear they may resemble those produced by disc protrusion.

Pain may be felt in the lumbar region or it may occur in root distribution in one or both legs. It is often severe, aggravated by movement and coughing, but unlike the disc case, not usually relieved by resting in bed. The pain may even appear to be related to recent muscular effort or strain, but recurrent episodes of sudden, immobilizing pain brought on by effort, are uncommon in tumour and much more likely to be a result of a prolapsed disc. Walking may relieve the pain. Generally speaking the pain in tumour becomes more or less continuous and less episodic than in disc lesions. Paraesthesiae—numbness, tingling or burning—may be described long before any objective sensory loss may be discerned. Sooner or later weakness and wasting of muscles appear; there may be fasciculation. Disturbance of micturition from pressure on sacral nerve roots may be quite late in appearing, even when there is bilateral sciatica. It is, of course, relatively uncommon with disc protrusions. Impotence occurs in the male.

On examination there may be no visible abnormality of the spine and straight leg raising may be adequate. Muscular weakness and wasting may be detected either proximally or distally in one or both legs. Wasting of the anterior tibial group of muscles should not escape detection, but it may not occur; wasting of the glutei may be missed because they are not inspected. The knee (L.2–4)

and ankle (S.1–2) reflexes may be lost if the tumour is placed high up in the cauda equina, but more commonly only the ankle jerks are lost. The distribution of the sensory loss depends on which posterior roots are involved. Compression of the upper lumbar roots produces sensory loss over the front of the thigh and the knee; involvement of the lower lumbar roots will affect the front and sides of the leg, the dorsum of the foot and the inner border of the sole of the foot. A saddle-shaped area of sensory loss over the buttocks and back of the thighs results from compression of the lower sacral roots.

The course of the illness is variable but although it is rarely as intermittent or episodic as in disc protrusion, remissions may occur and differential diagnosis largely depends on ancillary investigations. Diabetic neuropathy should not be forgotten. Lumbar puncture and myelography are essential. Narrowing of a disc space suggestive of a prolapse may only be incidental. A marked rise in the protein content of the spinal fluid is more likely to be due to tumour than disc protrusion.

Spina Bifida

This common developmental abnormality of the spinal cord results from defective closure of the neural tube and incomplete separation from the surface ectoderm. The defect is usually found in the lumbosacral region and there may or may not be any surface abnormality. In many of the severe forms of the malformation the infant does not survive, but in herniation of the meninges (meningocele and meningomyelocele) there are varying degrees of disability. A meningocele is often associated with hydrocephalus but there may be no significant abnormality of the lower limbs. In meningomyelocele there is paresis, sensory impairment, trophic changes in the extremities and sphincter disturbances.

The simplest type is spina bifida occulta. It is seldom associated with neurological disability. It is frequently only detected on radiographic examination. Sometimes the site of the defect may be marked by a change in the overlying skin—a dimple, an abnormal growth of hair, a naevus or a deposit of fat. The importance, neurologically speaking, of spina bifida occulta is that disability may arise during growth, adolescence or even in adult life. Intraspinal adhesions or lipoma may then compress the roots of the cauda equina or they may be tethered or stretched as a result of the differential rates of growth of the spine and spinal cord. An insidious cauda equina lesion then appears. The congenital nature of the disability may be suspected by a history of persisting nocturnal enuresis or by some lack of development of some portion of a lower limb. The feet and ankles may have always had a tendency to be cold and cyanotic; trophic disturbances are common, the toe nails may be deformed and callosities and ulcerations of the feet may have been troublesome.

Pain is unusual and although sensation is impaired, significant paraesthesiae are rarely complained of. The calf muscles may be poorly developed on one or both sides and there is often talipes or cavus deformity of the feet. The degree and pattern of reflex loss varies considerably, but in the majority of cases the ankle reflexes are impaired or lost. The general tendency is to a segmental distribution of the paralyses but in some cases sensory loss resembles that of nerve lesions or it may even be of a 'stocking' distribution.

When symptoms appear for the first time in adolescence or adult life, or when there has been a long period of apparent remission of disability, the possibility of surgical treatment should be kept in mind. Occasionally, an intraspinal tumour such as a lipoma or a dermoid may be successfully removed. There may not be any great degree of recovery of function, but the progression of disability may be halted.

Spina Bifida

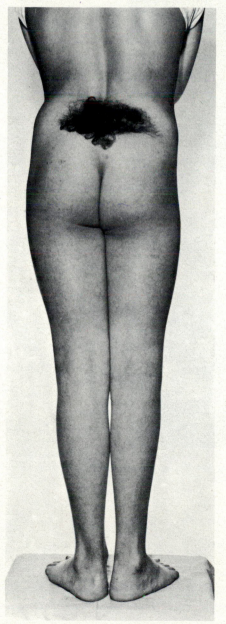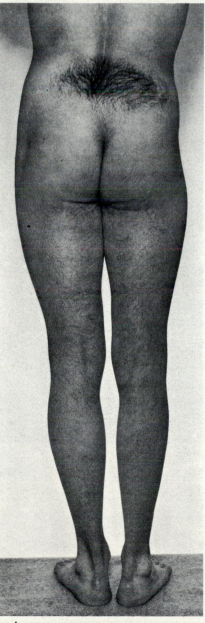

294a   294b

294. Spina bifida occulta
(a) Aged 13. Slight clumsiness since infancy; did not play games. Complaining of backache, weakness of right leg. Sphincters normal. Lumbosacral hirsuties. Disability slight. Right knee and ankle jerk absent, right plantar response extensor. Slight left pes cavus. Distal sensory impairment.
(b) Same patient, aged 20. Periodic shaving reduced the lumbosacral hair growth. Increasing weakness of right leg, which tends to give way; scuffing of toes of right foot. Paraesthesiae below knee. Right leg 1 inch shorter than left; thin thigh and calf. Reflexes unchanged. More extensive sensory loss in both lower limbs, including complete loss of vibration and position sense on the right. Bifid vertebrae; CSF protein 80 mg./100 ml.; myelography normal. Laminectomy (Mr. C. Langmaid) revealed mobile cauda equina roots, no bony peg (diastematomyelia) but a fibrous band between dura and conus and a fibrous tumour on S.2 root. Two years later there was no improvement in muscle power but the paraesthesiae in the right leg had subsided and sensation in the foot and leg was much improved.

Spina Bifida

295. Spina bifida with trophic changes in the feet   ▽

(*a*) No cutaneous lumbar abnormality. Atrophic paresis of the left lower limb with absent reflexes, distal (left) and sacral (right) sensory impairment. Note trophic changes on the right buttock and the sole of the small left foot (*b*).

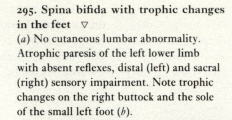

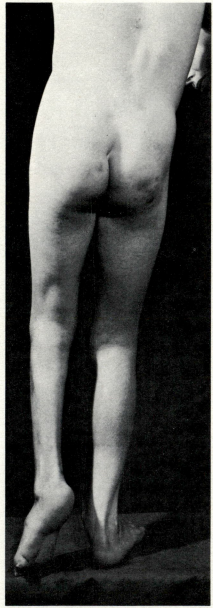

259b

295a

Spina Bifida

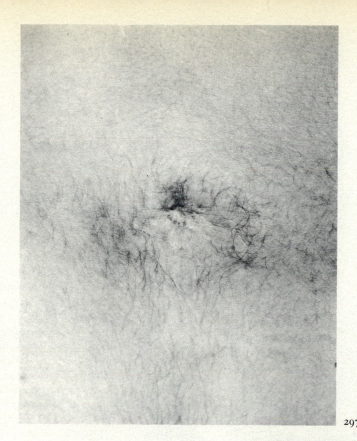

297a

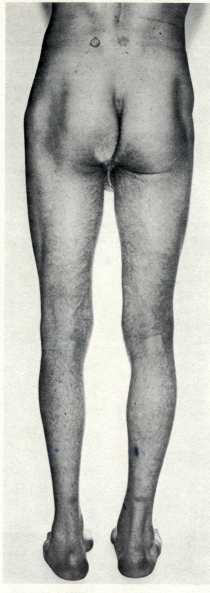

296. Spina bifida occulta △
Aged 40. Five year history of weakness, coldness and numbness of the left leg. Normal school activities and served in category A.1 for 6 years in the Second World War. Note small lumbosacral naevus with adjacent cutaneous tumour. Thin left thigh and calf, flaccid Achilles tendon and smaller left foot. Absent left ankle jerk, impaired left knee jerk. Distal superficial sensory impairment with vibration and postural loss in the toes.

297. Spina bifida with intraspinal tumour △ ▷
Male, aged 23. Slight clumsiness of gait and weakness of the right leg since infancy. Frequent falls and painless injuries to legs (note scars). Sphincters normal. Recent rapid deterioration in gait and increasing weakness of the right leg. Midline lumbar dimple surrounded by hair (*a*); bifid lumbosacral spine. Right leg smaller and weaker than left (*b*), impaired right knee jerk and absent right ankle jerk; bilateral extensor plantar responses with bilateral ankle clonus. Feet cold and cyanosed. Superficial sensation impaired below right knee; loss of temperature discrimination below L.1 on right. Vibration and postural loss in both feet. Myelography revealed a large central, space-occupying lesion, L.1– L.4, which proved to be an extradural lipoma.

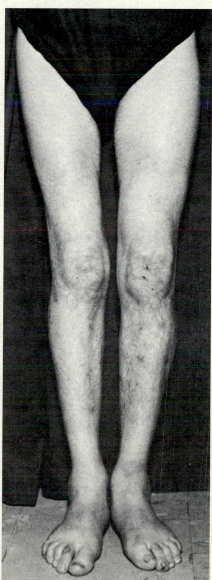

297b

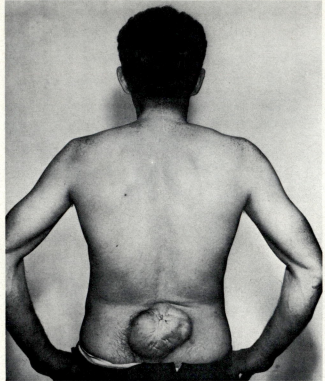

298a

Spina Bifida

298. Lumbosacral meningocele
Age 34. Wore a protective truss and without disability (apart from transient paraesthesiae when the meningocele was
compressed) until one year previously.
Then began to experience progressive
difficulty in walking, with paraesthesiae
in feet and occasionally in fingers.
Nystagmus, vertigo on extension of the
neck, absent biceps and radial reflexes
with hyperactive triceps jerks and brisk
finger jerks. Early pyramidal signs in lower
limbs. Sphincters normal. (*b*) Enlarged
foramen magnum; posterior spina bifida
of C.2–5 and 6; enlarged sagittal diameter
of the cervical spinal canal. No obstruction
on myelography. (*c*) Cervical laminectomy
disclosed a unilateral Chiari Type 1 malformation. Walking much improved.

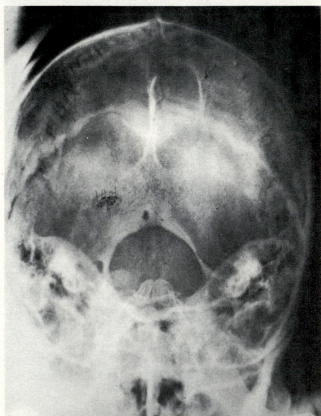

298b

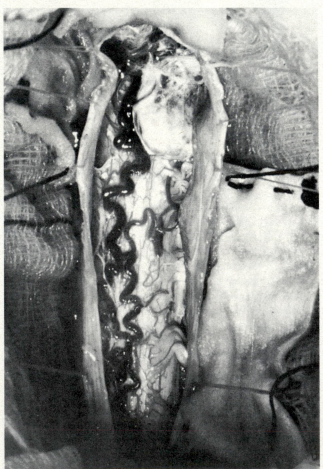

298c

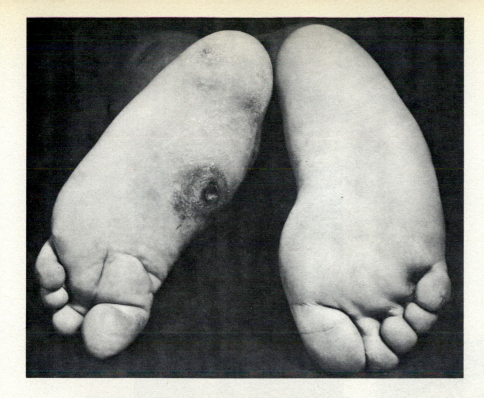

299. Trophic ulcer
Painless perforating ulcer on the sole of the left foot in a woman who had a lumbosacral meningocele removed in infancy. Note small, valgus-deformed left foot.

300. Diastematomyelia ▽
(*a*) Smallness of left leg since infancy. Recent progressive deterioration. No cutaneous lumbar abnormality but spinal movements limited, absent knee jerks and left ankle jerk. Plantar response extensor on left. Distal sensory loss below left knee.

[*continued overleaf*

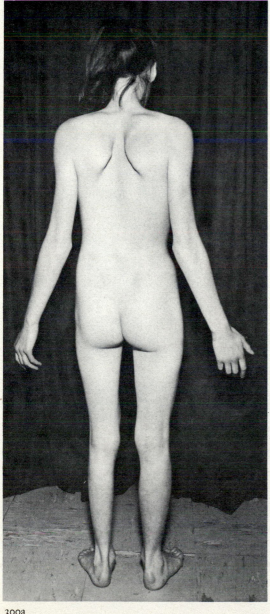

300a

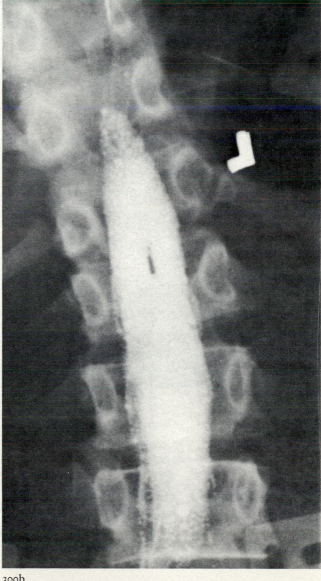

300b

300—*continued from p. 191*   *Spina Bifida*

Fusion of the bodies of the fifth, sixth and
seventh thoracic vertebrae; lumbosacral
spina bifida and on myelography a persistent central defect at L.1—a bony spur (*b*).
(*c*) Scoliosis and hirsuties in a child with
congenital dislocation of left hip and extensive spina bifida. Myelography (*d*)
showed the splitting of the spinal theca
around a central bony spur at T.12.
(Courtesy of Mr. C. Langmaid.)

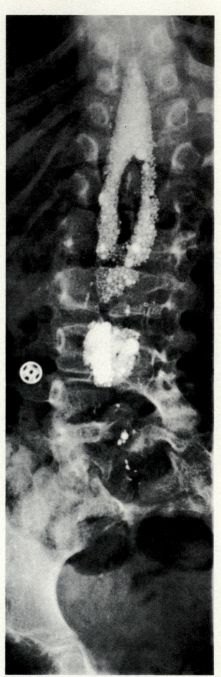

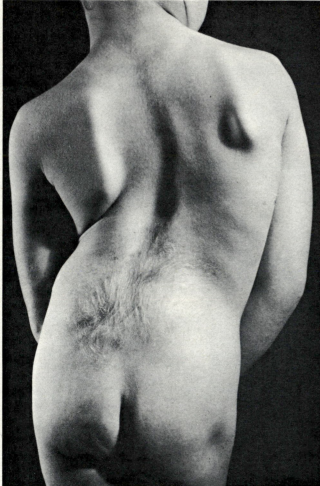

300c   300d

Spina Bifida

Backache

There are many causes of backache, but the majority of cases are due to either spondylosis or spondylitis. The pain is mostly of insidious onset. Acute backache may suggest prolapse of an intervertebral disc, a crush fracture of a vertebra due to osteoporosis, or spinal metastases. Backache is most often felt in the lumbar region; crush fractures are more common in the thoracic region. Pain from spondylitis usually begins in the lumbosacral region, but tends to extend upwards. Generally the pain in backache is of an aching character. Stabbing pain usually occurs when the onset is acute, as in disc lesions or crush fractures. Most patients with backache will say that it is aggravated by exertion and relieved by rest, but in ankylosing spondylitis the reverse is the case: the patient suffers at night and obtains relief on rising in the morning. Whatever the aetiology, the pain may radiate to the buttock regions. If it radiates to the lower limb, then there is nerve root irritation.

On examination it is important to inspect the spine and note the presence of any scoliosis or kyphosis. In acute disc prolapse a lateral scoliosis may be revealed only during forward flexion. Flattening of the normal lumbar lordosis is seen when there is chronic disc pathology and in ankylosing spondylitis. In nearly all cases of backache there is some diminution in the range of flexion and extension. A patient with a stiff lumbar spine may be able to touch his toes, provided that he has normal hip joints. The distribution of flexion between hips and spine should be observed. When ankylosing spondylitis is suspected, the sacro-iliac joints should be tested. This can be done with the patient lying supine and pressure being applied through the hands of the examiner on the anterior superior iliac spines. The joints are obliquely placed and will tend to 'spring' in this manoeuvre, which will be painful if they are diseased. When pain is referred to the lower limb, it is likely to be produced during the straight-leg raising test before 90 degrees' flexion at the hip is achieved. This test may cause pain in the lumbar region or, as a consequence of sciatic stretch, the pain may be referred in the distribution of the sciatic nerve. Lumbar pain on straight-leg raising is not a sign of actual nerve root irritation; it is merely an aggravation of the local pain by movement.

The patient's age is an important consideration in the analysis of backache. Pain of postural origin is mostly encountered in childhood; ankylosing spondylitis in the third decade; and prolapsed intervertebral discs in the third, fourth and fifth decades. In later life the responsible lesions are usually spondylosis, spinal metastases, osteoporosis and Paget's disease. In the younger age group, disc lesions tend to produce acute disability: a severe sharp stabbing pain which immobil-izes the patient and is slowly relieved by rest. There may or may not be sciatica. In older patients, degenerative disc lesions tend to produce chronic low back pain which is aggravated by exercise and which may from time to time be accompanied by symptoms and signs of root involvement. In female patients, gynaecological lesions are commonly considered and sometimes found, but what part they play in backache is not clear.

No patient with persistent backache is likely to go without a radiological examination, and in the majority of cases of spondylosis a narrowing of disc spaces, marginal sclerosis and osteophyte formation may be seen.

Spinal cord tumours do not always present with a progressive paraparesis. In children and adolescents abnormal posture, backache and a stiff spine may be the main features. Radiological investigation is then of extreme importance, and erosion of the pedicles, increase of the interpediculate width and scalloping of the posterior margins of the vertebral bodies must be looked for.

Persistent backache in the absence of spondylosis necessitates further investigations to exclude such lesions as prostatic carcinoma, reticulosis, myeloma, and the inflammatory arthropathies. Myelography is often an essential procedure when pain persists despite treatment, or when signs of a progressive root or cord lesion emerge. Persistent backache and vesical symptoms may arise from central prolapse of intervertebral discs.

Sciatica

In 'sciatica' we have a term which has been used for centuries to describe a well known clinical affliction. 'Thou cold sciatica' were words put into the mouth of Timon of Athens by William Shakespeare. But ancient a malady though it may be, its causation was only convincingly demonstrated 33 years ago when Mixter and Barr, of Boston, showed that rupture of an intervertebral disc was the commonest explanation.

The association of low backache or lumbago with sciatica had been known for some time. Lasègue (1816–1883), a Paris neurologist, drew attention to the importance of the straight-leg-raising sign in sciatica, later shown to be due to stretching of the sciatic nerve. The characteristic posture of the patient with sciatica was appreciated and sciatic scoliosis was described by Charcot in 1888. It was increasingly suspected that in some way or other sciatica was related to disturbance in the lumbar spine. The intervertebral discs were known since the days of Vesalius but the exceptionally intensive anatomical and radiological investigations by Schmorl of Dresden, 40 years ago, did not lead him to think that herniation of disc material posteriorly had any clinical significance. He was more impressed by disc herniation into the bodies of the vertebrae—Schmorl's nodes.

The first edition of Kinnier Wilson's *Neurology*, published in 1940, contains no mention of the role of the intervertebral discs in the causation of sciatica. Mixter and Barr did not discover either sciatica or the intervertebral discs, but as repeatedly illustrated in the history of medicine, their powers of observation were such that they grasped the significance of the role of intervertebral disc lesions in sciatica.

There is little or no evidence of 'neuritis' of the sciatic roots, plexus or the trunk of the nerve. Compression, of course, at any point along the course of the nerve through the pelvis and into the thigh, may produce the syndrome.

By definition the pain is referred along the course of the sciatic nerve, extending across the buttock, down the back of the thigh, the outer side and back of the calf and the outer border of the foot. It is usually due to herniation of the fourth or fifth lumbar disc. In the first case there is involvement of the fifth lumbar root; in the second the fifth lumbar or the first sacral root, or both are involved. Exceptionally, large midline herniations may involve the roots of the cauda equina and produce bilateral sciatica. Rupture of the annulus of a disc may occur while lifting a heavy weight or performing some awkward movement, or it may follow a direct blow to the lumbar region or a fall. In many cases there is no history of significant injury. It is thought that degeneration of the disc, with loss of resilience, is primarily responsible for the complication of herniation.

The cardinal feature of sciatica is pain of an episodic nature. The patient may present with low back pain, with sciatic pain or with both together. The lumbago may be acute, severe and incapacitating. On the other hand it may be gradual in onset, and consist of no more than a dull diffuse aching in the lumbar region, unattended with any muscle spasm. Both types of pain may be present or follow one another. Sciatic pain usually follows lumbar pain, but may precede it. As with the lumbago it may be acute and severe, or insidious and remittent. Commonly, pain is first felt in the buttock or back of the thigh; occasionally it is first felt on the outer side of the foot, ankle or calf. In the first attack, which usually subsides in a matter of weeks, motor, sensory or reflex signs in the affected limb may be absent. But lumbar spasm and abnormalities of posture and restriction of spinal movement are nearly always evident.

Recovery may be 'complete' and the subsequent progress varies greatly. There are many patients who have had only one severe attack of sciatica during a lifetime. Unfortunately there is a general tendency for symptoms to recur and in a minority, with increasing frequency, severity and regularity. Nevertheless, in the majority of patients symptoms are confined to one limb. Recovery is usually a matter of degree. The patient may no longer complain of sciatica or seek treatment, but he may nurse a 'lame' or stiff back and restrict his activities for the rest of his life. Mild chronic disability, in this sense, is very common.

During an attack of sciatica the pain may be described as sharp or dull and it may be relieved by lying down or standing, but nearly always it is aggravated by stooping, raising the leg or by coughing or sneezing. Sensations of tingling, pins and needles or numbness are often experienced; they are usually felt in the outer border of the foot and across the top of the toes or on the sole of the foot.

On examination, lumbar signs consist of spasm of the erector spinae muscles which may be visible and palpable, flattening of the spine in the erect position, and, perhaps, scoliosis. The latter is by no means constant; it varies from one attack to another, in degree and also in laterality. The convexity may be either towards or away from the side of the lesion. The mobility of the spine is generally reduced, but the movements of flexion and extension suffer most. With the knees straight and the arms extended, forward flexion principally takes place at the hips and in the dorsal region; the lumbar spine remains stiff. Movements of lateral flexion and rotation are much less affected. In some cases lateral flexion to the side of the lesion is impaired; in other cases this movement is reduced in the opposite direction. Flattening of the lumbar spine is probably not a reflex mechanism resulting from a local root lesion, but primarily a mechanical disturbance of the spine consequent on the local disc protrusion.

If the root lesion is entirely irritative, there will be no objective neurological signs by way of sensory loss or impairment of ankle jerk, but the straight-leg-raising test would be positive. With the patient lying in the supine position and the legs in extension, the examiner raises the leg by flexing it at the hip. Normally a leg may be raised through about 90 degrees without causing the patient much discomfort. In the presence of disc protrusion this angle is diminished. Lumbar and sciatic pain are felt if the examiner attempts to raise the leg still further. The pain is usually felt in the affected leg, but sometimes slight pain is felt in the sound leg; there may even be some pain and limitation of straight-leg-raising on the sound side. Raising of the sound leg may also cause pain in the affected leg. Dorsiflexion of the ankle of the affected side may produce pain when the limb has already been elevated without discomfort to a certain point.

Lasègue left no written account of his sign in his observations on sciatica; an account of it was later published by one of his pupils. Here the examiner flexes the affected limb at the hip and the knee. With the hip flexed to 90 degrees the knee is slowly extended. Normally the knee can be fully extended with the hip in this position without causing pain. Another modification of the straight-leg-raising test consists of flexing the cervical spine when the straight leg is raised just short of the point of tolerance. The mechanical basis for the test is in movement of lumbar roots. Experiments with cadavers have shown that raising the leg to its fullest extent evokes root movement of 2–8 mm. This movement takes place during the latter half of the manoeuvre. It seems likely that when a nerve root is stretched or displaced by a herniated disc, it reacts earlier, producing pain.

Objective neurological signs usually indicate a single root lesion. Herniation of the fifth lumbar disc compresses the first sacral root. Then, the ankle jerk is lost, the calf muscles are flabby, the glutei droop, and sensation is impaired along the outer border of the foot and along the outer half of the sole. Herniation of the fourth lumbar disc compresses the fifth lumbar root, so that the ankle jerk is not usually completely abolished and sensory loss is found on the outer side of the calf and the dorsum of the foot, perhaps involving the great toe. Herniation of the third lumbar disc, compressing the fourth root, is relatively uncommon; the knee jerk is not usually impaired and it is unusual to find any sensory impairment over the anteromedial aspect of the leg below the knee. If the third lumbar root is compressed by disc herniation at this level, the knee jerk is impaired but not usually abolished.

Fasciculation of the calf muscles may be seen in sciatica. Sphincter functions are not usually impaired.

Multiple disc protrusions, or massive protrusion of a large disc may produce more striking symptoms and signs. Indeed, paralysis of the cauda equina may result, either after a series of recurrent attacks, or in a progressive manner, as in tumour. The weakness of the legs may progress to complete paralysis of the anterior tibial group of muscles, with bilateral foot drop. There may be sensory loss over the saddle area and paralysis of sphincters. Although in the majority of these cases the paralysis follows bouts of bilateral sciatica, in some there is very little pain. Diagnosis may be difficult. In other cases, with the onset of paralysis, pain subsides dramatically. Paralysis of the sphincters may not be accompanied by any subjective sensory loss and if the buttocks are not examined for sensibility the neurogenic nature of urinary retention and overflow may not be appreciated. In an elderly man without obvious weakness of the lower limbs, or when bed rest obscures it, it may be thought that the troubles are prostatic. There is usually an elevation of spinal fluid protein and myelography reveals the site of the lesion.

When a patient with sciatica says that his pain only comes on after walking a certain distance, the possibility of intermittent claudication arises. This is nearly always due to peripheral arterial disease and then the absent ankle pulses, the evidence of ischaemia of the feet and the absence of neurological signs should clarify the diagnosis. When the vascular insufficiency is the result of an obstruction of the aortic or common iliac artery, the distinction may not be so easy. In both cases pain in the calf, thigh or buttocks, on exercise, is the common symptom. A previous history of lumbago or sciatica should be sought. Reflex and sensory impairment would point to a root lesion but in such cases myelography and even aortography may be essential. The notion of 'intermittent claudication of the spinal cord' has been considered for many years; namely, pain and discomfort in the feet and lower limbs during walking, in patients with pyramidal lesions. Ischaemia of the lumbar portion of the spinal cord has been postulated. A similar explanation has been suggested when pain on walking is the presenting symptom of a patient with a herniated lumbar disc. Hyperaemia of the nerve roots may occur, but it is more likely that the act of walking interferes in a mechanical way, as in straight-leg-raising, with the herniated protrusion and its relation with the adjacent nerve root.

It should not be necessary to stress that a herniated disc is not the sole cause of sciatic pain. The sciatic nerve is the largest in the human body and pain referred in its area of distribution may be arising in the spine, pelvis or hip. Lumbar osteo-arthritis, spondylolisthesis, primary and metastatic tumours and arthritis of the sacro-iliac joint or hip joint may all cause referred sciatic pain. This simulation of sciatica will vary considerably from one case to the next. It is rare for arthritis of the hip to cause referred pain below the knee. Spinal arthritis is characterized by persisting low back pain, often worse at night and relieved in the morning, less episodic than in sciatica and the referred pain down the limb is usually dull, aching and poorly localized. In spondylolisthesis there is usually a story of chronic backache, aggravated by movement and relieved by rest but occasionally root signs can be detected. Spondylolisthesis may cause symptoms which simulate claudication. In contrast with disc lesions the lumbar lordosis is increased. Rectal examination is vital in cases of referred sciatic pain and malignant metastases in spine and pelvis may not reveal themselves on radiological examination for some time.

We may leave this subject of sciatica by recalling the words of Cotugno, Professor of Surgery in Naples, who described the affliction in 1775.

'If the patient will but point out with his finger the track of the pain from the sacrum to the foot, we shall find him, like a skilful anatomist, tracing out the precise progress of the sciatic nerve. . . . In this nerve the pain is felt, in this nerve we should search for the cause of lameness, and from its affection the origin of the paresis and wasting.'

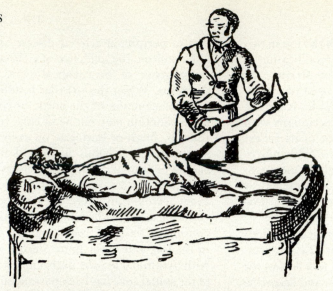

Sciatica

301. The Lasègue sign

The sciatic stretch test as illustrated by Forst, Lasègue's pupil, who first provided a written and illustrated account of this manoeuvre. Forst thought that the sciatic nerve was compressed by the muscles at the back of the thigh during this manoeuvre. He observed that when the knee was flexed pain did not occur.

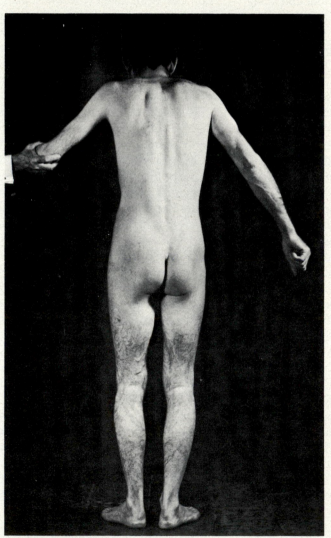

302. Acute sciatica (L)

Note flattening of the lumbar spine, spasm of the left erector spinae muscles and flexion of the left knee.

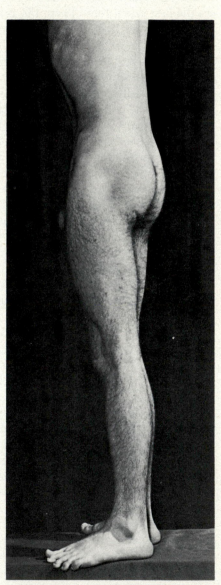

303. Recurrent sciatica (L)

Third attack. There is not only loss of the normal lumbar lordosis but it has been replaced by a slight kyphotic curve. Forward flexion was grossly reduced.

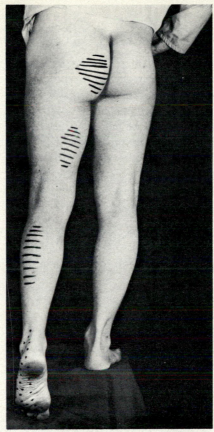

304b

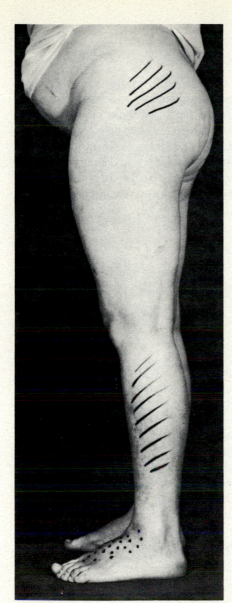

304a

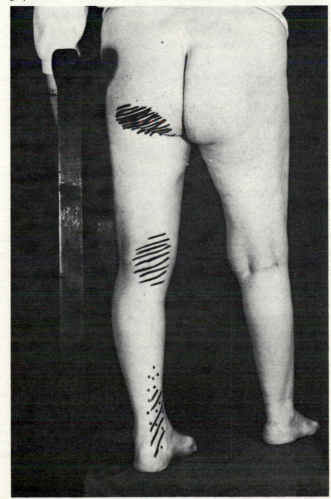

304c

304. Chronic recurrent sciatica
The zones of maximal pain and tenderness on pressure are indicated by lines; area of superficial sensory impairment indicated by dots.

(*a*) *L.5 root syndrome*. Pain was felt on the lateral half of the buttock near the great trochanter and the lateral side of the leg. Sensory impairment on the dorsum of the foot.

(*b*) *S.1 root syndrome*. Pain deep in the medial portion of the buttock, over the ischium, in the posterior thigh and calf. Sensory impairment behind the lateral malleolus and over the outer border of the foot and sole.

(*c*) *S.2 root syndrome*. Deep pain and tenderness in centre of buttock, behind the knee and on the inner side of the ankle, where there was also superficial sensory loss.

LUMBOSACRAL PLEXUS LESIONS

These are less common than brachial plexus lesions, both in civil practice and in war-time. But there is one particular variety which needs mention, namely, that which occurs in a mother after parturition. Weakness and numbness of one limb may be noticed immediately after a prolonged and difficult labour or when the foetal head has been large. Occasionally foot drop is only noticed when the mother resumes activity. When the lumbosacral cord is paralysed there is a dropped foot, but usually only minimal sensory impairment on the outer side of the leg in the distribution of the fifth lumbar dermatome. Obturator paralysis from compression of the nerve as it crosses the brim of the pelvis may be painless but there is usually numbness of the inner aspect of the thigh and the adductors are weak. These lesions may occur together and may even recur, but I have never seen one that did not fully recover, usually in a month or so.

LESIONS OF INDIVIDUAL NERVES

These also are less common in civil practice than those of the upper limb.

The Femoral Nerve (L.2, 3, 4)

This nerve supplies muscles and skin of the front of the thigh; one of its cutaneous branches, the saphenous, passes to the medial side of the leg and foot. The femoral nerve is deep to the inguinal ligament and as it enters the thigh divides into a number of branches, so that penetrating injuries often produce a partial paralysis. It supplies the iliacus, sartorius, pectineus and quadriceps, in that order. These muscles chiefly function as extensors of the knee and as an aid in flexion of the thigh at the hip. There is usually wasting of the anterior part of the thigh, difficulty in raising the foot from the bed and poor contraction of the quadriceps when the patient is asked to tighten the knee-cap. The knee jerk is lost. The patient is able to stand and to walk but experiences considerable difficulty in going up and down stairs. It is surprising how well a patient with a complete femoral nerve injury manages to walk on a level surface, albeit slowly. An acute idiopathic femoral nerve lesion is a rare occurrence; the onset is abrupt and accompanied by severe pain which subsides after a week or so. Recovery is slow but the prognosis is good. Isolated lesions of the saphenous nerve are also unusual; I have known it result from injury from a screw displaced from a metal plate used to pin a fractured femur.

The Lateral Femoral Cutaneous Nerve (L.2, 3)

This nerve is entirely cutaneous in its distribution, supplying the anterolateral aspect of the thigh. It usually enters the thigh by passing through a tunnel in the lateral attachment of the inguinal ligament to the anterior superior iliac spine. At first it lies beneath the deep fascia of the upper thigh but it soon becomes superficial. It is some disturbance in this nerve which is responsible for the condition called *meralgia paraesthetica*. The patient usually complains of a burning sensation in the anterolateral portion of the thigh; examination reveals an area of numbness of varying intensity and extent. In the majority there is no history of preceding trauma and the condition is thought to be due to compression or kinking or entrapment at some point in its course. Most probably the irritation occurs at the opening in the inguinal ligament. Not all patients experience pain; some only become gradually aware of an area of numbness or coldness on the thigh. It is rare in the female, except temporarily during pregnancy and although it is commonly said to be characteristically seen in obese men, one finds it in all physical types. It is occasionally seen after abdominal operations but despite the course of the nerve in the abdomen, descending behind the caecum on the right and the pelvic colon on the left, it does not seem to have any relationship to abdominal disorders. The numbness or tingling or pain may be intermittent or more or less constant; it is usually aggravated by standing or walking and in rare cases it is bilateral.

Whether factors other than the mechanical one are operative is not known. I have known it in diabetics and occasionally it is familial. (Sigmund Freud and one of his sons suffered from it.) It is important to recognize this condition because although it is relatively harmless, it is worrying. I have never known a patient who required section of this nerve.

The Sciatic Nerve (L.4, 5; S.1, 2, 3)

This nerve passes from the pelvis through the greater sciatic foramen to enter the thigh between the ischium and the femur. Its division into the common peroneal and tibial nerves takes place at any point between the pelvis and the lower portion of the thigh. It supplies the flexors of the leg, the adductor magnus and all the muscles below the knee. The nerve may be injured directly by penetrating wounds or misplaced intramuscular injections or indirectly as in fractures of the pelvis. The nerve may be compressed by primary or secondary pelvic tumours.

In complete paralysis the patient is able to stand and to walk, but there is foot drop, toe drop and complete inability to move the foot. The ankle reflex and the plantar reflex are lost. The muscles below the knee rapidly waste, sweating is deficient on the foot and the leg becomes oedematous if it is allowed to hang down. Trophic and vasomotor changes in the foot rapidly appear. Weak flexion of the knee is still possible through the action of the sartorius (femoral nerve) and gracilis (obturator nerve). The foot is anaesthetic except for a small zone over and distal to the internal malleolus, which is supplied by the saphenous nerve. The anaesthetic area extends up the outer aspect of the leg in its lower two-thirds, more evident posteriorly than anteriorly. The knee jerk is retained and there is no sensory disturbance above the knee.

Partial lesions of the sciatic nerve may affect both common peroneal and tibial divisions but it often happens that, although the injury occurs at a high level, one division escapes.

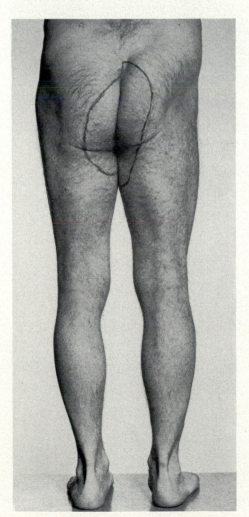

305. Fractured pelvis; lumbosacral plexus injury

Injury to pelvis 2 years previously. No apparent nerve injury. Current accident claim for alleged 'loss of libido'. Note moderate diffuse wasting of left lower limb and right buttock. No significant paresis; reflexes normal. Sensory loss in sacral 3, 4 and 5 dermatomes. The anal reflex (contraction of the external spincter ani in response to a scratch upon the skin in the perianal region) and the bulbocavernosus reflex (palpable contraction of this muscle beneath the root of the penis in response to squeezing the glans penis) were both absent. The anal reflex is through the fourth and fifth sacral roots and the bulbocavernosus reflex is dependent on the integrity of the second, third and fourth sacral roots. On enquiry it transpired that there was no complaint of 'loss of libido' but one of sexual impotence. This was complete. A case of 'accident neurosis' which proved to be otherwise.

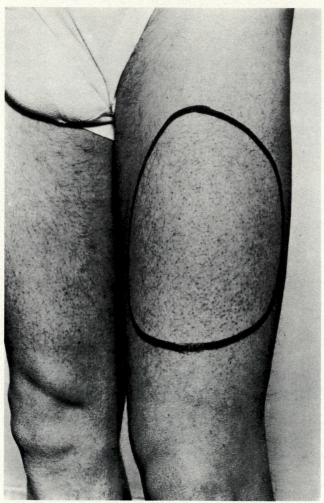

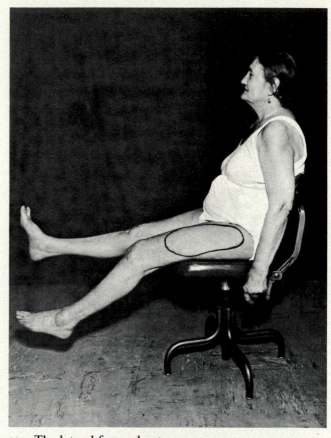

307. The lateral femoral cutaneous nerve
The area of sensory loss over the antero-lateral aspect of the thigh in a case of meralgia paraesthetica.

306. Femoral nerve
This patient, a robust lady of 70, experienced sudden, severe pain in the left thigh while gardening. Pain was excruciating for several days and was followed by difficulty in walking and a tendency for the left knee to give way when standing. There was severe paresis of the left quadriceps, loss of the left knee jerk and anaesthesia over the distribution of the lateral femoral cutaneous nerve (outlined in pencil). There was no impairment of sensation over the distribution of the saphenous nerve on the inner side of the limb. No cause was discovered and she slowly recovered.

The Common Peroneal Nerve

This nerve courses downward along the lateral border of the popliteal fossa to reach the head of the fibula where it winds around the neck and divides into the superficial and deep peroneal nerves. The former supplies the skin of the front and side of the leg and the dorsum of the foot and gives branches to the peroneus longus and brevis muscles. The deep branch supplies a triangular area of skin between the first and second toes dorsally, and it innervates the anterior tibial muscles, the long extensors of the toes and the peroneus tertius. A common site of injury is at the head of the fibula where the nerve may be involved in fractures or compressed by splints, tourniquets or bandages. Some individuals are particularly susceptible to pressure palsy of this nerve, experiencing numbness and foot drop of a temporary nature, sometimes induced by crossing the knees or taking part in some form of unusual physical activity. Such patients may also experience pressure palsy of other nerves such as the radial or ulnar. The tendency may even be familial so that some inherent metabolic factor plays a part.

There is wasting of the anterior tibial and peroneal group of muscles, the foot and toes cannot be dorsiflexed and eversion is lost. Sensory loss will depend on the level of the lesion. The ankle jerk is retained, the patient can naturally stand and walk, but his gait is altered as a result of the foot drop and although he can stand on his toes, he cannot stand on the heel of the affected side. He usually complains of a 'floppy foot' and the audible 'clop' of the foot as he walks will be described. When the foot drop is insidious in development, he will complain of scuffing of his shoe, the toe of which will tend to wear out.

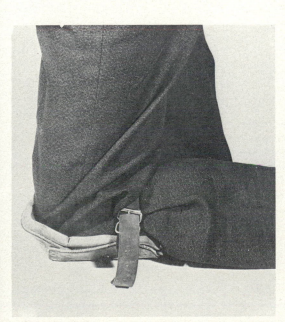

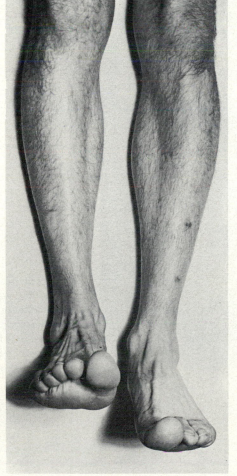

308. Common peroneal nerve palsy
A floor layer accustomed to using two thick leather knee pads strapped on as shown in (a). Painless partial left foot drop of 2 weeks' duration. Reflexes normal. No subjective numbness, but nevertheless there was impairment over the outer side of the calf and tenderness on percussion or compression just above the head of the left fibula. There was a conduction block in the common peroneal nerve well above the site at the neck of the fibula where compression commonly occurs. It corresponded to the point of compression by the strap.

308a   308b

The Tibial Nerve

This nerve supplies the calf muscles, the flexors of the toes and the small muscles of the foot. Paralysis most commonly results from penetrating wounds. The patient is able to walk but cannot stand on his toes; plantar flexion of the foot and the toes is impossible. The calf muscles waste and the ankle jerk is lost. Inversion at the ankle is impaired, not lost, as the anterior tibial muscle contributes to this movement. The patient has difficulty in lifting his heel from the ground as he walks. In complete lesions the foot becomes deformed owing to the paralysis of the small muscles with clawing of the toes and the posture of talipes calcaneovalgus. The sole of the foot is anaesthetic except along its inner border and on the plantar surface of the toes, and the flexor plantar response is abolished.

Partial or distal lesions of the tibial nerve are important because they can cause much pain with little outward disability. In the presence of an obvious foot drop, a mild injury to the tibial nerve may pass undetected. The Achilles tendon is less prominent and it may not be possible to grasp it between thumb and index finger. If the long flexors of the toes escape paralysis, there may only be paresis of the small muscles of the feet with a painful numb sole.

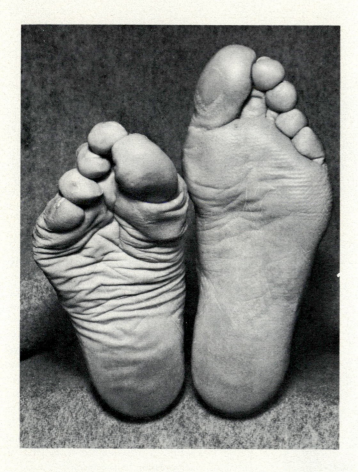

309. The tibial nerve
Right tibial nerve paresis from misplaced intramuscular thigh injection. The patient is supine and is trying to plantar flex both feet and toes. He is unable to do so on the right side. There was causalgic pain in the sole of the foot, especially on walking.

The Anterior Tibial Syndrome

Transient anterior tibial pain is a common experience after strenuous unaccustomed physical activity, such as a game of football, a long walk or cycle ride. It nearly always subsides and as training proceeds it does not recur. During the Second World War the term *anterior tibial syndrome* was used to describe a condition in recruits in which pain in the front of the leg was followed by ischaemic necrosis of the anterior tibial group of muscles. In the majority it followed strenuous activity such as marching, drilling and games. The pain did not subside after a night's rest and the patient was usually referred with signs of 'inflammation' on the front of the shin. The overlying skin was usually red, there was slight local oedema with tenderness on pressure over the anterior tibial muscle which felt firm and appeared to be swollen. The condition was usually unilateral. Soon there was weakness of dorsiflexion of the foot and toes; the peronei and the flexor muscles usually escaped. The muscles mainly affected were the anterior tibial and the long extensor of the great toe. The foot remained warm and the ankle pulses undiminished. When surgical decompression of the anterior tibial compartment was carried out, owing to the development of foot drop, it was found that the affected muscles were swollen, necrotic and the microscopic appearances were indistinguishable from those found in Volkmann's ischaemic contracture. Occasionally the anterior tibial (deep peroneal) nerve was damaged with paralysis of extensor digitorum brevis and sensory loss on the dorsum of the foot in the first interdigital cleft.

The condition usually subsides with rest but full recovery of function in the affected muscles may take some months; occasionally there is residual muscular fibrosis with slight disability. The syndrome has also been encountered after blood transfusion into the veins of the legs. Necrosis of the anterior tibial muscles may also follow arterial occlusion as the result of thrombosis or embolism. The patient is usually elderly and both legs may be affected. There is obvious ischaemia of the limbs and the prognosis is poor.

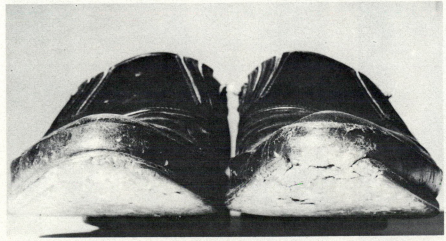

310a

310. Foot drop
(*a*) Wearing out of the toe of a left shoe as a result of foot drop.

[continued overleaf

310—*continued from p. 203*

(*b*) Left foot drop due to a lesion of the common peroneal nerve following injury at the knee. There is paralysis of eversion of the foot. On attempting dorsiflexion the foot inverts through the action of the anterior and posterior tibial muscles.

(*c*) Left foot drop. Healthy young man who developed left foot drop one month previously after sitting on floor watching television with his fiancée seated on his lap. Previous history of ulnar paraesthesiae and numbness when using arms, leaning on elbows and when using an electric drill. Recurrent numbness of thighs. Electromyography revealed widespread abnormalities of motor and sensory conduction in upper and lower limbs. His mother gets numb legs if she crosses her knees. Liability to pressure palsies of peripheral nerves may be a familial tendency.

311. Foot drop ▷
Partial right foot drop in sciatica. The droop of the right forefoot resembles that seen in pes cavus.

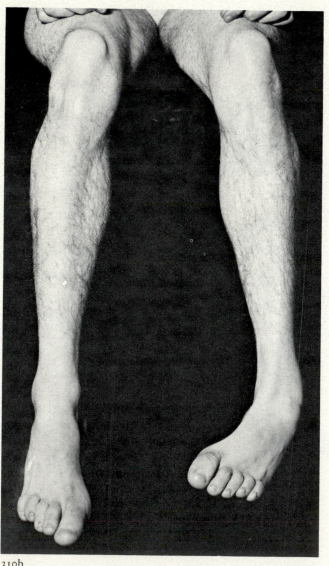

310b

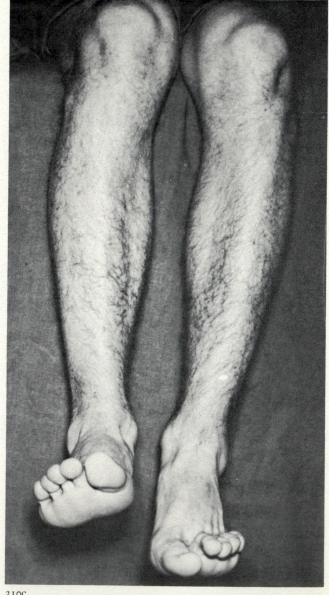

310c

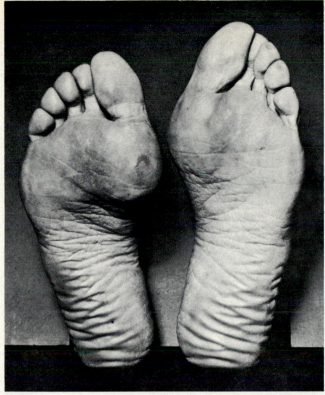

311

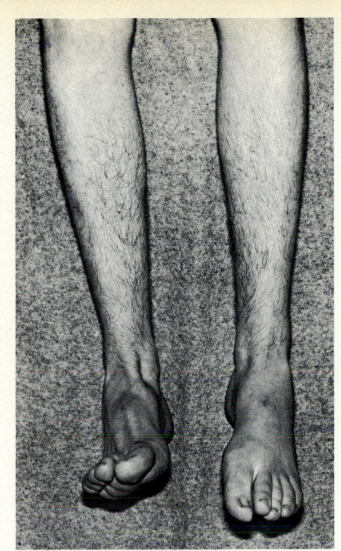

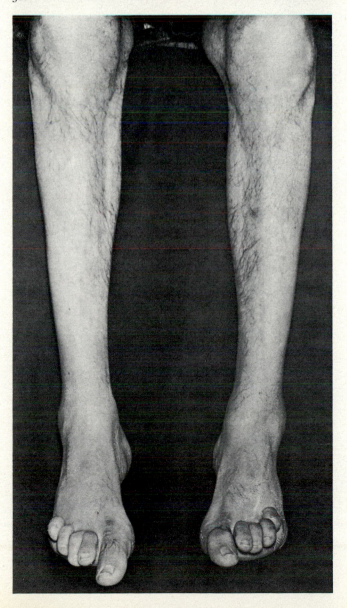

312. Foot drop △
Spastic left foot drop as the presenting
symptom in a youth with syringomyelia.
Three months previously he had accidentally discovered analgesia of the left thigh.
Weakness of the leg for one month with
drooping of the left foot and scuffing of the
toes. He is trying to dorsiflex his left foot.
Hyperactive knee jerks, normal ankle
jerks, flexor plantar response on the right,
no plantar reflex on the left. Spinothalamic
type of sensory loss on the left side below
T.2. Enlarged cervical spinal canal with
fusiform expansion of the cervical spinal
cord on myelography.

313. Foot drop ◁
Flaccid right foot drop in a cauda equina
lesion, probably angiomatous. The patient
is trying to dorsiflex his right foot and
toes; note drooping of the right hallux and
flattening of the anterior tibial muscles.
Similar signs were developing in the left
leg. The ankle jerks were absent, the right
knee jerk was absent and the left knee
jerk normal. There was L.4–5 and S.1
sensory impairment on the right. Myelography showed no block but the
appearances were those of angioma.

Miscellaneous

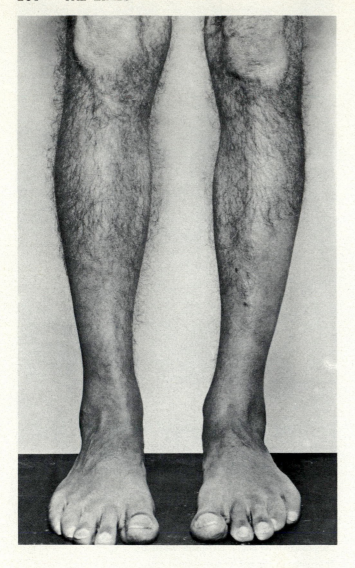

314. The anterior tibial syndrome ◁
A 20-year-old Army recruit who experienced acute shin pain on the right side after a cross country run. This photograph was taken 4 days later when there was swelling, redness and tenderness of the anterior tibial region. Dorsiflexion of the hallux and the foot was weak and painful. There was no sensory loss and the ankle pulses were normal. The condition subsided satisfactorily in 3 weeks with bed rest. On leaving hospital 1 month after onset discomfort on walking was still present, but the swelling had largely subsided.

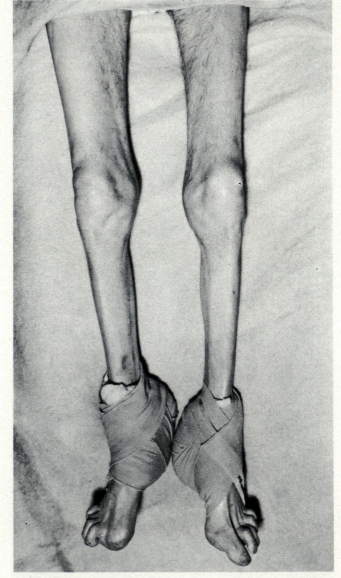

315. Aortic-iliac occlusion ▷
Male, aged 72, with a history of intermittent claudication. Recent weakness of lower limbs, bilateral footdrop and rest pain. Diffuse wasting of lower limbs, absent reflexes, vasomotor and trophic changes in the feet with previous loss of right hallux. Vascular occlusion of this nature can produce syndromes resembling lesions of the cauda equina.

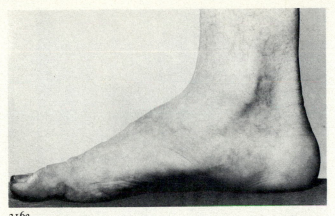

316a

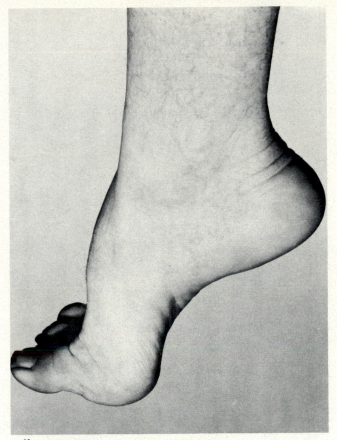

316b

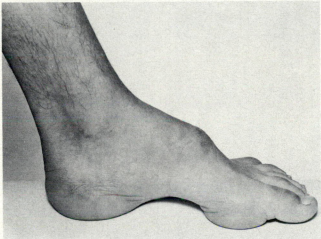

316c

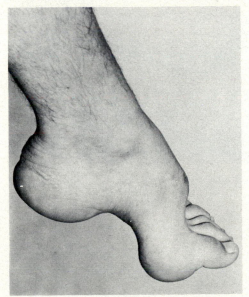

316d

316. Pes cavus

Abnormalities of the feet are often hereditary and are particularly common in the
hereditary ataxias. They may also occur
without any neurological abnormality or
only with absent lower limb reflexes. Pes
cavus (hollow foot) is the commonest type;
the longitudinal arch of the foot is accentuated. The toes may also be clawed. The
deformity may not be obvious when the
patient stands, as in (*a*), but is apparent
when the foot is dependent (*b*).

   In another case (*c*) the foot is seen to be
high-arched on standing; when it is in the
dependent position the fore-foot takes up
an equinus position (*d*). The mechanism
of the production of pes cavus is not
known. It may be stationary or progressive.
There is disturbance in the balanced function of the small muscles of the feet and in
the extrinsic muscles such as the anterior
tibial, the long extensors of the toes and
the peronei.

Miscellaneous

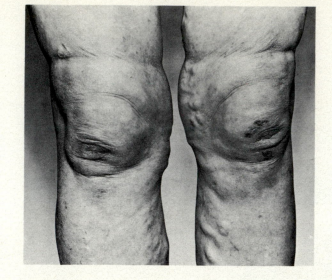

317. 'Drop attacks'
Scars on the knees in an elderly lady
who suffered from 'drop attacks' possibly
due to basilar artery insufficiency.

**318. Extensor plantar response in
pes cavus**
Patients with broad, stumpy, foreshortened
feet, a high arched instep and toes *en
griffe* often show this sign of dorsiflexion
of the hallux when the sole or the side
of the foot is stroked. There may be no
neurological disorder and the phenomenon must be in the nature of a false
Babinski sign. Such a toe seems incapable
of reflex plantar flexion.

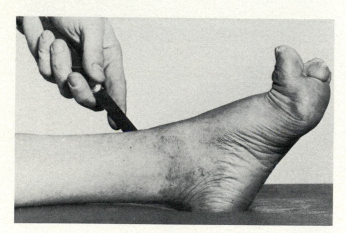

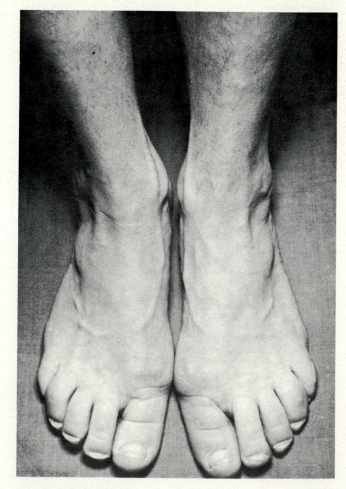

319. Acromegaly
The enlargement of the feet in acromegaly
is sometimes, as in this case, more obvious
than enlargement of the hands.

TINEL'S SIGN

This sign requires special comment because there have been varying expressions of opinion concerning its value as a clinical sign in the study of peripheral nerve injury.

Jules Tinel (1879–1952), whose father was Professor of Anatomy at Rouen, published a well known book, *Nerve Wounds*, based upon his experience of 639 cases in the First World War. He called the sign he described 'the sign of formication'.

'The all important sign is formication. We find that sudden pressure or percussion of the nerve trunk, below the lesion, calls forth a tingling sensation in the cutaneous region of the nerve. . . . It appears about the fourth or sixth week. . . . Then it gradually becomes more pronounced and it is possible to follow, week after week, in the course of the nerve, the progress of this provoked formication, *pari passu* with the advance of the axis cylinders. . . . The formication sign is thus of supreme importance since it enables us to see whether the nerve is interrupted, or in course of regeneration; whether a nerve suture has succeeded or failed, or whether regeneration is rapid and satisfactory, or reduced to a few significant fibres.'

It is obvious that only a clinician who has studied this sign in a large series of peripheral nerve injuries, over a period of time, can judge its value. This is usually only possible during war-time. Experience in the Second World War generally reaffirmed its value as a clinical sign.

The salient feature consists of the phenomenon of 'peripheral reference' which may be found in percussion of normal nerve, when a tingling sensation is referred to the appropriate peripheral zone. A common example is that which occurs when the 'funny bone' is knocked at the elbow and tingling is felt in the ulnar distribution. In a pathological nerve this phenomenon may be evoked more readily and may persist longer.

The sign came into disrepute when it was found to be positive when there was an anatomical gap at the site of the nerve injury. It is clearly no guide to the condition of the nerve at the site of the lesion, but it points to the presence of regenerating fibres. It may be used to localize the site of an injury. When it is persistently negative below the lesion in the presence of motor and sensory paralysis it is strongly indicative of a total division of the nerve. It may remain the only sign that the lesion is other than a complete interruption until such time as the early signs of motor or sensory recovery occur. If the sign is strongly positive at the level of the injury, but persistently absent distally, spontaneous regeneration cannot be expected. If the sign is strongly positive at the level of the lesion but is weak distally, poor regeneration follows. A strongly positive sign at the level of the lesion which steadily progresses peripherally is an indication of satisfactory spontaneous regeneration. A negative Tinel's sign has no value; recovery may be proceeding satisfactorily, or it may not.

CAUSALGIA

This term was coined by Weir Mitchell in 1867 to describe the burning pain (*kausos*, burning heat; *algia*, pain) which may be a sequel to nerve injury. He also coined the term 'phantom limb'. Weir Mitchell (1829–1914) made a special study of nerve injuries in an army hospital in Philadelphia during the American Civil War. He published his classic account of *Gunshot Wounds and Other Injuries of Nerves* in 1864. He wrote:

'Nerve injuries soon formed the majority of our patients. So complete was the field of study that it was not uncommon to find that at one time in the wards there were four or five cases of gunshot injuries of any single large nerve. . . . Never before in medical history has there been collected for study and treatment so remarkable a series of nerve injuries. . . . Nowhere were these cases described at length in textbooks and except in a single untranslated French book, their treatment was passed over in silence.'

He described causalgia in this way:

'It is a form of suffering as yet undescribed and so frequent and terrible as to demand from us the fullest description. . . . As a rule the burning arises later during the healing of the wound. . . . It's favourite site is the foot or hand. . . . The part itself becomes exquisitely hyperaesthetic, so that a touch or a tap of the finger increases the pain. Exposure to the air is avoided by the patient with a care which seems absurd, and most of the bad cases keep the hand constantly wet, finding relief in the moisture rather than in the coolness of the application. Two of the sufferers carried a bottle of water and a sponge, and never permitted the part to become dry for a moment. . . . The temper changes and grows irritable, the face becomes anxious and has a look of weariness and suffering. . . . The rattling of a newspaper, a breath of air, another's step across the ward, the vibrations caused by a military band, or the shock of the feet in walking, give rise to increase of pain. . . . In two cases the men found some ease through pouring water into their boots.'

He stressed that 'its intensity varies from the most trivial burning to a state of torture than can hardly be credited'. Some modern authors speak of minor and major causalgia. As in the lightning pains of tabes it is the character of the pain rather than its intensity which is peculiar. It is exceptional for the patient to deny that the pain has a burning quality.

It is interesting to note that in the same year, 1864, Sir James Paget (1814–1899) described this symptom after nerve injury in a clinical lecture entitled 'Some cases of local paralysis'. He wrote:

'In well marked cases the fingers which are affected are usually tapering, smooth, hairless, almost void of wrinkles, glossy, pink or ruddy, or blotched as if with permanent chilblains. They are commonly also very painful, especially on motion and pain often extends from them up the arm. In most of the cases this condition of the fingers is attended with very distinct neuralgia both in them and in the whole arm. . . . distressing and hardly manageable pain and disability.'

Causalgia is an exceptionally rare complication of a complete nerve injury; it is in partial nerve lesions that the syndrome develops. Its incidence is low, between 2 and 5 per cent. of all nerve injuries. It is most commonly encountered in lesions of the median and tibial nerves. It usually appears within the first 24 hours of the injury, the pain is severe, spontaneous, persistent, usually possessed of a burning quality and invariably aggravated by physical and emotional stimuli. The pain may spread beyond the territory of the injured nerve. It is commonly felt in the palm of the hand and the fingers and in the sole of the foot and the toes. Nevertheless it seldom prevents sleep. It persists for periods varying from a few months to a year or more. Improvement is slow and in some cases the pain persists for years. Weir Mitchell's son (Dr. J. K. Mitchell) studied many of his father's original patients and found some, 20 years later, still suffering from pain.

Vasomotor and trophic changes are common but not invariable. Immobility, resulting from the pain, is probably responsible for much of the smooth shiny skin, stiff joints and wasted muscles and finger pulps. Sometimes the affected hand or foot is warm and excessively moist. Examination of the part is resisted owing to apparent hyperaesthesia and hyperalgesia. However, if the confidence of the patient can be won, this apparent superficial hypersensitivity may fade and examination usually reveals impairment of sensibility, varying in degree according to the severity of the nerve lesion. Sympathectomy abolishes the hypersensitive state so that the painful sensations cannot be primarily due to the lesion of the somatic nerve fibres. Examination of motor function is beset with similar difficulties because movement provokes pain. There may be an intense osteoporosis consequent on the immobility of the affected part.

The general health of a patient with causalgia suffers considerably. There is usually loss of weight and appetite and the patient becomes irritable, withdrawn and depressed. The intense physical suffering is mirrored in the face. Inevitably, psychoneurotic factors are suspected, but there is no evidence that they play an important part. The disability is physical. Its aetiology is obscure. Although causalgia may follow injury to any peripheral nerve, the susceptibility of the median and tibial nerves is curious. These nerves carry most of the sympathetic fibres to the hand and foot and sympathectomy usually gives marked relief of pain in most cases. It is thought that as a result of the nerve lesion an artificial synapse is established between the sympathetic and somatic afferent nerve fibres. There is experimental evidence that electrical stimulation of an anterior root causes impulses to be transmitted to the sensory fibres in a crushed region of the nerve. Descending impulses are shunted to the sensory fibres and thus, returning to the spinal cord, give rise to the sensation of pain. Histological examination at the site of nerve lesions has shown that there are no changes which are peculiar to the causalgic state. Why causalgia is so rare in complete nerve lesions and after limb amputations is not understood.

THE PHANTOM LIMB

A phantom is a natural and almost inevitable sequel to amputation. It is not, really, a pathological disturbance. It should be regarded as a natural phenomenon characterized by the persistence of the missing part in consciousness. It is a positive sensation, usually described as numbness or tingling, which is not painful and which, occurring at first spontaneously, may also be induced by conscious thought.

Phantom limbs are very rarely encountered in congenitally limbless infants. They have not been described in the 'thalidomide babies'. Amputations in early life are not followed by phantom limbs; they are rare below the age of 6 years. From the age of 15 years and upwards they are an almost invariable phenomenon. They are seen in amputation of a limb and in injuries to spinal nerve roots and plexuses. They may be experienced in cases of traumatic paraplegia. Following amputation the phantom appears as soon as the patient regains consciousness. In paraplegia there is some delay. A phantom may last a few months or persist for 20 or 30 years. A cerebral lesion, such as a stroke, may abolish a phantom limb.

In the ordinary amputation phantom the limb usually tingles or 'feels asleep' but quite often the sensations are unnatural and described as 'vibrating, gripping, clenching or clutching'. Although these sensations may not be natural, they are not usually painful. The form of the phantom is not usually that of the whole of the missing limb; there are usually gaps in the phantom which cannot be felt. Peripheral parts of the limb persist more often than the proximal. Upper limb phantoms are more enduring than those of the lower limb. In the hand, the thumb and index are most obvious and persisting. In the foot it is the great toe which is most often felt. It thus appears that the phantom tends to consist primarily of those parts which have the most extensive representation in the cerebral cortex.

As time passes the phantom tends to weaken and the digits gradually approach the stump, the so-called 'telescoping' phenomenon. There is gradual shrinkage of the gap between peripheral and proximal parts of the limb, until finally the digits of the phantom may sink into the stump.

There may be illusions of movement in a phantom, more frequently those of adduction than abduction. Flexor movements predominate over extensor. In the upper limb the phantom hand may be clenched but not opened. In the foot flexion of the toes but not extension may be possible. In the phantom limbs of paraplegia the phantom coincides with the paralysed limbs. In the phantom of an amputated limb the patient may feel that the phantom can penetrate a solid object without any sensation of touch. For example, the lower limb phantom may hang through the mattress of the bed. After cervical root avulsion and lesions of the brachial plexus, the posture and illusion of movements of the phantom arm are much like those which occur following amputation. There is fading, diminution in size and telescoping of the phantom.

Pain in a phantom limb may be completely absent, but, rarely, it can be disagreeable and severe. It does not usually possess the burning qualities of causalgia and it is usually associated with distorted attitudes and involuntary spasmodic movements of the phantom. Operations on the stump and sympathectomy usually only provide transient relief. There is a strong suspicion that persisting pain in an amputated limb is psychologically determined. From time to time it has been suggested that the circumstances under which a limb was avulsed or amputated plays some part in the subsequent clinical history. But the role of the last moment of life of the limb is probably a popular misconception. This is not to deny that emotional factors involved in the loss of a limb or in the circumstances of amputation may not affect the individual. We may think of the phantom limb as a disturbance of the 'body scheme'. There is grief as well as physical loss. This was well described by Charles Lindbergh while reminiscing about his family as he flew the Atlantic. His grandfather injured one arm in a sawmill and it was amputated 3 days later. 'Lying in his bed in great pain he demanded to see his left arm before it was buried in the garden. It was brought to him in a small rough-board coffin. Taking the fingers in those of his right hand, he said slowly in broken English "you have been a good friend to me for 50 years. But you can't be with me any more. So good-bye, good-bye, my friend".'

The Phantom Limb

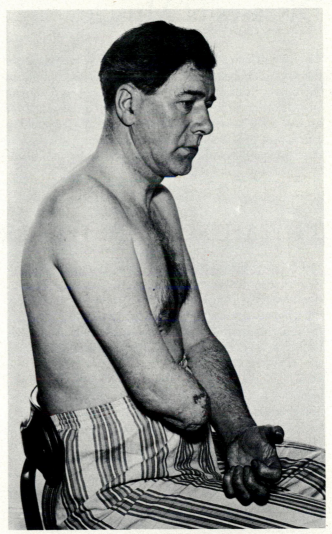

320. Phantom limb pain
The patient is indicating with his left hand the position of the painful phantom hand on the right side. He described it 'as like a vice squeezing the hand and the fingers on fire'. Two years after amputation; the 'telescoping' of the phantom hand was still proceeding. He was more acutely aware of the palm, thumb and index than of the remainder of the hand; he did not feel a wrist and there was a gap between the phantom and stump.

5 THE MUSCLES

Diseases of Muscles

The two principal types of primary muscle disease are the muscular dystrophies and polymyositis. The term 'myopathy' can of course be rightly used to designate any disorder in which the structure or function of muscle tissue is involved. The muscular dystrophies are a group of genetically determined, primary, degenerative myopathies; they may be clinically classified.

Polymyositis, on the other hand, is less clearly defined.

In addition there is a group of disorders which may be classified as metabolic myopathies—familial periodic paralysis, paroxysmal myoglobinuria, McArdle's syndrome and the so-called endocrine myopathies—thyrotoxic myopathy and the myopathy of Cushing's syndrome and Addison's disease.

THE MUSCULAR DYSTROPHIES

The muscular dystrophies are a group of heredofamilial disorders characterized by progressive degeneration of certain groups of muscles. There is a genetically determined, primary, degenerative myopathy. There is no abnormality in the nervous system itself. A number of clinical types have been distinguished according to the age of onset, the group of muscles first affected, the presence or absence of pseudohypertrophy, and the prominence of the hereditary factor. No rational scientific method of classification has yet been devised and eponymous titles are still used for the three principal varieties. These are: (1) the Duchenne pseudohypertrophic type (1868); (2) the limb girdle juvenile type of Erb (1884); and (3) the facioscapulohumeral type of Landouzy and Dejerine (1885). There is also a variety associated with myotonia (dystrophia myotonica) and another which is practically confined to the ocular muscles (ocular myopathy).

Their general characteristics include the presence of a family history, early age of onset, symmetrical involvement of proximal rather than distal muscles, disproportionate weakness as compared with the size of the muscle, and the presence of pseudohypertrophy in certain cases. There is no fasciculation nor wasting of subcutaneous fat—as in motor neurone disease. In general the earlier the development of the dystrophy the more rapid its progress. Severe forms of muscular dystrophy tend to have a sex-linked recessive mode of inheritance: milder forms may be due to a sex-linked recessive, an autosomal recessive, or an autosomal dominant mode of transmission.

The principal symptom in primary myopathy is weakness; the commonest signs are muscular atrophy and hypertrophy. Assistance in distinguishing whether muscular weakness and wasting are due to primary muscle disease or whether they are secondary to denervation may be obtained from electromyography, serum enzyme estimations and muscle biopsy. These studies also sometimes enable one to detect that apparently unaffected members of the family are, in fact, carriers of the disease.

In the Duchenne type of muscular dystrophy, the female carrier of the gene may transmit the disorder to 50 per cent. of her sons, and 50 per cent. of her daughters will themselves be carriers. If carriers can be identified, appropriate advice can be given. The identification of carriers in the other forms of muscular dystrophy is more difficult.

Of late there have been suggestions that the essential lesion in muscular dystrophies is not primarily myopathic but neuropathic. The low level of intelligence of many patients, the presence of E.E.G. abnormalities and the neuronal heterotopias seen in the brains of some patients have been taken to indicate the possibility of a lesion within the central nervous system. There are forms of dystrophy in mice and hens which seem to be neuropathic in nature. It is postulated that in human muscular dystrophy some defect in the motor neurones leads to the failure of some neuronal trophic factor necessary for the normal maintenance of muscle fibres.

The Pseudohypertrophic Type (Duchenne)

This occurs almost exclusively in young boys, beginning in the third or fourth year of life and steadily progressing. The child is observed to be clumsy, he falls frequently and has difficulty in rising. Although he looks sturdy the parents will say that he cannot jump or skip about with other children and has considerable difficulty in climbing stairs. At school it is soon appreciated that games and gymnasium classes are beyond him. His face is not affected, his speech and intelligence are usually normal, and he has no difficulty in using his hands.

Visible enlargement of some muscles is usually present when he is 5 or 6 years of age. It is most commonly seen in the buttocks and calves and infraspinati. Meanwhile other muscles are wasting, notably the latissimus dorsi and the lower part of the pectoralis major. The child stands with his legs apart, his abdomen thrust out in front of him and his shoulders thrown back, so that there is an accentuated lumbar lordosis. The latter may not be seen when he is sitting or lying. He walks with a waddling gait, his trunk moving from side to side and at each step his toes touching the ground before the heel. The mother will say 'he walks on his toes'. This gait is similar to that seen in bilateral congenital dislocation of the hip.

In rising from a chair he aids himself by pushing down on his own thighs or on the chair. Weakness of the proximal muscles of the thighs and of the glutei makes climbing stairs laborious. In rising from the supine position the child carries out a series of striking and well known manoeuvres. He cannot sit up in the normal manner and has first to turn over on his stomach. He lifts his head and chest with his arms and then gathers his knees underneath him. Raising his buttocks slowly he then places his hands on his knees and literally climbs up his thighs. The final erect posture is achieved with a jerk backwards and, if he is being watched, a grin. Minor variations of this sequence are common.

He is usually unable to walk by the time he is 10 years of age and is confined to a wheel chair. Progressive atrophy and shortening of muscles leads to flexion of the limbs, spinal curvature and talipes equinus. The deep reflexes disappear but sensation remains unaltered and there is no sphincter involvement. Death from respiratory infection or cardiac failure is common at about the twentieth year.

In some families the disease appears to start later and runs a slower course, so that the patient may survive into middle life. The mode of inheritance varies. A family history may not always be obtained, but usually several children are affected in each generation. In the classical form the disease is transmitted by a sex-linked recessive mechanism, transmitted by the females and manifest in the males. In the more benign form, and in the majority of cases which occur in females, inheritance appears to be by an autosomal recessive mechanism.

The Duchenne Type

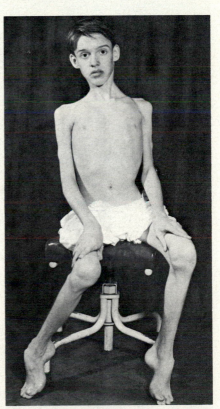

321. Muscular dystrophy: Duchenne type
Advanced stage of the disease in a boy of 17. Onset at 3, unable to walk in his twelfth year. Profound wasting of muscles of shoulder and pelvic girdles and proximal muscles of limbs. Lordosis and talipes. One brother similarly affected.

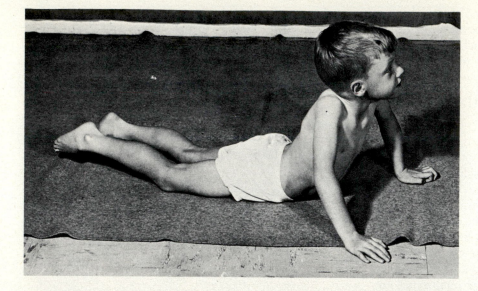

322. The Duchenne type of pseudo-hypertrophic muscular dystrophy Negative family history. Age 5; showing the characteristic method of rising from the floor. Observed to have difficulty in pulling himself up in the cot as an infant; did not start to walk until 20 months; disinclined to run. Diagnosis established when 3 years of age.

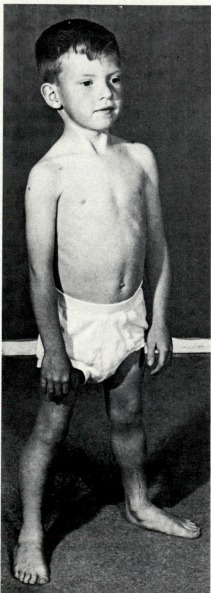

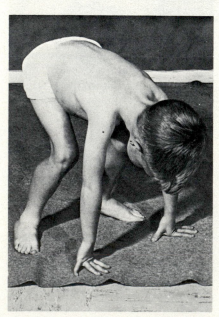

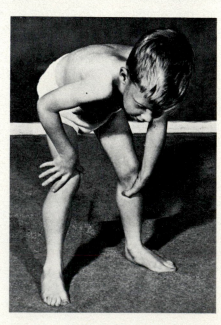

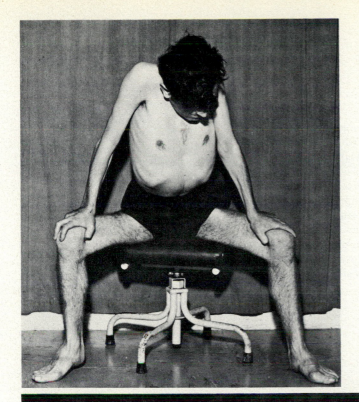
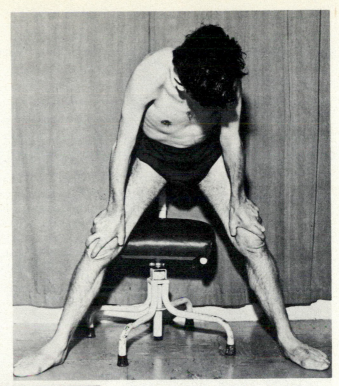

323. Muscular dystrophy: Duchenne type △

Age 24. One of three affected brothers. Mother with Addison's disease. Onset at 9 years of age; played football until 13 years of age. Earliest complaint was of difficulty in mounting stairs, jumping and playing games. Parents had noticed no abnormality in infancy or early childhood. Still able to work in a sheltered workshop. Note method of rising from a chair. Calves still fat and ankle jerks brisk.

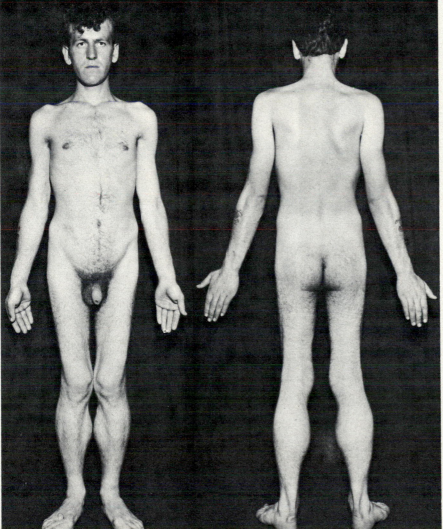

324. Muscular dystrophy: Duchenne type (brother of above patient) ◁

Age 23. Played football until the age of 14. No history of weakness until the age of 9 or 10 years. The first sign of trouble was when he repeatedly fell off his bicycle and found it difficult to pedal up hill. Several hospital admissions for bouts of vomiting due to acute gastric dilatation. This is a not uncommon symptom in this disease, but its explanation is unknown. Note wasting of buttocks and thighs and pseudohypertrophy of calf muscles.

The Duchenne Type

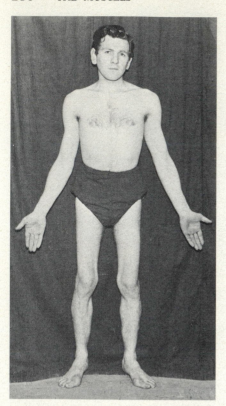

325. Muscular dystrophy: Duchenne type (brother of the two patients shown in Figs. 323, 324)
Age 21. Doing heavy labouring work in a paper mill; never previously examined. Upper limbs strong but probable early weakness about the shoulder girdles. Wasted thighs with characteristic waddling gait, pseudohypertrophy of the calf muscles and loss of knee jerks. Minimizes his disability and will shortly marry.

The Limb Girdle Type

326. Muscular dystrophy
Two brothers, aged 21 and 23 respectively, with profound weakness of pelvic girdle and thigh muscles and moderate weakness of shoulder girdle muscles. Distal power in the limbs excellent; both patients thought that their calves had increased in size during adolescence. Both had very high serum creatine–phosphokinase levels. It is often difficult to distinguish a limb girdle dystrophy of the Erb type from the benign X-linked Becker type. In the limb girdle, autosomal recessive type, serum enzymes are usually normal or only slightly raised. The family history here was compatible with either type; no consanguinity. The brothers have 3 normal children: 2 boys and 1 girl. The boys should remain healthy, but the daughter will be a carrier if this is an X-linked disorder.

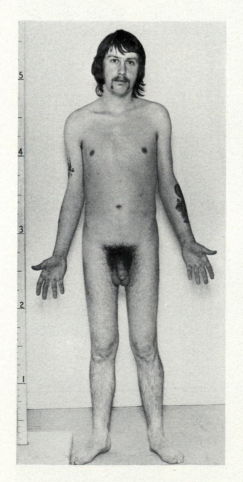

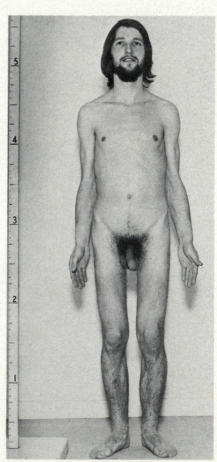

The Limb Girdle Type (Erb)

This is a less serious form of muscular dystrophy which may affect shoulder girdle or pelvic girdle. It can affect either sex and begin at any age, but usually does so in the second decade. It is inherited by an autosomal recessive mechanism. Pseudohypertrophy is less common, it progresses more slowly and atrophy may be confined to a group of muscles in either girdle for many years. The upper limbs tend to be affected before the lower limbs, but there is considerable variation from one family group to another. On the whole a greater degree of disability ensues when the pelvic girdle is first affected.

In both groups there is a tendency for some muscles to suffer early and for others to be spared. In the upper limbs the lower part of the pectoralis major, the latissimus dorsi, trapezius and rhomboids, and the serratus magnus are usually affected. The deltoid and spinati usually escape. Spinal and abdominal muscles may be involved and in the lower limbs the glutei, the flexors of the hip and the extensors of the knee are usually atrophied. The muscles below the elbows and knees tend to escape.

When the disease begins in childhood, deterioration is very slow; there may be little actual disability even until middle life. In other cases the onset may be delayed until middle age. Quite frequently the disease appears to become arrested or at least it remains confined to a restricted group of muscles.

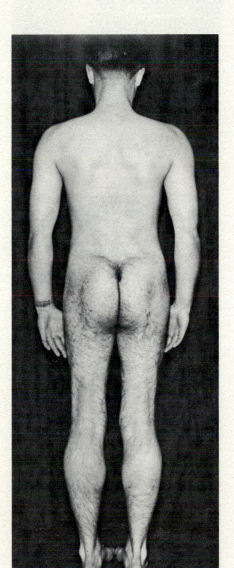

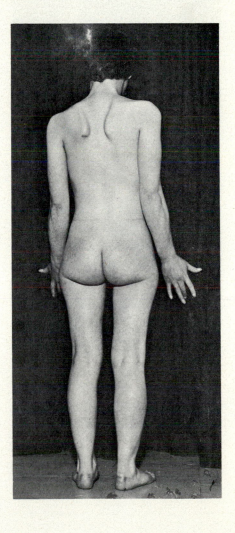

327. Muscular dystrophy; limb girdle type (pelvic) ◁
Age 20. Negative family history. Two year history. Played football until 16, tennis until 19. Gradual onset of weakness of the thigh muscles. Early weakness of shoulder girdle muscles. Disability slight, mainly in climbing stairs; working as a carpenter. Note thin thigh muscles and fat calves. Pseudohypertrophy of deltoid muscles which were weak; early weakness and wasting of latissimus dorsi muscles.

The Limb Girdle Type

328. Muscular dystrophy: limb girdle type (shoulder, followed by pelvic girdle weakness) ▷
Age 30. Drooping of left shoulder at 13; weakness of right shoulder at 19. Difficulty in mounting steps at 20. Very slowly progressive. Married with children and still able to do housework. Moderate weakness of all shoulder girdle muscles; profound weakness of glutei and muscles of thighs.

329a

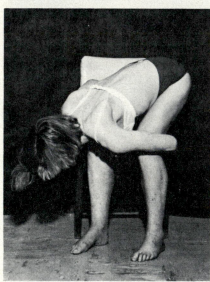

329b

The Limb Girdle Type

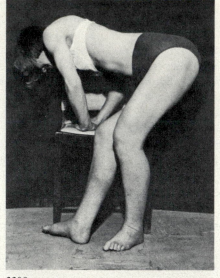

329c

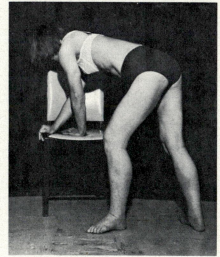

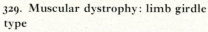

329d

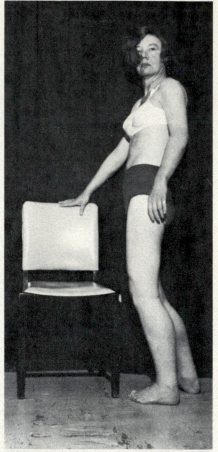

329e

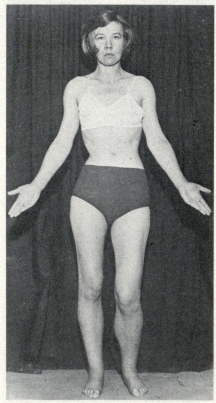

329f

329. Muscular dystrophy: limb girdle type

Age 42 years. Onset of leg weakness in mid teens. Bulky calves noted in childhood, waddling gait at 18, proximal upper limb weakness at 20. Note severe weakness of hip extensors and great diffculty in rising from chair as a result of atrophy of the posterior spinal muscles. 'Wasp' waist; pseudohypertrophy of calves.

Parents normal, no brothers, one affected sister. This patient, first seen by the author when she was 39, thought she had some muscular weakness of 4 or 5 years' duration. An amateur ballet dancer until aged 29. Shoulder girdle and limb girdle dystrophy with pseudohypertrophy of calves. Four children (three sons aged 15, 13 and 4 years, one daughter aged 8 years), all healthy so far.

The Limb Girdle Type

330. Muscular dystrophy: limb girdle type (pelvic and shoulder girdles) ▷
Age 40. Negative family history. Three year history of progressive weakness of muscles of thighs and shoulders, with wasting of calves, thighs and upper arms. Note pseudohypertrophy of deltoids, winging of the scapulae and wasting of lower portion of pectoralis major.

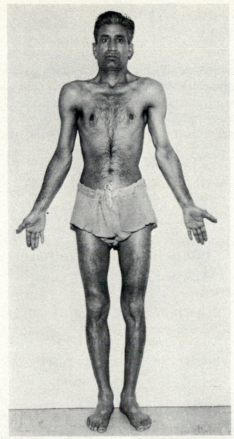
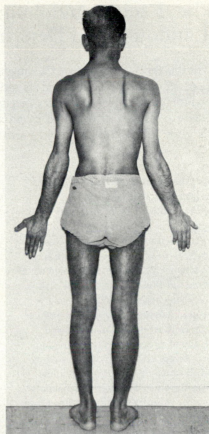

331. Muscular dystrophy: limb girdle type (scapulohumeral form: Erb) ▽
Age 29. Negative family history. Onset at 13 years of age. The first symptom was difficulty in brushing her hair; slowly progressive and in the past 2 years early weakness of thigh muscles. Note sloping shoulders and raised scapulae at rest with 'winging' on forward raising of the upper limbs.

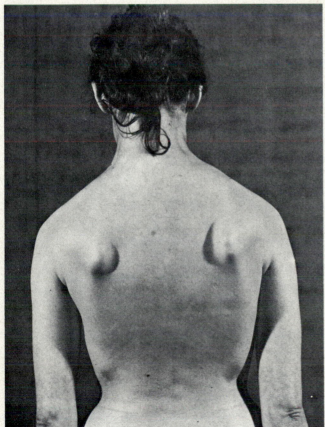
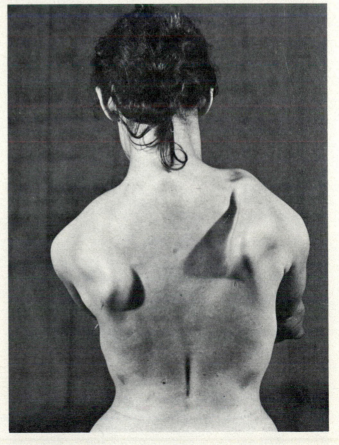

The Facioscapulohumeral Type (Landouzy and Dejerine)

In this form of the disease the muscles that are affected are mainly those of the face and shoulder girdles. As with the limb girdle types, either sex may be affected and the disease is usually transmitted by an autosomal dominant gene. Mild and apparently arrested forms of the disease may be encountered. The majority of patients are less disabled than in the limb girdle type. The involvement of the facial muscles gives to the patient a dull, unlined, expressionless face with lips that are usually open and slack. The movements of smiling, whistling and closing the eyes are impaired. Speech may be affected because of the difficulty in the articulation of labial consonants. The disease is one of the causes of the 'myopathic facies'.

332. Muscular dystrophy: facio-scapulohumeral type ▽
Age 39. Mother similarly affected but lived until she was 70 years of age. Two nephews with winged scapulae. Onset of muscular weakness in early twenties. Moderately disabled. Said he could never blow a wind instrument or use a pea-shooter in childhood. Weakness of eye closure; cannot puff his cheeks. Still no lower limb weakness. Weakness and wasting of trapezii, pectorals, latissimus dorsi, biceps and triceps. Note winging and elevation of right scapula and the wasp-like waist. Several hospital admissions for episodes of abdominal pain and vomiting. No cause found but probably due to episodes of acute gastric dilatation.

Facioscapulohumeral Type

333. Muscular dystrophy: facio-scapulohumeral type ▷
Onset of the disease at the age of 9 with weakness of shoulder girdle muscles. He had never been able to whistle, his smile was always 'funny' and he could not puff out his cheeks. In (a) and (b) he was 15 years of age. In (c), (d), (e) and (f) he was 28 years of age. In (c) he is trying to close his eyes and bare his teeth. Note the open mouth, the pouting 'tapir' lips (b) and (d), the expressionless face, and (e) and (f) the profound wasting of the muscles of the thorax with winging of the scapulae, atrophy of the pectorals and latissimus dorsi and the muscles of the upper arms. Lordosis and the 'wasp-like' waist. One maternal uncle affected.

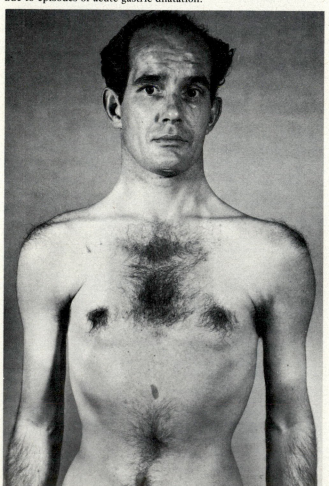

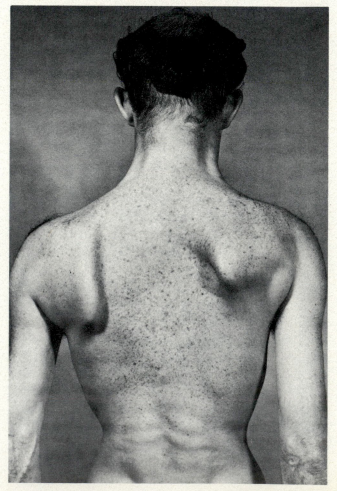

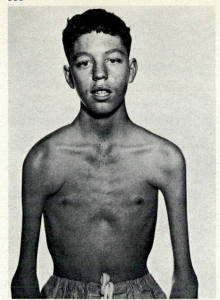

333a

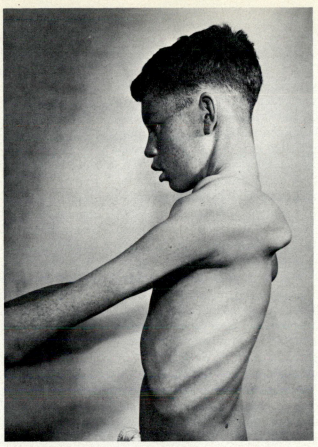

333b

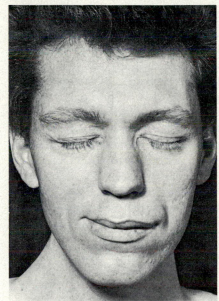

333c

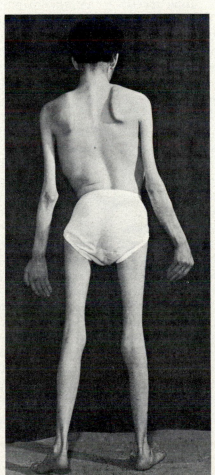

333e

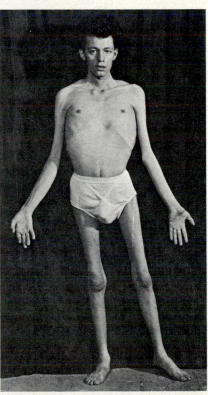

333f

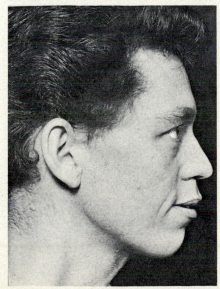

333d

Differential Diagnosis

Although there is general recognition of the classification of muscular dystrophies into three main types—Duchenne, limb girdle and facioscapulohumeral—the main difficulty in clinical practice is that family histories are often unknown or incomplete and sporadic cases are common. Studies of the 'floppy infant' have shown that certain old terms are better dropped, for example amyotonia congenita and benign congenital hypotonia. These are descriptive of symptoms and do not represent definable diseases.

The Duchenne type of muscular dystrophy is characteristically seen in males, being inherited as a sex-linked recessive factor. From time to time it has been suspected that the disease might occur in young girls, but investigations have always revealed certain differences in the clinical pattern, in the enzyme pattern, or in the electromyographic or histological changes. In these female cases male sibs are never affected, so that for the present the diagnosis of Duchenne type muscular dystrophy should be confined to the male sex.

Cardiac muscle involvement is common in the Duchenne type and uncommon in the other two types. Serum enzyme levels are markedly increased in the Duchenne type but may be normal in the others.

In infancy and early childhood there is a variety of congenital myopathies in which biopsy, using special techniques, is essential for diagnosis. These disorders are often familial but are not necessarily progressive, and their classification is determined by certain ultramicroscopic features. Examples are central core disease, nemaline myopathy and myotubular myopathy. In infants we also find examples of glycogen storage disease which may affect muscles. There are various varieties of this.

Muscular atrophy in childhood may be of spinal origin and there are fatal and benign forms. Because some of them so closely resemble muscular dystrophies, they are sometimes referred to as 'pseudomyopathic spinal muscular atrophy'. In one variety the onset is soon after birth and the disease is fatal within two years. In a second type the onset is later and the patient may survive for a decade. It is in a third variety, with onset during the first few years of life and a slow progression, that muscular dystrophy may be suspected. The presence of tremors or fasciculation should suggest a neuropathic process, but estimation of serum enzyme levels, electromyographic abnormalities and even muscle biopsy studies do not always enable one to establish whether the process is myopathic or neuropathic. This is not just an academic exercise, because whereas the Duchenne type of myopathy is invariably progressive and fatal, some forms of spinal muscular atrophy may undergo temporary or even prolonged arrest and thus have a much better prognosis. There are obvious implications for genetic counselling.

Dystrophia Myotonica

This is a type of heredofamilial disorder which gives rise to selective atrophy of muscles, myotonia and various other lesions such as cataract, alopecia, testicular atrophy and premature senility. Males are more commonly affected than females and the disease is thought to be transmitted by an autosomal dominant gene. Various members of the family may be affected in a remarkably varying degree. Presenile cataracts may have been the sole indication of the disorder in preceding generations.

Symptoms usually appear in the twenties and the onset and progress is slow and insidious. Myotonia, defective relaxation of a muscle after use, is often the first symptom. It is usually first noticed in the upper limbs. The workman has difficulty in handling his tools and the housewife her household appliances. Failure to relax the grip prolongs a handshake, delays the putting down of an object and renders rifle drill impossible for the recruit. Myotonia may interfere with chewing movements and when it develops in the lower limbs it may cause the patient to stumble and fall inexplicably. Myotonia may be present for years before there is any muscular wasting or other manifestation of the disorder. It is best recognized by the failure to disengage the hand on handshaking. It varies greatly in degree and distribution and it fluctuates under the influence of fatigue, emotion and cold. The slow relaxation of myotonic muscles may be seen on percussion, for example, of the muscles of the thumb or tongue. There is a slow filling-in of the dimple or depression induced by the percussion hammer. Muscular atrophy is most conspicuous in the facial muscles and the sternomastoids. Again we have the sad, listless myopathic facies which, with the baldness and scraggy neck give a most characteristic appearance. Sooner or later the muscular wasting involves the upper and lower limbs; it is usually symmetrical and tends to involve the anterior tibial group, the thighs and the muscles of the forearms. The deep reflexes are diminished or lost, but sensation remains unaltered.

No lesion within the nervous system has yet been described, but I think many patients show some deterioration of intellect or personality. There may be a decline of achievement in successive generations of an affected family. The endocrine failure may lead to childless marriages and impotence. Frequently the presence of cataract is not suspected as there is no visual complaint. It tends to develop at an increasingly early age in succeeding generations.

The heart is frequently involved in this disease. A small pulse, a relatively low blood pressure, and splitting of the first heart sound in the mitral area are common clinical findings. The electrocardiogram may reveal low P waves and prolongation of the P–R interval. Sudden death is not uncommon.

Dystrophia Myotonica

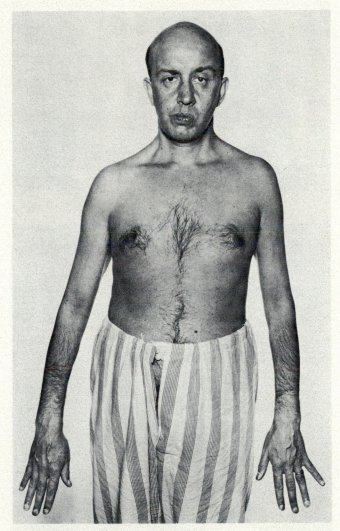

334. Dystrophia myotonica
Age 33. Sudden episodes of tripping, stumbling and falling. A schoolteacher who had difficulty in writing on the blackboard and putting down his chalk. Diffuse myotonia. Note baldness, left ptosis and the facial asymmetry. Weakness of right deltoid and wasting of posterior cervical muscles.

When it presents in infancy or childhood the disease may go unrecognized, since there may only be some generalized hypotonia, poor sucking and swallowing, and feeble intellect. Delay in opening the eyes after crying has been described. In addition to the characteristic electromyogram and the histological changes in the muscles, there may be a low level of IgG.

It has been found that in early onset dystrophia myotonica the mother is nearly always the affected parent. As the disease is generally considered to show simple autosomal dominant inheritance, one would expect a 1/1 sex ratio of affected parents. It has been suggested that there may be intra-uterine factors at work to produce the distinctive features of the early onset type of the disease. As in the pure muscular dystrophies, early detection and genetic counselling are important. Unaffected relatives may have myotonia detected only on electromyography, and cataracts detected only on slit lamp examination. But these and other features are not pathognomonic of the disease, and efforts have turned to studies of genetic linkage in an attempt to recognize individuals carrying the abnormal gene. This gene has been found closely linked to the gene responsible for the secretion of ABH blood group substances in saliva and other body fluids. These substances can be recognized in the amniotic fluid as early as the ninth week of gestation. A firm antenatal diagnosis may then allow selective abortion.

Dystrophia myotonica must be distinguished from the more benign disorder of myotonia congenita (Thomsen's disease). Thomsen, a Danish physician who described the disease in 1876 as he had observed it in himself and in five generations of his family, is said to have written his treatise on the subject to convince the Prussian occupiers of Denmark that his son suffered from the disease and was unfit for military service. The cardinal feature is a stiffness of the muscles after resting which tends to improve with exercise. This may be aggravated by cold weather. The myotonia is more widespread than in dystrophia myotonica and often affects the grip and ocular movements. Percussion myotonia may be observed on the thenar eminence, the deltoid or the tongue. There may be some degree of diffuse muscular hypertrophy. The myotonia tends to subside with age, and the majority of patients learn to avoid circumstances likely to provoke any serious or disabling myotonia.

The term paramyotonia congenita is used to describe a condition which is characterized by myotonia aggravated by exposure to cold but with episodes of generalized muscular weakness. These episodes are similar to those which occur in familial periodic paralysis and are often accompanied by a rise in serum potassium. In other cases the serum potassium falls or remains unchanged.

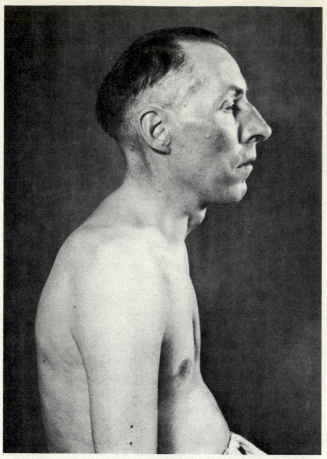

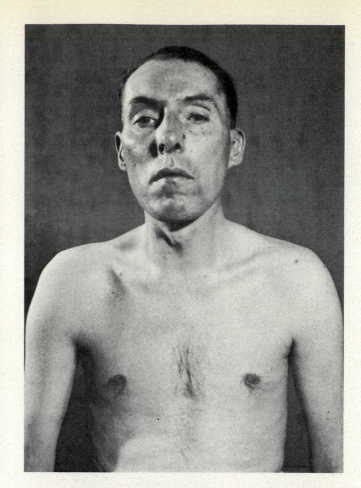

335. **Dystrophia myotonica** △

Dystrophia Myotonica

335. **Dystrophia myotonica** △
Age 34; presenting symptom, impotence. Married 7 years, no children. No other complaints but admitted to clumsiness of limbs. He could not understand why he could never throw a dart; the quick separation of index and thumb was impossible. Typical myopathic facies with ptosis, drooping mouth and sad, lifeless expression. Prominent larynx, atrophic posterior cervical muscles and sternomastoids.

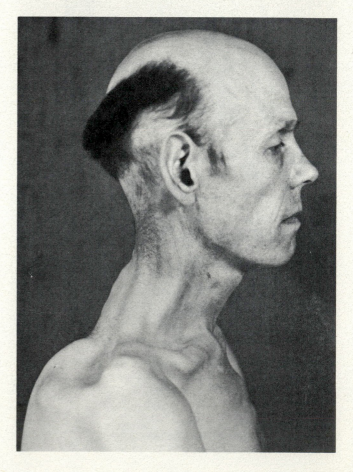

336. **Dystrophia myotonica** ▷
Age 51. Weakness, wasting and clumsiness of the muscles of the distal portions of the extremities and of the neck and face. He died suddenly in bed in hospital during investigation of his neurological disorder. Characteristic changes in the electrocardiogram (low voltage P wave; prolonged P–R interval; notched QRS). The heart is often involved in dystrophia myotonica. There is often a small pulse, a low blood pressure, a splitting of the first heart sound in the mitral area. The heart is usually normal in size. These cardiac changes may not be present when the neurological features of the disease are already established.

Dystrophia Myotonica

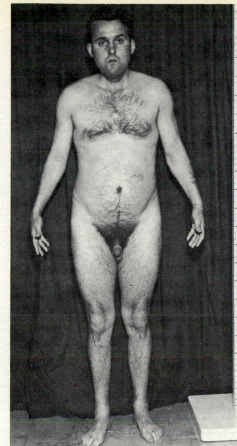

337. Dystrophia myotonica ▷
Age 30. Presenting symptoms were impotence and weakness of arms and legs. The first symptom occurred at the age of 19 when he found that he could not relax his grip on a tankard of beer; this often led to ribald comment. Serving in the Army at the time his clumsy rifle drill drew appropriate remarks from his superiors. Note the drooping mouth, the 'undercut' jaw, the small scrotum, the wasting of the distal muscles of the forearms and lower limbs.

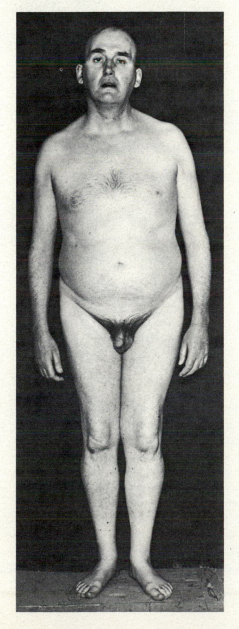

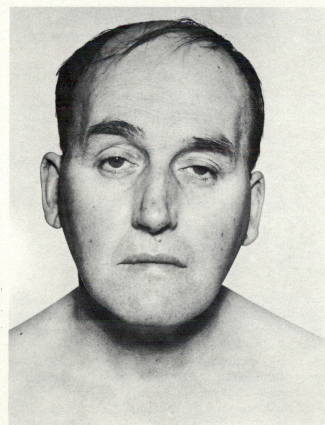

338. Dystrophia myotonica
Age 44. Frontal baldness in early twenties. Ten year history of failure to relax his grip. Three year history of difficulty in mounting steps. Playing Rugby until age 35. Maternal aunt with cataract. Semi-literate, low nasal voice. Absent knee and ankle jerks. Note wasting of left sternomastoid, bilateral ptosis, myopathic facies, small scrotum.

Dystrophia Myotonica

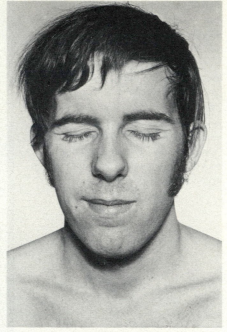

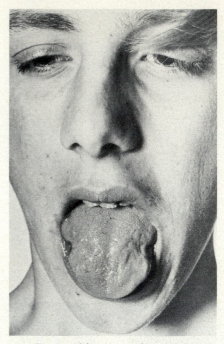

339. Dystrophia myotonica
Age 20. Athletic son of patient shown in
Fig. 337 (now aged 45 and very disabled)
who recently found himself 'slow off the
mark and in warming up' at football.
Several falls. He had diffuse myotonia,
but strong musculature and normal
reflexes. He has difficulty in opening
his eyes after firm closure.

340. Dystrophia myotonica
Age 15. 'Stiff hands' his only complaint.
Myopathic facies: dull expression, ptosis,
loose mouth. Percussion myotonia of the
tongue. Slowness in relaxing a handgrip.
The patient's father is completely disabled
with progressive dementia, paralysis and
diffuse myotonia. All of his 6 children
have the disease.

THYROTOXIC MYOPATHY

Muscular weakness is a common complaint in thyrotoxicosis, but it rarely dominates the clinical picture. In
acute thyrotoxic myopathy, a condition which must be
very rare, there is profound widespread muscular weakness sometimes complicated by respiratory and bulbar
paralysis. Fasciculation is said to occur and there may
be delirium and coma. Coincidental myasthenia gravis
is responsible for some of these cases and the existence
of the pure syndrome remains questionable. We are on
firmer ground in the case of *chronic* thyrotoxic myopathy. Many of the patients are elderly men in whom the
evidence of thyrotoxicosis may be slight. Proximal limb
muscles suffer most and fasciculation may be present.
The patient may not look ill despite the evident loss of
weight and muscular atrophy, in this respect differing
from the patient with carcinomatous neuromyopathy.
This form of chronic myopathy is most likely to be encountered when the thyrotoxicosis has passed unrecognized for some years. Chronic bulbar involvement
may suggest the presence of motor neurone disease.
The presence of auricular fibrillation in an elderly person with proximal limb weakness should raise the question of thyrotoxicosis. The electromyogram is said to be
commonly abnormal but muscle biopsy is unhelpful.

POLYMYOSITIS

The term polymyositis encompasses a group of muscular disorders in which weakness and wasting are accompanied by histological changes of degeneration and inflammation. The disorder may be acute, subacute or chronic in its development. It occurs in all age groups and it may be associated with dermatitis, arthritis, collagen diseases and malignancy. In the neurological clinic the type most often encountered is the chronic form occurring in middle or late life and without apparent association with the above-mentioned conditions. Muscular involvement tends to be asymmetrical and patchy, but usually affects the proximal muscles of the limbs. Complaints of pain and the finding of tenderness or hardness of the muscles are inconstant. The weakness is usually first evident in the lower limbs and the patient experiences all those difficulties of movement found in the young person with pelvic girdle dystrophy. Difficulty in rising from a chair, mounting steps, getting out of a bath and such like, usually suggest to the patient the onset of 'rheumatism'. With involvement of the shoulder girdle muscles such activities as pegging clothes on a line, brushing the hair and all those daily activities which require the person to reach upwards are impaired. There is often a complaint of general fatigue, joint pains, cold cyanosed hands, tightness of the chest muscles and although the skin may be normal when examined, there is often a history of transient rashes. Dysphagia is common.

No clear clinical pattern emerges from a study of these cases. There is a wide range of variation in the mode of onset, rate of progress, degree of muscular involvement, the effect on the general health of the patient and in the tendency for remissions and relapses. At one end of the scale is the patient gravely ill with acute dermato-myositis, with fever, rash and weak, tender, painful muscles. By contrast there is the middle-aged or elderly patient in whom the myositis is largely confined to the muscles of the pelvic girdle and thighs, which does not progress and which may fluctuate in a moderate manner for a few years before burning itself out.

When polymyositis is associated with malignant disease, most commonly a pulmonary carcinoma, there is usually progressive deterioration. Menopausal muscular dystrophy is a form of polymyositis.

Many of these patients respond to treatment with steroids, especially if the onset of the disorder has been acute. However, raised serum enzyme levels and the presence of inflammatory changes in muscle biopsy do not necessarily imply that the response will be satisfactory. Conversely, the response to steroid treatment may be surprisingly good when these signs are absent. One has the impression that the inflammatory phase of the disease has often subsided before the diagnosis is made. By then there may be little more to note than a patchy asymmetrical distribution of muscular weakness, with slight persisting pain or tenderness, and perhaps with some limitation of certain movements consequent on shortening of muscles. Evidence of cutaneous involvement may have subsided, but the patient may recall discoloration or oedema of affected areas of skin. There may be a history of mild Raynaud's phenomenon, of transitory joint pains and swelling, or of dryness of the eyes and mouth suggesting deficient lacrimal and salivary secretion as in Sjögren's syndrome.

Polymyositis may be classified into three types: (1) 'uncomplicated' polymyositis; (2) dermatomyositis and polymyositis associated with connective tissue disorders; (3) polymyositis associated with neoplasia.

POLYMYALGIA RHEUMATICA

It is convenient to mention this condition here, although it does not appear to be a primary muscle disorder. It can be readily confused with polymyositis. It is usually seen in middle-aged or elderly people and the principal symptom is of muscular pain. As in myositis the mode of onset and development vary considerably, but pain about the neck, shoulder, buttocks and thighs is invariable. There is often general malaise, muscular tenderness, loss of appetite and loss of weight. The course of the disease varies from case to case, but the majority of patients recover within a few years. An association with cranial arteritis has been claimed and I have seen it follow this disease in one case. The sedimentation rate is usually raised, but electromyography, serum enzyme studies and muscle biopsy are usually normal. There is some evidence that arteritis is the basis of the disorder. It certainly responds to corticosteroid therapy in a very satisfactory manner.

Polymyositis

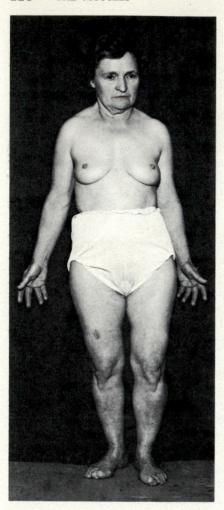

341. Polymyositis ◁

Age 57. Insidious onset with aching pains and weakness of the thighs and calves at the age of 45. Friends commented on her waddling gait. She could not mount steps without using a handrail; descends stairs backwards; could only get out of her bath by first turning over on to her hands and knees. Levers herself out of her chair with her arms. Could not sit up from the supine position. Calf muscles were hard; thigh muscles tender. Elevated sedimentation rate; muscle biopsy of calf normal; biopsy of quadriceps typical of myositis (degeneration and regeneration of muscle fibres; cellular infiltration, fibrosis). Poor response to treatment with corticosteroids.

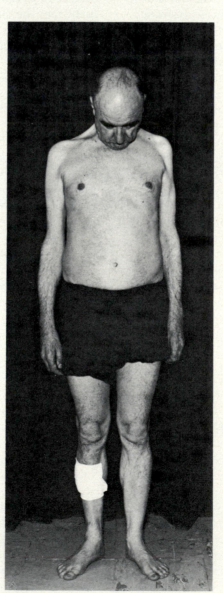

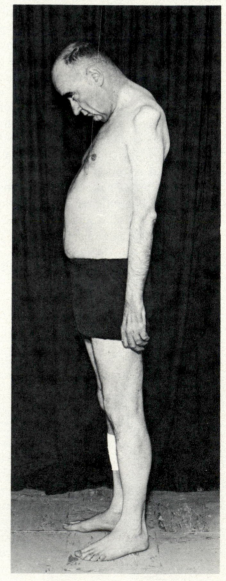

342. Polymyositis ▷

Age 52. Twenty-four-year history; under observation for 17 years. Proximal weakness of the arms, progressive weakness and wasting of the muscles of the neck and shoulder girdles, right foot drop. Relatively static for 12 years and then further weakness of the lower limbs. Profound wasting of the extensor muscles of the neck, shoulder girdles, upper arms, brachioradialis and intrinsic muscles of the hands. Moderate wasting of calf and anterior tibial muscles on the right side. Sensation normal; absent arm reflexes, preserved lower limb reflexes, coarse fasciculation in triceps and deltoid bilaterally. Muscle biopsy favoured myositis rather than myopathy. Electromyography showed denervation in the lower limbs but this may have been due to spondylolisthesis. Raised serum enzymes. A difficult case!

MYASTHENIA GRAVIS

Abnormal fatigability or variable paralysis is the essential feature of this well known and not uncommon disease. It especially affects those muscles innervated by cranial nerves. The ensuing symptoms are attributable to the excessive fatigability of the muscles; they appear after use and improve with rest; they are most marked in the evening and may be absent during the first hours in the morning. One or both eyelids begin to droop. The patient sees double. He is better after a night's rest but the symptoms return. He may find his voice is weaker and his family may comment on its nasal quality. At meal times he finds chewing an effort and may suggest the meat is tough. He complains of his throat because he has to gulp in order to swallow. There may be nasal regurgitation of fluids. Towards the end of a meal he may rest his sagging chin in his hand. The evening immobility of his facies may be the subject of comment and the 'snarling' quality of his smile noted. The young woman may find difficulty in applying lipstick, the man discovers he cannot whistle for his dog.

Although the muscles of the eyes, face, jaw and throat are those first affected, there may also be complaints of general fatigue or of weakness of the limbs. The young girl finds it an effort to brush her hair, the housewife to peg out her clothes on the line, the man may say that shaving is tiring, the typist that her neck is too weak to hold up her head at the end of the day. Generally speaking, the myasthenia is local at first before it becomes generalized, but existing weakness may be aggravated by exercise of a remote group of muscles. For example, in a patient of mine, a masseuse, ptosis was increased by vigorous exercise of the arms. I have also known swimming to induce diplopia. Weakness or hoarseness of the voice, complaint of discomfort and 'soreness' in the throat, and trouble at meal times, may all direct the patient to the laryngologist. If the tonsils happen to be infected they may be removed. Occasionally an upper respiratory tract infection produces an acute exacerbation of weakness and unmasks the disorder. Streptomycin and some related antibiotics, possessing a blocking action on neuromuscular transmission, may gravely aggravate existing paralysis and induce a respiratory crisis.

In a typical case diagnosis is not difficult, but in infancy or in old age or when the weakness mainly affects the muscles of the trunk and pelvic girdle diagnosis may be delayed. In ocular myasthenia ptosis is nearly always present, but it may be unilateral.

The edrophonium chloride (*Tensilon*) or neostigmine bromide (*Prostigmin*) test is not always easy to interpret. In this test a little lid retraction can occur in a normal person. In the chronic stage of ocular myasthenia, there may be little or no improvement in the range of ocular movements after *Prostigmin* or *Tensilon*. Photographs form a useful part of the clinical records. Not infrequently, years later, the diagnosis may be questioned or there may be a remission, so that a photographic record is useful.

Two medical women have played an important role in this disease. Dr. Harriet Edgeworth of Tucson, Arizona, began to suffer from the disease in 1918. Diagnosis was established in 1924 and by 1927 she was helpless. In 1929 while taking an ephedrine preparation for menstrual pain, she experienced remarkable relief from her muscular paralysis. For some years ephedrine remained the only form of treatment. Then in 1934 came the discovery by Dr. Mary Walker of London, that physostigmine had an even more beneficial effect. The exact nature of the defect that exists at the neuromuscular junction remains unknown.

Myasthenic fatigue may also be encountered in some forms of myopathy, in carcinomatous neuromyopathy and in thyrotoxic myopathy. A careful search for pulmonary carcinoma should always be made in the elderly myasthenic who is showing a poor therapeutic response. In primary myasthenia gravis the tendon reflexes are normal or even exaggerated but in the carcinomatous syndromes they are generally diminished.

It must be admitted that the early diagnosis of myasthenia can at times present great difficulty. A neurotic young lady and a zealous house physician can, between them, produce a story that seems classical. In the end an ampoule of distilled water may prove as effective as one of *Prostigmin*. The female myasthenic is often emotionally unstable so that management and nursing present problems.

There is considerable variation in the natural history of this disease. The onset is usually insidious but it may be quite acute. Remissions lasting months or rarely years may occur in some cases, while in others the course of the disease may be progressive and fatal. Onset is usually in the third decade and females are affected twice as commonly as males.

The nature of the essential defect in neuromuscular transmission which is responsible for the fluctuating muscular weakness remains undetermined. In affected muscles there are histological changes of a mild non-specific nature with lymphocytic infiltration and zones of fibre necrosis. There are pathological changes in the thymus gland in 70–80 per cent. of patients with myasthenia gravis. A tumour of the thymus is present in 10–20 per cent. of cases, the majority of these patients being male. It is suspected that the basis of the disorder is immunological as various types of antibodies may be found in the serum. The response to thymectomy is variable: sometimes it is remarkable, while in other cases improvement may be delayed for one or two years, but remissions are certainly more frequent in the operated cases. If a thymoma is present, the prognosis is worse regardless of whether the treatment is medical or surgical.

Crises are likely to occur in myasthenia, and these may be of two varieties. In the myasthenic crisis proper, there is an acute deterioration in the patient's condition. This may be spontaneous or it may be precipitated by an emotional upset, an infection, undue exertion or childbirth. A favourable response to the edrophonium test and the absence of cholinergic phenomena will indicate the true myasthenic nature of the crisis. On the other hand, the crisis may be cholinergic in character and there may then be collapse, confusion, vomiting, sweating, miosis and pallor. Signs of impending paresis of bulbar or respiratory muscles require the techniques of controlled respiration and injections of atropine until the danger has passed. This can be gauged when the normal myasthenic response to edrophonium has returned. At times it is exceptionally difficult to determine whether the collapsed myasthenic patient has been under-treated or over-treated. Withdrawal of all drugs, the insertion of a cuffed endotracheal tube and the introduction of positive pressure respiration are then vital. Tracheostomy may be necessary, depending on the duration of the paralysis. Coping effectively with a collapsed myasthenic patient is one of the most difficult of all neurological emergencies.

Myasthenia Gravis

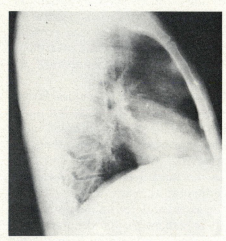

343. Thymoma in myasthenia gravis
Age 48. Five months' history of progressive oculofacial–bulbar paresis. Chest radiographs showed a large mass in the anterior mediastinum. Pneumomediastinography further outlined the tumour. The patient died 3 weeks after thymectomy.

344a

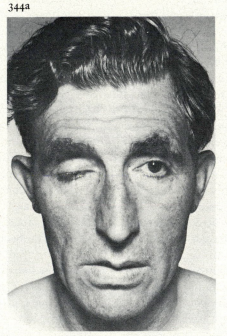

344b

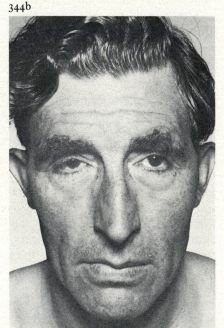

344. Myasthenia gravis: right ptosis
No other symptom or sign. (*a*) Before and (*b*) after *Tensilon*.

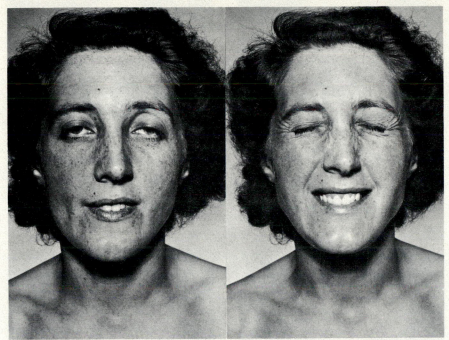

345a   345b

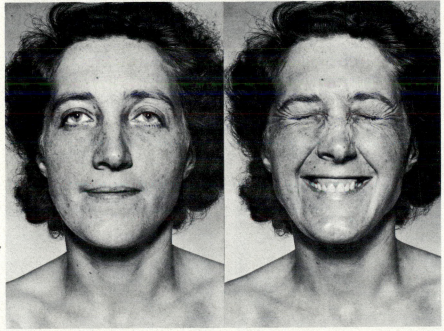

345c   345d

Myasthenia Gravis

345. Myasthenia gravis: bilateral ptosis and facial weakness
In (*a*) and (*b*) before *Prostigmin* (neostigmine bromide), 2 mg., intramuscularly: in (*c*) and (*d*) 20 minutes after injection. In (*a*) note the bilateral ptosis, the slack mouth and general lack of expression. In (*b*) she is trying to close her eyes and bare her teeth; note failure to bury the eyelashes and the weak retraction of the angles of the mouth. In (*c*) the upper lids are raised; the lips are not so slack and the face is livelier. In (*d*) there is a firmer contraction of orbicularis oculi so that the eyelashes are nearly buried and there is stronger retraction of the angles of the mouth.

Myasthenia Gravis

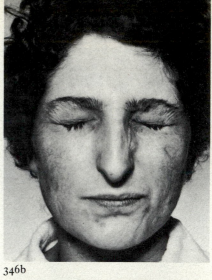

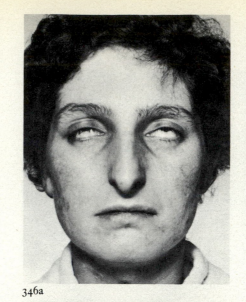

346a

346b

346. Myasthenia gravis: bilateral facial weakness
Afternoon fatigue, weakness of the voice in the evening, difficulty in applying lipstick and in chewing and swallowing. In (*a*) and (*b*) she is closing her eyes, before and after *Prostigmin*, respectively. In (*c*) and (*d*) she is trying to purse her lips, before and after *Prostigmin* injection, respectively.

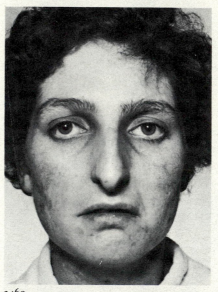

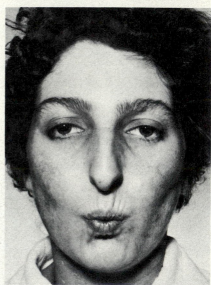

346c

346d

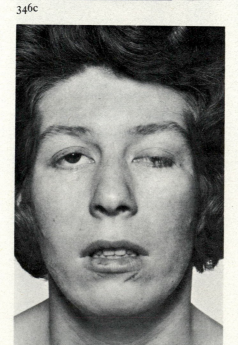

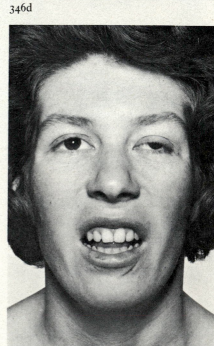

347. Myasthenia gravis: classical facies
Diagnosis is not difficult in this type of case; the *Tensilon* test is only confirmatory. There was ptosis, diplopia, a nasal voice and regurgitation of fluids through the nose on swallowing. Characteristic snarling appearance on smiling is well shown.

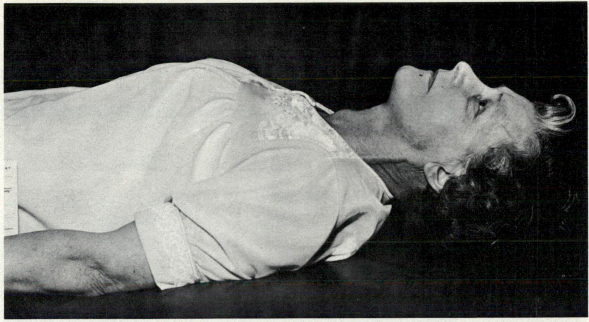

348a

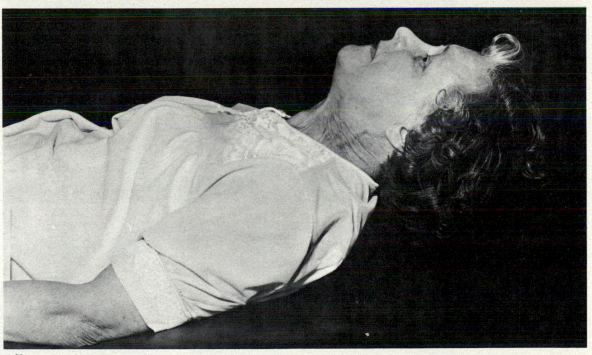

348b

348. Myasthenia gravis: weakness of the neck muscles
This is common in myasthenia and may account for discomfort and aching. In severe cases the head tends to drop forward on to the chest. In this case the patient is trying to raise her head; before *Prostigmin* in (*a*) and after *Prostigmin* in (*b*). Note complete failure to do so in (*a*); just able to raise it from the couch in (*b*).

Myasthenia Gravis

*Myasthenia
Gravis*

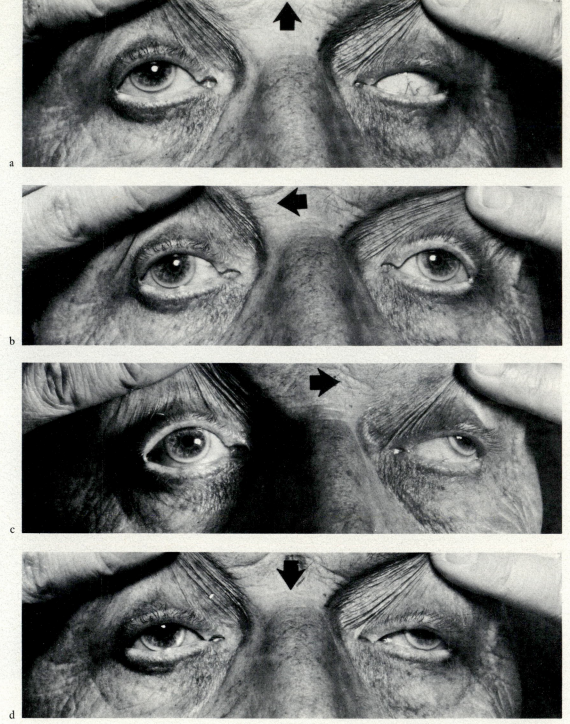

**349. Myasthenia gravis: bilateral
ophthalmoplegia**
Before *Tensilon*—(*a*), (*b*), (*c*), (*d*); after
Tensilon—(*e*), (*f*), (*g*), (*h*). Before *Tensilon*
little movement of the right eyeball was
possible; the left eyeball moved only upwards and outwards. After *Tensilon* movements of both eyeballs in all directions is
possible.

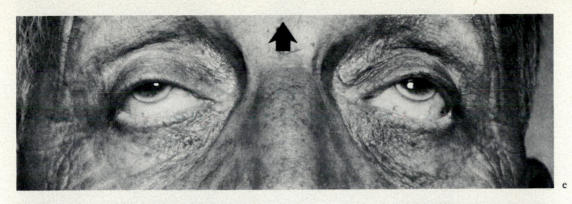

e

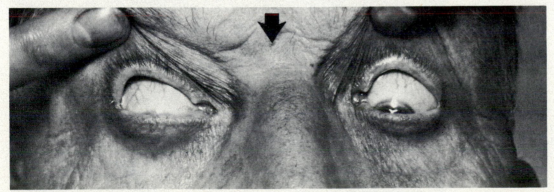

f

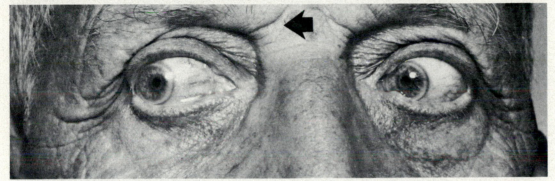

g

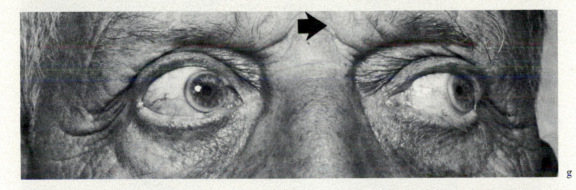

h

Myasthenia Gravis

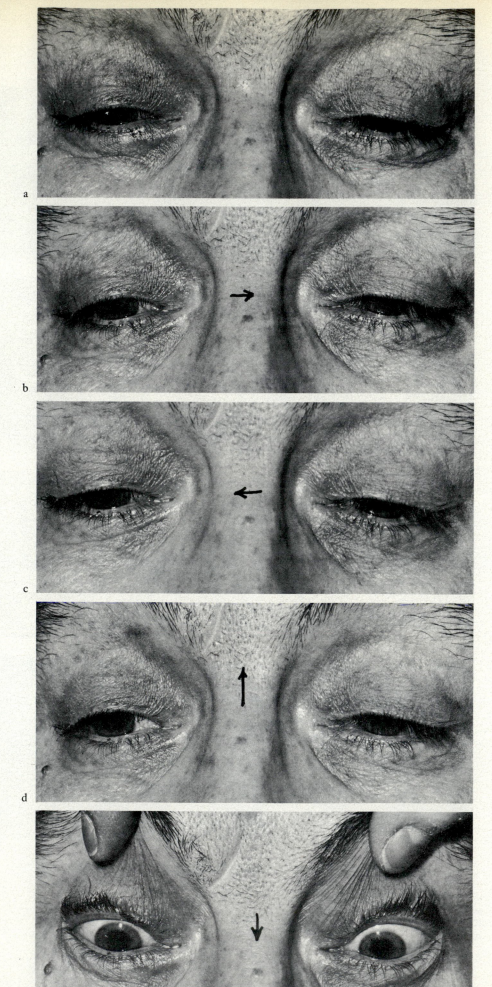

350. Myasthenia gravis: bilateral ptosis and ophthalmoplegia
Before *Prostigmin*—(*a*), (*b*), (*c*), (*d*), (*e*); after *Prostigmin*—(*f*), (*g*), (*h*), (*i*), (*j*). *Prostigmin* relieved the ptosis but did little to improve ocular movement. Clinical history was of 2 years' duration and the complaints were of ptosis and transient diplopia. There was nothing to suggest there had been a long-standing ophthalmoplegia with fibrosis of muscles to account for the failure to respond to *Prostigmin*.

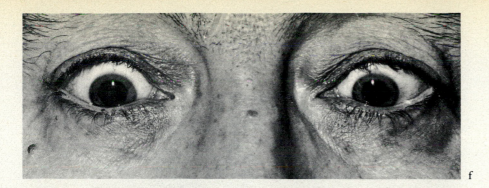

f

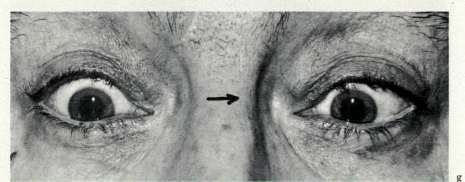

g

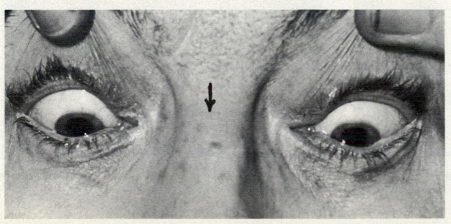

h

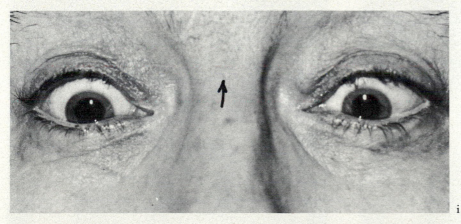

i

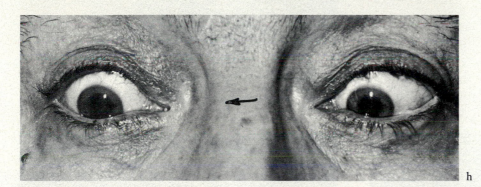

j

Myasthenia Gravis

351. Myasthenia gravis: neonatal myasthenia ▷
Four-day-old infant of a myasthenic mother, 3 years after thymectomy (Fig. 347). The infant was 'myasthenic' for 2 weeks and there was serious respiratory embarrassment. He responded to *Mestinon* and survived.

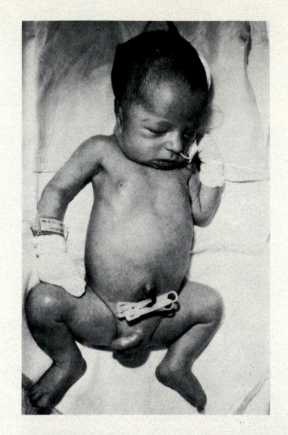

352. Myasthenia gravis: mandibular weakness ▽
Weakness of the muscles of the jaw and neck; drooping of jaw and head. He held his jaw up with a hand when talking or chewing. Initial symptom was hoarseness of voice and recurrent 'sore throats' for which tonsillectomy was performed.

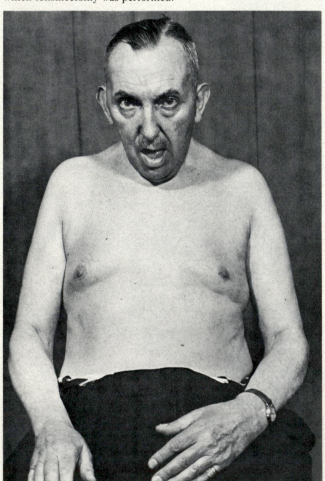

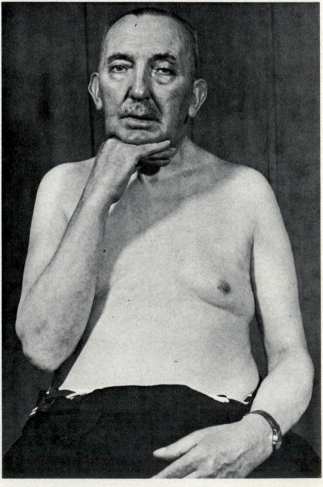

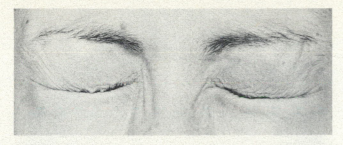

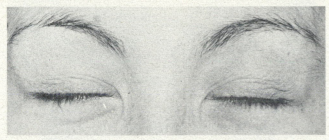

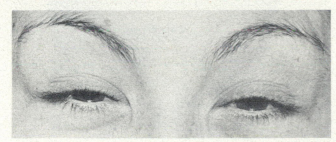

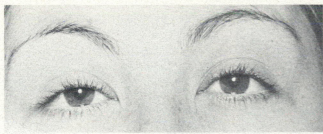

353a

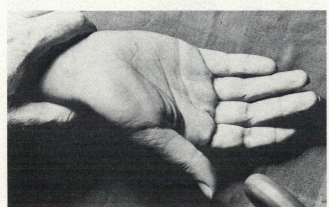

353b

Miscellaneous

353. Hyperkalaemic periodic paralysis with myotonia ◁

Female, aged 19. Father died aged 40 of 'a muscular disorder'. Brother aged 22 with same disorder as our patient; he had a respiratory arrest after an anaesthetic. Our patient suffered from muscle cramps and periodic paresis, both aggravated by exercise and cold. Longest period of weakness and stiffness was 24 hours. 'If soap gets in my eyes I screw them up and I can't open them for several minutes.' She showed myotonic lid lag and difficulty in opening her eyes after firm closure (*a*). She also showed percussion myotonia of the thenar muscles (*b*). A smile lingered on her face. On only one occasion, during an exercise-induced attack of paralysis, was a raised serum potassium level actually found (7 mEq/l.) In normal people a level of 8 mEq/l. is usually necessary before muscular weakness develops. (Courtesy of Dr. J. G. Graham.)

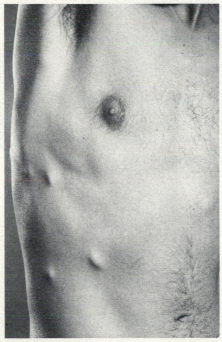

354. Cysticercosis

A Kenyan Asian student with epilepsy. Note subcuticular nodules. Muscle radiographs reveal calcified cysts in the majority of cases. Calcified intracranial cysts are seen in only about one-third. A coloured patient with epilepsy should always be examined carefully for evidence of cysticercosis.

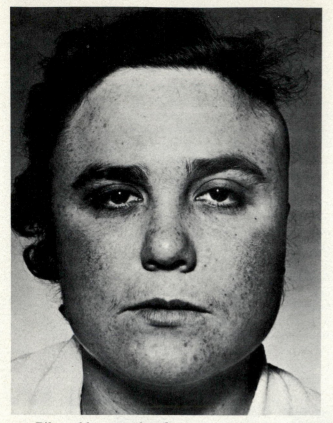
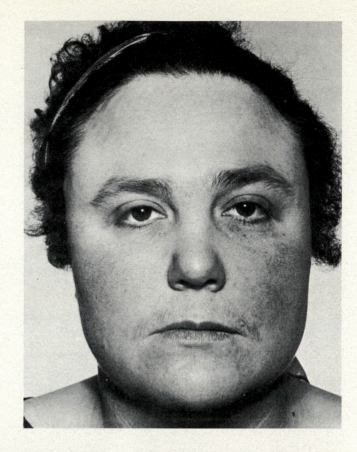

355. Bilateral hypertrophy of temporal and masseter muscles △
(*a*) In 1956; (*b*) in 1966. Negative family history. No other abnormalities. Swelling in temples noted by patient in mid-twenties. No associated muscular weakness. Electromyography normal. Biopsy refused. Apparently true isolated hypertrophy of temporal and masseter muscles. Hair shaved on left side in (*a*).

Miscellaneous

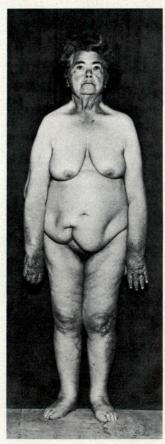
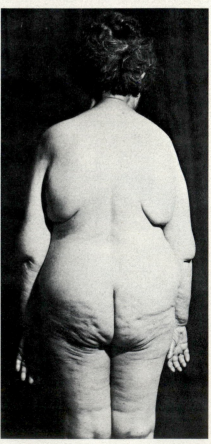

356. Complete flaccid paralysis of upper limbs ▷
Age 70; onset 18 years previously, slow and painless. Lower limbs normal. Only very weak movements of fingers remaining. No movements possible at wrists, elbows or shoulders. Arm reflexes absent. Sensation normal. Gross atrophy of deltoids. E.M.G., chronic partial denervation. Deltoid biopsy, ? polymyositis. Stationary for 15 years.

6 DISORDERS CHARACTERIZED BY INVOLUNTARY MOVEMENTS

Introduction

There is an exceedingly wide variety of involuntary movements, and their classification and pathogenesis present formidable problems. An involuntary movement may be confined to one small portion of a muscle, as in fasciculation, or it may embrace the whole body, as in a convulsion. It may consist of no more than a fine tremor of the outstretched fingers, or it may so contort the body that normal posture is impossible. Involuntary movements may occur only at rest or only when the patient is awake; they may be intermittent or continuous; their speed, intensity and duration may be equally variable. The majority are spontaneous, but some may be provoked by various sensory stimuli. An involuntary movement may be no more than a manifestation of passing psychological disturbance. On the other hand, it may appear soon after birth and constitute the first sign of a grave lifelong disorder such as congenital athetosis. Involuntary movements may result from lesions later in life which are vascular or degenerative in nature, or they may be manifestations of a systemic disease of the central nervous system. Finally, involuntary movements may be toxic in origin.

Descriptive terms have come into use which enable the clinician to recognize the major examples of these conditions. These terms are not definitions; they are not precise and they cannot be related to anatomical, physiological or pathological factors in aetiology. Nevertheless, they cannot be avoided and for the present they furnish the clinician with terms that have some practical meaning. They are tremor, chorea, myoclonus, tics, dystonia and athetosis.

Tremor

This is one of the commonest and the most distinctive of these abnormal movements, comprising a rhythmic, repetitive movement of some portion of the body consequent on alternating contractions of opposing muscle groups. Three types are recognized: tremor at rest, postural tremor and intention tremor.

The classic example of the first type is the tremor of Parkinsonism, but other diseases of the basal ganglia may cause tremor at rest. It may also be a constituent of essential, familial or senile tremor. Postural tremor is activated during attempts to sustain a posture, such as extending the arm, supporting the leg or holding up the head. A fine tremor of the fingers may occur in anxiety, hyperthyroidism, hepatic failure, and drug or alcohol toxicity. A benign, essential or familial tremor may be partially or wholly one of posture, with little or no tremor at rest. In Parkinsonism, on the other hand, tremor at rest often subsides during voluntary movement. Disease of the cerebellum may cause a postural tremor but, unlike the above conditions, it tends to involve the proximal and not the distal portion of the limbs. The outstretched arm shakes at the shoulder and perhaps at the elbow rather than in the fingers, and the tremor is slower in rate.

Intention or action tremor is induced by volitional movement. In its most characteristic form it is seen in disease of the cerebellum, but it can also occur in diseases of the basal ganglia such as Parkinsonism and Wilson's disease (hepatolenticular degeneration). It impairs the performance of voluntary movements, rendering some of them impossible. It is typically seen during the performance of the finger–nose test in multiple sclerosis.

Chorea

This denotes brief, jerky, abrupt movements that flit around the body in random, irregular and irrelevant fashion. At rest these may prevent relaxation, and during volitional movement they may interrupt or distort the performance. There is a general air of restlessness in choreic patients, an excess of motor activity. The pathological substrate of chorea is not known; the striatum and the cerebral cortex have been implicated.

241

Myoclonus

Myoclonic movements are sudden, brief muscular jerks which may be confined to one portion of the body or may be diffusely distributed. They are most commonly seen in epilepsy, in certain forms of subacute encephalitis, and in diseases affecting various levels of the nervous system—cortical, striatal, brain stem and spinal. Palatal myoclonus is an example of a discrete form in which there are more or less rhythmic contractions of the soft palate and pharynx, seen in certain lesions involving the inferior olivary nucleus and the olivocerebellar tracts. Myoclonic jerks often occur spontaneously, and some may be induced by stimuli such as startle or loud noise. In certain cases peripheral nerve stimulation evokes greatly enhanced cortical responses. Like tremor, myoclonic jerks may be a physiological phenomenon, as in sleep. Hemifacial spasm may be viewed as a form of myoclonus. In epilepsy, isolated or repeated myoclonic jerks may be a frequent complaint, usually in young persons in the morning. In petit mal, jerking of an upper limb at the breakfast table is quite common. A lower limb jerk may cause the patient to fall or may actually hurl him to the ground. *Progressive myoclonic epilepsy* is a serious inherited disorder which may lead to dementia. Fortunately it is rare. Myoclonus with dementia may be an aftermath of cerebral anoxia consequent on coma due to injury or attempted suicide.

Tics

The nervous tic or habit spasm is usually a benign disturbance particularly affecting children. It usually regresses. These movements mostly involve the face, neck, shoulders and upper limbs, with blinking, grimacing, sniffing, twisting of the neck or shrugging of the shoulder. In more serious persistent tics there may be a compulsive–obsessional state. Tics are generally regarded as psychogenic in origin. A rare disorder, the *syndrome of Gilles de la Tourette*, is characterized by persistent multiple tics beginning in childhood and often accompanied by inarticulate cries or barks or compulsive utterance of obscenities. Minor neurological abnormalities and electroencephalographic changes suggest the possibility that this unusual disease is not a psychological disorder.

Athetosis

This term was introduced by W. A. Hammond (1828–1900), a pioneer American neurologist whose textbook, published in 1876, was announced as the first on nervous diseases in the English language. Derived from Greek, the word athetosis means 'without fixed position'. Gowers used the expression 'mobile spasm'. The term athetosis is commonly employed to designate odd sinuous or writhing movements of the hands, feet and digits, which appear to be in continuous motion and unable to sustain a fixed posture. These movements are most frequently seen in the hands, but the face and tongue may be affected. The posture of the hand is characteristic: pronated, with flexion of the wrist and hyperextension of the fingers. The movements are superimposed upon the abnormal posture. Many choreic and dystonic movements are indistinguishable from athetosis. The latter disorder is most commonly seen in childhood, when it is often bilateral and results from anoxic, metabolic or developmental lesions in the striatum, usually the putamen. In adult life it is usually unilateral and follows a vascular lesion. In both types of case there may also be features of corticospinal disorder.

Dystonia

Dystonic movements are sustained spasms of some portion of the body, usually taking the form of a twisting or turning motion of the neck, the trunk or the proximal parts of the extremities. The movements are powerful and deforming, grossly interfering with voluntary movement and perverting posture. Torticollis is one of the commonest examples of torsion dystonia. There may be muscular hypertrophy. The basic pathology is not known, but in some cases the disorder is genetically determined.

Although the aetiology and pathology of these various disorders characterized by involuntary movements of one kind or another are not known, the majority are due to a disorder in the basal ganglia. This term has come to include not only the caudate nucleus, putamen and pallidum, but also adjacent structures such as the corpus luysi, the substantia nigra and the red nuclei. Alterations of tone and involuntary movements characterize diseases affecting these structures. Very little is known of their physiology and function and the manner in which disease produces such a rich variety of symptomatology. The relationship between these nuclear masses deep in the brain has always been a subject of considerable controversy, but recent biochemical and pharmacological discoveries indicate that a new era of research is at hand.

The striking demonstration that dopamine, a catecholamine normally found at high concentration in basal ganglia, tends to disappear in Parkinsonism, provided the first clue. The role of chemical transmitters in central neural mechanisms is now being studied in many types of involuntary movement disorders. As yet there is no useful drug to control intention tremor; Parkinsonian tremor responds to levodopa; propranolol is useful in benign essential tremor; reserpine and the phenothiazines are effective in Huntington's chorea, while tetrabenazine (a monoamine depletor like reserpine) benefits acute hemi-chorea or hemiballismus. Even the childhood tics and the more serious multiple tics of Tourette's syndrome may respond to haloperidol. These pharmacological developments have occurred at a time when a wide range of involuntary movements have been recorded as side-effects of drugs such as the phenothiazines, the butyrophenones and levodopa. Thirty years ago, when the importance of copper in the aetiology of Wilson's disease was discovered, it was widely hoped that this would lead to further knowledge of the basal ganglia and their diseases. But twenty years had to pass before the next discovery was made in this field, namely the importance of dopamine. Nevertheless one feels that the role of chemical transmitters and biological amines in brain mechanisms will prove to be more significant than that of trace metals.

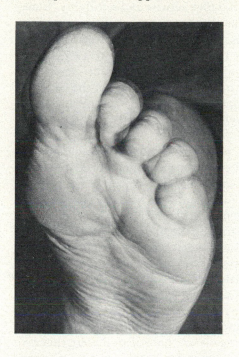

357. Painful legs and moving toes
Male aged 53. Referred by an orthopaedic surgeon whom the patient had consulted complaining of pain in the left foot, with involuntary movements of the toes, of 1 year's duration. Clinical examination was negative apart from the movements of the toes. These consisted of clawing and straightening, fanning and circular move-ments which could not be imitated voluntarily with the normal foot or by an observer. Nerve conduction studies normal; sural nerve biopsy normal. The patient could stop the movements for a few seconds by voluntary effort, but then they would return. Both the pain and the movements subsided at night and sleep was normal. The pain varied in intensity and fluctuated considerably, sometimes consisting of only moderate discomfort but at other times being a torment. Diazepam temporarily reduced the involuntary movements but did not affect the pain, and analgesics were ineffective. This syndrome resembles but is clearly different from Ekbom's syndrome of restless legs. In the latter the symptoms are worse at night and movements are voluntarily initiated in an attempt to abolish the discomfort and pain. (See Spillane, J. D., et al. (1971) *Brain*, **94**, 541.)

PARALYSIS AGITANS

(Parkinson's Disease; Parkinsonism)

James Parkinson (1755–1824) a general practitioner in London, wrote his famous essay 'on the shaking palsy' in 1817 when he was 62 years of age. Curiously, at no point did he describe the characteristic facies or 'mask' which has become associated with his name, but he vividly described the tremor, posture and gait and the course of the disease as he observed it in his patients.

'So slight and nearly imperceptible are the first inroads of this malady, and so extremely slow is its progress, that it rarely happens, that the patient can form any recollection of the precise period of its commencement. The first symptoms perceived are, a slight sense of weakness, with a proneness to trembling in some particular part; sometimes in the head, but most commonly in one of the hands or arms. The symptoms gradually increase in the part first affected; and at an uncertain period, but seldom in less than twelve months or more, the morbid influence is felt in some other part. . . . After a few more months the patient is found to be less strict than usual in preserving an upright posture; this being most observable whilst walking, but sometimes whilst sitting or standing. Sometime after the appearance of this symptom and during its slow increase, one of the legs is discovered slightly to tremble, and is also found to suffer fatigue sooner than the leg of the other side; and in a few months this limb becomes agitated by similar tremblings and suffers a similar loss of power.'

The end of the disease he describes in the following words:

'the chin is now almost immovably bent down upon the sternum. The slops with which he is attempted to be fed, with the saliva, are continually trickling from the mouth. The power of articulation is lost. The urine and faeces are passed involuntarily; and at the last constant sleepiness with slight delirium and other marks of extreme exhaustion, announced the wished for release.'

Parkinson also described the temporary disappearance of the tremor during a hemiplegic stroke.

This is a disease, of course, in which signs may precede symptoms, in which the condition is recognized rather than formally diagnosed after routine examination. It is for these reasons that it may be missed. The patient may complain of 'trembling' or 'shivering' in the trunk when there is no visible tremor in the limbs. I have not infrequently heard patients express a fear that they were developing the disease when signs were still dubious. I have learned not to dismiss the idea without careful review.

Although the coarse, rhythmic, rolling tremor of thumb and index and forearm, are the most conspicuous features of the malady, the earliest symptoms and signs are those resulting from the muscular stiffness and loss of elasticity. The patient nearly always looks depressed, so sad and immobile is his facies. The slightly staring eyes, the infrequent blinking, the loss of inflexion in his voice, his stoop and general stillness create an air of melancholy, yet if challenged he may smile quickly and seem surprised at the suggestion. This general poverty or economy of movement is always a prominent symptom; sitting in a chair one does not see the little shifts of movement, the folding of the arms, the crossing of the knees or the fingering of tie, handkerchief or cuff link. This akinesia may or may not be appreciated by the patient. If it is he may notice some vague constant bodily discomfort, sensations of fatigue, slowness in dressing and undressing, difficulty in writing, which becomes smaller as well as tremulous, lack of swing of one arm as he walks and loss of spring in his gait. He becomes self-conscious in public and disinclined to move. When he rises from his chair to answer a telephone, he may trip or stumble and be surprised at his lack of agility. His first steps are often hesitant. Surprisingly, despite the akinesia and slowness of voluntary movement, the patient may deftly catch a ball which is thrown to him.

The well known tremor usually first appears in the hand and forearm, but it may begin in the jaw or foot. In the latter case it may be seen only when he is lying on a couch. His wife will say that tremor ceases during sleep but is aggravated by excitement or self-consciousness. It is temporarily arrested by a voluntary movement such as lifting a teacup to the lips, only to reappear when it is replaced on the saucer. This, too, may be noticed by his wife and she wonders why he cannot hold his newspaper steady in his hands; but intention tremor occurs.

The patient will often find that if he hums a marching tune to himself as he walks, his step becomes livelier and his arms move more naturally.

Mental depression may be very real but as a rule mental symptoms are absent, although true organic dementia is occasionally encountered. I have seen several patients whose presenting symptom was a frozen shoulder. They have often had treatment for this and during the period of recovery, coldness, vasomotor changes, tremor and rigidity have made their appearance in the hand and forearm of the affected upper limb. In some male patients urinary disorders—frequency and hesitancy—have taken him to a genito-urinary surgeon. I have known prostatectomy to be performed.

Routine neurological examination shows normal muscular strength, reflex activity and sensibility. It may not be strictly true that 'tremor is rigidity spread thin' but there is often some antagonism between these two signs. There may be little or no tremor when rigidity is conspicuous; conversely, there may be severe bilateral tremor of hands and forearms, yet the patient is agile, moves quickly and passive movements of the limbs yield no feeling of the characteristic 'cog-wheel' rigidity.

There are two principal types of Parkinsonism—the degenerative and the postencephalitic. The latter commonly originates earlier in life, but there is not always a history of acute encephalitis. It tends to develop more quickly and becomes stationary, tremor is much less obvious than in the degenerative variety. Other encephalitic residua such as tics, spasms, oculogyric crises, respiratory disturbances and abnormalities of behaviour are common. Sialorrhoea is common in the postencephalitic variety but is not unknown in paralysis agitans. Increased sweating and a greasy skin seem to be peculiar to the postencephalitic patients. The pupillary reflexes and ocular movements are normal in the degenerative type of the disease but in the postencephalitic they may be defective and impairment of convergence is frequently encountered.

Parkinsonism may present in many ways and is sometimes detected during the investigation of some banal complaint such as constipation, 'rheumatism' or loss of weight. The patient may be subject to unexpected falls, or to faints caused by orthostatic hypotension, or may have urinary difficulties. Failure of the arm to swing automatically during walking may lead to presentation of the disease with a 'frozen' shoulder. The lack of arm swing will account for the self-winding watch that is always stopping. Some patients are afflicted with motor restlessness: they cannot remain seated for any length of time, but are for ever struggling to get up and totter about. This 'motor impatience' or akathisia was referred to by Gowers and Charcot as 'extreme' or 'cruel' restlessness.

Eye signs are common in all forms of Parkinsonism In addition to the familiar lack of blinking, there may be paresis of convergence, blepharoclonus, blepharospasm, a positive glabellar tap and, rarely, apraxia of lid opening (FIG. 89). Fleeting diplopia may be described, and convergence paresis may cause reading difficulties. Depression may be freely volunteered or firmly denied.

In the differential diagnosis it should be remembered that other diseases of the nervous system may have Parkinsonian features. In progressive supranuclear palsy there are in addition the ophthalmoplegia, the dementia and the bulbar signs; tremor is rare. In neurogenic orthostatic hypotension the autonomic failure reveals itself by low blood pressure, loss of sweating, incontinence and impotence; the background may be cerebellar and not Parkinsonian; tremor is not prominent. In normal pressure hydrocephalus the mild dementia, disturbance of gait and rigidity may suggest Parkinsonism, but tremor is not a feature. Other disorders which may involve the basal ganglia—Jakob–Creutzfeldt disease and striatal–nigral degeneration—are rare. In many forms of mild dementia there may be a slight element of Parkinsonism.

Whatever the mode of presentation in Parkinsonism, the clinician can expect that in the majority of his cases there will be a satisfactory response to treatment with levodopa, especially if it is combined with a decarboxylase inhibitor.

Paralysis Agitans

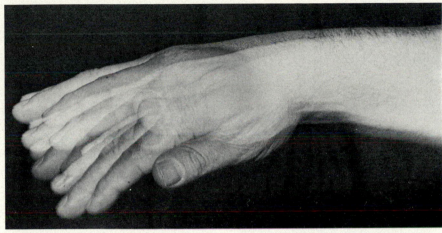

358. Parkinsonian tremor △
This is the initial complaint in the majority of patients with idiopathic Parkinsonism. It usually affects distal muscle groups such as those of the hand and foot. It is a coarse tremor, at a rate of 4–8 cycles per second, present at rest and often made worse by nervousness, excitement or fatigue. There are flexion and extension movements at the metacarpophalangeal joints of the fingers and thumb.

359

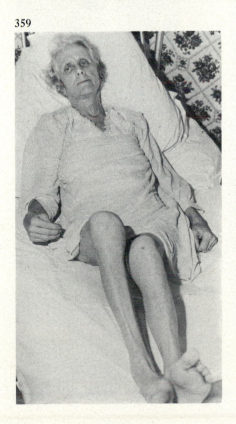

359. Parkinsonism: the 'on–off' phenomenon during levodopa therapy
Before levodopa therapy it was well recognized that in Parkinsonism a spontaneous fluctuation of symptoms and signs occurred. Since the introduction of levodopa these fluctuations have been more frequent and severe. They have been termed the 'on–off' effect, or akinesia paradoxica. Akinesia, distress and sometimes confusion and tremor are the main features and may last for minutes or for several hours at a time. This patient was ambulant, able to dress, cook and walk to nearby shops unassisted, 2 years after beginning levodopa therapy. In the third year, when taking 5 G. a day, she started to undergo episodes of helplessness. In one of these she was admitted to hospital, and when this photograph was taken she had been distressed, tremulous and in a state of profound hypokinesia for 5 hours. She recovered spontaneously but there were several further, shorter episodes.
The mechanism of this complication is not understood, but it probably represents a form of levodopa toxicity. It is usually seen in patients who have responded satisfactorily to treatment for a year or more.

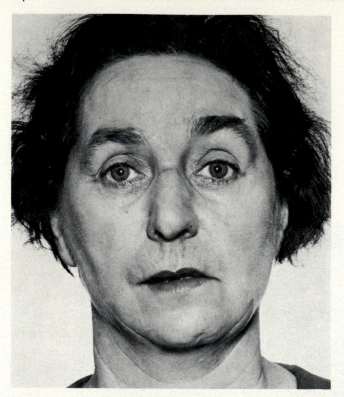

Paralysis Agitans

360. Paralysis agitans
'Frozen shoulder' on the left side;
followed by rigidity of left arm; no tremor.
Note fixed facial expression. When walking the left arm does not swing. Conscious
effort to swing the arm when walking fails
after a few steps; the arm may swing in
motion with the leg of the same side instead of the opposite. Automatic swinging
of the affected arm is possible if the
patient is encouraged to hum a marching
tune. The difference between walking and
marching is largely one of voluntary
swinging of the arms.

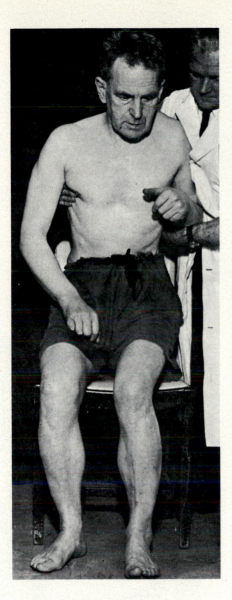

Paralysis Agitans

361. Paralysis agitans ◁
Initiating a movement is often difficult, as for example, in rising from a chair. Once on his feet he can walk. Note flexed posture of left upper limb. Akinesia and bradykinesia are terms used to denote the poverty and slowness of movement; there is no predictable relationship between the degree of rigidity and the slowness or poverty of movement. Despite his immobility this patient often said that he could not sit still; he endlessly requested to be assisted to his feet so that he could walk about for a few minutes—akathisia.

362. Paralysis agitans ▷
Loss of postural fixation of the trunk. This patient with paralysis agitans could stand semi-erect for only about 60 seconds; his head and trunk then sink forward until his spine is horizontal. In the terminal stages of Parkinsonism the postural change gradually worsens, all the limbs are drawn into a fixed attitude of general flexion.

Paralysis Agitans

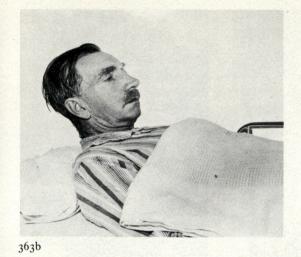
363b

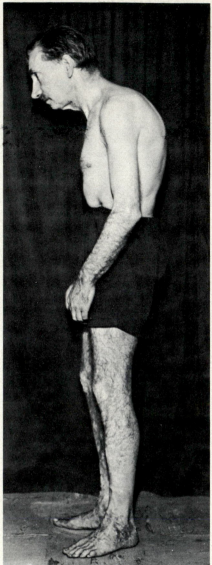
363a

363. Paralysis agitans ◁ △
Dementia accompanied the characteristic
features of paralysis agitans from the onset. Note the kyphosis and forward
position of the head in (*a*) and the absence
of a supporting pillow in (*b*). Such a
patient will lie for hours in the supine
position without a pillow. There is loss of
postural fixation of the head.

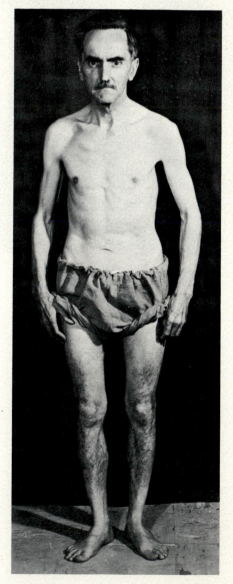

364. Post-encephalitic Parkinsonism ▷
Age 42; observed since onset when 30. No
history of encephalitis but occasional
oculogyric spasm with typical features of
progressive Parkinsonism. Marked
anorexia with severe loss of weight. Lower
limbs practically unaffected and his walking is excellent. Periodic gross tremor of
upper limbs with rigidity. Note staring
expression, position of fingers and forward
thrust of head.

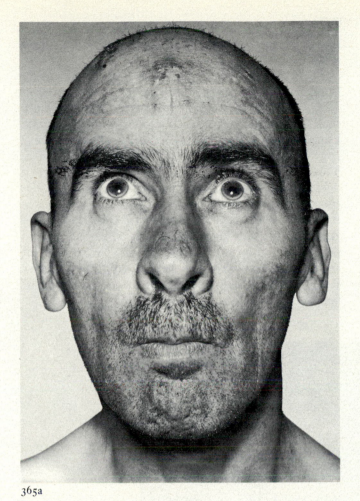

365a

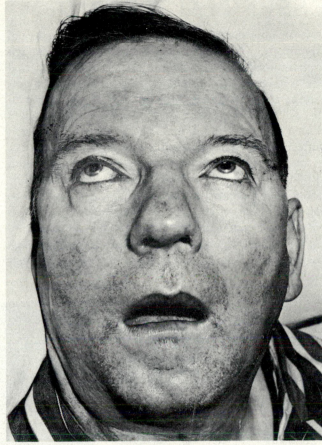

365b

365. Oculogyric spasms

(*a*) No previous history of epidemic encephalitis. Insidious onset of Parkinsonism with oculogyric spasms in his thirties. Episodes of upward deviation of the eyes lasting from 10 minutes to 3 hours. During them he rarely spoke but would sometimes mutter to himself in an incomprehensible manner. Rarely, the oculogyric spasms were associated with excitement, 'murderous thoughts' and restlessness.

(*b*) Age 50. Epidemic encephalitis when 15.

Mild chronic Parkinsonism with frequent oculogyric spasms, always lasting several hours. Normally pleasant and active; when he felt the onset of ocular discomfort he would retire to bed. There, he would lie in a state of stupor for most of the day. Rousable, but mute. Sometimes the head would deviate upwards and usually his mouth would open.

(*c*) Age 52; epidemic encephalitis at 17. Onset of Parkinsonism and oculogyric

spasms in her twenties. General disability was slight, but oculogyric spasms usually lasted 1 or 2 days and were associated with a strange mental state. She would feel 'dreadfully ill' and retire to bed. She was not mute or hallucinated or aggressive. An attack could usually be terminated by intravenous phenobarbitone. In (*c*) at the moment of injection the attack had been present for 2 hours; (*d*) 3 minutes later. Note inequality of pupils.

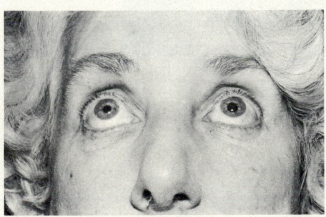

365c

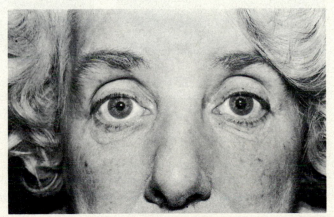

365d

ESSENTIAL TREMOR

It is important to distinguish hereditary essential tremor from Parkinsonism. It is a benign although embarrassing disorder, without rigidity or akinesia, and the tremor, rarely present at rest, appears on maintaining a posture and is aggravated by voluntary movement. It is this feature of the disease which makes dining in public such a trial. In contrast to the patient suffering from Parkinsonism, all voluntary movements, except raising a teacup or tumbler to the lips without spilling its contents, can be normally performed. The patient with essential tremor often thinks he is developing Parkinsonism and should be reassured. What is more, the various drugs used for the treatment of Parkinsonism are unhelpful and often upsetting. Most patients with essential tremor discover, sooner or later, that a couple of alcoholic drinks procure temporary relief before dining occasions.

The tremor may appear at any age, but it has usually been present for many years before advice is sought. This mostly occurs when the tremor has become a social embarrassment or when it interferes with writing. Usually there is no tremor at rest but a postural tremor appears when the patient holds his arms outstretched. This continues during voluntary movement, but it does not as a rule show the gross exaggeration encountered in cerebellar intention tremor. Occasionally there is a slight head tremor. Drug treatment is not very effective, but some patients who possess an anxious personality, or who have become very worried about their disability, may be helped by tranquillizers. Recently it has been found that propranolol may be beneficial. There is no known pathology.

Essential Tremor

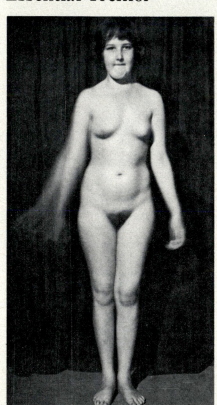

366. Tremor
Age 14; gross tremor of the right upper limb 3 months after 'encephalitis'. The latter was characterized by the subacute onset of right hemiparesis, confusion, headache, initial pyrexia, but a normal spinal fluid. E.E.G. showed a left parietal delta focus. The tremor subsided in 3 months and there was full recovery. A subsequent left carotid arteriogram was normal.

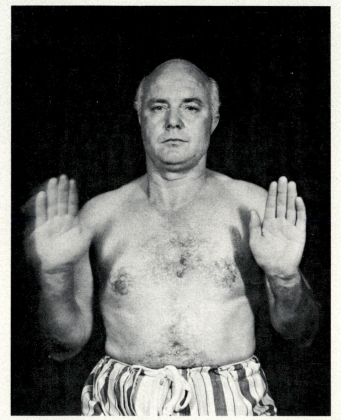

367. Tremor
Age 43; onset of temporal lobe epilepsy with uncinate phenomena at the age of 40. Coarse tremor of the right hand for 5 months. Minimal right lower facial weakness, weakness of right grip, spasticity at the right wrist. No other signs. Investigation showed that he had a large glioma of the left temporal lobe, spreading to involve the basal ganglia on the same side.

Essential Tremor

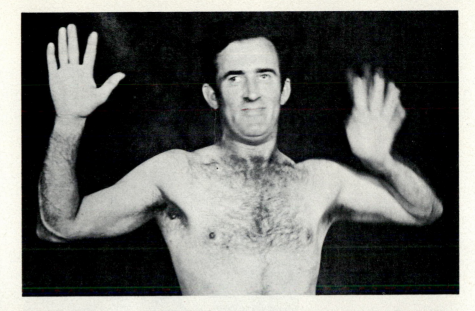

368. Tremor ▷
Age 33; head injury at 5 followed by right external strabismus and coarse tremor of left arm; similar slight tremor of left leg. Left limbs smaller than right, moderate left spastic hemiparesis.

369a

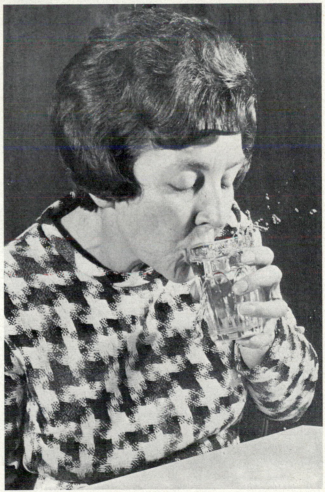

369b

369. Essential tremor
Onset at 12 years of age; no family history. Both hands affected; no tremor at rest; no tremor of head or lower limbs.

Raising a glass of water to her lips without spilling it was impossible. A moderate improvement was obtained with propranolol.

Athetosis

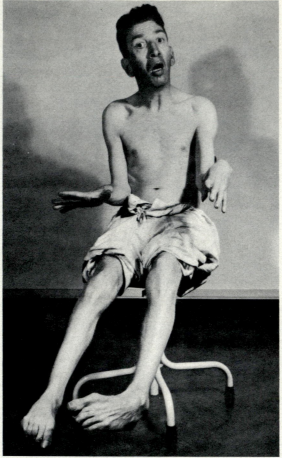

370. Double athetosis ◁
Age 41; negative family history, normal birth, no neonatal jaundice. Bilateral labile athetosis affecting all four limbs, face, neck and mouth. Increasing muscular rigidity has tended to produce flexion of upper limbs and extension of lower limbs in recent years. Dysarthria of 'pseudo-bulbar' type; extensor plantar reflexes; little muscular weakness but mobile spasm interferes with activity. Autopsy in this type of case usually shows a well localized marbled scar in the putamen on both sides.

372. Athetosis of right upper limb ▽
Age 11; premature birth, prolonged difficult labour. Clumsiness of right arm noticed in infancy. Writhing, twisting movements of the right arm and right side of face. Learned to write with the left hand; fair intelligence; mild spastic signs in lower limbs with slight dysarthria. A form of cerebral diplegia.

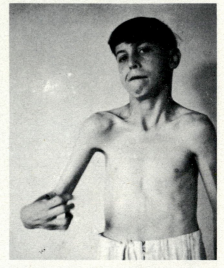

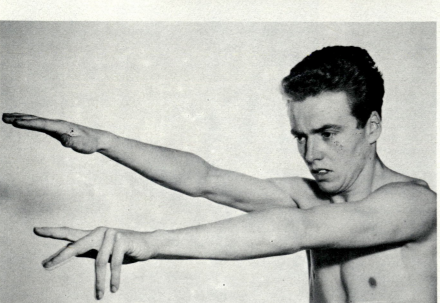

371. Athetosis of left arm △
Age 25; onset at age 15 of clumsiness of left hand. Voluntary movements of the limb were interrupted by tremor, grasping or extension movements of the fingers and wrist. Later these movements appeared spontaneously and there was increasing dysarthria. Slight progression over a period of 9 years; aetiology unknown. No evidence of Wilson's disease. With arms outstretched there are alternating movements of flexion and extension at left wrist and finger joints.

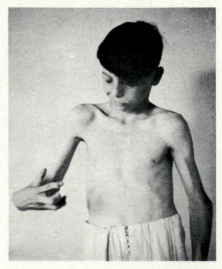

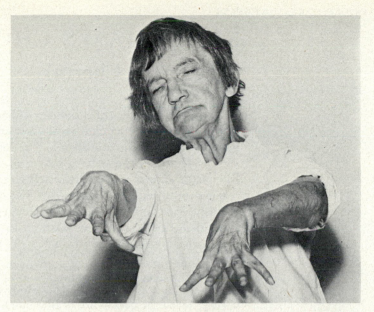

373. Pseudo-athetosis; carcinomatous neuropathy ◁

Age 70 years. Six months' history of 'numbness and uselessness' of her hands. As she described this she opened and closed her hands strongly. No complaints referable to the lower limbs. Absent upper limb reflexes; distal impairment of superficial sensation; complete loss of vibration and posture sense. With closed eyes and outstretched arms her fingers would wander and writhe. She was very disabled. The lower limbs became involved a year later, and she died 2½ years after the onset of the illness. Extensive investigations failed to reveal a carcinoma, but terminally her liver enlarged. Liver biopsy had been negative. No autopsy.

Athetosis

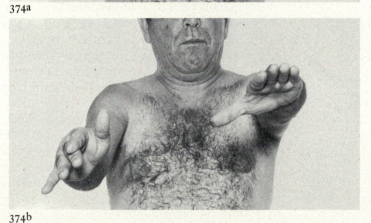

374a

374b

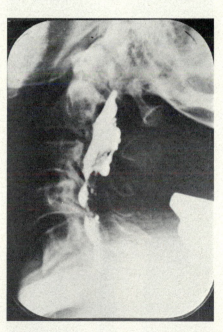

375. Myelogram in a case of pseudo-athetosis △

374. Pseudo-athetosis; left carotid artery stenosis △

Age 46 years; diabetic; progressive numbness and clumsiness of the fingers of the right hand for 4 months. Good general power in right upper limb; slight weakness of grip and of finger extension. Sensory examination: no impairment of appreciation of pain or temperature. Tactile appreciation, localization and discrimination slightly impaired; marked loss of posture sense and appreciation of passive movement; unable to appreciate the size, shape and form of an object in the hand with the eyes closed. Note sensory wandering or pseudo-athetosis of fingers of right hand when eyes are closed. Brain scan showed a large area of uptake in the left parietal region and on left carotid arteriography, there was a complete block of the internal carotid artery 0.5 cm. from its origin.

Age 64 years; male; 2 years' history of numbness and clumsiness of the hands. Good grips; slight superficial sensory loss but profound loss of posture, vibration and joint position sense bilaterally. Cervical spondylosis, narrow spinal canal, myelographic hold-up posteriorly, particularly in extension. Moderate improvement after decompressive laminectomy.

Athetosis

376. Choreo-athetosis
Age 22; asphyxia neonatorum. Retarded development, clumsy, stiff right limbs noted in infancy. Involuntary movements of both arms and right leg noticed at the age of 5. Grimacing face, tremor of lips and tongue, spastic dysarthria with athetoid and choreic movements of all limbs, particularly on the right which were less developed. Cerebral diplegia.

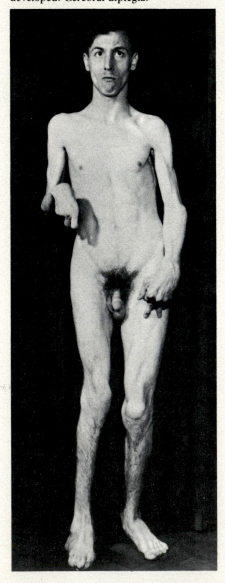

SYDENHAM'S CHOREA
(Rheumatic Chorea)

Two acute disorders of childhood which a neurologist of 30 years' experience now rarely sees are tuberculous meningitis and rheumatic chorea. The former was universally fatal and the latter a source of grave anxiety. Rheumatic chorea is now fortunately a rare disease.

Thomas Sydenham (1624–1689), one of the greatest English physicians, who said 'young man go to the bedside; there alone can you learn disease', described rheumatic chorea in these words:

'This disorder is a kind of convulsion, which chiefly attacks children of both sexes, from 10 to 14 years of age. It shows itself by a certain lameness, or rather unsteadiness of one leg, which the patient draws after him like an idiot and afterwards affects the hand of the same side, which being brought to the breast or any other part, cannot be held in the same posture a moment, but it is distorted or snatched by a kind of convulsion into a different posture and place, notwithstanding all his efforts to the contrary. If a glass of liquor is put into his hand to drink, he uses a thousand odd gestures before he can get it to his mouth; for not being able to carry it in a straight line thereto, because his hand is drawn different ways by the convulsion, as soon as it has happily reached his lips, he throws it suddenly into his mouth and drinks it very hastily, as if he only meant to divert the spectators.'

Even though its association with acute rheumatism and rheumatic heart disease has been well known, the pathological basis of the disorder was never fully understood. It probably took the form of a slight meningo-encephalitis. The essential feature of the disorder—emotional lability, involuntary movements and incoordination and hypotonia—are probably determined by the location of the lesions in the cortex, basal ganglia and cerebellum.

Rare and mild though it is in modern times, it is important not to miss, because vague ill health persisting for a year or so between the ages of 10 and 15, may interfere with education. The mother usually thinks the child is 'naughty' or just 'fidgety'; she, and subsequently the school teacher, are usually surprised by the diagnosis. On the other hand, nervousness and emotional lability may be so common in the family, that the onset of the illness goes unrecognized. The involuntary movements may be very slight indeed and formal examination may reveal little of note. But discreet observation will often reveal fleeting grimaces, brief twitches of the fingers, a certain abruptness about voluntary movements and some clumsiness while dressing or undressing. As Sydenham described, manifestations may be hemiplegic in distribution and when the affected limbs are paretic and choreiform movements are few or slight, cerebral palsy or tumour may be suspected. But the limbs are flaccid and not spastic, the paresis is never absolute and recovery is not long delayed.

A case of mild chronic chorea must be distinguished from one of multiple tics or habit spasm. The constantly repeated movements of the face seen in Huntington's chorea are rarely as obvious in rheumatic chorea but are prominent in tics. In chorea there is clumsiness, the child often drops things and his grasp is poorly sustained. When the onset of chorea is acute or has followed a sore throat or is accompanied by some form of erythema, the child may be sent to a hospital for infectious diseases with suspected encephalitis. The young practitioner may never have seen acute rheumatic chorea.

Lastly, rheumatic chorea may occur during the early months of pregnancy, with or without a previous history of rheumatic disease; it is an obscure but well known relationship and may recur with subsequent pregnancies. It does not seem to be any commoner in unmarried mothers.

The child with chorea may present as a case of behavioural disorder: there may be disobedience at home or in school, and periods of irritability or agitation may occur. The child may not look ill, there is no fever, and unlike a case of acute rheumatic fever, the erythrocyte sedimentation rate is not elevated. However, there may be some abnormality in the electroencephalogram, which may show periodic slow wave activity. On examination, in addition to the obvious choreic movements it may be noted that there is postural abnormality and a poorly sustained hand grip. The reflexes are normal.

Rarely, chorea may appear in thyrotoxicosis, primary polycythaemia and disseminated lupus erythematosus. Lastly, choreic movements may be a consequence of phenothiazine medication, and have also been reported in women with a past history of chorea who are prescribed oral contraceptives.

Sydenham's Chorea

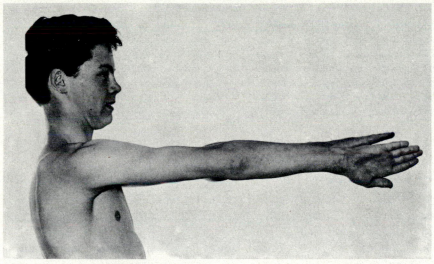

377a

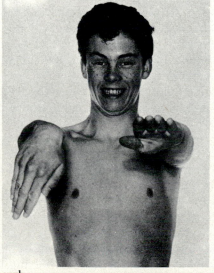

377b

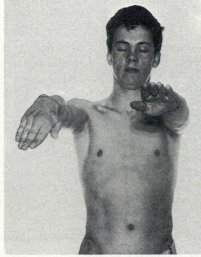

377c

377. Rheumatic chorea (Sydenham's) Choreic movements, posture and hypotonia of right upper limb. Note involuntary pronation of right hand in (a); flexion of wrist and grimacing in (b); deviation of arm when eyes are closed in (c).

These 'little signs' in chorea may persist when the characteristic spontaneous movements have subsided. (Courtesy of Dr. C. E. C. Wells.)

Sydenham's Chorea

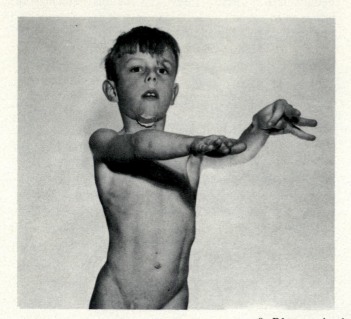 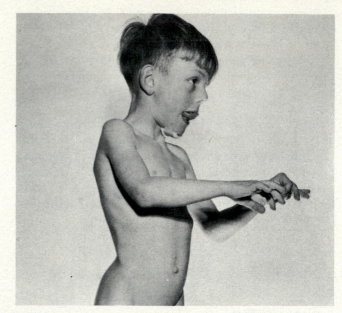

378. Rheumatic chorea (Sydenham's)
A continued endless series of movements of the hand and wrist, the lips, the face and the tongue; occasional movements of the right foot. Voluntary movements were all performed rapidly and smartly; the protruded tongue flies back into the mouth; the arms shoot out in front on request; he jumps out of bed like a 'jack-in-the-box'; he frequently falls (note dressing on chin). His limbs were hypotonic, posture was impaired and voluntary movements were clumsy.

HUNTINGTON'S CHOREA

It was in 1872 that George Huntington, a physician of Long Island, United States, gave the first distinctive account of the disease that has since borne his name. His father and grandfather before him had practised in the same locality and had observed the disorder and it is still interesting to recall the grandson's first acquaintance with the disease as he described it in an address to the New York Neurological Society in 1910.

'Over 50 years ago, riding with my father on his professional rounds, I saw my first case of 'that disorder', which was the way in which the natives always referred to the dreaded disease. I recall it as vividly as if it had occurred but yesterday. . . . We suddenly came upon two women, mother and daughter, both tall, thin, almost cadaverous, both bowing, twisting and grimacing. I stared in wonderment, almost in fear. What could it mean? My father paused to speak to them and we passed on.'

Genealogical studies in America disclosed that the disease was most common in the New England States, the majority having descended from a few individuals who emigrated to Boston in 1630 from a village in Suffolk, England, sailing in the fleet of the Puritan leader John Winthrop. It is a curious coincidence that the Huntingtons also hailed from East Anglia, and left Norwich in 1633, only 3 years after the tainted emigrating families had set sail, to settle in the New England States.

No causal factors other than heredity are known. There is a slowly progressive degeneration of the nerve cells of the basal ganglia and of the cerebral cortex. The disorder is transmitted directly by both sexes and the hereditary factor behaves as a simple Mendelian dominant. It affects both sexes and rarely if ever skips a generation. It may appear to do so if an affected member dies before the onset of the disease.

Signs of the disorder usually appear between the ages of 30 and 50 and it progresses slowly to a fatal termination in from 5 to 30 years.

The choreiform movements appear to differ in no essential way from those which occur in rheumatic chorea. The face is rarely still and blinking of the eyes, smacking and licking movements of the lips and tongue, sniffs and grimaces are usually to be observed. There is slurring articulation and general incoordination of movements and gait. The mental changes, whether they occur before, during or after the onset of the chorea, consist of a gradual disintegration of the psyche. The early symptoms are carelessness, slovenliness, peculiarities of behaviour and a general deterioration of habits. There is no particular form of insanity peculiar to the choreic patient. I have found that unaffected members of a family show no significant trace of abnormality and the incidence in them of such disorders as epilepsy and mental defect is low. The social consequences of the disease are obviously serious and important. Little has been done in the past 50 years to promote the adoption of some form of voluntary or legislative birth control. Every patient heterozygous for the disease, may expect an average of 50 per cent. of affected offspring. Few of them realize this and I can only recall one family in which eugenic advice was accepted and acted upon successfully.

In the classical form of the disease the progressive development of chorea and dementia is the cardinal feature. The condition may escape detection if the cerebral impairment precedes chorea, if the latter is minimal, or if the family history is not uncovered or is denied. The disease itself usually progresses insidiously, but the deterioration is sometimes alarming. The appearance of the patient may, despite the postural disturbances, lurching gait, grimacing face and slurred speech, distract attention from the choreic movements. A dementing person is often restless and unsteady. Muscular rigidity varies considerably between cases and families: in some it is slight or entirely absent, while in others it is a striking feature. The presence or absence of rigidity may, like the choreic movements, fluctuate during the course of the disease.

It is when the disorder begins in childhood or adolescence that diagnosis may be difficult. The juvenile form of the disease, affecting about 5 per cent. of all cases, presents with dystonic posturing and a tendency to mutism, depression, behavioural disorder and apathy. Dysarthria and ocular signs are common.

Schizophrenia may be suspected. In the majority of juvenile cases the father is the affected parent. Epilepsy is common, occurring in 60 per cent. of the juvenile cases. Petit mal status has been described.

Naturally the early detection of the disease is important, and clinical, genetic and biochemical studies are being made in this field. Among the early signs are disorder of upward gaze and 'viscosity' of ocular movements. Assessing the personality in a possible case is notoriously difficult, but a parent may have a shrewd suspicion which of the children will be affected. Levodopa has been used in presymptomatic detection of the disease because the movements it induces in patients with Parkinsonism so often resemble those of Huntington's chorea. Levodopa seems to provoke dyskinetic movements more frequently in afflicted families than in controls, but it is not known whether a positive result therefore means that Huntington's chorea will develop in the future. Moreover, this type of test raises ethical issues. As with the disease of myotonic dystrophy, genetic linkage is being studied in an endeavour to identify the abnormal gene. Biochemical studies have shown that drugs which deplete the brain of catecholamines, and particularly of dopamine, are of some therapeutic benefit in Huntington's chorea. Examples of such drugs are reserpine and tetrabenazine. It has also been shown that drugs which block the brain dopamine receptors, such as the phenothiazines and butyrophenones, have a therapeutic effect. It is therefore likely not only that early detection will become possible biochemically but that, as in Parkinsonism, an appropriate treatment will emerge. Such developments would have wide repercussions in all forms of dementia and also in senility. As yet there is no specific therapy, but many patients may be helped by neuroleptics such as chlorpromazine and haloperidol.

HEMICHOREA

Choreic movements may be seen in senility, in the absence of heredity or progressive dementia. This is rare. A more clearly defined syndrome is that of acute hemichorea or hemiballismus—apoplectiform chorea. The onset is sudden; the involuntary movements are unilateral and are often severe, of large amplitude and practically continuous except during sleep. The wild flinging movements may cause injury and exhaustion; they rarely subside spontaneously. Death may occur within a few days or weeks, but I have known a few patients survive for nearly a year. Despite the flagrant clinical picture, the commonest responsible vascular lesion is a small one in the subthalamic nucleus of the opposite side.

In contrast to acute hemichorea in adult life, there is another variety in which the hemichorea appears insidiously. Usually the patient is elderly and has recently had a stroke. Some days or weeks after the episode, with the return of power to the hemiplegic limbs, choreic movements appear. These may persist for weeks or months, but are not usually severe. They tend to respond, as in acute hemichorea, to tetrabenazine.

Huntington's Chorea

379a

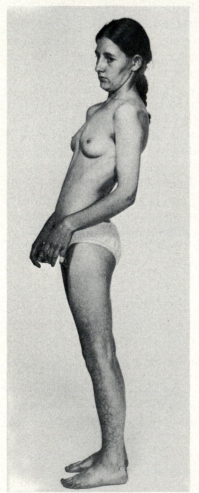

379b

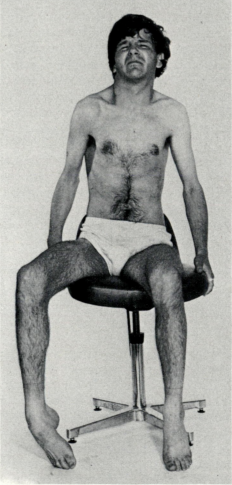

379c

379. Huntington's chorea

The father of the 3 children shown in (a) suffered from the classical form of adult Huntington's chorea and was under the author's care. He died at the age of 47 and at autopsy the characteristic features of striatal and cortical degeneration were found. His first child (not shown), a male now aged 28 years, is healthy. The second child, a male aged 23 years (in centre of group), has inferior intelligence and suffers from epilepsy.

(b) The third child, a girl aged 22, has shown signs of the disease since the age of 14. She presented with behaviour disorder, which was soon followed by slurring of speech and clumsiness of movement and gait. The photograph shows the facial expression and unusual posture. She moves slowly and awkwardly and all her limbs are rigid.

(c) The fourth child, a male now aged 20, presented at the age of 11 with slurring speech, clumsiness of movement and retardation. Nine years later he was demented and practically helpless; there were continuous generalized choreic movements. Forty-eight hours' treatment with levodopa had a very adverse effect. He became stuporous and rigid. The drug was withdrawn.

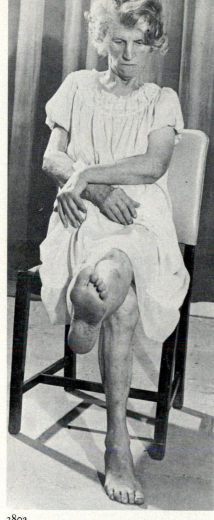

380a

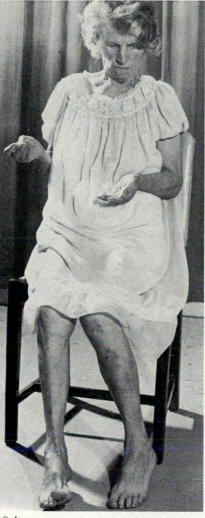

380b

380. Huntington's chorea ◁
Age 53 years. Characteristic features of chorea and dementia of 10 years' duration. Surprisingly alert, but with a bizarre gait, profound amnesia and disorientation. Speech slurred, slight facial grimacing. Tetrabenazine 75 mg. t.d.s. strikingly reduced the involuntary movements within 48 hours, but she became withdrawn and depressed. The photographs were taken before treatment. Six days after beginning treatment, she could sit quietly in a chair and her gait was less abnormal.

Hemichorea

381. Hemiballismus ▽
Age 70 years. Seven days previously, at 10 a.m., acute onset of wild thrashing movements of left arm and leg. No impairment of consciousness. The movements were reduced when she lay in bed, but were gross when she sat in a chair. She could scarcely walk. The movements disappeared during sleep. Tetrabenazine 50 mg. t.d.s. practically abolished the movements in 48 hours. This treatment was maintained for 1 month and there was no return of symptoms.

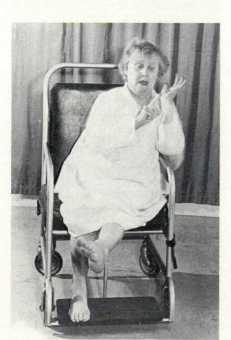

381a

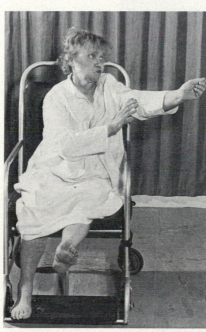

381b

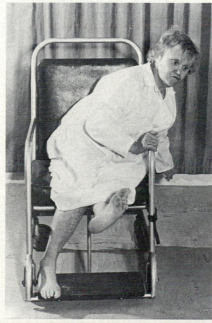

381c

TORSION DYSTONIA
(Dystonia Musculorum Deformans)

This is a rare syndrome due to disease of the basal ganglia and characterized by involuntary movements of a slow, powerful character, which produce torsion of the limbs and spine. It may be sporadic or familial and can occur as a sequel of acute encephalitis. The onset of the disease is gradual, the symptoms appearing in late childhood or early adolescence. The involuntary movements may first appear in a lower limb or upper limb. Not infrequently the child is observed to have difficulty in putting the heel on the ground when walking; there is spasmodic plantar flexion of the feet. Abnormalities of gait may be quite bizarre, with flexion of the knees and thighs, and twisting of the pelvis. Similar disturbances about the neck, trunk and shoulder girdles, produce bouts of torticollis, flexion of the arm and twisting, writhing torsion movements of the trunk. There may be dysarthria and facial grimacing and the movements are generally provoked by attempts to use the limbs. Muscular tone is variable, there is no wasting, reflexes and sensibility are unimpaired and there are no signs of pyramidal disorder. Mental changes only occur late in the disease which is progressive but may remain stationary for many years.

In chorea and athetosis the involuntary movements most commonly affect the peripheral portions of the limbs, rather than the proximal as in torsion dystonia. In chorea they are more rapid and brief and in athetosis, though the movements are slow and writhing, they are not so powerful and twisting and rarely implicate the trunk. In torsion dystonia there is usually an increased lumbar lordosis. Hysteria is often suspected when an involuntary movement increases during observation or under the influence of excitement or emotional situations. But this is true of all organically determined involuntary movements—in Parkinsonism, chorea, essential tremor and hemifacial spasm. The bizarre nature of the early movements in torsion dystonia may be indistinguishable from hysteria and only a period of observation will decide the diagnosis. It is customarily said that hysteria can only be diagnosed when there is other evidence of 'an hysterical personality' but, although this may be theoretically correct, it is often otherwise in clinical practice.

Torsion dystonia usually appears without any recognizable cause but, as with other types of abnormal movement disorder, it may be but one expression of an identifiable disease. It may accompany athetosis in a child with cerebral palsy due to anoxia at birth or kernicterus (bile pigmentation of the basal ganglia in neonatal jaundice). In the latter condition there may in addition be bilateral central deafness. Dystonic movements may also occur in Wilson's disease and in juvenile Huntington's chorea. Spasmodic torticollis is one of the commonest dystonic disorders, and there is little genuine evidence that it is of psychological origin. Some clinicians would include conditions such as writer's cramp and blepharospasm as manifestations of fragmentary dystonia. Certainly the term dystonia is merely a descriptive one, and although occasionally dystonia may be the sole manifestation of some idiopathic disorder of the nervous system, it can have many causes. The iatrogenic category should not be forgotten (see page 422).

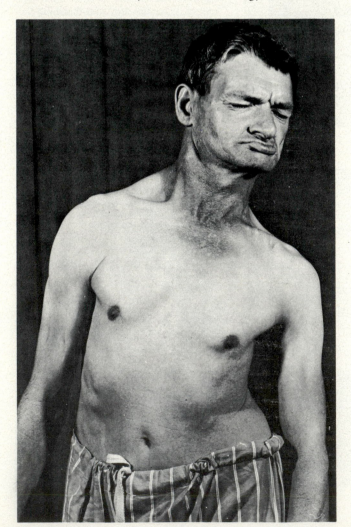

382. Torsion dystonia
Age 50; onset of dysarthria at 16; torticollis at 20; torsion of trunk at 25. Spasms greatly intensified by willed movement; lordotic posture and gait; hands and feet spared. Hypertrophy of right sternomastoid. Eye closure and jaw closure accompanied the neck spasms and speech was nearly incomprehensible. No history of encephalitis.

Torsion Dystonia

383. Torsion dystonia ▽
Powerful muscular spasms flexing the toes and feet and turning the head and opening the jaw. There were twisting movements of the neck, shoulder and pelvis, with lordosis. The disease began in childhood with clumsiness of gait and hands. For many years there were no visible spontaneous involuntary movements. No history of encephalitis.

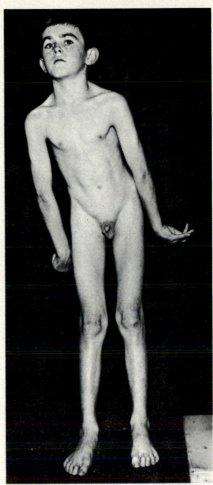

384. Torsion dystonia △
Age 10; onset of fidgety movements and clumsiness at age of 6; frequent falls, awkward gait, athetoid and choreic movements of limbs were followed by torsion movements of head and trunk. Head pulled back or to one side, trunk arching backwards or to the right. Spasms in arms; extended at the elbows rotating them internally and often bending them behind his back. Voluntary movements such as walking induced a variety of contortions. No history of encephalitis; no evidence of Wilson's disease.

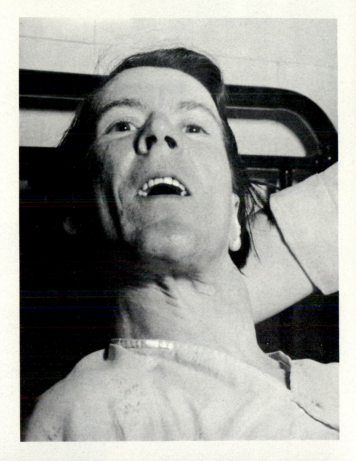

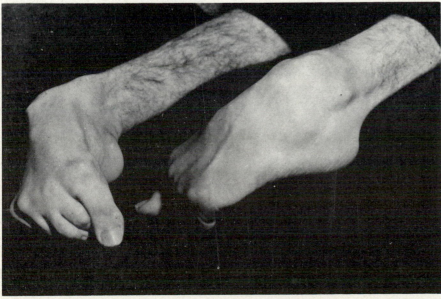

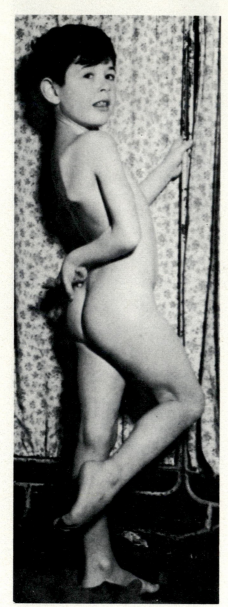

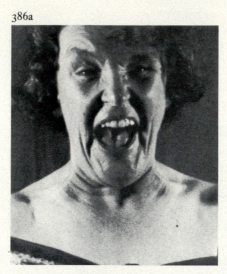

386a

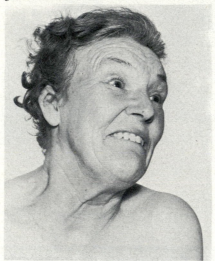

386b

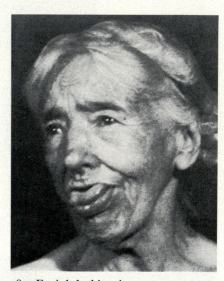

385. Habit spasm
Age 9; onset of involuntary movements of right arm and leg at 8 years. Normal intelligence, no previous illnesses, no evidence of Wilson's disease. Muscular development, strength and tone were normal. Periodic flexion of right elbow and wrist, right knee and ankle; arm would twist behind his back. Torsion dystonia considered likely but movements gradually subsided and ceased by the time he was 12 years. Further development normal and last seen when he was 20. Delinquent behaviour in his teens, unstable family background, subsequently suggested the original movements were psychologically determined.

386. Facial dyskinesia
Age 50; onset of dysarthria at the age of 40 with visible abnormality of the movements of lips and tongue during speech. Then followed facial grimacing, spasmodic torticollis and twisting movements of trunk. Age 43 in (*a*); age 50 in (*b*).

387. Facial dyskinesia
Mother of patient in Fig. 386. Age 73. Progressive dysarthria and dysphagia with involuntary movement of lips, tongue and palate; 16 years' duration. Palatal myoclonus; spasms of diaphragm. Cerebration normal; limbs normal. In neither mother nor daughter was there any history of prior medication with phenothiazines.

FACIAL DYSKINESIA

This term is used to describe cases exhibiting complex, involuntary, stereotyped movements of the face, especially the lower half. There are repetitive smacking, grimacing, champing, chewing and swallowing motions involving the lips, tongue and jaw. The tongue may be constantly thrust out (FIGS. 386 and 387) and may actually hypertrophy. Speech, eating and even respiration may be affected by these abnormal movements. Sometimes they are associated with distal choreic movements or restlessness (akathisia).

Facial dyskinesia may occur as a spontaneous disorder or may follow treatment with phenothiazines or levodopa. It is most commonly seen in inmates of chronic mental hospitals, usually over the age of 50, and is more frequent in females. The majority of these patients have had various forms of treatment including phenothiazines, but a substantial number have had no such therapy. All gradations of severity may be encountered. The most extreme examples are often elderly and demented patients who have previously been treated by leucotomy or extensive electroconvulsive therapy. This syndrome does not include the *acute dystonic* reactions to phenothiazines which are essentially an idiosyncratic response, but in chronic phenothiazine-induced facial dyskinesia, the movements may worsen when the drug is withdrawn. They tend not to respond to treatment with other neuroleptic drugs and may persist indefinitely. It is possible that in the spontaneous and iatrogenic variety of facial dyskinesia there are permanent changes in the midbrain, the brain stem and the substantia nigra.

HEPATOLENTICULAR DEGENERATION (Wilson's Disease)

Kinnier Wilson (1878–1937) of the National Hospital, Queen Square, described this disease in 1912, when he was 33 years of age, in a doctoral thesis entitled 'Progressive Lenticular Degeneration; a Familial Nervous Disease associated with Cirrhosis of the Liver'. This work was the beginning of the modern study of the anatomy, physiology and disorders of the basal ganglia which Wilson called the 'extrapyramidal system'. Although it is a rare disease its importance is that it results from an inborn error of metabolism of unknown aetiology. The historical landmarks are interesting. In 1902 Kayser described corneal pigmentation in a case diagnosed as 'multiple sclerosis', and in 1903 Fleischer associated it with obscure neurological disorder and cirrhosis of the liver. But it is only in the past 20 years that the characteristic biochemical manifestations of the disease have been described. Copper deposits in the liver, brain and corneal ring were mentioned in the 1930's; the discovery of amino-aciduria by Uzman and Denny-Brown of Boston was made only in 1948. In that year also Cumings of London, after a detailed study of the accumulation of copper in the brain in health and in Wilson's disease, suggested the therapeutic use of B.A.L. (British Anti-Lewisite; dimercaprol). In Sweden, in the same year, Laurell and Holmberg identified the copper-carrying serum protein caeruloplasmin. Beard and Kunkel were the first to show the increased absorption of copper from the gut and the diminished amounts of caeruloplasmin in the blood. Finally, Walshe introduced the oral method of treatment with penicillamine. There is no other neurological disorder in which these two biochemical abnormalities—accumulation of copper and amino-aciduria—have been found. Thirty years ago their discovery led to great expectations that similar inborn errors of metabolism might be found in other diseases of the extrapyramidal system, such as Parkinson's disease, torsion dystonia and Huntington's chorea. They remain obscure disorders, but the discovery of dopamine has renewed our hopes.

The disease is not congenital, although several siblings may be affected. Usually the disorder appears in childhood, adolescence or early adult life. Untreated, it is invariably fatal, usually within a few years. Although there is a progressive subacute hepatitis leading to nodular cirrhosis of the liver, in many cases this is not apparent during life. But, as in some of Wilson's original cases, there may be a story of jaundice, haematemesis, anaemia, ascites and various gastro-intestinal symptoms. Nausea and vomiting are particularly common in some patients, but these prodromal signs may be so slight that they are only interpreted as manifestations of hepatic disease when the appearance of neurological symptoms and signs reveal the true nature of the disorder. But in any case of juvenile cirrhosis the family history should be taken, the Kayser–Fleischer ring should be looked for and the serum copper oxidase (caeruloplasmin) should be estimated.

Wilson described the general neurological features as 'generalized tremor, dysarthria, dysphagia, muscular rigidity and hypertonicity, emaciation, spasmodic contractions, contractures and emotionalism'. Pyramidal function remains intact and there are no sensory disturbances. The onset is usually insidious and it may be some time before the parents realize that something is amiss. Their attention may be drawn by emotional lability, peculiarities of movement or gait, by deterioration in handwriting or by the appearance of some form of involuntary movement. The latter may take the form of regular, rhythmical tremor at rest, which is aggravated by excitement. In other cases there is no tremor at rest, except perhaps for a fine one affecting only the head, but on volitional movement sudden tremors of the limb, often violent and of large amplitude, make performance difficult. In writing, for example, the child may be observed to pick up his pen and handle it in a normal fashion until the moment is reached when it touches the paper. Then the arm may fling out in an uncontrolled wild manner and jerk about for several seconds before it can be brought under control. He may jerk about as he sits in his chair, and when asked to stand and walk, the interference with normal motion is seen. There is hypertonicity of the muscles and spasmodic movements of tonic and clonic variety in addition to the static and action tremors. There is often a fixed vacuous smile, some indistinctness of speech or gross dysarthria, salivation and bouts of emotional disturbance, sometimes with involuntary laughter and crying.

When the disorder appears in adult life the process is more protracted and there may be little wrong for some time apart from tremor. The face may take on an immobile Parkinsonian expression. There is no nystagmus or cerebellar symptomatology and the reflexes are unaltered. Hypertonicity is usual in the terminal stages of the disease. All movements become difficult, the patient stumbles and falls, the limbs adopt abnormal postures, usually of flexion, and there may be superimposed tonic or clonic spasms.

There is invariably some change in intellect and personality from the outset. There may be transient psychotic episodes, but usually it is the childishness and emotional overacting which are most obvious. The disease does not often present as a case of progressive organic dementia. The Kayser–Fleischer ring is a zone of golden-brown pigment, a few millimetres in width, with a very narrow area of clear cornea peripheral to it. Unless it is complete it is not likely to be identified with the naked eye; slitlamp microscopy is essential. It is rarely present in the absence of other signs of the disease and it may subside with treatment.

Hysteria may be suspected because of the florid nature of the involuntary movements and the smiling, apparently indifferent facial expression. When multiple sclerosis is attended by progressive dysarthria, gross action tremor and euphoria in an adolescent, the resemblance to Wilson's disease may be considerable, but examination will disclose the presence of nystagmus, cerebellar ataxia and involvement of the pyramidal and posterior tracts of the spinal cord. In hepatic failure, with tremor and cerebral deterioration, there are no abnormalities of copper metabolism and there will be no Kayser–Fleischer ring. These signs will also be absent in cases of torsion dystonia and juvenile Parkinsonism.

Hepatolenticular degeneration is a rare disease with a prevalence rate of only a few cases per million of the population, but it is one of the few hereditary metabolic disorders for which there is an effective treatment. Hence early diagnosis is all-important. Experience has shown that the presenting (not necessarily the dominant) symptoms in childhood are abdominal. In adolescence and early adult life they are usually neurological. It has been said there is no such thing as a typical case of Wilson's disease. The diagnosis must always be considered in any juvenile, adolescent or young adult with a chronic progressive lesion of the nervous system (or of the liver) for which there is no very obvious diagnosis. The one pathognomonic sign is the Kayser–Fleischer ring. The three important screening tests are for urinary copper, serum copper and serum caeruloplasmin. It is generally acknowledged that the pathology of the disease results from the gradual accumulation of copper in the tissues, but the mechanism of this is unknown; it could be increased absorption, or decreased excretion via the bile—the normal route of copper excretion in man.

Copper excretion is promoted by administration of the chelating agent penicillamine. This is a powerful chemical liable to give rise to toxic reactions, but treatment must be continued for life. 'Decoppering' is accompanied by clinical improvement, and neurological signs tend to subside in a few years. Complications of treatment are the nephrotic syndrome, thrombocytopenia and skin rashes.

Wilson's Disease

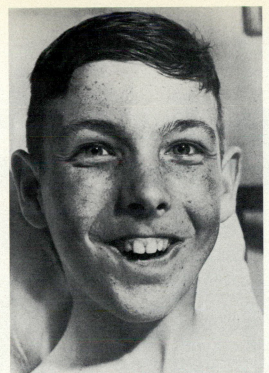

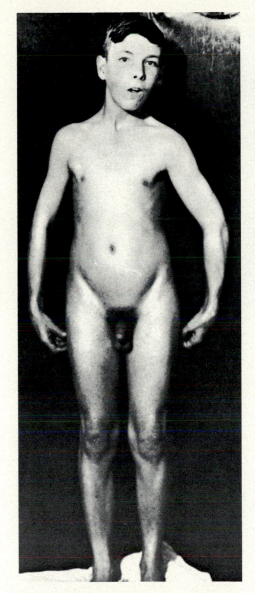

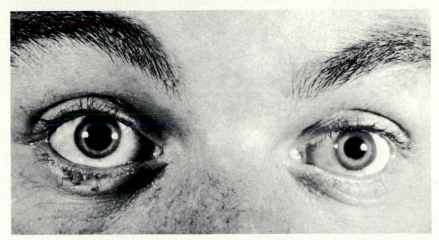

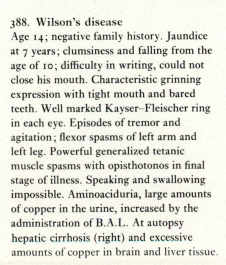

388. Wilson's disease
Age 14; negative family history. Jaundice at 7 years; clumsiness and falling from the age of 10; difficulty in writing, could not close his mouth. Characteristic grinning expression with tight mouth and bared teeth. Well marked Kayser–Fleischer ring in each eye. Episodes of tremor and agitation; flexor spasms of left arm and left leg. Powerful generalized tetanic muscle spasms with opisthotonos in final stage of illness. Speaking and swallowing impossible. Aminoaciduria, large amounts of copper in the urine, increased by the administration of B.A.L. At autopsy hepatic cirrhosis (right) and excessive amounts of copper in brain and liver tissue.

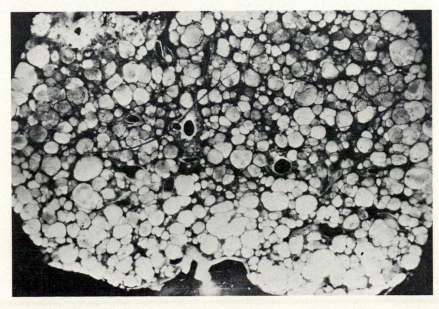

Focal Epilepsy

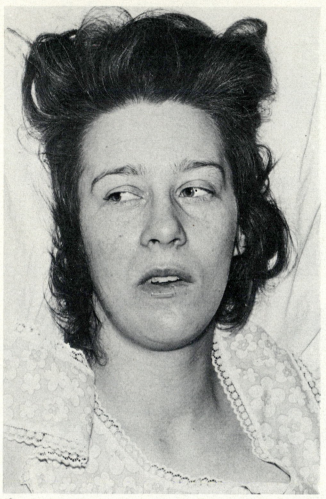

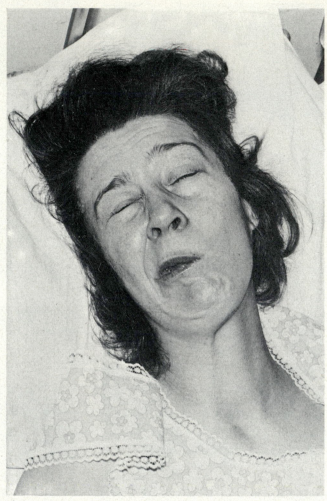

389a   389b

389. Focal epilepsy

Age 30 years. Onset of major and minor epilepsy at age of 20. Calcified focus, 1 cm., in left parietal region. Ten-year period of observation disclosed no evidence of tumour. Following parturition there was a striking increase in her minor attacks. For a period of some weeks she had right-sided focal attacks every 5 minutes; each attack lasted 30–60 seconds and was characterized by deviation of the eyes to the right and by clonic spasm of the right side of the face and often of the right arm. Anticonvulsive medication had only a minimal effect on these serial minor seizures and eventually all medication (phenobarbitone, phenytoin, *Valium* and carbamazepine) was withdrawn. The seizures subsided during the next few days and did not recur.

Focal Epilepsy

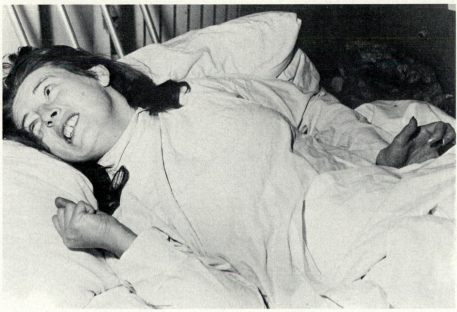

390a

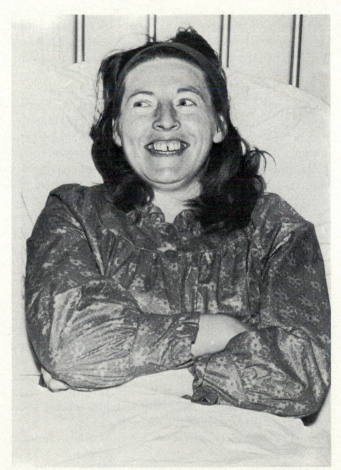

390b

390. Focal epilepsy
Age 36 years. Onset of epilepsy at age of
24. Status epilepticus at 30 and 36 years
of age. During ensuing months had
repeated episodes of right-sided focal
motor attacks, with turning of head and
eyes to the right and jactitation of the
right upper limb (*a*). No apparent loss of
consciousness, and the attacks usually
lasted 30 seconds. Residual dysphasia and
weakness of the right upper limb. All
investigations normal.

Following these focal attacks (*b*) she
experienced a state of 'wonderful, beautiful happiness' which lasted for several
hours. 'I feel wicked, glorious, sexy.'
The focal attacks followed her second
episode of status epilepticus and may
have resulted from temporal or limbic
lobe anoxia.

7 DIFFUSE AND SYSTEMIC DISORDERS

Motor Neurone Disease
(Progressive Muscular Atrophy; Amyotrophic Lateral Sclerosis)

This terrible and invariably fatal disease is characterized pathologically by degeneration of the upper and lower motor neurones. The term 'motor neurone disease' is not strictly correct because the degenerative process is not entirely confined to them. But the posterior columns of the spinal cord are invariably spared. There is profound loss of anterior horn cells of the spinal cord, particularly in the cervical enlargement, and in the homologous motor nuclei of the brain stem, namely, the hypoglossal, trigeminal and facial nuclei; the oculomotor nuclei are rarely involved. Pyramidal degeneration is patchy and unevenly distributed; it is never total. There is a fall out of Betz cells in the precentral cortex with distal degeneration in the pyramidal axons. As a consequence of this diffuse degenerative process within the nervous system, the anterior nerve roots and the peripheral nerves degenerate with resulting atrophy of voluntary muscles.

There are three main clinical varieties of the disease. The commonest type is that designated by Charcot, *amyotrophic lateral sclerosis*. It is characterized by wasting of the upper limbs and spasticity of the lower limbs. In the second type, *progressive bulbar paralysis* there is wasting of muscles innervated by the motor nuclei of the brain stem. In the third type, the *purely atrophic form* of progressive muscular atrophy, pyramidal signs do not develop and the wasting, beginning in upper or lower limbs, may progress very slowly or advance rapidly. Not all cases run true to type and there are transitional forms; amyotrophic lateral sclerosis and bulbar palsy are often combined.

The prevalence rate of the disease in many countries is about 4 per 100,000. Amyotrophic lateral sclerosis is commoner in the male (3 male to 1 female), but bulbar paralysis is probably commoner in the female (2 female to 1 male). The maximum incidence is between the years 30 and 50. A family history of the disease is very unusual.

The onset is usually gradual and painless. When it begins in the upper limbs weakness is first noticed in the hand or shoulder region. In the former the patient may notice the wasting before he has appreciated any weakness, but wasting of shoulder girdle muscles or other covered parts escapes notice for a time. Although the disease is essentially a painless one, many patients describe various forms of discomfort and aching or coldness or numbness in the affected limb. Actual 'pins and needles' are not described except in the advanced stages of the disease in a dependent arm or in the wasted lower limb of a patient confined to bed or chair. Painful cramps on the other hand are commonly experienced, although the patient may not at first mention them. In the lower limbs they may occur at rest or when the patient is walking; in the hands they may cause twisting or locking of fingers. Fasciculation of muscles may be localized or widespread, slight or gross and is usually not felt or observed by the patient, although there are exceptions.

The global nature of the atrophy of the intrinsic muscles of the hand is apparent in the flattening of the palm, due to the wasting of the thenar and hypothenar muscles, the 'clawing' of the fingers, the 'guttering' of the back of the hand from interosseal wasting and the exposure of the long flexor tendons in the palms from lumbrical wasting. The deltoid muscle is usually the first affected at the shoulder girdle and the wasting spreads to the spinati and biceps. For some reason the upper half of the trapezius, the triceps and the latissimus dorsi may escape for a time. It is unusual for the wasting to begin in both upper limbs simultaneously but it soon spreads to the opposite side. Despite the wasting the deep reflexes of the arms are hyperactive, brisk finger jerks, supinator clonus, exaggerated pectoral reflexes and a general hyperexcitability of the muscles to percussion are commonly found. Together with striking fascicular play, these signs combine to provide the most characteristic features of the disease.

The wasting, of course, is not confined to the muscles; the subcutaneous tissues are also involved. The way in which the bony framework of the hand or shoulder is gradually revealed by the wasting of muscles and fat may be striking. I have the impression that this is commoner in the male; in the female muscular wasting at the shoulder girdle may be partly hidden by the apparent sparing of subcutaneous tissues.

Meanwhile in one or both lower limbs symptoms and signs of pyramidal disorder may be appearing. Occasionally they precede the atrophic involvement of the upper limb. Generally speaking severe forms of spastic paraplegia with flexor spasms and contractures do not develop. Sphincter control is seldom seriously disturbed but sexual power is usually lost. The abdominal reflexes are often retained until a late stage of the disease.

I have seen ophthalmoplegia in motor neurone disease on only one occasion. No gross changes usually take place in the face, but a mild weakness of the lower half is not uncommon.

When bulbar palsy supervenes there is weakness of the muscles of the tongue, palate, pharynx and often of the larynx. It may come on at any stage of the disease and may precede, accompany or follow the limb manifestations. It is usually heralded by some alteration in voice or of articulation. A slight indistinctness may be evident only when the patient is tired, or he may find that he can no longer sing or shout or that his voice has lost its modulation. Labial and lingual consonants are imperfectly pronounced. The processes of chewing and swallowing begin to fail. Saliva collects in the mouth and may appear at the corners of the lips; while the patient talks he may be seen to pause periodically while he gulps the secretions that meanwhile have accumulated in his pharynx. Many female patients, of course, with other ailments carry a handkerchief in one hand while telling their clinical history. They clutch it in an anxious manner and if they lose it momentarily they may trot quickly across the consulting room to retrieve it before lying on the examination couch. The male patient rarely does this and when he is seen to hold a handkerchief in his hand during the preliminary stages of a consultation, he is usually either suffering from Parkinsonism or bulbar palsy. He requires it to periodically wipe his lips. The appearances of the tongue have already been described. Usually it is wasted, wrinkled, thrown into folds and increasingly motionless. Alternatively, in the spastic form of bulbar palsy it is small, tight and pointed. The progressive dysarthria and dysphagia are not infrequently accompanied by emotional lability. Explosive episodes of laughing and crying occur and are as a rule unaccompanied by the appropriate emotion. This state of affairs in a patient wasting away from lack of nourishment, as well as from the disease process itself, no longer able to feed himself or swallow or communicate with his family, presents one of the most difficult therapeutic situations that a doctor can face. There is usually a brisk jaw jerk.

In the third type, the atrophic form, wasting and fasciculation of the muscles of the upper or lower limb, are accompanied by progressive loss of deep reflexes. When this form of the disease appears in one lower limb diagnosis may be delayed. The onset and progress of the disease in the atrophic form is slower and the patient may live for many years. On the other hand, it may spread in a rapid manner and cause death within a year. I have never actually seen a remission but certainly the disease process can appear to be stationary for a time or remain localized to one limb. Final stages may also be rapid.

The relatively painless nature of the complaint and the negative sensory examination usually enable the clinician to exclude other causes of wasting of the hand muscles, such as ulnar or median nerve lesions, the carpal tunnel syndrome, syringomyelia and cervical spondylosis. In the last named condition, obvious wasting of the small muscles of the hands is uncommon while fasciculation is rarely widespread as in motor neurone disease. Muscular tenderness, pain and paraesthesiae may be noted and the pattern of reflex activity in the affected upper limb may indicate a midcervical cord lesion. A bilateral chronic ulnar palsy may be insidious in development, without pain or tenderness of the elbow, and the characteristic sensory impairment may pass unnoticed by the patient.

When the initial weakness is in one lower limb diagnosis may present certain difficulties. Slight spasticity without wasting or sensory loss may raise the suspicion of multiple sclerosis or spinal cord tumour. Careful search for fasciculation of the trunk muscles should be made. The retention of the abdominal reflexes is not uncommon. When the presenting feature consists of a flaccid foot drop with wasting of the anterior tibial and peroneal muscles and there is a feeling of heaviness and aching about the foot and ankle, the nature of the illness may be obscure for a time. A similar disturbance arising in the opposite leg may raise the question of a cauda equina syndrome. Another mode of onset in which diagnostic difficulties may be encountered is that where weakness begins in the tongue and remains confined there for some time. The characteristic vermicular movements in the tongue may be slight or pass unnoticed. An important differential diagnosis in this early bulbar type of case is from myasthenia gravis. There may be no fatigue phenomenon which can be elicited from the clinical history in some cases of this disease, while the response to a *Prostigmin* or *Tensilon* test is not always obvious. In early bulbar palsy articulation and swallowing may at first be so influenced by fatigue as to suggest the possibility of myasthenia gravis.

Dementia occasionally precedes the symptoms and signs of motor neurone disease. It is indistinguishable from that which is found in other forms of cerebral atrophy.

Fasciculation is never as apparent in syringomyelia

and peroneal muscular atrophy as it is in motor neurone disease. It is occasionally seen in the wasted limbs of old poliomyelitis and indeed it is an old clinical observation that in some cases of motor neurone disease there is a previous history of poliomyelitis. I have seen fasciculation and apparently new muscular wasting in patients with old poliomyelitis but I have never witnessed the actual development of motor neurone disease in such cases.

There is no evidence that trauma causes motor neurone disease but naturally enough, from time to time, this question arises. A blow to a hand, a fall on a shoulder or an injury to a lower limb is, sooner or later followed by the typical symptoms and signs of the disease. The history of trauma is often not elicited on the first exami-

nation; it emerges after interrogation. Quite frequently it is trivial and can be discounted, but sometimes the possibility of spinal cord or root injury has to be carefully investigated. I have never seen a case where clear evidence of nerve root or cord injury has been followed by this disease. It is when there is a history of trauma to a limb that repeated inexpert examinations seem to suggest the presence of sensory loss. Quite probably there is the matter of compensation. Sensory testing becomes unreliable, diagnosis is confused and delayed.

Arthritic muscular atrophy should rarely cause trouble. In an old burnt out case of arthritis of the first metacarpophalangeal joint there may be flattening of the thenar muscles and hollowing of the interspace between thumb and index. There may even be fasciculation of

Motor Neurone Disease

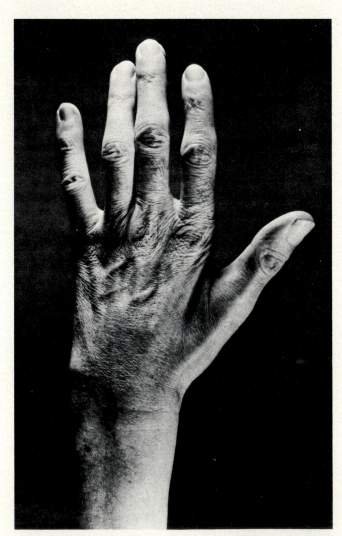
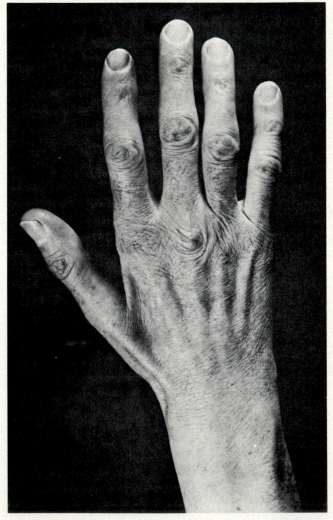

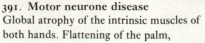

391. Motor neurone disease
Global atrophy of the intrinsic muscles of both hands. Flattening of the palm, straightening of the hypothenar border and 'simian' attitude of the thumb. Deepening of the interosseal grooves.

the wasted first dorsal interosseous, but the abnormality of the joint and the restricted movement and crepitus should point the way to the correct interpretation. Fasciculation is not seen in the wasted deltoid or spinati that may follow arthritis of the shoulder. Chronic arthritis of the elbow may result in marked restriction of the range of movement but biceps and brachioradialis rarely atrophy to any degree and the only fasciculation which is seen is confined to the hypothenar muscles innervated by the irritated ulnar nerve.

Nothing is known of the aetiology of motor neurone disease. No biochemical lesion has been discovered. It is therefore of great interest that in Guam, a small island in the Pacific Ocean, amyotrophic lateral sclerosis is fifty times more common than in the United Kingdom. The disease is clinically similar but tends to occur earlier and last longer. A second progressive and fatal neurological disorder also occurs on this island—the Parkinsonism–dementia syndrome, which appears to be uniquely confined to the Chamorro-speaking people. In this disease there is progressive organic mental deterioration and extrapyramidal disorder taking the form of akinesia, rigidity or tremor. In both disorders, amyotrophic lateral sclerosis and the Parkinsonism–dementia syndrome, there is depressed dopamine synthesis in the nervous system. These observations may, one hopes, provide a clue to the nature of motor neurone disease.

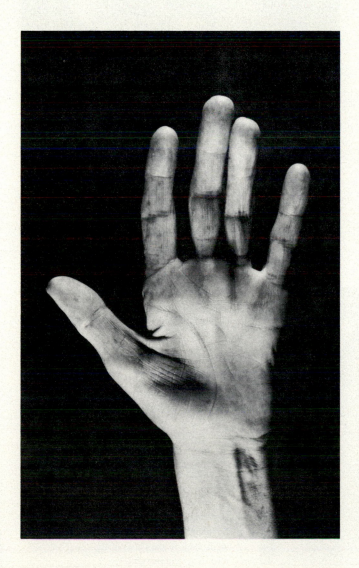

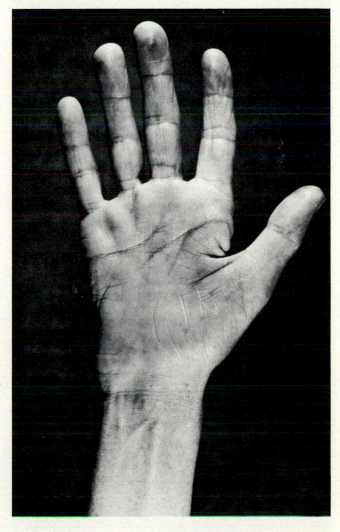

Motor Neurone Disease

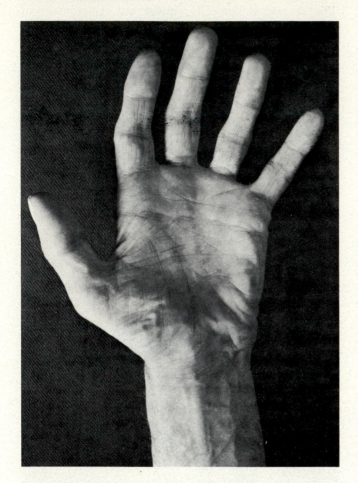

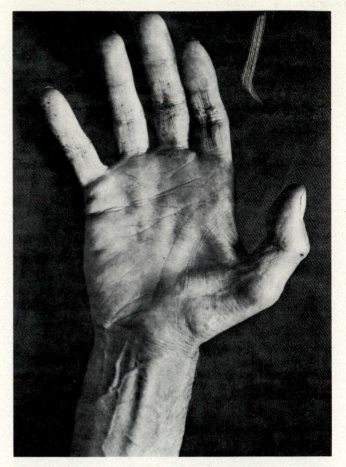

392. Motor neurone disease △
Moderately advanced atrophy in the right hand, early atrophy in the left. On the right there is thenar atrophy with early exposure of the flexor tendons in the palm from lumbrical atrophy. Early atrophy of thenar group on left. The contour of the ulnar border of the hand is sometimes preserved although atrophy of the hypo-thenar muscles may be detected by palpation.

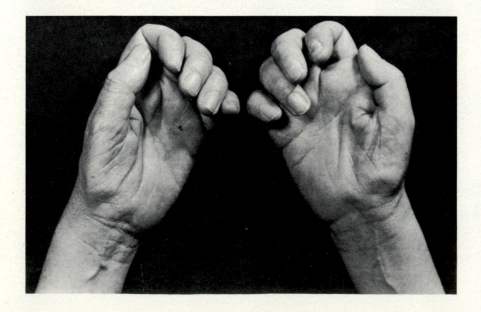

393. Motor neurone disease ◁
Bilateral *main en griffe*. Contractures of atrophic muscles are not marked in motor neurone disease and the involvement of the long flexors of the fingers prevents the development of the severe type of *main en griffe* seen in paralysis of the ulnar nerve and in syringomyelia.

Motor Neurone Disease

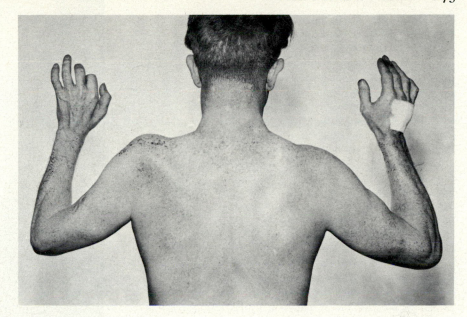

394. Motor neurone disease ▷
Diffuse wasting of left upper limb involving small muscles of the hand, the muscles of the forearm and upper arm, the deltoid and spinati. Note position of the fingers on the left.

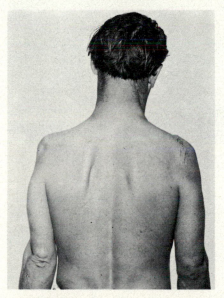

395. Motor neurone disease ◁ ▽
Bilateral atrophy and fasciculation of both deltoids, weakness of the spinati, the left biceps and left brachioradialis. This man reported to his doctor with weakness of the left arm the day after a girder had fallen across the left side of his neck and shoulder. No complaints about his right arm.

396. Motor neurone disease ▽
Motor neurone disease in a woman, age 23, which presented with slight spastic weakness of the right lower limb which was soon followed by flaccid wasting and weakness of both upper limbs and later by weakness of the neck muscles, shoulder girdles and progressive bulbar palsy. There was complete anarthria, severe dysphagia, profound weakness of the extensor muscles of the neck and of the deltoids.

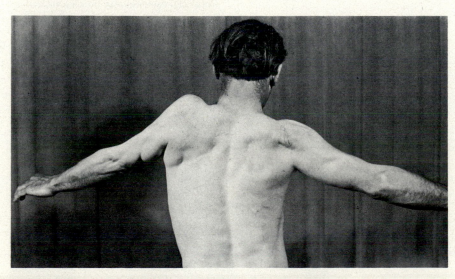

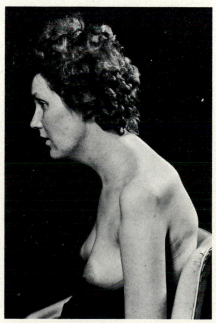

397. Motor neurone disease ▷
Flaccid weakness and wasting of the
anterior tibial and peroneal muscles of the
right leg. Note weakness of dorsiflexion.
Impaired right knee jerk, absent right
ankle jerk. No fasciculation or sensory loss.
Very slow progression and no involvement
of left leg for 2 years. Subsequently more
typical features of motor neurone disease
appeared in both upper limbs.

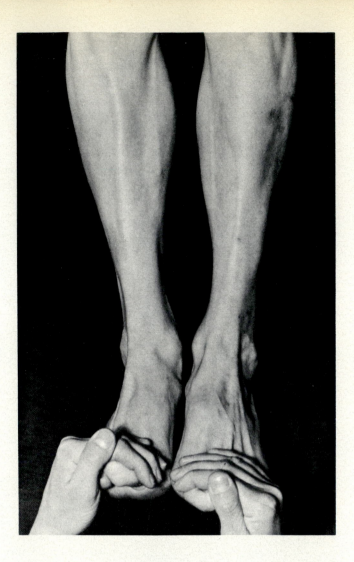

398. Motor neurone disease ▽
Early diffuse wasting of muscles of right
lower limb in a male aged 40 complaining
of cramp in right calf at rest and during
walking. Moderate weakness of leg, scuffing
of toes, impaired right knee and ankle
jerks, fasciculation of right thigh muscles;
no sensory loss. Note loss of contour of
outer side of right thigh and inner side of
right calf. There was also flattening of
right gluteal muscles.

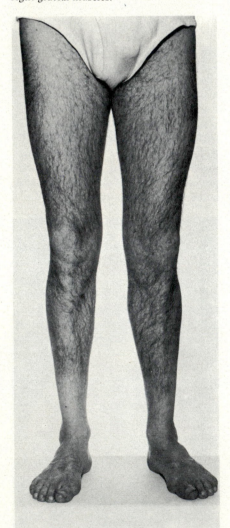

399. Right parietal lobe glioma ▽
Slight diffuse atrophy of the small muscles
of the left hand with corresponding weakness. Note flattening of left thenar eminence and loss of contour of ulnar border
of the hand. This form of unexplained
wasting of the small muscles of the hand
in parietal tumours may be very misleading.

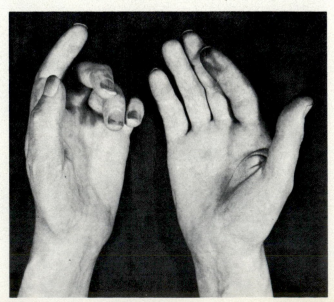

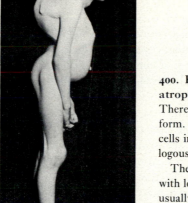

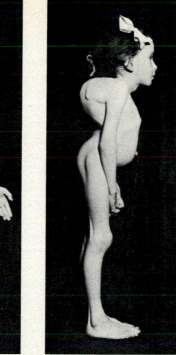

Miscellaneous

400. Progressive spinal muscular atrophy of children ◁

There is an infantile form and a juvenile form. Progressive loss of anterior horn cells in the spinal cord and in the homologous motor nuclei of the brain stem.

There is progressive flaccid paralysis with loss of deep reflexes; sensation is usually preserved and the function of the sphincters is unimpaired. Fasciculation may be seen. The face is unaffected but bulbar paralysis may occur. Note the normal facial appearance in this child, the gross kyphoscoliosis, the thin limbs and the extreme hypotonia which allows her to adopt abnormal attitudes.

The infantile form of the disease is fatal but the juvenile form is not usually fatal and becomes arrested in late childhood. (Courtesy of Professor A. G. Watkins.)

402. Rheumatoid arthritis ▽

Arthritis of first metacarpophalangeal joint with atrophy of adjacent first dorsal interosseous muscle.

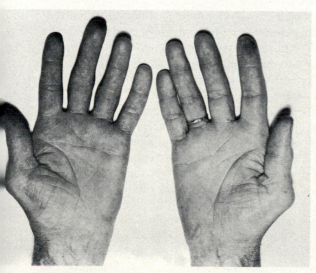

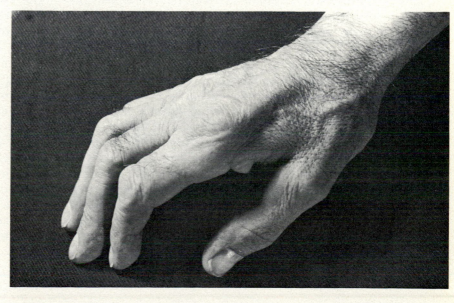

401. Rheumatoid arthritis △

Bilateral atrophy of abductor pollicis brevis as the result of chronic arthritis of the first metacarpophalangeal joint of each hand.

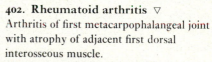

The Hereditary Ataxias

This term comprises a group of heredofamilial disorders in which there are various combinations of degeneration in the tracts of the spinal cord, the olives, the cerebellum and the optic nerves. There are predominantly spinal forms, spinocerebellar forms and predominantly cerebellar forms. The age of onset ranges from childhood to middle life and they are slowly progressive. Hereditary transmission may occur either as a dominant or a recessive. They are probably the result of some defect in enzyme systems. Within an affected family the clinical picture may be remarkably stereotyped, but ataxic and spastic forms may vary in degree and extent, while apparently unaffected members of the family may show reflex or skeletal abnormalities, such as scoliosis or pes cavus.

In the past hundred years the descriptions of the pathological and clinical features of these obscure disorders have been associated with some of the greatest names in German, French, and English neurological literature—Friedreich, Charcot, Marie, Dejerine, Alajouanine, André Thomas, Gowers and Holmes.

FRIEDREICH'S ATAXIA

In a series of papers from 1861 to 1876 Friedreich of Heidelberg laid the groundwork of our knowledge of hereditary degenerations of the spinal cord, brain stem and cerebellum. His claim that he had described a new disease gained slow recognition and for some time patients with hereditary ataxia continued to be confused with sufferers from multiple sclerosis or tabes dorsalis.

The disease is transmitted through both sexes, usually indirectly, and sporadic cases occur. The spinal cord is unusually small and degeneration is most marked in the posterior columns. The pyramidal and dorsal spinocerebellar tracts also degenerate and there is reactive gliosis. The anterior horn cells suffer little but there may be involvement of the dorsal root fibres. The cerebellum is usually normal. Various lesions in the brain stem have been described, including degeneration of the nuclei of the vestibular, ninth, tenth and twelfth cranial nerves.

In the great majority of cases the first signs of ataxia are noted in childhood and take the form of an awkwardness of gait and a tendency to stumble and fall. Not infrequently these observations are made after an incidental illness. The rate at which the disease progresses varies greatly in different families, but tends to be similar in the siblings of a family. By the age of 20 the patient is usually noticeably ataxic and may be chair-bound at 30 years of age. Exceptions are encountered and I have seen patients still up and about in their forties. The average duration of the disease is about 30 years.

At first the ataxia of gait is to some extent corrected by the patient walking with his legs further apart than normal, but he tends to stumble when he turns quickly. Later he swerves and reels and has difficulty in maintaining a straight path. He raises his arms to help him in balance and both upper and lower limbs tend to tremble and shake. He is clumsy at the table, fumbles and drops things and his head tends to shake. There is nystagmus, and speech is invariably dysarthric. It may be slow and slurred or scanning and explosive. A difficult word may stop him completely and the observer may hear 'inspiratory whoops' indicating the lack of co-ordination of respiration with phonation. The nystagmus is often slow and coarse and may be observed before formal examination is carried out. Knee and ankle jerks are absent and the plantar responses extensor. Subjective sensory symptoms are seldom encountered but there is usually some loss of sense of position in the limbs with diminished vibration sense. The small muscles of the feet and hands tend to waste. Intelligence may be inferior and during the course of the disease there is often some degree of deterioration, intellectually and emotionally. The sphincters usually escape. Optic or retinal atrophy is a rare complication.

Few patients with this disease possess a normal spine; scoliosis or kyphoscoliosis is the rule and as the disease advances may be severe. Pes cavus is present in nearly all cases, although Friedreich did not include it in his original account. The feet are short, high arched with the toes *en griffe*. Pes cavus may be present from childhood, but in other cases it seems to develop during the course of the disease. The characteristic outline of the foot is best seen in the dependent position; on standing it may not appear very abnormal, but as the disease progresses the deformity becomes fixed. The deformity of the feet may be a developmental abnormality present from infancy or one becoming evident later in life as the effects of muscle imbalance are established. Spinal curvature may be also interpreted in this way.

Unaffected members of the family may show slight signs of abnormality in the lower limbs, chiefly pes cavus and absent reflexes. The fully fledged syndrome of Friedreich's ataxia is much rarer than these mild forms of ataxia. Similar observations may be made in families afflicted with peroneal muscular atrophy.

As in myotonia atrophica sudden death from heart failure is well known; E.C.G. abnormalities are common and the heart is often enlarged.

Juvenile tabes dorsalis, with which Friedreich's ataxia used to be confused, is now a practically unknown disease. In patients with mild forms of heredofamilial ataxia who do not present with disability until the thirties, distinction from tabes dorsalis should not be difficult. The family history may not be known, but the tell-tale abnormalities of the feet, the spinal curvature, the normal pupils and the extensor plantar reflexes, with normal sensibility to pain and deep pressure, should serve to exclude a syphilitic origin. Multiple sclerosis, on the other hand, may be much more difficult to exclude in the early stages of Friedreich's ataxia. In multiple sclerosis heredity plays a small part, the onset of the disease is rare before the age of 15, the deep re-flexes are invariably exaggerated and the spine and feet are normal. Remissions in Friedreich's ataxia are practically unknown.

For some obscure reason a certain proportion of patients suffering from Friedreich's ataxia develop diabetes mellitus. There are no unusual features about the diabetes, but when it develops the patients are already severely disabled with the neurological disorder.

Friedreich's Ataxia

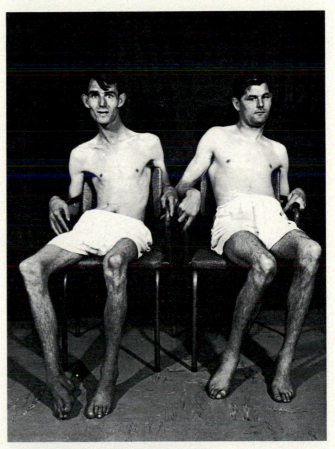

403. Friedreich's ataxia (brothers aged 30 and 32 years)
Negative family history. Onset with ataxia and tremor at 10 years of age. Confined to wheel chairs at 20 years. Nystagmus, scanning speech, tremors, ataxic limbs with signs of involvement of pyramidal path-ways and posterior columns. Kypho-scoliosis. The elder brother also suffers from diabetes mellitus.

Friedreich's Ataxia

404. Heredofamilial ataxia (father and son)

Son, age 12. Pes cavus since infancy. Increasing clumsiness of gait for 6 years. Episodes of vertigo with obvious oscillation of the eyeballs. Constant fine nystagmus on ophthalmoscopy. Slight dysarthria, mild dorsal kyphosis, weakness of the small muscles of the hands and the peronei. Absent knee and ankle reflexes and extensor plantar reflexes. Sensation normal apart from impairment of vibration in feet and shins. Air myelography and encephalography normal. Feet (*b*). *Father, age 40.* He has typical peroneal muscular atrophy; speech and eyes are normal and his disability is moderate; he never had the ataxic difficulties experienced by his son. Feet when standing (*c*). He says his toes were always clawed, never straight like his son's.

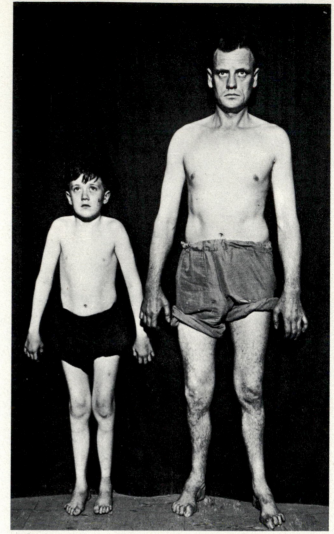

404b

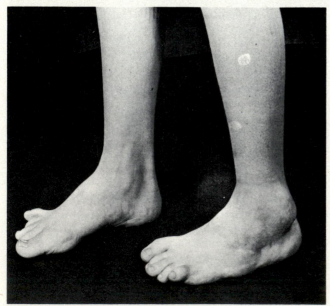

404a

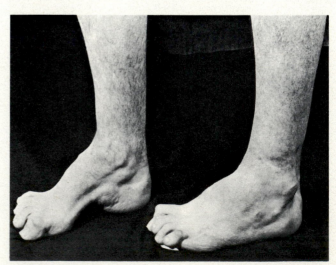

404c

PROGRESSIVE CEREBELLAR DEGENERATION

No satisfactory classification of these disorders is possible. Cerebellar degeneration may occur in sporadic or familial form. It may begin in childhood, in middle life or in late adult life. It may be purely cerebellar or spinocerebellar. From the pathological point of view there are two main forms—olivopontocerebellar atrophy and cortical cerebellar atrophy. Either form may be associated with degeneration in the posterior columns, the spinocerebellar or pyramidal tracts. These and other transitional varieties provide the connecting link with Friedreich's ataxia.

Clinical differentiation is rarely possible. Onset in adult life is commoner than in childhood or adolescence. Cerebellar symptoms predominate—dysarthria, tremor, ataxia of upper and lower limbs—and mental deterioration is common. Such patients may first complain that after a pint of beer their speech becomes slurred; they are accused of over-indulgence and usually have to forgo alcohol in a couple of years. Rarely, nicotine may grossly aggravate the ataxia. Syncope from orthostatic hypotension, consequent on degeneration of sympathetic cells in the spinal cord, may occur. Mental deterioration is common; nystagmus is rare. Formal examination on a couch may reveal little more than some hyperactivity of deep reflexes. The degree of the ataxia may only be appreciated when the patient is asked to walk.

It may be difficult to distinguish the disease from late developing multiple sclerosis. I have made the diagnosis of progressive cerebellar degeneration in a woman of 60, who, when she died 10 years later, proved to have literally hundreds of plaques in her brain. In multiple sclerosis nystagmus is commoner, signs of spasticity and posterior column loss more evident and there may be pallor of the optic discs, but there may be no remission and little fluctuation of disability when multiple sclerosis appears in middle-age or later. On the whole, in these spinocerebellar degenerations, disturbances of speech and gait are more conspicuous.

It must be remembered that progressive cerebellar degeneration may result from chronic alcoholism or visceral carcinoma. It is probable that in the past many recorded examples of sporadic cerebellar degeneration in middle-age were due to carcinoma.

HEREDITARY SPASTIC PARAPLEGIA

This is a rare disease which usually affects several siblings with or without an hereditary background. It is commoner in the male and usually begins in childhood; rarely, it may present in the thirties but usually not later. Degeneration of the pyramidal tracts is most marked in the lumbar segments and can seldom be traced above the level of the medulla. Although at autopsy slight changes may be found in the posterior columns and spinocerebellar tracts, during life there is little or no sensory loss or ataxia to be detected. The salient feature comprises the gradual development of spastic weakness in the lower limbs. The child has difficulty in placing his heels on the ground, his knees tend to rub against each other and his gait is generally stiff and awkward. There is little if any wasting to be observed and characteristic pyramidal reflex changes are found. There may be some degree of pes cavus and contractures of the knees and hips are inevitable. In some patients the upper limbs are spared for many years. Optic and retinal atrophy which may be difficult to distinguish from acute retrobulbar neuritis has been described. Mentality is not usually affected. When the disease develops in childhood it has to be distinguished from cerebral diplegia, in which case the onset can be traced to infancy, mental retardation and epilepsy are common and the spasticity of the lower limbs not so relentlessly progressive. Unilateral or bilateral optic atrophy of rapid onset in a person with hereditary spastic paraplegia would have to be distinguished from multiple sclerosis. Nystagmus, intention tremor, dysarthria and evidence of sensory spinal ataxia should be looked for. Sphincter complaints are commoner in multiple sclerosis.

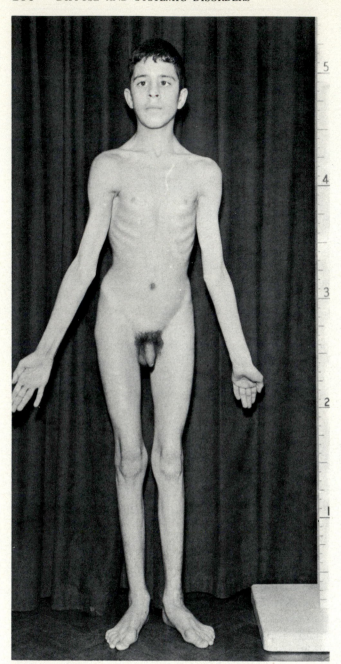

405. Progressive cerebellar degeneration △

Age 15. Maternal uncle died at 13 of cerebellar ataxia. Father suffers from Parkinson's disease. Tremors and clumsiness of voluntary movement first noticed at the age of 5; ataxic gait by the age of 11; dysarthric at 12, diplopia and squint at 15. Titubation of the head, static and intention tremors of all four limbs. Note squint due to left sixth nerve palsy. Diffuse hypotonia, normal reflexes and sensation. Bedridden at 17; died at 18. No autopsy.

406. Hereditary spastic paraplegia ▽
Age 65. Observed for 15 years. Maternal grandfather had 'paralysed legs'; maternal aunt and uncle ataxic; three siblings alive and well. Onset of spastic weakness of the lower limbs at the age of 45. Steady progression for 20 years; now can only walk a few steps; urinary incontinence. Cranial nerves normal, minimal disability in the upper limbs. No cerebellar signs. Loss of vibration sense in feet and shins in recent years. Valgus deformity of the knees and pes planus were probably incidental.

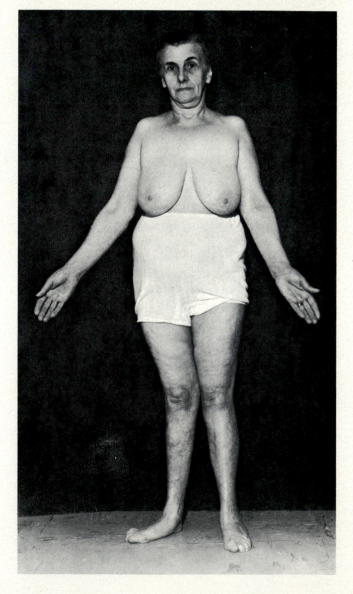

PERONEAL MUSCULAR ATROPHY

(Charcot–Marie–Tooth Disease)

The peculiar clinical features of this form of muscular atrophy were originally described at the Salpêtrière in Paris by Charcot and Marie in 1886, and independently by Tooth of St. Bartholomew's Hospital, London, in the same year. Thus it did not figure in the first edition of Gowers' famous *Diseases of the Nervous System* published in that year. It was originally thought to be some form of muscular dystrophy, but later reports revealed involvement of the peripheral nerves and spinal cord, so it came to be reclassified as a neural muscular atrophy. The muscular atrophy is a result of degeneration of the motor nerves, especially the common peroneal and the posterior tibial. It is not known whether this degeneration begins in the distal portions of the axones, the ventral nerve roots or in the anterior horn cells within the spinal cord. At autopsy degeneration is often not confined to these motor structures but may also be seen in the dorsal roots and in the columns of Clarke and the tracts of Goll. Slight pyramidal degeneration is commonly also found.

There are two distinctive clinical features of the disease. First, the muscular atrophy has a very peculiar distribution and mode of development. It attacks the distal portions of affected muscles in the lower and upper limbs. The muscles do not shrink and waste in a global manner as in motor neurone disease or muscular dystrophy. The atrophy literally creeps up the limb inch by inch involving all muscles. It is this peculiar process which gives to the lower limbs, according to the stage of the disease, the characteristic appearances described as 'stork' or 'spindle' legs, 'fat bottle' calves, and 'inverted champagne bottles'. The second distinctive clinical feature is that in spite of the remarkable deformities the degree of disability is commonly surprisingly slight.

With few exceptions peroneal atrophy begins in childhood or youth. An hereditary basis is evident in many cases, but the mode of transmission varies. Sporadic examples of the disorder are not uncommon. It progresses in a very slow manner and usually becomes arrested in middle life. As with other heredofamilial disorders of the nervous system, there are many variants of the classical disease. Thus, although the atrophy usually begins in the feet and only involves the hands years later, in some cases they are involved simultaneously from the onset. Again, although the progress of the disease is extremely slow and finally tends to become arrested, in some families cases are encountered in which there is relentless deterioration in later life.

Lastly, sensory complaints are usually slight or absent in the classical form of the disease but sometimes after many years these symptoms may be very troublesome.

In the typical case attention is first drawn to the feet of the child by troubles in fitting shoes as a result of a high instep, hammer toes and wasting of the small muscles of the feet. Later, the thin legs are noted and there may be comments about clumsiness and awkwardness of gait. With the progress of the disorder the latter becomes 'steppage' in character, but from the onset the appearance of the legs is much more abnormal than their performance. In the male with trousers hiding the atrophy, outward disability is often slight. The girl usually dances well, although shoe fitting is a problem.

Some degree of atrophy of the small hand muscles is usually evident by the time the patient is 20. The fingers tend to curl up and the patient has difficulty in straightening and abducting them. There is wasting of the thenar and hypothenar muscles and a 'guttered' appearance of the dorsum of the hand. Both feet and hands are commonly cold and cyanosed but trophic ulceration is rare.

The muscles of the face and limb girdles are unaffected and sphincter function remains intact.

The degree of toe retraction, pes cavus, talipes and deformity of the feet varies considerably. When the patient stands before the examiner there is often little abnormality. In the supine position the hollowing of the feet, the pes cavus and the weakness of the extensors of the toes and feet are usually more apparent. Wasting and weakness are not always parallel and loss of deep reflexes may precede obvious atrophy. The ankle jerks are usually absent, but it is not true to say that the knee jerks are always retained. The plantar reflexes are usually absent. I have never encountered an extensor plantar response in this disease.

Accounts of sensory involvement vary considerably as do descriptions of cramp and paraesthesiae. Usually there is only slight distal involvement of superficial modalities of sensation. Some writers have found that deep sensibility is normal or only minimally lost, while others have reported that it is commonly impaired or lost. No doubt there is a genuine variation of sensory involvement from case to case and family to family and according to the stage of the disease.

Intolerable cramps and paraesthesiae may be most troublesome in later stages of the disease. Rarely, dissociated forms of sensory loss may supervene, resulting in digital trophic ulceration as in the primary degenerative lesions of the dorsal root ganglia.

Minor signs of peroneal muscular atrophy may be observed in apparently healthy members of affected families. They usually consist of pes cavus and absent ankle jerks. Similar abortive, intermediate forms, or *formes frustes* are seen in the general group of the hereditary ataxias.

Peroneal Muscular Atrophy

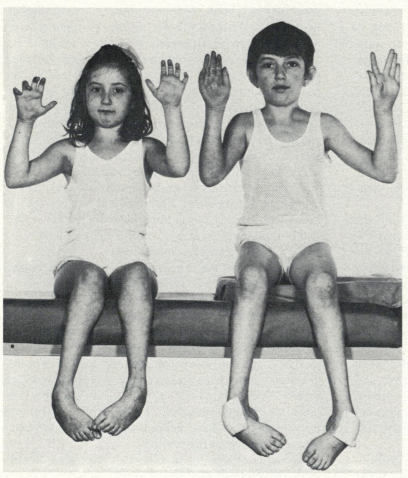

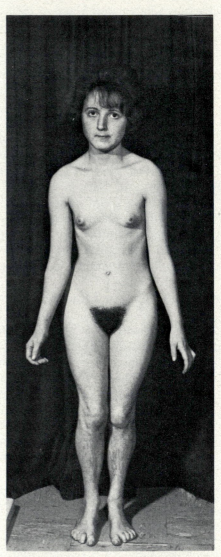

407. Peroneal muscular atrophy in a brother and sister
Negative family history; parents normal. The girl, aged 10, developed signs of disease at the age of 5; the boy, aged 11, at 7 years of age. The disease began with deformity of the feet which led to orthopaedic surgery, but involvement of the hands followed 2 years later in each case. Now profoundly disabled.

408. Peroneal muscular atrophy
Age 17. Three year history of clumsiness of the hands, difficulty in straightening the fingers and early clawing. No complaints about her feet but she was aware of a tendency to hammer toes. All deep reflexes of upper and lower limbs were absent; plantar reflexes absent. Slight impairment of superficial sensation over the feet; deep sensibility normal. Note atrophy of peronei and the appearance of the feet in the supine position. There were callosities on the toes.

Peroneal Muscular Atrophy

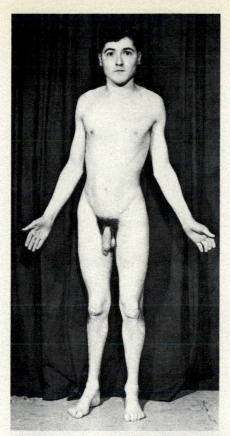

409. Peroneal muscular atrophy
Age 20; brother of patient in Fig. 408.
Bilateral foot drop, steppage gait, distal
muscular atrophy of the lower limbs, pes
cavus and early wasting of the intrinsic
hand muscles. All deep reflexes absent;
slight distal sensory impairment but
vibration sense completely absent below
knees. One other sibling was normal;
father known to have had the disease.

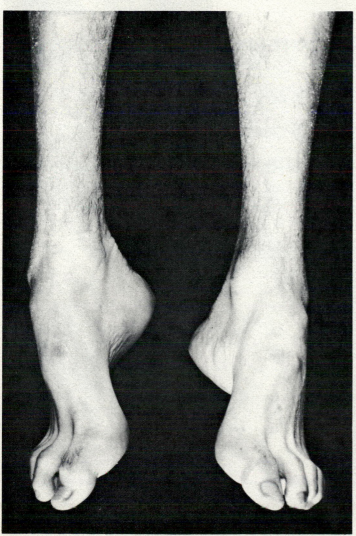

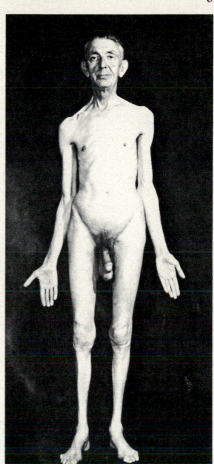

410. Peroneal muscular atrophy
Age 65. Arrested form of the disease.
Entered hospital with peptic ulcer. Father
and one paternal uncle affected. Hammer
toes in teens, 'spindle' legs in his twenties,
hands affected in his thirties. Disability
slight despite gross muscular atrophy.

Peroneal Muscular Atrophy

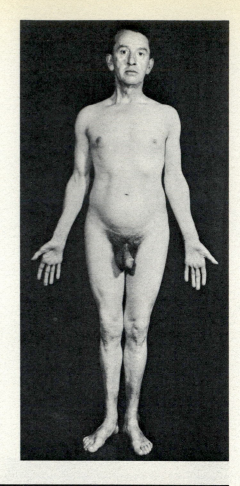

411. Peroneal muscular atrophy

Age 45. Late onset; negative family history. Weakness of feet first noticed in early thirties; hands affected at 40. Disability slight. Normal thighs, brisk knee jerks; absent ankle jerks. Inconspicuous distal sensory impairment. Occasional cramps in calf muscles. No fasciculation. Note wasting of distal portion of upper and lower extremities including small muscles of hands.

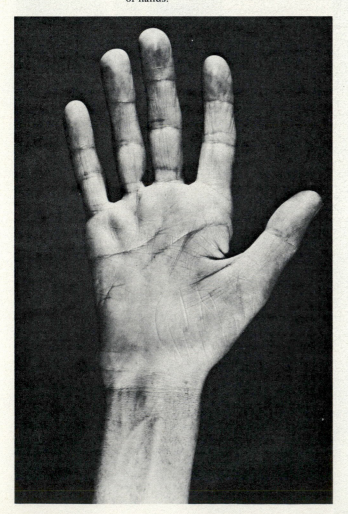

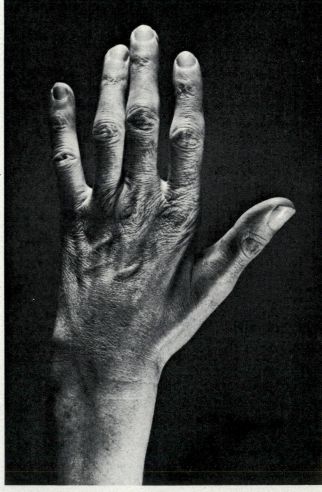

Peroneal Muscular Atrophy

Neurofibromatosis of von Recklinghausen

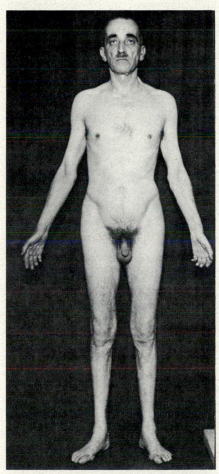

412. Peroneal muscular atrophy
Age 56. Positive family history (mother, maternal grandfather, two maternal aunts). High arched feet and thin legs since his teens. Led an active life, without disability until he was 50. Then, troubled by painful cramps in calves and hands, paraesthesiae in hands and feet and unsteadiness of gait. All deep reflexes absent; superficial sensation normal; vibration sense profoundly impaired below midthoracic level; joint position sense normal. Fasciculation of thigh muscles.

Some medical names become famous because they are unusual as well as being associated with a disease or syndrome, symptom or sign. They sound good. Such a one is von Recklinghausen, the pathologist from Strasbourg, whose name generations of medical students have no difficulty in remembering. But the clinical features of the disease whose histology he defined in 1882, were unquestionably described by R. W. Smith of Dublin in 1849, in his monograph entitled *A Treatise on the Pathology, Diagnosis and Treatment of Neuroma*. One suspects that Smith, even had he also described the histopathology of neurofibromatosis, would have had little chance of immortality in competition with a 'von Recklinghausen'.

The complete picture is one of considerable complexity and characterized by multiple tumours of peripheral nerves, spinal nerve roots, cranial nerves and by cutaneous tumours and pigmentary changes. There may be skeletal abnormalities and defects of development and malformation of the nervous system. It is a disease of congenital origin, hereditary or familial, whose manifestations vary greatly in extent and degree, so that it is difficult to say just when it is proper to speak of von Recklinghausen's disease.

The cutaneous features of the disease are usually the first to appear. They may be present at birth or early in infancy, or develop or increase throughout life. The patient's skin as a whole may be darker than other members of his family, and scattered about the body, especially the trunk and face, may be numerous spots, freckles or patches, café-au-lait in colour, varying in hue and size. There may also be numerous cutaneous tumours or fibromata, soft, sessile or pedunculated, which tend to appear in childhood and may increase greatly in number during life. They are usually painless, more numerous about the trunk, varying in size from a few millimetres to several centimetres. They may develop beneath the nails, subungual, and at times take on a naevoid appearance.

The neurofibromata are subcutaneous, found along the course of superficial nerves, especially of the limbs and are sometimes painful or tender. They vary in size, but they are commonly about a centimetre in diameter and may be movable across but not along the course of the nerve trunk. When they arise from spinal nerve roots, they may lead to compression of the cord. The term 'plexiform neuroma' is used to describe the condition when an entire nerve trunk and all its branches are involved in diffuse neurofibromatosis. It is often associated with an overgrowth of the skin and subcutaneous tissues. Favourite sites for these plexiform neuromas are the temporal or frontal region of the scalp or neck, but they may occur on any part of the body. Local overgrowth may be such that the term 'elephantiasis' is applied.

The commonest cranial nerve to be involved is the auditory, but the average auditory neuroma of adults is rarely associated with the cutaneous signs of neurofibromatosis. On the other hand the bilateral auditory neuromata of adolescence are strongly familial and may be associated with the fully developed clinical picture of von Recklinghausen's disease. Other intracranial tumours which tend to occur are gliomas of the optic nerves and chiasma, and cerebral gliomas and meningiomas. Tumours may also occur in the sympathetic

nervous system and paroxysmal hypertension in neurofibromatosis has resulted from the presence of pheochromocytomata.

Numerous skeletal deformities have been described of which the commonest is kyphoscoliosis. This itself may be severe and cause compression of the spinal cord. Localized zones of hyperostosis about the face, skull and long bones have been described. Scalloping of the posterior surfaces of the bodies of the vertebrae occur and they are important because they might be taken to indicate erosion by spinal tumour. More often they are a congenital defect, symptomless, and sometimes associated with anomalous development of the meninges.

Defects in the skull may occur in the occipital and temporal regions and when they are found in the posterior wall of the orbit, there may be proptosis, pulsating

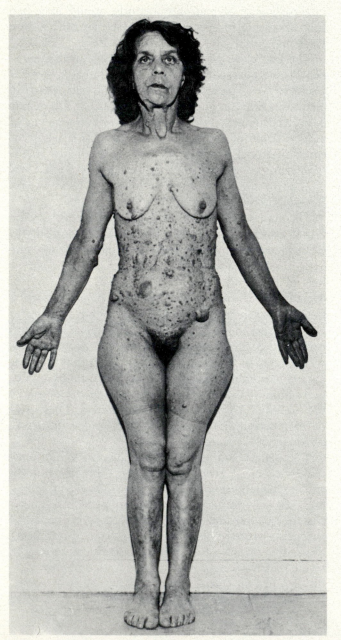

413a

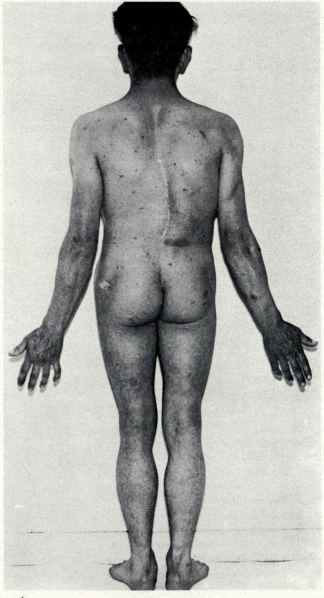

413b

exophthalmos, or bulging of the squamous temporal bone. Exophthalmos may also be due to an orbital tumour or a glioma of the optic nerve.

Various congenital defects of development of the skeleton have been described, such as spina bifida occulta, congenital elevation of the scapula and in some patients there is mental retardation and epilepsy. The retinal tumours or phakomata, seen in tuberous sclerosis, are said to occur in neurofibromatosis but I have never seen them.

The majority of patients with this disease are not seriously disabled, as the peripheral nerves are much more commonly involved than the spinal or cranial nerves, although malignant changes can occur in peripheral tumours. Neurofibromatosis should be suspected when there are *numerous* café-au-lait spots. There may be no significance in the presence of a few.

Neurofibromatosis

414. Neurofibromatosis ▽

Scoliosis in a child of 12 with a dark skin and scattered café-au-lait patches. No fibromata or palpable neurofibromata. Associated spina bifida occulta.

Paroxysms of left trigeminal pain and paraesthesiae. Cerebellar ataxia of left arm and leg. Left extensor plantar response. Radiography normal. CSF normal. Unchanged 10 years later but moderate right nerve deafness.

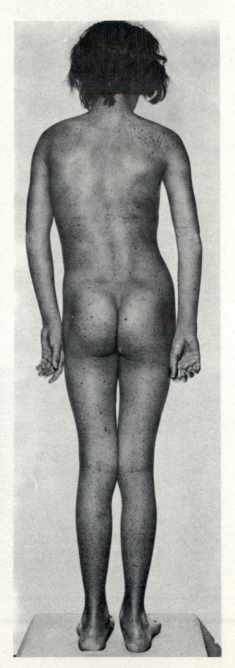

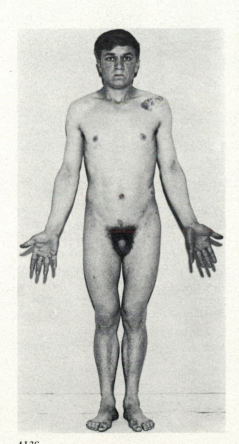

413c

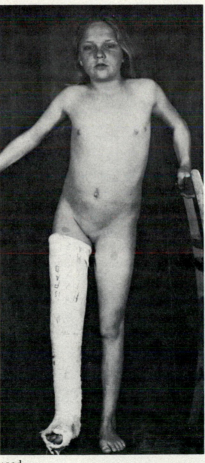

413d

413. Neurofibromatosis

A family with neurofibromatosis. Mother (*a*); first son (*b*); note scar of operation for correction of gross scoliosis. Second son (*c*); note angiomatous naevus on left shoulder. Daughter (*d*); bowing of right tibia noted in infancy; localized hyperostosis and spontaneous fracture when 9 years of age.

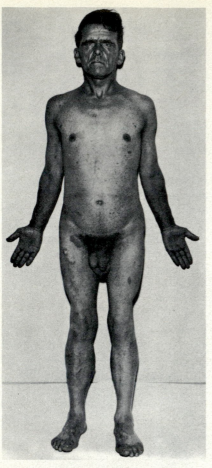

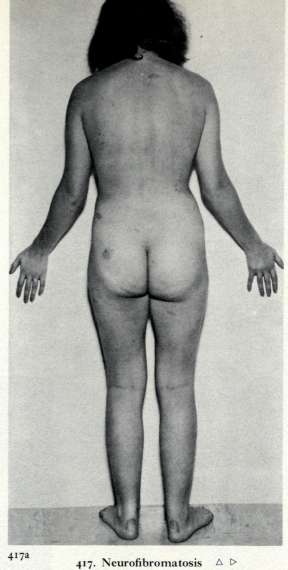

415. Neurofibromatosis △
Mental defective, age 44. Hoarse voice 2
years; paralysis of right vocal cord. Intermittent diplopia. Plexiform neuroma of
right calf causing pains and paraesthesiae,
weakness of limb when walking.

417a

417. Neurofibromatosis △ ▷
(*a*) Dark skinned girl with café-au-lait
patches and transient backache.
(*b*) Radiographs of the lumbar spine disclosed extensive scalloping of the posterior
bodies of the lumbar and sacral vertebrae.
No evidence of a cauda equina lesion;
spinal fluid and manometry normal;
opaque myelography (*c*) revealed the
presence of a capacious spinal canal with
pouching of the meninges.

416. Neurofibromatosis ▽
Recent epilepsy in a man of 37 with mental
retardation, kyphoscoliosis, a plexiform
neuroma on the right shoulder, a naevus
in the right supraclavicular region and
generalized neurofibromatosis. Nystagmus,
increasing ataxia and slight right nerve
deafness, but extensive investigations failed
to demonstrate an auditory neuroma.

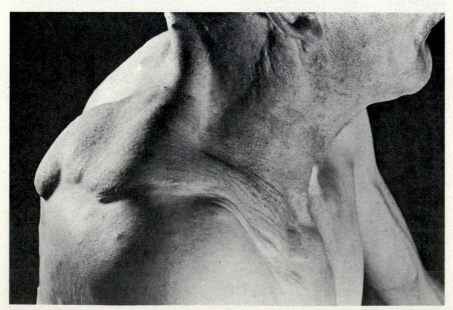

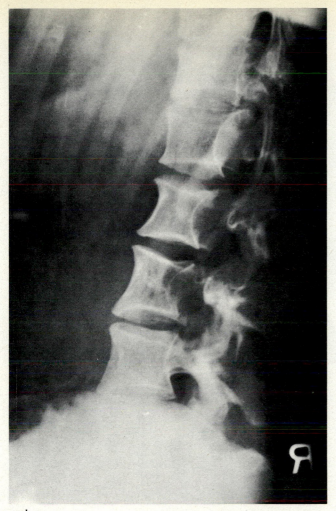

417b

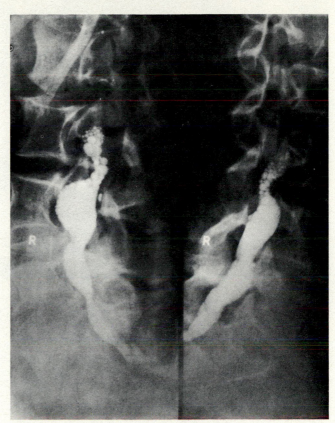

417c

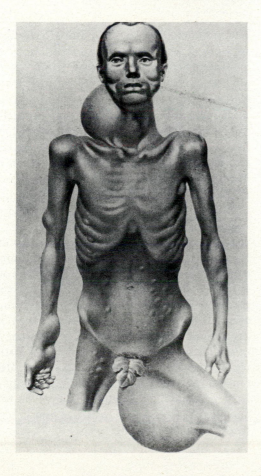

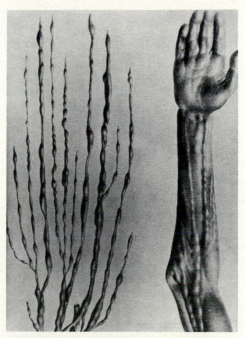

418. Neurofibromatosis
Illustrations from R. W. Smith's monograph entitled *A Treatise on the Pathology, Diagnosis and Treatment of Neuroma*, published in Dublin in 1849, 33 years before von Recklinghausen's classical report.

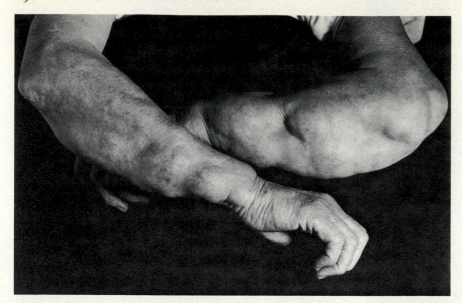

419. Lipomatosis
A woman of 70 with focal epilepsy resulting from a calcified parasagittal meningioma in whom there were multiple subcutaneous tumours of the forearms. They proved to be lipomata and not neurofibromata.

Tuberous Sclerosis

This rare congenital condition derives its title of 'tuberous' or 'tuberose' sclerosis because of the nodular sclerotic masses or 'tubers' found in the brain. The clinical features comprise mental retardation, epilepsy and cutaneous lesions—sebaceous adenomas. Tumours of other organs often coexist and the disorder is one of blastomatous malformation especially involving the neuro-ectodermal system. It presents analogies with the neurofibromatosis of von Recklinghausen. It may occur sporadically or in a familial or hereditary manner. Incomplete forms of the disease tend to occur with one or more of the main ingredients of the syndrome lacking.

Mental retardation in some degree is constant; it may range from feeblemindedness to idiocy and is often progressive. Various psychotic manifestations may occur and institutional treatment is often necessary. Epilepsy makes its appearance in the early years of life and there is nothing unusual about its manifestations; major convulsions are the rule. There are various cutaneous lesions which may not appear until late childhood. The most characteristic of these are seen on the face, appearing as a collection of papules and nodules distributed in a butterfly fashion over the cheeks and the bridge of the nose. Apparently they are not ordinary sebaceous adenomas but are minute tumours more analogous to neurofibromata. They are yellowish or brownish in colour, a few millimetres in diameter and often covered by a fine network of capillaries. Other skin lesions include café-au-lait spots, areas of depigmentation, pigmented naevi and 'shagreen' patches—areas of roughened thickened skin usually in the lumbosacral region. Protruding from under the finger-nails there may be small angiofibromatous growths—subungual fibromata. Small tumours may also be seen in the retina—phakomata—small oval whitish lesions on or near the optic disc or in the retinal periphery. Various types of major and minor congenital malformations and stigmata have been described and visceral and cerebral tumours, apart from the glial nodules, occur from time to time.

Minor forms of this disorder are not uncommon and disability may be slight. In the past there has been a tendency to describe only the major forms of the disease. Intracranial calcification occurs in about 50 per cent. of cases; it is more common in those with mental retardation. The calcification is usually seen in the basal ganglia and adjacent regions. The lungs may be involved in the disease, but this is rare. Affected patients present with exertional dyspnoea; 50 per cent. develop spontaneous pneumothorax. The chest X-ray appearances vary from a fine reticular infiltration to multicystic changes. Tuberous sclerosis was first described by von Recklinghausen in 1862.

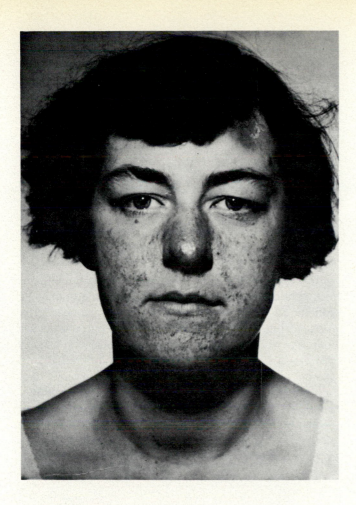

420. Tuberous sclerosis

Age 19. Mental defective with psychotic symptoms (negativism, apathy, episodes of excitement and catatonia). Major and minor epilepsy; adenoma sebaceum was present from infancy but accentuated at the age of puberty.

421. Tuberous sclerosis

Age 64. Premature retirement at 55 owing to mild organic dementia. Epilepsy in youth but not since. Facial appearance said to date from adolescence. Bilateral grasp reflexes, bilateral extensor plantar responses, disorientated and mildly catatonic. Intracranial calcification in the region of the thalami and basal ganglia. Characteristic adenoma sebaceum, with subungual fibromata of toes.

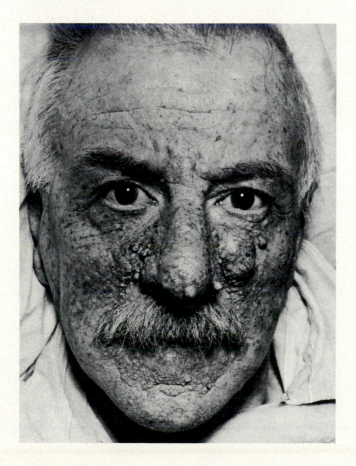

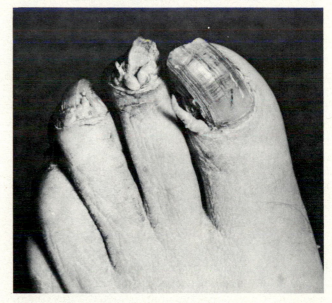

Cerebral Diplegia

(Little's Disease)

The various manifestations of cerebral diplegia result from damage to or imperfect development of the neurones of the cerebral cortex, basal ganglia or cerebellum. Agenesis, trauma at birth or asphyxia are usually responsible; the rubella virus is responsible for some cases of diplegia with congenital deafness.

The resulting clinical picture varies considerably, depending on the degree and extent of involvement of face, trunk and limbs by spasticity, ataxia, involuntary movements and of mental retardation. There may be a cerebral spastic paraplegia (Little's disease), congenital choreo-athetosis, cerebellar ataxia or various combinations of these syndromes. In many cases the parents notice some weakness, stiffness or abnormality of posture in the first year of life. There may be convulsions, delay in learning to sit up, walk and talk.

In the neurological clinic those patients who reach adult life are usually ambulant and betray varying degrees of paresis, spasticity, ataxia and abnormality of posture. The lower limbs suffer most from spasticity; involuntary movements are more frequently observed in the upper limbs. Facial grimacing, a staring expression, an open mouth and peculiar attitudes are common. The gait may be ungainly, grotesque or of the 'scissors' variety as in the classical congenital spastic paraplegia.

Involuntary movements are often the principal disability. Chorea, athetosis and intention tremor, interfere with willed movements as well as distorting the body at rest. The tendon jerks are usually brisk but may be difficult to elicit in the presence of severe spasticity. Affected limbs remain small and thin, contractures are common. Much of the disability is due more to spasticity than to muscular weakness and the abdominal and plantar reflexes are often normal. The parents of a mildly affected child may feel that disability is increasing, whereas the probable explanation lies in the gradual revelation of incapacity as the result of a widening range of activities. By the seventh or eighth year a stationary condition is often reached.

Infantile Hemiplegia

The term 'infantile hemiplegia' is restricted to those forms of hemiplegia which develop during the first 3 years of life. Rarely, it is congenital, the result of agenesis, prenatal lesions or birth trauma. It usually appears acutely or suddenly and there are two principal varieties. In the first the hemiplegia is a complication of an acute infective disorder, pertussis, measles and scarlet fever being the commonest of these. The cerebral lesion is usually vascular. In the second variety, which is commoner, there is no obvious predisposing cause and the hemiplegia is probably a manifestation of an encephalitis or toxic encephalopathy.

When it follows an acute infection the hemiplegia usually appears at the end of the first or during the second week of the illness; occasionally in convalescence. In a large proportion of cases it is ushered in by a series of convulsions and consciousness is often lost for a day or so. There may be a series of fits or actual status epilepticus; the convulsions are commonly generalized but they are sometimes predominantly unilateral. With the cessation of convulsions and the return of consciousness, signs of cerebral damage emerge—hemiplegia, aphasia, hemianopia. When convulsions have not occurred and consciousness is not lost, hemiplegia appears without warning.

The next phase of the illness varies considerably from case to case. There may be rapid surprising recovery in a matter of days or weeks. Fits do not recur and in a month or so there is no residual hemiparesis. In other cases recovery is slower and incomplete. The originally flaccid paralysed muscles become spastic and the characteristic signs of an adult hemiplegia gradually emerge. A greater degree of recovery often takes place in the lower limb of the affected side.

When recovery is incomplete contractures develop, there is arrest of growth on the affected side and the hemiplegic limbs may be the site of spontaneous involuntary movements of a choreic or athetoid character. Epilepsy is a common sequel and the convulsions usually begin upon the affected side. The degree of cerebral retardation is determined by the extent of the original involvement of the cerebral cortex. It is important to stress that in some cases the ultimate abnormality in an affected limb may be slight indeed and escape notice. It may consist of nothing more than a smallness of hand or foot, a thinness of forearm or calf, a clumsiness of the fingers or some contracture in the Achilles tendon. In other cases the arrest of growth on the affected side may be minimal and diffuse, giving rise to an imperceptible degree of general body asymmetry. Focal convulsions appearing in an otherwise healthy child or adolescent should always raise the possibility of a minimal infantile hemiplegia. It is only by inspecting the completely undressed patient as a whole that such slight abnormalities may be detected.

The behaviour of a child with infantile hemiplegia may present a problem. It is not directly associated with his physical disability, but as a rule it is related to the degree of mental retardation he has suffered and to the liability to epilepsy. The child is often inattentive, disobedient and aggressive.

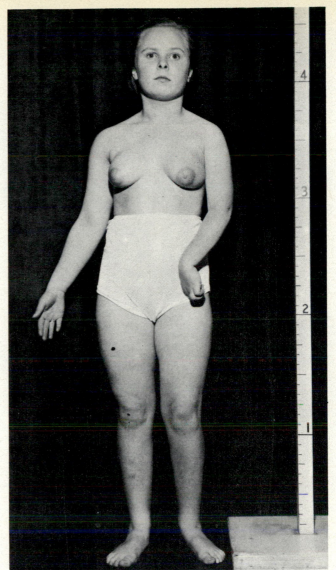

422a

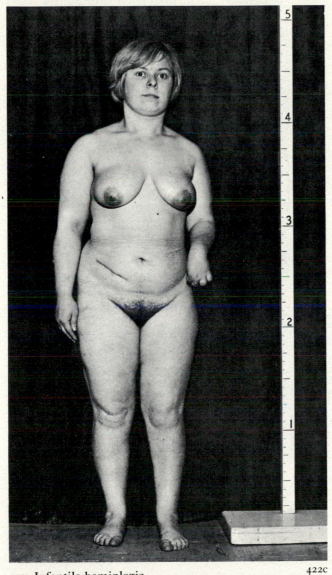

422c

422. Infantile hemiplegia
Acute tuberculous meningitis at age of 3 years. Ten years of age in (*a*); 13 years of age in (*b*). Precocious puberty. Left-sided focal epilepsy since age of 7; often 20 attacks in a day. I.Q. 81; left homonymous hemianopia with left spastic hemiparesis; small contracted left hand and forearm. Behaviour problems. Right hemispherectomy (Mr. Wylie McKissock) at $13\frac{1}{2}$ led to complete and immediate cessation of epilepsy. No recurrence in 5 years. No adverse or beneficial effect on the affected limbs. Note obesity in (*c*), at $16\frac{1}{2}$.

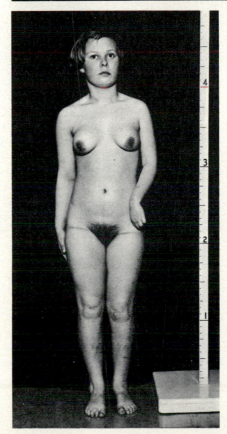

Infantile Hemiplegia

422b

Infantile Hemiplegia

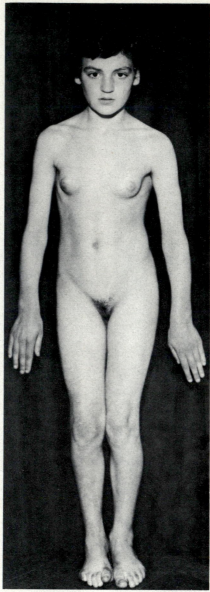

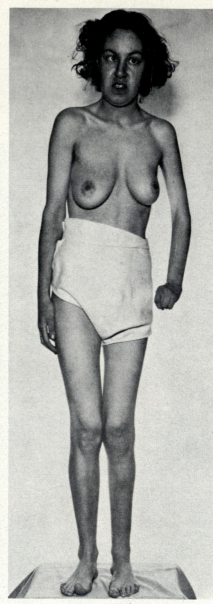

423. Infantile hemiplegia
Age 12. Began to limp at 3; slight deformity of the right foot noticed. No fits, normal intelligence, speech normal. The right upper limb normal. Right spastic crural monoplegia; hypoplasia of calf muscles; slight equinovarus deformity of the right foot, hyperactive right knee jerk, right ankle clonus, right extensor plantar response. Sensation normal. Air encephalogram normal. Note the asymmetry of the trunk; smaller on right.

424. Infantile hemiplegia
Age 19. Born 6 weeks prematurely, weight 2½ lb., toxaemic pregnancy. Three convulsions during first year of life; first at 6 weeks. Left hemiparesis noted at 1 year; delayed milestones. Recurrent epilepsy; grand mal, and sensory Jacksonian attacks on left. Right convergent squint, jaw clonus, spastic dysarthria, hypoplasia of left arm and leg, spasticity and contractures. Left ankle clonus and extensor plantar response. Diffuse impairment of sensation on the left side of the body. Air encephalogram showed marked localized dilatation of the right lateral ventricle in parietal region. Note asymmetry of thorax. Right half of skull smaller than left.

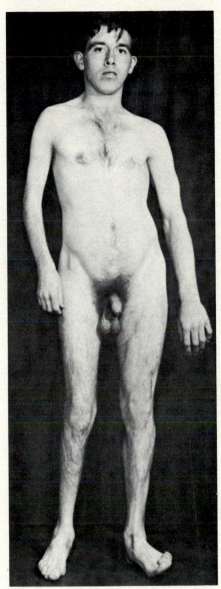

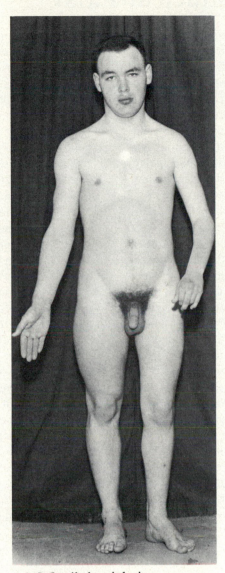

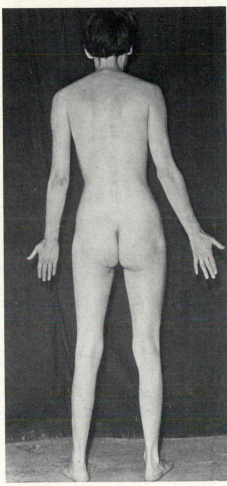

425. Infantile hemiplegia
Age 23. Normal birth, meningitis at 3 months (type unknown), delayed milestones, retarded mental development. Epilepsy began at 7 years. Right hemiparesis noted at 1 year. Several attacks of status epilepticus. Recent increase in hemiparesis. Behaviour disorders.

426. Infantile hemiplegia
Age 18. Left spastic hemiparesis following post-vaccinal (Jennerian) encephalitis at 4 months. Focal epilepsy since the age of 3 years. Normal intelligence; partial left homonymous hemianopia; small spastic left upper limb, left leg less affected. Impaired postural sense left hand and left foot. Air encephalogram showed diffuse dilatation of right lateral ventricle.

427. Cerebral angioma
Female aged 40 years. Sudden loss of consciousness of 5 minutes' duration, followed by stupor lasting 1 hour and a residual left hemiplegia. Right carotid arteriography revealed a large parasagittal angiomatous malformation. Good return of function on the left side, but occasional focal seizures during the subsequent year. The photograph illustrates the asymmetry —a smallness of the left side of the body compared with the right—of which she had always been aware. This was not altered by her hemiplegia. No carotid or intracranial bruits. This is not a true infantile hemiplegia; there had been no weakness of the left side before the apoplexy.

Progressive Supranuclear Palsy

This not uncommon disease of middle and later life has only gained recognition during the past ten years. It is a sporadic and not a familial disorder, usually beginning in the sixth decade of life with unsteadiness of gait, a tendency to fall, altered vision, slurred speech or difficulty in swallowing, and vague changes in personality. The characteristic clinical picture may take several years to develop, but eventually comprises supranuclear ophthalmoplegia, pseudobulbar palsy, muscular rigidity, and axial dystonia in extension. There is often a fatal outcome within seven years.

In many patients there is a spasticity of the facial musculature and a rigidity of the trunk and limbs, with difficulty in initiating volitional movement and a minimal degree of pyramidal signs, so that a diagnosis of Parkinsonism may be made. Other cases present with ocular difficulties and defects of gaze. The most constant feature is ophthalmoplegia for vertical gaze; defects of lateral gaze may also occur. Paresis of downward gaze may be particularly distressing and cause the patient to fall. The supranuclear nature of these gaze palsies becomes evident when examination discloses that there is a loss of gaze to command and in following movements, but not when the head is passively moved. Thus, the patient may not be able voluntarily to direct his gaze upwards or downwards or to follow the examiner's finger in an upward and downward direction, yet when his head is flexed or extended passively by the examiner, he can retain visual fixation. The pupils are usually normal, but ocular convergence may be impaired. The dystonic feature may be obvious about the neck and upper trunk, so that the patient's head is tilted upwards and backwards. The slowness, clumsiness and generalized muscular rigidity may suggest Parkinsonism, but Parkinsonian tremor does not appear. Pseudobulbar palsy is common and there may be trismus. Speech slowly deteriorates.

This striking clinical picture is accompanied by equally remarkable signs of degeneration in the brain stem and the diencephalic and cerebellar nuclei, with corresponding gliosis. The aetiology of the disease is unknown, but in some cases treatment with levodopa has resulted in improvement.

It is interesting and instructive to recall that when the first paper on this disorder was read at a meeting of the American Neurological Association in 1963, the general impression was that it must be a rare disease with a geographic location, and indeed the authors were advised to look for some local toxic cause which would account for their unusual experience. The authors—Richardson, Steele and Olszewski—came from Toronto, Canada, and the disorder is now often referred to as the Richardson–Steele–Olszewski syndrome. However, in the past ten years the disorder has been described in most countries of the world and we have come to regard it as not uncommon. In retrospect, most neurologists can recall having seen cases in which gaze palsies developed against a background of Parkinsonian-like rigidity and mild dementia. As another Canadian neurologist (Dr. F. McNaughton, Montreal, who had also seen a case) said at the above meeting, 'Classical neurology is still growing and changing, even in 1963'.

428. Parkinsonism ◁
This photograph appeared in the series of 28 volumes published from 1888 to 1918 under the direction of Charcot and entitled *Nouvelle iconographie de la Salpêtrière : Clinique des maladies du système nerveux*. It was used to illustrate the fact that occasionally in this disease the postural abnormality is one of extension and not flexion of the trunk and neck. This patient had 'immobile eyes', so that one wonders whether she had a progressive supranuclear palsy, of which Parkinsonism, external ophthalmoplegia and dystonic neck retraction are features. However, the term 'immobile eyes' may have been intended to mean only a staring expression.

429. Progressive supranuclear palsy ▷
Age 64 years. Five years' history of unsteadiness, impairment of memory, depression, slurring of speech, sialorrhoea and periodic tremor of hands; cogwheel rigidity. Treated for Parkinsonism (benzhexol). Then developed difficulty in swallowing, stiff neck, visual difficulties, and inability to open his mouth fully. On examination: unsteady but good limb power, normal reflexes and flexor plantar responses. No sensory loss or cerebellar signs. (*a*) Mildly staring expression, spastic facial and neck muscles and trismus (he is trying to open his mouth). (*b*) Ophthalmoplegia. Impairment of upward gaze and loss of conjugate lateral gaze to command and in following movements. (*c*) and (*d*) Gaze remained fixed when the head was passively moved in a vertical or horizontal plane. No therapeutic effect from levodopa.

Progressive Supranuclear Palsy

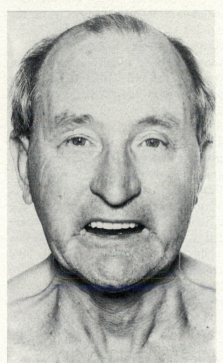

429a

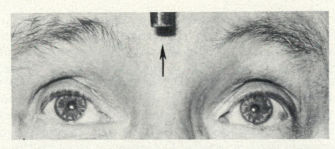

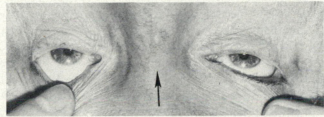

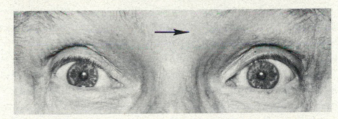

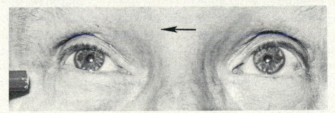

429b

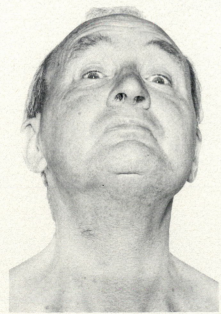

429c

429d

Primary Neurogenic Orthostatic Hypotension

This is another disorder which has received general recognition only during the past decade. It is sometimes known as the Shy–Drager syndrome. For many years it has been known that orthostatic hypotension can develop in neurological disorders which interfere with reflex circulatory control. This may happen in transection of the spinal cord which interrupts the descending sympathetic fibres. Orthostatic hypotension is likely to occur if the transection is above the level of D.5 where there is sympathetic outflow to the abdominal contents. With the passage of time there is improvement, but the basis for this is ill understood. Orthostatic hypotension may be present in diabetic polyneuritis and in acute forms of polyneuritis. It is also an old observation in tabes dorsalis. In all such disorders the orthostatic element may cause fainting, loss of consciousness and falling, and these events may be attributed to weakness or ataxia if the orthostatic element is not recognized.

In recent years it has been learnt that idiopathic autonomic degeneration may develop in a person with no known neurological disease. It presents with orthostatic hypotension, loss of sweating and sexual impotence. The outcome may be fatal. In other cases the autonomic failure is followed or accompanied by signs of progressive neurological disorder. Dementia, extrapyramidal rigidity and tremor, spinocerebellar ataxia, and upper and lower motor neurone disorders have been associated with the autonomic failure. Again the falls may be incorrectly attributed to ataxia, vertigo or weakness. A patient with progressive spinocerebellar degeneration may sometimes fall because of ataxia and at other times because of syncope. Only careful history taking would enable one to identify the orthostatic element. At autopsy the autonomic failure has been found to be due to loss of cells in the intermediolateral columns, namely the cell bodies of preganglionic sympathetic fibres. It appears, therefore, that there is a group of primary neuronal degenerations in which these cells of the autonomic system may be involved. Loss of the normal circulatory reflex is demonstrated by the invariably abnormal Valsalva response. Loss of sweating in response to indirect body heating also suggests that the autonomic defect is central or on the efferent side of the reflex.

In normal circumstances the blood pressure is maintained by hormonal and neurological mechanisms. The former are mainly concerned with sustaining the general level of vascular tone, while the latter are more concerned with the adjustments necessitated by changes in the condition of the body. When a healthy person stands up, there is little if any fall in the blood pressure. Several compensatory reflexes quickly counter the effects of blood leaving the thorax. The afferent pathway from these reflexes begins in the baroreceptors in the carotid body and aortic arch. The efferent pathways include the sympathetic downflow through the brain stem and spinal cord to the intermediolateral columns and to the effector cells of the sympathetic ganglia. The effect of change of posture on the blood pressure can be tested at the bedside, and in orthostatic hypotension the cardiovascular reflex response to Valsalva's manoeuvre may disappear. Postural hypotension in the elderly may be a serious or even a dangerous disability. It may account for obscure falls, accidents or episodes of amnesia. In Parkinson's disease there is a tendency for hypotension, but the cardiovascular reflex responses are usually intact.

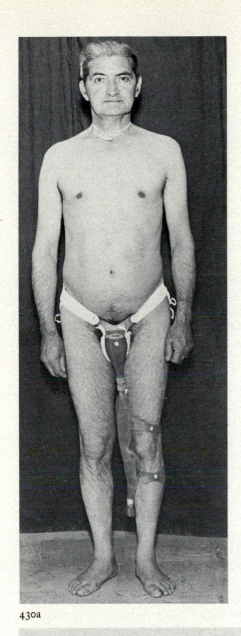

430a

430. Neurogenic orthostatic hypotension

(*a*) Age 57. Lack of sweating for 7 years; postural syncope and impotence for 5 years; episodes of stridor, culminating in bilateral abductor paralysis of the vocal cords requiring tracheostomy, 8 months previously. Urinary incontinence for 6 months. Recently in a mental hospital with depression and alleged hysteria. Treated for epilepsy for several years. Examination: left Horner's syndrome, hoarse voice, tracheostomy, portable urinal. Routine neurological examination was negative. In erect position, only very feeble pulsation of the radial arteries could be felt, and no blood pressure could be recorded. Supine, the blood pressure was 110/70.

(*b*) *Valsalva test.* Normally the blood pressure (recorded on a manometer with an intra-arterial catheter) shows a small rise consequent on compression of the aorta as the intrathoracic pressure rises. The arterial pressure then falls due to the reduction of venous return and the fall in cardiac output. The pulse pressures then cease to fall and may rise as a consequence of reflex vasoconstriction. On release of intrathoracic pressure, the diastolic and systolic pressures rise above their original values and in consequence the heart is reflexly slowed. There is an overshoot due to the persistence of the reflex vascular constriction. Note that in this patient, when the intrathoracic pressure is released, there is no overshoot and the blood pressure rises gradually.

(*c*) *Tilting test.* The stystolic pressure usually alters little when a normal subject stands up, but in a third of cases it falls 10–15 mmg. of mercury. In orthostatic hypotension, however, the pressure falls. The speed and degree of the fall may be sudden, so that consciousness may be lost. Note the falling pressures when the patient is tilted upwards from the horizontal position.

Idiopathic autonomic degeneration may occur as a primary disease or as a syndrome in spinocerebellar degeneration and striatal disorders.

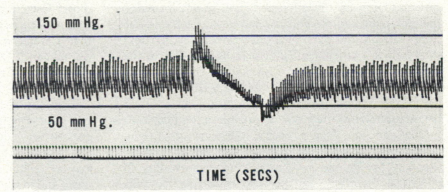

430b

TILT FEET DOWN ↓   TILT HORIZONTAL ↓

150 mm Hg.

50 mm Hg.

TIME (SECS)

430c

8 SYRINGOMYELIA

The term 'syringomyelia' (*syrinx*, a pipe or tube) was first used by Ollivier in 1824, in his monograph on diseases of the spinal cord, to denote cavity formation. The syrinx fills with fluid which may be clear or yellow and usually involves the cervical and upper thoracic segments; it may extend to or begin in the brain stem (syringobulbia) but whether it ever begins in the lumbosacral segments is doubtful. The majority of patients with 'lumbosacral syringomyelia' are in fact examples of sensory neuropathy.

Cavitation appears to arise in the midline behind the central canal or at the base of a posterior horn. There may be more than one cavity. There is surrounding gliosis with compression and secondary degeneration of cells and tracts, notably of the crossing axons which convey pain and temperature sensations. The process spreads longitudinally and transversely slowly involving the grey matter of the anterior and posterior horns, the spinothalamic and pyramidal tracts and, lastly, the dorsal columns. In the medulla the process may destroy the nuclei or emerging fibres of the ninth, tenth, eleventh and twelfth cranial nerves, producing a chronic bulbar palsy and it may also abolish all forms of sensation below the level of the lesion if it involves the fillets.

One can say that a cavity, whatever its origin, developing in the lower cervical and upper thoracic levels of the spinal cord, expanding it, spreading in a vertical direction, and perhaps rupturing its walls and developing secondary cavities, will inevitably produce a characteristic clinical picture. This could be designated the syringomyelia syndrome. In recent years it has come to be recognized that there are two main types of syringomyelia—the communicating and the non-communicating. In the former type the syrinx communicates with the CSF pathways; in the latter it does not. The majority of cases belong to the communicating variety in which abnormalities at the foramen magnum, developmental or acquired, frequently coexist. The commonest developmental anomaly is cerebellar ectopia or the Chiari malformation. The non-communicating type may result from trauma, or it may be associated with spinal arachnoiditis, neoplasms of the cord, or spinal cord vascular disease.

A hydrodynamic theory of origin of the communicating variety of syringomyelia has been proposed. At operation and at autopsy, communications have been noted between the floor of the fourth ventricle and the syrinx within the cord. It is thought that the syrinx originates in embryonal life as a result of over-distension of the neural tube. Thus the syrinx may be considered to be merely a dilatation of the central canal of the cord—hydromyelia. More commonly it is a ramifying cavitation communicating with the central canal and the fourth ventricle and dissecting along paths of least resistance among the fibre tracts of the cord. It has been demonstrated by a variety of methods that the cord cavities are usually in communication with the central canal. Isotope injected into the syrinx can be detected in the cisterns of the brain within a few hours. Dilatation and expansion of the central canal of the spinal cord is thought to occur when the exit foramina do not develop in the normal way in the roof of the fourth ventricle. Cerebrospinal fluid is then thrust down into the central canal, and arterial pulsation from the choroid plexuses may well be transmitted so that a water hammer effect is developed within the central canal. Distension, rupture and ramification may then ensue. This is the hydrodynamic hypothesis of syringomyelia.

The natural history of the classical, communicating type of syringomyelia is that of a lesion which progresses very slowly. Age at onset bears no positive correlation with rapidity of progress. At first the latter may be relatively rapid, but the process tends to slow down and in roughly half the cases it becomes stationary and may remain so for a decade or more. The majority of patients, although disabled, manage to work for twenty years or longer. Deterioration can be episodic, sometimes following an accident or a fall, so that one can visualize a lesion within the cord which periodically advances by small dissections. Obviously it will therefore be many years before the results of decompressive operations in the region of the foramen magnum can be evaluated. However, there is no other treatment, except the tapping of the cyst itself, which is likely to be useful. Radiotherapy, so long used for syringomyelia, was never shown to be of proved worth. The new surgical approach to the treatment of this disease necessitates considerable neuroradiological and other investigations. The surgeon requires to know the size and position of the cystic expansion of the spinal cord, the state of the spinal subarachnoid pathways, whether they are free or blocked, conditions at the level of the foramen magnum, the position and size of the fourth ventricle, and whether there is any hydrocephalus.

The disease begins in early life and the majority of patients present with symptoms before the age of 30. It runs a very chronic course and signs often exceed symptoms. Few patients survive into the 60's. The classical picture combines dissociated anaesthesia and muscular atrophy in the upper limbs with some degree of spastic paraplegia. In addition there are usually trophic and vasomotor disturbances.

The first complaints usually refer to one or both hands. There is loss of feeling or weakness, or both. Subjective sensory disturbances such as pains and paraesthesiae do occur but are not conspicuous. Usually the patient inadvertently discovers that he does not possess normal sensibility. Failure to appreciate heat with the hands is usually discovered in the bathroom or at the kitchen stove. The cigarette smoker burns his fingers without feeling pain and they become deeply stained. The patient may notice that this insensitivity affects some or all fingers of one or both hands. The housewife may first notice it along the ulnar or radial border of the forearm which she burns as she reaches into her oven. This dissociated sensory loss may be found in the peripheral or proximal distribution of several adjacent segments. In the early stages loss of pain and temperature sensibility may be unequal in degree and in extent, while thermal defect may not always involve both modalities; cold stimuli may be perceived when warm are not. The gradual destruction of the spinal commissures in the lower cervical and upper thoracic regions eventually produces the characteristic suspended zone of dissociated sensory loss, extending from the upper cervical to the mid-thoracic region—an area which would be covered by a sleeved bodice. Involvement of the spinothalamic tracts will produce analgesia and thermoanaesthesia in one or both lower limbs. There is often an area of normal sensibility over the lower half of the trunk intervening between the area of thoracic analgesia due to interruption of the commissural fibres and the area of sensory loss on the lower limbs resulting from spinothalamic tract involvement. Only in the later stages of the disease are the posterior columns involved with loss of appreciation of posture, passive movement and vibration.

Manifestations of involvement of the spinal motor system take the form of muscular weakness and wasting due to atrophy of the anterior horn cells and spastic paraparesis from pyramidal degeneration. In the early stages of the disease and for many years the former are more marked than the latter. As the disease usually begins in the cervicothoracic region of the cord, muscular wasting usually first appears in the small hand muscles. The fingers begin to curl, the patient has difficulty in abducting and adducting the fingers and

there is flattening of the muscles of the ulnar border of one or both forearms. The upper limb reflexes are almost invariably absent but conspicuous fasciculation is uncommon. The muscular atrophy is rarely as severe as in motor neurone disease and although contractures develop they rarely reach the severe 'claw hand' degree seen in ulnar paralysis. Occasionally wasting and weakness is first seen, not in the hand, but about the shoulder. Nystagmus is the commonest sign of bulbar involvement. In the lower limbs weakness and spasticity with extensor plantar responses are later in their appearance and for many years there is little difficulty in locomotion. The sphincters usually function normally.

Trophic and vasomotor disturbances are almost invariable. The patient himself may have noticed areas of loss of sweating or excessive sweating about the face neck or upper limbs. The female patient is often embarrassed by the ugly appearance of her hands which are usually cold, puffy and cyanosed, with stumpy swollen fingers, pudgy soft palms—la main succulente. In other cases the hand or even one upper limb is mildly hypertrophied and the skin of that hand is coarse and thickened with callosities over the knuckles, and scars from old injuries. Healing is slow, septic infection and indolent ulceration of the digits is common. Despite this and the often accompanying total analgesia of the hands, absorption of the terminal digits may be long delayed. In contrast with such conditions as leprosy and the ganglionic sensory neuropathies, radiographs of the hand usually reveal normal terminal phalanges. Likewise, Charcot's arthropathy rarely affects the joints of the hands, but is seen at the elbow and shoulder. It is not seen in the lower limb. Painless muscle rupture may occur spontaneously or follow trivial trauma.

Syringomyelia is one of the commonest causes of a Horner's syndrome in a young adult. It is symptomless and may pass undetected if it is incomplete or bilateral.

Not uncommonly the patient with syringomyelia possesses poor physique or may exhibit various congenital abnormalities or stigmata—short neck, asymmetrical thorax, sternal depression or prominence, cervical ribs, unequal development of the mammary glands. Some degree of spinal curvature is very common. Scoliosis or kyphoscoliosis may show itself in childhood and must be regarded as an associated bony abnormality and not the result of paralysis of the trunk muscles as may occur later in life. Spina bifida and pes cavus are occasionally encountered but, like the foregoing defects, they are by no means conspicuous in other members of the family.

Diagnosis

Syringomyelia is one of those diseases of the nervous system in which at a stage when complaints are slight and few, careful examination often reveals extensive physical signs. The young person may only be troubled by one hand, yet there may be nystagmus, hypoglossal paresis, loss of all arm reflexes and dissociated sensory loss of segmental distribution. On the other hand early diagnosis may be difficult or wellnigh impossible owing to the insidious nature of the development of the characteristic analgesia and thermo-anaesthesia.

A young woman with cold, blotchy, cyanosed hands, who can handle hotter objects than the examiner, may have to be examined over a period of years before the diagnosis can be established or rejected.

The disease may mimic an ulnar nerve palsy very closely for a time, as the atrophy may be confined to the hypothenar muscles and interossei, while the sensory impairment is restricted to the fifth finger and the ulnar border of the hand. It may be difficult to be certain whether the sensation of touch is impaired as well as pain.

Progressive muscular atrophy affects older patients, the muscular atrophy proceeds relentlessly and is usually accompanied by widespread fasciculation. There is no sensory loss.

A syringomyelic syndrome is seen in intramedullary tumours of the spinal cord and in haematomyelia. The latter condition is rare and should not be diagnosed merely because the syringomyelic picture has followed an injury. In gliomas of the cord deterioration is more rapid than in syringomyelia. In craniovertebral anomalies a syringomyelic syndrome is not uncommon.

There may be particular difficulty when a cervical rib is present in association with atrophy of the small muscles of the hand, sensory impairment and vasomotor changes in the hand. As in the case of ulnar palsy careful repeated examination over a period of time may be necessary before these two conditions can be distinguished. Nystagmus, a Horner's syndrome, mid-thoracic sensory loss or spinal curvature should indicate the presence of syringomyelia. A lateral radiograph of the cervical spine is sometimes helpful; in many young patients with syringomyelia there is an increase of the sagittal diameter of the cervical spinal canal.

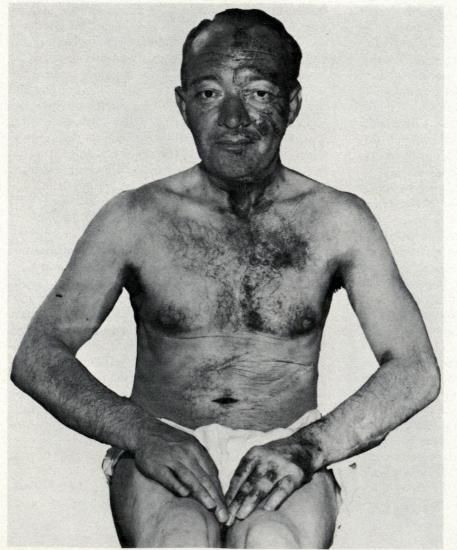

Syringomyelia

431. Syringomyelia; sweat test
Age 35. Excessive sweating on left side of face, neck, thorax and left hand for 1 year. No other complaint but burn scars on left upper abdomen and left forearm disclosed long-standing dissociated sensory loss. Left Horner's syndrome, absent arm reflexes but no muscular atrophy or lower limb signs.

432. Syringomyelia

Age 14 on first hospital admission for tendency to drag the left leg. Despite minimal disability there were extensive physical signs including a partial left Horner's syndrome, fasciculation of the tongue, brisk jaw jerk, dissociated behaviour of upper limb reflexes and characteristic pyramidal signs in the lower limbs with clonus and bilateral extensor plantar responses. All modalities of sensation were normal. Syringomyelia suspected because of increased sagittal diameter of the cervical spinal canal (*a*).

Three years later, when the photograph was taken (*b*), he complained of loss of temperature sensation in the right foot, clumsiness of the left hand, and diplopia. Wasting and weakness of the muscles of the left shoulder girdle and of the left upper limb. Zone of dissociated sensory loss from C.2 to T.4 bilaterally and loss of appreciation of temperature in the whole of the right lower limb. Normal sensibility in intervening thoracic and lumbar dermatomes. Myelography confirmed the presence of a syrinx (*c*) and there was some improvement in function of lower limbs following its evacuation.

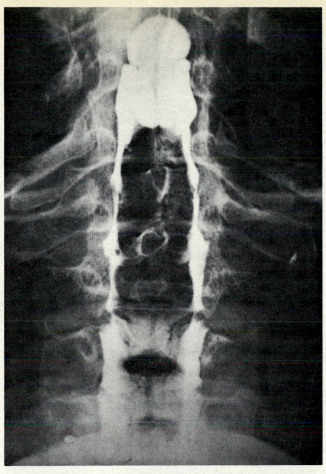

432c

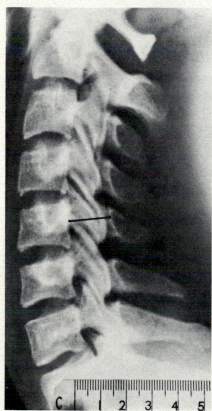

432a

Normal

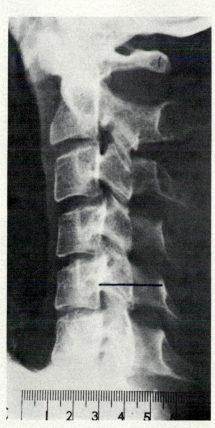

Syringomyelia

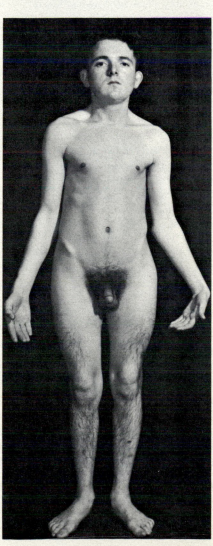

432b

Syringomyelia

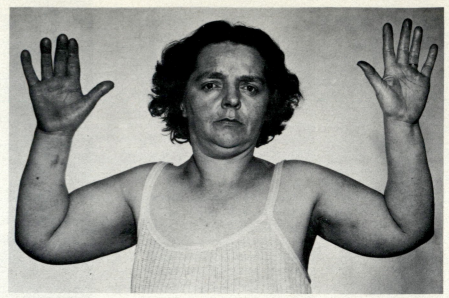

433a

433. Syringomyelia

(*a*) Age 41. 'Congenital' hypertrophy of right upper limb, loss of temperature sensibility recognized at 20. Weakness of right hand for 1 year; cyanosed, atrophy of small muscles, burn scars; absent right arm reflexes. Impairment of all modalities of sensation on the right side from C.2 to C.8. Early dissociated sensory loss in thumb, index and middle fingers of left hand. Lower limbs normal.

(*b*) Age 52. Disability affecting right upper limb relatively unchanged; still weak and clumsy and numb. Recent episode of severe pain in the whole limb. Essential signs unchanged, but sensory loss on the right side now extended from C.2 to D.5. Lower limb reflexes on the right were hyperactive and there was a probable right extensor plantar response.

(*c*) Age 61. Right upper limb unchanged; slight weakness in right leg with clonus at ankle joint and a brisk extensor plantar response.

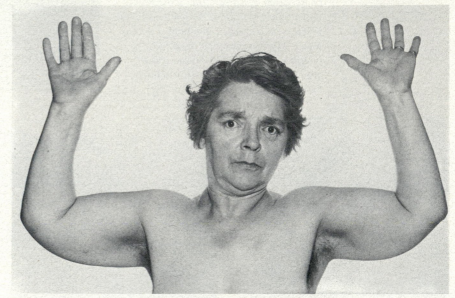

433b

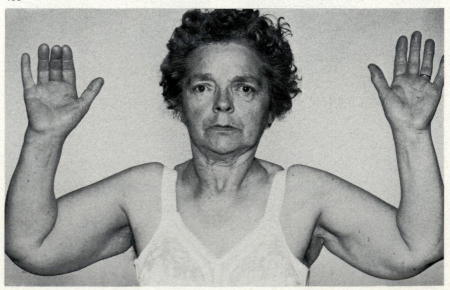

433c

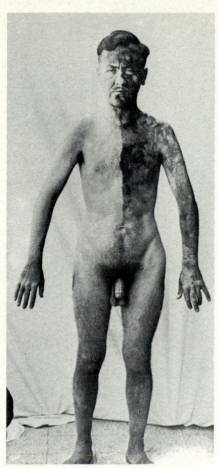

434. Syringomyelia △

Loss of sweating over right side of face and trunk and the right upper limb in an early case of syringomyelia.

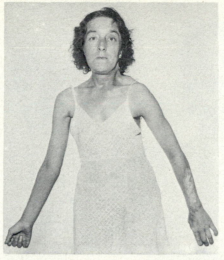

435. Syringomyelia △

Age 45. Scoliosis in childhood; spastic right leg at the age of 17, loss of pain and temperature sensations in right arm at 25, and in left arm at 35. Recent dysphagia, nasal regurgitation of fluids, hoarse voice.

Partial right Horner's syndrome, horizontal nystagmus, anaesthetic palate and pharynx, paralysis of right palate and right vocal cord; tongue normal. Wasting and weakness of right sternomastoid, trapezius and muscles of the right shoulder girdle. Lower motor neurone signs in the arms and characteristic pyramidal signs in the lower limbs. Suspended zone of dissociated sensory loss C.2 to T.3 bilaterally and below T.3 on the left. Joint position sensation absent in the fingers, normal in the toes. Vibration sensation impaired in all limbs. Note clawing of the fingers of the right hand and burn scars on the left forearm.

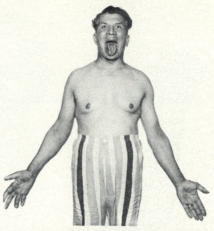

436. Syringomyelia △

Age 51. Acute onset of numbness and clumsiness of the right hand at 20. Progressed for 2 years to involve right arm, right side of neck and face, then stationary for 20 years. At 40 onset of temporary dysarthria and weakness of the right leg. Recent painless effusion into right elbow joint.

Right hypoglossal nerve palsy, dissociated sensory loss of right side of face, neck, right upper limb and on chest to T.4 Absent arm reflexes, wasting and weakness of small muscles of right hand, atrophy of right deltoid with abnormal mobility of right shoulder joint; atrophic arthropathy of right shoulder and elbow joints. Slight over-all disability.

437. Syringomyelia ▷

Age 44 years. Four months' history of weakness, clumsiness and paraesthesiae in the right hand. Since childhood she had known that her right hand and forearm were larger than the left. She had always regarded her right hand as 'ugly, unsightly', but there had been no disability. On examination, the only abnormalities were in the right upper limb. Skin of right hand coarser and darker; global atrophy of intrinsic hand muscles with corresponding weakness. No fasciculation. Right arm reflexes were present but perhaps not as brisk as those on the left. No obvious sensory loss in the right hand except probable impairment of appreciation of pain and temperature.

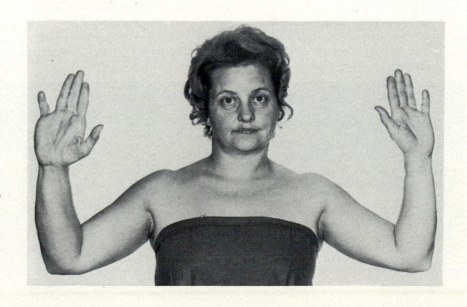

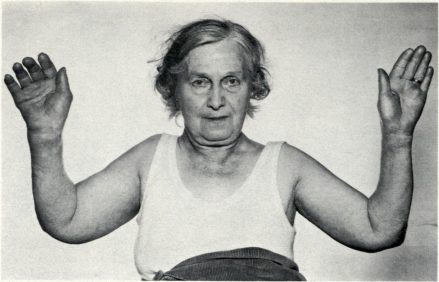

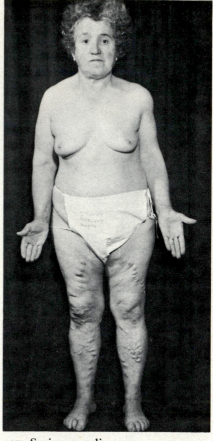

438. Syringomyelia △

Age 65. 'Congenital' diffuse hypertrophy of right upper limb. As a schoolgirl discovered she could not feel the vibration of a tuning fork below the clavicles nor appreciate hot and cold in the right hand. No further disability until the age of 50 when spastic weakness developed in the lower limbs. Right hand puffy, cyanosed and weak; absent right arm reflexes. No arthropathy. Dissociated sensory loss on right from C.2 to C.8; pain sense impaired over the third division of the right trigeminal nerve. Impaired reflexes in left arm, pyramidal signs of moderate degree in lower limbs. Vibration sense practically absent below both clavicles. Marked postural loss in fingers of right hand. Radiographs of the craniovertebral junction showed asymmetry of the foramen magnum, slight basilar impression, occipitalization of the atlas with spina bifida at C.2.

439. Syringomyelia △

Age 65. Slight weakness and numbness of right arm and shoulder at 30; pains and weakness above both shoulder joints for 10 years. Short neck. Minimal weakness of right upper limb with absent tendon reflexes in both upper limbs. Lower limbs normal. Dissociated sensory loss over right forequarter and right side of neck, but not the right side of the face. Charcot's arthropathy in both shoulder joints, with wasting and weakness of deltoid muscles. No pyramidal signs in lower limbs. Wide sagittal diameter of the cervical spine; syrinx on myelography.

440.   Syringomyelia ▽

Age 62. Observed over a period of 30 years. Weakness of right upper limb following a fall from a cycle at the age of 20; never able to distinguish cold from warm with the right hand. At 30 years of age there was weakness of the right side of the palate, dysphagia, slight diffuse weakness of the right upper limb with absent reflexes, sausage-shaped fingers, callosities over the knuckles, with dissociated sensory loss of the right forequarter. Progressive deterioration, bedridden for 10 years. Nystagmus, dysarthria, spastic tetraplegia with gross sensory loss to all modalities below C.3, but denser loss to pain and temperature in upper limbs and thorax.

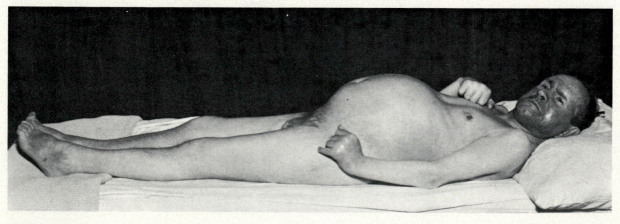

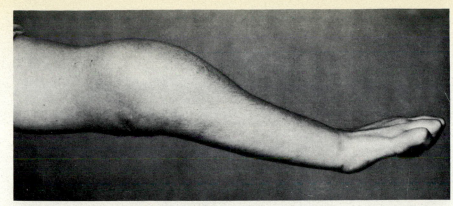

441a

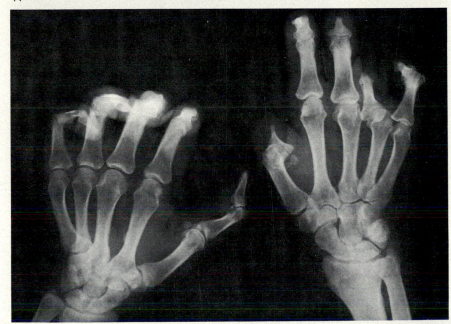

441d

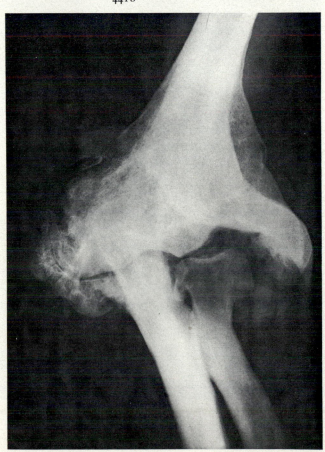

441b

441c

Syringomyelia

**441. Syringomyelia: Charcot arthro-
pathy**

(*a*) Right elbow joint in a young woman.
Note wasting of the muscles of the hand
and forearm and clawing of the fingers.
Effusion into the elbow joint occurred
following a mild injury.

(*b*) and (*c*) Left elbow in advanced syringomyelia with phalangeal osteolysis (*d*).

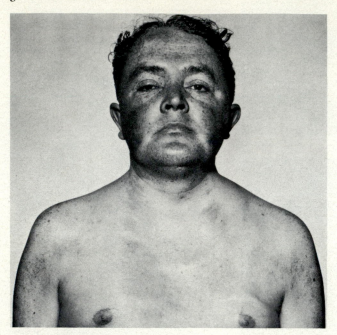

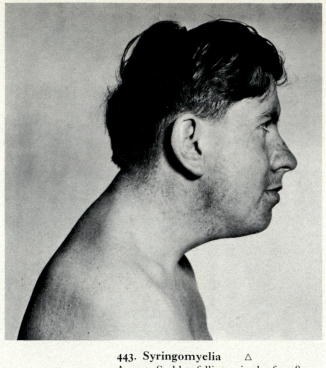

442. Syringomyelia △
Bilateral Horner's syndrome, short neck
and weakness and wasting of both deltoid
muscles in a syringomyelic syndrome
associated with basilar impression.

443. Syringomyelia △
Age 19. Sudden falling episodes for 18
months. Oscillopsia, burning paraesthesiae
left side of face and scalp, clumsiness of
left hand.

Head thrust forward, tilted to left, short
neck with restricted movements. Nasal
voice, weak palatal movements, vertical
nystagmus, wasting and fasciculation of
the tongue. Bilateral atrophy of the sternomastoids. Lower motor neurone signs in
the upper limbs, pyramidal signs in the
lower limbs. Loss of pain and temperature
sensation involving the head, neck and
upper limbs to T.4 level bilaterally.
Vibration sense impaired in the left upper
limb; joint position sense intact
throughout.

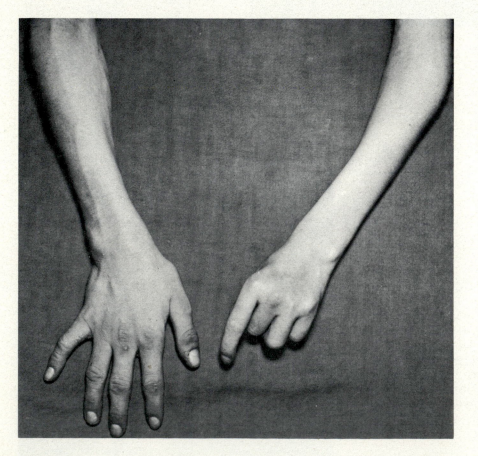

444. Syringomyelia syndrome ◁
Age 20. Syringomyelic syndrome present
at the age of 10. Cervical cord glioma with
syrinx formation. Capacious cervical
spinal canal, CSF protein 250 mg./100 ml.;
myelographic block. Initially presented
with weakness and spasticity of left lower
limb. Note clawing of fingers of left hand
and wasting of the muscles of the left
forearm.

Syringomyelia

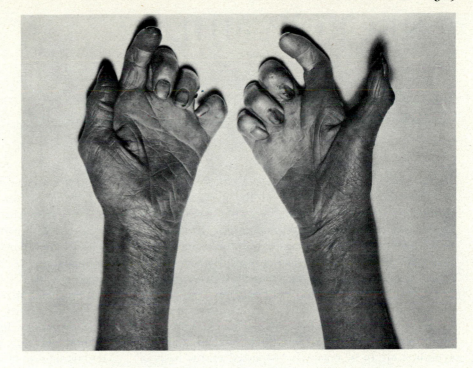

445. Syringomyelia
Age 67. Syringomyelia of at least 40 years' duration but able to work in the bottling department of a brewery for 45 years. Global atrophy with claw hand, nail changes and scarring. Mild spastic paraparesis.

446. Syringomyelia. Charcot's arthropathy of right shoulder ▽
Age 47. Twenty-year history of impaired sensibility in the hands; 10-year history of unsteadiness of gait. Recent fall led to effusion into the right shoulder joint; relatively painless but radiography revealed gross disorganization. Slight generalized disability despite dissociated sensory loss in the upper limbs, posterior column loss in the lower limbs and bilateral extensor plantar responses. Serology negative in blood and spinal fluid.

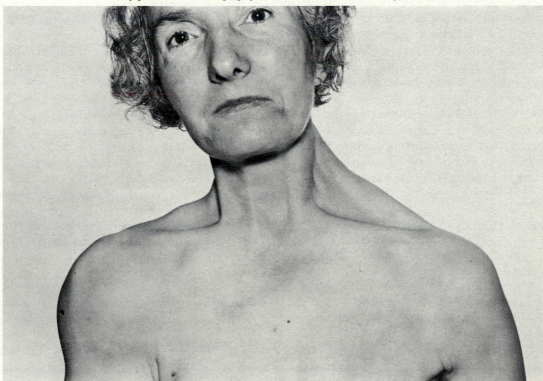

9 NEUROSYPHILIS

In one form or another syphilis was formerly one of the commonest causes of disease of the nervous system throughout the world. The discovery of the responsible spirochaete in the brain in general paresis, by Noguchi in 1913, marked the end of a century of theorizing as well as of clinical and pathological studies. By the middle of the 19th century it was increasingly appreciated that in general paralysis of the insane there were organic changes in the brain and that the paralysis was not merely a complication of the mental illness. Gradually its recognition as a disease entity was achieved and its syphilitic origin increasingly suspected on the basis of purely clinical observations. For a long time, however, like hypertension and arteriosclerosis today, there were many who thought that in some vague way or other 'civilization' was responsible. Urbanization, ambition, competition, 'venery and spirituous liquors' and other similar phrases figured prominently in the textbooks of the time. The peculiarities of the gait and the reflex changes in the lower limbs in both tabes dorsalis and general paresis were well known by the turn of the century and a syphilitic aetiology was accepted. Schaudinn and Hoffmann discovered the spirochaete in primary syphilitic lesions in 1905; Wassermann described his test in 1906 and found it positive in a high percentage of cases in blood and spinal fluid in all forms of neurosyphilis. Since 1890 examination of the spinal fluid obtained by lumbar puncture had been studied by Quincke although Corning, a New York physician, first performed a spinal puncture in 1885. (He did it, strangely enough, so that he could cocainize the spinal cord of a man with excessive sexual habits!)

TABES DORSALIS

The medical student of today will appreciate the frequency and importance of this disease in former years when it is recalled that Pierre Marie in his *Lectures on Diseases of the Spinal Cord*, published in Paris in 1892, devoted no less than 213 pages, out of a total of 474, to this particular disease. It was one which was rich in symptoms and signs, with exceedingly varied modes of presentation; it could be diagnosed at a glance or missed for years, and few clinicians grew tired of demonstrating its peculiarities to generations of students. 'A case of tabes' was a standby in the examinations. But this is a scene that has passed and in the modern clinic it is the old burnt-out cases of tabes, often presenting with Charcot's arthropathy or urinary difficulties, which are encountered. Such patients are usually in their 50's or 60's, a history of syphilis or its treatment is usually wanting, and apart from a complaint of 'rheumatism' or 'neuritis' they have enjoyed fair health. They are usually underweight and may appear older than their years and despite the paucity of symptoms the characteristic signs of tabes may be present—Argyll Robertson pupils, ptosis and ataxic gait with a positive Romberg test, loss of appreciation of vibration and passive movement, loss of pain sense in the Achilles tendon, and hypotonia. But even though the gait is ataxic one is rarely able to demonstrate the traditional wide-based, high stepping gait, nor the zones of cutaneous analgesia with delayed perception of pain, the laxity of ligaments that allow extreme degrees of movement of the lower limbs or a perforating ulcer on the sole of the foot. While, as if these were not enough, the only pain the patient will acknowledge is a vague ache about a joint, nothing that resembles the 'lightning' pains of yore. Every now and again an old tabetic is admitted to hospital with acute abdominal pain or urinary difficulties. These symptoms rarely turn out to be due to a visceral crisis or an insensitive bladder. Twice, in recent years, I have seen acute abdominal pain in a tabetic prove to be due to a perforated peptic ulcer. Prostatic enlargement is the commoner explanation for the urinary difficulties in an elderly tabetic. But, to whatever department of a hospital the tabetic is directed, to the eye department because of optic atrophy, to the department of physical medicine or orthopaedics because of a crumbling joint, to the genito-urinary department because of bladder troubles or to the psychiatrist because of impotence —a history of lightning pains, if obtained and recognized, is virtually diagnostic.

As their name indicates, they are pains which pass away like a flash of lightning, but as in those of trigeminal neuralgia, which they closely resemble, their intensity varies greatly. The term 'lightning' reflects their momentary or fleeting nature, the stabbing, shooting or dart-like quality; it does not mean that the pains are necessarily excruciating. Indeed, they may constitute a nuisance and not a torment to the patient who may use such words as 'funny' or 'peculiar' to describe them. On the other hand they can be intolerable, difficult to relieve by ordinary analgesics, and a cause of drug addiction. In the lower limbs, where they are most commonly felt, they may appear to stab into the limb or up or down its length. They may be superficial or deep, in the shaft of the limb or about its joints, but whatever their location, quality and severity, they tend to occur in bouts with intervals of complete freedom. A bout may last days or weeks, during which time single momentary pains or clusters of them, recurring quite irregularly, every few minutes or hours, plague the patient. But not all his pains are lightning in character; there may be various aching, boring or 'wrenching' pains, especially about the knees, ankles and feet, which, when they are aggravated by cold and damp weather, are likely to be attributed to rheumatism or neuritis. Various forms of girdle sensations around the trunk, band-like feelings in the lower limbs and burning paraesthesiae and numbness in the feet may be complained of. They may resemble those of diabetic neuropathy. Cutaneous hyperaesthesia may coexist with analgesia. These and other sensory symptoms characterize the early, pre-ataxic stage of the disease; they may persist for some years before entirely subsiding and are sometimes long forgotten by old tabetics.

A neuropathic joint may constitute the only disability. Effusion, spontaneous or following a blow or fall, takes place into a knee, hip or ankle joint and is subsequently followed by articular disorganization. This process is not always entirely painless but it may proceed to a severe degree before advice is sought. The possibility of a neuropathic origin of a disorganized joint should not be excluded because there is pain. The latter is always relatively slight in comparison with the degree of joint destruction, but it is not always entirely absent. Dislocation and spontaneous fractures may occur. Fractures following trauma to the affected limb may unite poorly and indeed sometimes provide a new site of arthropathy. Fractures in non-syphilitic paraplegic limbs heal satisfactorily.

Primary optic atrophy can occur by itself or in association with other manifestations of tabes. In its early stages there may be little loss of visual acuity because central vision is the last to suffer. No patient with primary optic atrophy should fail to have a full battery of modern serological tests for syphilis. No one, as yet, has found it possible to culture *Treponema pallidum* and the name of August von Wassermann who was born in Bavaria, just 100 years ago, in 1866, is likely to be perpetuated in the 'W.R.' for many years to come.

Two conditions—diabetic neuropathy and the Holmes–Adie syndrome—require to be differentiated from tabes dorsalis. In the former although the pain in the lower limbs may be peculiarly disagreeable and graphically described and associated with sensory ataxia,

Tabes Dorsalis

447. Tabes dorsalis
Age 35. One course of penicillin for primary syphilis during National Service. Ten years later lightning pains with progressive loss of weight. The pains were considered to be 'rheumatic' for 5 years. Diffuse hypotonia allowing abnormal range of limb movements.

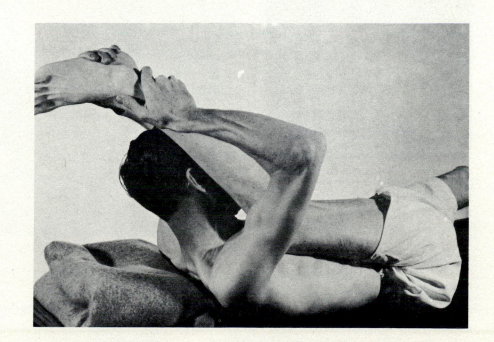

cutaneous hypersensitivity, impotence and loss of tendon reflexes, the muscles are often tender, the pupils are usually normal, the neuropathy is not steadily progressive and other evidence of diabetes is present. The patient with the myotonic pupil and absent reflexes of the Holmes–Adie syndrome, on the other hand, has no tabetic symptoms of any kind. The abnormality of the pupil is either noticed accidentally or at the time of onset when there is blurring of vision. Years later, when the originally dilated pupil is constricted, or when the other pupil is also involved, serological tests are necessary to distinguish it from tabes dorsalis.

Tabes Dorsalis

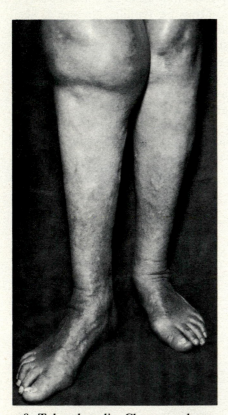

448. Tabes dorsalis: Charcot arthropathy of right knee △
Female, aged 57. Unsteady gait for 2 years with painless effusion into the right knee joint. Argyll Robertson pupils. Positive Romberg test, ataxic gait, cutaneous analgesia, absent deep pain sense, vibration sense and appreciation of passive movement. Serology negative in blood and spinal fluid. Radiographs, surprisingly, revealed no bony changes in the right knee joint.

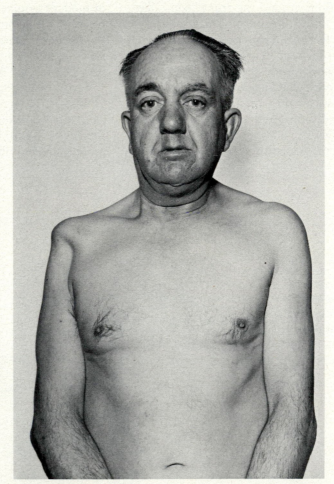

449. Tabes dorsalis; Charcot arthropathy of right shoulder

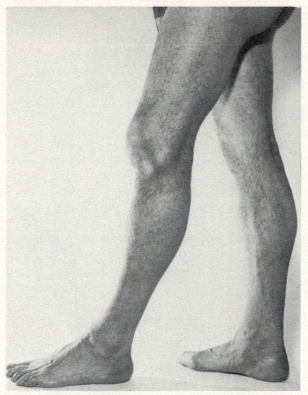

450a

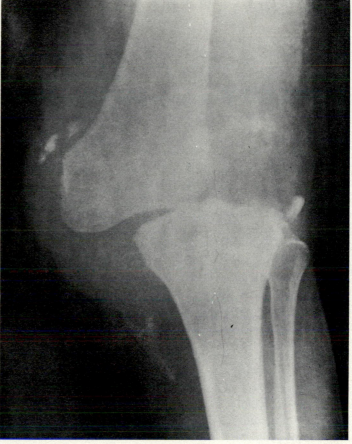

450b

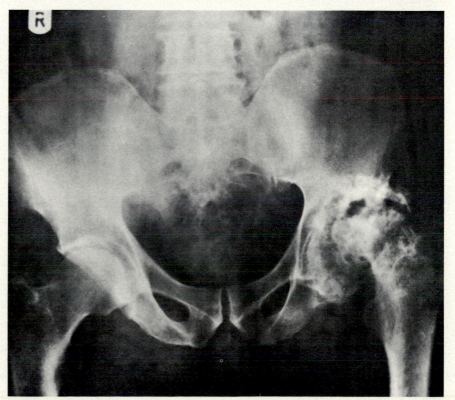

450c

450. Tabes dorsalis

(*a*) Charcot arthropathy of left knee. Painless effusion, no injury; normal radiograph. Negative serology. Postural hypotension was the presumed explanation of syncopal attacks. Argyll Robertson pupils. Complete areflexia.

Radiographic appearances of Charcot arthropathy of a knee (*b*) and of left hip (*c*) in two further cases of tabes dorsalis.

GENERAL PARESIS

This disease is also now comparatively rare. The dementing patient, smiling, fatuous, given to airy explanations for his deficiencies, who is brought, protesting to the doctor, is much more likely to be suffering from cerebral tumour or presenile dementia. The tremor of the hands, lips and tongue, the hesitant, slurred speech or feeble voice, may be seen in the chronic alcoholic, in agitated depression and in diffuse cerebral arteriosclerosis. In general paresis change in temperament usually precedes any evidence of intellectual decline, but the patient's complaints, if any, cannot be distinguished at this stage from those of an anxiety state or depression. They may be quite reasonably attributed to business or domestic worries. Formal examination may reveal no more than slight pupillary abnormalities and brisk reflexes. Something more serious is not usually suspected until there has been some failure of memory, lapse in social refinement, errors of judgement or grotesque expressions of opinion or untoward behaviour. Occasionally the first manifestation is a fit or seizure. The first symptoms may follow a concussion and the presence of a subdural haematoma may be suspected. An episode of confusion following an anaesthetic or an upper respiratory tract infection may disclose the presence of the disease. In general it may be said that in contrast to tabes dorsalis symptoms and signs may be very few indeed. On the other hand serological tests of blood and spinal fluid are more often positive.

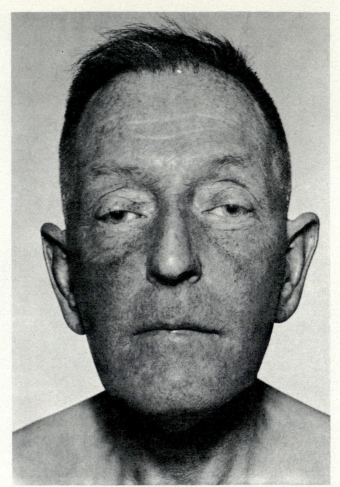

451. General paresis △
Age 60. Unusual financial speculations, dysarthria and declining efficiency for 6 months. Demented, bilateral ptosis, dilated pupils with impaired light reflex, 'trombone' tremor of the protruded tongue, fine tremor of lips and fingers. Serology positive in blood and spinal fluid; the latter contained 53 white cells per mm.[3]; protein 95 mg./100 ml., and a paretic colloidal gold curve.

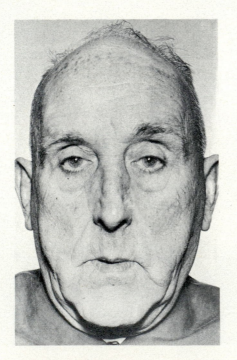

452. Neurosyphilis; general paresis ◁
Age 66 years. Mild dementia with occasional minor epilepsy. Forty years previously, this patient was treated for general paresis with malaria and silver salvarsan by the author. He made a complete recovery, has worked regularly, and only in the last 18 months has shown some memory loss, disorientation and epilepsy. Neurological examination was otherwise negative, and although his pupils were small and unequal they reacted briskly to light.

General Paresis

453a

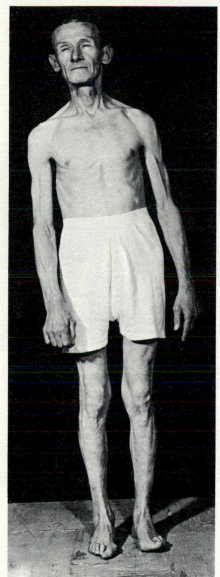

453b

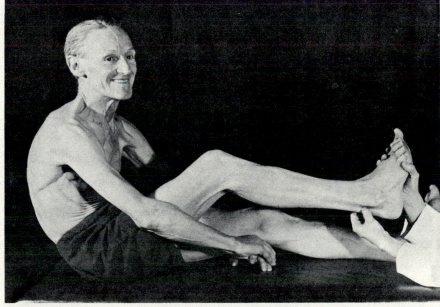

453c

453. Taboparesis
Age 59. A classical instance of a 'fresh' case of neurosyphilis with a history of primary infection 40 years previously. Lightning pains of 1 year's duration; no other symptom. Argyll Robertson pupils; diffuse hypotonia (a); Rombergism (b); impairment of vibration sense; normal appreciation of passive movement of the toes; absent deep pain sensation in the Achilles tendon (c). Positive serology.

MENINGOVASCULAR SYPHILIS

The virus has largely replaced the spirochaete in the aetiology of acute meningitis, encephalitis and myelitis. The young man with a stroke, convulsive seizure or episode of stupor with meningism, due to syphilis, is now rarely seen. An isolated third nerve palsy is nearly always painful and due to intracranial aneurysm. But the odd case of meningovascular syphilis still occurs although it is rarely recognized before the results of examination of blood and spinal fluid are known. A subacute paraparesis, the rapid onset of bilateral nerve deafness, an isolated external rectus palsy, and post-traumatic delirium are recent examples which I recall.

Syphilophobia, like neurosyphilis, is declining but it may still provide a trap. Usually the blood Wassermann has been proved negative on many occasions but the phobia is not always without foundation and examination of the spinal fluid is occasionally surprising.

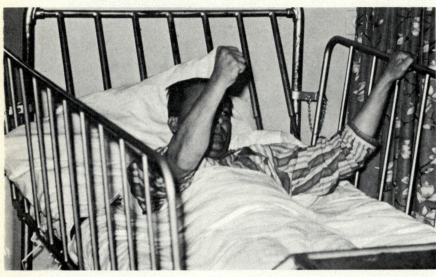

454a

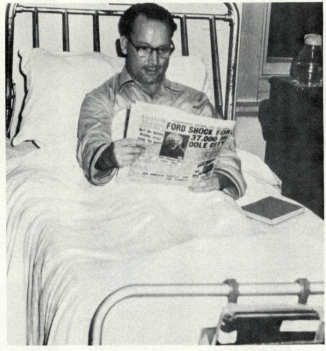

454b

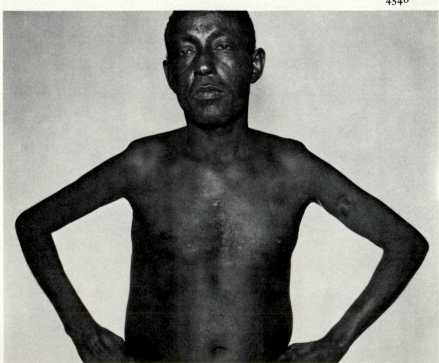

454. Acute meningovascular syphilis △
Age 40. Emergency admission following bizarre behaviour, confusion and pyrexia of one day's duration. Subsequent history of altered personality following a concussion one year previously. Suspected sub-dural haematoma but characteristic evidence of neurosyphilis in spinal fluid. Rapid recovery on penicillin. During illness (*a*); 6 days later (*b*).

455. Syphilitic amyotrophy ◁
Age 54. Primary syphilis at 45. Pain in the shoulder and weakness and wasting of right arm for 5 years; similar symptoms in left arm for 3 years; unsteady gait 6 months. Slight bilateral ptosis; normal pupils. Diffuse amyotrophy of upper limbs with impaired reflexes. Brisk lower limb reflexes; left extensor plantar response. No fasciculation. Cutaneous hypalgesia on right, C.4–T.1; on left C.6–T.1. Positive serology in blood and CSF. Cells 20 per mm.[3]; protein 70 mg./100 ml.

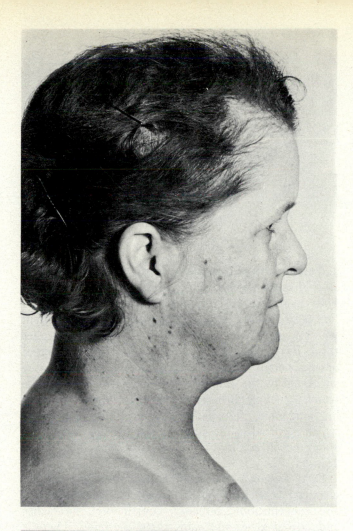

Congenital Syphilis

456. Congenital syphilis ◁
Age 47. Old history of interstitial keratitis; epilepsy in adolescence. Always
ataxic. Recent recurrence of epilepsy.
Optic atrophy, nystagmus, unsteady gait.
Marked bossing of frontal and parietal
bones, clinically and radiographically.
Blood Wassermann positive; CSF
negative. No evidence of hypothyroidism.

457. Congenital syphilis ▽
Age 50. 'Saddle nose', bilateral corneal
opacities (*a*), interstitial keratitis at the age
of 10 years. Eleven siblings, seven of
whom died. Four-year history of spastic
tetraparesis. Bilateral anosmia; unequal
inactive pupils; positive serological tests
for syphilis in blood and spinal fluid. Old
gummatous lesion of the palate (*b*). Air
encephalography and opaque myelography
were normal. In mild tabes in adults due
to congenital infection the serology is
usually negative. In this case no other explanation for the tetraparesis was obtained.

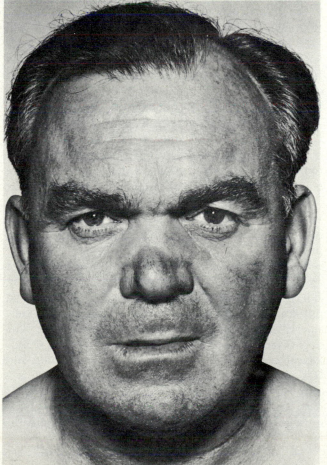

457b

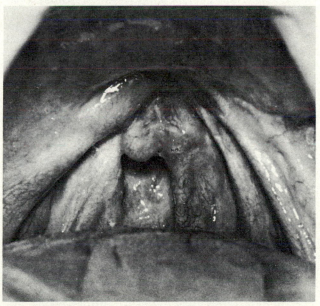

457a

10 DISORDERS OF ENDOCRINE GLANDS

HYPOTHYROIDISM

Not all patients suffering from hypothyroidism are myxoedematous in appearance. The latter term, introduced by Ord in 1878, implies a subcutaneous infiltration, probably with mucin. Myxoedema may be localized, as pointed out by Sir William Gull in 1873 in his classical account 'On Cretinoid State Supervening in Adult Life in Women'. His description of his first case is an excellent example of the powers of clinical observation by a man, who said of himself, 'if I am anything I am a clinical physician'.

'Miss B., after the cessation of the catamenial period, became insensibly more and more languid, with general increase of bulk. This change went on from year to year, her face altering from oval to round, much like the full moon at rising. With a complexion soft and fair, the skin presenting a peculiarly smooth and fine texture was almost porcelainous in aspect, the cheeks tinted of a delicate rose-purple, the cellular tissue under the eyes being loose and folded, and that under the jaws and in the neck becoming heavy, thickened, and folded. The lips large and of a rose-purple, alae nasi thick, cornea and pupil of the eye normal, but the distance between the eyes appearing disproportionately wide, and the rest of the nose depressed, giving the whole face a flattened broad character. The hair flaxen and soft, the whole expression of the face remarkably placid. The tongue broad and thick, voice guttural, and the pronunciation as if the tongue were too large for the mouth (cretinoid). The hands peculiarly broad and thick, spade-like as if the whole texture were infiltrated.'

The severity of the condition varies considerably, depending on the duration and the degree of thyroid deficiency. As in the case of Parkinsonism the disease may be recognized rather than diagnosed. There must be few clinicians who cannot recollect missing a case of myxoedema. The manner in which the true diagnosis comes to light varies greatly. Formal history-taking and examination may have revealed little. Complaints are few and often vague. The physician may only be alerted by some chance observation or remark offered by patients or relatives. Many such examples may be quoted. A middle-aged woman with recent onset of epilepsy who remarked as she was leaving that 'my doctor is also sending me to the dermatologist because of my dry skin'. The patient with deafness and vertigo and clumsiness of gait, whose husband said 'her skin is as cold as the kitchen table'. The lady with headache, body pains and lethargy who said that 'she could no longer sing in the choir'. There was the female patient who said that 'when I answer the telephone the caller thinks it is my husband and may ask for me'. Intolerance of cold is often not mentioned by the patient but may be suggested by the amount of clothing that is worn; the woman, peeling off her carapace of cardigans, the man, his 'long johns'. The bedsocks and the electric blankets which are used in the summer one usually only learns about on direct inquiry after suspicions have been aroused.

Early diagnosis is difficult because of the non-specific character of so many of the symptoms—poor memory and concentration, lethargy, constipation, headaches and various aches and pains about the body. There is nothing particular about the headache, but it may be prominent and in describing it some patients will add that they feel dull and slow; they often attribute their lethargy to the headache. The voice is often low pitched and takes on a nasal or catarrhal quality. It may be husky or harsh. Articulation may suffer, speech becoming slow and slurred. As the history and examination proceed the slowness of thought and speech and movement become apparent.

Because of the varied nature of the presenting symptoms, the patient may attend any department of a large hospital. He may find his way to the neurologist for many reasons. Epilepsy, mental deterioration, deafness and vertigo, acroparaesthesiae (the carpal tunnel syndrome) or ataxia. There may be a rise in cerebrospinal fluid protein.

The condition should be borne in mind in cases of epilepsy of late onset. It should be remembered in elderly people whose complaints are general but sound physical. Only too often this type of case may be considered an example of cerebral arteriosclerosis. The hypothyroid patient is often a poor historian and neurological examination is limited by the retardation and lack of co-operation. Sensory testing when there is a complaint of acroparaesthesiae may be unrewarding. It may be difficult to judge the strength of the proximal muscles of the lower limbs. Frank peripheral neuropathy and myopathy are not common. The hypothyroid patient complains of aching and tiredness in his limbs and examination may reveal proximal weakness, but the degenerative myopathic changes are not such that they result in visible atrophy. Yet the clumsiness of their movements is no doubt attributable in some measure to the myopathic weakness. I have never felt confident that I could feel any change in affected muscles on palpation.

Frank cerebellar symptoms and signs are uncommon in hypothyroidism but they do occur and may be quite striking and misleading. Nystagmus and ataxia of upper and lower limbs may be detected.

Apart from the diagnostic value of the facial appearance, the most reliable neurological sign of hypothyroidism is the altered ankle reflex. The contraction may be slow or normal, but the relaxation is delayed, suspended or 'hung up.' It is best demonstrated when the patient is kneeling on a chair. It is of course only a physical sign and must be sought for. The responsible fault seems to lie in the muscle and not in the reflex arc. William M. Ord, physician of St. Thomas's Hospital, London, appears to have been the first to write of this sign in hypothyroidism, in 1884. He said that 'the reflex actions are produced with considerable delay'—not mentioning any particular reflex. He also referred to loss of the senses of taste and smell, and incoordination of movement, in this disease.

Personality changes may be slight or marked. As a cause of organic dementia I think exaggerated claims have been made for myxoedema. It is much rarer than cerebral atrophy and cerebral arteriosclerosis. But when one case of 'myxoedematous madness' has been found the search is renewed, as in vitamin B$_{12}$ deficiency.

Myxoedema coma is a grave development of chronicity and lack of treatment. It occurs mostly during cold weather and is characterized by hypothermia of a remarkable degree. In the only case I have seen the flesh was fish-like to the palpating hand.

Disease is a process, so that hypothyroidism must be a question of degree. The thyroid gland fails gradually. Clinical and biochemical correlation shows that when there is overt clinical hypothyroidism, conventional tests of function are abnormal. But the recognition of minor degrees of hypothyroidism presents many difficulties. Complaints are nonspecific; signs such as hair loss, constipation and dryness of the skin are not uncommon in middle-aged women, so that the interpretation of biochemical tests is essential. Hypothyroidism may be asymptomatic and only recognized biochemically. With mild hypothyroidism, measurements of circulating thyroid hormone concentration may be within the normal range, but the concentration of thyroid-stimulating hormone (TSH) is usually raised. The presence of circulating thyroid antibodies is important in diagnosis. However, the value of all these tests cannot be appreciated if the clinician has not suspected the possibility of thyroid failure.

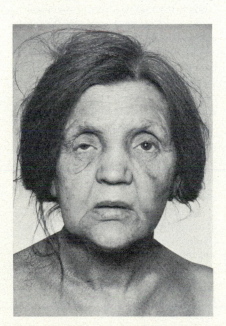
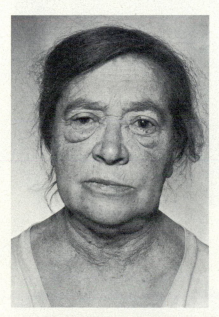

Myxoedema

458. Myxoedema: characteristic facial appearance
In examples such as these diagnosis is not difficult. Not only are there the characteristic changes in hair and skin and subcutaneous tissues, but there is a dull lifeless look that goes with cerebral impairment.

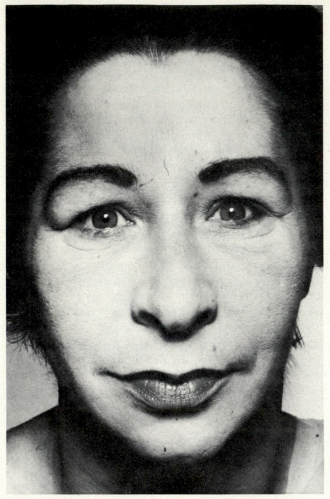

459a

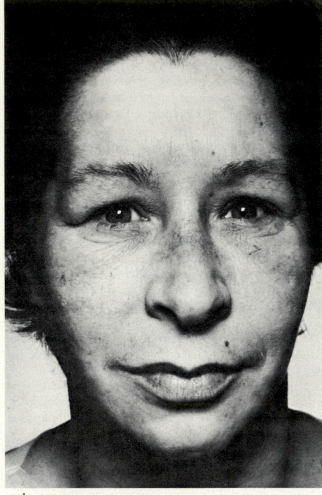

459b

459. Myxoedema △

Relapse of symptoms of the carpal tunnel syndrome after surgical treatment. Symptoms of myxoedema were only elicited on inquiry; these were characteristic. Cosmetics can disguise or minimize the facial appearance of myxoedema. In (a) she has applied her make-up; in (b) she has removed it. After treatment with thyroxine she said that, in retrospect, her acroparaesthesiae should have been the least of her complaints. She had not realized how 'sluggish' she had been.

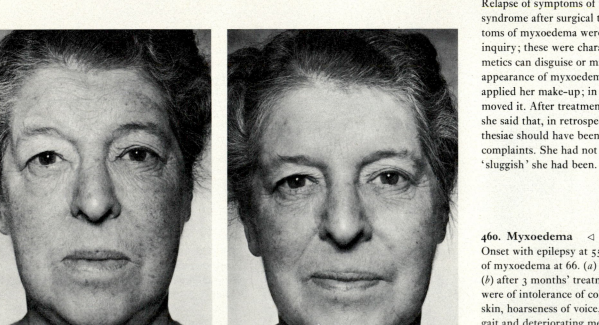

460b

460. Myxoedema ◁

Onset with epilepsy at 55 years. Diagnosis of myxoedema at 66. (a) Before treatment; (b) after 3 months' treatment. Complaints were of intolerance of cold, dryness of the skin, hoarseness of voice, unsteadiness of gait and deteriorating mental faculties. Her sister suffered from epilepsy and her mother from organic dementia.

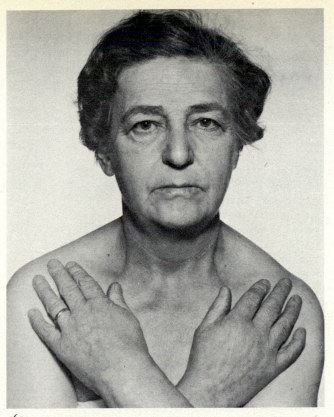

461a

461b

461. Myxoedema
The only complaints were of depression, lassitude and constipation. The diagnosis was suggested by the characteristic 'slow' ankle jerks; the facial appearance was then recognized—not before.

(a) Before treatment; (b) after 6 months' treatment.

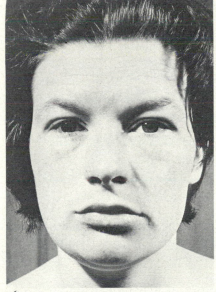

462a

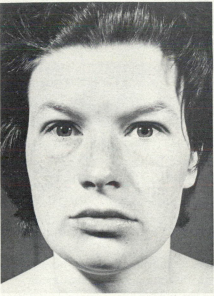

462b

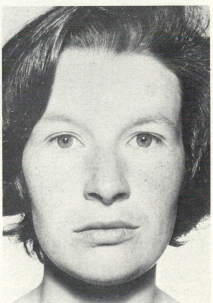

462c

462. 'Myxoedematous madness'
Age 26; married; 3 children aged 6 years, 4 years and 3 months. One month previously, mumps in second child; one week later, mumps in first child and mother. Children recovered. Mother developed strange symptoms. Periods of weakness in lower limbs, fluctuating, at times so severe that she could only crawl upstairs. G.P. suspected encephalitis or hysteria.

On examination: giggling, fatuous, vague, with an almost total areflexia. Polyneuritis suspected; admitted to hospital. Twenty-four hours later frankly psychotic; garrulous and hallucinated. Porphyria suspected. This was excluded. On third hospital day, hypopituitarism was suspected from the facial appearance, but there was active lactation. Re-examination disclosed the characteristic slow ankle jerks of hypothyroidism. Only then was the subnormal temperature—down to 35°C—noticed. No bradycardia (pulse always between 80 and 90).

Investigations: E.E.G. showed normal alpha rhythm. E.C.G. showed flat T-waves and low voltage QRS complexes. C.S.F. protein 60 mg./100 ml. Serum cholesterol 195 mg./100 ml. Rapid response to treatment with thyroxine.

(a) On third hospital day when psychotic; vacant expression, puffy eyelids, thickened lips and nostrils, malar flush with yellow tinge to the skin. (b) After 18 days' thyroxine therapy. Alert with improving facial appearance. (c) After 6 weeks' treatment.

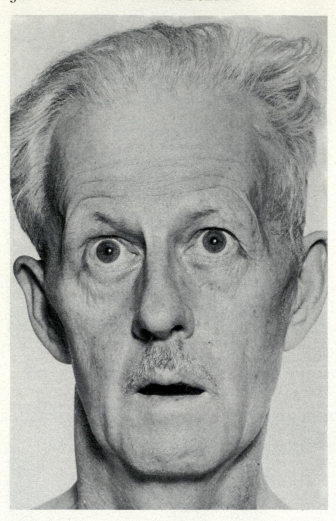

Hyperthyroidism

463. Thyrotoxicosis and cerebral ischaemia
Age 60 years. Referred to a neurological clinic with a diagnosis of Parkinsonism because of bilateral *gross* hand tremors. Previous pulmonary tuberculosis. One year's history of weight loss (2 stone), weakness, unsteadiness of gait and tremulous, clumsy upper limbs. Examination: thin, sweating, agitated, *coarse* tremor of upper limbs, slightly ataxic gait, sluggish limb reflexes, equivocal left extensor plantar responses. Pulse 120; atrial fibrillation; enlarged liver. Lid retraction and lid lag. Confused, erratic, hyperkinetic. E.E.G. showed diffuse high-voltage slow delta activity with occasional left temporal phase-reversals. Cerebral scan was normal. Left carotid arteriogram normal. Thyroid function tests confirmed hyperthyroidism. At no time was there any visible or palpable thyroid enlargement; no neck bruits. Treatment for his thyrotoxicosis and cardiac failure gave good results: mental confusion subsided, E.E.G. returned to normal, extensor plantar responses disappeared. He was left with an amnesia for about 1 week.

HYPOPITUITARISM

Adult panhypopituitarism (Sheehan's syndrome; Simmonds' disease), which results from infarction of the pituitary gland as a result of severe obstetrical haemorrhage and shock, is not often seen in the neurological clinic. There, the commonest cause is tumour—the suprasellar tumour or cyst (craniopharyngioma) or the intrasellar neoplasm (chromophobe adenoma). Hypopituitarism may also be a late result of an eosinophilic tumour in acromegaly. In some cases the pituitary lesion is a granuloma—a tuberculoma, a xanthoma or a sarcoid or non-specific granuloma. Sometimes compression from an aneurysm of the internal carotid artery is responsible for the pituitary destruction. Pituitary failure is an occasional consequence of severe head injury. It may follow surgery or radiotherapy to the pituitary or hypothalamic region. Hypopituitarism is occasionally iatrogenic, e.g. a result of steroid treatment.

The clinical features of hypopituitarism are mainly determined by the pattern of deficiency of the various pituitary hormones, but will be influenced by the age and sex of the patient and the rate of progress of the disease. The anterior pituitary gland secretes six hormones: corticotrophin (ACTH), thyrotrophin (TSH), gonadotrophin, growth hormone (GH), prolactin, and melanocyte-stimulating hormone (MSH). The gland itself is under the control of the hypothalamus, in which stimulating or inhibitory factors are synthesized. These pass down the pituitary stalk through the portal vessels to the anterior lobe of the pituitary. Loss of any of these factors due to lesions affecting the appropriate nuclei of the hypothalamus will lead to various degrees of secondary hypopituitarism. The hypothalamus is also concerned with temperature regulation and with food and water satiety, and takes part in the control of the cardiovascular system. Disease of the hypothalamus may therefore cause not only hypopituitarism but such disorders as diabetes insipidus, precocious puberty, obesity, various types of somnolence and disturbances of temperature regulation, and galactorrhoea or inappropriate secretion of milk. Hypothalamic lesions may result from severe head injury, meningitis or intracranial haemorrhage, but are most commonly caused by tumours. They are to be suspected in other conditions such as anorexia nervosa, disturbed sleep rhythms and some types of severe behavioural disorder.

In hypopituitarism there may be clinical signs indicating a lack of one or more of the six pituitary hormones, but laboratory tests are nearly always necessary to identify these. It is possible to measure the plasma levels of some of them, but more frequently the clinician has to rely on tests based on deficiencies of the hormones secreted by the target organs. Lack of growth hormone produces shortness of stature, the bone age is retarded, muscle growth is limited and there is an increase of subcutaneous fat. In the male, gonadotrophin deficiency causes impotence and loss of libido; in the female there is oligomenorrhoea or amenorrhoea and there may be infertility. The lack of skin pigmentation in hypopituitarism, often with pallor of the nipples, is due to deficiency of MSH. The myxoedematous state of the skin and subcutaneous tissues in primary hypothyroidism is rarely seen when there is TSH deficiency. Polyuria and polydipsia from ADH deficiency seldom occur in pituitary tumours. Postpartum hypopituitarism of serious degree is now fortunately rare; prolactin deficiency is responsible for the failure to initiate lactation and for the resumption of menstruation. A deficiency of ACTH may be responsible for the general lack of wellbeing, the lassitude, the depression and the gastro-intestinal symptoms —features which are not particularly distinctive and may be masked by other complaints.

Loss of pituitary trophic hormones results in failure of gonadal, thyroidal and adrenocortical function. The clinical manifestations occur in that sequence.

Tumour being the commonest cause, headache may be a feature, but this is rarely severe. It may be persistent, fluctuating, at times bursting. It may be frontal, temporal or even occipital in location. Commonly it is fairly nondescript but persistent. Visual field defects may be symptomless, and unilateral loss of visual acuity may have developed to a marked degree before it is detected. Whenever there is the slightest suspicion of hypopituarism, the visual fields must be charted and

the skull X-rayed. Ballooning of the sella turcica, a double contour to the floor of the sella, erosion of the anterior or posterior clinoid processes, and calcification may be demonstrated. Air encephalography is often necessary.

Hypopituarism can occur at any age. The child with a craniopharyngioma usually complains first of headache and vomiting and, later, of failing vision. Papilloedema is much commoner in the child than in the adult with this type of tumour. The child is often fat and listless; growth and sexual development are retarded. Although often small in stature, the child is not a dwarf, and intellect is usually normal. Puberty and the menarche are delayed or do not occur. The degree of endocrine disorder in craniopharyngioma varies considerably. Although the craniopharyngioma is of developmental origin, it may remain symptomless for many years. In adult life it may present with visual defects, and in the elderly patient it is an occasional cause of dementia.

The adult patient may be primarily eunuchoidal or myxoedematous. The general appearance may be as diagnostic as in primary myxoedema or acromegaly. General symptoms include asthenia, apathy and abnormal sensitivity to cold. The patient is often forgetful, listless, indifferent, with slow speech and sluggish movements. The skin is thin, atrophic, inelastic and often covered with very fine wrinkles. It is usually pale or yellowish resembling parchment. This pallor is usually taken to indicate anaemia, but if this is found to be present it does not usually respond to therapy with iron or vitamin B_{12}. It may only respond to hormonal substitution therapy. The pallor is also in part due to lack of melanophore-stimulating hormone. The generalized and vague character of many of the symptoms and the absence of anaemia often lead to an incorrect diagnosis of neurosis. The patient rarely offers the information that he only shaves once or twice a week or that he has become impotent. But the female patient with amenorrhoea usually volunteers this information. The scalp hair is usually normal, but there is progressive loss of body, pubic and axillary hair over the years. With the onset of thyroid failure, some of the features of myxoedema may be noticed. Signs of adrenal failure are slight and late.

The patient with hypopituitarism may naturally consult the doctor for a variety of reasons—general ill health, symptoms and signs of raised intracranial pressure, visual failure or episodes of syncope, confusion or fits. Although the outward evidence of hypopituitarism may be apparent, the presenting symptoms are many and varied. Even if the hypopituitarism is obvious, there may be no complaint of general ill health. I have known such patients continue to do hard work for many years and then to fail suddenly or rapidly. Chiasmal compression may be symptomless until vision is in jeopardy. On the other hand the complaint may be of sudden failure of vision in one eye.

Suprasellar extension of a tumour may result in diplopia from ocular palsy, mental deterioration from invasion of the frontal lobes, or uncinate epilepsy from temporal lobe involvement. There may be episodes of prolonged syncope, confusion or disorientation lasting hours or days. Recovery is spontaneous and apparently complete.

Stupor or coma in the course of hypopituitarism cannot always be explained in terms of hypothermia, hypoglycaemia, or hyponatraemia. Involvement of the hypothalamus is probably responsible for some of these

episodes. Not uncommonly hypopituitarism is first suspected when there has been such an episode following an injury or an infection.

Pituitary apoplexy is not uncommon in pituitary tumours. There is acute violent headache with collapse and unconsciousness. A clinical diagnosis of meningitis or subarachnoid haemorrhage is usually made. If the outward manifestations of hypopituitarism are obvious or if the patient is known to have a pituitary tumour the diagnosis can be made on clinical grounds. If the infarct is white the spinal fluid resembles that in meningitis, but if it is red a diagnosis of intracranial aneurysm may appear to be confirmed. Rapid enlargement within a pituitary tumour may cause an acute ophthalmoplegia,

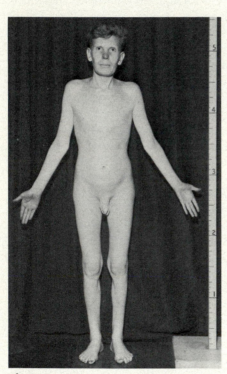

464a

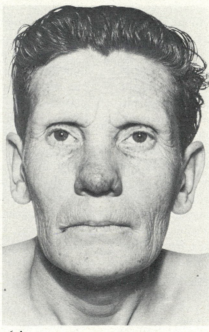

464b

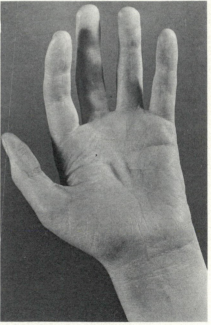

464c

464. Familial hypopituitarism, amyotrophy and sarcoidosis

First seen in 1947, aged 21 years. A collier with 1 year's history of general fatigue with weakness of left lower limb. Examination: cranial nerves normal; diffuse wasting and weakness of musculature of both upper limbs, including global wasting of hand muscles. Generalized reflex hyperactivity with bilateral extensor plantar responses. No fasciculation; no sensory loss. C.S.F. protein 180 mg./100 ml. Suspected amyotrophic lateral sclerosis. Not seen again until 1958, aged 33 years (a). No neurological deterioration; neurological signs unchanged. Now showed clinical appearance of hypopituitarism:

dry, yellowish skin; no facial, axillary or pubic hair. Sexually impotent since his late teens. Nocturnal emissions until aged 22. Small testes. Still showed generalized hyper-reflexia, absent abdominal reflexes, bilateral extensor plantar responses with ankle clonus. Normal cranial nerves. Radiology: skull normal; air encephalogram normal; pulmonary tuberculosis. Sputum negative. Strongly positive Mantoux test 1/1,000. Antituberculous and endocrine replacement therapy was instituted, but subsequently he required a right upper lobectomy. Caseating tuberculosis was revealed in the biopsy specimen, in which acid fast bacilli were seen. A few years later, a skin lesion on one foot

was biopsied and proved to be lupus vulgaris. Seen again in 1966, aged 40 years (b). Became sexually potent, married but no children. Still general fatigue, but neurological signs unchanged. Diffuse weakness of limbs; generalized hyper-reflexia with ankle clonus, bilateral extensor plantar responses and absent abdominal reflexes. Global atrophy of hand muscles (c). No fasciculation or sensory loss. Electromyography and nerve conduction studies normal. C.S.F. normal. Serum proteins and electrophoretic strip normal. W.R. negative in blood and C.S.F. He now had lupus pernio; his nose was swollen and purple; biopsy revealed a histology suggestive of sarcoidosis. Positive Kveim test.

most commonly a third nerve palsy. Pituitary infarction is probably related to the peculiar portal type of circulation which is readily occluded by pressure. Pituitary swelling, with rapid failure of vision, severe headache, but without loss of consciousness may be mistaken for cranial arteritis. I have known ACTH prescribed in one such case give rapid relief of headache and recovery of vision. The tumours of the pituitary which undergo apoplexy are usually chromophobe and eosinophilic adenomas, with perhaps a preponderance of the latter. This complication has not been described in basophilic tumours.

Diabetes insipidus may be the presenting symptom, but not necessarily the dominant one, in pituitary tumours and craniopharyngiomas. It may also ensue from head injury or from granulomatous disorders in this region. It is necessary first to establish that both thirst and polyuria are present. In urinary frequency, only small volumes of urine are usually passed at a time and there is no polydipsia. Thirst may be merely due to a dry mouth because of salivary gland disease. In diabetes insipidus, the specific gravity of the urine will be 1·005 or less, and plasma osmolality tends to be high. The 24-hour intake and output during unrestricted access to fluid must be measured. Fluid deprivation tests are sometimes necessary. Occasionally diabetes insipidus proves to be an idiopathic disorder, and in some cases even a familial one. Tumours remain the commonest cause.

Familial Hypopituitarism

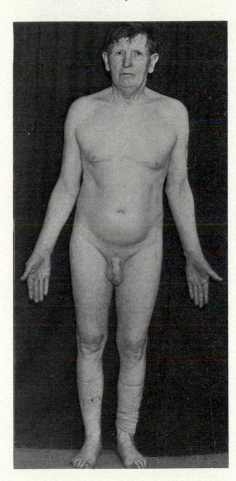

465. Familial hypopituitarism
Age 62 years; father of patient shown in Fig. 464. A retired collier who enjoyed good health until the age of 50. Married. 2 sons. In recent years complained of general tiredness, susceptibility to cold, increase in weight, diurnal sleep. Had never shaved more than once per week. Never had any pubic or axillary hair. Sexual potency normal until early fifties. Examination: nervous system normal except for bilateral ring scotomata; normal discs; visual acuity 6/9 bilaterally. E.E.G. normal. Skull X-ray: normal sella turcica but multinodular intrasellar calcification. Typical clinical appearance of hypopituitarism—dry wrinkled yellowish skin, hairless. Cerebration normal. Characteristic biochemical findings of hypopituitarism. Replacement therapy; general improvement, but died of a myocardial infarction 2 years later.
His second son was also studied: he only shaved once a week but was clinically normal and there was no biochemical evidence of hypopituitarism.

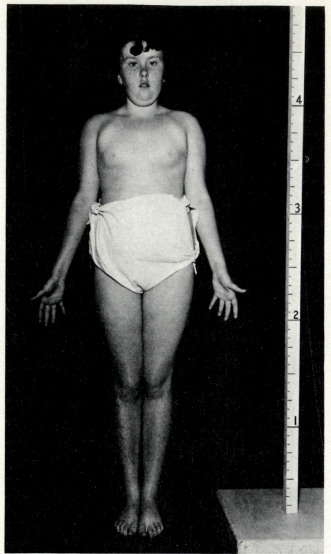

466a

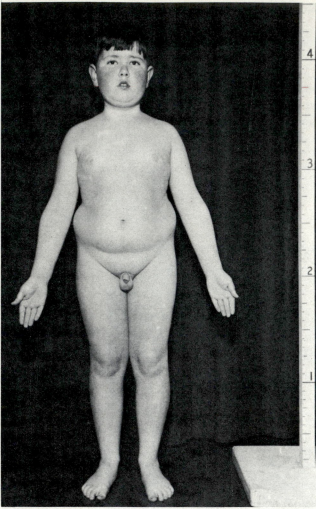

467a

Craniopharyngioma

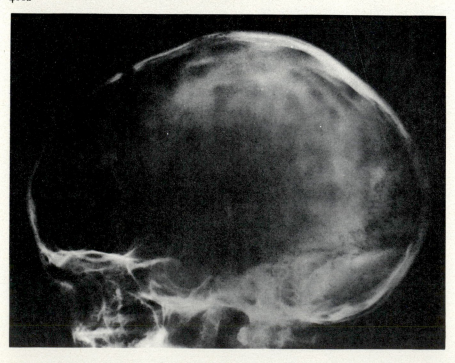

466. Craniopharyngioma
Age 15. Failure of the menarche, headache, primary optic atrophy, obesity and hypogonadism (*a*). Suprasellar calcification (*b*).

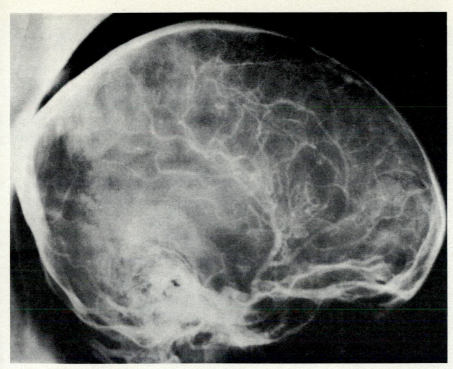

467b

467. Craniopharyngioma
Age 12. Headache for 4 years. Bilateral papilloedema. Bitemporal hemianopia. Obesity, infantilism, skin pale, thin and hairless (*a*). Suprasellar calcification. Carotid arteriogram (*b*) showed upward displacement of the terminal portion of the carotid siphon and the origins of the anterior and middle cerebral arteries.

468. Chromophobe adenoma; impotence
Age 35. No other voluntary complaint but there was mild chronic headache, lethargy and fatigue. Note the bodily configuration, faint abdominal striae, the smooth, pale, hairless skin (*a*). Testicular atrophy. Vision normal. Enlarged sella turcica (*b*).

Chromophobe Adenoma

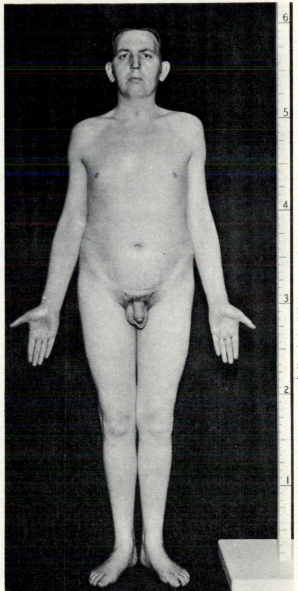

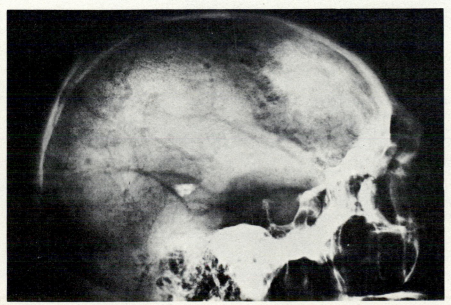

468b

468a

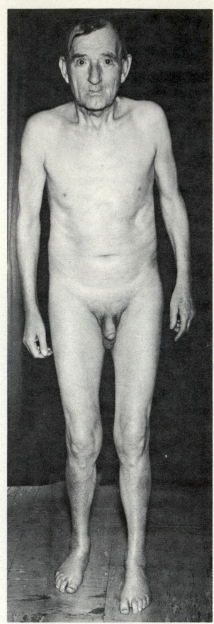

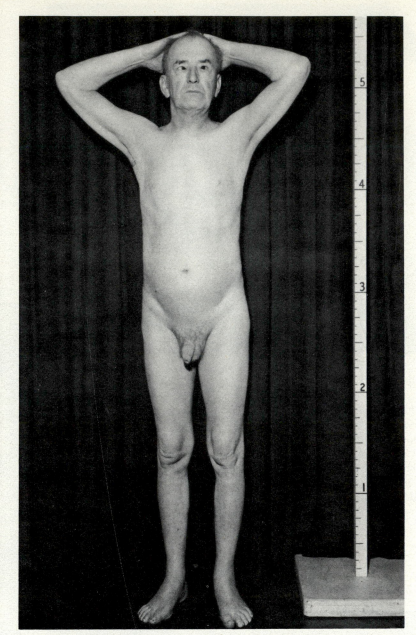

469. Chromophobe adenoma; sudden visual failure

Three episodes of amaurosis in one month; blind for several days on each occasion. Moderate visual recovery. No other complaints, but he was old, forgetful and paranoid. His skin was dry, wrinkled and yellow. Anaemia often suspected but never revealed. No body or axillary hair; sparse pubic hair. He still shaved twice weekly.

470. Chromophobe adenoma; progressive visual failure

Age 66. Failing vision on right, with internal strabismus for 2 years; failing vision on left with internal strabismus 1 year. Recent episodes of loss of consciousness. Bilateral optic atrophy, bilateral sixth nerve paresis. Eroded and enlarged sella turcica. His skin was pale, fine and parchment coloured; trunk and limbs were hairless; sparse pubic hair, no axillary hair. Scalp hair fine and silky. Shaved once weekly. Intracranial pressure was normal and the bilateral sixth nerve palsies must have been due to extrasellar extension of the tumour.

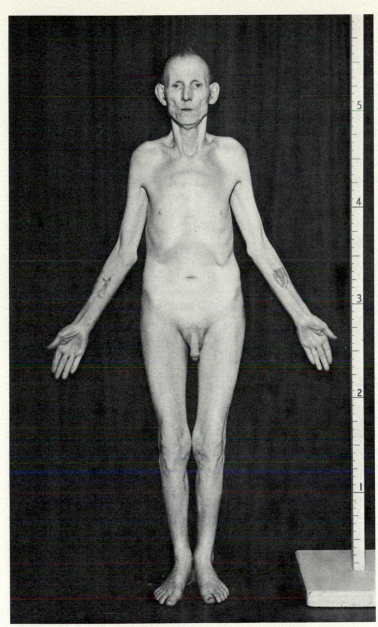

471. Chromophobe adenoma; acute stupor

Age 62. Labourer until 6 weeks before admission. Sudden physical weakness without loss of consciousness; recovery in 1 week. Admitted in stupor 1 month later. Recovery in 3 days. Left optic atrophy. Enlarged sella turcica. B.M.R.—25. Air encephalography revealed a large extra-sellar extension of the tumour. No hypothermia, hypoglycaemia, or serious electrolyte disorder. Impotent 30 years; no pubic or axillary hair since he was shaved as a prisoner of war in Germany in the First World War. Shaved his face once a week. Skin yellow and atrophic. A general labourer for 40 years.

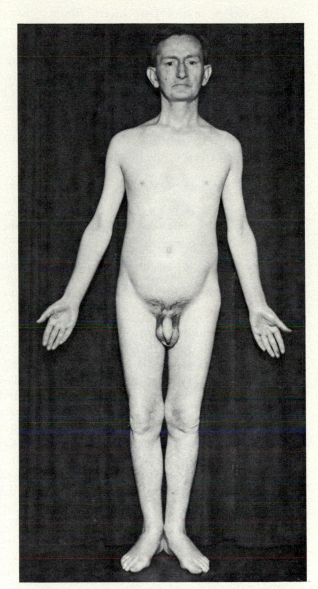

472. Pituitary apoplexy

Age 47. Sudden headache with loss of consciousness; diagnosis of meningitis. Turbid cerebrospinal fluid, protein 280 mg./100 ml.; polymorphs 2,000 per mm.³; sterile. Recovery but with right ophthalmoplegia. Subsequent story of impotence 15 years, headache 10 years, failing vision of right eye 3 years. Enlarged sella turcica which was virtually empty on craniotomy.

ACROMEGALY

It was a neurologist, Pierre Marie (1853–1940), assistant and successor to Charcot at the Salpêtrière in Paris, who first recognized this disease and gave it its title in 1886. Although he noted the enlargement of the pituitary gland he thought that this was a part of the general hypertrophy of the tissues. In the first of his two cases he described the amenorrhoea, the acroparaesthesiae, the headaches and the enlargement of the distal parts of the extremities. The facial appearance of his first case he described in the following words:

'Briefly, the face presents the appearance of a lengthened ellipse, with the diameter from above downwards. The centre of this ellipse is situated on a level with the bridge of the nose, and its greatest diameter is opposite the malar prominences. The cranial vertex is of nearly the same size as the end of the chin. The lower jaw is well developed. The complexion is pale and the eyelids a little pigmented. The patient's thirst is intense, obliging her to beg tea of her friends in order to satisfy it. The quantity of urine is excessive.'

The well known features of acromegaly usually develop so insidiously that neither the patient nor his family may be aware of the changes that are taking place. On the other hand there are well authenticated cases in which symptoms and signs have appeared and progressed in a rapid manner. Probably the commonest complaint is one of headache which may be persistent and intractable. It seems to fluctuate in intensity with the activity of the acromegaly. It has not been shown that it is due to increased intracranial pressure and treatment by surgery or deep X-ray therapy does not necessarily relieve it.

In the majority of female patients irregularity of menstruation or amenorrhoea are first noticed. In the male there is loss of sexual potency. The female patient usually notices the increase in the size of the hands and feet; the male patient may not do so.

In an established case the patient's appearance is characteristic and does not go so long unnoticed as in myxoedema. The nose, lips and tongue enlarge and the whole face takes on a coarse, enlarged and elongated appearance. The mandible is prominent and the lower teeth separated by growth of the jaw. The ears enlarge and their cartilages thicken and harden. The corrugations of the forehead are exaggerated and the frontal sinuses overgrown. The skin is darker and the hair coarser. The patient complains of excessive perspiration, acroparaesthesiae, depression and fatigue. The character of the voice alters from changes in the pharynx and larynx; it may be deep and husky.

Dr. Leonard Mark* (1912), a sufferer from the disease, was amazed to learn, at the age of fifty, when he realized that he was acromegalic, that his family and friends had known it for many years. Tinnitus, facial aching and periods of fatigue were his earliest symptoms.

As in the case of myxoedema the patient with acromegaly may visit many departments of a hospital. Thirst and polyuria may take him to the diabetic department or visual failure from optic atrophy to the ophthalmological department. Kyphosis and limb pains may suggest some form of arthritis. Changes in the synovial membranes, articular cartilages and in the bone ends themselves are no doubt responsible. Compression of peripheral nerves may be a presenting feature. Changes in the wrist lead to the carpal tunnel syndrome. In acromegaly the carpal tunnel syndrome is not so predominantly a female complaint as in the idiopathic variety. There may be ulnar or peroneal symptoms and signs due to compression. As with the headache these peripheral nerve manifestations may come and go.

One of the greatest difficulties in acromegaly is in assessing the activity of the disease. I have seen several patients in whom it had been thought the disease was 'burnt out' but in whom, years later, symptoms and signs progressed or were renewed. On clinical grounds alone it does not appear possible to assess activity and the only certain guide to successful treatment is the restoration of normal levels of circulating growth hormone. Newer methods of pituitary irradiation suggest that effective treatment may result in remarkable restoration of normal facial appearances.

Enlargement of the sella turcica is seen in 90 per cent. of patients with acromegaly. Life expectancy is reduced in this disease. The main causes of death are cardiovascular, cerebrovascular and respiratory. There is no satisfactory form of medical treatment, and surgical methods are now undertaken before headache and chiasmal compression develop. Yttrium implantation of the tumour is commonly used, but replacement therapy is necessary in 25 per cent. of cases.

* Mark, Leonard P. (1912) *Acromegaly: A Personal Experience*, London.

Acromegaly

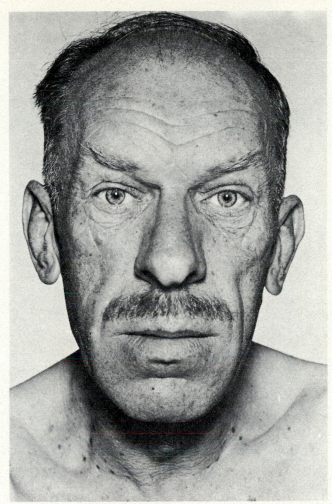

473. Acromegaly

This patient was a professional photographer and was wholly unaware of the change that had been taking place in his facial appearance. His wife was also unaware of it. The only symptoms were of three episodes of loss of consciousness in the previous few weeks. Retrospectively he realized that his hands and feet had enlarged and that he had suffered fatigue. Note the great enlargement of his heels. Thickness of the heel pad may be determined radiologically and is a good guide to the acromegalic state.

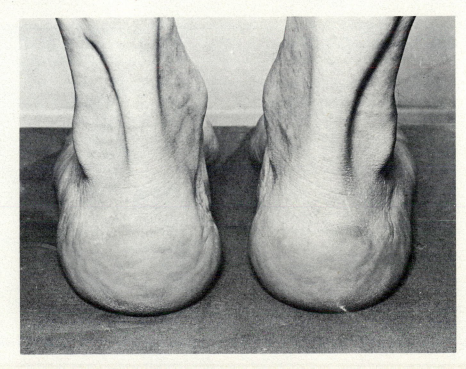

Acromegaly

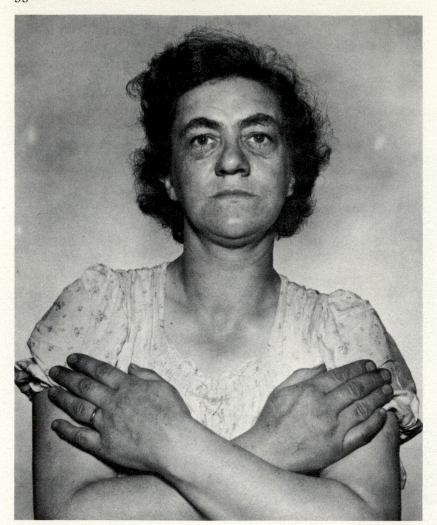

474. Acromegaly
Irregular menstruation 6 years; two increases in shoe size in 2 years; similar increase in glove size. Embedded wedding ring. One year headache, 6 months' failing vision. Bilateral optic atrophy with bilateral superior temporal quadrantanopsia. Visual acuity 6/60 bilaterally. Galactorrhoea. Enlarged sella turcica.

475. Acromegaly
Amenorrhoea for 30 years. General ill health but little specific complaint, the chief changes taking place in the soft tissues. Note hypertrophied folding skin of the hands.

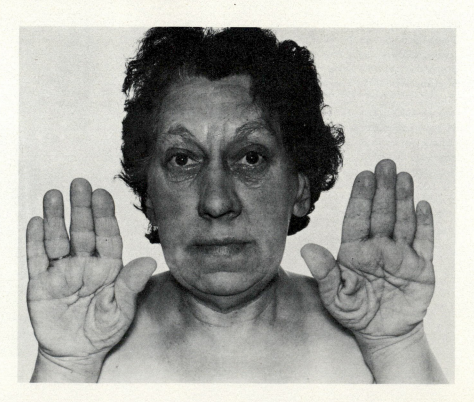

476. Acromegaly ▷

Kyphosis, arthritis, headache and depression. Later developed diabetes mellitus. Limb pains, stiffness and acroparaesthesiae remained her main complaints for many years.

477. Acromegaly ▽

In contrast to the preceding illustration, the main changes here are in the facial bones. Age 50. Goitre since 9; deep voice since 20; facial change since 20 years of age; enlarged hands and feet since 25; operation for carpal tunnel syndrome at 40. Diabetic at 45. Vision normal.

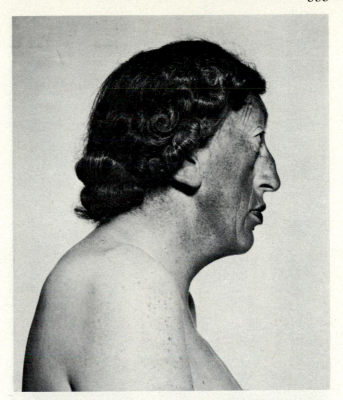

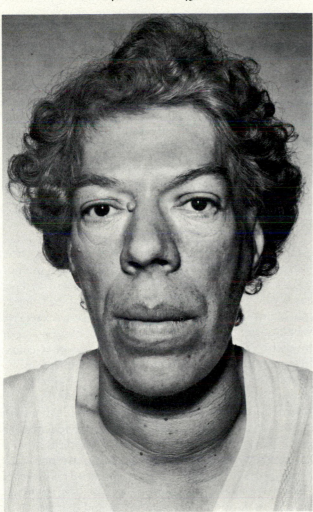

478. Acromegaly: pituitary apoplexy ▷
Age 28. Amenorrhoea 15 months, galactorrhoea 2 weeks. Admitted to hospital with suspected acute meningitis. Headache, stiff neck, cells and protein increased in cerebrospinal fluid. Bilateral papilloedema, bilateral sixth nerve palsies. Slow recovery. Enlarged sella turcica. Photograph shows residual left external rectus palsy.

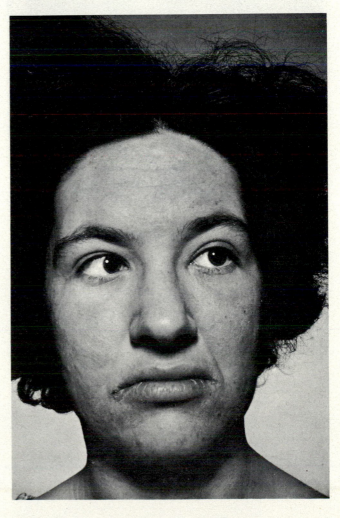

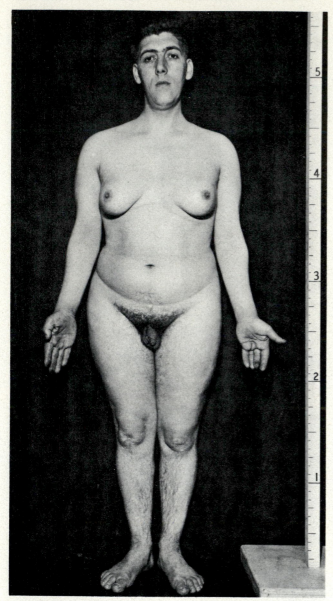

479. Acromegaly
An acromegalic patient who had received
prolonged 'glandular' therapy.

CHRONIC ADRENAL INSUFFICIENCY
(Addison's Disease)

Thomas Addison (1793–1860) described both pernicious anaemia and disease of the adrenal glands in 1849 when he was 56 years of age. His monograph *On the Constitutional and Local Effects of Disease of the Suprarenal Capsules*, published in 1855, is one of the classics of medicine. His eleven case reports were illustrated with coloured portraits depicting the cutaneous pigmentation of his patients and with drawings of the diseased adrenal glands at autopsy. He vividly described the progressive failure of health and physical exhaustion of the patient and the characteristic discoloration of the skin:

'sufficiently marked indeed as generally to have attracted the attention of the patient himself, or of the patient's friends. This discolouration pervaded the whole surface of the body, but is commonly most strongly manifested on the face, neck, superior extremities, penis and scrotum and in the flexures of the axillae and around the navel. It may be said to present a dingy or smoky appearance, of various tints or shades of deep amber or chestnut brown; and in one instance the skin was so universally and so deeply darkened that, but for the features, the patient might have been mistaken for a mulatto.'

He found that the adrenal glands may have been destroyed by tuberculosis, atrophy or malignant tumour.

We can understand him when he said, of one case, 'it was to me a matter of much regret that I had not an opportunity of employing an artist to make an exact representation of the singular discolouration observed upon the skin'—thus stressing the superiority of a colour drawing over the most elaborate verbal description.

Nowadays the most common cause is atrophy of the adrenal gland, the origin of which is obscure. Formerly tuberculosis was the commoner cause. Metastatic adrenal deposits, particularly from a bronchial carcinoma, occur. Whatever the cause pigmentation is usually the first manifestation and in the atrophic form it usually antedates any other symptom by many years. There is progressive weakness, weight loss, anorexia, nausea, vague abdominal discomfort and diarrhoea. On the other hand the patient may remain relatively well for a long time. He may not seek advice or suspect any form of illness and his friends and relatives may not notice the deepening pigmentation. Such a patient may present in an acute adrenal crisis with collapse, hypotension, abdominal pain and diarrhoea leading to dehydration.

It is an uncommon disease, but minor degrees of chronic adrenal insufficiency must occur from time to time, without the obvious manifestations of Addison's disease, and requiring steroid assays to establish the diagnosis. Chronic asthenia without obvious pigmentation may readily suggest an anxiety state. The pigmentation must be distinguished from that due to racial factors, malignant disease and hepatic cirrhosis. It may take the form of a diffuse tan of the skin, brownish coloration over exposed parts or on pressure points, or in palmar creases or scars. The skin may be dotted with multiple freckles and the lips and gums may be pigmented. Addison himself observed vitiligo or leucodermia.

Weakness may be profound. One patient was referred to me with suspected myopathy. Muscular pains and cramps are sometimes the result of sodium depletion. Recurrent syncope is another reason why the patient may be referred to a neurologist. The personality may alter; the patient becoming more quiet, seclusive and apathetic. Although the onset is usually insidious and

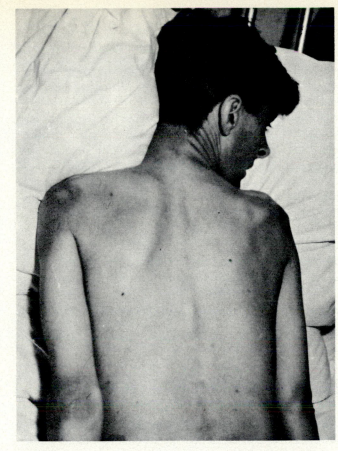

480. Addison's disease; post-operative syncope

Age 30. Three syncopal attacks in hospital ward following tonsillectomy. No previous symptoms of any kind. Deeply pigmented; note dark nipples, pigmentation on shoulders, elbows, palm creases and in appendicectomy scar. No radial pulse in erect posture. B.P. in supine position

75/40. Conjunctivae blanched on sitting up. No adrenal calcification. Listless, apathetic but was at full work until the day prior to his tonsillectomy. E.E.G. showed an absence of alpha rhythm with diffuse high voltage delta activity in all leads; prompt return to normal on treatment.

Plasma sodium 120 mEq./l.; potassium 5·9 mEq./l.; chloride 86 mEq./l. Subsequently a study of photographs revealed that his pigmentation had been developing for 10 years, but he was never ill and the only time he had ever fainted was when he saw a man remove his false arm!

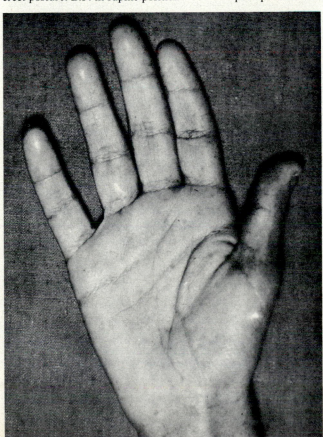

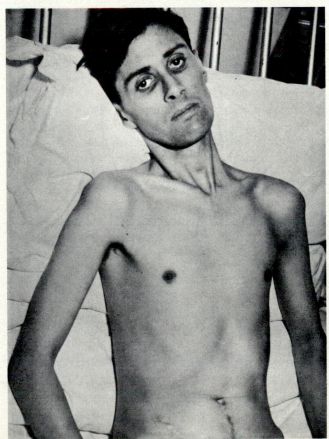

slowly progressive, an acute infection or an operation may precipitate acute symptoms. Acute adrenal insufficiency from lack of aldosterone and glucocorticoids, will cause hypotension and circulatory collapse, hypoglycaemia, stupor and coma. Abdominal pain, nausea, vomiting, confusion and delirium might suggest, not adrenal insufficiency, but porphyria.

The response to the oral administration of cortisone is usually so striking as to be diagnostic. The patient may literally sit up and take notice.

Hypoadrenalism is due to disease of the cortex of the gland. Failure of the adrenal medulla is not associated with any specific clinical syndrome. The cortex secretes three main groups of hormones. (1) The glucocorticoids, the secretion of which is controlled by the adrenocorticotrophic hormone (ACTH) of the anterior pituitary gland. Cortisol (hydrocortisone) is the most important of these glucocorticoids. (2) The mineralocorticoids, of which aldosterone is the most powerful. The term corticosteroid is used to include glucocorticoids and mineralocorticoids. (3) The androgens.

The clinical features of Addison's disease are largely due to deficiency of glucocorticoids and mineralocorticoids. Deficiency of the former is responsible for the anorexia, nausea, hypotension and hypoglycaemia. Mineralocorticoid deficiency causes sodium depletion with dehydration and hypotension. The pigmentation is due to the overproduction of ACTH and the other anterior pituitary hormone, melanocyte-stimulating hormone (MSH), as a consequence of the low levels of circulating cortisol.

HYPERADRENOCORTICISM (Cushing's Syndrome)

Harvey Cushing (1869–1939) described this syndrome in 1932 when he was 63 years of age and about to retire. In his pioneer work entitled *The Pituitary Body and its Disorders*, published in 1912, he had drawn attention to a special group of patients with the 'polyglandular syndrome', in whom it was difficult to say which of the endocrine glands was primarily at fault. They did not exhibit chiasmal compression or signs of raised intracranial pressure and none had come to autopsy. Until 1930 Cushing had not seen a basophilic tumour of the pituitary but he had often suspected that such might occur. In his search for basophilic tumours of the pituitary he actually arranged for the exhumation, three days after the funeral, of one of his former patients, and found a well-circumscribed basophilic adenoma. His concept of 'pituitary basophilism' had been stimulated by the publication of the photographs of a patient from a Prague clinic 'which were so striking and bore such a close resemblance to the appearance of a patient at the same time under observation in my own ward that I felt little doubt that they had been afflicted in all certainty with the same disorder'.

We now know that the syndrome results from the excessive secretion of glucocorticoids from the adrenal cortex and is characterized by truncal obesity, hypertension, diminished glucose tolerance, increased protein catabolism, amenorrhoea and an increased liability to infection. It is much commoner in women and in the majority of cases there is bilateral hyperplasia of the adrenal glands, induced by hypersecretion of ACTH and associated with a basophil or chromophobe adenoma of the pituitary gland. The syndrome may also be caused by an adenoma or carcinoma arising in the adrenal cortex and, very rarely, it may result from a hormone-secreting bronchial carcinoma. The term Cushing's disease is now usually applied to those cases in which there is a basophil adenoma with bilateral adrenal hyperplasia.

The clinical picture of Cushing's syndrome results from the excessive secretion of glucocorticoid hormones. The most striking feature is protein depletion which is evident in skin, muscle, blood vessels and bones. There is marked weakness due to the wasting and also to associated potassium depletion. Impaired glucose tolerance and in some cases frank diabetes mellitus are due to increased gluconeogenesis.

The onset of the disease is usually gradual. The patient complains of increase in weight, backache, general weakness and swelling of the face. Impotence in the male and amenorrhoea in the female are common. Fragility of the skin and blood vessels is revealed by the development of livid purple striae over the abdomen, thighs and upper arms, and by increased susceptibility to bruising. Backache results from osteoporosis; dorsal kyphosis and compression fractures of the vertebrae are not uncommon. On two occasions I have seen the disease present with a convulsion resulting in compression fractures of already osteoporotic vertebrae.

Although Cushing's syndrome is another example of a condition which may be recognized at sight, it must be admitted that since the development of modern methods of assessing adrenocortical function, it has been realized that a purely clinical diagnosis is often impossible. The classical appearance is absent. In the florid case there is a striking redistribution of fat with the obesity confined to the face, neck and trunk. The face is swollen and plum coloured. There is acne and hirsutism. But many obese females may have a 'buffalo hump' and red striae and in Cushing's syndrome the obesity is by no means always truncal in distribution. In Cushing's syndrome the striae are broad and livid whereas in obesity they are usually thin and red. Amenorrhoea is much commoner in Cushing's syndrome than in obesity.

Mental symptoms may be the presenting manifestation in Cushing's syndrome. The commonest symptom is depression, but mild mania, paranoia and schizoid symptoms are encountered. Mental symptoms have been reported in as many as 60 per cent. of cases. I have known one patient commit suicide 6 months after the onset of symptoms. Polyneuritis of the Guillain-Barré variety has been reported several times in association with this syndrome. Myopathic weakness chiefly affects proximal limb muscles. It is rare for local signs of pituitary tumour to occur in Cushing's syndrome, but after bilateral adrenalectomy this may happen and necessitate surgical treatment.

Symptoms related to hypertension or diabetes mellitus are naturally common. Polycythaemia is not as common as formerly considered, occurring in about 20–25 per cent. of patients. The actual diagnosis of Cushing's syndrome requires establishing that there is adrenocortical hyperfunction by steroid assays. There is an increased urinary excretion of 17–oxogenic steroids, a raised level of plasma cortisol without the normal diurnal variation—a high level in the morning and a lower level at night. In differentiating bilateral adrenal hyperplasia and an adrenal adenoma, difficulty may be encountered. An intravenous pyelogram may reveal the presence of a suprarenal tumour. Radiography after presacral insufflation of oxygen may show bilateral adrenal enlargement or a unilateral tumour. An adrenal adenoma or carcinoma, being autonomous, may not be stimulated by ACTH nor suppressed by dexamethasone.

Cushing's syndrome is a diagnosis which is often suggested but not confirmed. An emotionally unstable, obese, adult female, with a hump, fat limbs, thin red striae and hypertension is not usually suffering from Cushing's syndrome. It should be suspected when there is evidence of a *recent* change in physical appearance, with the onset of weakness, emotional distress and when the striae are broad and livid.

Clinical diagnosis is only possible in the florid examples of the disease. Laboratory diagnosis can now be made in patients in whom few of the classical features are present.

Cushing's original concept was one of hyperpituitarism; then came the discovery of hyperadrenocorticism, but now we appreciate that in Cushing's syndrome we see the clinical picture of hypercortisolism. Cortisol excess may be iatrogenic (the Cushing's syndrome of steroid therapy), or it may be a manifestation of an adrenal tumour or of ACTH-producing tumours, the commonest of which is pulmonary carcinoma. Thus, in a physiological sense, Cushing was correct in his concept of hyperpituitarism.

Progress often leads to difficulties of nomenclature. Some feel that the term 'Cushing's syndrome' should be abandoned, while others think that 'Cushing's disease' should be used when the syndrome is associated with spontaneous bilateral adrenal hyperplasia. Cushing's disease represents approximately 75 per cent. of the cases of Cushing's syndrome. The treatment of choice is said to be bilateral total adrenalectomy; pituitary tumour occurs in 10–20 per cent. of these patients post-operatively.

There are thus two main groups of conditions included in Cushing's syndrome: (1) those which are ACTH-dependent, such as Cushing's disease, ectopic ACTH syndrome and results of ACTH therapy; (2) those which are not dependent on ACTH, such as adrenocortical adenomata and carcinomata and results of corticosteroid therapy. The particular cause is identified by tests of the pituitary–adrenal axis functions.

The story of Cushing's syndrome, which I do not pretend to have fully outlined, affords the modern medical student an excellent example of the importance of the historical approach to the understanding of disease.

Cushing's Syndrome

481. Cushing's syndrome; before and after pituitary irradiation
(1) At the age of 18 years; (2) 1 year later;
(3) 6 months later. Headache, hypertension
(240/150) truncal obesity, purplish face,
livid striae. Pituitary irradiation (6,000 r
in 32 days). Apparent full recovery.
(4) Shows his appearance 1 year after
completion of irradiation. Three years
later gradual onset of blindness from optic
atrophy and progressive organic dementia
from cortical atrophy. Air encephalography
showed progressive cerebral atrophy, presumably the result of radionecrosis.

**482. Cushing's syndrome presenting
with psychosis**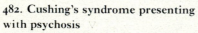
Age 44. Six months' history of depression,
paranoid delusions, attempted suicide.
Fairly rapid change in physical appearance. Purple, moon-shaped face with
hirsutism. Headache, diplopia and hypertension (170/100). Bilateral adrenal
hyperplasia confirmed at operation. Subtotal (90 per cent.) adrenalectomy (Mr.
D. B. E. Foster). No improvement. Died 1
year later of pulmonary embolism after
removal of remaining adrenal fragment.
Small basophil adenoma of the pituitary
gland found at autopsy.

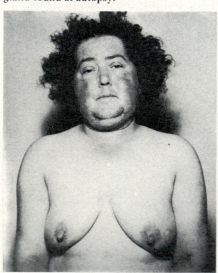

483. Cushing's syndrome ▷
Age 25 in 1952. Rapid obesity and change
in appearance following a pregnancy. Note
distribution of obesity, abdominal striae,
moon-shaped face and acne. Subtotal
(90 per cent.) adrenalectomy 18 months
later; little change apart from improvement of acne. The disease progressed and
was not controlled by radiotherapy to the
pituitary gland. By 1962 she was deeply
pigmented and had an enlarging sella.
Pituitary implantation of yttrium-90
resulted in no improvement, clinically or
biochemically (Professor A. P. M. Forrest).
Gold implantation in 1963 caused a remission with disappearance of pigmentation
and reduction of the levels of circulating
melanocyte-stimulating hormone in the
serum.

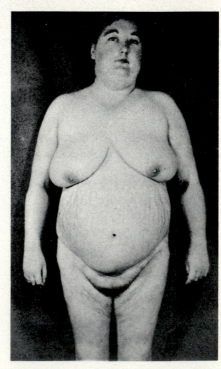

Cushing's Syndrome

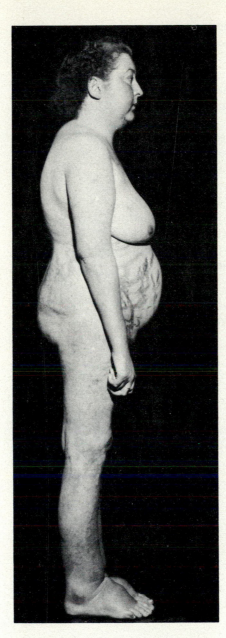 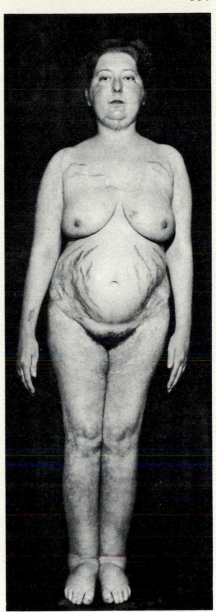

484. Cushing's syndrome
Age 21. Three-year history of amenorrhoea, facial hirsuties, obesity and oedema
of the lower limbs. Hypertension (220/
150), bilateral papilloedema, with multiple
spontaneous fractures and collapse of two
vertebrae. Improvement after subtotal
adrenalectomy (Mr. D. B. E. Foster).
Died 1 year later of cerebral haemorrhage.

HYPERINSULINISM

Hypoglycaemia may be either induced or spontaneous. In the former case it is usually iatrogenic in
origin but occasionally it is self-induced with the aid of
either insulin or excessive doses of one of the sulphonyl-
urea drugs. Barbiturates and alcohol may also cause
hypoglycaemia. By far the commonest form of spontaneous hypoglycaemia is that which occurs a few hours
after a meal—reactive hypoglycaemia. The patient is
often unstable and complains of faintness, weakness,
trembling, visual disturbance and failure of concentration. The attacks subside spontaneously even though no
food is taken. The fasting blood sugar is normal and
attacks are not provoked by fasting. Neurological disturbances do not occur but the condition may be
mistaken for minor epilepsy or narcolepsy.

The most important cause of spontaneous hypoglycaemia is hyperinsulinism—overproduction of insulin by an islet cell tumour of the pancreas. Although a
rare disease it is a fascinating and important one because of the many ways in which it presents and because
surgery can provide a cure.

Recurrent disturbances of consciousness or odd be-

haviour or both are the commonest forms of presentation. These may vary from transient syncope to status
epilepticus and coma, from passing irritability and
restlessness to an outburst of violence with hallucinations
and delusions. Between attacks the patient may be quite
normal or there may be signs of intellectual deterioration
which in some cases progresses to dementia. The
patient may have very mistaken notions concerning the
duration of his attacks. It is essential to interview witnesses. Only then may the unusual and bizarre nature
of the attacks be appreciated. They may last minutes or
hours and may be predominantly 'neurological' or
'psychiatric'. In either case there may be no evident
association with food or exercise. Nevertheless they may
occur early in the morning or before breakfast and
although at the time the patient may instinctively take

Hyperinsulinism

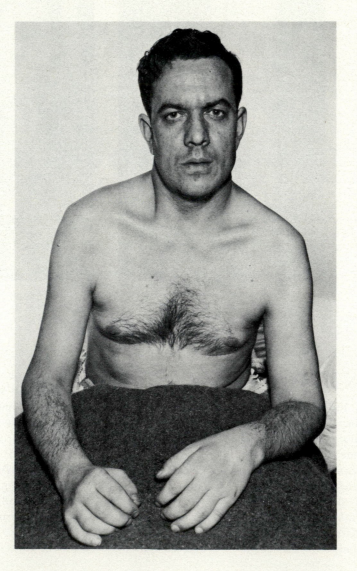

485. Hyperinsulinism: adenomata of pancreas and parathyroids
Age 32. Two year history of episodes of various kinds; anxiety and panic; excite-ment and elation; aggression; confusion and amnesia; stupor or coma. Severe stammer since childhood, unstable. Mother and sister schizophrenic.

Recent episodes of transient paresis of both upper limbs, usually recovering in a few hours. While under investigation in a mental hospital he woke one morning with profound paralysis of both upper limbs, associated with paraesthesiae in hands and fingers. The photograph was taken one week later when some recovery had taken place. There was wasting of the left del-toid, the left biceps and both brachio-radialis muscles. Upper limb reflexes were absent and there was no fasciculation. There was weakness and slight wasting of all the small muscles of both hands, especially the interossei. There was distal hyperaesthesia and hyperalgesia; vibration sense was absent in both hands and present at elbows and clavicles; postural sensibility impaired in the fingers. The lower limbs were normal and reflexes were brisk.

Blood sugar during a subsequent epilep-tic attack was 35 mg./100 ml. On fasting for 20 hours he became restless and aggressive, complaining of 'weakness'. His knee and ankle jerks were observed to be absent and there was a right extensor plantar response. Prompt recovery follow-ing intravenous dextrose.

Subsequently four islet-cell adenomata of the pancreas were removed (Mr. A. S. Aldis).

Routine investigations had meanwhile revealed an increased serum calcium level (14·4 mg./100 ml.) and a lowered serum phosphorus level (0·7 mg./100 ml.). There had been weight loss, weakness, thirst and polyuria. A second operation resulted in the removal of four parathyroid adeno-mata (Mr. A. S. Aldis). He made a good recovery from both operations, regained practically full power in the upper limbs, the arm reflexes returned as did vibration sensibility.

some form of nourishment he may not remember this when interviewed. Inevitably diagnoses such as epilepsy, narcolepsy, cerebral ischaemia or brain tumour are considered when there are attacks of impaired consciousness, while odd behaviour will suggest neurosis, hysteria, schizophrenia or some form of drug intoxication. The case notes may reveal that in the clinic or ward, widely varying impressions of the patient were gained by different observers. To one clinician the patient appears polite but slow and inattentive, while to another he is rude, garrulous or paranoid. If the clinician is fortunate enough to observe an attack, he may see flushing, sweating and tremor before there is any disturbance of consciousness or behaviour. When consciousness is lost there may be convulsive phenomena, incontinence and extensor plantar reflexes.

Occasionally there are symptoms and signs of damage to the spinal cord and peripheral nerves. There are complaints of fluctuating weakness and paraesthesiae of the extremities which may lead to permanent weakness and wasting of musculature. It was the appearance of such symptoms in a mental hospital patient which led to the correct diagnosis in the patient illustrated in FIGURE 485.

The effects of hypoglycaemia are many and varied. They are not a simple reflection of the degree and duration of the fall in blood glucose concentration. The effects within the nervous system, commonly termed 'neuroglycopenia', may be acute, subacute or chronic, whatever the origin of the disorder. In the newborn the results may be catastrophic. Neonatal hypoglycaemia can seriously affect subsequent brain development and is usually due to defective gluconeogenesis together with increased glucose utilization. Babies born prematurely or of mothers suffering from pregnancy toxaemia are particularly at risk. In children, spontaneous hypoglycaemia may be associated with recurrent episodes of ketosis, particularly during intercurrent infections. In the adult, acute neuroglycopenia is characterized by an anxiety state, nausea or hunger, tachycardia, sweating and unsteadiness; these autonomic features may progress until there is disturbance

of consciousness. In subacute neuroglycopenia the picture is one of progressive impairment of consciousness with minimal objective signs. In chronic neuroglycopenia the cardinal features comprise alteration of personality and progressive cerebral impairment. In any of these clinical states of neuroglycopenia, coma may ensue and there is nothing characteristic about it although hypothermia may provide a clue to its nature. Modern techniques for estimating blood glucose concentration are now more reliable, and hypoglycaemia is proved when the blood glucose concentration is less than 40 mg./100 ml.

In practice the majority of patients who experience transient symptoms in association with hypoglycaemia turn out to have the functional or reactive type. The patient is usually an emotionally labile young woman whose symptoms occur during the mid-morning and are often provoked or aggravated by exercise. In such cases it can rarely be demonstrated that the symptoms are due to hypoglycaemia. The syndrome is ill understood.

Only too often a diagnosis of hypoglycaemia is made on inadequate evidence. When the condition is suspected, the effects of fasting should be studied in hospital. Where there is an insulinoma, fasting overnight for 12–16 hours causes the blood glucose concentration to fall to subnormal levels in about 90 per cent. of cases. After such a fast the plasma insulin concentration is usually raised. Further tests are sometimes necessary to determine the effects of intravenous glucagon and tolbutamide, although the latter procedure is dangerous. Glucose tolerance tests give unpredictable results. Investigations sometimes show that the patient with an insulinoma is also harbouring adenomata in other endocrine glands—the pituitary or the parathyroid—or that he is in addition suffering from a peptic ulcer (the Zollinger–Ellison syndrome). Hypoglycaemia also occurs in patients with a variety of large mesenchymal tumours such as sarcomata, fibromata and mesotheliomata. Its cause in such cases is not known.

HYPOPARATHYROIDISM

Parathormone has two separate and distinct actions. It reduces reabsorption of phosphates by a direct effect on the renal tubules and it also mobilizes calcium from bone. In hypoparathyroidism there is a rise in the serum phosphorus level and a fall in the serum calcium concentration. The latter is responsible for the increased

excitability of nervous tissue and for certain changes in ectodermal tissues. Hypoparathyroidism is usually due to the accidental removal of or injury to the parathyroid glands during thyroidectomy. It may also occur as an idiopathic disorder and is then occasionally familial.

After thyroidectomy it usually manifests itself during the first post-operative week. Symptoms may be slight and transient, consisting of no more than paraesthesiae in the extremities and around the lips and perhaps some restlessness and anxiety. Such symptoms may subside spontaneously. In other cases symptoms are more marked and consist of painful cramps involving the hands (carpopedal spasm), and facial and laryngeal spasms. The latter may cause hoarseness and stridor. These well known manifestations of tetany are nowadays rarely seen, but temporary hypocalcaemia may result in a latent form of tetany in which the excitability of nervous tissue is revealed by the presence of the well known signs described by Chvostek and Trousseau. The former test is said to be positive when tapping over one facial nerve induces a contraction of the lips and facial muscles of that side; the latter sign is said to be positive when inflation of a sphygmomanometer cuff just over the systolic blood pressure level for 3 minutes induces carpopedal spasm.

But if the recognition of post-operative tetany is not difficult it is otherwise with chronic hypoparathyroidism. Not only may there be no tetany but the chronic hypocalcaemia may induce a state of general ill health difficult to diagnose. Moreover, changes in the skin, hair and nails may take the patient to a dermatologist, cataracts to the ophthalmologist, dysphonia to the laryngologist, anxiety and depression to the psychiatrist and epilepsy or papilloedema to the neurologist. It is thought that the latter manifestations are related in some way to cerebral oedema but their exact pathogenesis remains unknown. In the few cases of papilloedema in hypoparathyroidism which I have seen, disturbance of vision was slight but the cerebrospinal fluid pressure was raised. Tetany is not necessarily present when there is epilepsy.

The middle-aged female with a thyroidectomy scar is a well known patient. She is usually complaining of lassitude, vague bodily symptoms, and anxiety or depression. Her symptoms could result from parathyroid or thyroid insufficiency, or they could be manifestations of a personality disorder which were originally thought to be due to thyroid over-activity. The concept of chronic mild parathyroid insufficiency is one that I find difficult to accept. Experience with the families of such patients rather suggests that we are dealing with a personality disorder. If the thyroid gland were not so readily accessible to the surgeon, one suspects that there would be fewer thyroidectomized neurotic women.

Idiopathic hypoparathyroidism is very rare. The patient is often short but normally proportioned. He may be mentally subnormal and have cataracts and ectodermal defects. Tetany, papilloedema or epilepsy may suggest the possibility of cerebral tumour. Symmetrical calcification of the basal ganglia on a skull radiograph should direct attention to the serum calcium level.

The plasma calcium level is normally regulated by the activities of the parathyroid hormone and vitamin D. The precise way in which the former manages this is not known, but vitamin D stimulates the gastrointestinal absorption of calcium. Recently a new hormone concerned with calcium homeostasis has been identified. This is calcitonin. It lowers the serum calcium, but it is not known whether in man this hormone is important to calcium homeostasis. It may be overproduced in patients with medullary carcinoma of the thyroid, and this overproduction may be associated with pheochromocytoma or with neurofibromatosis and may thus present to the neurologist. Calcitonin is useful in treating Paget's disease and may relieve headache in that condition. It reduces the serum alkaline phosphatase.

In pseudohypoparathyroidism there is an inherited renal tubular defect with failure to respond to parathyroid hormone. There are phosphate retention and hypocalcaemia. The patient is usually round-faced, short and stocky, with short metacarpals and metatarsals; often mental retardation, poor dentition, and calcification of the basal ganglia and the cerebellum are present. The syndrome of pseudohypoparathyroidism is characterized by end-organ resistance; there is failure to respond to parathyroid hormone. The patient not infrequently presents to the neurologist as a case of epilepsy.

Trousseau observed his sign by chance. 'I was present when a woman suffering from contractions was being bled from the arm and I saw a paroxysm return in the hand on the same side when the bandage was applied around the arm.' He used to call the condition 'rheumatic contraction occurring in nurses', referring, not to members of the nursing profession, but to nursing mothers and wet nurses. No doubt these were examples of hypocalcaemia resulting from low calcium intake and vitamin D deficiency consequent on lactation. The term 'tetany' was suggested by Corvisart (Lucien, not Jean-Nicolas, Napoleon's favourite physician) in 1852. Trousseau described his sign in 1868; Chvostek in 1879. The latter sign has often been noted in healthy children.

One of the first accounts of infantile tetany was written by John Clarke, the London obstetrician, in 1815, in his *Commentaries on Some of the Most Important Diseases of Children*. He described the 'spasmodic inspiration—the squeaking noise—opisthotonos—a bending of the toes downwards, clenching of the fists and the insertion of the thumbs into the palm of the hands'.

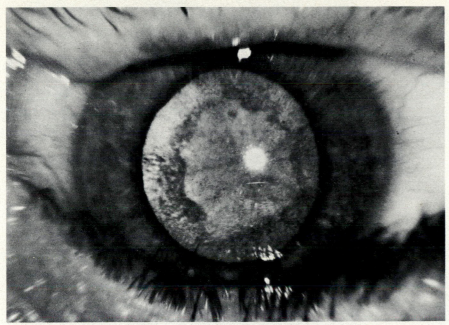

486a

**486. Post-thyroidectomy
hypoparathyroidism**
Cataract (*a*) and carpopedal spasm (*b*) of
right hand.

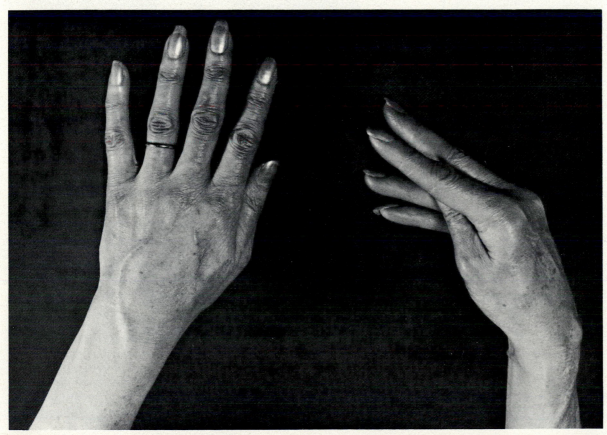

486b

Hypoparathyroidism

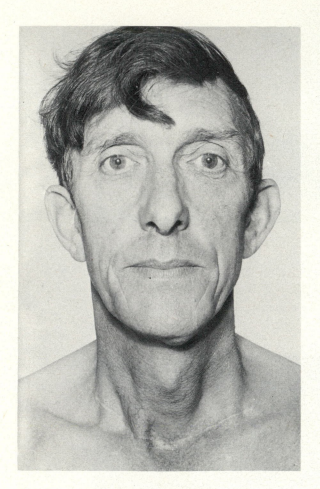

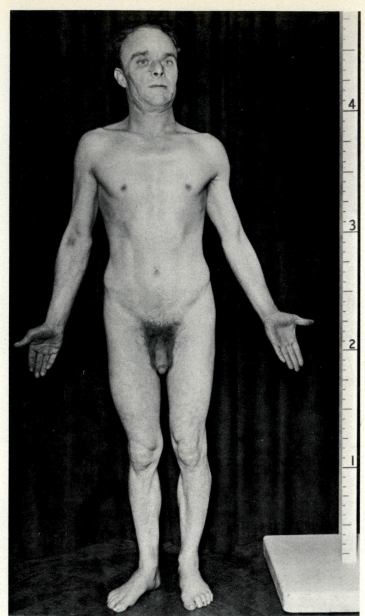

488a

487. Suspected hypoparathyroidism
Age 55 years. Partial thyroidectomy for
thyrotoxicosis in 1940; subsequent
thyroid operations in 1948, 1953 and
1970. Since the last operation, had complained of hoarse voice, general fatigue,
and paraesthesiae in the limbs. Clinical
examination revealed no evidence of
hypothyroidism or hypoparathyroidism.
Left vocal cord paresis. Serum calcium,
phosphorus and alkaline phosphatase
levels were normal. Twenty-four-hour
urinary calcium excretion normal. Sodium
E.D.T.A. infusion test normal. In the
writer's experience, 'neurasthenia' is a
commoner explanation than hypocalcaemia
for continuing vague symptomatology
after thyroid operations.

488. Suspected hypoparathyroidism
Age 43. Mental defective, dwarf (height
4 ft. 8 in.). I.Q. 78. Admitted to hospital
with sudden headache, vomiting and
questionable focal epilepsy involving left
arm. Skull radiographs (*b*) and (*c*) showed
bilateral calcification of the basal ganglia.
Air encephalography and carotid arteriography normal. Serum calcium 9·9 mg./
100 ml., serum phosphorus 3·4 mg./100 ml.
No radiological signs of rickets or osteomalacia; no evidence of renal failure
or steatorrhoea. One brother developed
Parkinsonism at the age of 23, but skull
radiographs were normal as also were the
serum calcium and phosphorus levels.
Diagnosis was idiopathic calcification of
the basal ganglia. Ten years later the
brother also showed calcification of the
basal ganglia.

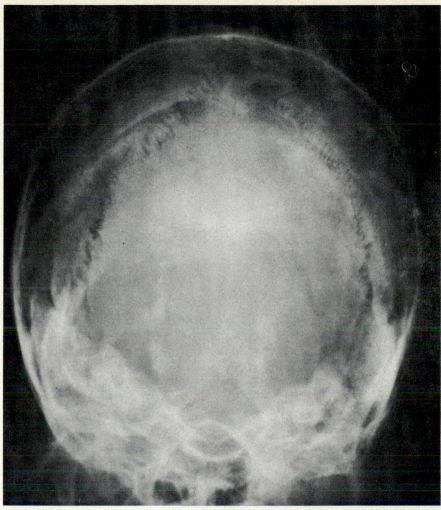

488b

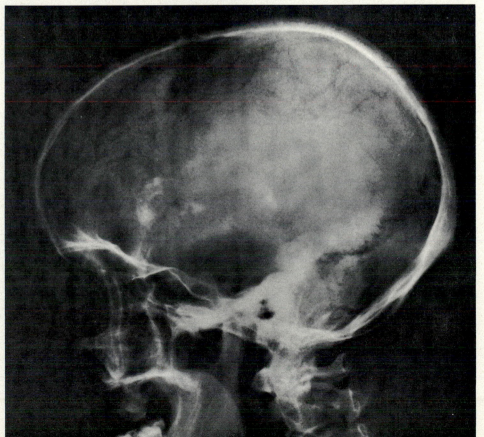

488c

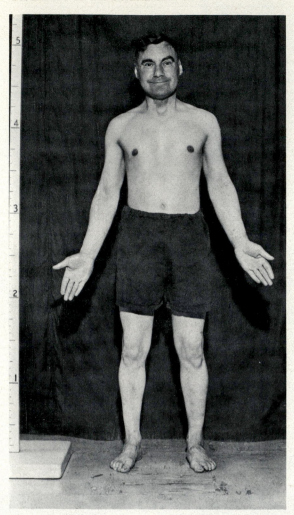

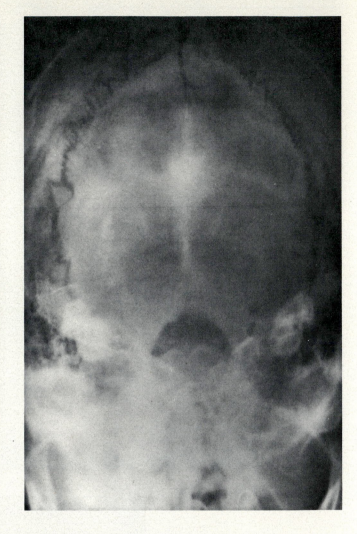

489. Idiopathic hypoparathyroidism
Age 35. Mental defective, short stature
(5 ft. 1½ in.), round face, dental hypoplasia. Referred because of episodes of
weakness and clumsiness involving the left
arm and left leg; occasional dysarthria. No
paresis, reflexes normal, no sensory loss.
Chvostek's and Trousseau's signs were
both strongly positive. Clumsiness of
voluntary movements and painful cramps
of the left upper limb. Optic fundi normal;
early cataracts. Serum calcium 5·6 mg./
100 ml. Serum phosphorus 6·9 mg./100 ml.
Normal response to *Parathormone*. Normal metacarpals. Skull radiograph showed
bilateral calcification of the basal ganglia.
Good therapeutic response to vitamin D
and calcium. (Courtesy of Dr. L. H.
Howells.)

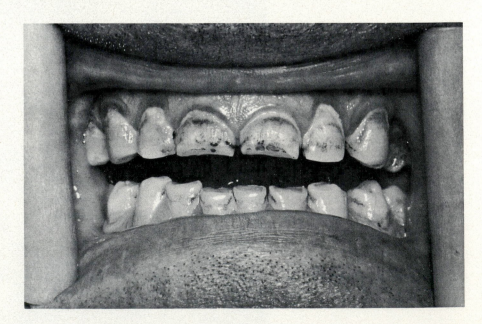

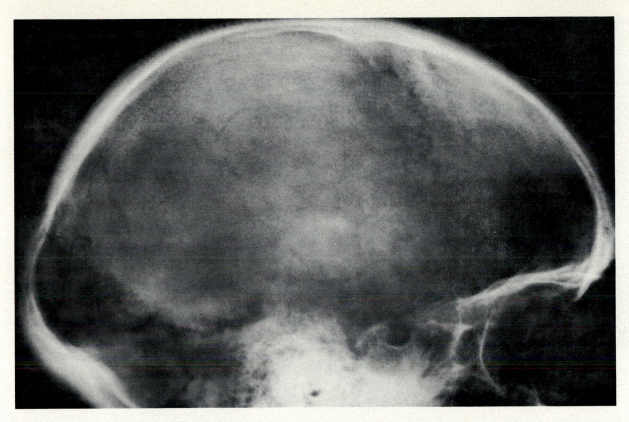

HYPERPARATHYROIDISM

Endocrine disorders have a habit of masquerading in different guises and although the neurological repertoire of parathyroid over-activity is limited, one aspect of it deserves mention in this context. Hyperparathyroidism was first identified as the cause of von Recklinghausen's disease of bone (generalized osteitis fibrosa cystica). It was subsequently found that osteomalacia might occur without bone cyst formation. It was also discovered that renal calculi were common and that renal lesions could occur without the classical bone disease. Finally, the general effects of hypercalcaemia were appreciated, namely anorexia, nausea, weakness, loss of weight, drowsiness, thirst and polyuria. To these general symptoms may be added chronic constipation and mental symptoms. Of these three forms of presentation—bony, renal and general—the bony form of the disorder is now known to be the least common.

The general symptoms of hypercalcaemia are of particular interest to the neurologist because, with the complaints of fatigue, lassitude, headache and loss of appetite, there may be profound muscular weakness and hypotonia. The possibility of Addison's disease may thus arise. The patient may walk in a waddling manner so that muscular dystrophy is suspected. On the other hand the striking polyuria and polydipsia may suggest diabetes insipidus. There is an increased excretion of water consequent on the increased excretion of calcium. Episodes of mental confusion in a person complaining of excessive thirst and polyuria should suggest investigation of the serum calcium level. This is raised while the serum phosphorus level is lowered. Hyperparathyroidism is usually due to a parathyroid adenoma.

It should not be forgotten that the general effects of hypercalcaemia may be seen in a wide variety of disorders. It can result from excessive administration of vitamin D or calcium. It can occur in sarcoidosis, or can be a consequence of osteolytic bone disease. Malignant tumours may produce hormones which modify calcium metabolism and raise the plasma calcium without invading the bones: these tumours include carcinoma of the breast, bronchus, kidney, stomach and uterus, as well as the lymphomata. Corneal calcification is said to be the most striking physical sign of hypercalcaemia, occurring in 25 per cent. of parathyroid tumours; it is best seen with a hand lens and appears as a granular or gritty collection close to the corneal–scleral junction.

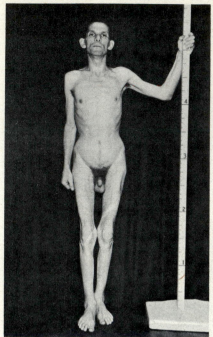

490a

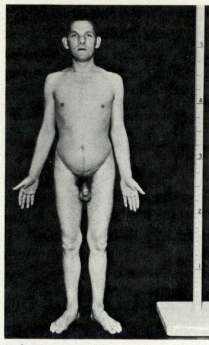

490b

Hyperparathyroidism

490. Hyperparathyroidism: parathyroid adenoma
Age 37. Generalized weakness and wasting with polyuria and polydipsia. No renal or skeletal lesions. Serum calcium 17·0 mg./100 ml.; serum phosphorus 3·3 mg./100 ml. (*a*) Before operation; (*b*) 1 year after removal of parathyroid adenoma. (Courtesy of Professor H. Scarborough.)

ENDOCRINE COMPLICATIONS OF CANCER

The neurologist is familiar with the neurological complications of cancer which include neuropathies, myelopathies, myasthenic syndromes and encephalopathies. The tumours most often concerned are those arising in the bronchus, breast, cervix, ovary and colon. These syndromes have been described over the past twenty years, but their cause is still unknown although humoral agents have been suspected. Simultaneously it has been realized that cancer cells are capable of secreting polypeptide hormones which have biological properties indistinguishable from those of the hormonal polypeptides produced by the endocrine glands themselves, and which are generally referred to as ectopic hormones. These para-endocrine syndromes do not seem to be as common as the neurological syndromes of cancer, but they are often overlooked and may cause difficulties in diagnosis. Of particular interest to the neurologist are the cases of Cushing's syndrome due to bilateral adrenal hyperplasia arising in cancers of the bronchus and other organs secreting corticotrophin. Weakness, thirst and polyuria are a consequence of the ensuing hypokalaemic alkalosis. When Cushing's syndrome appears in a man, carcinoma should be suspected.

A second example of these disorders is the inappropriate secretion of the antidiuretic hormone. This is also seen in carcinoma of the bronchus and in lymphomata. The continued secretion of the hormone leads to overhydration with resulting cerebral oedema. This may present as irritability, confusion, drowsiness and disorientation. It may culminate in epilepsy and coma. The hyponatraemia is dilutional as opposed to depletional in type, so that all other plasma constituents will also be diluted by the increased plasma content of water.

A third example is the hypercalcaemia of osteolytic metastases in bone. This may arise in carcinoma of the breast, prostate, lung and kidney and also in the leukaemias, myelomata and lymphomata. The symptoms of hypercalcaemia are the same whatever the cause—thirst, polyuria, lethargy, muscular weakness, vomiting, constipation and psychotic changes.

Fourthly, the neurologist should not forget the carcinoid syndrome which occurs in malignant argentaffin tumours of the intestine. Here the cyanotic flushing of the face and chest is accompanied by attacks of abdominal pain, diarrhoea and perhaps bronchospasm. But in carcinoma of the bronchus the episodes may present with anxiety, tremor, hypotension and flushing. There are said to be differences in the syndromes according to whether the serotonin is released primarily into the portal or the systemic circulation.

11 POSTURE AND GAIT

Posture

The manner in which an individual carries his body depends on mechanical, reflex and psychic factors.

The structure and tilt of the pelvis and hip joints influence the whole alignment of the spine and lower limbs and the erect posture in general. The maintenance and regulation of posture or attitude depends on muscle tone, which is reflex in origin. This reflex tonus of muscles is an aspect of the activity of the proprioceptive system of the body, which includes the eyes, the labyrinth, the muscle spindles and the cerebellum. The muscle spindles are innervated by the gamma efferent fibres in the anterior spinal roots, so that segmental reflex 'servo-mechanisms' are continuously at work in the regulation of muscle tone and posture. A vital role in this co-ordinated activity is played by the cerebellum which Sherrington described as the 'head ganglion of the proprioceptive system'. The boy riding 'no hands' on his cycle, the girl perched on stiletto heels picking her way through a crowded thoroughfare, are everyday performances which excite no comment. But it is the wonderfully integrated activity of the same proprioceptive systems of the body which permits the underwater swimmer, the 'free falling' parachutist and the astronaut, to execute voluntary movements of high accuracy. It is not surprising that circuit defects will arise as a result of disease, producing symptoms and signs of particular significance.

Lastly, there is a psychological aspect of posture. It is common knowledge that an habitual posture may be a reflection of personality. The odd attitude of the bored or maladjusted child, the queer tricks of movement or gait of the obsessional child, the dejected attitude of the depressed, the slouching one of the indifferent individual are examples which come to mind. The physiotherapist is perhaps more consciously aware of these observations than the clinician. Muscle tone may reflect the emotional state of the patient.

MUSCLE TONE

The nature of normal muscle tone has been extensively studied by physiologists. Clinicians are mainly concerned with detecting abnormalities of tone. The one uses fine techniques and the other has to content himself with crude methods of assessment. Nevertheless, it is something more than an impression which enables an experienced clinician to detect an increase of muscle tone, as for example, at the wrist of a patient with early Parkinsonism. When he holds the wrist of the patient in one hand and the fingers in his other hand, and gently flexes and extends the wrist, he is estimating and measuring in a skilled way. What he is trying to measure is the state of continuous tension of the muscles of the forearm—the muscle tone. It is normally maintained by an asynchronous discharge of impulses in the motor neurones which supply the muscles. Basically it is a spinal segmental reflex so that it is abolished when any part of the reflex arc is the site of injury or disease, as in polyneuritis, nerve and root injuries, tabes dorsalis, anterior horn cell disease and, of course, disease within the muscles themselves. But muscle tone is also affected by supraspinal mechanisms. Until the effects of shock pass off, the hemiplegic limbs in a stroke and the paraplegic limbs in spinal injury, are hypotonic or flaccid. Hypotonia is also seen in disease of the cerebellum and in chorea. Sudden accesses of hypotonia occur in cataplexy and in the 'drop attacks' of the elderly individual.

Muscle tone is estimated by observation and by the execution of passive movements. The droop of the jaw in myasthenia, the sag of the shoulders in muscular dystrophy, the fall of an outstretched arm in cerebellar disease are examples of visually recognizable hypotonia. Hypertonicity, a release phenomenon, may also be a visible sign, contributing to the posture of the hemiplegic or paraplegic individual. Passive manipulation of a limb by the examiner is the most important method of assessing tone. It may be performed in a limb with normal power or one which is paralysed. The examiner is attempting to measure the resistance of the muscles to his passive manipulation of the limb. Hypertonicity is seen in disease of the pyramidal and of the extra-pyramidal motor systems, but with some difference. In pyramidal disease, as in the arm of the hemiplegic patient, there is so-called 'clasp-knife' spasticity; resistance to passive movement at the elbow or wrist is maximum at the onset and suddenly subsides. The spasticity of a pyramidal lesion is usually more evident in the flexor muscles of the upper limb and in the extensor muscles of the lower limb. In extrapyramidal disease, as in Parkinsonism, the rigidity is said to be of the 'cogwheel' or 'lead pipe' type. Extrapyramidal rigidity is more uniformly distributed to the opposing muscle groups of the affected limbs. Here agonists and antagonists are both involved, either intermittently or continuously, throughout the movement. Extrapyramidal rigidity results from impulses arising above the level of the brain stem. So-called pyramidal spasticity results from an imbalance of the inhibitory and facilitatory centres in the lower brain stem. The traditional 'release'

explanation for pyramidal rigidity is an over-simplification and it is well known that power, tone, and reflex activity may be variably affected in a pyramidal lesion.

In a hypertonic limb the deep reflexes are usually brisk or obviously exaggerated. These reflexes are muscle stretch reflexes. The sensory organs of muscles—the muscle spindles—when stretched, excite the muscles' own motor neurones. It is the selectivity of action in the alpha and gamma fibres of this self-regulating circuit which probably explains the paradox of a hypotonic limb with hyperactive reflexes. In judging reflex activity the clinician notes the briskness of the response, the range of the movement and its duration. This also is a matter of experience and interpretation. To the inexperienced, brisk finger reflexes or a jaw jerk, might suggest an upper cervical or pontine lesion; both may occur in normal people. Asymmetry of reflex action is important to note, but it must be confessed that although one knee jerk may respond more briskly than its opposite, the range of movement of the latter may be greater. It is then difficult to say which reflex is the more hyperactive.

ABNORMALITIES OF POSTURE

Posture thus largely depends on the harmonious integration of those factors which influence muscle tone. A disorder of the nervous system which alters muscle tone would influence posture. We have seen that tone may be altered in pyramidal, extrapyramidal and cerebellar disorders. Abnormalities of posture may be slight or gross, and may be seen in the conscious or unconscious person and in the erect, seated or supine positions of the body. The posture of the patient in bed will be considered in Chapter 12.

The patient entering a consulting room may be noticed to hold his head to one side or thrust forward, as in cerebellar or extrapyramidal diseases respectively. Pain or discomfort in the neck could equally explain this abnormal posture. A visual field defect may be responsible for an unusual position of the head. There is the relatively immobile flexed upper limb of the hemiplegic or Parkinsonian patient.

Sudden loss of posture is a feature of cataplexy and 'drop' attacks. In cataplexy, which is often associated with narcolepsy, there are abrupt attacks of muscular hypotonia and weakness which cause the patient to

slump or fall helplessly to the ground. Sometimes the hypotonia appears only to affect the neck muscles so that the head falls forward. Attacks are usually provoked by an emotional stimulus such as mirth, surprise or anger. The nature of the lesion in cataplexy and the 'drop' attack is unknown, but presumably some brain stem reflex mechanism is suddenly lost.

Sherrington thought that the 'knock out' in boxing was due to concussion of the labyrinth, which 'reduces in a moment a vigorous athlete to an unstrung bulk of flesh whose weight alone determines its attitude, if indeed a reactionless mass can be described as possessing attitude at all'.

In catatonia the patient may adopt an odd posture for a time or maintain one which was imposed by the examiner. There is a 'waxy' resistance to passive movement and the abnormality may be a manifestation of schizophrenia or of a frontal lobe disturbance such as tumour. A limb elevated by the observer may be maintained in that position for several minutes. Bizarre attitudes may be adopted by the hysteric and the malingerer.

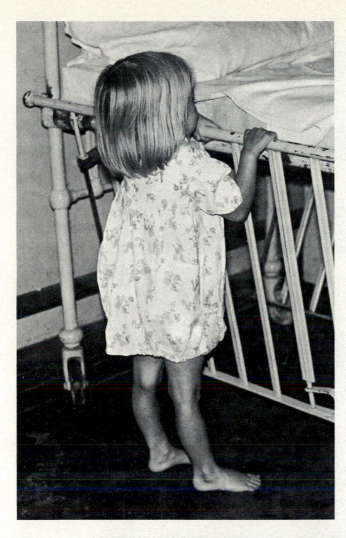

491. Cerebellar medulloblastoma
Progressive cerebellar ataxia led to falling and fright so that the child would not try to stand unsupported. She was happy in bed but would not let go of the bed rail if she was stood on the floor. Bilateral papilloedema; no nystagmus.

492. Multiple sclerosis ▽
Only slight incoordination on the finger–nose test on the left side. Gross intention tremor on the right, blurring the outline of the forearm. Head and shoulders would shake when she tried to use the right arm.

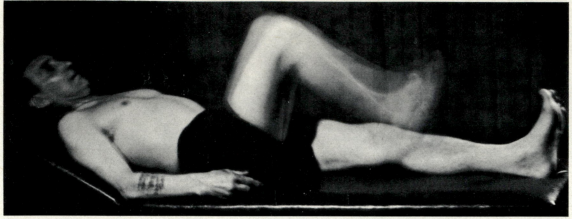

493. Cerebellar ataxia
Ataxia of the lower limbs revealed on the heel–knee test. Progressive spinocerebellar degeneration. He has difficulty in placing one heel on the opposite knee and running it up and down the shin of the leg.

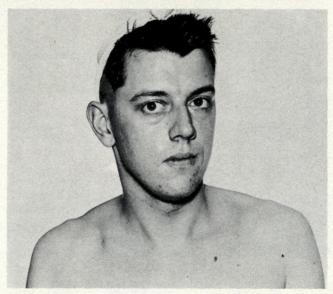

494. Left cerebellar astrocytoma
(*a*) Head turned to the left. (*b*) With arms outstretched and eyes closed the left arm droops; it was hypotonic and clumsy.

494a

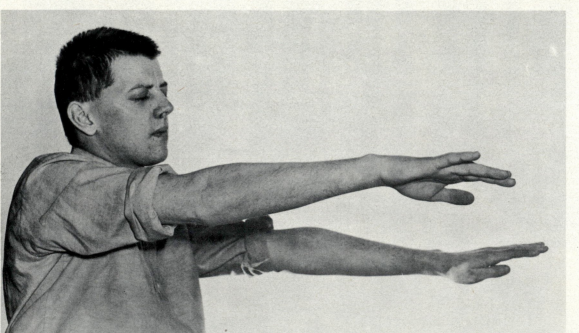

494b

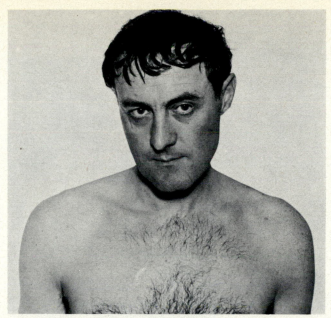

495. Left cerebellar haemangioblastoma

Occipital headache, stiffness of the neck and clumsiness of movement. In unilateral cerebellar disease there may be deviation of the head and body towards the affected side. But the position of the head may be determined by pain and stiffness of the neck. Here the head is tilted forwards to the right. There was nystagmus only on left lateral gaze associated with ataxia of the left upper limb and gait.

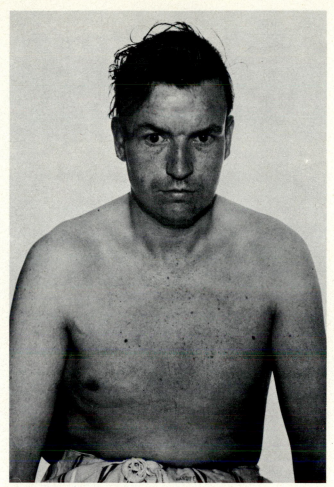

496. Occipital meningioma

Head tilted slightly downwards especially when he walked, because of bilateral superior altitudinal hemianopia.

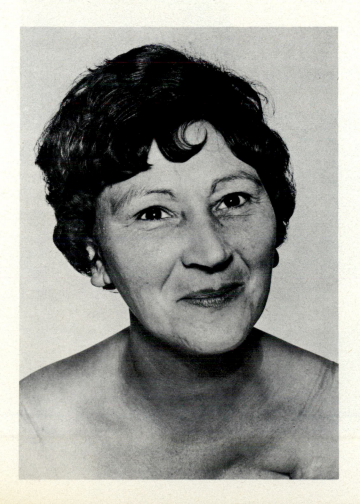

497. Left homonymous hemianopia

Four months after sudden occlusion of the right posterior cerebral artery in a patient without mitral stenosis, hypertension or peripheral arteriosclerosis. Head turned to left to compensate for deficient field of vision on the left.

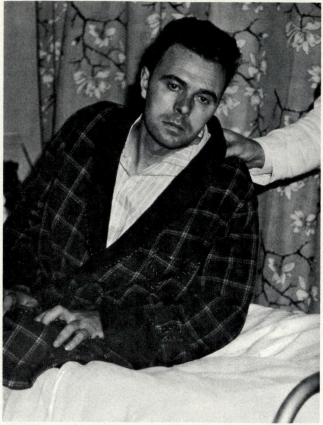

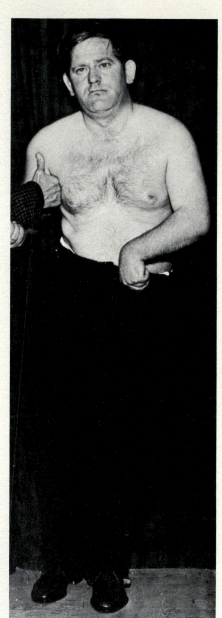

498. Acute encephalitis △
Cerebellar ataxia was a striking feature of
this case. Nystagmus, gross dysarthria and
disturbance of stance and gait. Ataxia of
the trunk, with falling to the left, occurred
when he sat up.

**499. Left cerebellar metastatic
carcinoma** ▽
The primary lesion was in the lung. When
he sits his head and trunk deviate backwards and to the left. The left outstretched arm droops when he closes his
eyes.

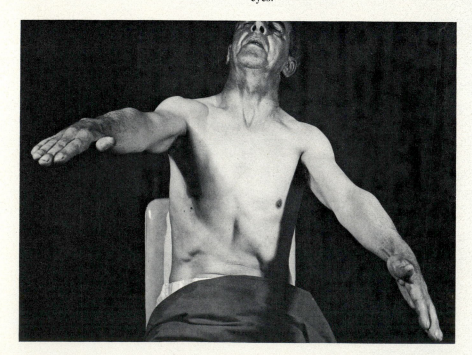

500. Left post-traumatic hemiplegia △
In the hemiplegic arm paralysis of extension is more marked than that of flexion;
the reverse is the case in the lower limb.
The arm is consequently held in a position
of adduction with flexion and pronation at
the elbow and flexion of wrist and fingers.
The clenched fist is the gravest disability
in the hemiplegic arm.

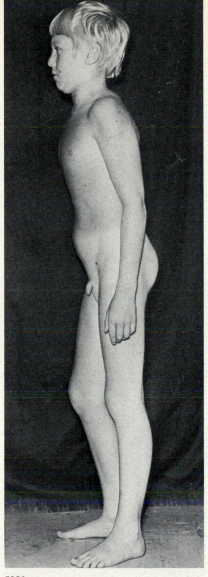

501a

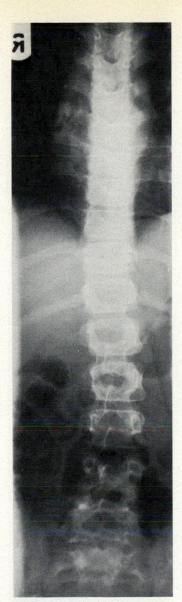

501c

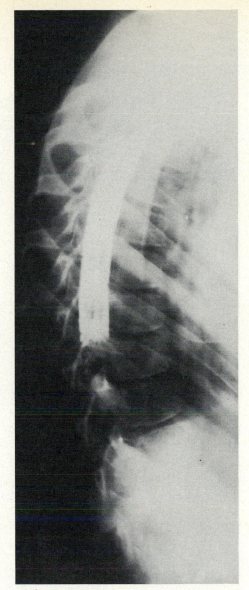

501d

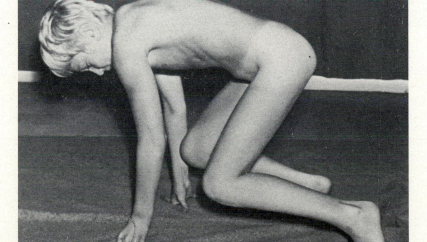

501b

501. Spinal cord tumour

Age 13 years. Patient uncomplaining, but father concerned about boy's poor posture. Tended to slouch and could not brace his shoulders. No pain, no symptoms referable to head, neck or upper limbs. Admitted that at times his thighs were 'sort of numb'. No familial muscular dystrophy. Examination: (a) stiff straight spine, slight wasting of thigh muscles; (b) he could not rise from a prone position on the floor. Arms normal. Weakness of extensors of hips and knees; diminished knee jerks, brisk ankle jerks, flexor plantar responses. Distended urinary bladder. (c) Radiograph: erosion of pedicles in dorsolumbar region with scalloping of posterior margins of bodies of vertebrae, D.11 to L.2. C.S.F. xanthochromic, protein 2·4 G./100 ml. (d) Cisternal myelography, complete block at D.8. Laminectomy: ependymoma.

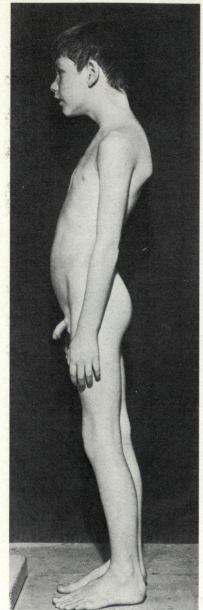

502a

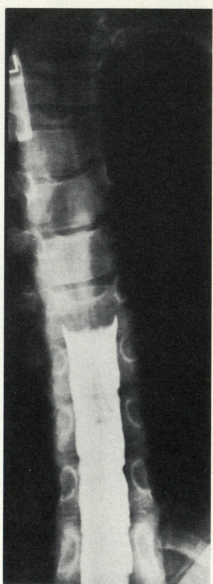

502b

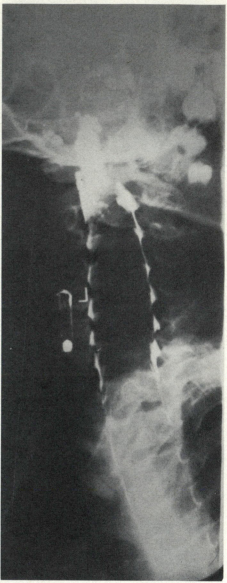

502c

502. Spinal cord tumour
Age 8 years. Poor posture noted at school clinic. Corrective exercises. In orthopaedic hospital for 3 months; cervical traction and collar. Radiographs of cervical spine normal. No improvement; after 6 months began to walk with a 'floppy' right foot.

(*a*) Neurological examination showed thin general musculature, abnormal posture, impaired left upper limb reflexes, normal right upper limb reflexes. Left abdominal reflexes impaired. Lower limbs: hyperactive reflexes, left ankle clonus, left extensor plantar response. Spine radiographs reviewed; erosion of inner margins

of pedicles and scalloping of posterior margins of vertebral bodies from C.6 to D.7. (*b*) Lumbar myelography showed a block at D.6. (*c*) Cisternal myelography showed expansion of the cord from C.2 to D.6. Laminectomy revealed an inoperable intramedullary tumour.

Gait

When a healthy person gets up from a chair or bed he is normally able to walk immediately. Assumption of the erect posture requires voluntary muscular activity, but its maintenance is a passive affair. Electrical studies have shown that there is surprisingly little activity taking place in the muscles of the thighs and trunk when standing. If his trunk moves, however, as when he sways or is jostled, there sets in reflex compensatory muscular activity which restores his poise. Falling is halted by the reflex contraction of the antigravity muscles of the lower limbs, the extensors, which keep the limbs straight and thrust them to the ground. It is obvious that maintenance of this erect posture is essential for locomotion and that anything which disturbs the activity of the stretch receptors in the trunk and lower limbs and the receptors in the labyrinths and eyes, will impair stance and hence locomotion.

When the individual starts to walk another set of reflexes comes into action. They are concerned with the well known phenomenon of reciprocal innervation. Against a background of static reflex activity there now emerge dynamic reactions which are co-ordinated in such a manner that walking may appear to be effortless and automatic. The muscles engaged in this activity include those which preserve the erect posture, such as the glutei medius and minimus, and those which are concerned with forward propulsion, such as the gastrocnemii. The correct position of the feet is maintained by the tibial and peroneal muscles. The normal sequence of movements is initiated by a slight flexion of the trunk on the hip joints, which is almost immediately followed by a lifting of the heel from the ground and flexion at all joints in that limb. The resulting lengthening of extensor muscles brings into action the stretch reflexes which operate to inhibit flexors and extensors. The toes and ankles are dorsiflexed so that the foot clears the ground and there is active extension of the knee and flexion of the hip joint. As the foot is thrust to the ground there is a positive supporting reaction in the other limb; the combined contraction of the flexors and extensors stiffen the limb so that it can support the weight of the body. Walking becomes a pattern of successive flexions and extensions of the lower limbs.

The biological engineer views walking just as he would view any form of locomotion. The object being to move the body from one place to another. He notices that the centre of gravity of the body, which is roughly at the second sacral vertebra, moves in a smooth path which curves slightly in both vertical and horizontal planes. There is a certain economy of movement.

DISORDERS OF GAIT

Difficulty in walking is found in a wide variety of conditions; it is not necessarily an indication of neurological disorder. Mechanical factors may be obvious, as in the case of ankylosis of one of the joints of the lower limb, a short lower limb or a curved spine. Slight abnormalities such as a lumbar lordosis, a tilted pelvis or a shortened Achilles tendon, may not be observed until the patient is unclothed. Examination of the feet should not be neglected. A corn or sore heel, a rigid hallux or a fallen arch may cause pain and limping. Pain in such conditions as polyneuritis, sciatica and intermittent claudication may alter the gait. Minor irregularities may be habitual and difficult to account for on either a mechanical or functional basis. A mother may say of her son 'he has always walked funny' or 'he walks the same as his father'. A person's gait is peculiar to himself; the dog recognizes the footsteps of his master, the secretary those of her employer. The members of a family of a patient may notice a change in his gait at a time when it is not apparent to the clinician. A patient of mine with an occipital lobe infarction, who could not recognize the face of his wife (prosopagnosia), was able to identify her footsteps as she approached him in the ward. Occasionally, minor abnormalities are misleading. An arm that does not swing when the person is walking does not necessarily mean the onset of Parkinsonism; an unusual degree of inversion of a foot may not result from muscular weakness, and allowance must always be made for the age of the patient; a little unsteadiness is more or less inevitable in the elderly.

We have seen that the integration of voluntary and reflex activities of the nervous system during the act of walking are exceedingly complex and are liable to be disturbed at various levels of the nervous system and situations on the reflex arcs. It is obvious that walking will suffer if there is muscular weakness of a flaccid or spastic nature, which impairs maintenance of the erect posture and voluntary movement of the lower limbs. On the sensory side, proprioceptive deficiency will impede voluntary movement by reducing the patient's knowledge of the position of the various parts of his body; alternate forward motion of the lower limbs is disturbed as a result of spatial disorientation. Cerebellar deficiency will impair the harmonious co-operation of synergic muscles. Lastly, locomotion will be affected if there is any lesion at spinal or supraspinal level which interferes with the activity of the reflexes, muscle tone, posture and stance.

Disturbance of gait may be obvious when the patient enters the consulting room or gets up from his chair or bed. The nature of the disturbance may also be suggested by the manner of his progress. Initial impressions are often vital and if missed, as in early Parkinsonism, cerebral arteriosclerosis or disseminated sclerosis, diagnosis may be delayed because formal examination in such cases may reveal little. Indeed, studied inspection of the gait itself may be less revealing than observation when the patient moves about the room or ward. A request to 'let me see you walk' may induce a self-conscious pose and form of movement or it may enable the patient to temporarily correct a deficiency.

One should notice whether the patient adopts a broad base, watches the ground, drags his legs in a stiff manner or lifts them unduly. Is he steady or unsteady? A gait may be slow and laboured, the limbs only moving through the use of accessory muscles, the trunk deviating from one side to the other, yet progress is unswerving. On a hard floor before the patient removes his shoes, the sound of his footsteps may be a clue to the nature of his trouble. A flopping sound suggests a foot drop; a scraping or dragging sound may indicate a hemiplegia or paraplegia; stamping sounds will result from postural deficit, as in subacute combined degeneration or tabes dorsalis.

Facial expression should also be noticed. There is the determined look of the person trying to overcome muscular weakness, the tearful depressed appearance of the shuffling arteriosclerotic, the anxious look of the ataxic patient, fearful of falling, and the labile, smiling face of the young woman with multiple sclerosis.

Minor faults of stance and gait may only be identified when the patient performs certain simple tests. Sensory ataxia may only be disclosed when the patient is requested to stand with his feet together or with one foot in front of the other. Unsteadiness may appear or be increased when he closes his eyes—the Romberg test. Naturally, there is a wide range of variation, anxious individuals and elderly patients may feel quite insecure in such positions and sway or hesitate. The patient should be asked to walk in a straight line, to turn quickly, to stop suddenly, to walk around a chair or table and, if necessary, to climb stairs. Walking on the toes or the heels and in heel–toe fashion should be performed.

Certain abnormalities of gait are of diagnostic importance. It must be confessed, however, that many of the more florid examples have largely disappeared from the medical scene. The stamping, high-stepping tabetic or sufferer from subacute combined degeneration of the spinal cord; the 'drunken' reeling patient with the cerebellar tumour and the bilateral foot-drop gait of the patient with alcoholic or diphtheritic polyneuritis, are now rare spectacles. On the other hand, the spastic walk of the patient who has injured his spinal cord in an accident and the shuffling gait of the old person are, if anything, increasingly seen and, as always, there is the spastic-ataxic gait of the person with multiple sclerosis; the stiff gait of the workman who has injured his back; and the temporary, though dramatic, disturbance of locomotion, which afflicts the hysteric. Indeed, glaring disorders of locomotion are nowadays more likely to be seen in a mental hospital. In the neurological clinic only the occasional example of Huntington's chorea, the postencephalitic state, choreo-athetosis or dystonia, provide the modern medical student with a glimpse of florid disorders in this field.

The three most characteristic forms of gait in diseases of the nervous system are the spastic, the ataxic and the high stepping.

The Spastic Gait

The disability may be unilateral as in hemiplegia or bilateral as in paraplegia. The characteristic attitude and gait of the person who has had a stroke is well known. There is an increase of flexor tone in the arm and of extensor tone in the leg. This accounts for the adducted flexed posture of the arm which the patient appears to hold tightly to his side, folded and with his fist clenched. The lower limb is often less affected, but when he walks the weakness, rigidity and difficulty he has in flexing his hip and knees become apparent. With each step he tilts his pelvis to the other side in an endeavour to clear the toe from the ground; the paretic limb is swung in a semicircle around his hip but rarely without scraping the toe on the floor. The forefoot flops to the ground before the heel. During the process of recovery the leg usually recovers before the arm and power tends to return to the proximal portion of the limbs before the distal.

Incipient hemiparesis may only noticeably affect gait when the patient has walked some distance, but even then loss of swing of the affected arm and the worn toe of the shoe on that side may be observed. The patient may notice difficulty in wiggling his toes in the bath or manipulating his foot when putting on his socks, or raising his leg to negotiate a curb or step or in placing his foot on a foot pedal in his car. The disturbance of gait may be intermittent when there are periods of cerebrovascular insufficiency.

When both lower limbs are spastic, as in all forms of paraparesis, the labour of movement is obvious. The steps are slow and short; the feet appear glued to the ground. The gait is stiff-legged and the patient tends to lean forward. Additional disability may arise when there is adductor spasm. This may be prominent in the spastic diplegias of childhood. There is difficulty in placing one foot in front of the other; the feet tend to cross in 'scissors' fashion. When spasticity and contracture affect the muscles of the calves the patient has difficulty in placing his heel to the ground as he walks.

When paraparesis is developing in an insidious manner, visible abnormality over short distances may be slight. A few steps across a consulting room may be insufficient to reveal the disability. The patient should be observed as he walks the length of the ward or along a corridor. It may be necessary to fatigue the muscles. But in any case, what the patient and his family have to say about walking is important. Trouble may only come at the end of the day, or after sitting down for a long time or when the patient has to hurry. The sensation experienced may be likened to that 'when wading in the sea'.

The Ataxic Gait

There are two types of ataxic gait—sensory and cerebellar.

Sensory ataxia used to occur in its most flagrant form in tabes dorsalis as the result of the interruption of the proprioceptive pathways in the posterior spinal roots and posterior columns of the spinal cord. Nowadays it is most commonly seen in multiple sclerosis (with cerebellar ataxia), cervical myelopathy, chronic polyneuritis and in vitamin B_{12} myelopathy. Stance and walking are unsteady because there is lack of appreciation of the senses of position and motion of the lower limbs. Information from muscles and joints is insufficient for correct localization and control of the limbs. To some extent this deficiency can be compensated by visual attention. The patient watches the ground and his feet as he walks. To maintain his balance he widens his base. His feet tend to 'throw' and he will say that they are not under normal control. Both the heels and the toes seem to slap on the ground. When he stands with feet together and his eyes closed he sways and in the dark his ataxia is worse (many an old tabetic has fallen in his garden at night in the days of outdoor lavatories). In recent years the gait in tabes dorsalis is by no means diagnostic; unsteadiness is usually slight and nondescript. A smooth surface is negotiated better than a rough one and removing the shoes may aggravate the ataxia. The oscillations of the feet and movement of the tendons may be observed during the Romberg test. The incoordination of the lower limbs may also be observed when the patient is lying in bed.

Cerebellar Ataxia

Knowledge of the localization of function in the cerebellum has not yet reached the stage obtaining in the cerebrum and anatomically and phylogenetically there is much to be learned. In the primates that part of the posterior lobe known as the neocerebellum has developed in an elaborate manner and established connexions with the brain stem which are not seen in lower animals. The clinical effects of cerebellar disease in man have proved to be more subtle and difficult to analyse than those resulting from experiments of stimulation and ablation in animals. The clinician's contribution to localization of function rests on two observations. First, a hemisphere lesion affects the same side of the body. Secondly, a midline lesion of the cerebellum tends to affect the trunk more than the limbs. The ataxia which results in each case may be clinically distinguishable, but the difference between truncal ataxia from a lesion of the vermis and limb ataxia from a hemisphere lesion, cannot be explained in terms of the function of the phylogenetically older and newer portions of the cerebellum respectively.

The differences are best seen when one considers examples of cerebellar ataxia in childhood and adult life. Persistent ataxia in a child may be due to a cerebellar tumour. This may arise in the midline and the ataxia presents chiefly as a swaying of the trunk while the child is sitting, standing or walking, with a titubation of the head. The latter bobs and weaves, standing is impaired and the child tends to fall in any direction. The instability is not markedly worse when he performs with his eyes closed. Apart from this obvious instability there may be no other sign. His mother and teacher will describe his clumsiness and tendency to fall, while abrasions and scars will bear witness to their statements. For a time, naughtiness, not ill health, may be suspected.

Tumours of the cerebellum in childhood are not, of course, confined to midline structures and involvement of the hemispheres produces symptoms and signs as in the adult. In childhood also the cerebellum may be involved as the result of encephalitis or degeneration.

In the adult with a unilateral lesion of the cerebellum the signs are mainly to be found on the same side of the body. There are disturbances of posture and of voluntary movement. There may be a tilt of the face towards the opposite side, a droop of the shoulder and hypotonia of the limbs on the side of the lesion. A looseness of movement may be discerned. His gait is reeling, irregular, and swaying. He looks, and sometimes has been suspected of being, drunk. He rarely confesses this; he should be asked. Although he sways to and fro he may tend to veer to the side of the lesion. When circling a chair he stumbles to the affected side. If the ataxia is not obvious it may be elicited when he is asked to walk in heel–toe fashion or along a line on the floor. Alcohol, and sometimes nicotine, aggravate his unsteadiness.

The performance of voluntary movements of the upper and lower limbs is impaired. There is decomposition of movement, as if it were being broken up into separate stages. There is lack of co-ordination between the muscles executing the movement, namely the prime movers, the antagonists and the synergists—asynergia. There are errors in the execution of movements in respect of direction, range and force—dysmetria. These signs are usually best seen in the upper limbs, but with the patient in bed they may also be identified in the lower limbs. The patient with cerebellar ataxia is often conspicuously tremulous. Some degree of tremor may be observed at rest, or when the patient is walking, but it is most conspicuous when the affected part is used in a voluntary movement—intention tremor. In the upper limbs this may be disclosed by tests of tapping, spinning and finger-nose touching. One side should be compared with the other. In an early stage of cerebellar ataxia movements of alternate motion may appear to be well done, but the patient cannot be made to speed up the movement. This may precede overt incoordination. Early signs may pass undetected. In cerebellar ataxia it is not only the posture and gait which suffer from this incoordination. The eyes (nystagmus) and the speech (a slow, slurred, jerky, lalling, staccato, scanning or explosive dysarthria) may testify to the widespread nature of the disturbance of muscle function.

The High-stepping Gait

Steppage gait may be unilateral or bilateral and is a consequence of foot drop resulting from weakness or paralysis of dorsiflexion of the feet.

The patient, unable to lift his foot in the normal manner, has to flex the limb as a whole at hip and knee so that the foot will clear the ground. This movement is an exaggeration of the normal stepping process. But unlike the strutting of the playing child, or drum majorette, the foot is thrown forward and slaps the ground in an uncontrolled manner. When asked to stand or walk on his heels, the paresis of dorsiflexion may be seen. Walking on the toes is not impaired.

In unilateral cases incipient weakness may only be noted on careful observation. The only abnormality may consist of the way in which the foot reaches the ground—toes and forefoot before heel. It may result from a lesion affecting the anterior horn cells or roots in the lumbosacral region, as in motor neurone disease and sciatica, from tumours of the cauda equina or from a lesion of the common peroneal nerve.

When the fault is bilateral the same cord and root lesions may be responsible, while in peroneal muscular atrophy the thin legs and pes cavus are likely to be present. Any form of polyneuritis may present in this manner and is likely to be associated with complaints of numbness and paraesthesiae.

Other Gaits

Reference has already been made to the shuffling gait of the person with Parkinsonism or cerebral arteriosclerosis and the waddling gait in muscular dystrophy. It only remains to say that in some diseases the gait may be disturbed in more than one manner. In multiple sclerosis there is often both spasticity and ataxia; the latter, sensory, cerebellar or both. In motor neurone disease a degree of spasticity may accompany bilateral foot drop. In subacute combined degeneration of the spinal cord, spastic and ataxic difficulties may be combined.

The hysteric can mimic all types of abnormality of gait and invent those of his own. They are not always theatrical and bizarre and sometimes they are an addition to some genuine disturbance. On the other hand every neurologist possesses his own collection of cases in which a gait, apparently hysterical, turned out to be of organic origin. My own include a child with a medulloblastoma of the vermis of the cerebellum, a youth surreptitiously taking a phenothiazine drug, a girl with porphyria and a man with myxoedema. It is not always that the true cause of disability is ascertained by formal attention to detail. Suspicion may originate in a chance remark by a patient, a relative or nurse, or in a fleeting observation. This is one of the reasons why clinical experience can never be complete nor errors wholly avoided.

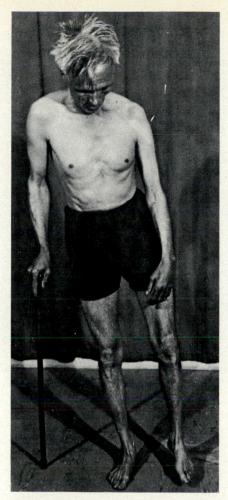

503. The gait in hemiplegia ◁

The weakness and increased extensor tone of the lower limb causes difficulty in flexing the limb at hip and knees and dorsiflexing at the ankle. The pelvis is tilted to the other side with each step in an endeavour to clear the toes from the ground; the affected limb is swung in a semicircle around the hip and the forefoot flops to the ground before the heel.

504. The gait in paraplegia ▽

Lathyrism. One of the 'purest' forms of pyramidal lesion due to a toxic or deficiency effect from the ingestion of bread made from flour contaminated by certain peas of the genus *Lathyrus*. It is now mainly seen in India. The stiff-legged progress of the patient is seen. The cervical cord is rarely affected in lathyrism.

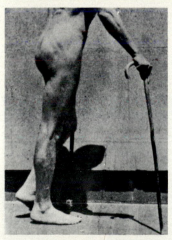
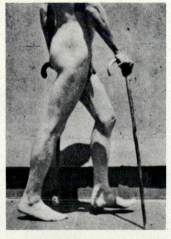
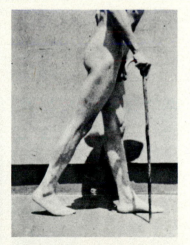
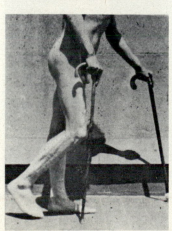

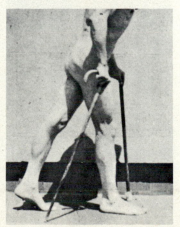

505a   505b   505c   505d

**505. Ataxic gait: left cerebellar
tumour** △ ▷
(a) Romberg test—he sways to the right;
(b) He can stand on the right leg;
(c) Is unsteady on his left leg.

In (d), (e), (f), (g) and (h) he is walking
in heel–toe fashion and his ataxia is evident. His trunk sways to left and right and
he uses his arms in balancing. When he
walked normally he could usually correct
his tendency to lurch or reel, but when he
turned he always staggered.

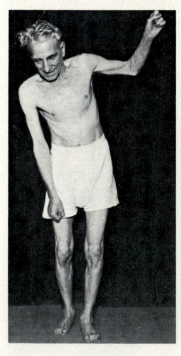

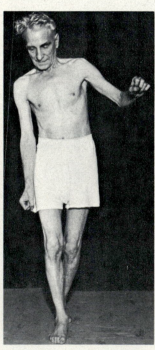

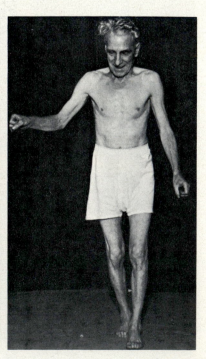

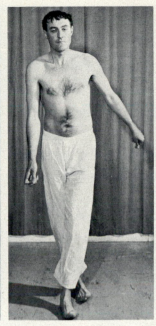

505e   505f   505g   505h

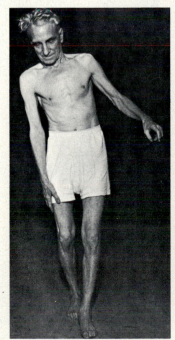

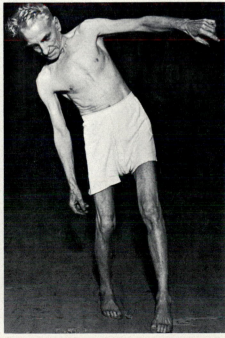

506. Subacute combined degeneration of the spinal cord (vitamin B$_{12}$ neuropathy) ◁

Ataxia revealed on attempting to walk in heel–toe fashion. The gait of spinal sensory ataxia is caused by lack of appreciation of the senses of position and motion of the lower limbs. He watches the ground as he walks; there was a positive Romberg test.

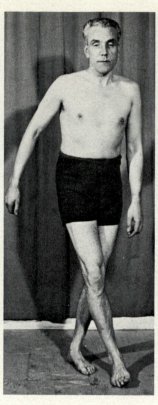

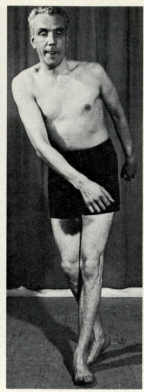

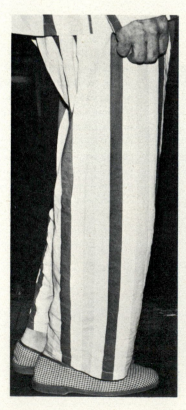

507. Multiple sclerosis ◁

He is trying to walk in a straight line towards the camera. There is spasticity and ataxia in his lower limbs. The incoordination was partly cerebellar and partly sensory in character. In the upper limbs it was primarily cerebellar; in the lower limbs there was marked proprioceptive sensory loss contributing to any cerebellar ataxia.

509. The gait in foot drop ▷

(a) Diabetic neuropathy. Partial left foot drop. As he raises his left foot to take a step there is little dorsiflexion of the forefoot. As the left leg reaches the end of its stride the ankle is not dorsiflexed and the forefoot reaches the ground before the heel.

(b) Left foot drop due to L.5 root lesion from disc prolapse.

508. Cerebral arteriosclerosis ◁ ▽

A shuffling gait, also seen in Parkinsonism. The steps are short and mincing, irregular and hesitant. The patient has difficulty in starting to walk when he rises from a chair and may make little dancing movements before he sets off—*marche à petit pas.*

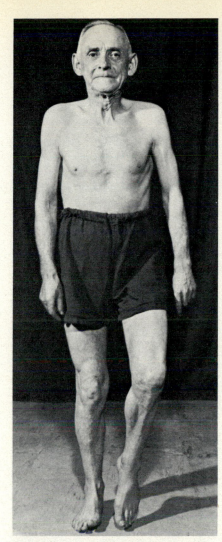

509a

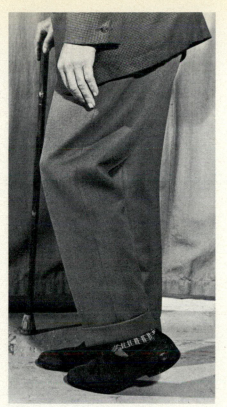

509b

510. Muscular dystrophy ▽

A 'waddling' gait due to difficulty in fixation of the pelvis. The gait has a rolling or throwing character and is broad based. A waddling gait may also be seen in a child with congenital bilateral dislocation of the hips. Brothers aged 6 and 8 years.

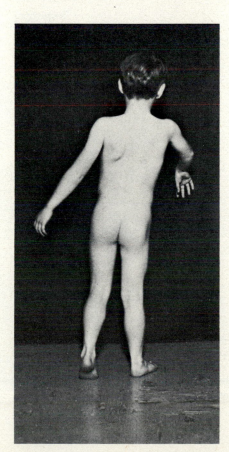

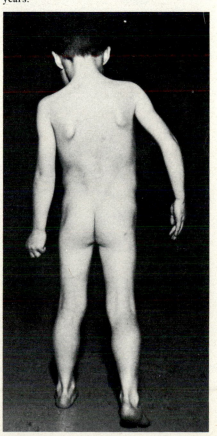

Hysterical Gait

511. Hysterical gait
Here the stiff-legged gait might be taken for the spasticity of a paraplegia.

512. Hysterical gait
He is asked to walk in heel–toe fashion. He used his arms in an exaggerated manner and although the body swayed to and fro in a dramatic fashion, he could toe the line in an accomplished manner.

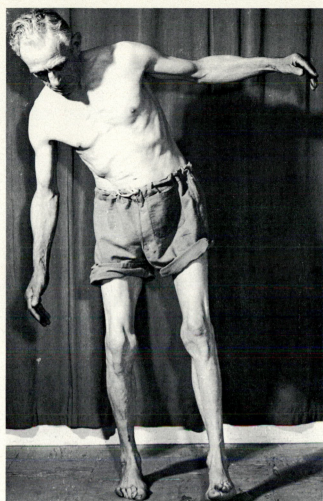

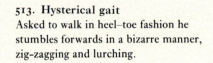
513. Hysterical gait
Asked to walk in heel–toe fashion he stumbles forwards in a bizarre manner, zig-zagging and lurching.

514. Hysterical gait
A casual ward visit is sometimes more rewarding when observing a gait. This man, although he used to stumble and stagger in a nondescript manner, would at the same time suddenly reach for the overhead curtain rail and proceed down the ward in a rapid fashion.

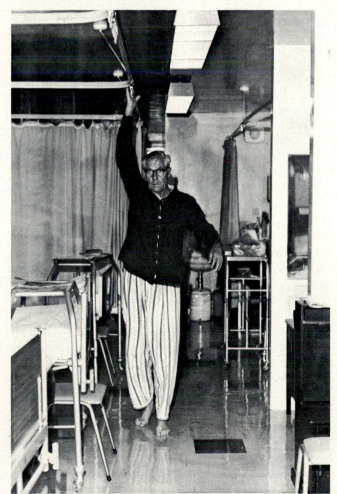

12 THE PATIENT IN BED

In this chapter it is convenient to consider some aspects of the physical and mental state of the patient who is confined to bed because of neurological disorder. He may be there, of course, because of vertigo, sciatica or some other complaint, or for the convenience of the clinician. But the conditions I have in mind are those which render him helpless in varying degrees, such as disorders of consciousness, paralysis and allied states.

Disorders of Consciousness

It is easier to think of disorders of consciousness than of consciousness itself. The word 'consciousness' is an abstract noun. The word 'conscious' is an adjective of quality. To be conscious means to be conscious *of something*. Consciousness is a person's awareness of himself and his environment. As a physiological concept the state of consciousness cannot be dissociated from its content. More is known of the pathology of consciousness than of its physiology and chemistry.

There are several aspects of the conscious state. There is the *range* of consciousness, something that varies between individuals, between the infant and the adult, the dolt and the intelligent. There are also different *levels* of consciousness in the same person depending on the degree of his alertness. Sleeping and waking are variations in the form of consciousness. When we speak of the *stream* of consciousness, we refer to the continuous variations in the activity underlying consciousness. Lastly, the awareness and responsiveness of the state of consciousness indicate the essential sensory and motor nature of its basic physiological processes.

On the anatomical side we know that the central reticular formation of the brain stem is the anatomical basis of an alerting system, which, by modifying the activity of the cerebral cortex and the afferent pathways, influences the state of consciousness. Consciousness may be profoundly disturbed by a small, isolated brain stem lesion while it may be unaltered by major surgery such as bilateral frontal lobectomy or hemispherectomy.

On the other hand, discharging cortical lesions, as in epilepsy, may cause loss of consciousness. The maintenance of consciousness seems to require a fine balance of activity between the cerebral cortex and the central reticular formation.

The clinician recognizes four major states of consciousness. First, there is the normal state in which awareness and responsiveness, subjectively and objectively, are the same for clinician and patient. Secondly, there is sleep, a state in which awareness and responsiveness are reduced, but from which the person can be roused and is able to resume normal activity. Thirdly, a state of impaired or lost consciousness in which the patient cannot be roused to a normal state. Fourthly, there are states in which the patient, though awake and responsive, is imperfectly aware of himself, his actions and his environment and of which he usually has no subsequent recollection; such states are seen after concussion, in epilepsy, and in certain cases of delirium.

'Heightened consciousness', a phrase which recurs in the literature of drug addiction, is possibly a fifth category.

Electroencephalographic studies of normal sleep have shown that it is not, as was formerly supposed, a continuous state lasting several hours, but an alternating one in which two different kinds of sleep have been identified. The rhythms or cycles which govern our waking life also extend to sleep. In passing from wakefulness to sleep, the alpha rhythm of the electroencephalogram at about 10 cycles per second disappears, and sleep spindles at about 14 cycles per second appear with large slow waves at about 1 cycle per second. This phase of orthodox sleep lasts about an hour in the normal person. The next phase, of paradoxical or rapid eye movement (R.E.M.) sleep, has a low voltage electroencephalogram without spindles. It comprises only about one quarter of the normal night's sleep, but profound physiological changes take place during it, including a greatly increased flow of blood to the brain. The rapid eye movements which characterize paradoxical sleep occur in brief bursts and seem to be associated with dreaming. The two kinds of sleep alternate. Sleeping pills, such as barbiturates, suppress paradoxical sleep. Patients suffering from narcolepsy are said to pass initially not into orthodox sleep but, for a period of about 15 minutes, into paradoxical sleep. This probably has something to do with the well known complaint in narcolepsy of vivid dreams and awareness of paralysis as the patient awakens. Disturbances such as nocturnal enuresis, night terrors and sleep-walking occur during orthodox sleep. It is in the dreaming phase that the elderly dementing patient is most likely to wake up, clamber out of bed and wander round in a confused fashion. Human growth hormone is released during orthodox sleep.

Thus, we should no longer regard sleep as a simple state of physical rest and passivity, but as one in which there is continuing, altered and even increased organic activity.

Full conscious behaviour requires not only intact cerebral hemispheres but also a normal brain stem. Clinical and experimental investigations have shown that within the brain stem there is an activating system or arousal mechanism. Defects of arousal characterize stupor and trauma. These states may occur in bilateral lesions of the upper part of the brain stem. Such lesions may be relatively small and localized. By contrast, lesions of the cerebral hemispheres have to be extensive before consciousness is impaired. Both in the brain stem and in the hemispheres, an acute lesion is more likely to influence consciousness than a slowly developing one. In progressive diffuse cerebral degeneration there may be profound dementia with retention of normal waking and sleeping patterns. In large unilateral hemisphere lesions, for example subdural haematoma, consciousness is usually retained until intracranial hypertension compresses or displaces the diencephalon.

Loss of consciousness may be episodic, and its cause does not always lie within the nervous system. It is commonly caused by disorders of the cardiovascular system. These include simple syncope, postural hypotension, cough syncope, micturition syncope, aortic stenosis, cyanotic heart disease, tachycardia, bradycardia, heart block and ventricular fibrillation. On the other hand, the brain may be deprived of oxygen as a consequence of anaemia, hypoglycaemia or arterial occlusion. Epilepsy is the commonest primary neurological disorder that produces loss of consciousness. The mechanism of its loss in concussion is still unknown. Narcolepsy is a rare form of loss of consciousness.

Age is an important consideration when investigating a case of recurrent episodes of unconsciousness. In childhood, epilepsy is the most usual cause. In the young adult, syncope and epilepsy are common. In middle and old age, cardiovascular lesions, cerebral arterial disease, postural hypotension, and cough and micturition syncope are frequent explanations. Certain drugs—phenothiazines, imipramine and hypotensive agents—are liable to cause hypotension. A detailed history usually provides some clue or clues to the aetiology of the episodes.

The Investigation of the Unconscious Patient

Loss of consciousness may develop during the course of an illness, after a head injury or suicide attempt, or in other circumstances which render diagnosis relatively straightforward. It is another matter when loss of consciousness is the presenting clinical feature, as when a child drifts into a state of stupor in a few hours, or when an adult is found unconscious in bed or on the floor. The clues must be sought for in a deliberate manner.

In the patient's home there is nearly always evidence to hand concerning the mode of onset or the nature of any premonitory symptoms. A few minutes' inquiry may disclose that the unconscious child has had minor fits in the past, or that he has had meningeal symptoms for a few days; that the young woman has been unstable and depressed, taking sedatives; that the middle-aged patient has recently been slower, forgetful and often waking with headache and nausea in the morning; that the elderly person was last seen to be hale and hearty a few hours previously, but was known to have hypertension. On the other hand it may not be known that the child has diabetes, the young woman has chronic renal failure, the middle-aged person has cirrhosis or that the elderly person has recently had a minor head injury. The problem of diagnosis may be rendered more difficult because some of the evidence is misleading. It is common knowledge that an alcoholic breath does not necessarily mean alcoholic coma, nor a bottle of sedatives at the bedside mean narcotic coma, nor a contusion or laceration of the scalp mean concussion. Moreover, there may be more than one factor at work. Thus the patient with hypertension may have a cerebral tumour, the diabetic may have sustained a stroke and the patient with outward signs of head injury may have fallen in an epileptic or apoplectic attack.

In the Casualty Department one may or may not be able to obtain a useful history. Witnesses should be interrogated before they leave. In the hospital ward all possible lines of inquiry should be continued while routine investigations and management proceed. A telephone call to a known contact may be more rewarding than analysis of a sample of blood or spinal fluid.

There are infinite gradations of loss of consciousness but the terms *drowsiness*, *stupor* and *coma* usefully describe the three major stages which can be clinically recognized.

In *drowsiness* there is a state of abnormal sleepiness, but what is abnormal is not the appearance of the patient, which may be indistinguishable from normal sleep, but the way in which it is prolonged. The patient may be rousable and his co-operation temporarily obtained so that a more or less satisfactory examination is possible, but when stimulation is withdrawn, he sinks back or curls up and returns to sleep. While he is awake he is able to make appropriate verbal and motor responses. Drowsiness may be caused by a wide variety of cerebral disturbances, but it is often a striking feature of raised intracranial pressure, particularly that resulting from a tumour or subdural haematoma.

In *stupor* also the patient may look as if he is asleep—but he cannot be fully roused. He may be immobile or restless. There are no consistent reflex abnormalities and he is not usually incontinent. His responsiveness varies with the degree of stupor, but he can usually be stimulated to open his eyes, protrude his tongue and move his lips. He is oblivious of his surroundings, incapable of much co-operation and readily relapses into his former state when left to himself. Cerebral anoxia, metabolic disorders, drug intoxication, brain injury and compression or disease of the upper brain stem may all cause stupor. In the variety called akinetic mutism, or, more correctly, akinesia with mutism, the patient lies motionless and speechless but with open eyes and relaxed limbs, as if awake. He is not unresponsive or resistive and his eyes may appear to gaze about him. Yet there is always an amnesia for the duration of this state. It is most commonly seen in association with lesions in the neighbourhood of the third ventricle.

The term 'akinetic mutism' was coined by Cairns and his colleagues in 1941. They observed the disappearance of the syndrome on tapping a cyst of the third ventricle. Further episodes occurred when the cyst refilled. It is a type of stupor seen in subacute encephalitis and encephalopathies and it may or may not be associated with evidence of decorticate rigidity. In all likelihood it is a consequence of involvement of the reticular formation in the upper brain stem. It illustrates the dissociation which may occur between wakefulness and awareness.

In *coma* loss of consciousness is complete. The patient cannot be roused, he makes no voluntary movements and his reflexes may be completely abolished. He is usually incontinent of urine. The degree and extent of loss of reflexes naturally depend on the depth of the coma. Pupillary, corneal and swallowing reflexes may be abolished. In some profound states of coma the deep reflexes are hyperactive and there may be extensor plantar responses.

It is obvious that, depending on the nature of the lesion, a patient may suddenly fall unconscious and remain comatose, as in a cerebral haemorrhage, or pass gradually through the transitional states of drowsiness

515. Concussion; duration of loss of consciousness and amnesia
Retrograde amnesia 24 hours; post-traumatic amnesia 6 days. Loss of consciousness 48 hours. The patient believes he has been unconscious for 6 days because he has no recollection of events between the time he regained his senses and his memory. He does not recall visiting the X-ray department, the E.E.G. department, or talking to his family. The duration of post-traumatic amnesia (P.T.A.) is the most reliable index of the severity of concussion. A suggested classification is as follows; slight concussion, P.T.A. under 1 hour; moderate, P.T.A. 1–24 hours; severe, P.T.A. 1–7 days; very severe, P.T.A. over 7 days.

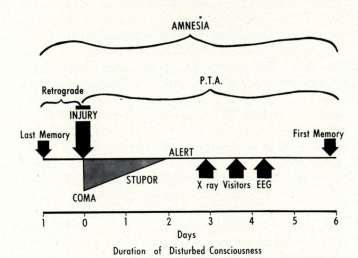

Duration of Disturbed Consciousness

and stupor, before finally becoming comatose. Coma is found in a wide variety of conditions in which there is cerebral damage; the cortex or the central reticular formation may be primarily involved. The state of consciousness may fluctuate, as for example in subdural haematoma, and in the intervals of relative lucidity there may be few significant signs.

Having established the state of unconsciousness the next step is to make a physical examination. It is vital to check whether there is any immediate danger to life. Is there a heart beat? What is the pulse rate and volume? Is the patient breathing? Is the airway patent? What is the blood pressure? Cardiac and respiratory arrest constitute the most immediate threats to life; the brain can survive only a few minutes without blood flow. Emergency measures may be necessary before anything further is done. If examination can be resumed, a preliminary survey should be made with particular attention to certain points which may indicate the cause of the coma.

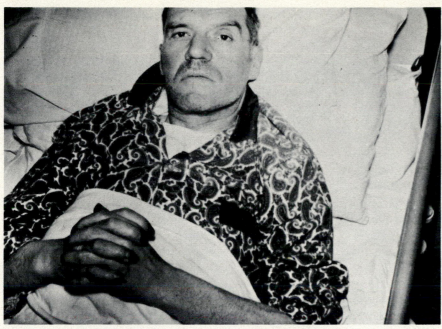

516a

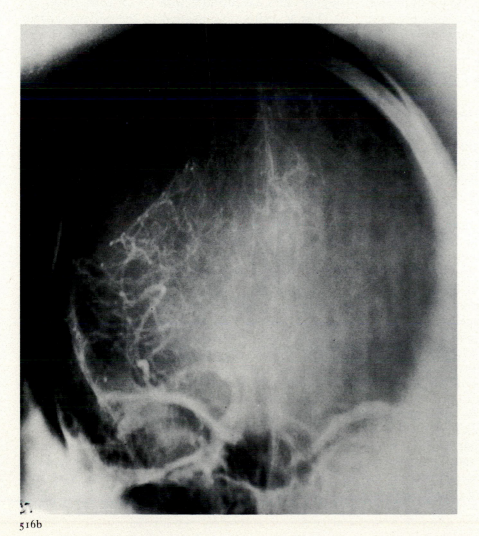

516b

516. Subdural haematoma

(*a*) Headache and fluctuating drowsiness
for 6 weeks. Mild concussion 3 months
previously. This picture was taken on
admission to hospital, the day before
craniotomy. He was quiet, drowsy and
rousable. Slurred speech, pulse 60, partial
left third nerve palsy (note ptosis) and
minimal right hemiparesis. Fluctuation of
the level of consciousness is characteristic
of subdural haematoma.

(*b*) Carotid arteriogram in another patient
with a right subdural haematoma. Displacement of vessels away from inner table
of skull.

The head and face should first be examined for signs of injury, infection or bleeding in the ears, or a bitten tongue. The odour of the breath should always be noted. In diabetic coma it will smell of acetone; it may be alcoholic; in uraemia it may be ammoniacal. The face may be suffused in alcoholism, cyanosed in epilepsy or where there is respiratory obstruction, or white and clammy in states of shock. A subconjunctival haemorrhage may be the only evidence of head injury. When the bedclothes are stripped away the state of the skin and the posture of the body should be noted. A cherry-red colour occurs in carbon monoxide poisoning. Hepatic coma is usually accompanied by some degree of jaundice. Small haemorrhagic lesions, petechiae and ecchymoses, should always be looked for. They may occur in meningococcal meningitis, in bacterial endocarditis, in various blood diseases and drug intoxications.

The position of the body and the disposition of the limbs should be observed. When there is meningeal irritation, as in meningitis or subarachnoid haemorrhage, the neck may be retracted and the patient curled up on one side, resisting attempts at movement. In children with meningitis there may even be some degree of opisthotonos. When there has been a stroke the presence of hemiplegia may be suggested by the puffing out of one cheek with each expiration, and by the external rotation of the lower limb of the same side. The affected upper limb may be folded across the body but is more likely to lie extended at the side.

In some cases of coma or stupor the limbs may be disposed in a manner resembling the decerebrate and decorticate postures of the experimental animal. It will be recalled that section of the brain stem between the superior colliculus and pons produces a degree of spasticity of the antigravity muscles of all four limbs which enable the animal to 'stand'. In the human patient decerebrate rigidity is often incomplete, but in varying degree and distribution, rigid extension of the four limbs may be seen. The upper limbs are internally rotated at the shoulders, the elbows extended and the wrists flexed. The legs are straight and, if there is spasm of the adductors, they may be crossed. A midbrain, suprapontine lesion, as in haemorrhage, encephalitis or tumour, may produce the decerebrate state.

In decorticate rigidity, although the legs are extended and adducted, the arms are flexed. This posture may be seen after carbon monoxide poisoning or in various forms of encephalitis and encephalopathy.

Abnormal tonic neck reflexes may be seen in patients with 'high' decerebration or decortication. They are most likely to be encountered in children with meningitis, encephalitis or brain stem tumour. The posture of the limbs may be altered, by flexing, extending or turning the head. If the head is raised the arms fold up and the legs extend. The reverse may be the case if the head is extended. Turning of the head to one side accentuates the extensor tone of the arm on that side, with flexion of the opposite arm.

At this stage of the examination of the unconscious patient it may be appreciated that there are involuntary movements. Twitching tremors of the lips, face or fingers are common in young children with encephalitis. There may be periodic stiffening of the body and limbs, as when there is tentorial herniation from raised intracranial pressure. Convulsions may be minor, focal or major. If they are persistently one-sided, even though slight in degree, they indicate a lesion of the contralateral cerebral hemisphere. Myoclonic jerks are common in some forms of subacute encephalitis and encephalopathy. They may be confined to the face and upper limbs and consist of sudden, brief movements of varying frequency, amplitude and distribution. They may occur singly, in small groups or in runs lasting several minutes, both spontaneously and in response to various forms of sensory stimulation. In hepatic coma muscular twitching may persist for a time after the characteristic slow flapping tremor of the hands and upper limbs has subsided with the onset of coma.

Lastly, before examination of the nervous system, pulse, blood pressure and respiration should be recorded. The pulse may be surprisingly normal in many types of coma; in cerebral haemorrhage it is often full and bounding and associated with stertorous breathing; when there is raised intracranial pressure it is usually slow; in brain stem lesions it may be weak and irregular.

The limited examination of the nervous system which is possible in states of stupor and coma should, in the first place, be directed towards detecting signs of meningeal irritation, raised intracranial pressure, or hemiplegia. In testing for neck rigidity the pillows should be removed and in addition to assessing the state of muscular spasm in the posterior cervical group of muscles, attention should be paid to the facial expression and any reflex movement of the limbs which may occur when the head is raised in the examiner's hand. It may be necessary to repeat this examination at intervals, as in some cases of meningitis and subarachnoid haemorrhage neck rigidity is late in appearing. Ophthalmoscopic examination must be as complete as possible; if the patient is noisy and restless it may have to be postponed, but patience is necessary. Paralysis of a limb can usually be detected by lifting it and allowing it to fall. The paralysed limb falls heavily, the unparalysed limb falls in a less abrupt manner. In deep coma it may not be possible to detect the presence of a hemiplegia as all limbs fall heavily to the bed. But stimulation of the soles of the feet often causes a withdrawal of the unparalysed leg, while the paralysed leg remains motionless.

In many states of coma, examination of the deep

reflexes yields little of diagnostic value. The plantar responses may be extensor in any case of deep coma, whatever its origin. Asymmetry of reflex activity should nevertheless be sought, and a unilateral extensor plantar response may be of more significance than bilateral responses. Tonic palmar or plantar grasp reflexes may occur in stupor from frontal lobe lesions.

The examiner should seek for evidence of structural lesions within the nervous system. Attention to respiration, to the pupils and to ocular movements is vital.

One of the commonest disorders of respiration is the periodic (Cheyne–Stokes) type in which there is alternating hyperpnoea and apnoea. This usually indicates a bilateral cerebral or high brain stem lesion. Brain stem lesions may also cause hyperventilation or ataxic irregular breathing patterns. The latter are most commonly seen in lesions of the medulla and lack the rhythmical waxing and waning of breathing which is a feature of the periodic Cheyne–Stokes type.

Examination of the pupils should be directed to their size, shape and responsiveness. Pupils of medium size which are inactive to light may result from midbrain lesions. Small fixed pupils, which may even be pinpoint, occur in lesions of the tegmentum of the pons, being most characteristically seen in pontine haemorrhage. A fixed dilated pupil on one side is generally indicative of a lesion of the third nerve. In a comatose patient, it usually indicates herniation of the medial portion of the temporal lobe through the tentorial hiatus. This occurs in tumours and haematomata.

The position of the eyes and their response to movements of the head should be noted. A frontal lesion may cause deviation of the eyes towards the side of the lesion, whereas a pontine lesion may produce conjugate deviation to the opposite side. Downward deviation of the eyes suggests a lesion of the midbrain. Skew deviation of the eyes may result from either a pontine or a cerebellar lesion. Cerebral hemisphere lesions do not affect the oculocephalic reflexes. The examiner turns the patient's head briskly to one side or the other and flexes or extends the neck. With an intact oculocephalic reflex response, the eyes turn in the opposite direction to that of the head movement, pausing like dolls' eyes, and then return to their primary position. Also in cerebral hemisphere lesions, caloric stimulation of the ears—with iced water for example—produces normal evoked nystagmus.

These observations are of particular value in distinguishing structural lesions of the cerebral hemispheres from those of the brain stem. However, most cases of coma seen in hospital are not due to either of these causes. The lesions are diffuse or metabolic. The majority are of endogenous or exogenous toxic origin: cerebral anoxia, poisoning by drugs or alcohol, and the

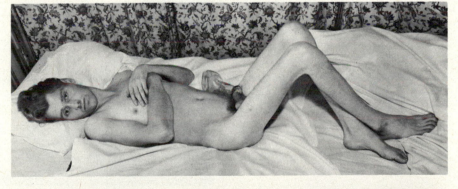

517. Post-traumatic dementia ▷
Road accident, immediate loss of consciousness, coma for 2 weeks; stupor 6 months. This photograph was taken 5 months after injury when he was in a state of akinesia with mutism. He moved his limbs, looked around the ward, often appeared to be about to say something but remained completely mute.

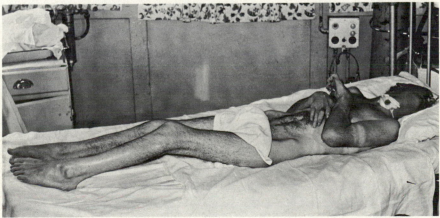

518. Post-traumatic dementia ▷
Decorticate rigidity 6 months after a head injury. Consciousness not immediately lost. Onset of stupor several hours later. Fatal outcome. Note retracted neck, flexed posture of upper limbs and extended legs.

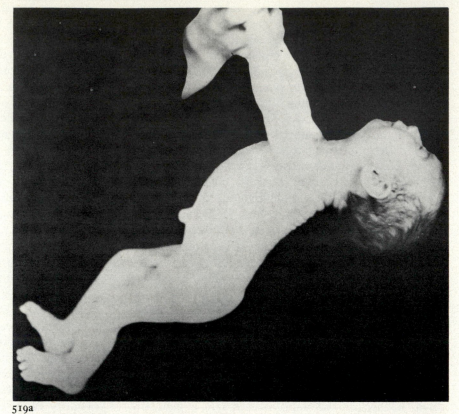

519. Acute meningitis

(*a*) Meningococcal meningitis. Opisthotonos. This was the author's first clinical
photograph 40 years ago.

(*b*) Acute pneumococcal meningitis in 1966.
Twenty-four-hour history of headache,
vomiting, culminating in drowsiness, confusion and noisy delirium. This picture
was taken 36 hours after onset. Note the
curled up position in bed and the evidence
of restlessness. With antibiotic treatment
he was conscious next day and made a full
recovery, in contrast to the fatal outcome
of the infant in (*a*).

519a

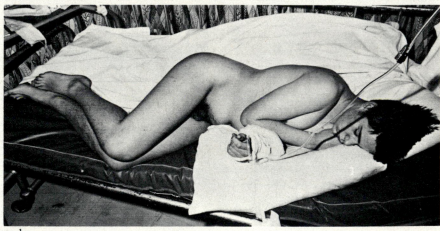

519b

coma of diabetes, uraemia and liver disease are
examples. In most of these cases the pupillary light
reflexes are spared; unilateral pupillary or oculomotor
palsies are rare, but hypoventilation and hyperventilation are common.

The commonest structural lesions which cause coma
are intracranial haematomata (subdural or intracerebral)
and brain stem infarctions.

In many cases the cause of coma remains unknown
after full clinical examination. Many investigations may
be necessary before a diagnosis is made; while urine,

blood and spinal fluid are being examined, the proper
management of the patient should be proceeding. In
narcotic poisoning, for example, the person who induces vomiting and washes out the stomach as soon as
the diagnosis is suspected may save a life. Such immediate treatment is infinitely more important than anything that can be done hours later.

It is obviously vital for the student and young doctor
to know the causes of coma, but he should concentrate
less on memorizing a list of causes than of appreciating
the general features of coma and the procedure of

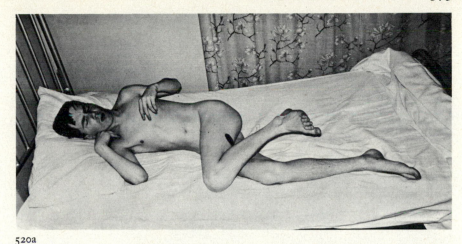

520. Epilepsy

(*a*) Status epilepticus. Progressive organic dementia, increasing fits, uncontrolled by anticonvulsants. Days of freedom and then serial fits and status. Naevus on left thigh.

(*b*) Partial continual epilepsy in a case of cerebral tumour. Twitching of left thumb and left side of face for hours at a time. Note spasm of facial muscles and orbicularis oculi on left side.

520a

identifying the cause. When confronted with coma he may be tempted to reach for the needles at the expense of the clinical scrutiny. In a case of stupor, the degree of co-operation by the patient may wax and wane in such a manner that the house physician is bewildered and disheartened. If he stays at the bedside and thinks, instead of hurrying around arranging investigations, he may win through. I know of no better test for the new intern.

The outcome of coma is notoriously difficult to predict. Few experienced clinicians have not had occasional surprises. Recovery of consciousness following severe head injury, anoxia or poisoning may be unexpectedly complete. The patient's age is an important factor in prognosis: the young brain has a capacity for recovery which does not exist in the elderly. The quality of recovery after severe head injury with prolonged loss of consciousness is related to age and to the duration of the unconsciousness. Evidence of brain stem injury worsens the prognosis. If recovery is seen to take place, it is still impossible to estimate how far it will continue.

The remarkable advances achieved in maintaining the life of an unconscious person have led to the physical survival of 'brainless' individuals. Their existence is purely reflex and vegetative. When the cerebral hemispheres and the brain stem are irreversibly destroyed, we speak of 'brain death'. This cannot be diagnosed until all signs of cerebral and brain stem function have disappeared for several hours—the exact length of time has not yet been determined. In such cases the pupils are inactive, the oculovestibular responses are absent, spontaneous respiration has ceased, and no cerebral electrical activity can be recorded for 60 minutes. Meticulous care is necessary in this field because of the seemingly miraculous recoveries which have been recorded. The brain that is profoundly depressed by hypothermia or by drug action may, to all intents and purposes, seem quite dead.

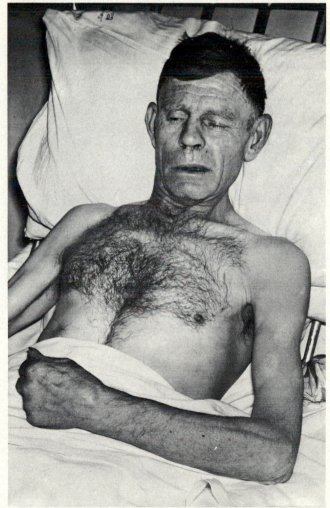

520b

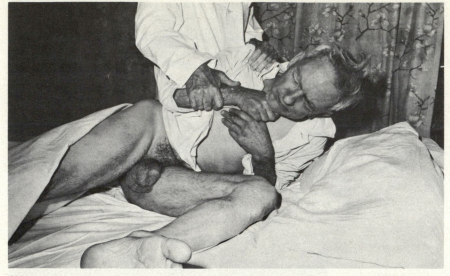

521a

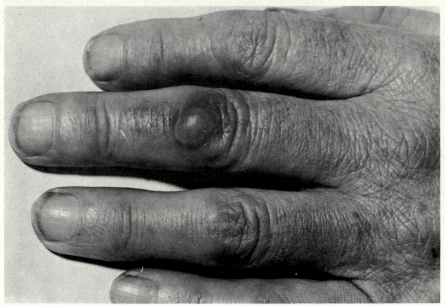

521b

521c

521. Barbiturate intoxication

Stupor; noisy and restless. (a) Long history of previous episodes of drowsiness and stupor, necessitating lengthy in-patient hospital investigations with negative results. The clue to the diagnosis in this case was a blister on the dorsum of the left middle finger (b). Barbiturate blisters are uncommon in this type of coma, but when present they may be very helpful in diagnosis. (c) Barbiturate blister scars in a patient 3 weeks after episode of coma due to overdose.

The cause of blisters in barbiturate coma is still being debated. Some think they are the result of central effects in coma; others view them as manifestations of pressure and hypoxia, while still others consider that barbiturates have a direct effect upon the skin. Barbiturates are usually incriminated because they are a frequent cause of coma, but similar blisters have been described in other drug-induced comas.

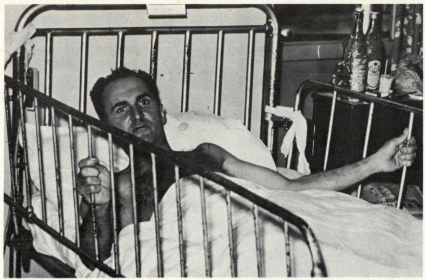

522a

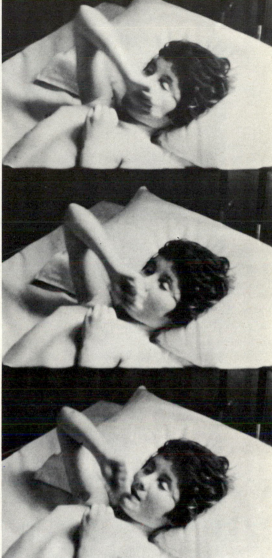

522. Acute encephalitis △ ▷
(a) Headache, fever, confusion, disorientation and noisy delirium. Virological studies normal. Residual psychosis with profound amnesia.
(b) Post-vaccinal encephalomyelitis. Twelve years of age; 18 days after primary vaccination. Onset of illness on thirteenth day. Decorticate rigidity, incontinent, bilateral extensor plantar responses. Frames from a ciné film showing involuntary movements of right arm. Complete recovery.

522b

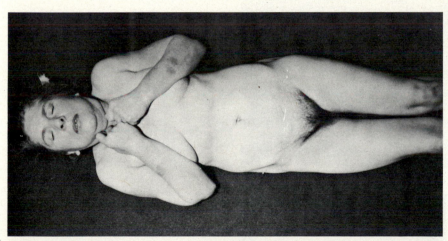

523a

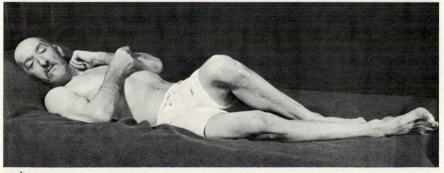

523b

523. Subacute encephalopathy ◁
(a) Age 53. Insidious onset of personality change, disturbance of speech, stiffness of limbs and myoclonus. Decorticate posture, akinesia with mutism. Trismus, fluctuating bilateral pyramidal signs. Fatal in 10 weeks.
(b) Age 57. Progressive cerebral impairment with occasional major convulsion and considerable post-ictal stupor. Mutism, jerking movements of head and upper limbs and insidious development of decorticate posture. Fatal in 15 weeks.

The clinical picture in subacute encephalopathy of adult life resembles that of subacute inclusion-body encephalitis. It is usually fatal and the cause is not known. Status spongiosus is found in the cerebral cortex and a vascular aetiology is suspected.

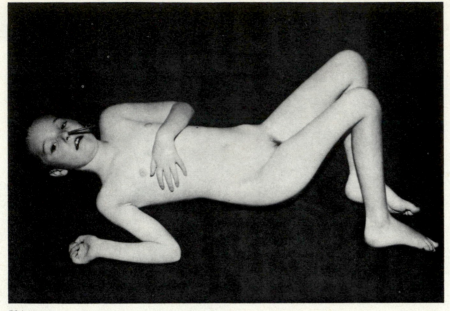

524

524. Subacute encephalitis

Onset with minor epilepsy, behaviour disturbance and deterioration at school. Followed by dysarthria, lethargy, tremors and myoclonic movements of limbs. This photograph was taken in the fifth month of the illness which was fatal in 9 months. Complete mutism. Note gazing eyes. Paretic colloidal gold curve; electro-encephalogram characterized by periodic symmetrical complexes of high-voltage slow waves.

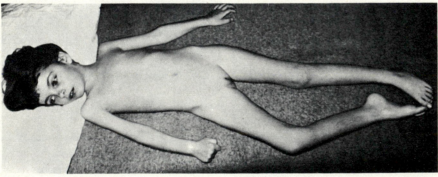

525a

525. Subacute encephalitis

Subacute onset with malaise, anorexia, bed-wetting and drop attacks. A few major convulsions but prolonged periods of petit mal. Akinesia with mutism, myoclonic jerks, decerebrate posture and tonic neck reflexes. In the 8th month of the illness, when these photographs were taken, there were still periods of responsiveness. Note (b and c) the squint and eyelid movements which were manifestations of petit mal status.

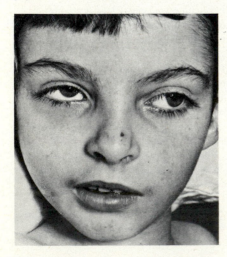

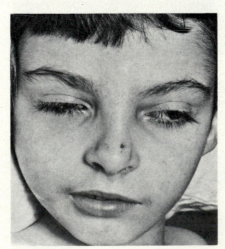

525c

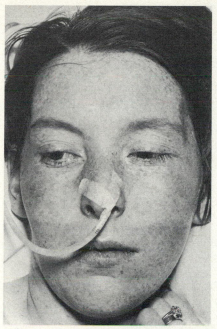

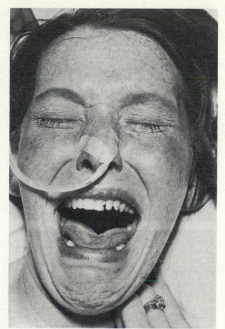

526a   526b

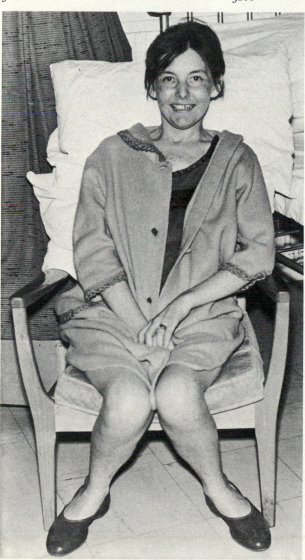

526. Acute multiple sclerosis

Age 23 years, married, with an infant aged 2 months. Two weeks previously she became listless and handled her baby in a clumsy fashion. She complained of tingling sensations in her limbs and was unsteady. Three days before admission she was unable to rise from bed, and on admission she had been in a deep stupor for 48 hours. Examination: afebrile, immobile, mute, unresponsive, incontinent. Bilateral grasp reflexes, reflex hyperactivity, bilateral extensor plantar responses. C.S.F. normal apart from a raised protein content (96 mg./100 ml.).

(a) Eyes deviated to the right; later it became apparent that she had conjugate paralysis of left lateral gaze.

(b) Outbursts of emotional lability, with laughter and crying.

A diagnosis of acute multiple sclerosis was made when we learned that we had seen her 9 years previously with a transient paresis of the right lower limb with ataxia following a polio vaccination, and 4 years previously with an episode of numbness and paraesthesiae of both lower limbs that was considered to be due to multiple sclerosis.

In the third episode she responded remarkably to the administration of ACTH. She came out of her stupor in 3 days.

(c) Four weeks after admission. Five years later there had been no relapse and she was quite well and without abnormal neurological signs.

526c

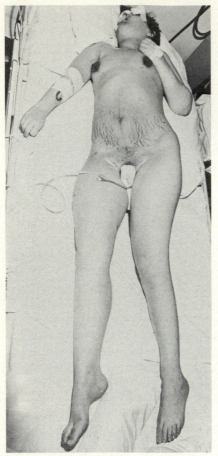

527a

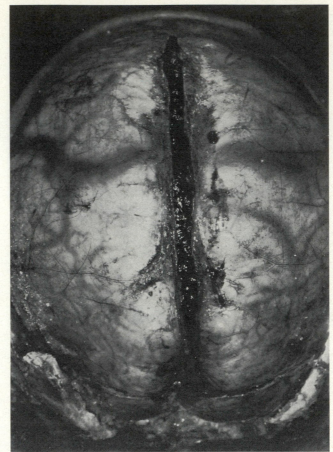

527b

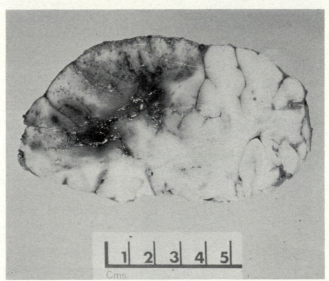

527c

527. Intracranial thrombophlebitis
(*a*) Age 22 years. Emergency admission
with serial major convulsions 2 weeks after
childbirth. Well on leaving Maternity
Department 10 days after delivery, but
soon developed headache, vomiting and
apathy. Then ensued jerking movements
of her limbs followed by general convulsions. On examination: febrile, comatose,
no neck stiffness, normal fundi. Marked
generalized rigidity of limbs with bilateral
extensor plantar responses; flexed posture
of upper limbs. E.E.G.: diffuse high
amplitude slow waves from all areas
except the right parietal region, where
there was marked suppression of all
activity; the left frontal region showed
the highest amplitude delta waves, with
phase-reversals. C.S.F.: xanthochromic,
protein 200 mg./100 ml.; cells, 30 WBC,
900 RBC per c.mm. Right carotid
arteriography: no displacement or pathological circulation, but the arteries were
stretched and tight, the circulation time
was extremely slow and no dural sinuses
were demonstrated. She died 5 days later.
(*b*) and (*c*) Brain at autopsy showing
thrombosis of venous system (*b*) and
cerebral infarction (*c*).

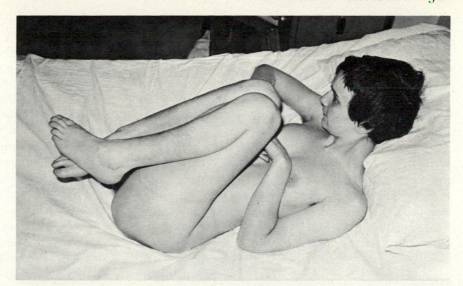

528. Cerebral lipidosis
Age 20. Onset of epilepsy at 6. Progressive organic dementia with pyramidal signs in limbs, dysarthria and incontinence. Now nearly bedridden and adopting a flexed posture. Cortical biopsy revealed lipidosis.

529. Catatonia
Insidious, progressive, organic dementia in a middle-aged man, who showed grasp reflexes and catatonia. The right leg has been raised by the examiner and the patient maintains this posture for several minutes. Catatonia is met with in many diffuse organic cerebral disorders. In this case air encephalography showed widespread cortical atrophy.

Paralysis

The motor pathways originate in the precentral convolutions of the cerebral hemispheres and end in the voluntary muscles. The debates which in recent years have been carried on concerning the organization of the motor system, though fundamental in nature, have never seriously modified the interpretation of the classical neurological signs which the clinician has found useful in the localization of faults within the motor system. Despite arguments concerning premotor cortical areas, the origin, and even the existence, of the pyramidal tracts, the doubts about the extrapyramidal

system as an anatomical or physiological entity, and the discovery of the so-called 'suppressor areas' of the cerebral cortex, the impact on clinical neurology has been slight. The concepts of upper and lower motor neurone lesions remain clinically important. It is clear that the pyramidal or corticospinal tracts are not the sole neural mechanisms conducting impulses to the spinal cord which are responsible for both reflex and willed muscular activity. The extrapyramidal system may still be viewed as one which plays an important part in voluntary muscular activity. The corticospinal tract innervates the prime movers engaged in a muscular action. The extrapyramidal system also innervates these same muscles, together with the synergists and antagonists on whose activity effective movement depends. The pyramidal system is more highly developed in man than in the experimental animal and there is an infinite gradation in the degree of disability which may be encountered in pyramidal lesions.

The lower motor neurones, which transmit impulses from the anterior horn cells of the spinal cord to the voluntary muscles, are subjected to a wide variety of impulses which arrive from the cerebral cortex and brain stem. The role of the pyramidal system in this respect was probably over-emphasized in the past because the effects of pyramidal lesions were more readily discerned. The naming of a few of the extrapyramidal tracts such as the vestibulospinal, reticulospinal and bulbospinal tracts, and the way in which, in diagrammatic sections of the spinal cord, there appear to be no unfilled spaces, should not be taken to mean that there are no remaining descending motor pathways to be identified.

From the precentral motor cortex the fibres of the pyramidal tract converge through the corona radiata to reach the internal capsule lying between the lenticular nucleus laterally and the thalamus and caudate nucleus medially. The corticobulbar fibres (those destined for the motor cranial nuclei) occupy the genu and the corticospinal fibres the anterior two-thirds of the posterior limb of the internal capsule. Thus, even within this compactly arranged group of projection fibres, discrete lesions may have different effects; represented anteroposteriorly are projections from face, upper limb and lower limb, with, most posteriorly, fibres subserving control of the bladder and rectum. Behind the pyramidal tract, in the internal capsule, are the ascending sensory tracts from thalamus to parietal lobe with, behind them, the auditory and optic radiations and the temporopontine fibres. Mingled with the pyramidal fibres are extrapyramidal fibres, both excitatory and inhibitory. It is clear that a lesion in the internal capsule can produce widespread motor and sensory disturbances.

The pyramidal tracts enter the midbrain via the cerebral peduncles. In the pons they are broken up into a series of scattered bundles by the pontine nuclei and crossing fibres. At this level localization within the pyramidal tract puts the face medially, the lower limb laterally, and the upper limb in the intermediate position. In the medulla, where its pyramids were first located over 100 years ago, the tract becomes compact again, the main decussation taking place in the lower part of the medulla. The crossed pyramidal fibres occupy the lateral columns of the spinal cord and terminate by synapsing with internuncial neurones in the grey matter of the spinal cord; these in turn relay to the anterior horn cells. The uncrossed pyramidal fibres descend in the anterior column and their precise destination is not entirely known. Some of them are thought to remain uncrossed and are responsible for the ipsilateral innervation of certain muscle groups.

The final common pathway of motor activity is made up of the lower motor neurones which transmit the impulses from the anterior horn cells of the spinal cord to the voluntary muscles. A motor unit, so-called, is made up of an anterior horn cell, its axone and the muscle fibres which it supplies.

In an upper motor neurone lesion weakness is likely to affect movements rather than individual muscles; 'the brain knows nothing of muscles.' Thus, a muscle may not be able to act as a prime mover, yet it may function usefully when used as a synergist. For example, a man with a slight stroke may be unable to voluntarily extend his wrist, but this movement automatically takes place when he clenches his fist. Fine, highly skilled movements are more severely impaired than coarse proximal movements of a limb. A patient who has had a stroke may be able to put on his jacket but is unable to button it up. Manipulation of the fingers is particularly impaired. This loss of voluntary movement in a lesion of the upper motor neurones is followed by the development of increased muscle tone, hyperactivity of deep reflexes and the extensor plantar response in the lower limb. Muscle wasting is slight, delayed and usually due to disuse; there is no fasciculation.

In a lesion of the lower motor neurones, as we have described in previous chapters, paralysis is likely to involve specific muscles or groups of muscles for all movements. A muscle deprived of its motor nerve supply is completely paralysed, becomes flaccid, loses any deep reflex, and wastes. Fasciculation occurs during the process of denervation and contracture occurs in the fibrosed muscles.

HEMIPLEGIA

Since the days of Hughlings Jackson (1835–1911) the phenomena of hemiplegia have been taken to exemplify the chief modes of disorder of motor function. The sequence of events in a capsular haemorrhage are all too familiar; coma or apoplexy—flaccid hemiplegia—spastic residual hemiplegia. Loss of consciousness is due to cerebral paralysis or 'shock'. This is followed by paralysis of voluntary movements consequent on destruction of pyramidal fibres. If the patient survives the 'release' phenomena of hypertonicity and reflex hyperactivity will appear. (Hughlings Jackson's studies of epilepsy and the 'discharging' lesion added the fourth category of motor disturbance which we recognize, namely convulsion, due to excessive activity of cortical motor neurones.) A hemiplegia may appear suddenly, intermittently, or slowly and although it is most commonly met with in elderly people, it may also be seen in childhood and in all decades of adult life.

Hemiplegia of Acute Onset

Cerebral haemorrhage, infarction and embolism are responsible for most cases of acute hemiplegia in adult life. Haemorrhage is responsible for almost half of the autopsy-verified cases of stroke. Primary cerebral haemorrhage, as opposed to the subarachnoid haemorrhage which results from a ruptured aneurysm, usually occurs in hypertensive and arteriosclerotic subjects. It may take place during sleep or while the patient is awake, and may occur with or without any premonitory disturbance. In haemorrhage and infarction, warning symptoms such as headache, vertigo, transient confusion or lethargy are not uncommon. There may be fleeting focal symptoms such as clumsiness or numbness of a limb, difficulty in holding a conversation, or blurring of vision.

Loss of consciousness occurs in about 50 per cent. of cases of cerebral haemorrhage, but it is uncommon at the onset of infarction or embolism. Early loss of consciousness in cerebral infarction usually accompanies myocardial infarction or cardiac arrhythmias, but any form of acute stroke may be followed by impairment or loss of consciousness due to pulmonary, cardiac or metabolic complications.

Mitral stenosis with atrial fibrillation, and myocardial infarction remain the commonest sources of cerebral embolism, but the incidence of the former, like that of bacterial endocarditis, is declining; the onset is usually abrupt and associated with maximum disability.

If consciousness is lost the posture of the limbs and the asymmetrical distribution of flaccidity may indicate the side of the lesion. During recovery it may be possible to deduce the level of the lesion in the pyramidal pathway. A capsular lesion usually affects the contralateral side of the face, as well as the arm and leg. Involvement of the sensory and optic fibres of the internal capsule, often leads to impairment of postural sensibility in the affected limbs and homonymous hemianopia. The latter is sometimes the only residual physical sign in a person who has suspected he has had a mild stroke but in whom there was no loss of speech or paralysis of limbs. He may describe that he experienced a headache and a period of mental confusion and he may or may not have come to recognize that there was a visual disturbance. Loss of postural sensibility in a hand may be singularly disabling in itself despite good power, as when extracting coins from a pocket or purse or, for example, when using toilet paper. The arteries involved in a capsular hemiplegia are usually the perforating branches of the middle and anterior cerebral arteries; rupture of the posterior communicating and anterior choroidal arteries may also destroy the internal capsule.

In hemiplegia of cortical origin, because of the wide distribution of the head and limb areas in the pre-central convolution, paralysis may be incomplete. There may be a facial, brachial or a crural monoplegia. Occlusion of cortical branches of the middle cerebral artery commonly produce a faciobrachial monoplegia; the leg and foot zone occupy the superior aspect of this convolution and the medial surface of the hemisphere and is supplied by the anterior cerebral artery, so that occlusion of one or more of its distal branches may produce a crural monoplegia. Cortical vascular lesions often cause focal motor convulsions in association with the hemiparesis. The convulsive movements may be of a minor but a continuous nature, confined to hand or foot for several hours or days at a time; hemiplegia is not inevitable.

An acute unilateral lesion in the brain stem may cause a contralateral hemiplegia with an ipsilateral cranial nerve palsy. In the midbrain, for example, the third nerve nucleus may be involved on the side of the lesion; in the pons the fifth, sixth and seventh nerves may be implicated; in the medulla the twelfth nerve. In these 'crossed' or 'alternate' hemiplegias, the facial signs on the side of the lesion will comprise a drooping eyelid with a fixed dilated pupil, an internal squint, a sagging face, weak jaw muscles and unilateral paresis of the tongue. In pontine lesions facial paralysis may be incomplete or complete, that is of upper or lower motor neurone type, on the same or opposite side of the hemiplegia. In the pons, also, ascending sensory tracts may be affected; a lateral lesion may involve the spinothalamic tract so that the paralysed limbs are also anaesthetic to pain and temperature appreciation; involvement of the medial fillet, may render the paralysed limbs insensitive to vibration and passive movement.

In unilateral medullary lesions acute hemiplegia may be associated with ipsilateral paralysis of a vocal cord and soft palate, with a Horner's syndrome, trigeminal analgesia and thermo-anaesthesia and with spinothalamic type of sensory loss in the opposite limbs. There may also be ipsilateral cerebellar signs. When there is isolated occlusion of a posterior inferior cerebellar artery, the pyramidal pathways escape and there is no hemiplegia. But in the majority of cases of the lateral medullary syndrome there is occlusion of the vertebral artery and pyramidal signs commonly appear.

An acute hemiplegia is rarely due to a lesion which is not primarily vascular. In cerebral tumour hemiplegia may develop rapidly, but when it is acute in onset haemorrhage into the tumour is the usual explanation. Occasionally in multiple sclerosis a hemiparesis may develop within 24 hours, but the paralysis is rarely as profound as in a stroke. Aside from traumatic extradural haemorrhage and subdural haematoma, an acute hemiplegia means intracranial haemorrhage, infarction or embolism or cerebrovascular insufficiency. In primary cerebral haemorrhage the onset is nearly always sudden but consciousness is not always lost. In subarachnoid haemorrhage the onset is almost inevitably sudden and signs of meningeal irritation and a bloody spinal fluid point to the correct diagnosis. Nowadays primary intracerebral haemorrhage is not necessarily fatal; survival, with a hemiplegia, does not mean that there must have been a thrombosis or embolism.

The differential diagnosis in acute hemiplegia must be based on the history, physical signs and the results of the examination of the spinal fluid. Without a known source of embolus formation cerebral embolism cannot be diagnosed. A cerebral haemorrhage may be impossible to distinguish from infarction if there has been no loss of consciousness and the spinal fluid remains clear. A hemiplegia developing during sleep or soon after waking is more likely to be due to thrombosis than haemorrhage. Hypertension and renal failure favour haemorrhage.

For many years it was known that a patient might suffer one or more 'little strokes' before being struck down with an acute hemiplegia. Small thromboses or spasm of the cerebral arteries were considered the likely explanations. In recent decades, largely through the development of arteriography and autopsy study of the carotid and vertebral arteries in the neck, a more dynamic view of the cerebral circulation, and the ways it fails, has emerged. Ischaemia of a cerebral hemisphere, or in the territory of the anterior, middle or posterior cerebral arteries, may result from stenosis or occlusion in the arteries of the neck. The effects of reduction of blood flow may be influenced by the level of the blood pressure and the state of the collateral circulation. An acute hemiplegia may thus be viewed as an expression of the failure of the intracranial circulation as a whole. We now know that occlusion of a carotid or vertebral artery may be symptomless. A fully developed and healthy circle of Willis helps to ensure distribution of blood to the hemispheres, provided extracranial occlusion has not suddenly occurred.

The clinical features of recurrent cerebral ischaemic attacks are an outcome of this newer knowledge. They are attacks of focal disorder of brain function—hemiparesis or hemiplegia, tetraparesis, vertigo, ataxia and transient disturbances of vision, speech and sensation. They often herald a stroke. Some idea of the territory involved in the ischaemia may be suggested by the nature of the symptoms. Carotid insufficiency is likely to cause motor and sensory symptoms in the contralateral limbs, perhaps with transient ipsilateral amaurosis and, when the dominant hemisphere is affected, dysphasia. Vertebrobasilar insufficiency is characterized by episodes of brain stem and posterior cerebral disturbance—vertigo, diplopia, drop attacks, hemianopia and dysarthria.

The precise cause of these intermittent ischaemic symptoms is not known but embolism and altered cerebral haemodynamics play a part. The passage of retinal emboli during ischaemic attacks has been observed with the ophthalmoscope. The importance of haemodynamic factors has been shown by the demonstration of the reversal of blood flow in the vertebral artery when there has been stenosis or occlusion of the first part of the subclavian artery or of the innominate artery. The consequent diversion of blood from the brain to the upper limb has been graphically termed 'subclavian steal', and symptoms of vertebrobasilar ischaemia may arise spontaneously or may be precipitated or aggravated during exercise of the affected arm.

Because of the difficulties the clinician encounters in identifying the nature of the pathological process that causes an acute stroke, terms have come into use which are essentially descriptive. Thus we speak of transient cerebral ischaemia, a stroke in evolution, and a completed stroke. A certain number of patients with transient cerebral ischaemic attacks are shown by carotid or vertebral arteriography to have atherosclerotic lesions in one or more of the major cervical arteries, and these lesions may be responsible for the shedding of micro-emboli from an ulcerated plaque. The local lesions can also cause stenosis and reduce blood flow. Episodes of cerebral ischaemia are a consequence of these phenomena. However, atheromatous stenosis of the major cervical arteries is relatively common after middle age, and occlusion of one artery is a not infrequent finding at autopsy. The lumen of a carotid artery has to be reduced by nearly 90 per cent. before the rate of blood flow through it is seriously diminished. If one of the arteries of the circle of Willis is seriously diseased, the danger of ischaemia is greatly increased. Ischaemia itself may impair the physiological mechanisms regulating the flow of blood to the brain, so that the cerebral blood flow may be in a precarious state for some hours. A transient stroke may then become a completed stroke. Many transient strokes are followed by completed strokes at a later date, but it is not possible to identify those patients who will go on to a completed stroke. Epidemiological reports have varied: one showed that fewer than 10 per cent. of patients with cerebral infarction had had a preceding transient cerebral ischaemic episode, whereas another gave a figure of 80 per cent.

In the hypertensive patient a completed stroke is often the result of a localized cerebral haemorrhage. Consciousness is usually lost. The intracerebral bleeding is from micro-aneurysms which are now considered to be a feature of long-standing hypertension. The presence of hypertension in patients undergoing cerebrovascular episodes adversely affects the prognosis. An abnormal electrocardiogram is another grave sign.

Pathological studies have shown that cerebral vascular lesions occur twice as frequently in the hypertensive as in the normotensive brain. It therefore seems possible that in strokes we are seeing the consequences of two processes: (1) the ischaemic effect on the brain of progressive atherosclerosis of major arteries, and (2) the effect on smaller intracerebral arteries of long-standing hypertension with the production of micro-aneurysms. The value of hypotensive therapy in reducing the incidence of strokes is now generally agreed. The patient admitted to hospital deeply unconscious with a stroke usually dies within 48 hours. Most of the patients who are semi-conscious on admission die within a few weeks. The person with a stroke who remains mentally alert does not usually die during that episode. About half the immediate survivors of acute strokes recover satisfactorily. Right-sided cerebral lesions have a less favourable prognosis—a fact for which there is no satisfactory explanation. Ischaemic episodes affecting the vertebrobasilar territory have a better prognosis than those affecting the carotid territory.

Before leaving this subject of the acute stroke it is important to remember that the final condition of survival is not solely determined by the density or extent of the hemiplegia. The factors which impede rehabilitation are impairment of intellect and speech, apraxia, agnosia, incontinence, forgetfulness, emotional lability and depression. The weak and spastic limbs may not be the major disability and physiotherapy not the sole requirement.

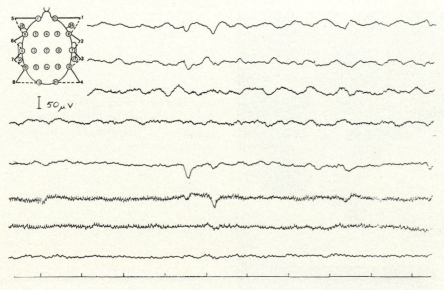

530a

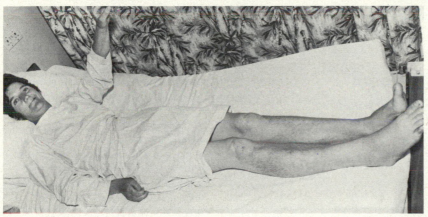

530b

530. Hemiplegic migraine
Age 37 years. Twenty years' history of classical migraine with teichopsia, scotomata and paraesthesiae. This photograph was taken 24 hours after the onset of acute left-sided hemiplegic migraine. (a) She has been asked to raise both arms and bare her teeth. Note left facial weakness and paralysed left arm. The left leg paresis was less marked. (b) E.E.G. taken on the same day, 24 hours after onset. Marked asymmetry; moderate voltage irregular slow delta waves from the right hemisphere.

Hemiplegia of Insidious Onset

The gradual development of a hemiparesis usually requires more than routine history-taking and clinical examination before a diagnosis can be confidently made. In a young person it may be due to diffuse and progressive demyelination in the centrum ovale of a hemisphere. The weakness of the affected limb may fluctuate or remit as in cerebral ischaemia. Usually, however, in multiple sclerosis, sooner or later, symptoms and signs make their appearance which denote the presence of other lesions. But even in the absence of new symptoms there may be signs on the apparently unaffected side of the body, such as loss of abdominal reflexes, hyperactive deep reflexes and an extensor plantar response, which indicate silent involvement of the other pyramidal pathway. Symptoms do not always precede signs.

Neurosyphilis is now a rare cause of progressive hemiparesis and a positive Wassermann reaction in the blood does not necessarily exclude a cerebral tumour or arterial disease.

An expanding lesion within the skull, such as tumour or subdural haematoma, may cause the gradual development of a hemiparesis in the absence of any evidence of raised intracranial pressure. Occlusion of a major artery in the neck may also result in a progressive hemiparesis. Even a cerebral haemorrhage may present in a gradual manner. Distinction between these causes can never be certain without neuroradiological studies.

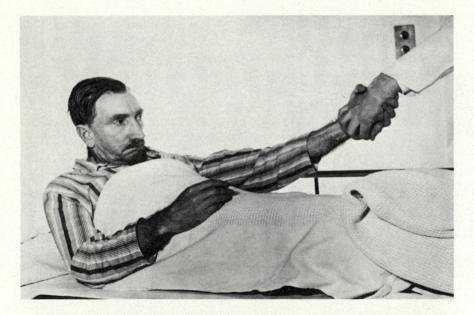

531. The grasp reflex
The examiner's fingers are placed in the palm of the patient's hand. There is reflex closure of the patient's hand around the examiner's; an exaggeration of the normal palmar reflex. If the reflex response is marked the patient's grasp increases as the examiner tries to withdraw his hand. The patient may be lifted from the bed in this manner. This is known as tonic perseveration, or the forced grasping reflex. In the groping response, the patient will reach for the examiner's hand if he sees it, or, if the patient's eyes are closed he will grope at the touch of a hand. Normally an infantile response, they are found in frontal lobe disturbances in the adult. It is essentially a contralateral response. This patient suffered from diffuse cortical atrophy with dementia and Parkinsonism.

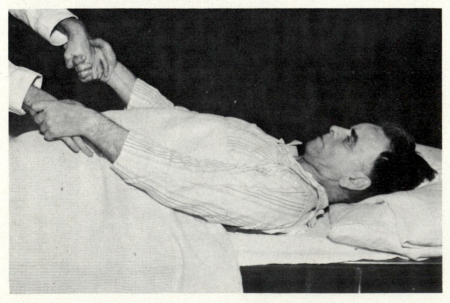

532. Bilateral grasp reflexes
This patient had a large frontal meningioma, mainly left sided. There was progressive dementia.

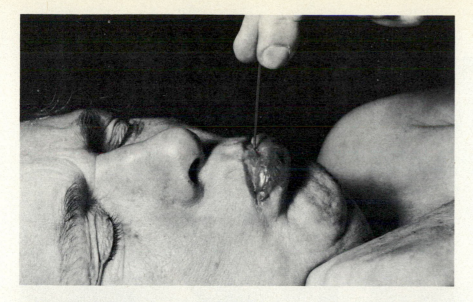

533. Pouting – sucking reflex
Touching the lips induces reflex pouting and sucking movements. Normal in infancy, in adults it is seen in diffuse cerebral degeneration. This patient died of a subacute encephalopathy.

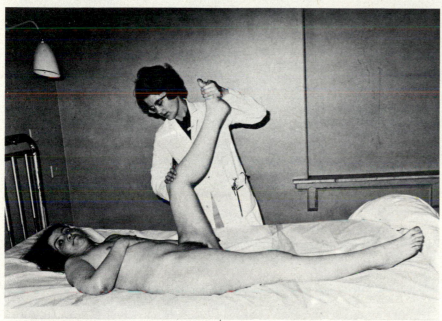

534. Kernig's sign
The examiner flexes the patient's thigh to a right angle and then attempts to extend the leg on the thigh. There is a reflex spasm of the hamstring muscles which limits extension at the knee and causes pain and discomfort. Like Lasègue's sign it is seen in meningeal irritation and in sciatica. The meningeal irritation in this patient was due to a subarachnoid haemorrhage.

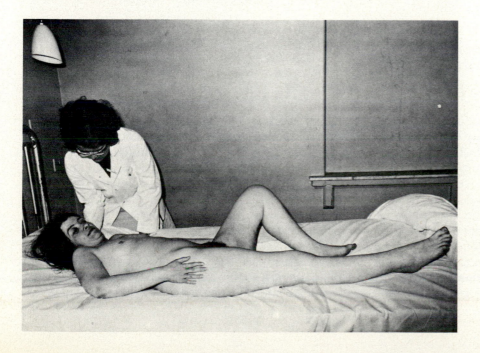

535. Brudzinski's neck sign
Passive flexion of the head on the chest causes reflex flexion of one or both thighs. Note flexion of left leg. Same patient as in Fig. 534.

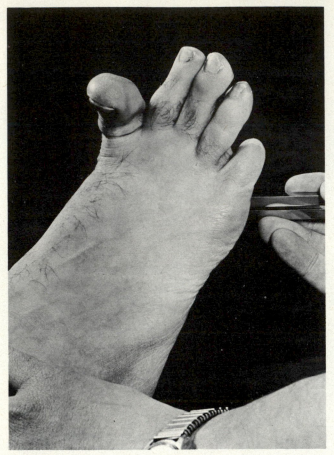

536. The Babinski sign
One of the most famous signs in clinical neurology. Plantar stimulation leads to dorsiflexion of the great toe; fanning of the other toes is inconstant. It may be associated with reflex withdrawal of the limb; a sign of pyramidal disorder.

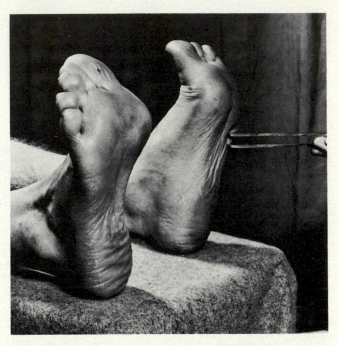

537. A crossed extensor plantar response
Plantar stimulation causes reflex dorsiflexion of the toes of both feet.

PARAPLEGIA AND TETRAPLEGIA

In affections of the spinal cord we see in operation the same modes of disturbance of nervous function which occur in the brain—shock, 'negative' effects (paralysis) and 'positive' or 'release' effects (spasticity, hyper-reflexia and the extensor plantar reflex). In the spinal cord there is no phenomenon equivalent to the 'discharging' lesion of the cerebral cortex, but muscular fasciculation does represent the abnormal electrical activity of diseased lower motor neurones. We may see in the hospital bed the clinical counterpart of the 'spinal' animal, although, as Sherrington said, 'the spinal man is more crippled than the spinal frog'.

Spinal shock is now less fatal than it used to be and patients often survive complete transection of the spinal cord. There is immediate loss of all function below the level of the lesion—a flaccid paralysis with loss of reflexes. With the passing of shock reflex activity returns first to the flexor muscles and there is a tendency to the development of paraplegia-in-flexion. In progressive lesions of the spinal cord, there is a predominance of extensor over flexor tone with the development of paraplegia-in-extension. Spread of the lesion beyond the pyramidal pathways to involve the vestibulospinal tracks leads to the appearance of flexor-withdrawal re-

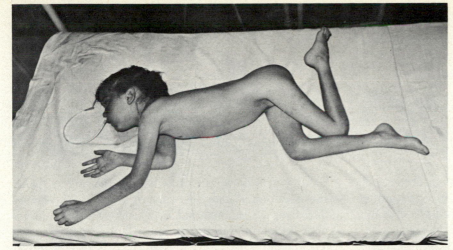

538a

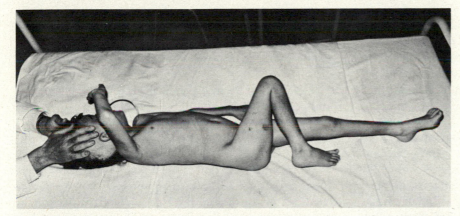

538. Subacute encephalitis; tonic neck reflexes
(*a*) The flexed position she normally adopted.
(*b*) Turning her head to the left induced extension of the ipsilateral limbs.
(*c*) Turning her head to the right induced extension of the right leg, but her right arm remained flexed. (Courtesy of Dr. O. P. Gray.)

538b

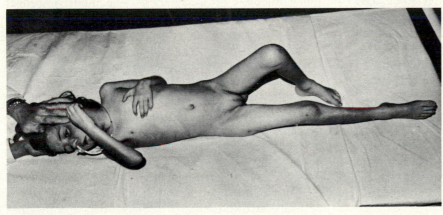

538c

flexes and paraplegia-in-flexion. This is seen in cord compression from tumour and in multiple sclerosis. A paraplegia may remain flaccid as in poliomyelitis, where the anterior horn cells of the lumbosacral region of the cord have been destroyed or it may continue to be predominantly flaccid in motor neurone disease. As described in previous chapters a flaccid paraplegia may also result from lesions of the cauda equina and from polyneuritis.

The effects of a lesion of the spinal cord depend on its mode of onset, its extent and position. Paraplegia may

therefore be acute, subacute or insidious and it may be incomplete or complete. Detecting the level of the lesion is a matter of interpreting the segmental arrangements derived from the original neural tube.

The spinal lesion may be small but complete, as in trauma; diffuse as in myelitis and vascular lesions; multiple, as in demyelination; or systemic in nature, predominantly affecting certain motor pathways, as in hereditary spastic paraplegia and motor neurone disease, or sensory pathways, as in tabes dorsalis. In some types of system degeneration within the spinal cord, motor and sensory pathways are involved, as in subacute combined degeneration and in certain nutritional myelopathies.

Topographical Diagnosis

Accurate localization of a lesion of the spinal cord may require the assistance of plain radiographs and myelography, but in many cases a fair degree of localization may be achieved on clinical examination. A lesion of the spinal cord will have two main effects. First, there may be sensory and motor phenomena at the level of the lesion. Second, there may be sensory and motor disturbances below it. The ensuing symptoms and signs, which may comprise root pains and paraesthesiae, weakness, numbness and disturbance of sensation in the extremities, may be accompanied by abnormalities of reflex behaviour. At the level of the lesion a reflex whose arc passes through the segment involved will be impaired or lost; below the lesion, cutaneous reflexes will be impaired or lost, while the deep reflexes will be exaggerated. Naturally, the total effect will vary considerably from one case to the next.

Pain is often an early symptom of spinal cord tumour. It is most commonly of a radicular character, due to irritation of a posterior nerve root. It is usually but not always sharp and severe; it may be dull and aching. It may not be felt in the entire area of the affected dermatome. It may be restricted to the distal portion of a limb so that its root origin may not be suspected. Root pains are often worse at night and aggravated by coughing, sneezing or straining at stool. Thoracic root irritation may cause pain like that of pleurisy or 'stitch'. If bilateral it may be described as 'like a tight belt'. In intramedullary lesions a diffuse pain of a burning or boring character, below the level of the lesion, may be a manifestation of involvement of the spinothalamic tracts. This occurs in syringomyelia. Localized vertebral pain is uncommon in benign tumours of the spinal cord but may be severe in secondary tumours. Local tenderness of a spinous process on percussion or pressure may of course also result from root irritation at a higher level.

Paraesthesiae are another frequent early symptom of spinal lesions. They may be described as numbness, pins and needles, tingling, burning, stinging, coldness or crawling and they may be felt in the dermatomes at the level of the lesion or below it. They may be unilateral or bilateral and, as with pain, they are frequently perceived only in the distal portions of the affected dermatomes. Simple loss of awareness of sensation may pass unnoticed; it is most commonly detected in the hand, least commonly on the trunk. Loss of temperature appreciation may be noticed when the patient takes a bath, especially if it has developed rapidly, as in multiple sclerosis. Loss of pain sense may be marked before it is accidentally discovered as a result of a cut or burn. There

may be no objective sensory loss in multiple sclerosis at a stage when paraesthesiae are persistent. Hyperaesthesia at the level of a root lesion may be described by the patient as a form of irritation and soreness, aggravated by the contact of clothes.

A complaint of weakness may be referred to a limb as a whole or to one part of it. In the lower limbs there is usually a story of undue fatigability or stiffness in walking when the corticospinal tracts are involved. In the upper limbs spastic weakness of the fingers makes the execution of many movements clumsy and difficult. The flaccid weakness and hypotonia of a lower motor neurone lesion, in upper or lower limb, usually leads to a complaint of difficulty in performing a specific movement. There is weakness of grip or elevation of the shoulder; in the lower limb complaint of dragging of the toes or lifting of the foot on walking, weakness in rising from a chair or in raising the legs when mounting stairs.

Weakness of the muscles that innervate the shoulder and pelvic girdles is often insidious, tends to be neglected by the patient or dismissed as 'rheumatism', and unless specifically looked for may be missed by the examiner.

Sensory examination is particularly important when there is the possibility of cord tumour. It may denote the level of the lesion more accurately than motor or reflex methods of localization. The modern student needs to be reminded that spinal cord tumours were accurately localized and successfully removed for many years before myelography was developed. A clear upper level of sensory impairment, confirmed by repeated examinations, is the best clinical indication of the level of a compressing lesion of the spinal cord. This level may be quite definite even though the sensory loss is incomplete; it is often missed for this reason. The upper limit of a hypalgesic zone may be just as definite as that of an analgesic one. In the interpretation of objective sensory loss, one must take into account factors such as the overlapping of adjacent dermatomes, the two routes by which tactile sensibility is transmitted upwards and also the delayed crossing of the fibres conveying pain and temperature sensation. The latter take several segments to cross in the cervical and lumbosacral regions. In the mid-thoracic region they cross in about one segment. Loss of vibration and postural sense arising from involvement of the posterior columns is not usually of much value in localization of the level of a lesion. But loss of vibration sense may be complete in the lower limbs and over the vertebral spinous processes up to a more or less definite level. In the cervical region there may be loss of posture in the fourth and fifth fingers bilaterally with sparing of the thumbs, indicating a lesion at C.7.

The distribution of the dermatomes in the upper and

lower limbs has been described in previous chapters. In segmental diagnosis by sensory testing it is helpful to recall certain features. The first cervical nerve does not reach the surface. The second cervical dermatome is contiguous with the trigeminal dermatome on the face and scalp. The segments C.5 to T.1 are almost wholly distributed on the upper limbs and not on the neck or chest. C.4 and T.2 segments overlap in the infraclavicular region. When a sensory level is detected at T.2 the examiner should proceed to investigate sensation in the upper limb and not continue directly upwards over the clavicle and to the neck. Useful landmarks are the nipple (T.4) the costal margin (T.7, 8) the umbilicus (T.10) and the groin (T.12, L.1).

The segmental interpretation of muscular weakness and wasting in the limbs has also been referred to in previous chapters. It will be recalled that the grasp of the hand will be affected in a lesion at C.8; the small muscles of the hand at T.1. In standing and walking, actions such as bracing the knee (L.4) and lifting the foot and toes (L.5) are naturally important.

The segmental level of reflexes in common use is as follows. The jaw, pons; biceps and radial, C.5–6; triceps, C.6–7; finger, C.8; abdominal: upper, T.8–9; lower, T.11–12; cremasteric, L.1–2; knee, L.3–4; ankle, S.1; and plantar, S.1.

It is not often that autonomic disturbances are noted in chronic disease of the spinal cord, but they may be seen in syringomyelia and, of course, in acute transverse lesions. Impairment of bladder function may result from suprasegmental or segmental lesions of the cord. In the former involvement of inhibitory fibres causes urgency and precipitancy of urination, as in multiple sclerosis. Implication of those fibres concerned in the voluntary act of urination may cause retention. Lesions of the conus and cauda equina interrupt the sacral reflex arc concerned in evacuation of the bladder with resulting retention. In spinal cord transection, from injury or disease, reflex evacuation of the bladder may be established.

There are particular difficulties which may be encountered from time to time in the localization of the level of the spinal cord lesion. Some are due to faulty interpretation, others to incomplete examination and still others are due to the operation of factors which are ill-understood or unknown. A few examples may be quoted.

The distribution of pain, as previously noted, may have a myotome as well as a dermatome distribution; pain in the ribs or vertebrae may be of sclerotome origin. Facial pain or hypalgesia may result from involvement of the spinal trigeminal nucleus in the upper cervical cord. Then there are signs which are considered abnormal in a particular case but which, actually, are normal but misleading variations. Asymmetry of the face may be interpreted as facial weakness, so that, if the limb signs are unilateral, a cerebral rather than a spinal lesion is suspected. Ill-sustained nystagmus or a jaw jerk may similarly mislead; neither are necessarily pathological. Errors may arise through the faulty interpretation of reflex activity; normally, the deep reflexes may be lively or sluggish and they cannot all be elicited in every individual. The biceps reflexes are usually brisker than the triceps reflexes, while the knee jerks may be sluggish in the presence of brisk ankle jerks. Reflex flexion of the fingers occurs in some normal individuals when the radial or supinator reflex is elicited; this does not necessarily mean a mid-cervical cord lesion. The lower abdominal reflexes are often sluggish in comparison with the upper.

In cervical cord lesions dissociated sensory loss does not necessarily mean that the lesion is intramedullary; it may result from compression of the cord. It is in this region of the cord that sensory levels are least accurate. A high cervical cord lesion may sometimes produce wasting of the small muscles of the hand. Interference with the downward flow of blood in the anterior spinal artery may be responsible for this complication and for similar segmental discrepancies in cervical myelopathy with spondylosis. The direction of flow of blood in the lower portion of the two posterior spinal arteries is upward and it is possible that ischaemic changes may arise some distance from a compressing lesion. The cord is richly supplied with blood in an intricate pattern, but clinical and pathological studies suggest there are areas which are specially vulnerable to ischaemia; the fourth thoracic and first lumbar segments are examples. Sensory examination may reveal an area of normal sensibility within a widespread zone of sensory loss below the level of a lesion. Thus, 'sacral sparing' in an intramedullary lesion of the cervical or thoracic cord may occur and is probably due to the laminar arrangement of the fibres in the spinothalamic tracts; those from the sacral segments come to lie in a lateral position in the spinothalamic tracts. Many lesions of the cord are incomplete so that there may be an area of normal sensation between that which results from segmental involvement and that which derives from interruption of ascending sensory tracts.

The Mode of Onset of Paraplegia and Tetraplegia

In clinical neurology there is no better example of the importance of the time factor in diagnosis than that which the clinician encounters in a case of paraplegia. Interpretation of the signs can only be made in the context of the clinical history. A pair of weak lower limbs in which the muscles are found to be spastic and associated with exaggerated deep reflexes and extensor plantar responses may be the result of a lesion which has developed suddenly, or grown insidiously or intermittently, and the nature of which varies considerably with the age of the patient. Thus, acute paraplegia in a child is usually due to myelitis; in an elderly person it may be due to thrombosis of the anterior spinal artery or to secondary carcinoma of the spine. In middle age an insidious onset may result from compression by tumour or from multiple sclerosis, a disease which, at an earlier age, is usually characterized by acute, subacute and remitting symptoms and signs. Although a paraplegia is nearly always due to a spinal lesion, it should not be forgotten that it occasionally results from lesions involving the leg areas of the cerebral cortex. The latter may be compressed by a tumour such as a parasagittal meningioma or softened as a result of arteriosclerosis. The diagnosis of spinal paraplegia may be usefully approached in terms of its mode of onset.

Paraplegia of Acute Onset

A paraplegia (or tetraplegia) of sudden onset is most commonly due to injury; occasionally the lesion is vascular—thrombosis or haemorrhage in the cord substance. Paralysis appearing in a matter of hours may also be vascular in origin or the result of acute myelitis.

Traumatic Lesions

In civilian life injury to the spinal cord usually results from indirect violence as in the case of falls, diving accidents and road accidents. Direct violence may occur in crushing injuries as in many industrial accidents. In war-time it is the penetrating wound which so frequently injures the cord. Stab wounds, of course, are commoner in certain parts of the world than in others and I cannot refrain from mentioning that the first two cases of the Brown-Séquard syndrome that I ever encountered, many years ago, were both civilians; one was stabbed in an Eastern bazaar and the other as he drove his taxi in New York. Compression injuries are most often seen in the lower thoracic and lumbar region, as in mining accidents. In road accidents sudden forcible flexion of the spine, especially in the cervical region, is frequently associated with fracture-dislocation of the vertebrae and is responsible for damage to the cord. In many cases of tetraplegia the degree of injury to the cervical vertebrae as subsequently revealed by radiography may appear to be surprisingly small. The sudden displacement of the vertebrae was transient and perhaps largely restored, but the effects on the enclosed spinal cord are only too often permanent. On the other hand initial radiography may not have been adequate enough to reveal the true state of affairs. Hyperextension injuries are most frequently seen in the cervical region. Flexion or hyperextension injuries to the cervical cord may cause paresis which is greater in the upper than in the lower limbs, and for some weeks the patient may be greatly distressed by painful, stinging, burning sensations in the chest and upper limbs, with hyperpathia.

The phenomena of spinal shock, flaccid paralysis and paraplegia-in-extension and in-flexion have been referred to earlier. They largely depend on the severity of the injury.

There are several aspects of mild injury which require stressing. Transient spinal paralysis which passes off completely in a few hours has been termed 'spinal concussion'. Weakness and paraesthesiae of the limbs are presumably due to some reversible cord lesion. Another type of case is that in which an obvious head injury has masked a mild cervical cord injury. On recovery of consciousness or when the patient becomes ambulant, symptoms are noted such as pain in the neck and weakness and numbness of the extremities, which lead to further examination. It is in such a case, where there has been a mild mid-cervical cord lesion, that the pattern of reflex activity in the upper limbs points to the level of the lesion. The long tract signs in the lower limbs are often associated with impairment or loss of the biceps reflexes, inversion of the radial reflexes (brisk flexion of wrists and fingers replacing flexion at the elbows, with preservation or exaggeration of the triceps reflexes). Variations of this pattern may be encountered in symmetrical and asymmetrical fashion.

When a trivial or mild injury is followed by tetraparesis or paraparesis, a pre-existing vertebral abnormality should be suspected. A small spinal canal, congenitally fused vertebrae or spondylosis may be present, especially in the cervical region. Such abnormalities are often symptomless until the injury occurs. In cervical spondylosis the injury is usually indirect; the elderly person trips over a mat and strikes his head on the floor. In other instances, spinal manipulation or over-extension under anaesthesia is sufficient to injure the cord. In one patient of mine micturition syncope was followed by a tetraparesis; the patient, a healthy young man, struck his head on the urinal as he fell and was unable to rise on regaining his senses. Subsequently, radiography disclosed an abnormally narrow cervical spinal canal.

Vascular Lesions

Whereas a cerebral stroke is an everyday affair, a spinal stroke is a rare event. It may take the form of a thrombosis of the anterior spinal artery or a haemorrhage from an angioma. The spinal arteries, the anterior and the two posterior spinal, receive their blood supply, in the upper regions, from the two subclavian arteries, mainly via the vertebrals, and, lower down, from the aorta via the intercostal and lumbar arteries. There are six to eight anterior radicular arteries, the largest usually in the lumbar region, which enter the spinal canal through the intervertebral foramina. The upper thoracic region of the cord represents the arterial watershed between the two main sources of blood supply; anoxia of the spinal cord may show here.

In thrombosis of the anterior spinal artery there is infarction of the anterior two-thirds of the cord. The posterior third, including the posterior horns and columns, are supplied by the two posterior spinal arteries. The patient is usually middle-aged or elderly and the onset may be abrupt and painful or it may take several hours before paralysis develops. There is a flaccid tetraplegia or paraplegia, dissociated sensory loss to the upper level of the lesion, double incontinence and, with the passing of spinal shock, the emergence of pyramidal signs. Destruction of the anterior horns of the thrombosed segments will result in flaccid paralysis of corresponding muscles. The cerebrospinal fluid is normal or may show an increased protein content.

A similar syndrome may arise as a result of occlusion of a radicular artery, in which case there may also be unilateral loss of deep sensation. Infarction of the spinal cord may thus result from aortic atheroma or dissecting aneurysm. Aortic surgery is sometimes responsible.

Haemorrhage into the substance of the cord, haematomyelia, may follow trauma or occur spontaneously. The haemorrhage tends to plough through the grey matter for several segments. In the past the role of trauma has probably been overemphasized; the majority represent a leak from an angioma. This vascular malformation can occur at any level in the cord, but the largest are to be found in the thoracic region. Haemorrhage within the spinal canal usually presents in a sudden manner, with pain and a meningeal reaction as in an intracranial subarachnoid haemorrhage, or as an abrupt syringomyelic syndrome, from haematomyelia. In other cases the formation of an extramedullary haematoma causes cord compression. Spinal aneurysms are exceptionally rare.

The diagnosis of spinal angioma can only be proved by arteriography, but it may be suspected on clinical grounds when episodes of paralysis are accompanied by pain and evidence of spinal bleeding. A cutaneous naevus or a spinal bruit would be important clues, but they are usually absent. A spinal angioma, of course, may also mimic chronic diseases of the spinal cord and never present with abrupt or acute paralysis.

Paraplegia of Subacute Onset

When paralysis of the lower limbs, or of all four limbs, appears over the course of a few days, the lesion is usually inflammatory—a myelitis or abscess. Formerly, the commonest form of myelitis was anterior poliomyelitis and the commonest spinal abscess was tuberculous, two diseases now fortunately rare. In poliomyelitis paralysis is usually maximum within 24 hours and shows the characteristic features of a lower motor neurone lesion. Subjective sensory disturbances are common but objective sensory loss, if present, is slight and transient. Spinal caries used to present in childhood with increasing deformity of the spine and paraplegia was a complication of cord compression by abscess and tuberculous granulation tissue. Weakness of the legs in a person who is known to have caries of the spine should present no diagnostic difficulty. Nevertheless, it is a condition which should be remembered in all cases of paraplegia in childhood and may still be encountered in the elderly. Twice, in recent months, a paraplegia of subacute onset in an elderly person proved to be due to spinal tuberculosis. There was no previous history of tuberculosis, pain was minimal, and there was no outward sign of clinical deformity of the spine.

In myelitis or myelopathy paralysis usually reaches its maximum severity in a few days, but it may be sudden or acute in onset; there is considerable variation. The cause of the syndrome is not known and probably includes several different entities. It is not usually fatal and about a third of patients make a good recovery. It may be a manifestation of multiple sclerosis or a virus infection. The patient is usually a young adult. A history of recent infection is not as commonly obtained as in the case of acute polyneuritis. The first symptom is often pain in the back, followed by numbness and weakness of the feet and lower limbs. There is often fever, spinal tenderness and root pain. There is usually retention of urine which, if not relieved, goes on to overflow incontinence. In some cases a clear sensory level is apparent from the onset, but in others it may appear to ascend. There is flaccid paralysis with loss of reflexes and impairment or loss of all forms of sensation below the level of the lesion. The patient usually looks and feels ill and he may be alarmed and distressed early in the illness.

There is usually an increase of cells and protein in the spinal fluid and manometry is usually normal, occasionally the Queckenstedt test showing signs of slight obstruction in the subarachnoid space. Signs of return of function and sensation in the lower limbs usually make their appearance after a few weeks. As in acute polyneuritis, there may be a remarkable degree of recovery, although many patients, about a third, remain gravely disabled. In those who recover the question of multiple sclerosis always arises. Certainly, this disease may present as a myelitis, but many of these patients live many years without any further neurological illness.

When confronted with a patient with acute or subacute paraplegia the question of spinal epidural abscess always requires consideration. It is not a common disease but it may closely resemble a myelitis. There is pain, spinal tenderness, a stiff neck, constitutional upset with fever, abnormal spinal fluid and signs of a transverse lesion of the spinal cord. Absence of back pain and maximum paralysis in 24 hours favour a diagnosis of myelitis. Complete subarachnoid block, which should be followed by myelography, favours abscess; recent bacterial infection also suggests abscess. In all cases radiography is necessary and any sign of vertebral osteomyelitis excludes myelitis.

An increasingly important cause of acute and sub-acute paraplegia is the malignant epidural spinal tumour. Just as a small pyogenic abscess in this position may have very serious consequences so also may the small deposit of carcinoma from lung, breast or prostate. Pain is an almost invariable symptom, often of girdle distribution or distributed to a limb in root fashion. It may be accentuated by coughing, sneezing or straining and unrelieved by simple analgesics. The rate at which paraplegia develops varies considerably; in some it is abrupt, in others it is spread over several weeks. Lumbar puncture and radiography are essential, but a long search for a primary lesion should not be undertaken in the face of advancing paralysis. Normal manometry should not be taken to imply that myelography is unnecessary. When compression is suspected laminectomy should be undertaken, as in the case of epidural abscess.

Paraplegia of Insidious Onset

Many affections of the spinal cord develop slowly and some remain undiagnosed during life. Syphilitic paraplegias are now rare and subacute combined degeneration (vitamin B_{12} neuropathy) is uncommon. Clinical vigilance in respect of these two causes of spinal cord disease is still necessary and the possibility of compression paraplegia must always be entertained. Cervical spondylosis with myelopathy is important to recognize because it may be mistakenly confused with such conditions as multiple sclerosis, motor neurone disease and spinal tumour.

A chronic paraplegia may be predominantly flaccid as in motor neurone disease, lesions of the cauda equina, peripheral neuropathy and myopathy, subjects which we have previously discussed. Spastic paraplegia and tetraplegia may arise from compression by tumour or cervical spondylosis or from a degenerative lesion such as amyotrophic lateral sclerosis or multiple sclerosis. In many cases there is spasticity and ataxia of the affected limbs as in multiple sclerosis and subacute combined degeneration. Thus ataxia may be cerebellar or sensory in character, or both.

Cervical Spondylosis

This is a condition, common in middle-aged and elderly people, which is characterized by degeneration of the cervical intervertebral discs and the production of osteophytes which tend to project into the intervertebral foramina and the spinal canal. Its particular importance lies in the fact that involvement of the spinal cord and nerve roots may occur in a silent manner. Neurological signs may precede the development of symptoms. A paraplegia may insidiously develop with or without symptoms referable to involvement of the cervical segments. If the weakness of the lower limbs follows a story of repeated pain and stiffness in the neck and upper limbs, cervical spondylosis is naturally suspected. But in many cases movements of the neck remain painless and free while referred cervical root pain and paraesthesiae may not have been experienced or else they occurred sometime previously and are not recalled. The paraplegia is not always steadily progressive but may come to a halt for a time or even improve, but there is a general tendency to deterioration and a fall or a blow may aggravate the disability.

In many cases there are signs of a mid-cervical cord lesion, as previously described. In others the level of the lesion may not be apparent from clinical examination and myelography is essential. An atheromatous vertebral artery, in its ascent through the transverse foramina of the cervical vertebrae, is liable to compression by osteophytes particularly on movements of the neck. In elderly subjects, to the radicular and cord signs of the disease, may therefore be added symptoms of intermittent brain stem or cerebellar ischaemia. The predominant clinical feature lies in the hyperactivity of the lower limb reflexes, often with extensor plantar responses. Spasticity often exceeds weakness. On the sensory side considerable variation is met with. In some there is merely some impairment of tactile sensation in the fingers, but in others a degree of postural loss which makes for much clumsiness in use of the hands. In the lower limbs signs of posterior column disturbance are common and are associated with ataxia of stance and gait.

In attributing paraplegia to cervical spondylosis with myelopathy there are obvious difficulties. Radiographic evidence of cervical spondylosis is insufficient for it is common and may be found in a person with undoubted multiple sclerosis, amyotrophic lateral sclerosis, spinal tumour or with subacute combined degeneration. Each case must be considered on its merits; it is not a diagnosis which should be based on a radiograph.

In the differential diagnosis from multiple sclerosis the absence of remissions and of any evidence implicating the cranial nerves together with the late age of onset, are features in favour of cervical myelopathy. But we know only too well that multiple sclerosis beginning in middle life often confines itself to the spinal cord in a manner suggesting compression paraplegia from spondylosis or tumour. On the other hand, many cases previously labelled multiple sclerosis, which remained more or less stationary for many years, have been shown to be due to cervical myelopathy. In amyotrophic lateral sclerosis fasciculation is usually widespread; if present in cervical spondylosis it tends to remain confined to one or more muscle groups. It is often said that global atrophy of the small muscles of the hand does not occur in spondylosis as they are largely innervated by C.8 and T.1 segments. But it does occur, although it may not reach gross proportions, and is presumably a result of vascular charges in the cord below the lesion. Cervical spondylosis is not uncommonly associated with the carpal tunnel syndrome. A cervical cord tumour may not only be clinically indistinguishable from cervical myelopathy, the myelographic appearances may be identical. The manner in which the spinal cord is damaged in cervical spondylosis is not clearly understood. There are mechanical and vascular factors involved, but whatever the mechanism, in my own experience, it is the sagittal diameter of the spinal canal which has seemed so important. A person with a narrow canal who develops spondylosis is in more danger of myelopathy than one possessing a roomy canal. The spondylotic process itself tends to narrow the canal as well as the intervertebral foramina.

Multiple Sclerosis

If cervical spondylosis is the commonest cause of paraplegia over the age of 50, multiple sclerosis remains the commonest cause before that age. Practically nothing is known of the cause of this enigmatic demyelinating disorder of the nervous system, except that it is rare in tropical climates. It may present acutely, subacutely, remittently or in an insidious form; spinal paraplegia may be its first and is usually its terminal feature. Few diseases are so puzzling in the diversity of symptoms and signs and in the unpredictability of its course. Essentially a disease of the white matter of the central nervous system, there are nevertheless few neurological symptoms and signs which it may not produce. Involvement of the anterior horn cells is exceptional so that, fortunately, muscular atrophy is not a feature of the disease. Neither is pain, usually, with the exception of trigeminal neuralgia and that resulting from flexor spasms. The peripheral nervous system is virtually spared, but at times the symptoms and signs in the distal portions of a limb may suggest some form of neuritis. It is indeed simpler to state what is uncommon or rare in this disorder than to list its many features. Among the cranial nerves those that are usually spared are the lower cranial pairs; the vestibular portion of the eighth nerve may be affected, but deafness is rare. In a spinal paraplegia multiple sclerosis is likely if there is: (1) a history of remission and relapse; (2) evidence in the history or on physical examination of affection of the brain or cranial nerves; or (3) ataxia of gait out of proportion to the degree of motor weakness. Long before paraplegia is established, fleeting motor and sensory signs may have been experienced. They may have comprised no more than some clumsiness of the hands and a tendency to drop things, undue fatigability of the lower limbs; paraesthesiae of various forms, sometimes spreading rapidly from the lower limbs on one or both sides to the trunk. Urinary difficulties and impotence may long antedate the paraplegia. Indications that there is a supraspinal lesion or lesions may be recorded in a history of acute retrobulbar neuritis, diplopia, or in the presence of nystagmus or internuclear ophthalmoplegia. Facial numbness is common; facial weakness is not so common. It is not always possible to be certain about the significance of a jaw jerk. Nystagmus is very common and may be fine or coarse, horizontal, vertical or rotary. It may be monocular. I have seen ill-sustained, so-called 'nystagmoid jerks' too often in the early stages of this disease to ignore this sign. Sometimes the only indication of supraspinal involvement lies in the mood of the patient or in a slight disturbance of speech. Certainly, euphoria can be mistaken for optimism or courage, but there is no gainsaying that it can be very striking. In its early stages dysarthria is rarely noticed by the patient. Most commonly seen in young adults there is no particular group of symptoms and signs nor any laboratory test which is diagnostic of multiple sclerosis. The disease is often suspected for a time; it reveals its identity by its behaviour. It is the manner in which its manifestations are displayed and not the manifestations themselves that are so characteristic.

But in the middle-aged person the story may be rather different. It may present as an insidious paraplegia and distinction from cord compression may not always be clinically possible. Myelography is essential. Cervical spondylosis and tumour may otherwise remain undisclosed. In this form of the disease the only indication that the cord lesion is a manifestation of multiple sclerosis may lie in the impairment of alternate motion rate and incoordination of an upper limb. In the lower limb also signs of ataxia should be particularly sought. Bilateral pyramidal signs are often noted at a stage when the patient is only complaining about one lower limb. There is a tendency for the abdominal reflexes to disappear when pyramidal signs are developing, but there are exceptions.

Sensory signs may be scanty at a time when sensory symptoms are a main complaint. They are usually first detected in the distal portions of a limb and are superficial in character, affecting touch and pain. Vibration and postural loss may persist for a time and then recede with the subsidence of symptoms. A sensory level on the trunk is usually indefinite, but occasionally a partial Brown-Séquard phenomenon is observed.

Lhermitte's sign, while not diagnostic of multiple sclerosis, is most commonly caused by it. It is a sensation that the patient feels when he bends his head forward. He usually describes it as a 'tingling', 'electric feeling', or 'funny sensation' which passes down his spine and perhaps into his lower limbs. It rarely passes upwards or in a reverse direction from the neck. It is seen in cervical cord tumour and spondylosis and in subacute combined degeneration of the cord. It may occur at various stages of the disease, but it is often an early and sometimes indeed, a presenting symptom. In a young man who feels it in a barber's chair it is usually due to multiple sclerosis; in a middle-aged man playing bowls, it is usually the result of cervical spondylosis.

Although scattered zones of demyelination characterize the autopsy findings, it is by no means certain that the successive episodes of clinical disorder in this disease are actually due to new plaques. The correlation of clinical and pathological findings is not always convincing. It is probable that new clinical phenomena are due to more subtle changes within the white matter of the nervous system than can be observed at autopsy. The exacerbation of symptoms by fatigue or by a rise in body temperature is too transient to suggest that demyelination is the basis for this. Blurring of vision, and even the appearance of transient scotomata to red, may be provoked by a hot bath. The symptoms of multiple sclerosis are not necessarily multiple or disseminated at any given time; examples of mono-symptomatic presentation are trigeminal neuralgia and abducens palsy, facial paresis, postural vertigo, and a progressive spastic paraplegia. In some cases, sensory symptoms are persistent and widespread and yet no objective sensory deficit can be demonstrated. It seems, therefore, that more subtle tests must be devised before early defects within the nervous system can be identified in this disease. The value of examining the visual evoked responses has already been shown. A delay in cortical responses may be demonstrable when ordinary methods of examination reveal no evidence of lesions in the visual pathways. Transient conduction defects in the spinal cord might be similarly disclosed.

Multiple sclerosis has been called 'the great imitator'. In many instances, of course, the remitting nature of the multiple complaints points only too readily to the disease. Yet it may mimic other diseases very closely. In adolescence it may present in a manner resembling acute encephalitis. A cerebral tumour may be suspected because of the development of focal epilepsy, or a progressive hemiparesis. An insidious spastic tetraplegia, associated with cerebellar signs may produce a picture very difficult to distinguish, without myelography, from a tumour at the foramen magnum. The spinal demyelination of multiple sclerosis may be clinically indistinguishable from spinal cord tumour. Lastly, in its early stages, it may be confused with neurosis. Ill-defined complaints of tiredness, dizziness, periodic unsteadiness, fleeting visual symptoms and, in the male, impotence, may for some years precede any neurological signs. Evidence of emotional instability may seem to confirm the suspicion of 'hysteria'. It is a mode of presentation of the disease which may fox the most wary clinician. When a patient with such complaints actually expresses a fear of multiple sclerosis it should not be lightly dismissed. The patient may be right.

Spinal Cord Tumour

Unfortunately, the commonest form of spinal tumour, the meningioma or neurinoma, is a much less common cause of paraplegia than multiple sclerosis and cervical spondylosis. Unfortunately, for their removal can lead to complete recovery. Symptoms almost invariably develop slowly and steadily; it is surprising how often the history in tumour is about 18 months. Symptoms rarely appear in an acute manner, although I have known a case in which the onset consisted of sudden paresis of the legs when the patient was running for a bus. Remissions are certainly not a feature of the paralysis of the lower limbs, although they can occur. The less common intramedullary tumour, usually some form of glioma, presents in the same general way as those which compress the cord.

Symptoms and signs of a local lesion at the spinal cord comprise those resulting from involvement of structures at the level of the lesion and those following interruption of tracts in the cord. There are several ways in which root and tract symptoms and signs may develop.

Pain may of course be of cord or root origin. Root pains are sharp, shooting and superficial and tend to radiate in a clear fashion. They may be aggravated or precipitated by coughing, sneezing and straining and by certain movements. They may be relieved by rest. Pain of cord origin is different in both its quality and its location. It may be entirely aching in character, or described as deep and boring. There may be a constant burning sensation, and night pain is not uncommon. Pain of this character in the back and lower limbs may result from cord compression and not from lumbosacral root involvement.

Most commonly root pains are followed by ipsilateral motor and contralateral sensory disturbances. Unilateral sensory symptoms may be followed by gradual loss of contralateral power and sensation. There may be spinal pain of long duration before cord symptoms appear. Whatever the mode of presentation, the steady loss of power and sensation in the lower limbs, with loss of sphincter control, is the essential feature. In intramedullary tumours dissociated sensory loss is likely to be found, unilateral or bilateral, suspended in distribution, or below the level of the lesion. There is less likely to be root pain in the intramedullary tumour and a greater likelihood of muscular atrophy from involvement of anterior horn cells.

The level of the tumour in the spinal canal will determine the ultimate extent of the motor and sensory paralysis. Its position within the canal, in relation to the spinal cord, may influence the clinical picture. The benign extramedullary neurinoma and meningioma is most commonly seen in the thoracic region. The intramedullary glioma is most commonly found in the lumbar cord.

In general, a midline extramedullary tumour tends to cause symmetrical motor and sensory loss. If the tumour is posteriorly placed, ataxia from posterior column disturbance is likely to develop. A tumour lying anterior to the spinal cord may exert a predominantly motor disturbance, without pain. Posterolateral compression produces a partial Brown-Séquard disturbance. When superimposed vascular changes or contralateral pressure effects occur at the level of the lesion, clinical localization of the tumour may be impossible.

The most important indications of tumour are root pain, progressive paralysis and a sensory level. An elevated spinal fluid protein, a positive Queckenstedt test and a myelographic block complete the picture.

Vitamin B$_{12}$ Neuropathy

Formerly a familiar disease to clinicians, subacute combined degeneration of the cord is a less satisfactory name than vitamin B$_{12}$ neuropathy, because we now know that the brain and the peripheral nerves are liable to be implicated. It is one of the few 'degenerative' conditions of the spinal cord about the origin of which something is known. It is a nutritional disorder, due to deficiency of vitamin B$_{12}$. It usually arises through lack of intrinsic factor in the stomach but it may also be a manifestation of malabsorption from the ileum or, rarely, from an inadequate diet. The modern medical student will see few patients with frank pernicious anaemia and paralysed lower limbs. He is unlikely to see a strict vegetarian who takes no dairy products, but he may see a chronic psychotic who takes no food of animal origin or an elderly person with declining vitamin B$_{12}$ reserves, on an inadequate diet. He is more likely to see vitamin B$_{12}$ deficiency arising in a patient long after gastrectomy or gastro-enterostomy or in one with strictures, blind loops, short circuits or multiple diverticula of the small intestine.

The student may not encounter an example of the classical combination of anaemia, glossitis and progressive ataxic paraparesis. He is more likely to be confronted with an underweight individual with one or more laparotomy scars on his abdomen and symptoms of 'neuritis' in his lower extremities; or a confused elderly person, unsteady and weak, who is not quite sure when the illness began. The 'lemon-yellow' or 'biscuit-coloured' pallor and the smooth red tongue, the low fever and breathlessness are now rare in this disease.

Not all patients with a megaloblastic anaemia and signs of degeneration in the lateral and posterior columns of the spinal cord are suffering only from vitamin B$_{12}$ deficiency. In idiopathic steatorrhoea and in disease of the small intestine, the neurological disorder may not respond satisfactorily to treatment with vitamin B$_{12}$. There must be some other deficiency as well.

In the classical case the patient first complains of disturbance of sensation in the lower limbs—pins and needles, tingling, numbness in the toes, later in the feet and legs and in the fingers and hands. They are felt first and most persistently in the lower limbs. Numbness and clumsiness of finer movements of the fingers leads to difficulty in holding objects and in buttoning up clothes or in sewing or writing. At this stage of the illness the signs may be indistinguishable from those of a mild chronic polyneuritis. The gait becomes unsteady, the legs weak and the muscles flaccid and hypotonic. Signs of pyramidal disorder are seldom marked in the early stages, although examination may reveal extensor plantar responses. Sensory loss of varying degree, in a characteristic glove and stocking distribution, is a frequent finding. The ankle jerks are reduced or absent and there is profound loss of postural sensibility in the limbs and pelvis. Vibration sensation may be absent below the lumbar spine; tenderness of the calves is inconstant. Bladder disturbances are relatively late in appearance, but impotence is an early symptom in the male. There may be associated mental symptoms, progressive enfeeblement of intellect and memory or episodes of confusion or paranoia. The patient with chronic vitamin B$_{12}$ deficiency is often difficult and uncooperative but frank dementia is not often seen. Optic atrophy is rare.

When vitamin B$_{12}$ deficiency is suspected in a neurological disorder, it cannot be excluded merely because the blood film and bone marrow are reported as normal; the changes may be very slight and overlooked. The serum B$_{12}$ level is usually below 80 $\mu\mu$g./ml. It is still not understood why so many of these patients are not anaemic.

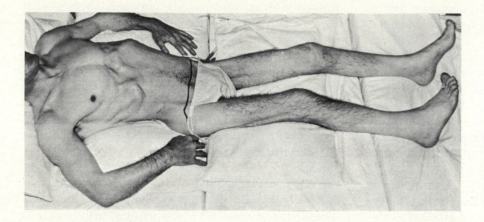

539. Traumatic paraplegia
A crush injury to the lower thoracic spine in a mining accident. Note injury to ribs. Sensory level at T.12. Eleven years after the accident. (In Figs. 539 to 544 the sensory level is indicated by a line.)

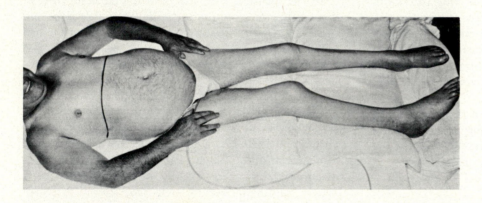

540. Paraplegia in acute transverse myelopathy
Sudden onset of paralysis of legs as he walked across a room. An acute spontaneous vascular lesion at T.7. One year after onset.

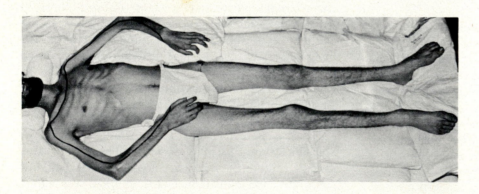

541. Traumatic tetraplegia
Direct injury to neck. Sensory level on trunk at T.1. Atrophic paralysis of small muscles of hands (T.1). Impaired movements of abduction of the shoulders and flexion of the elbows (C.5–6). Six months after accident.

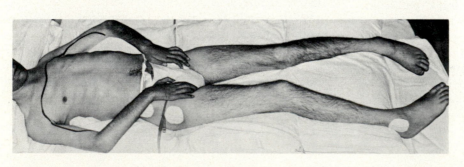

542. Traumatic tetraplegia
Motor cycle accident. Fracture dislocation of C.4–5. Sensory level at T.1–2. Four years after accident. (Courtesy of Dr. D. R. Thomas.)

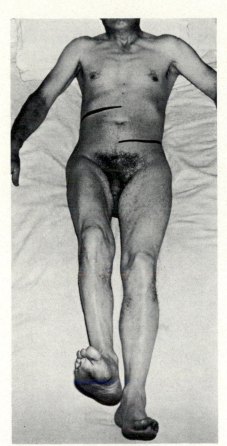

543. Spinal cord tumour
Brown-Séquard phenomenon in a T.8 meningioma on the right side. The right limb was weak, spastic, with hyperactive reflexes and an extensor plantar response; postural and vibration loss; sensory level at T.8. His left leg was much stronger but there was spinothalamic sensory loss to T.11. He is trying to raise his right leg.

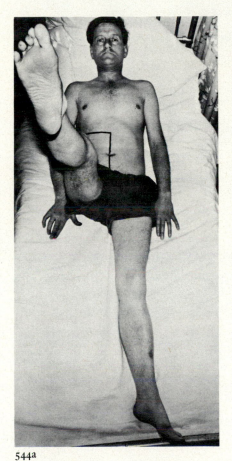

544a

544. Spinal cord tumour
Brown-Séquard phenomenon in a C.2 meningioma on the left side. The left lower limb was weak and spastic; both knee and ankle jerks were hyperactive and there was ankle clonus on the left side. Both plantar responses were flexor. The abdominal reflexes were absent. The arm

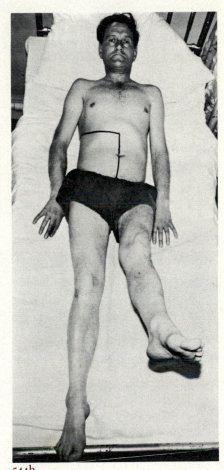

544b

reflexes were hyperactive and there were brisk finger jerks on each side. There was loss of sensation in the right lower limb and the trunk to T.7, mainly affecting appreciation of pain and temperature. His right leg was strong (*a*) but he could only raise his left leg a short distance (*b*).

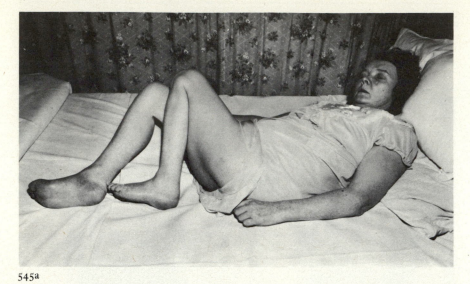

545a

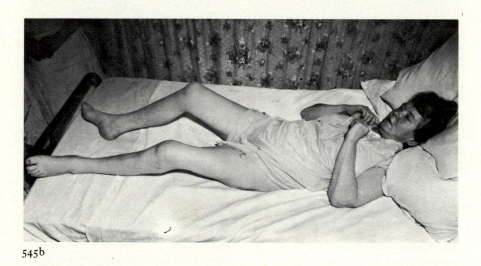

545b

545. Multiple sclerosis
Paraplegia in flexion. (*a*) Before intrathecal
phenol injection; (*b*) improved posture of
the limbs 4 weeks later.

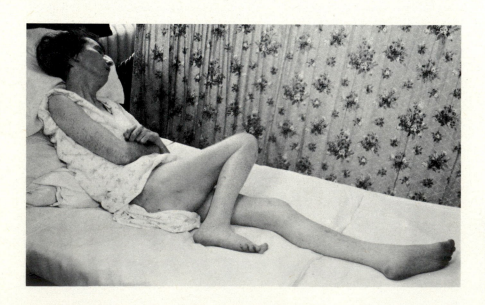

546. Multiple sclerosis
Repeated flexor spasms of the right leg. A
persisting flexion reflex ultimately results
in the limb remaining in the flexed posture
for increasing intervals. The right leg in
this case could still be passively extended.

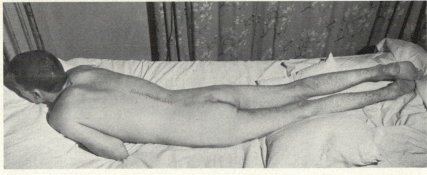

547a

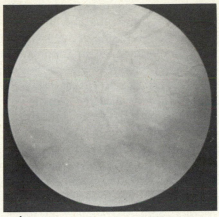

547b

547. Traumatic paraplegia D.12–L.1; bilateral papilloedema
Mining accident; fracture dislocation at D.12–L.1. Open reduction and plate fixation the same day. Moderate paraplegia. Five weeks later blurring of vision, transient diplopia. Gross bilateral papilloedema. Skull X-ray, E.E.G. and CSF normal. No explanation forthcoming. Optic discs returned to normal in 3 months. Two years later slight residual paraparesis.

548. An early walking aid
'Go-cart' used by paraplegics at the hospital of Bicêtre, Paris, for many years. (From *Lectures on Diseases of the Spinal Cord* by Pierre Marie, 1892.)

Agnosia and Apraxia

It is not uncommon to find that a patient in bed because of a neurological disorder seems to be confused, clumsy or relatively helpless, although he is conscious, speaks normally and is not paralysed. His difficulties may arise from the presence of agnosia or apraxia.

AGNOSIA

This is a defect of recognition which may be primarily tactile, visual or auditory. While the patient can feel with his hands, see and hear, he fails to appreciate the significance of the sensory stimulus. The patient with tactile agnosia, or astereognosis, cannot recognize a familiar object placed in his hands if his eyes are closed. In visual agnosia there is impairment of recognition of familiar objects, symbols or persons. In auditory agnosia he cannot appreciate the significance of well known sounds. Agnosia is usually found in only one of these spheres of sensory appreciation. In astereognosis, for example, the object in the hand which cannot be identified when the eyes are closed is immediately recognized when they are open. In visual agnosia, a patient may not be able to recognize a penknife by sight, but may identify it at once when handling it. In auditory agnosia the sound of a telephone, a voice or music may only be appreciated when touch or vision come to the patient's assistance.

Visual agnosia may lead to difficulties in spatial orientation. There may be defective visual localization of objects on one side of the visual field; agnosia of one half of the immediate environment; loss of topographical memory, so that objects are not seen, mislaid or lost; or the patient may lose himself in familiar surroundings.

In autotopagnosia the patient has difficulty in perceiving or identifying the various parts of his body; he may be unaware or deny the existence of the left half of his body. Autotopagnosia is often associated with anosognosia in which the patient is unable to appreciate a disability such as hemiplegia or blindness.

Visual agnosia arises from a lesion in the parieto-occipital area, particularly in the left hemisphere of right-handed persons. In auditory agnosia the responsible lesion is in the temporal lobe of the dominant hemisphere. In tactile agnosia the lesion is in the posterior part of the opposite parietal lobe. In anosognosia and autotopagnosia there is usually a left hemiplegia in a right-handed person.

These various forms of agnosia are usually encountered in middle-aged patients suffering from tumour, cerebral arteriosclerosis or some degenerative disease of the brain. Consequently they may only be identified in an early stage of illness; they cannot be recognized when deterioration has progressed, but points in the history may indicate they were responsible for certain of the patient's difficulties. Clumsiness of movement and in handling objects, disregard or inattention may have been suspected; failure of topographical memory may explain why the patient was 'losing himself', unable to find his car parked in the city centre, or losing his way home. Witnesses will say that he appeared to be 'confused' and if the latter is viewed as a disturbance of behaviour and not one of consciousness, an agnosic handicap may be missed. In the hospital ward defects of recognition may be first noticed by the nursing staff who may report that the patient cannot tell the time on the ward clock, or identify his bed or belongings, or recognize the ward sister; he may lose himself in a corridor or another department of the hospital.

APRAXIA

Whereas in agnosia we have a defect of recognition, in apraxia the difficulty is in execution. Thus, with unimpaired perception and in the absence of motor and sensory paralysis and ataxia, the patient is unable to perform certain familiar activities, either spontaneously or on request. Apraxia may affect movements of the face, trunk and limbs. The patient may be quite unaware of his disability until it is revealed during formal examination.

In facial apraxia the patient may be unable to carry out such voluntary movements as closing his eyes, whistling, or putting out his tongue. In upper limb apraxia he has trouble in handling common objects, such as a fountain pen, comb or toothbrush. He may find difficulty in extracting his spectacles from their case and putting them on, in winding his watch, in replacing his dentures or in dressing and undressing. These difficulties, in themselves, may be quietly tolerated for some time, the patient's main complaints being concerned with such symptoms as headache or failing memory. Confronted with a packet of cigarettes and a box of matches he may be quite unable to light up. There may be disturbance in special manual skills such as writing, drawing and construction. In constructional apraxia the patient is unable to lay out simple geometrical figures, such as a triangle, square or cross, with matchsticks. Apraxia of the lower limbs may mimic weakness or ataxia; the patient hesitates, he appears unable to lift one foot in front of the other and in bed he moves the legs clumsily. In apraxia of the trunk the patient has difficulty in seating himself on a chair or lavatory seat, in turning over in bed or on getting on to an examination couch.

As with agnosia the lesions associated with apraxia are frequently diffuse, as in tumours and cerebral atrophy; the topographical significance of apraxia may be difficult to determine. The corpus callosum, the parietal lobes and the premotor areas tend to be involved. A lesion of the dominant hemisphere may produce bilateral apraxia; a lesion in the right posterior parietal region may cause contralateral apraxia; a lesion of the corpus callosum in a right-handed individual may cause apraxia on the left side. In apraxia for dressing the lesion is usually in the right parieto-occipital region.

The patient with a parietal lesion may be ataxic, hemiparetic or have profound astereognosis. In parietal hemiparesis the limbs are often hypotonic rather than spastic and the plantar response may be absent; the limb muscles are often flaccid and may even waste as in a lower motor neurone lesion. There is often a disinclination to move the affected limb, rather than actual paralysis.

549. Apraxia: left parietal glioma ◁
Presented with a tube of toothpaste and a toothbrush she was unable to brush her teeth. The only thing she did correctly was to unscrew the cap from the tube. She made many errors and her difficulties are obvious.

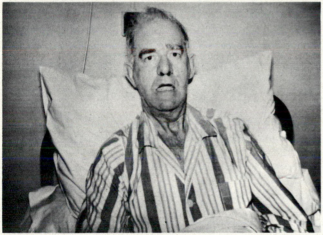

550a

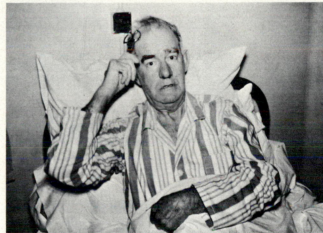

550b

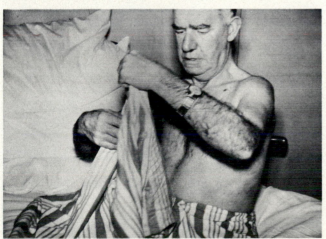

550c

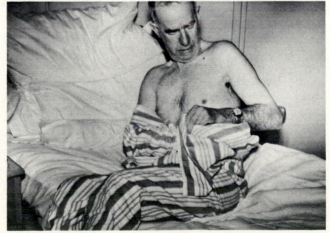

550d

550. Apraxia: right parieto-occipital glioma

(a) His upper dentures have not fallen; he has inserted his lower dentures upside-down.

(b) Presented with a scissors and asked to use them he attempts to comb his hair.
(c) and (d) Apraxia for dressing. His

pyjama jacket was removed and returned to him; he was requested to put it on; he had great difficulty and became irate.

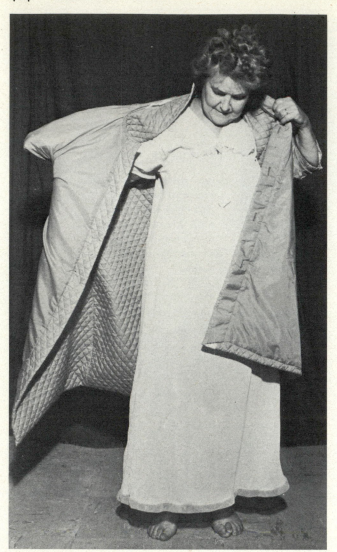

551. Presenile dementia; dressing apraxia △

Age 60 years. Failing memory, concentration and orientation. Unable to cook and shop and great difficulty in dressing and undressing, which caused her great distress. Unassisted she would take an hour to get up in the morning or retire to bed at night. Physical examination negative; no evidence of hypothyroidism or vitamin B_{12} deficiency. CSF normal. E.E.G. showed diffuse slow irregular delta activity. A.E.G. revealed dilatation of lateral ventricles and pooling of air over the cortex in widened sulci.

552. Right parietal glioma
Specimen of handwriting. Note the crowding into the lower right-hand corner of the page.

553. Right parieto-occipital glioma
The patient was asked to mark in the hours in a clock face and to copy a drawing of a flower, an arrow and a house. Note the neglect of the left half of the clock face, the crudity of the copies of flower and arrow and the evidence of spatial disturbance in the copy of the house.

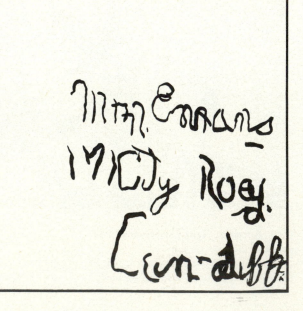

13 HYSTERIA

In the language of illness there is no word more difficult to define than 'hysteria'. There is little to be gained by attempting to do so. Freud considered it a 'conversion neurosis'; Head said it was a 'morbid mental state accompanied by physical manifestations and certain forms of aberrant conduct'. However we regard it, it has played an extraordinary role in the history of medicine. It derived its name from the view of the ancients that it resulted from disorder of the womb. Spasms of that organ caused *furor uterinus*; its upward wanderings and ascent caused 'hysterical suffocation'. Hysterical states were characterized by convulsions, paralyses and anaesthesias, but in all ages the diversity and complexity of the symptoms in hysteria were recognized. Sydenham called it 'that Proteus that cannot be laid hold of'. The modern doctor, looking for evidence of hysteria in anaesthesia of a patient's pharynx, is in some respects copying the witch-hunter of the Middle Ages, who searched for evidence of 'the devil's claw', that insensitive patch which was a certain sign of demoniacal possession. Like the modern hysteric the possessed person was unaware of her anaesthesia and the suggestibility of the hysteric was one of the features which early led to the belief that the illness was a neurosis.

We may feel we are on safer ground when we talk of the 'hysterical personality' or 'the manifestations of hysteria'. The former we regard as characterized by emotional immaturity which leads to over-dependence, attention-seeking, histrionic behaviour and undue suggestibility. Such people are prone to hysterical forms of illness, but it is generally agreed that not all people so afflicted show these particular traits of personality.

The major manifestations of hysteria, convulsions, paralyses, contractures and anaesthesias are now less common. Moreover, we know that such manifestations are not always the outward expression of some emotional conflict; they may arise from injury or disease of the body, including the brain, or they may be a manifestation of a psychotic illness.

In some respects the difficulties which face us when we talk of hysteria we also encounter in 'hypochondriasis'. There may be no such disease as hysteria or hypochondriasis but there are patients who behave hysterically or in an hypochondriacal manner. It may well be that the person who complains endlessly about pain in the head, neck or abdomen is suffering from some form of anxiety or depression. The distinction between 'functional' and 'organic' is clearly artificial but not wholly avoidable. A neurosis may be as much an expression of some inborn constitutional defect as epilepsy.

Pain is one of the commonest symptoms and many physicians believe it can be hysterical in nature. It is common in the face and head and is resistant to treatment. It is usually described by the patient in the language of metaphor and simile. On this interpretation of pain there is wide divergence of opinion. Thus a famous neurosurgeon can write 'I should record that after a long experience of patients with facial neuralgia, I do not think I have seen one case of truly psychogenic facial pain'. Others, myself included, would say that psychogenic facial pains are much commoner than trigeminal neuralgia (FIG. 569).

But all agree that the hysteric may describe symptoms and exhibit signs which at times make it impossible to distinguish between mental and physical illness. When, in addition, it is appreciated that the abnormality of behaviour which we call hysteria may result from organic disease of the nervous system, the difficulties and dangers confronting the physician are obvious. The modern student is not likely often to encounter flagrant examples of hysteria reminiscent of those described in the textbooks 50 years ago. The declining incidence of hysteria in this century was particularly revealed during the Second World War. Hysteria was such a problem in the First World War that Sir William Osler was able to write that 'our hospitals swarm with cases of aphonia, dumbness, deafness, amnesia, anaesthesia, spasms, tremors and with the subjects of hitherto unknown or rarely seen incoordinations'. It is as if hysteria was once a primitive and crude way in which the patient demonstrated his distress and sought relief, whereas nowadays things are subtler.

We should look upon hysteria as a clinical phenomenon which may occur both in health and in disease. In the young person, hysterical symptoms are generally seen against a background of physical health and without overt evidence that the pre-morbid personality was in any way exceptional. The hysterical person's capacity for dissociation is usually only disclosed by the attack itself. On the other hand, in the middle-aged or elderly person the development of hysterical symptoms should always alert the clinician to the possibility of some other illness—neurological or psychological.

HYSTERICAL PARALYSIS

This varies considerably both in degree and distribution. In the face it is rare, although hysterical ptosis may be seen; paralysis of the muscles of the eyeballs, the face and of the tongue do not occur. Paresis of the cervical muscles with resulting drooping of the head on the chest or difficulty in elevating the head from the pillow is occasionally seen. Paralysis of the trunk muscles is rare. Thus in hysterical paralysis it is usually a matter of weakness or complete loss of power in one or more limbs. Probably the commonest variety are those which result in paralysis of one upper limb or paresis of both lower limbs.

If the patient is ambulant, the manner in which he moves, dresses and undresses, and mounts an examination couch should be noted. In hysterical hemiparesis the face is not affected and the paretic lower limb is dragged rather than circumducted in walking. In organic hemiparesis the arm is often more affected than the lower limb; in hysterical hemiparesis it is often the reverse. In hysterical paralysis the patient appears to be more helpless, making little effort to overcome his disability and relying wholly on others to assist him. His calm unconcern contrasts with the distress of the patient with organic paralysis.

In hysteria we are not dealing with paralysis of individual muscles but with paralysis of movements. The hysteric may complain that all movements at one joint are affected, for example, at the knee or shoulder. The object of the examination, therefore, must be to note the distribution of the paralysis, the muscles affected and to discover whether the patient can still use the affected muscles to perform movements which he does not realize entail their use.

The muscle tone of the affected limb is usually normal. Sometimes it is unduly flaccid as in paralysis of an upper limb, while in the case of the lower limb excessive rigidity may be present. The limb may be held firmly in an odd position and when attempts are made to alter it the resistance encountered may be remarkable and in proportion to the efforts of the examiner to overcome it. Grimacing and protests of pain usually accompany this resistance. There is no true muscular atrophy but in long-standing defects slight diffuse wasting of the limb is often seen. There are no pathological reflexes and the common general hyperactivity of the deep reflexes is usually shown, not so much by the speed of response, as in organic paralysis, but in the range of movement. Other limbs may take part in the 'reflex' response. In the upper limb there is no sign comparable to the Babinski sign of pyramidal disease affecting the lower limb. Ankle clonus in hysteria is usually poorly sustained and irregular and jerky.

When testing muscle strength in hysteria, it is often evident that the patient is not exerting himself. A request to grasp the examiner's hand is usually accompanied by a 'shunting of effort', so that the muscles of the upper limb, shoulder and face are brought into powerful play, but the fingers of the affected hand remain limp and useless. The grimacing, clenching of the teeth and holding of the breath are characteristic. When the patient is in bed a request to raise a limb is followed by a preliminary ritual in which the patient takes a breath, holds it, clutches the side of the bed with his upper limbs and strains with effort before finally collapsing back, puffing and 'exhausted'. If the affected limb is weak but not paralysed and the patient is requested to resist a passive movement by the examiner, his cooperation is short-lived and he suddenly gives up.

The examiner should look for discrepancies which indicate that movements and not muscles are paralysed. Thus a patient in bed who is apparently unable to dorsiflex or plantarflex his feet may be able to walk on his heels or toes. A latissimus dorsi muscle which fails to contract on request to depress an arm, may do so when the patient coughs. When a lower limb is paralysed a test devised by Babinski is often very useful. A patient, lying in bed, is asked to raise himself to a sitting position, while holding his arms across his abdomen. Normally, to do so the heels are pressed into the bed. In organic hemiplegia there is involuntary elevation of the paretic limb, as the heel cannot be pressed downwards. In hysteria the sound leg may be raised, the paralysed one pressing into the bed. If the examiner's hand is placed under the heel of a paralysed leg in hysteria, there may be no response when the patient is requested to press upon the observer's hand; but when he is asked to raise his sound limb, pressure may be felt.

But aside from these observations and devices which suggest exaggeration, deceit, pretence of effort and cooperation, and discrepancies in muscle action, it must be admitted the most striking feature of hysterical paralysis lies in the contraction of antagonistic muscles in the performance of a movement. There may be little response in the prime movers and a considerable one in adjacent antagonists. Thus, when the patient is requested to abduct an arm at the shoulder a visible contraction of his pectoral muscles may be seen. A request to flex the elbow is attended by a powerful contraction of the triceps, making the movement impossible. In testing the grip of a paralysed hand, the contraction of the forearm extensors may be seen and palpated.

In hysterical paraplegia the sphincters are usually un-affected but occasionally transient retention of urine may occur in the female.

HYSTERICAL ANAESTHESIA

Loss of sensation in a limb or limbs, or of one half of the body, is common in hysteria. At the first examination, however, the patient may be quite unaware of this anaesthesia. The complaint may be only of headache, for example, and the hysterical hemianaesthesia is dis-covered or induced during routine examination. On the other hand the complaint may be of weakness or paraly-sis of a limb which, on examination, proves to be anaes-thetic. Certainly the suggestibility of the hysteric is well shown in sensory testing; anaesthesia of the nose, pharynx or umbilicus may be induced in many cases.

As with paralysis the degree and extent of the sensory loss varies greatly. Most commonly it is a limb, or a portion of a limb, which is anaesthetic. The zone of anaesthesia commonly extends upwards to one of the joints—knee or elbow, hip or shoulder. The upper limit of the sensory loss encircles a limb and it may vary considerably from one examination to the next. It thus does not conform to any organic distribution of peri-pheral nerve, nerve root, or spinal nerve. When there is a glove-and-stocking distribution of sensory loss, the upper limit is abrupt, not gradual, as in polyneuritis. When the sensory loss is confined to one side of the body, the zone of demarcation is at the midline or to the anaesthetic side of it in hysteria, whereas in organic lesions, owing to the bilateral overlapping representation of midline structures, the line of demarcation is slightly to the normal side of the midline. The hysteric may allege that he cannot feel the vibration of a tuning fork on the anaesthetic side of his skull or sternum; bone conduction makes this impossible on an organic basis.

All modalities of sensation may suffer in hysteria, but light touch and cutaneous pain are most commonly lost. At the first examination the appreciation of temperature, passive movements and vibration may be unimpaired, but with repeated examination these may also come to be involved. True dissociated anaesthesia in which there is retention of tactile sense with loss of superficial pain and temperature sensations, is uncommon. The patient's notion of sensation is that it comprises only touch, pain and temperature; he does not understand the signi-cance of vibration and postural loss. Thus, he cannot know that with complete loss of vibration and posture in his fingers he would be unable to identify an object in his hands when his eyes are closed, nor perform skilled movement with those fingers, as in tying a knot, or

buttoning a jacket in a normal fashion. He would not know that his numbness should be accompanied by clumsiness.

In practice, of course, hysterical paralysis of motor and sensory functions may accompany or even mask an underlying organic disability. Particularly does this apply in cases of accident neurosis. An obvious ulnar nerve injury is accompanied by sensory loss which extends on the inner side of the forearm as far as the elbow; numbness of the whole limb may accompany an injury to the common peroneal nerve. Naturally, the tests we use to distinguish between hysteria and malin-gering are much the same. In sensory testing the 'Yes' and 'No' test is helpful. The patient is asked to say 'Yes' when he feels the prick of a pin and 'No' when he does not. In hysteria, at the first examination, he will say 'Yes' when he feels it and say nothing when he does not. The malingerer, on the other hand, will say 'Yes' when he feels it and 'No' when he thinks he should not. But this test is not a certain way of distin-guishing the hysteric from the malingerer and in due course the patient or claimant may say that the test con-fused him; the judge may nod in sympathy.

THE HYSTERICAL ATTACK

Normally there is little difficulty in distinguishing between an hysterical and epileptic fit. The classical sequence of the major convulsion is not seen; cyanosis of the lips, tongue biting and incontinence do not usually occur in the hysteric. The hysterical fit often begins with a period of excitement or mounting tremor and may be staged with obvious intent, as at the door of the home, or consulting room, or during a hospital ward round. The patient may slump to the ground with folded knees or fall in a dramatic fashion after a few preliminary lurches in which furniture or clothing are disturbed.

Two types of case present particular difficulty. There is the young person, usually a girl, with proven epilepsy, whose 'attacks' begin to increase in frequency and severity and remain uncontrolled by increased medica-tion. Such a patient, in hospital, often proves to have both hysterical and epileptic fits and it may be exceed-ingly difficult to know which is the more frequent. If the patient is confined to bed it may be impossible and it is best to keep the patient ambulant and to note all happen-ings. The second type of case is that in which the possi-bility of temporal lobe epilepsy arises. The patient may be unable to give a satisfactory account of the attacks and the statements of witnesses may be biased because they do not appreciate the wide variety of disturbance of consciousness and behaviour which may occur in temporal lobe epilepsy. This applies even in hospital. Only on the basis of a history should diagnosis be considered; too often elaborate tests are undertaken, including electroencephalography, without the basic data of the history ever having been obtained. Not that the distinction between hysteria and temporal lobe epilepsy will always be achieved when this is known, but in many cases it will settle the case and even serve to correctly interpret the result of some unreliable laboratory investigation.

HYSTERICAL AMNESIA

In hysterical amnesia the patient's loss of memory may be of short or long duration. It may extend over a well defined period of one or two days, the most common duration, or over a prolonged period of time. A complaint of persistent amnesia for all life events is usually spurious. Indeed, it is often impossible to prove that a period of amnesia was hysterical and not feigned. In hysterical amnesia the memory loss is rarely complete; it mainly centres around loss of memory of personal events and, at times, of personal identity. It is usually a conversion symptom related to some form of recent stress, commonly a fear of disclosure. On the other hand, the escape mechanism may be an attempt to flee from an intolerable state of anxiety or depression. There is a process of inward flight. In an hysterical fugue the patient may wander in a state of restricted awareness of time, place and identity. A fugue usually ends abruptly with a sudden realization that a long period has elapsed for which there is no memory. When an offence has been committed, loss of memory does not constitute grounds for unfitness to plead. The patient in an hysterical fugue may appear exhausted and ill, but he has usually managed to care for himself satisfactorily. Hysterical amnesia may be repeated; indeed, it has been found to be more common in those patients who have already suffered from post-concussional amnesia, as though the experience of the first episode in some way facilitated the development of the second.

Hysterical amnesia must be distinguished from the episodes of amnesia which may occur in epilepsy or encephalitis, and from transient global amnesia.

In epilepsy the amnesia is usually post-ictal and transient, but occasionally it is the principal manifestation of a temporal lobe fit. The amnesia may precede the fit. In such cases, however, features such as automatism, depersonalization and other abnormalities of behaviour are present. The amnesia is rarely the sole manifestation.

Amnesia may be an early or main manifestation of encephalitis involving the temporal lobes. This has been observed in herpes simplex encephalitis and also in acute tuberculous meningo-encephalitis.

Transient global amnesia is much commoner. It usually affects middle-aged men and begins abruptly. There is no loss of perception or of personal identity, and during the bout the patient repeatedly asks questions about where he is or what he should be doing. The retrograde amnesia may at first extend over several years, but it shrinks gradually until, after a few minutes or hours, it remains only for the period between the onset and full recovery. There is no memory of events occurring during the attack itself. During the attack, behaviour is normal. Exposure to cold, as in taking a shower or a bath or bathing in the sea, may provoke the episode. Some patients show signs of cerebrovascular disease, and there may be transient E.E.G. changes during or shortly after an attack. In all probability transient global amnesia is due to bilateral temporal lobe ischaemia, possibly consequent on vertebro-basilar disease. We may regard it as an amnesic stroke. In contrast with the young unstable person with hysterical amnesia, whose indifference may be evident, the elderly man with an amnesic stroke immediately complains of his loss of memory and, by his questions, reveals its severity.

ANOREXIA NERVOSA

Anorexia nervosa is rare in the male. It has three distinctive features: (1) a characteristic attitude towards food—determined avoidance or actual revulsion; (2) endocrine disturbance—in the female usually amenorrhoea, and in the male loss of libido and potency, with a reduced output of pituitary gonadotrophin; (3) a morbid preoccupation with ideas of obesity or of what the patient conceives should be her normal weight. The existence of centres in the hypothalamus concerned with sexual behaviour, menstruation and feeding suggests that in anorexia nervosa there may be some hypothalamic disorder. The numerous clinical signs—dry skin, lanugo hair, slow pulse, low blood pressure, ankle oedema, acrocyanosis, and reduced basal metabolic rate—are probably consequent on the nutritional deficiency. Despite this, most patients are very lively and active.

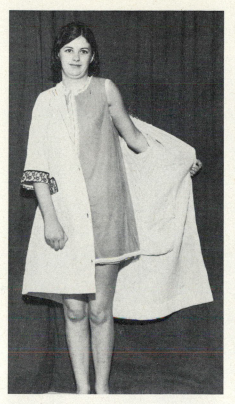

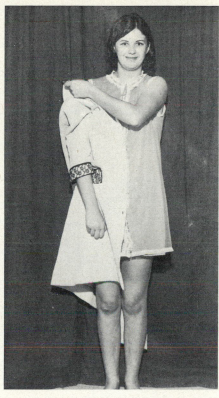

554. Hysterical paralysis of right upper limb

Age 18 years; a student. Had an episode of pain in the right hand and forearm followed by loss of use of the arm 2 years previously. Physiotherapy and recovery in 3 weeks. Recurrence 2 years later, again with onset of pain in the hand and forearm. Complete paralysis of the upper limb within 48 hours. The only voluntary movements were shrugging of the right shoulder and feeble flexion of the fingers. Brisk reflexes. Sensation: normal tactile sense, joint position sense and appreciation of cold. Loss of pain and heat appreciation to the elbow; vibration sense impaired in the hand. Rapid recovery with reassurance and firm suggestion. Note her happy indifference to her disability. The act of undressing often helps in differentiating between an organic and an hysterical paralysis of an upper limb: when it is organic the patient's efforts to overcome the disability are obvious, while the hysteric manages quite neatly with the opposite limb.

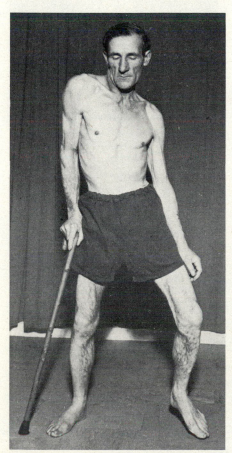

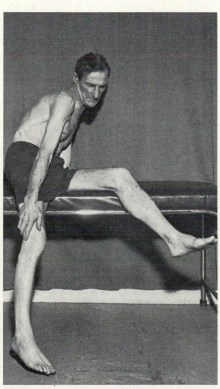

555. Hysterical paralysis of left arm and right leg

Age 46 years. Two minor injuries at work, to his right leg and left arm, on successive days 5 years previously. No work since. Paralysis of left arm and right leg with a gross stammer (post-traumatic). Face and tongue unaffected, reflexes normal, no muscular wasting. Hysterical anaesthesia of the affected limbs.
(a) Bizarre gait with immobile left arm and dragging motion of right leg. Rate of propulsion nevertheless excellent.
(b) Mounting a couch was laborious, 'exhausting', and a glass of water was always requested before he 'recovered'. No *belle indifference* here, only a fanatic determination to achieve compensation. Difficult to believe that this type of 'hysteria' is at all subconscious.

555a   555b

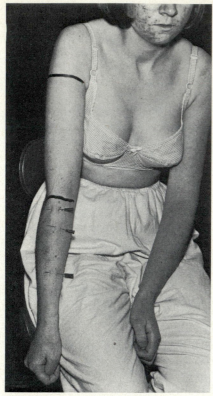

556. Hysterical anaesthesia
Acute paralysis with anaesthesia of the
right arm in a schoolgirl. Onset while
actually packing her books into her satchel
the evening before returning to school,
with 'O' level examinations only a few
days away. Note the disfiguring facial acne.
Variable upper levels of anaesthesia could
be obtained. (An over-zealous houseman
thought three needles were necessary to
demonstrate the anaesthesia!)

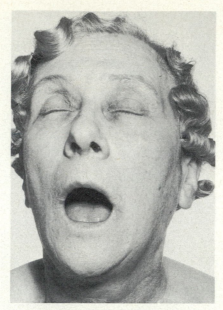

557. Hysterical blepharospasm
Age 65. Headaches, vertigo, unsteadiness
and many bizarre visual complaints,
prominent among which were 'attacks
when I can't open my eyes'. Neurological
examination was negative. After firm
closure of her eyes she was unable to open
them. Much facial grimacing during her
attempts at voluntary opening. Resisted
passive elevation of lids by the examiner.
This symptom subsided after investigation
in hospital, but other complaints
continued.

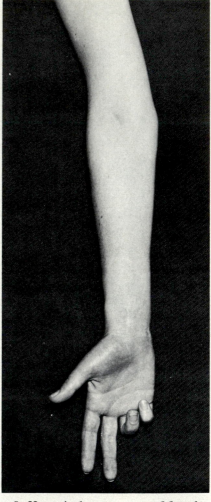

**558. Hysterical contracture of fourth
and fifth fingers**
A young woman sustained a blow to her
right elbow at work. 'I fainted with the
pain'. There were transient ulnar paraesthesiae and within a few days the fourth
and fifth fingers began to curl up. There
were no clinical or electromyographic
signs of ulnar nerve injury. Sensation was
normal. Note that flexion occurred not
only in the interphalangeal joints, but
also at the metacarpophalangeal joints.

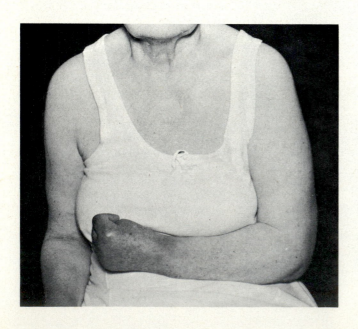

**559. Hysterical paralysis of the left
upper limb**
Duration 6 years. She had had a series of
minor operations of a gynaecological
nature and, 'my arm got weaker after
each until it was paralysed'. The arm was
held across the abdomen with the thumb
enclosed by the fingers. Note the wasting
of the left deltoid and the swollen and dis-
coloured left hand. No sensory loss. The
fist could still be opened by the examiner
but movements at the shoulder were
reduced and 'frozen'. Her husband had
noted that in her sleep her hand opened.

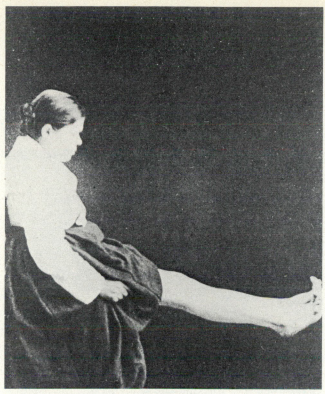

560. Hysterical fixation at the knees
An illustration from *Nouvelle iconographie de la Salpêtrière : Clinique des maladies du système nerveux*, published in 28 volumes from 1888 to 1918 under the direction of Charcot. Compare this photograph with that of my own patient in Fig. 562.

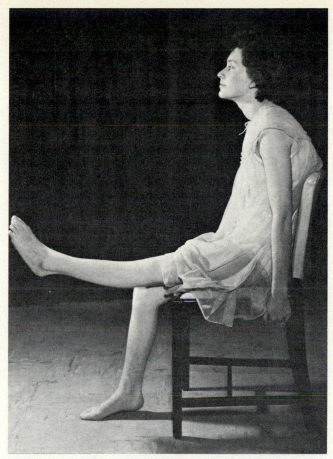

562. Hysterical fixation of the left knee
Onset with pain in the left thigh and knee at the age of 15 years. Prolonged orthopaedic treatment failed; a full range of movement of the knee was obtained under general anaesthesia. She sat and stood, supported, with the left leg rigidly extended; it could not be forcibly flexed at the knee. She spent 2 years in hospital. No cause was discovered; there had been previous psychological exploration. Treatment was aimed at the knee, not her psyche, and consisted of 'physiotherapy'. She made a complete recovery.

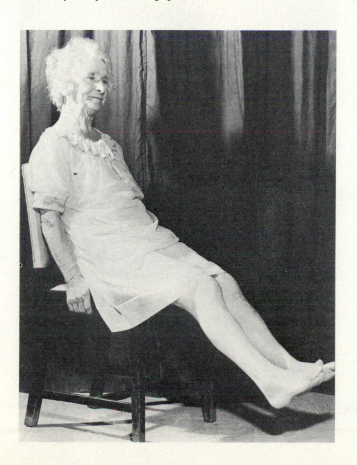

561. Hysterical fixation of both knees
Widow aged 74 years, living alone. Recent burglary. Sudden onset shortly afterwards of inability to bend her knees. First noticed on getting out of bed in the morning. No evidence of any organic neurological disorder. She could wiggle her toes and move her ankles and hips, but held her knees rigidly extended and strongly resisted strenuous efforts to flex them passively. No sensory loss; sphincters normal. When she sat in a chair her legs remained extended. The condition persisted for 2 weeks and then gradually subsided.

563. Hysterical hemiplegia (left) ▽
The histrionic pose (*a*) is evident and when asked to try and take a step forward he clutches his left trouser leg and attempts to lift the limb with his arm (*b*). One year's duration.

565. Post-traumatic hysteria ▽ ▷
An invalid for 10 years, following a 'strained back' at work, and a subsequent lumbar laminectomy 5 years later.
(*a*) Trying to sit up. Note 'effort'.
(*b*) The stiff 'railway spine' and the bizarre gait.

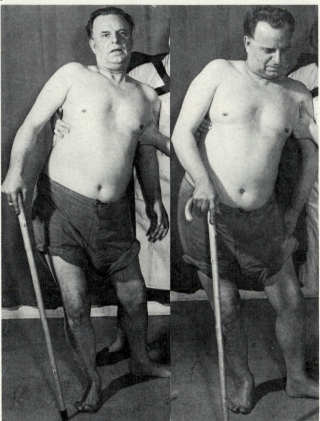

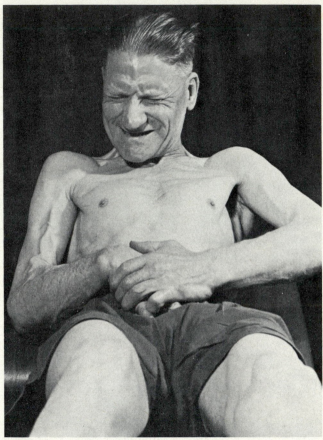

565a

564. Hysterical paraplegia ▷
Two years' duration, with pain in back and limbs. Sphincters normal, reflexes normal, limbs flaccid. No sensory loss. He is responding to a request to try to lift either foot from the bed. Note the shunting of effort; teeth clenched, eyes closed, hands clutching the mattress.

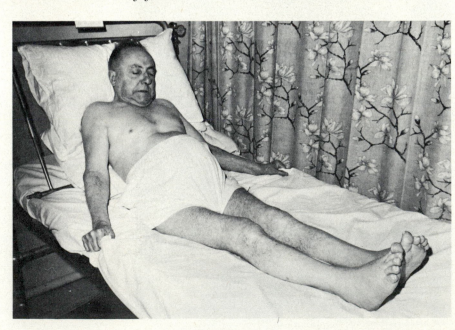

565b

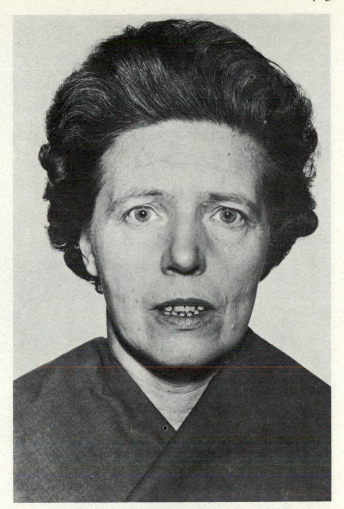

567. Hysterical trismus △
The patient was unable to open her mouth
fully for the past 6 years. Onset with acute
pain in the left temporomandibular joint
while biting a biscuit. Articulation and
swallowing were normal. She had had
manipulation of the jaw under general
anaesthesia on four occasions; repeated
injections into the left temporomandibular
joint, various wiring and bite-altering dental procedures and finally, exploration of
the right temporomandibular joint. She
also had a Caldwell-Luc operation,
months of orthopaedic treatment for
backache, 25 years' treatment, with many
operations, for pain in the right wrist and
many minor neurotic complaints. The
photograph indicates the full extent to
which she can open her mouth.

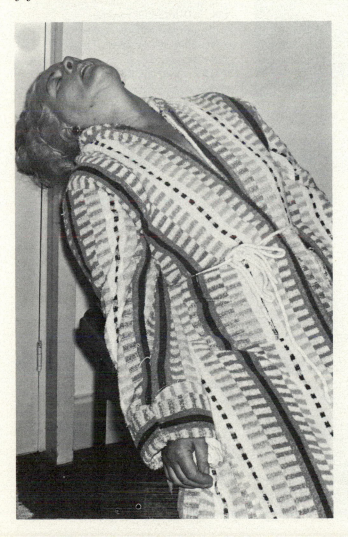

566. The hysterical fit ◁
The patient repeatedly fell backwards from
chair or examination couch in a dramatic
fashion during the first interview. Recovery was equally abrupt and followed
by laughter and tears.

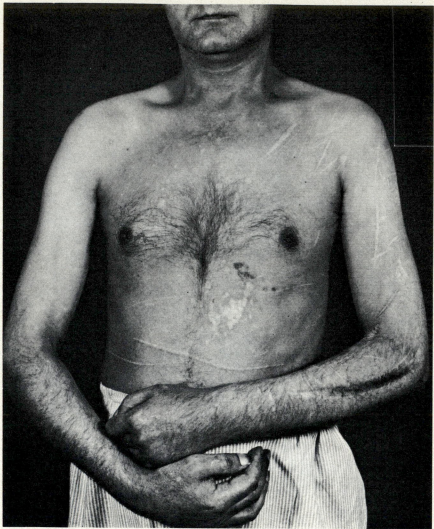

568a

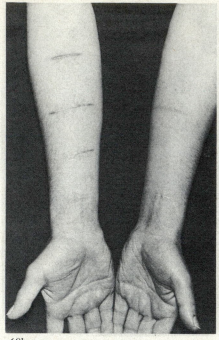

568b

568. Self-inflicted wounds
(*a*) In a patient admitted to hospital for investigation of 'epilepsy'. This was excluded.
(*b*) In a patient admitted to hospital for investigation of 'hypoglycaemic' attacks. Periods of amnesia and stupor were hysterical.

569. Psychogenic facial pain
Age 67 years. History of facial pain, usually on the left side, for 37 years. Diagnosed as trigeminal neuralgia, but no response to medical treatment. General health excellent. The history revealed that her current account of characteristic paroxysms of trigeminal neuralgia had evolved over the years after interminable consultations. At the clinic she had in her handbag 15 sets of dentures and 15 pairs of spectacles, none of which she could use because 'they brought on the pains'. In all she had 26 sets of dentures. She was happy with her pain and said cheerfully, 'I am still going to the Dental Hospital, I will fight it to the end'.
(Courtesy of Dr. J. G. Graham.)

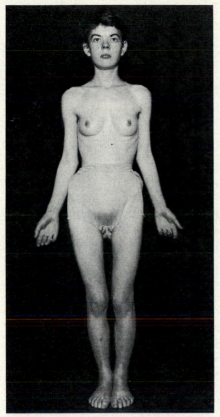

570a

570. Anorexia nervosa

Nervous malnutrition. (*a*) Profound weight loss following an attempt at slimming. Unstable family background. Feet and hands were cold and cyanosed; a growth of downy hair covered the extensor surfaces of the extremities and the dorsal region. The breasts are often well preserved in anorexia nervosa. (*b*) The anorexia nervosa in this case was only one manifestation of psychiatric illness.

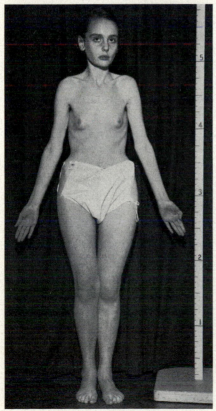

570b

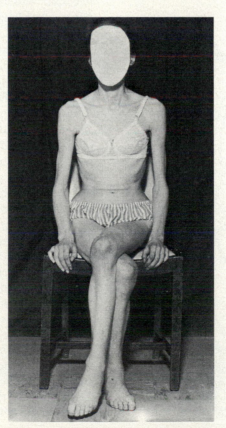

571

571. Anorexia nervosa and foot drop

Age 28 years. Left foot drop of 6 months' duration. Characteristic signs of left common peroneal palsy with positive Tinel's sign at head of left fibula and a motor conduction block. Thin, weight 5 st. 6 lb., amenorrhoea for 6 months. Profound anorexia. Facial hirsutism. Investigations revealed no evidence of steatorrhoea or malabsorption. Good response to treatment with chlorpromazine with a high protein, high calorie diet.

14 IATROGENIC NEUROLOGICAL DISORDERS

HAZARDS OF DIAGNOSTIC PROCEDURES

In this last chapter I wish to remind the student that the nervous system, in common with other systems of the human body, may be damaged during the course of investigation or treatment of a complaint. The toxic effects of many modern drugs are now well known and appreciated, and there are hazards in many procedures routinely used for the investigation of disease. But it should not be forgotten, that aside from any physical damage, there is always the possibility of psychological hurt when a patient is admitted to hospital. Common courtesy should ensure that the patient knows why he is there and why certain investigations are being undertaken. It is unlikely that the patient or his family will not be informed of the nature of a positive diagnosis, but when the results of investigations are all negative misunderstandings may arise. There may be a failure of communication between doctor and patient, misinterpretation of what has been stated, or inadequate explanation. In some patients the seeds of neurosis may be sown at this time. We all know that there are some patients who are incapable of grasping or remembering the simplest statements of information or advice, but the dangers tend to increase in this respect in proportion to the number of investigations which have been undertaken. Many of them are unpleasant in themselves and require a certain amount of fortitude on the part of the patient. Others are harmless but look formidable. A great deal of unnecessary suffering and neurosis may be avoided if the patient and family understand what has and what has not been revealed by these examinations.

Although many of the diagnostic neurological procedures are potentially dangerous, it is remarkable how attention to technique minimizes complications. When cerebrospinal fluid is withdrawn, or replaced by air or *Myodil*, infection is an ever present danger. Such investigations should never be considered as routine procedures. The indications should be clear. A lumbar puncture is not necessary in migraine or sciatica, nor in the majority of patients suffering from multiple sclerosis. Air encephalography may demonstrate cerebral atrophy, but in many cases this can be inferred on clinical grounds. The technique of cerebral angiography may be similarly abused and, moreover, is sometimes harmful. An elderly, hypertensive or arteriosclerotic individual may suffer a stroke in consequence of trauma and ensuing spasm of the wall of the injected artery.

The intern should take pride in explaining to the patient the reasons for and the nature of the proposed tests and he should master the technique of those procedures which he himself has to carry out. A lumbar puncture can be converted from a relatively painless procedure to one of torment, solely because of improper positioning of the patient or because the point of a needle was not inspected before use.

572. The wound man
The 'wound man' of Paracelsus, 1493–1541, described as the 'Luther of Medicine'. This Swiss physician was one of the great medical figures of the Renaissance. In this illustration he depicted the various injuries from the weapons of the day.

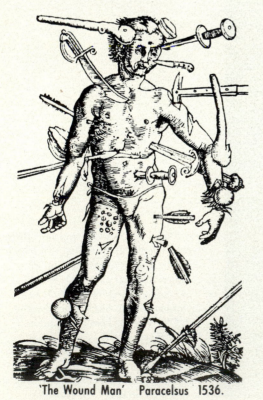

'The Wound Man' Paracelsus 1536.

ADVERSE EFFECTS OF NEW DRUGS

Ill health due to treatment is not of course a new phenomenon, and from time to time the story of the horrors of purgation, blistering and bloodletting is retold as historical papers come to light. It is the former advocacy of these methods by the eminent which particularly disturbs the modern reader. What will our successors think of our own era in which, for example, in this country there are twenty million prescriptions a year for barbiturates? Harmful side-effects of drugs may go unnoticed for decades, as was the case with aspirin and the alimentary tract, phenacetin and the kidney, and amidopyrine and the leucocytes. It is said that some 10 per cent. of the beds in our general hospitals are occupied by patients suffering in some degree from our efforts to treat them. But side-effects are not always adverse, and it would be more accurate to speak of unwanted effects. The observation of unexpected side-effects has occasionally led to the development of a new drug. Some examples of this may be quoted. The occurrence of polyuria when mercury was used to treat syphilis led to the introduction of mersalyl; the hypoglycaemia observed during sulphonamide therapy led to the use of the sulphonylureas in the treatment of diabetes; and the euphoria noted in patients with tuberculosis treated by iproniazid proved to be due to the ability of this drug to inhibit monoamine oxidase and led to its employment as an antidepressant.

Unwanted effects of drugs can be predicted by pharmacologists on the basis of their chemical structure or by analogy with animal experiments.

The establishment of registries where clinicians can record the adverse effects that they encounter has proved of immense value. It was the realization in the U.S.A. in 1952 that chloramphenicol was liable to cause aplastic anaemia which led to this development. On the other hand, it was personal clinical observations which disclosed that thalidomide could produce phocomelia, that ileal obstruction might result from administration of enteric-coated potassium chloride, that the incidence of deaths from asthma increased with the introduction of pressurized aerosols, that steroid contraceptives could cause thrombo-embolism, and that monoamine oxidase inhibitors could provoke fatal hypertensive crises.

Obviously a rare phenomenon—for example, phocomelia—would be more readily traced to the operation of a new agent than would some common condition such as cerebral haemorrhage if a new cause for it arrived on the scene. In this country spina bifida is common, while cranium bifidum is rare. If the latter condition became epidemic, one would suspect that some new factor was operating. It is clear that the keen awareness of the clinician as well as the establishment of a central registry is vital in this increasingly complex field of medical activity. At times the problem may even have a geographical aspect. In Switzerland, for example, as everywhere else, primary pulmonary hypertension was a rare disease until an appetite depressant (aminorex fumarate) was introduced on the Swiss market. This drug subsequently gave rise to dyspnoea, syncope and signs of right-sided cardiac failure within 6–12 months. It was withdrawn. In Japan, clioquinol, a drug which has been widely used for 30 years in many countries in the treatment of gastro-enteritis, has been found to be neurotoxic and to be involved in a disease called subacute myelo-opticoneuropathy. More than 10,000 alleged cases of this disease have been recorded in Japan, yet it is rare everywhere else in the world.

THE METABOLISM OF DRUGS

It has long been known that individuals vary greatly in their response to both the therapeutic and the toxic action of drugs. The rate of absorption of the drug from the alimentary tract and the degree of protein-binding are less important in determining the plasma level than the rate at which the drug is metabolized. The metabolism of many drugs takes place in the liver. Oxidation is carried out by enzymes in the endoplasmic reticulum of liver cells. The activity of these enzymes may be increased (enzyme induction) or reduced (enzyme inhibition) by the presence of other substances. The concentration of a drug in the plasma is continuously affected by the processes of absorption, distribution, metabolism and excretion. But it is the rate of drug metabolism which varies most from one individual to another, and the influential factors are both genetic and environmental. For example, there may be genetically determined differences in the amounts of drug-metabolizing enzymes in the liver. An enzyme which metabolizes a particular drug may be present in one individual and lacking in another. Thus the rate of acetylation of isoniazid is genetically determined, the slow acetylators being deficient in certain liver enzymes. In the United Kingdom the gene governing slow acetylation is three times more frequent than that governing rapid acetylation, while in Japan the reverse is the case. The high plasma levels of isoniazid reached in slow acetylators render tham much more prone to the complications of isoniazid neuropathy and dementia. Failure to hydroxylate phenytoin is also genetically determined but is fortunately rare; in such cases dysarthria, ataxia and nystagmus may occur when normal doses produce a high plasma level.

Studies of the plasma levels of drugs achieved in identical and non-identical twins confirm that both genetic and non-genetic factors are involved in the rate of drug metabolism. An important factor has proved to be the concomitant administration of another drug. For example, phenobarbitone increases the rate at which certain drugs are oxidized, thus causing their more rapid removal from the blood and thereby lowering the plasma levels. The anticoagulant effect of warfarin may be lost in this way when phenobarbitone is prescribed. Less is known about the ways in which one drug may inhibit the metabolism of another, as in the case of tolbutamide which, if given with a sulphonamide, can cause marked hypoglycaemia. It is suspected that alcohol inhibits the metabolism of some drugs, including that of warfarin.

However, it is in the use of the monoamine oxidase inhibitors (M.A.O.I.'s) that so many examples of drug interaction have been encountered. These drugs block the synthesis of certain sympathomimetic amines including dopamine, tyramine, serotonin and, to a lesser extent, noradrenaline and adrenaline.

Lastly, it should be remembered that drug interaction can occur at receptor sites. It has long been known that two drugs may compete with each other for a pharmacological effect. For example, there is danger in some hypotensive and antidepressant combinations. The tricyclic antidepressants such as imipramine and amitryptyline are potent inhibitors of the amine pump which takes up circulating catecholamines. Hypotensive agents—for instance, the adrenergic blocking drugs guanethidine and bethanidine—are concentrated in adrenergic nerve endings, so that the combination of antidepressant and hypotensive drugs may result in a rise in blood pressure.

All these dangers of drug prescribing are even more important in the elderly. Here we are dealing not only with reduced tolerance of drugs in general and their impaired renal excretion, not to mention the interactions between sedatives, tranquillizers, antidepressants and anticoagulants, but also with the consequences of failing intellect, confusion and forgetfulness. A precise schedule of treatment may be impossible to arrange. Mental confusion may be aggravated, while the patient's general unsteadiness and tendency to vertigo may be accentuated by hypotension. In treating the elderly one should not hesitate to withdraw a drug if no clear benefit has been obtained from it, and should avoid combinations of drugs as far as possible. The elderly patient may have many complaints, but to prescribe a drug for each is madness.

NEUROLOGICAL COMPLICATIONS OF MEDICAL TREATMENT

For centuries the commonest form of medical treatment has been the administration of a drug by mouth. Twenty years ago the commonest form of ill health due to drugs was drug addiction. This seems to be increasing, but we now also have to contend with the harmful effects of drugs used in orthodox treatment. Formerly, therapy was simple, safe, but relatively ineffective. Nowadays it tends to be complex, beneficial, but increasingly dangerous. The danger derives from the toxicity of many modern drugs.

The therapeutic effect of the majority of drugs which we use is achieved by interference with some biological process, in the patient or in some invading organism. In reality this pharmacological action is a toxic one which the physician endeavours to control by precision of dosage and selectivity of action. The more potent the drug the greater the necessity for accuracy in both of these fields.

The side-effects of drug therapy may be conveniently considered in a manner outlined in the accompanying table.

SIDE-EFFECTS OF DRUG THERAPY

1. Drug allergy	e.g. methyldopa induced haemolytic anaemia
2. Exaggerated pharmacological effect	Anticoagulants Hypotensives
3. Subsidiary pharmacological effect	Antihistamines Antibiotics Steroids
4. Genetic circumstances	Primaquine anaemia Suxamethonium apnoea Porphyria: sulphonamides, barbiturates Diabetes: steroids Favism: broad beans
5. True toxicity	Absolute: e.g. anticonvulsants and drugs used in the treatment of Parkinsonism Relative: e.g. renal impairment (streptomycin; nitrofurantoin)
6. Interaction of drugs	Alcohol and hypnotics Monoamine-oxidase inhibitors and morphine, pethidine, amphetamine Phenobarbitone and phenytoin Phenobarbitone and phenylbutazone Phenobarbitone and warfarin

1. Hypersensitivity reaction or drug allergy. Drug allergy is a loosely used term for the multiplicity of sensitivity reactions which include fever, skin eruptions,

oedema, joint swelling, lymphadenopathy and haematological abnormalities. In the majority of cases these reactions cannot be proved to involve an antigen-antibody mechanism as in the case of methyldopa-induced haemolytic anaemia. It is possible, however, that in some examples of drug-induced polyneuritis and encephalitis there is an allergic arteritis.

2. Exaggerated therapeutic effect. Examples of this type of reaction are provided by the alarming and sometimes fatal misuse of the anticoagulants and hypotensive drugs.

3. Subsidiary pharmacological effect. Side-effects may represent no more than another pharmacological property of the drug prescribed. There are many examples of these, such as the soporific effect of the antihistamines, the disappearance of the normal intestinal flora during antibiotic treatment and the hormonal imbalance during steroid treatment.

4. Genetic circumstances. In other instances the side-effect is genetically determined. Here we are in the field of 'pharmacogenetics' and we already have the examples of primaquine-induced haemolytic anaemia and suxamethonium-induced apnoea. In both cases we are dealing with the consequences of inherited enzyme deficiency; glucose-6-phosphate dehydrogenase in the former and pseudocholinesterase in the latter. There will be others, and chance clinical observation may provide the first clue as in the case of the Japanese surgeon who noticed that occasionally hydrogen peroxide did not foam in the mouth. This proved to be due to the absence of the enzyme catalase in human saliva and blood.

In diabetes mellitus and porphyria we are dealing with inherited abnormalities the symptoms of which may appear spontaneously or through the intervention of some agent. In the case of diabetes mellitus it may be steroid treatment; in porphyria, barbiturates or sulphonamides. More interesting still is the possibility that the agent precipitating the crises in these inherited abnormalities may not be a drug but a normal article of diet. In favism, in which again there is a deficiency of glucose-6-phosphate dehydrogenase, broad beans are the agent responsible for the onset of the acute haemolytic anaemia. Some similar mechanism may be at work in lathyrism (epidemic spastic paraplegia).

5. True toxicity. Here we are often dealing with the results of prolonged treatment. Two not uncommon examples are of the over-treated epileptic child and the elderly person with Parkinsonism. The child may be taking three or four different anticonvulsants and not only do the fits continue but the child is noticeably retarded and often clumsy. The old person is trying to take one or two drugs which have little if any therapeutic effect and reduce him to a state in which he feels muddled and depressed.

At other times the cumulative toxic effect of a drug is brought about because of impaired renal function. Elderly patients or those with renal disease are specially susceptible to drugs such as streptomycin, nitrofurantoin and the ganglionoplegic hypotensive drugs.

6. Interaction of drugs. It has long been known that alcohol and hypnotics may summate in cerebral depression; they may also result in a potentiation that can be fatal. More recently it has been discovered that the monoamine-oxidase inhibitors may potentiate the action of a number of drugs, including morphine, pethidine and the amphetamines. There may be severe hypotension. The patient taking a monoamine-oxidase inhibitor may also suffer a hypertensive crisis on eating varieties of strong cheese or meat extract preparations, probably because of their content of tyramine.

A number of drugs, of which the best known is phenobarbitone, can stimulate the production of drug-metabolizing enzymes in the liver microsomes (enzyme induction). Thus the rate of metabolism of phenytoin is enhanced by phenobarbitone. The latter drug similarly increases the rate of breakdown of warfarin so that the desired anticoagulant effect is not obtained. The patient discharged from hospital on warfarin and phenobarbitone may bleed dangerously when the phenobarbitone is subsequently withdrawn or replaced by some sedative which does not stimulate liver enzymes.

Neurotoxicity may occur at all levels of the nervous system. Thus the clinical manifestations comprise epilepsy, extrapyramidal syndromes, cranial nerve dysfunction, neuropathy and myopathy. Drugs responsible for these harmful effects are given in FIGURES 574, 575, 576 and 577. Instead of presenting them in table form I have chosen to adorn my dull words with the beautiful wood cuts from Vesalius' *De Humani Corporis Fabrica Libri Septem*, published in 1543. In the opinion of many medical historians it is the greatest medical book ever written and its illustrations those of a great artist.

Drug-induced Epilepsy

There are many drugs which, if given in sufficient quantity, will cause convulsions and coma. Particularly important are the phenothiazines; chlorpromazine and thiopropazate may aggravate an epileptic tendency or even induce an epileptic fit for the first time. Reserpine is another drug widely used as a tranquillizer or antihypertensive agent which may cause epilepsy. It is one of the most potent depressant drugs in common use.

The antituberculous agent isoniazid, is another occasional convulsant. It may also cause a psychotic disturbance. Chlorambucil, a nitrogen mustard derivative, has epileptogenic properties.

Cycloserine is another antituberculous agent which may cause epilepsy and mental disturbance. A patient may safely take cycloserine for several years before any fit occurs and unless the clinician is aware that she is taking this drug, he may think there is a tuberculous or other lesion of the brain.

Intravenous or intrathecal penicillin may cause epilepsy if the concentration in the CSF exceeds ten units per millilitre. The dangerous neurotoxic effect of penicillin has also been encountered in patients undergoing open heart surgery for cardiopulmonary bypass.

Toxic Disorders of the Cranial Nerves

1. The Retina and the Optic Nerve

Optic atrophy from arsenicals and amblyopia from quinine are now very rare. Pigmentary degeneration of the retina may occur after some of the phenothiazine derivatives such as thioridazine. Chloramphenicol, the only effective drug in the treatment of typhoid fever, and very liable to cause depression of the bone marrow, may also produce optic atrophy.

Optic atrophy with or without blindness has been observed in patients given isoniazid for the treatment of pulmonary tuberculosis. Papilloedema due to benign intracranial hypertension may follow prolonged steroid therapy, especially in children.

A particularly important drug in this connexion is chloroquine. This drug is a quinine derivative widely prescribed for rheumatoid arthritis and lupus erythematosus. It can produce both corneal and retinal changes. The former are usually symptomless and regress with the withdrawal of treatment. A characteristic symptom is the appearance of haloes around naked lights. On the other hand the retinal changes are largely irreversible and consist of arterial attenuation, oedema and pigmentary disturbances. There may be changes in the retina similar to those found in retinitis pigmentosa and there may be night blindness. Routine testing of visual acuity during chloroquine treatment is not sufficient to exclude the development of toxic retinal changes because foveal vision is affected comparatively late. Regular examination of the optic fundi and the visual fields should be made during prolonged chloroquine therapy.

Corneal injury may result from the use of corticosteroid drops in the presence of herpes simplex keratitis. Prolonged adminstration of corticosteroids may lead to cataract formation. Small opacities, which usually begin at the posterior pole of the lens bilaterally, may be seen in such patients with the ophthalmoscope; they rarely progress if the corticosteroids are withdrawn. Ethambutol, an antituberculous drug, can disturb colour vision and produce scotomata. In children, nalidixic acid and the tetracyclines have been reported to cause papilloedema due to benign intracranial hypertension. When the hypertension develops in children who have received prolonged treatment with corticosteroids, withdrawal should be gradual since papilloedema may appear at this stage of management.

The principal drugs which may initiate or aggravate glaucoma are antispasmodics, antihistamines, psychotropic drugs and those used in Parkinson's disease. Angle-closure glaucoma has been seen in the treatment of Parkinson's disease with benzhexol. This drug has a mydriatic effect, and the insidious angle-closure glaucoma which develops may pass unrecognized because the eye is not painful or red.

Less serious are the instances of blurred vision that are liable to occur with many of the atropine-like drugs which cause mydriasis and cycloplegia. Ganglion blocking agents may impair accommodation, and anti-

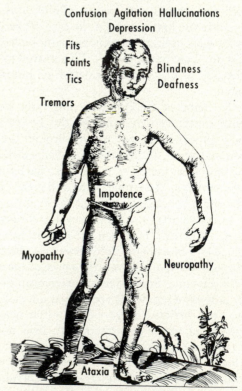

573. Toxic man
The 'toxic man' of 1968. The medieval weapons have gone. Modern man can now be rendered blind, deaf, mad, epileptic, paralysed and impotent by drug therapy.

CONVULSANTS

Cycloserine
Reserpine
Chlorpromazine
Isoniazid
Chlorambucil

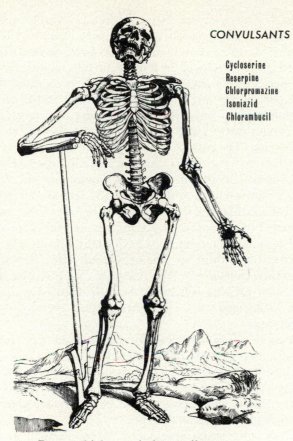

CRANIAL NERVES

II	Chloroquine
	Chloramphenicol
	Thioridazine
	Isoniazid
	Steroids
VII XII	Phenothiazines
VIII	Streptomycin

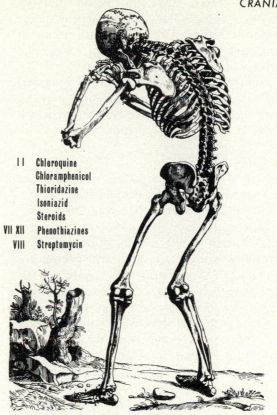

574. Drugs which may induce epilepsy

575. Drugs which may cause cranial nerve lesions

576. Drugs which may cause neuropathy

577. Drugs which may cause myopathy

NEUROPATHY

Isoniazid
Nitrofurantoin
Butazolidin
Heavy Metals

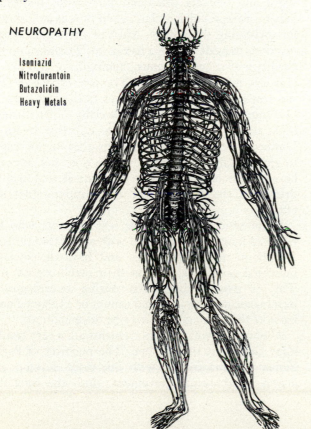

MYOPATHY

Triamcinolone
Dexamethasone
Chloroquine

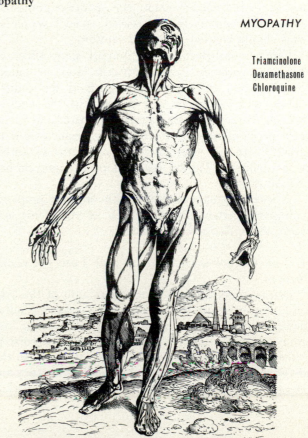

depressants may affect focusing. Certain diuretics (acetazolamide), sulphonamides and tetracyclines may cause a transient myopia. Temporary alterations of refraction are not uncommon in women taking oral contraceptives.

Ocular conditions such as cataract, glaucoma and retinitis due to cytomegalovirus infection may be complications of the imunosuppressive therapy which is necessary after renal transplantation.

2. The Auditory Nerve

Streptomycin is the most important drug likely to disturb the function of the vestibular and cochlear divisions of this nerve. They were noted a year after the discovery of this effective antituberculous drug in 1945. The onset of vertigo occurs usually during the first month of treatment and signs of vestibular damage are present in about half the patients who receive 1 G. of streptomycin daily. It seems that a prolonged course of streptomycin with a small daily dose is just as damaging as a short course with high dosage. In young subjects the vertigo clears almost completely within a few weeks when medication is stopped. In older subjects recovery may be slower and incomplete. It is rare to find that streptomycin causes any delayed vestibular damage, presenting months after cessation of therapy. On the other hand loss of hearing may be insidious and the possibility of deafness must be reckoned with, not only throughout the period of treatment with streptomycin, but also for some months afterwards. In elderly people with impaired renal function, the incidence of ototoxic effects of streptomycin is increased. In such people the drug should be used with great caution.

Other aminoglycoside antibiotics may affect the auditory apparatus. Streptomycin and gentamicin mainly attack the vestibular branch of the auditory nerve, and neomycin and kanamycin the auditory branch. Parenteral adminstration of neomycin is now rare because the risk of producing deafness is much greater than with streptomycin and because kanamycin is less ototoxic. Topical applications of neomycin have caused deafness.

A second group of drugs with ototoxic properties comprises certain diuretics such as ethacrynic acid. Here again, deafness may occur.

3. The Oculomotor, Facial and Lower Cranial Nerves

Disturbances in the motor innervation of the eyes, face, mouth, throat and neck may be seen as a result of treatment with phenothiazine. They may appear soon after treatment is begun, and represent a personal idiosyncrasy, or they may be delayed in onset, so that they are less readily recognized. In either case they may be associated with the features of drug-induced Parkin-sonism—expressionless facies, muscular rigidity and tremor, salivation and alteration of gait. There may be peculiar dystonic movements and spasms particularly affecting the muscles of the mouth and lips, tongue, face and neck. There may be oculogyric crises, spasms of torticollis or sensations in the mouth and throat un-accompanied by any visible abnormality, but causing the patient distress and affecting speech, chewing and swallowing. The patient with drug-induced Parkinson-ism does not also suffer from oculogyric crises. The Parkinsonian syndrome is much commoner in the female and is related to the dosage and length of treatment. Facial and oral dyskinesias, on the other hand, are unrelated to the dosage and symptoms usually arise at the beginning of treatment. They usually subside when treatment is withdrawn, but occasionally they persist, apparently indefinitely. The risk seems to be greater in demented patients, where the brain is diseased or has been subjected to electroconvulsive therapy or leucotomy.

Phenothiazines are now so widely used that any patient, especially a middle-aged female, who complains of unusual sensations of tightness or discomfort about the lips, mouth and throat, accompanied by involuntary movements in this region, should be questioned about previous phenothiazine therapy.

These phenothiazine-induced extrapyramidal syndromes may be reversible or irreversible. Parkinsonian reactions, akathisia (syndrome of motor restlessness) and dystonia are largely reversible. Parkinsonism is often slight and scarcely disabling. But motor restlessness may be interpreted as agitation and thus as an indication for increasing the dosage. Most of the acute dystonic reactions subside within a day or so. Trismus and neck rigidity may suggest tetanus, meningitis or encephalitis. Hysteria may be suspected. The irreversible dyskinesias constitute a serious drawback to the long-term use of tranquillizers. They may be socially embarrassing or quite disabling, and there is no effective treatment. Unlike the acute dystonic reactions, they do not respond to anti-Parkinsonian drugs. There does not appear to be any correlation between the clinical response to a drug and the development of extrapyramidal side-effects.

From time to time I have seen patients who have received long-term treatment with major tranquillizers, usually in mental hospitals, and have developed an increased protein content in their cerebrospinal fluid. This is usually discovered during neurological or psychiatric investigation and cannot be explained on the basis of their illnesses. It may be drug-induced.

Abnormal involuntary movements are a very trouble-some side-effect of levodopa. The majority of Parkinsonian patients treated with this drug develop some degree of abnormal movement. Both the total daily dose and the total cumulative dose are important in determining the onset of these movements. After two years, most of the patients thus treated show some disturbance. The type of movement disorder varies considerably. There are three main varieties.

(1) *Head movements*: these resemble the dyskinesias of phenothiazine; they are sniffing, grimacing or chewing movements, rolling of the tongue, clicking sounds, and dislodging of dentures.

(2) *Body movements*: these are less frequent and may affect the chest, abdomen or diaphragm.

(3) *Limb movements*: there may be increased gesticulation, flapping of the arms, jerking of the fingers, spasms and restlessness of the lower limbs, rocking movements of the feet, or rhythmic spreading of the toes.

These effects of levodopa administration are not seen either in normal control subjects receiving the drug or in patients, treated with comparable dosages, who are suffering from non-striatal neurological disorders. They do occur, however, when levodopa is given for dystonias, Huntington's chorea, Wilson's disease, or progressive supranuclear palsy. These observations suggest that damage to brain stem–striatal systems or to actual striatal receptors is necessary for the development of levodopa-induced involuntary movements.

Peripheral Neuropathy

As already mentioned the heavy metals such as arsenic, lead and mercury are rare causes of polyneuritis today. Thalidomide neuropathy was mainly of a sensory kind and paralysis was rare. Many patients continued to suffer from paraesthesiae long after they had ceased taking the drug. Two important drugs are isoniazid and nitrofurantoin.

Isoniazid has been used for the treatment of tuberculosis for more than 10 years and in ordinary dosage there is a remarkable lack of toxic effects. The incidence of toxicity is largely a reflection of the size of dosage and the duration of treatment. Symptoms are infrequent during the administration of isoniazid, 5–10 mg./kg. body weight daily. Isoniazid neuropathy is a form of conditioned pyridoxine deficiency. Simultaneous administration of this vitamin prevents the development of neuropathy. There is evidence that differences in the rates of metabolism of isoniazid are genetically controlled. The slow inactivators are more prone to polyneuritis as a complication of prolonged treatment.

Nitrofurantoin is widely used as an antibacterial agent in infections of the urinary tract. The drug may cause a peripheral neuropathy but by what mechanism is not known. It is most likely to occur when the patient has impaired renal function. A daily dose of 400 mg. should not be given for more than 2 weeks, but a small daily dose can probably be given safely for a longer period.

A recent addition to the list of drugs which cause peripheral neuropathy is vincristine sulphate, an indole alkaloid obtained from the periwinkle plant. It is used in acute leukaemia and cancer chemotherapy.

Ethoglucid (*Epodyl*) is an alkylating agent given by intra-arterial injection or regional perfusion in the treatment of cancer; it may induce neuropathy. This may also follow local treatment with nitrogen mustard. Most of these cancer chemotherapeutic agents impair bone marrow function, but to some extent this impairment is avoided by regional perfusion. Neuropathy has been described following imipramine, glutethimide and disulfiram; the last named drug (*Antabuse*) is used in treating alcoholics. There have been recent suggestions that methaqualone causes a neuropathy: it is a constituent of the popular hypnotic, *Mandrax*.

Muscular paresis may develop during therapy with certain antibiotics because of their neuromuscular blocking action. Streptomycin, neomycin and viomycin have a curare-like effect, whereas polymyxin and kanamycin have a depolarizing neuromuscular blocking action. Respiratory paralysis is a dangerous complication of antibiotic-induced neuromuscular block.

Suxamethonium, a muscle relaxant, is another potent neuromuscular blocking agent of the depolarizing type. It is activated by the pseudocholinesterase in serum. Prolonged apnoea after its use results from the absence or low level, or an atypical form, of pseudocholinesterase in the serum.

Myopathy

This is a rare complication of medical treatment but prolonged steroid therapy may cause weakness and wasting of the muscles of the shoulder and pelvic girdles. Triamcinolone and dexamethasone have been implicated in many of these cases.

Chloroquine is another drug found to cause a myopathy or neuromyopathy. Like the corneal changes in the eye, the muscular lesions seem to be largely reversible.

Carbenoxolone sodium (*Biogastrone*) has been used for several years to treat gastric ulcer. It can produce muscular weakness as a result of hypokalaemia. Episodes of hypertension, oedema and potassium loss have been reported, and the latter may cause flaccid tetraparesis, in some cases with myoglobinuria. Serum muscle enzymes may be raised. In some reports the muscle paresis developed acutely a week or so after the cessation of *Biogastrone* therapy.

Emetine is another drug that occasionally induces myopathy. It is an effective agent in the treatment of amoebic disease, but it has widespread toxic effects when large doses are given over long periods of time. The heart may be involved.

The Neurological Complications of Injections and Inoculations

Examples under this heading comprise local nerve injury at the site of injection, the neurological reactions to prophylactic immunization and the sequelae of intrathecal medication.

In the first category may be cited damage to the ulnar or median nerve at the elbow or wrist during intravenous therapy. Not uncommonly the patient is recovering from the effects of a general anaesthetic and the pain which would warn of nerve irritation is not felt until consciousness is restored. Serious and permanent damage to these nerves can occur under such circumstances. Improperly placed intramuscular injections are another cause. Injections into the buttocks may damage the sciatic nerve and an injection intended for a deltoid muscle may injure the radial nerve.

All levels of the nervous system may react to the injection of foreign protein, so that polyneuritis and radiculitis, myelitis and meningo-encephalitis may be encountered. Serum sickness after the injection of foreign protein usually occurs about 12 days later with the appearance of an itchy rash, fever, urticaria and joint swellings. In a small minority of these cases some form of acute neuropathy follows. Such complications may occur after the administration of antisera for tetanus and other infections. Serum sickness is essentially an anaphylactic vasculitis. The majority of neurological reactions associated with serum sickness are in the nature of a radiculitis—a shoulder girdle neuritis, indistinguishable from the spontaneous form of this disease. Polyneuritis is uncommon and myelitis and encephalitis are rare complications.

Similar disorders may follow prophylactic vaccination, against typhoid, tetanus, pertussis, diphtheria, rabies and smallpox. They usually follow a week or so after the injection, but in pertussis, convulsions, coma and hemiparesis may follow in a day or so. Following T.A.B. inoculation there is a higher incidence of damage to the central nervous system. The effects of inoculation against rabies may result in acute demyelination resembling that seen in multiple sclerosis.

The introduction of infection or a chemical irritant into the theca by lumbar or cisternal injection may lead to serious and even fatal infection of the nervous system. Scrupulous attention to aseptic technique is always necessary. The irritant effect of penicillin introduced into the subarachnoid space should never be forgotten.

In fulminating meningitis the injection of more than 10,000 Units of penicillin in 10 ml. of saline is never safe. In the vast majority of cases of meningitis, penicillin injections should be made parenterally.

NEUROLOGICAL COMPLICATIONS OF SURGICAL TREATMENT

There are two major categories here. First, some portion of the nervous system may be damaged at the time of operation. Second, there may be a delayed neurological complication of surgery.

Paresis of a group of muscles or a limb may be a consequence of malposition on the operating table. Various compression palsies may arise if the limbs of an anaesthetized person, under the effects of a muscle relaxant, are not sufficiently protected. Compression of the outstretched arm may result in a wrist drop or an ulnar paralysis. Pressure of the leg-rest in the lithotomy position may cause a common peroneal palsy with foot drop. In the Trendelenburg position the brachial plexus may be compressed as the result of pressure at the root of the neck by a shoulder-rest.

Spinal manipulation is another danger. The spine may be manipulated during the course of an operation or as a form of therapy. In the former case excessive flexion of the lumbosacral spine and hips may result in foot drop due to prolapsed intervertebral disc. Excessive movement of the neck of an elderly patient with cervical spondylosis under general anaesthesia has been known to produce a tetraparesis. It may occur during operations in the pharynx or when hyperextension of the neck is necessary for the passage of endoscopic instruments.

Cerebrospinal fluid rhinorrhoea after nasal surgery and impotence after sympathectomy are further examples of complications resulting directly from operation. Surgery, particularly for head and neck cancer, may cause carotid occlusion with cerebral infarction or bilateral jugular occlusion with papilloedema. In general, the neurological complications of modern cancer therapy appear to be increasing with the more aggressive and effective methods now employed. In addition to the direct and indirect consequences of surgery, we have the effects of radiation and of powerful chemotherapeutic agents such as steroids, methotrexate and vincristine. Neuropathy may be a consequence of dialysis treatment in renal failure.

Even surgical procedures which are in themselves of a minor nature, such as lumbar puncture or carotid arteriography, can give rise to complications. Repeated lumbar punctures lead to the development of spinal epidermoids; carotid arteriography can cause cerebral infarction. Patients are still being encountered who had an injection of thorium dioxide (*Thorotrast*) many years previously. This radiographic contrast medium was introduced in 1928 to outline cavities such as the renal pelvis and the cerebral ventricles and for the visualization of blood vessels. Twenty years later, tumours of the liver may still develop.

An example of a dangerous complication arising after a 'safe' medical procedure is that of malignant hyperpyrexia after a general anaesthetic. This is a genetically determined condition in which the patient has an asymptomatic myopathy and reacts with hyperpyrexia and muscular rigidity to various anaesthetic agents. The mortality rate is 60 per cent. and some survivors have been left with neurological and renal sequelae. The biochemical basis of the disorder is not known.

In the second category the nervous system suffers as a delayed consequence of surgical treatment. It is obvious that in resection of cervical or axillary glands or in abdomino-perineal operations, nerves or plexuses may be injured. But more important are those cases in which there has been no direct injury, but the treatment has indirect effects. A few examples may be quoted.

Vitamin B_{12} neuropathy may follow total and partial gastrectomy, gastro-enterostomy, and anastomoses and blind loops in the small intestine. The neuropathy presents in the form of subacute or chronic polyneuritis or subacute combined degeneration of the spinal cord. Rarely, it presents in the form of an organic dementia.

The vitamin B_{12} deficiency is due to a failure of secretion of intrinsic factor as a consequence of atrophic gastritis in the gastric remnant. But deficiency of vitamin B_{12} is not invariably responsible for neurological disorders after gastrectomy. There may continue to be normal absorption and normal serum levels of this vitamin. The myelopathy and peripheral neuropathy which then develop are similar to those that occur in adult coeliac disease, the aetiology of which is still not known.

In partial gastrectomy, between two-thirds and three-quarters of the stomach is removed. It is an effective form of treatment for gastric and duodenal ulcer and the majority of patients are relieved of their symptoms, but the radical alterations in the normal gastro-intestinal physiology may in turn cause trouble. Usually there is weight loss, and steatorrhoea may develop with malabsorption of the fat-soluble vitamins A, D and E. Deficiency states—anaemia, B_{12} deficiency and folate deficiency—are generally of late onset. Bone disease may develop years after gastrectomy. In osteoporosis there is actual loss of bone tissue, but that which remains is normally calcified. There is a proneness to fractures. In osteomalacia there is a loss of calcium from bone, probably due to a lack of vitamin D. There are bone pain and tenderness and muscular weakness. Blood calcium and phosphate levels are often low and the serum alkaline phosphatase (bone) is raised. Patients who have had a gastrectomy and who seem to be poorly nourished should receive calcium and vitamin D treatment.

Thyroid surgery may ultimately be followed by hypothyroidism which may present in a neurological manner as previously described. Thyroid surgery may also be responsible for hypoparathyroidism. Another example of a metabolic disorder or deficiency state following surgical operations is that in which a subacute encephalopathy or myelopathy follows a portacaval anastomosis. The operation has usually been performed for hepatic cirrhosis or splenic anaemia. In such cases the encephalopathy usually runs a subacute course and is characterized by intermittent disturbances of consciousness and of the motor system. Less commonly there is a steadily progressive course in which cerebral, cerebellar and spinal phenomena appear.

The operation of bilateral ureterocolostomy may result in hypokalaemia. This may reveal itself by periodic, fluctuating paralysis of the limbs with loss of reflexes and paraesthesiae. It may mimic familial periodic paralysis and myasthenia gravis.

Two final examples come from the new field of vascular surgery. We have the paraplegia which may follow an operation upon the aorta and the cerebral complications of cardiac surgery. Infarction of the spinal cord and brain is common in both cases. Aortic surgery may deprive a section of the spinal cord of blood. Cerebral emboli are the probable explanation for the oedema and ischaemia of the brain after cardiac surgery. Cardiac arrest during operations may also be responsible for permanent cerebral injury. It is estimated that the upper limit for the period beyond which serious if not irreversible changes will occur in the nervous system is about 4 minutes. The neurological sequelae range from slight impairment of intellect, memory or vision, to epilepsy, dementia, decerebrate rigidity and death.

NEUROLOGICAL COMPLICATIONS OF DEEP X-RAY THERAPY

The brachial plexus may be damaged following radical mastectomy and subsequent radiotherapy, the spinal cord may be damaged during treatment for nasopharyngeal carcinoma and the brain may be injured following irradiation for tumour. It is often impossible to apportion the blame between surgery and radiotherapy in a case of chronic progressive brachial plexus palsy. In cervical cord irradiation injury, symptoms may not appear for 6 to 18 months, when signs of a focal lesion rapidly develop. Irradiation myelopathy is most frequently seen following treatment for malignant disease of the pharynx, the oesophagus and neck. Irradiation encephalopathy is characterized by a short latent period of weeks and the rapid onset of neurological symptoms and signs which are often similar to those encountered in multiple sclerosis. A few months after radiation the patient complains of nausea, vertigo and ataxia and on examination there are signs of cerebellar ataxia and nystagmus. The pathological picture is often one of demyelination rather than blood vessel damage. The rapid return of symptoms may naturally lead one to suspect the recurrence of tumour.

Radiation myelopathy may present as a transient sensory disturbance a few months after therapy, tending to disappear after a further three months. In a second variety there appears to be selective damage to anterior horn cells producing a flaccid paresis of the limbs. A third variety is that in which there appears to be an acute spinal cord infarction. But the most common form is a chronic, progressive myelopathy of which the pathological basis is ill understood.

Perhaps the Hippocratic injunction to refrain from harming our patients has been best expressed in modern times in the words of Sir Robert Hutchison (1871–1960). He wrote:

'From inability to let well alone; from too much zeal for what is new, and contempt for what is old; from putting knowledge before wisdom, science before art, and cleverness before common sense; from treating patients as cases; and from making the cure of the disease more grievous than its endurance, good Lord deliver us.'

Neurological Complications of Medical Treatment

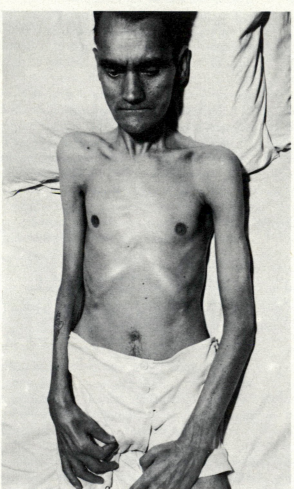
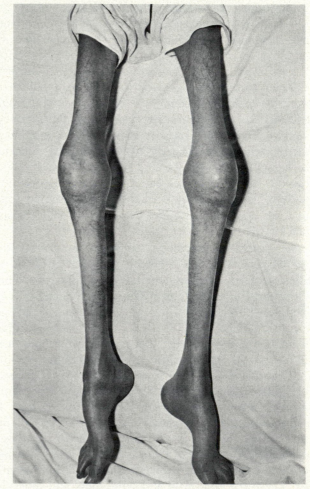

578. Neuropathy and epilepsy
A patient with ankylosing spondylitis, arthritis and pulmonary tuberculosis. Epilepsy resulted from cycloserine and neuropathy followed isoniazid and phenylbutazone.

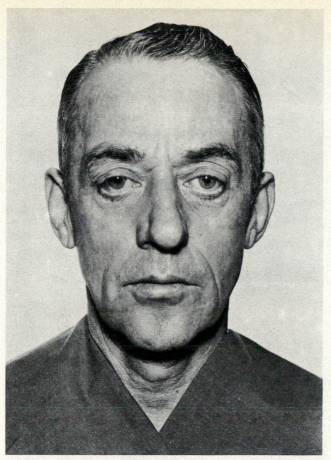

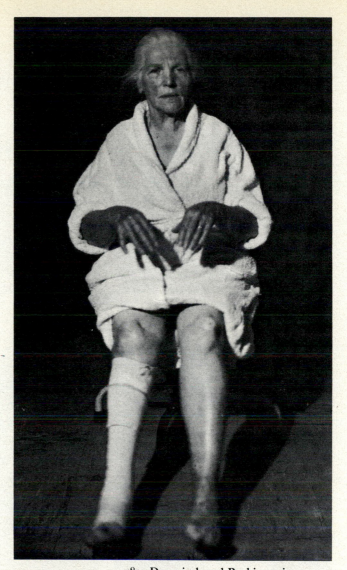

579. Drug-induced Parkinsonism
Referred with a diagnosis of Parkinsonism by a medical tribunal dealing with the effects of an industrial accident. Had not worked for 3 years, no physical disability. Staring, immobile, unblinking facial expression due to phenothiazines. He had been taking 'twenty tablets a day' for several years.

580. Drug-induced Parkinsonism
Coarse tremor and rigidity of the extremities in a patient who had been taking promazine, 50 mg. t.d.s. for 16 days. Eczema of right leg. Symptoms appeared on the tenth day and disappeared within 3 days on withdrawing the drug. The blurred outlines of hands and feet are the result of the tremor.

581. Drug-induced oculogyric crisis
A mental hospital nurse was given two intramuscular injections of perphenazine, each of 5 mg., during an episode of migraine. The following day she felt dazed and experienced oculogyric crises. 'I found I was looking at the ceiling all the time'. She had difficulty in speaking 'my tongue and throat seemed swollen'; there was stiffness of the hands and of the muscles at the back of the neck. These symptoms subsided in the next 12 hours after an injection of procyclidine, 10 mg. intravenously.

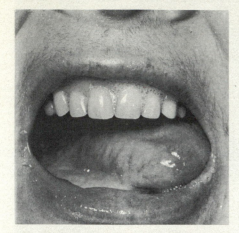
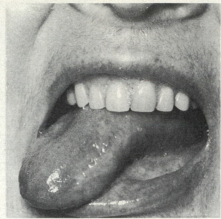

582. Drug-induced involuntary movements of mouth and tongue

A patient suffering from an agitated depression and treated for 15 months with imipramine, 50 mg. t.d.s.; trifluoperazine, 5 mg. daily, and benzhexol, 2 mg. b.d. There was dysarthria, difficulty in chewing, smacking movements of the lips, opening and closing of the mouth and dyskinetic movements of the tongue. These photographs were taken after the drugs had been withdrawn for 2 months. There was little improvement and 12 months later the involuntary movements were still present but less marked.

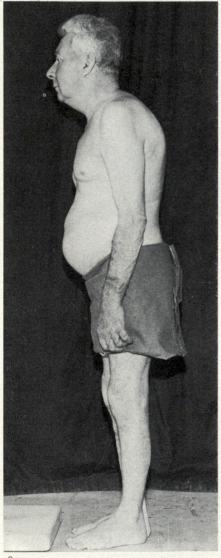

583a

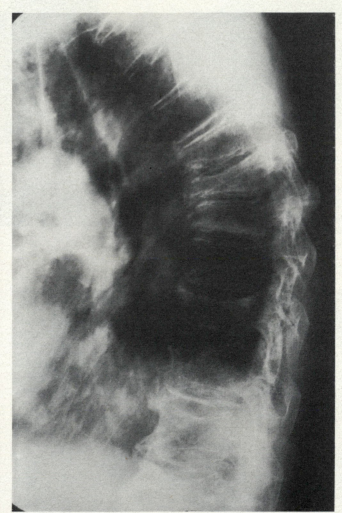

583b

583. Steroid-induced Cushing's syndrome, myopathy, osteoporosis and vertebral collapse

Age 62 years. Chronic beryllium disease (berylliosis). Progressive respiratory illness in a worker in a plant manufacturing alloys. Steroid treatment for 7 years. Progressive myopathy affecting shoulder and pelvic girdles; painless rupture of one Achilles tendon; purpura; bruises; thin atrophic skin with florid face and kyphosis. No neuropathy. (*b*) Lateral radiograph of dorsal spine showing osteoporosis and vertebral collapse. (Courtesy of Dr. J. G. Graham.)

584. Depigmentation of scalp hair; a side-effect of mephenesin carbamate
The manner in which this drug affects melanogenesis is not known. In the photograph the middle zone of dark hair represents 6 weeks' growth when the patient was not taking mephenesin. Note blonde roots and ends of hairs which grew while she was taking mephenesin. A patient with multiple sclerosis. (For further details see Spillane, J. D. (1963) *Brit. Med. J.*, 1, 997.)

Neurological Complications of Medical Treatment

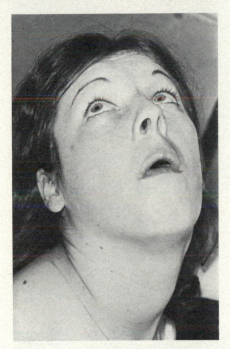

585. Acute dyskinesia; drug-induced
Age 16 years. Emergency admission with recurring episodes of dystonic movements of the head and neck and oculogyric crises. Duration several hours. It transpired that she had been inadvertently prescribed a phenothiazine preparation (fluphenaxine hydrochloride). Her doctor had intended to give her 'a tonic' when she consulted him earlier in the day with a sore throat and malaise. This dystonic reaction was a true idiosyncratic response, because she had taken only 4–5 mg. of the drug. It ceased overnight and on the following morning she was well. (Courtesy of Dr. J. G. Graham.)

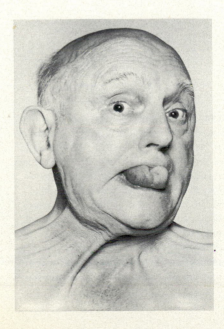
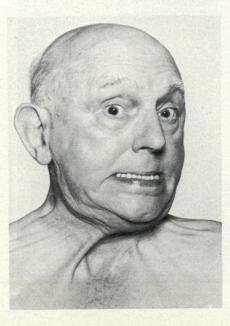

586. Parkinsonism
Facial dyskinesia in a patient taking L-dopa 4 G. daily for 1 year. His rigidity, tremor and akinesia were completely abolished by the drug. There was only a slight return of general disability, and an almost complete disappearance of the facial movements and grimacing, on reducing the dose of levodopa by 1 G. daily.

*Neurological Complications
of Medical Treatment*

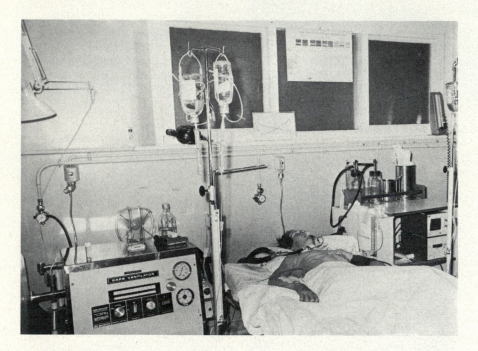

587. Penicillin encephalomyelopathy
One hour after intraspinal injection of 300,000 units of undiluted crystalline penicillin (instead of the prescribed 10,000 units), this patient with suspected viral meningitis (but with a turbid, sterile CSF) developed convulsions, coma and respiratory arrest. He showed fixed dilated pupils, opisthotonos and decorticate rigidity; diabetes insipidus developed and he died on the tenth day. The CSF penicillin level was 256 units/ml. At autopsy the brain was soft and showed extensive cortical necrosis; there was liquefaction of the mid-dorsal spinal cord, with extensive fibrinous exudate. The pituitary gland was necrotic and haemorrhagic.

Convulsions and coma have been known to follow intraventricular, intracisternal and intraspinal penicillin injections. Massive intravenous penicillin may cause fits and coma if there is renal failure. Intravenous penicillin in large doses may also produce status epilepticus and coma after cardiopulmonary bypass operations. The neurotoxic effects of penicillin are such that there are nowadays few indications for intrathecal penicillin in the treatment of meningitis.

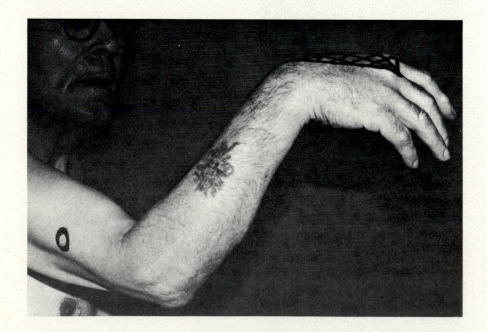

588. Radial nerve palsy
Injection of penicillin into the radial nerve at the point marked with a circle, instead of into the deltoid muscle. Pain and paraesthesiae immediately referred to the territory of the cutaneous distribution of the nerve. Note wrist drop and extensive area of anaesthesia on the dorsum of the hand, more than is seen in compression palsies of this nerve. No recovery by the time this photograph was taken, two weeks after the injection. (Courtesy of Dr. J. G. Graham.)

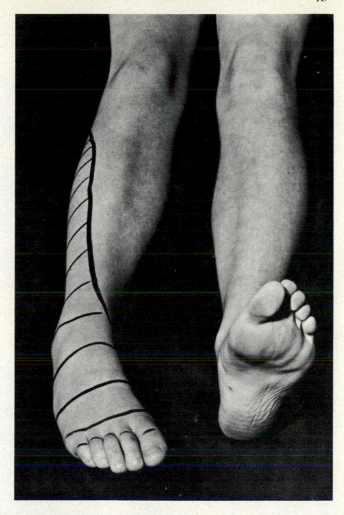

589. Sciatic nerve palsy
Female aged 20 years. Barbiturate overdose. Coma 48 hours. Paralysis of right leg below knee on recovering consciousness. Absent ankle jerk. Knee jerk present. Sensory loss as outlined. Sciatic nerve injured during intramuscular tetracycline injections into the buttock. Photograph taken eight weeks after injury. Patient cannot dorsiflex the right foot. (Courtesy of Dr. C. E. C. Wells.)

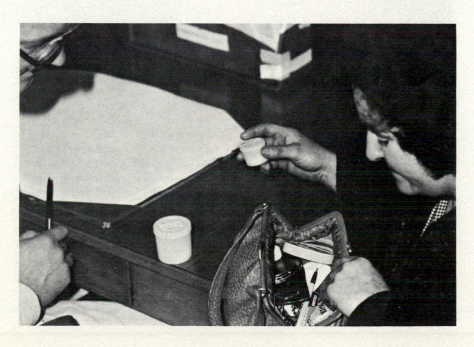

590. The pills in the handbag
The clinical history should include details of previous treatment. The pills in the handbag may reveal the source of a complaint where intensive investigation proves negative.

Neurological Complications of Surgical Treatment

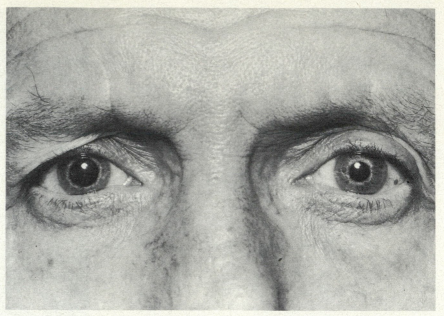

592a

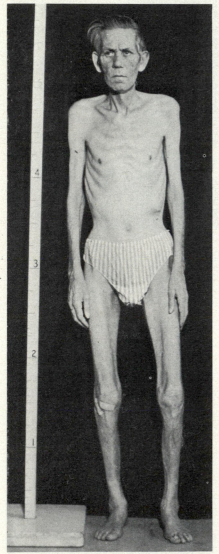

591. Malabsorption syndrome
Chronic sensorimotor polyneuropathy of 3 years' duration in a patient who had a gastro-enterostomy 14 years previously.

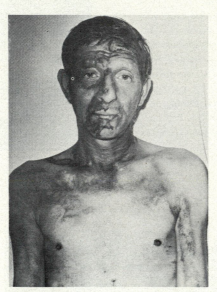

592b

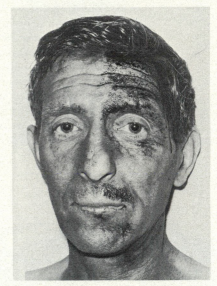

592c

592. Gustatory sweating; post-operative
Age 45 years. Resection of upper lobe of left lung for tuberculosis 10 years previously. Since then he had noticed an abnormality of sweating on the left side of his face. Generally when he perspired the *left* side of his face remained dry. On the other hand, the odour or taste of spicy foods caused profuse sweating on the *left* side of his face. The thought alone of such foods did not cause this, but even standing outside a fish and chip shop would initiate the sweating.
(*a*) Left Horner syndrome.
(*b*) Thermoregulatory sweat test: note absence of sweating on left side of face and left shoulder.
(*c*) Gustatory sweating: fish, chips and a sauce caused reflex sweating on left side of face. Gustatory reflex sweating may be a congenital abnormality, or an idiopathic complaint in adult life, or it may follow facial paralysis or operations in the region of the parotid gland (the auriculotemporal syndrome). It has been described in syringomyelia and after operations such as cervical sympathectomy and thoracotomy. In general, gustatory sweating following nerve damage is thought to result from aberrant regeneration of nerve fibres.

INDEX

Numbers in ordinary type are page numbers and refer to the text;
those in heavy type are the figure numbers of the illustrations.